PHILOSOPHY OF MIND

Philosophy of Mind: Contemporary Readings is a comprehensive anthology that includes classic and contemporary readings from leading philosophers. Addressing most major topics within the philosophy of mind, O'Connor and Robb have carefully chosen articles under the following headings:

- Substance Dualism and Idealism
- Materialism
- Mind and Representation
- Consciousness

Articles by the following thinkers are included:

Zimmerman	Swinburne	Lowe	Robinson
Smart	Kripke	Zuboff	Lewis
Putnam	Block	Chalmers	Fodor
Dretske	Searle	Davidson	Dennett
Churchland	Levine	McGinn	Jackson
Carruthers	Harman	Hasker	Lockwood
Unger	Kim		

Each section is prefaced by an introductory essay written by the editors, which aims to guide the student gently into the topic. The book is highly accessible and provides a broad-ranging exploration of the subject including discussion of leading philosophers in the field. Ideal for any philosophy student, this book will prove essential reading for any philosophy of mind course.

Timothy O'Connor is Associate Professor of Philosophy at Indiana University. He is editor of *Agents, Causes, and Events: Essays on Indeterminism and Free Will* (1995) and author of *Persons and Causes: The Metaphysics of Free Will* (2000).

David Robb is Assistant Professor of Philosophy at Davidson College. He is the author of several articles on metaphysics and the philosophy of mind.

Routledge Contemporary Readings in Philosophy

Series Editor: Paul K. Moser,
Loyola University of Chicago

Routledge Contemporary Readings in Philosophy is a major new series of philosophy anthologies aimed at undergraduate students taking core philosophy disciplines. It is also a companion series to the highly successful Routledge Contemporary Introductions to Philosophy. Each book of readings provides an overview of a core general subject in philosophy offering students an accessible transition from introductory to higher-level undergraduate work in that subject. Each chapter of readings will be carefully selected, edited, and introduced. They will provide a broad overview of each topic and will include both classic and contemporary readings.

Philosophy of Science
Yuri Balashov and Alex Rosenberg

Metaphysics
Michael J. Loux

Epistemology
Michael Huemer with introduction by Robert Audi

Philosophy of Mind
Timothy O'Connor and David Robb

PHILOSOPHY OF MIND

Contemporary Readings

Edited by
*Timothy O'Connor and
David Robb*

Routledge
Taylor & Francis Group

LONDON AND NEW YORK

First published 2003
by Routledge
11 New Fetter Lane, London ECP4 4EE

Simultaneously published in the USA and Canada
by Routledge
29 West 35th Street, New York, NY 10001

Routledge is an imprint of the Taylor & Francis Group

Editorial matter © 2003 David Robb and Timothy O'Connor

Typeset in Sabon and Trade Gothic by
Florence Production Ltd, Stoodleigh, Devon
Printed and bound in Great Britain by
MPG Books Ltd, Bodmin, Cornwall

British Library Cataloguing in Publication Data
A catalogue record for this book is available from
the British Library

Library of Congress Cataloging in Publication Data
Philosophy of mind: contempory readings/edited by
Timothy O'Connor and David Robb.
p. cm. – (Routledge contemporary readings in philosophy)
Designed to be used with: Philosophy of mind/John Heil.
Includes bibliographical references and index.
1. Philosophy of mind.   I. O'Connor, Timothy, 1965–
II. Robb, David, 1966–   III. Heil, John. Philosophy of mind.
IV. Series.
BD418.3.P47 2003
128′.2–dc21   2002044532

ISBN 0–415–28353–1 (hbk)
ISBN 0–415–28354–X (pbk)

CONTENTS

CONTENTS

CONTENTS

vii

CONTRIBUTORS

Ned Block is Professor of Philosophy and Psychology at New York University.

Peter Carruthers is Professor of Philosophy at the University of Maryland.

David J. Chalmers is Professor of Philosophy and Director of the Center for Consciousness Studies at the University of Arizona.

Paul M. Churchland is Professor of Philosophy at the University of California, San Diego.

Donald Davidson is Willis S. and Marion Slusser Professor of Philosophy at the University of California, Berkeley.

Daniel C. Dennett is University Professor, Austin B. Fletcher Professor of Philosophy, and Director of the Center for Cognitive Studies at Tufts University.

Fred Dretske is Senior Research Scholar at Duke University and Emeritus Professor of Philosophy at Stanford University.

Jerry A. Fodor is State of New Jersey Professor of Philosophy at Rutgers University.

Gilbert Harman is Stuart Professor of Philosophy at Princeton University.

William Hasker is Emeritus Professor of Philosophy at Huntington College.

Frank Jackson is Professor of Philosophy in the Philosophy Program, Research School of Social Sciences at the Australian National University.

CONTRIBUTORS

Jaegwon Kim is William Herbert Perry Faunce Professor of Philosophy at Brown University.

Saul A. Kripke was McCosh Professor of Philosophy at Princeton University until his retirement in 1998. He is currently Visiting Professor of Philosophy at the City University of New York Graduate Center.

Joseph Levine is Professor of Philosophy at Ohio State University.

David Lewis was, until his death in 2001, the Class of 1943 University Professor of Philosophy at Princeton University.

Michael Lockwood is Lecturer in Philosophy in the Department for Continuing Education at Oxford University.

E.J. Lowe is Professor of Philosophy at the University of Durham.

Colin McGinn is Professor of Philosophy at Rutgers University.

Hilary Putnam is Emeritus Professor of Philosophy at Harvard University.

Howard Robinson is Professor of Philosophy at Central European University and Honorary Research Fellow in the Department of Philosophy at the University of Liverpool.

John R. Searle is Mills Professor of the Philosophy of Mind and Language at the University of California, Berkeley.

J.J.C. Smart was Professor of Philosophy at the Research School of Social Sciences at the Australian National University from 1976 until his retirement at the end of 1985. He is currently an Honorary Research Fellow in the Department of Philosophy at Monash University.

Richard Swinburne is Emeritus Nolloth Professor of the Philosophy of the Christian Religion and Emeritus Fellow of Oriel College, Oxford University.

Peter Unger is Professor of Philosophy at New York University.

Dean W. Zimmerman is Associate Professor of Philosophy at Rutgers University.

Arnold Zuboff is Lecturer in Philosophy at University College London.

PREFACE

The sciences of the mind have grown rapidly since the mid-twentieth century. There is now a sizeable body of empirical knowledge concerning the structures and processes in the human brain which underpin, e.g., thought, sensation, and emotion. More generally, the interdisciplinary field of cognitive science is burgeoning on several fronts. Contemporary philosophical reflection about the mind – which has been quite intensive – has been influenced by this empirical inquiry, to the extent that the boundary lines between them are blurred in places.

Nonetheless, the philosophy of mind at its core remains a branch of metaphysics, traditionally conceived. Philosophers continue to debate foundational issues in terms not radically different from those in vogue in previous eras. The present volume gathers together some of the best recent writing on such issues. This metaphysical orientation is shared by John Heil's *Philosophy of Mind: A Contemporary Introduction* (Routledge 1998; a second edition is forthcoming). We have designed the anthology as a companion to Heil's book, although it could also serve as a stand-alone anthology for those who prefer to teach without a textbook.

Our volume is intended for use in a mid-level undergraduate course in the philosophy of mind, so we have selected readings that should be accessible to undergraduates who have taken only one or two courses in philosophy. We have shied away from writings that are heavy in formalism and dense argumentation. The selections are also fairly self-contained and both engage and motivate foundational issues, rather than working out details of a presupposed framework. Each of the four main sections opens with an essay in which we lay out the central problems and locate the selections within that context (O'Connor authored the Introductions to Parts II and IV, Robb the Introductions to Parts I and III).

We want to thank two anonymous referees for detailed, useful comments on an early version of our list of readings. Special thanks also are due to Siobhan Pattinson at Routledge for her advice and encouragement at every stage of this project.

Timothy O'Connor
and David Robb

PART I

SUBSTANCE DUALISM AND IDEALISM

INTRODUCTION

I. The mental–physical contrast

Philosophical reflection about the mind begins with a curious, even unsettling fact: the mind and its contents – sensations, thoughts, emotions, and the like – seem to be radically unlike anything physical. Consider the following:

- The mind is a conscious subject: its states have phenomenal feel. There is something that it is like to be in pain, say, or to imagine eating a strawberry. But what is physical lacks such feel. We may project phenomenal qualities, such as colors, on to physical objects. But the physical realm is in itself phenomenally lifeless.
- The mind's contents lack spatial location. A thought, for example, may be about a spatially located object (e.g. the Statue of Liberty), but the thought itself isn't located anywhere. By contrast, occupants of the physical world are necessarily located in space.
- Some mental states are representational: they have *intentionality*. Now it is true that parts of the physical world, such as the words printed here, can have intentionality. But what is physical is representational because we bestow meaning on it. It is due to our semantic conventions that the words on this page stand for something, so the intentionality of the physical is in this way derived. But the mental has original – that is, underived – intentionality. My thought about the Statue of Liberty is in itself about something in a way that no physical representation is.

These (alleged) differences are all metaphysical: they point to a fundamental difference in nature between the mental and physical. The mind–body divide can also be drawn epistemologically: we know about the mental – at least our own minds – in a way that is quite different from the way we know about the physical. For example:

3

- Our primary means of discovering truths about the physical world is perception (sight, hearing, and so on). But our primary means of discovering truths about our own mental states is introspection. And whatever the exact nature of introspection, it seems to give us a much more direct, intimate knowledge of the mental than outward perception gives us of the physical.
- Our knowledge of our own minds is more secure than our knowledge of the external, physical world. While you may have doubts about whether you are reading a book right now – perhaps you're hallucinating or dreaming – you cannot doubt that it seems to you as if you're reading a book, that your mind contains this sort of appearance. Mental states are "self-illuminating" in a way that no physical states are.
- The mental is private: your own mental states are uniquely your own, directly accessible only to yourself. But the physical world is public: in principle, it is equally accessible to everyone.

All six of the features just listed could use further elaboration, and each is controversial. But they do create a prima-facie puzzle. Do they divide reality into two fundamentally distinct realms, or are these apparent differences merely apparent, so that the mental and physical are really just parts of the same world? These questions form the traditional mind–body problem, and philosophical responses to them fall into two broad camps, monism and dualism.

Monists insist that one of the realms is, despite appearances, really just subsumed by the other. Monism comes in two varieties: materialists believe that the mental can be reduced to the physical. Reality is fundamentally physical in nature; minds and their contents are ultimately composed of the same sort of stuff composing baseballs, bridges, and the like. Idealists, on the other hand, believe that the physical can be reduced to the mental. Here reality is fundamentally mental in nature; baseballs and bridges are ultimately composed of mental items, out of "ideas," to use an old-fashioned term. While materialists and idealists disagree about the exact nature of reality, as monists they agree that the mental and physical are not distinct parts of it.

Dualists, on the other hand, take the apparent differences between the mental and physical to reflect a fundamental division in reality. The mental and physical comprise distinct realms, neither reducible to the other. And dualism also comes in at least two varieties: substance dualists believe the mind itself is a non-physical substance. (A substance, as philosophers use the term, is what we might ordinarily call a thing or object, something that bears properties and persists through time.) Property dualists believe that, while the mind may be a physical substance, such as the brain, its mental properties are not physical.

4

In contemporary philosophy of mind, materialism dominates, and much of philosophy's recent history has been devoted to articulating and defending materialist theories of the mind. Most of the selections in Parts II–IV of this anthology come from the materialist program. Yet the alternatives to materialism, idealism, and dualism have never disappeared from the intellectual scene. Both positions have contemporary philosophical defenders, and dualism in recent years has even enjoyed something of a renaissance. The selections in Part I are drawn from this important contemporary work.

II. Substance dualism

Chapters 1–4 are about substance dualism. (Property dualism will appear in later selections, most prominently in Part IV.) Substance dualism in its most radical form is called Cartesian Dualism, after its most famous modern proponent, René Descartes. Descartes held that the mind (or the self – he took these to be the same) is an immaterial soul, a substance the essence of which is consciousness. All of the mind's properties are conscious mental states, expressions of this essence. By contrast, all of a material substance's properties are physical, expressions of extension, the essence of bodies. Mental and physical substances (and their properties) are thus radically distinct.

This is, roughly, the content of Cartesian Dualism – but why believe the view is true? Descartes was impressed by some of the mental–physical differences listed earlier. But his most powerful argument for dualism, and the one that has historically received the most attention, proceeds from the mere conceivability of one's own disembodied existence. While it is true that I have a body, this appears to be a contingent fact about me, for I can clearly conceive of myself existing in a purely disembodied state, one in which I lack physical properties. It is thus possible for me to exist in such a state, since what is clearly conceivable is at least logically possible. But if I were a material thing, such as a brain or a living human body, this would not be possible: every physical substance is essentially physical, and so could not exist without physical properties. It follows that I am not a material thing. This argument (or one quite like it) appears in Descartes' *Meditations on First Philosophy* (Descartes 1642/1996) and has been enormously influential among dualists ever since.

Central to the Cartesian argument are (1) the claimed conceivability of my own disembodiment and (2) the move from the conceivability of this state of affairs to its genuine possibility. But both of these are problematic. First, what is it to conceive of some state of affairs? What sort of cognitive act am I engaging in when I conceive of my own disembodiment? And second, under what conditions is conceivability a guide to what's genuinely possible? Might we be subject to systematic illusion about modality – about what's possible or necessary – or do our powers of conception reliably track the modal truth? These questions are not easy to answer; here I just touch on some of the main issues.

Conceiving of a state of affairs S involves, at a minimum, considering S and not discerning any impossibility in it. Following Van Cleve (1983), call this weak conceivability. Some states of affairs are not even weakly conceivable: there being a square circle, for example, or there being an object that is red all over and green all over. Other states of affairs are weakly conceivable for some people but not for others. For example, many find Russell's Barber weakly conceivable – this is a man who shaves all and only those men who do not shave themselves – but careful thought reveals a contradiction in such a notion, rendering it inconceivable even in this weak sense. Now it looks as if we must grant Descartes at least this: my disembodied existence – call this state of affairs DE – is weakly conceivable; we can discern no contradiction in it. But does this give us reason to think that DE is possible? The traditional worry here is that I may fail to perceive a contradiction in DE because I do not fully understand my own nature, just as many find Russell's barber weakly conceivable because they do not fully understand his nature. I may in fact be a material being – and so essentially material – but not being aware of this, I find DE weakly conceivable.

Cartesians can take a number of different routes at this point. They may say that the mere possibility of modal error does not undermine our prima-facie evidence for DE's possibility, evidence we take from its weak conceivability. But, more likely, Cartesians will insist that we can conceive of DE in a way that is more robust than weak conceivability. Descartes speaks of "clear and distinct perception," and here he has in mind a kind of intellectual insight or intuition. This corresponds to what Van Cleve (1983) calls "strong" conceivability. While the weak conceivability of S involves merely not discerning any impossibility in S, strong conceivability involves a higher cognitive achievement: intuiting that S is in fact possible. (Compare: a detective may at first simply lack evidence that a suspect is guilty, but after some investigation, he may move to a higher epistemic state, having gained evidence that the suspect is innocent.) Applying our distinction to the present case, Descartes' claim is that I can intuit that DE is possible, that I can just (intellectually) *see* that I could exist in a disembodied state.

Whether this move to strong conceivability will help the dualist depends on the exact nature of this cognitive act. It appears to be a kind of internal "vision," where one forms a mental image of a state of affairs and, inspecting this image, sees that it is possible. Alternatively, it could be a kind of non-imagistic insight into the nature of the state of affairs, perhaps depending on – fanciful as it might sound – a faculty for discerning metaphysical truths. In any case, such questions about the nature of conceivability are relevant, not just to the Cartesian argument, but to a wide variety of conceivability arguments in the philosophy of mind, many of which appear in this anthology. (For some recent work on conceivability and possibility, see Hart 1988, Yablo 1990, and Gendler and Hawthorne 2002.)

In Chapter 1, Dean Zimmerman reconstructs and critically examines the Cartesian conceivability argument. He concludes that at best the argument shows that there could have been *a* disembodied mind, not that *I* could have existed in such a state. This leaves us without any reason to think that dualism is true of our world, that our minds are immaterial substances. One of Zimmerman's targets is the contemporary dualist Richard Swinburne, who also has defended a conceivability argument in the Cartesian tradition. But in Chapter 2, Swinburne explores a different line. Here he claims that only the dualist can account for certain facts about personal identity. He imagines a case in which the left and right hemispheres of my brain are removed from my body, then separated and placed, still functioning, into different bodies. There must be a clear fact of the matter, Swinburne argues, about whether I continue to exist after the transplant, and if so, which body is mine. But a complete enumeration of the relevant physical facts leaves these questions unanswered. Thus there must be more to me than what is physical: this is an immaterial soul. (A more detailed version of Swinburne's argument, along with a materialist's reply, can be found in Shoemaker and Swinburne 1984.)

III. The problem of interaction

However one evaluates arguments for substance dualism, the view must confront a number of problems (for a survey of these, see Smith and Jones 1987, Chapter 4). Perhaps the most serious is the *Problem of Interaction*. The mind clearly seems to causally interact with the body: damage to the skin causes a pain (body-to-mind), a decision causes an arm to go up (mind-to-body), and so on. But how are such commonplace causal relations possible if mind and body have radically distinct natures? Descartes was well aware of this problem; it was forcefully put to him by Princess Elizabeth of Bohemia, who in a 1643 correspondence asked Descartes to tell her

> how the human soul can determine the movement of the animal spirits in the body so as to perform voluntary acts – being as it is merely a conscious substance. For the determination of movement seems always to come about from the moving body's being propelled – to depend on the kind of impulse it gets from what sets it in motion, or again, on the nature and shape of this latter thing's surface. Now the first two conditions involve contact, and the third involves that the impelling thing has

extension; but you utterly exclude extension from your notion of soul, and contact seems to me incompatible with a thing's being immaterial (trans. E. Anscombe and P. Geach in *Descartes: Philosophical Writings*, New York: Bobbs-Merrill Co., 1954).

Elizabeth's point may be put this way: causation requires a mechanism or nexus. When *A* causes *B*, there must be some interface between them via which *A* exerts its causal influence. If *A* and *B* are material substances, a likely nexus is spatial contact: one body directly moves another through being in contact with it. Yet this interface is not available for mind–body interactions, at least if dualism is true, for Cartesian minds cannot literally be in spatial contact with any body. And to put the point more generally, if minds and bodies are so radically different, it is hard to see what *could* be the mechanism of mind–body interaction. If the two sorts of substance have nothing in common, what possible nexus could serve to join them? Indeed, a dilemma confronts the Cartesian: any nexus the dualist might propose – call it *N* – will be either spatial or non-spatial. But in either case, *N* will be unable to perform its assigned role. If *N* is spatial, it will fail to link on to a Cartesian mind; if *N* is non-spatial, it will fail to link on to any material substance.

A dualist may try to evade this problem by rejecting the demand for a causal nexus. Following the British empiricist David Hume, a dualist might insist that the notion of a causal nexus, at least at the most basic level, is unintelligible. It is true that we can understand the mechanisms for causal connections at the macro level, as when we explain the interactions of two chemicals by appealing to their microstructures. But when we are considering causal relations at the most basic level, those between simple material substances, the demand for a mechanism or nexus becomes pointless. And, the argument goes, we should expect it to be no different in the case of basic mind–body causal interactions. Whether this move can be successful takes us deep into the metaphysics of causality. (For some helpful general discussions of Hume's theory of causality, see Strawson 1987 and Blackburn 1990.)

Even if the dualist could make the mind–body nexus intelligible (or at least reject the need for one), there would still be another problem to face: we have, or so it is often claimed, good empirical reasons to think that the physical world forms a *causally closed* system. Trace the causal history of anything physical, and you will find only physical causes. At no point does the immaterial causally break into the physical world. This version of the Problem of Interaction sometimes makes a direct appeal to conservation laws in physics. If a Cartesian mind were to exert an influence on a body, then its doing so would violate the conservation of, say, momentum. And while the laws of conservation are not known to be true a priori – and indeed may turn out to be false – we have good empirical reasons to think they hold in our world, and thus that Cartesian mind–body interaction is nomologically impossible. Since mind–body interaction manifestly *does* occur, the argument goes, the mind must be wholly material.

In Chapter 3, E.J. Lowe confronts this version of the Problem of Interaction. Lowe presents a novel picture of dualist interaction on which, he claims, no conservation laws are violated. Lowe's idea, roughly, is that a Cartesian mind could influence the body by structuring causal pathways in the brain without actually causing any particular neural events, and thus without violating conservation laws. Such structuring is comparable to the way a web structures a spider's movements without ever causing any particular movements a spider makes (this analogy appears in Lowe 1996). In Chapter 4, Jaegwon Kim exploits the apparent lack of a mind–body nexus to motivate a more recent version of the Problem of Interaction, the "pairing problem." Since Cartesian minds cannot bear spatial relations to anything, Kim argues, causation between minds and bodies, or even between two minds, becomes problematic. If minds are not within a spatial network, there is nothing in virtue of which the activities of a mind could be causally paired with any other substance. (For further discussion of the pairing problem, see Foster 1991.)

IV. Idealism

As I mentioned earlier, dualism is not the only contemporary rival to materialism. Idealism, though not enjoying the same renewed attention as dualism, is still a significant position supported by its own set of philosophical arguments. Like its rivals, idealism comes in several varieties, but all these agree that the physical is reducible to the mental. Idealism is most often associated with another British empiricist, George Berkeley. Berkeley believed that reality consists solely of minds (or "spirits") and their ideas. Physical objects, such as trees and telephones, are merely collections of ideas in minds. This includes my own body and any part of it, such as my brain. In one sense, then, Berkeley is a mind–body dualist, for he believes that minds and bodies are different in kind: a mind is a spiritual substance, while a body is a collection of ideas. But idealists are nevertheless classified as monists, for, while bodies are not mental substances, they are still wholly mental, composed entirely of ideas.

Idealism may seem to be a bizarre view, and Berkeley and his followers must confront a number of prima-facie difficulties from common sense, including the following:

(1) Much of the physical world exists unperceived by any mind. Rocks buried deep below the earth's surface, planets in an unobserved, uninhabited solar system, and sub-atomic particles are all examples of objects that

exist but are not and never have been perceived by minds. But ideas cannot exist outside of a mind, so how could the above objects be collections of ideas?

(2) Even ordinary, local, macroscopic objects are mind-independent in the sense that they continue to exist when we do not perceive them. The chairs in a classroom, for example, do not disappear at night when there's no one around to perceive them.

(3) Where do our ideas come from? That is, what is their causal origin, and why are they in general so orderly? Materialists and dualists have a ready explanation of the origin and order of our ideas: they come from a world of external, stable, law-governed, material objects. But this explanation is not available to the idealist. Berkeley anticipated all these objections and others. His answers to them are in his *Three Dialogues Between Hylas and Philonous* (Berkeley 1713/1979).

Even if the idealist can successfully answer these objections, there is still the question of whether a positive case can be made for idealism. In Chapter 5, Howard Robinson updates and strengthens Berkeley's positive argument (see also Foster 1982). Robinson first makes a case for the traditional distinction between the *empirical* world and the *transcendental* world, the latter being the world (if there is such) that exists independently of our minds and is causally responsible for our experiences. Even if there is a transcendental world, Robinson argues, it could not be our physical, empirical world of tables, baseballs, stars, and planets. It is part of our concept of the physical world that it is, at least in principle, open to investigation by empirical science. But there is no guarantee that the transcendental world has the characteristics that science tells us the physical world exhibits. Thus, it is at least *possible* that the transcendental world is not the physical world. But identity propositions are necessarily true if true at all: if it is even possible that *A* is not the same as *B*, then *A* is in fact not the same as *B*. So the physical world, Robinson concludes, is not in fact the transcendental world. The physical world is, rather, entirely mental, constituted by the directly experienced world of ideas.

FURTHER READING

Berkeley, G. (1713/1979) *Three Dialogues Between Hylas and Philonous*, ed. R. Adams, Indianapolis: Hackett.

Blackburn, S. (1990) "Hume and Thick Connexions," *Philosophy and Phenomenological Research* 50, Supplement: 237–50.

Corcoran, K. (ed.) (2001) *Soul, Body, and Survival: Essays on the Metaphysics of Human Persons*, Ithaca: Cornell University Press.

INTRODUCTION

Descartes, R. (1642/1996) *Meditations on First Philosophy, With Selections from the Objections and Replies*, ed. and trans. J. Cottingham, Cambridge: Cambridge University Press.

Foster, J. (1982) *The Case for Idealism*, London: Routledge.

—— (1991) *The Immaterial Self*, London: Routledge.

Gendler, T. and Hawthorne, J. (eds) (2002) *Conceivability and Possibility*, Oxford: Oxford University Press.

Hart, W.D. (1988) *Engines of the Soul*, Cambridge: Cambridge University Press.

Hoffman, J. and Rosenkrantz, G. (1991) "Are Souls Unintelligible?," *Philosophical Perspectives* 5: 183–212.

Lowe, E.J. (1996) *Subjects of Experience*, Cambridge: Cambridge University Press.

Shoemaker, S. and Swinburne, R. (1984) *Personal Identity*, Oxford: Blackwell.

Smith, P. and Jones, O.R. (1987) *The Philosophy of Mind: An Introduction*, Cambridge: Cambridge University Press.

Strawson, G. (1987) "Realism and Causation," *Philosophical Quarterly* 37: 253–77.

Van Cleve, J. (1983) "Conceivability and the Cartesian Argument for Dualism," *Pacific Philosophical Quarterly* 64: 35–45.

Yablo, S. (1990) "The Real Distinction Between Mind and Body," *Canadian Journal of Philosophy*, Supplement 16: 149–201.

IA

SUBSTANCE DUALISM

1

Dean W. Zimmerman, "Two Cartesian Arguments for the Simplicity of the Soul"

I. Arguments for the existence of the soul

There are many reasons that have been given for thinking that *I* – the thing now thinking about what to write next, and watching this sentence appear – cannot be simply identical with any part of the 140-pound hunk of matter sitting in front of my computer. Some of these reasons have been theological: We may believe that God has told us that, when we die, we come into His presence; but since our bodies are obviously not going anywhere, there must be something more to us than just bodily parts. Other reasons have been of an empirical sort: For instance, ostensible memories of earlier lives have been said to be best explained by appeal to reincarnation; now, a reincarnated person must overlap somehow with her previous self; but since the bodies involved do not share any parts, there must be some other sort of part which survives the first body's death. It has also been argued (famously by Kant) that, for *ethical* reasons, we must suppose that the soul is immortal.

There are also what could be called purely metaphysical reasons for believing that the thinker is not identical with the body. What I have in mind are philosophical arguments which begin by noting certain alleged facts about our mental lives which are supposed to be obvious *a priori* or evident to reflection, but which seem to raise difficulties for the supposition that the thing which does our thinking is an extended material object.

There have been several noteworthy purely metaphysical arguments for the conclusion that thinking things cannot be extended bodies. In the 18th and 19th centuries, many philosophers propounded arguments for the simplicity of the soul which appealed to the "unity of consciousness."[1] Even more familiar, however, are those arguments for simplicity based upon the

Dean W. Zimmerman, "Two Cartesian Arguments for the Simplicity of the Soul," *American Philosophical Quarterly*, 28(3) (1991): 217–26.

logical possibility of disembodiment. Descartes introduced this sort of argument into modern philosophy (he had a kind of unity of consciousness argument as well[2]), and it continues to have its supporters today. Although careful analysis of Descartes's *Meditations* does not produce a convincing proof that thinkers must be unextended, it does help to show what is wrong with a more recent argument of Richard Swinburne's which appeals in a similar fashion to the logical possibility of disembodiment.

II. My body, my soul, and I

The Cartesian conclusion, "I am a soul," raises a host of questions. What are souls supposed to be like, and how do they differ from ordinary physical things? What is the relationship between my body, my soul, and the thing I refer to when I use the first person pronoun, "I"? At least a few of these questions must be answered if the following arguments are to appear at all plausible.

There have probably been almost as many distinct doctrines about the nature of the soul and its relationship with the body as there have been different arguments for the soul's existence. Some have claimed that the soul is an extended ghostly substance – a sort of "astral body" – superimposed upon and interacting with a physical body. Others have meant by "the soul" a simple substance – that is, a substance having no proper parts, no upper and lower, left and right halves – which possesses all of a person's psychological properties. Both arguments to be considered here have as their conclusion that the thinker is a soul in this latter sense: An unextended substance, indivisible not because its parts are especially durable and tightly knit together, but because it has no parts at all.[3]

Sometimes people who have held one or the other of these views have gone on to say that, although the soul does all my thinking and sensing – it is the bearer of all my "purely psychological" properties,[4] – nonetheless I am not identical just with my soul. I, the whole *person*, am a compound including both a physical and a spiritual part. Even Descartes feels a certain pressure in this direction, and is willing to grant that, from the fact that my soul has "sensations of pain, hunger, thirst, and so on," I should conclude that "I am not merely present in my body as a sailor is present in a ship, but that I am very closely joined and, as it were, intermingled with it, so that I and the body form a unit."[5] Many contemporary philosophers go further to assert that we typically use the word "I" to refer not merely to whatever thing is the subject of the speaker's mental states (be it a soul, a brain, or some larger physical object), but also to the speaker's whole physical body. However, in the typically Cartesian arguments considered here, "I" is used in an extremely narrow way to refer just to the subject of the thinker's present thought – i.e., to that thing, whatever it is, that possesses all of her purely psychological properties. If in fact we mean by "I": "my whole body and whatever does my thinking"; then this narrow Cartesian use of "I" is illegitimate, and the statement "I am not a body" is a contradiction.

There is no need, for present purposes, to take a side in the dispute about whether or not by "I" or "the whole person" we generally mean "whatever does my thinking, together with every part of the physical body that is most closely linked with that thinking thing." When considering statements in the first person which figure as premises in the following arguments – statements such as "I am possibly such as to be unextended," – let us simply stipulate that "I" is being used to refer to whatever it is that has my psychological and phenomenal properties at the present moment. In fact, I think we do not stray far from ordinary usage if we take "I" in this way to mean "the thinker of *these* thoughts" or (equivalently) "whatever it is that exemplifies *these* psychological properties." But those who disagree may feel free to replace "I" with one of these longer definite descriptions at every occurrence.

Since "I" is restricted in this way to refer to the thinker of just one's *present* thoughts, questions about the nature of personal identity over time need not be raised. The arguments considered here try to show that a thing must be unextended in order to have mental properties. It is then inferred that whatever has my psychological properties now must therefore be unextended. But obviously such considerations could not tell us much by themselves about the relationship between the thing that has my psychological properties today and the thing that will have them tomorrow.

III. Descartes's argument

Perhaps the most well known purely metaphysical argument (or arguments) for the conclusion that I am a simple, thinking substance is found in Descartes's second and sixth meditations. Here is the passage from the sixth meditation which contains, according to his "Synopsis,"[6] the *real* argument for the conclusion that I am unextended:

> First, I know that everything which I clearly and distinctly understand is capable of being created by God so as to correspond exactly with my understanding of it. Hence the fact that I can clearly and distinctly understand one thing apart from another is enough to make me certain that the two things are distinct, since they are capable of being separated, at least by God. Thus, simply by knowing that I exist and seeing at the same time that absolutely nothing else belongs to my

17

nature or essence except that I am a thinking thing, I can infer correctly that my essence consists solely in the fact that I am a thinking thing. It is true that I may have a body that is very closely joined to me. But nevertheless, on the one hand I have a clear and distinct idea of myself, in so far as I am simply a thinking, non-extended thing; and on the other hand I have a distinct idea of body in so far as this is simply an extended, non-thinking thing. And accordingly, it is certain that I am really distinct from my body, and can exist without it.[7]

It is not immediately obvious how this argument is related to an earlier argument in the second meditation which seems quite similar. But whatever their precise relationship, it is clear that the correct interpretation of this passage depends upon our understanding what Descartes means by "nature or essence." And a brief account of the discussion in the second meditation will help explain what Descartes means by the claim that my essence is to be a thinking, unextended thing.

The notion of "essence" in Descartes is never clearly defined, but he does say things which allow us to draw conclusions about at least some of the things implied by statements of the form appearing in the above passage: "P belongs (does not belong) to the essence of x." In the second meditation, in the context of the evil demon hypothesis, Descartes discovers that he can doubt that he has a body or any physical attributes at all. However he cannot similarly doubt that he has his current set of purely psychological properties. He concludes that thinking – or having psychological properties – is his essence: "this alone is *inseparable* from me" [my italics].[8] By this, he seems to mean that he is possibly such that he still exist without any physical properties, including *being extended* (these are "separable" from him); but that he is not possibly such that he still exist after having ceased thinking (this is "inseparable" from him). Similarly, he claims that the essence of a body is to have shape, location, and take up space.[9] Since these are essential to every material object, no material object could possibly fail to be extended.

After making these claims about his own essence and the essences of bodies in the second meditation, Descartes grants that, for all he has said so far, it may "perhaps be that these very things [i.e., a body, a wind, etc.] are in reality identical with the "I" of which I am aware."[10] He seems to be reserving his formal proof that he is not a body until the sixth meditation.

Now in the light of his second meditation statements about essences, his claims in the sixth meditation with respect to the essences of himself and physical things can be "boiled down" to these:

18

(a) "Thinking belongs to my essence" = "I am not possibly such as to not be thinking"
(b) "Being extended does not belong to my essence" = "I am possibly such as to be non-extended"
(c) "Being extended belongs to the essence of body" = "No body is possibly such as to be non-extended"

Without even having to rely upon the peculiarly Cartesian (and highly dubious) claim that I can never exist without thinking, we can formulate a sixth-meditation-inspired argument using equivalences (b) and (c) as follows:

(1)   I am possibly such as to be non-extended.
(2)   No body is possibly such as to be non-extended.
_____

(3)   Therefore, I am not a body.[11]

Descartes also assumes that anything having psychological properties is a substance,[12] and that anything extended is a body.[13] Thus he may conclude from (3) that he is a non-extended substance – i.e., a simple substance having no proper parts.

Although the argument for (3) is clearly valid, neither premise is without its problems. Premise (2), for instance, must be taken to imply that no individual thing could pass from being extended to being simple.[14] If (2) did not imply this, then premise (1) could be true in virtue of the fact that, though I am now extended, I may become unextended in the future. This interpretation would render the argument invalid, so (2) must rule out the possibility of dwindling into simplicity. But is this really impossible? Or could a thing slowly lose parts until all that is left of it is an unextended "atom"? Suarez considered the possibility of a cone being obliterated from its base up until the only part remaining was an unextended point – its "tip."[15] Is this possible? In particular, could some thinking thing be an extended body now, but eventually be reduced to a simple? More needs to be said in defense of premise (2).[16]

Setting aside the questions that arise concerning the second premise, what do we find Descartes saying in favor of (1), the proposition that he, Descartes, is possibly unextended? Simply that it follows from the fact that he can *doubt* whether or not he is an extended body, that he can *imagine a case* in which someone would have all of his current psychological properties, but lack extension. But is this enough to establish the truth of (1)?

I believe that Descartes is right about the conceivability of a simple, unextended thing possessing psychological properties. Furthermore, I agree that conceivability is our main test of logical possibility.[17] So we may conclude that it is logically possible for an unextended thing to have all of the psychological properties that I now possess. Does it follow that *I* am possibly an unextended thing? No. This inference would be of the following fallacious form:

(A) It is possible that some things having *P* also have *Q*.

(B) *x* has *P*.

_____

(C) Therefore *x* is possibly such that it have *Q*.

To see the problem, replace *P* with "being bespectacled," *Q* with "being made of wax," and let *x* be me.

There is the suggestion of another argument in the sixth meditation for the conclusion that I am possibly such as to be non-extended.[18] It can (with quite a bit of reconstructive surgery) be given a valid form, but unfortunately depends upon extremely implausible premises. As we noted at (a) above, Descartes says that thinking belongs to his essence – that is, that he is not possibly such as to not be thinking. He also claims (in the passage from the sixth meditation quoted at the beginning of this section) that any two "things" that can be distinctly conceived apart from one another are possibly such that they exist apart from one another. This principle is clearly intended to apply to the two "essences," thinking and being extended. Because of these two truths, he says, he can conclude that "my essence consists solely in the fact that I am a thinking thing." This conclusion seems to imply that he is necessarily a thinking thing but not necessarily an extended thing – and thus that premise (1), "I am possibly such as to be non-extended," is true. Does the line of argument suggested here provide a substantial reason for accepting premise (1)?

Descartes's claim about the separability of thinking-as-an-essence from being-extended-as-an-essence yields premise (A′) in the following argument, and his views about his own essence noted in (a) above provide premise (B′):

(A′) Anything which is necessarily such as to be thinking is possibly such as to be non-extended.

(B′) I am something which is necessarily such as to be thinking.

_____

(C′) Therefore, I am possibly such as to be non-extended.

This argument, though valid, is quite unconvincing. (A′) is a sweeping claim, and the only support Descartes adduces for it (at least in the *Meditations*) is his ability to clearly and distinctly understand *being necessarily thinking* apart from *being necessarily extended*. If we grant that it is conceivable for something to have either one of these properties without having the other, then we have reason to believe that it is possible for something to be necessarily thinking and not necessarily extended, and vice versa. But this is a far cry from (A'), the assertion that *anything* necessarily thinking is *not* necessarily extended.

(B') is even more problematic. Ordinarily, we suppose that our conscious lives are interrupted by frequent periods of unconsciousness during which no thinking occurs. Why does Descartes deny that it is even possible for him to exist while not thinking? His statements in the *Meditations* proper are not very helpful.[19] And although his discussion of the concept of a "complete thing" in the reply to Arnauld throws some light on his reasons for accepting both (A') and (B'), his arguments there are extremely sketchy and dubious. There he supports (A') and (B') by arguing for the doctrine that whatever thinks is necessarily such that it thinks and possibly such that it be non-extended, and that whatever is extended is necessarily such that it is extended and possibly such that it fail to think. Of course if this is true, then nothing that thinks is extended and nothing that is extended can think. Although Descartes's reasons for holding this view are worth examining (but not in this paper),[20] they are far from being sufficient to overthrow the nearly universal conviction that thinking things sometimes take a break. The argument from (A') and (B') does not, then, lend much support to premise (1). We have no reason to think that (A') is true, and every reason to think (B') is false.

There is a further difficulty for Descartes's argument. For it seems perfectly conceivable that an extended object have psychological properties. But if this is so, it provides the same sort of evidence for believing that it is logically possible for an *extended* thing to have a mental life just like mine. So, just considering the evidence provided by the fact that I have psychological properties, I would seem to be at an impasse with respect to premise (1) of Descartes's argument. I can imagine cases in which something has all of my psychological properties and is unextended, but I can also imagine cases in which something has them and is extended. Thus whatever support Descartes's imaginary scenarios may provide for thinking that I am possibly simple is counterbalanced by support for the conclusion that I am possibly a body. And, given premise (2), if I am a body I could not fail to be one. As a result, Descartes can have no more reason to believe premise (1) than its negation. Of course, Descartes may deny that it is possible for an extended thing to think.[21] But if he does so, he hardly needs the above argument to prove that whatever thinks must lack extension.

The 19th century Austrian philosopher, Franz Brentano, was making essentially these same points when he said that, although inner perception of our own mental states does not show us that whatever thinks and perceives must be extended, "there is a difference between not showing something and showing that something does not exist."[22] Although whenever I have a particular sensory experience or make a judgment, I can be certain that this thinking thing has the properties of sensing or judging; still I cannot be certain that this thinking thing has *only* the properties which are revealed in this self-evident manner. So although it seems possible from the evidence afforded by "inner perception" that I may be an unextended thinking thing, this evidence alone does not rule out the possibility that I am in fact an extended thinking thing.[23]

IV. Swinburne's argument

Richard Swinburne formulates an argument in his recent book, *The Evolution of the Soul*, which has much in common with the Cartesian argument from premises (1) and (2).[24] Like Descartes, he begins by asking us to imagine certain possibilities involving unextended psychological subjects, and he eventually reaches the conclusion that all of us are unextended thinking things. Although the defects in Swinburne's argument are not as obvious, they are of precisely the same sort as those that plagued Descartes's.

Swinburne conducts plausible thought-experiments meant to show us that we can imagine what it would be like to become a disembodied thinking thing. We can clearly conceive of a being like ourselves, whose sensations and causal powers are correlated with states of a single physical body, but who continues to have sensory experiences and produce physical effects apart from this or any other particular body. The ease with which such thought-experiments may be performed provides strong evidence for the logical possibility of a thinking thing's becoming disembodied. Swinburne, however, takes these thought-experiments to have established the logical possibility of *any* thinking thing's "becoming disembodied." This stronger claim is essential for the success of his argument. Its plausibility will be examined below.

Swinburne also assumes that a substance cannot persist from time t_1 to time t_2 without being composed of at least some of the same "stuff" ("or stuff obtained therefrom by gradual replacement").[25] He calls this the "quasi-Aristotelian assumption,"[26] and it is a persistence principle which seems compelling (although there are those who would not accept it).[27]

Swinburne's argument proceeds briskly from these two assumptions:

> Given the quasi-Aristotelian assumption, and given, that for any present person who is currently conscious, there is no logical impossibility, whatever else may be true now of that person, that that person continue to exist without his body, it follows that that person must

now actually have a part other than a bodily part which can continue, and which we may call his soul – and so that his possession of it is entailed by his being a conscious being. For there is not even a logical possibility that if I now consist of nothing but matter and the matter is destroyed, that I should nevertheless continue to exist. From the mere logical possibility of my continued existence there follows the actual fact that there is now more to me than my body; and that more is the essential part of myself. A person's being conscious is thus to be analysed as an immaterial core of himself, his soul being conscious.[28]

This argument, though valid, should not convince us if Descartes's argument did not. It can be put in a similar form, and suffers from similar defects:

(1*) I am now possibly such that I survive the destruction of all my physical parts and persist as a non-extended thing.

(2*) Nothing entirely made of my physical parts is possibly such that it survive the destruction of all my physical parts and persist as a non-extended thing.

_____

(3*) Therefore, I now have a part that is not a physical part.

Swinburne's support for premise (1*) is of the same sort as Descartes's support for his premise (1): I can conceive of a psychological subject having the sorts of psychological properties I now have, and then becoming disembodied. Since whatever I can distinctly conceive is logically possible, it is logically possible that such a subject become disembodied. Now *I* am a subject having these sorts of psychological properties. Therefore I am possibly such that I survive my death in disembodied form. Clearly, this is an instance of the fallacious inference form noted above: It's possible that something with a mental life like mine survive in disembodied form; I am something with a mental life like mine; therefore I am possibly such as to survive disembodiment.

In conversation, Swinburne has responded to this objection by claiming that his support for (1*) does not come by way of this fallacious inference. I represented his argument as beginning with the quite plausible move from: It is conceivable that a psychological subject having mental states like mine survive death, to: It is possible that a psychological subject having mental states like mine survive death; and then proceeding on (fallaciously) to the conclusion that *I* am possibly such that I survive death. However, he intends to go directly from the fact that it is conceivable that I survive my death, to the conclusion that I am possibly such that I survive my death.

In general we can go from conceivability to logical possibility; why not in this case?

Again, comparison with Descartes's argument is instructive. Just as in that case, I can conceive of states of affairs logically incompatible with the one asserted to be possible in the first premise. It is conceivable in the same way that I be identical with my body, or some part of it – this is a state of affairs which I can imagine easily enough, and with as much clarity and detail as Swinburne's favored alternative. Therefore, if this sort of conceivability invariably leads to logical possibility, it must be logically possible that I be identical with my body. But, since (by the quasi-Aristotelian assumption) it is necessarily the case that a substance cannot persist through the complete loss of all its parts, it follows that it is possible that I am not possibly such that I survive my death. But what is possibly possible is possible.[29] So, contrary to premise (1), I am *not* now possibly such that I survive the destruction of my body and persist as an unextended thing. If the move from conceivability to possibility suggested by Swinburne is justified, then this one must be as well. Since together they lead to a contradiction, we cannot rely on either of them.

It might be suggested that my surviving my death is somehow "more conceivable" than my being identical with a part of my body, and thus that I am more justified in believing that I could survive my death than that I am possibly a physical thing.[30] A story about my seeing my body disappear below me as I drift through the ceiling of my hospital room has much more charm and appeal than a story about my tallying up all of my parts and finding only hunks of matter on the list. But does the greater degree of attractiveness or "luminosity" associated with the disembodiment story suggest that I am better able to form a distinct conception of the state of affairs it describes?

The phenomenology of *a priori* knowledge is a complicated and intricate affair, one which cannot be explored in any detail here.[31] However, the confusion at the root of this objection may be detected even without a subtle analysis of *a priori* justification: the conceivability of a kind of experience is being mistaken for the conceivability of an extremely complicated state of affairs. The experience of seeming to "float out of one's body" may be described in great detail. Such an experience is eminently conceivable, more distinctly conceivable surely than my being identical with my brain. We can *know* that such an experience is possible; perhaps we can even produce it deliberately by practicing some kind of meditation or taking certain drugs.

The conceivability of *disembodied-seeming experience*, however, is not at issue, but rather the conceivability of *my becoming disembodied*. The experiences described as accompanying disembodiment are entirely irrelevant to this question. After all, someone else could have the experience of seeming to remember events in my life, seeming to see my body fall away, and so on, without having been me. Or I might survive as a disembodied amnesiac or perpetual dreamer who never has conscious recollection of events in my embodied life. To really assess the conceivability of my disembodiment, I must consider this state of affairs itself, and not be distracted by the ease with which I can imagine disembodied-seeming experiences. And if the Aristotelian assumption is, as Swinburne believes, a necessary truth, then the supposition that I become disembodied is equivalent to the supposition that I now have a non-physical part interacting with my body which comes to have psychological properties "all by itself" after my body is destroyed. The aura of attractiveness surrounding my conception of *this* complex state of affairs is much weaker than that surrounding my imagination of an experience that feels like "leaving my body." And it is the degree of conceivability of the former, and not the latter, which is to be compared with the conceivability of my being identical with some physical thing.

Once the conditions necessary for my becoming disembodied are considered by themselves, the halo of plausibility lent by the conceivability of disembodied-seeming experience fades away and the real complexity of this supposition becomes clear. It is perhaps no less attractive or distinctly conceivable than the supposition that I am identical with my brain. But it is certainly no better or more distinctly understood. So Swinburne, too, is left at an impasse: There are precisely parallel reasons for accepting both his premise (1*) and the proposition that I am possibly wholly physical. But then there are, as shown above, parallel arguments leading to both his conclusion and its negation. Swinburne has provided no more justification for believing the one than the other.

The investigation of these two Cartesian arguments reveals, then, a powerful objection to any argument that includes as a premise the proposition that "I" am possibly such as to be unextended, disembodied, or in some other way non-physical. Although I may recognize the logical possibility of a psychological subject with a mental life like mine surviving its death, and though I may be able to conceive of myself as unextended, I may still be an extended thing *for all I know*. Conceivability provides only defeasible evidence for possibility. And if one assumes (as Descartes does) that whatever is extended is essentially extended, and whatever is unextended is essentially unextended, then it also follows that I may for all I know be *necessarily* an extended thing.[32]

Notes

1 In the early 18th century, for example, Samuel Clarke and Bishop Butler formulated such arguments. See Clarke's *A Discourse Concerning the Unchangeable Obligations of Natural Religion and the Truth and Certainty of the Christian Revelation* in Vol. II of *The Works* (New York and London: Garland Publishing Co., 1978; reprint of 1738 edition), pp. 648–49; Butler's *The Analogy of Religion* (New York: Frederick Ungar, 1961; first published in 1736), p. 15. Kant considers a similar argument in his second paralogism of rational psychology, which, he says, is "no mere sophistical play . . . but an inference which appears to withstand even the keenest scrutiny and the most scrupulously exact investigation." (See Kant, *Critique of Pure Reason*, trans. by Norman Kemp Smith [New York: St Martin's Press, 1965], p. 335; A 351.) In the 19th century the "Bohemian Leibniz," Hermann Lotze, advanced a similar unity of consciousness argument in his *Microcosmus: An Essay Concerning Man and His Relation to the World* (see Vol. I, trans. by Elizabeth Hamilton and E.E. Constance Jones [New York: Charles Scribner's Sons, 1894], p. 158.) So did Franz Brentano near the turn of the century (see Brentano's *On the Existence of God*, ed. and trans. by Susan F. Krantz [Dordrecht: Martinus Nijhoff Publishers, 1987], pp. 290–301).

2 See Descartes, *Meditations on First Philosophy*, in *The Philosophical Writings of Descartes*, Vol. II, trans. by John Cottingham, Robert Stoothoff, and Dugald Murdoch (Cambridge: Cambridge University Press, 1984), p. 59. All references to the *Meditations* are to this volume.

3 Swinburne holds the even more radical view that the soul not only lacks extension but *every other physical property* as well. Souls possess only "purely mental properties." (See Richard Swinburne, *The Evolution of the Soul* [Oxford: Clarendon Press, 1986], pp. 145–55.)

4 For the purposes of the Cartesian arguments to follow, we may define psychological properties in this way: Property F is a *psychological property* if and only if, necessarily, for any S, if S exemplifies F, then S is the only person who is in a position to know without evidence that S exemplifies F. (This is a variation on a definition proposed by Jaegwon Kim; see his "Materialism and the Criteria of the Mental," *Synthese*, vol. 22 [1971], pp. 323–45. Kim goes on to introduce amendments to this definition which are needed to circumvent difficulties arising from the occurrence of variables in opaque epistemic contexts.) This comports well with Swinburne's characterization of mental properties as the "ones to which one subject has privileged access, which he is necessarily in a better position to know about than anyone else" (Swinburne, p. 6). Since the arguments at hand attempt to prove that the soul is *simple*, physical properties may be defined in the true Cartesian spirit as those properties which are necessarily such that, if they are exemplified, then something is spatially extended. (Note that, by this standard, many psychological properties – e.g., seeing a rabbit – are also physical properties.) *Purely* psychological properties, then, are those mental properties which do not logically imply that something has a physical property. (For a somewhat different characterization of the physical and the purely psychological, see Swinburne, pp. 6–7.)

5 *Meditations*, p. 56. If Descartes accepts the (admittedly controversial) central thesis of mereological essentialism – namely, that if x is a whole composed of

    y and z, then x is necessarily such that it is composed of y and z, – and also believes, as I think he does, that he is possibly such that his body not exist, but not possibly such that his soul not exist, then he cannot say that *he* is the "unit" composed of soul and body. For Descartes has a property which that whole lacks, namely being possibly such that his body does not exist.

6 *Meditations*, p. 9.

7 *Meditations*, p. 54.

8 *Meditations*, p. 18.

9 *Meditations*, p. 17.

10 *Meditations*, p. 18.

11 Apparently Bernard Bolzano advanced a similar argument in his *Athanasia*. For discussion, see Roderick M. Chisholm's "Bolzano on the Simplicity of the Soul," in *Traditionen und Perspektiven der analytischen Philosophie*, ed. by W. Gomboscz, H. Rutte, and W. Sauer (Vienna: Hölder-Pichler-Tempsky, 1989), pp. 79–88; and Chisholm's "On the Simplicity of the Soul," *Philosophical Perspectives*, vol. 5 (1991).

12 This becomes clear when Descartes says, with respect to "certain special modes of thinking," that they could not occur "without an intellectual substance to inhere in" (*Meditations*, p. 54). His view that the concept of a thinking thing is that of a "complete substance" are further developed in his reply to Arnauld (*Objections and Replies*, in *The Philosophical Writings of Descartes*, Vol. II, pp. 138–44).

13 "[B]y a body I understand whatever has a determinable shape and a definable location and can occupy a space in such a way as to exclude any other body . . ." (*Meditations*, p. 17).

14 This proposition that nothing can pass from being extended to being simple is a theorem of mereological essentialism, according to which, strictly speaking, nothing can gain or lose parts. Leibniz was a mereological essentialist, but it is not entirely clear what Descartes thought about the possibility of identity through the gain and loss of parts.

15 I owe the example from Suarez to Roderick M. Chisholm. More recently, Lewis Carroll countenanced the possibility of a three-dimensional object gradually fading away into a two-dimensional object: At a certain point all that remained of the Cheshire Cat was his grin.

16 In "Mind–Body Interaction and Supervenient Causation" (*Midwest Studies in Philosophy: Vol. IX:* Causation and Causal Theories, ed. by Peter A. French, Theodore E. Uehling, Jr, and Howard K. Wettstein [Minneapolis: University of Minnesota Press, 1985], pp. 271–81), Ernest Sosa argues that "anything, x, not three-dimensional but located in space must be located superveniently on the location in space of something y such that (a) y is three-dimensional and (b) (the existence of) x supervenes on (the existence of) y" (p. 273). If this principle (with the parenthetical portions) is correct, then cones and Cheshire Cats cannot disappear leaving only points and grins.

17 Sometimes philosophers seem to use "conceive" as a sort of "success" verb, so that if one can conceive of something, then that state of affairs must be metaphysically possible. At other times the phrase "such-and-such is conceivable" seems to be used to describe a way in which the contemplated state of affairs strikes one – a sort of "plausible-seeming" quality about it which provides merely prima facie justification for concluding that the state of affairs

really *is* possible. Such justification may be overridden by further evidence, and comes in various degrees. I am using "conceivable" in this latter sense.

18 I was prompted to look for this argument by the comments of Richard Purtill and an anonymous referee for *American Philosophical Quarterly*.

19 In the second meditation, while considering what he can and cannot doubt, he points out that "it could be that were I totally to cease from thinking, I should totally cease to exist" (*Meditations*, p. 18). The other most relevant passage is the sixth-meditation paragraph presently under scrutiny.

20 In the reply to Arnauld he argues that, since the concepts of mental substance and physical substance are "complete" and distinct, and since completely different kinds of substance "mutually exclude one another," it is impossible for something to be both a thinking thing and a body. This argument, although it would yield (A'), depends upon the very slippery and ill-defined notion of a "complete thing," a concept which also helps explain his adherence to (B'). My notion of myself as a thinking thing is the notion of a "complete" substance, that is, one which can exist "without any of the forms or attributes by which we recognize that body is a substance." Now a thing cannot exist without *some* properties. But since "all the attributes which belong to a body can be denied of [the mind]," I must always possess psychological properties (Descartes, *Objections and Replies*, pp. 156–60).

21 As he does in the reply to Arnauld (*Objections and Replies*, pp. 156–60).

22 Franz Bretano, *Psychology from an Empirical Standpoint*, ed. by Oskar Kraus, English edition ed. by Linda L. McAlister, trans. by Antos C. Rancurello, D.B. Terrell, and Linda L. McAlister (New York: Humanities Press, 1973; first published in 1874), pp. 165–66.

23 Brentano, *On the Existence of God*, pp. 290–91. (The German edition of this volume is entitled *Vom Dasein Gottes* [Hamburg: Verlag von Felix Meiner, 1968]; the relevant passage appears on pp. 415–19.)

24 Swinburne, pp. 145–60 and pp. 314–15.

25 Swinburne, p. 154.

26 Locke seems to have made a similar assumption, at least with respect to human beings and other animals; he says that the "Idea of a Man" requires that whatever persists as a human being must be "the same successive Body *not shifted all at once . . .*" (my italics) (Locke, *An Essay Concerning Human Understanding*, ed. by Peter H. Nidditch [Oxford: Clarendon Press, 1985], p. 335 (Bk. II, Ch. xxvii, §8)).

27 In particular, anyone enamored of a certain kind of teletransportation will reject the Aristotelian assumption. For example, some would say that a person, S is "transported" at time t from planet A to a distant location B if there is a machine which destroys S at t and simultaneously assembles a molecule-for-molecule copy of S as he or she was just before t, but made from particles in and around location B. If people are substances and they may persist through such a process, then the Aristotelian assumption must be false.

28 Swinburne, p. 154; for his formalization of the argument, see pp. 314–15.

29 This principle follows from the plausible assumption that logical possibilities do not change from one possible world to the next. It is a theorem of the modal systems S4 and S5.

30 This objection was suggested by some questions put to me by C. Stephen Evans.

31 The subject is given a careful and illuminating examination in Chapter 6 of Alvin Plantinga's book, *Warrant and Proper Function* (Oxford: Oxford University Press, 1993).

32 Roderick M. Chisholm furnished me with unpublished material on the simplicity of the soul, and both he and Ernest Sosa offered many helpful comments and suggestions. I am grateful to both. This paper is also better for the criticisms and suggestions of an anonymous referee for this journal, and the questions of audiences at Mankato State University and Wheaton College (Illinois). I particularly benefitted from discussion at the Wheaton College Philosophy Conference with Larry Lacy (my commentator), C. Stephen Evans, George Mavrodes, Richard Purtill, and Richard Swinburne.

[Author's note added in 2003: I remain unconvinced by the sort of Cartesian arguments for dualism discussed here, but there is a kind of "emergent dualism" that holds considerable attraction for me. For its advantage over materialism, see my chapter "Material People," in the *Oxford Handbook of Metaphysics*, ed. by Michael Loux and Dean Zimmerman (Oxford: Oxford University Press, 2003); and "Should the Christian Be a Mind–Body Dualist?", in *Contemporary Debates in Philosophy of Religion*, ed. by Michael Peterson (Oxford: Basil Blackwell, 2003).]

2

Richard Swinburne, "The Soul"

In writing loosely in the last chapter [of *Is There a God?*] of evolutionary processes causing the existence of animals and humans, I glossed over something all important. Evolutionary processes certainly cause the existence of animal and human bodies in virtue of the laws of nature discovered by the physical sciences (sustained, I claim, by God). But there is more to humans than their bodies. Humans (and the higher animals) are conscious beings. They have thoughts and feelings; atoms do not have thoughts and feelings. But consciousness, I shall be arguing, cannot be the property of a mere body, a material object. It must be a property of something else connected to a body; and to that something else I shall give the traditional name of soul. At some time in evolutionary history bodies of complex animals become connected to souls, and this, I shall be arguing, is something utterly beyond the power of science to explain. But theism can explain this – for God has the power and reason to join souls to bodies. First, however, I need to describe the phenomena, and to bring out that humans (and the higher animals) consist of two parts – a body which is a material substance, and a soul which is an immaterial substance and to which the conscious life of thought and feeling belongs. I shall make my case with respect to humans, and then point out briefly that the same holds for the higher animals.

Human souls

The world consists of substances. Tables and chairs, persons, nerve cells, and bones are all substances. Substances have properties such as being brown or square, and relations to other substances such as being 10 feet away from another desk or coming into existence after it. A particular substance having

Richard Swinburne, "The Soul," Chapter 5 (originally titled "How the Existence of God Explains the Existence of Humans") of *Is There a God?* (Oxford University Press, Oxford, 1996), pp. 69–94.

a particular property or relation at a particular time is an event – for example, my tie being green at 8 a.m. on 1 January 1995, or a certain neurone (a nerve cell) firing (i.e. quickly discharging electricity) at 2 p.m. on 2 January 1994. Anything is a substance if it can cause an event, or if something can cause a change in it. So, as well as material substances, substances which occupy volumes of space, there may be immaterial ones as well, which do not occupy space. I am arguing in [*Is There a God?*] that there is a God who is such an immaterial substance; and, if there are ghosts and poltergeists, they too are immaterial substances. I am going to argue in this chapter that the essential part of each one of us is a soul which is an immaterial substance.

The history of the world is just the sequence of all the events which have ever happened. If you knew all the events which had happened (which substances existed, which properties and relations they had to which other substances when), you would know all that had ever happened.

Properties and events may be physical or mental. I shall understand by a physical event one such that no one person is necessarily better placed to know that it has happened than is any other person. Physical events are public; there is no privileged access to them. Thus my desk being square is a physical event because, even though I may be the only person to have observed this, anyone else could check that it is square just as well as I can. Among physical events are brain events. Whether a certain neurone in the brain fired at a particular time is something which could be observed equally well by many different observers, and so the firing is also a physical event. Mental events, by contrast, are ones which just one person has a special way of finding out about – by actually experiencing them. The person whose events these are has privileged access to them, a means of finding out about them which no one else can share.

Evidently – more evidently than anything else – there really are mental events, as we know from our own experience. They include patterns of colour in one's visual field, pains and thrills, beliefs, thoughts and feelings. They also include the purposes which I try to realize through my body or in some other way. My being in pain at midday yesterday, or having a red image in my visual field, or thinking about lunch, or forming the purpose of going to London – are such that if others could find out about them by some method, I could find out about them by the same method. Others can learn about my pains and thoughts by studying my behaviour and perhaps also by studying my brain.

Yet I, too, could study my behaviour: I could watch a film of myself; I could study my brain – via a system of mirrors and microscopes – just as well as anyone else could. But, of course, I have a way of knowing about my pains, thoughts, and suchlike other than those available to the best other student of my behaviour or brain: I actually experience them. Consequently,

31

they must be distinct from brain events, or any other bodily events. A neuro-physiologist cannot observe the quality of the colour in my visual field, or the pungency of the smell of roast beef which I smell. A Martian who came to earth, captured a human being, and inspected his brain could discover everything that was happening in that brain but would still wonder "Does this human really feel anything when I stamp on his toe?" It is a further fact beyond the occurrence of brain events that there are pains and after-images, thoughts, and intentions. Likewise, such events are to be distinguished from the behaviour to which they typically give rise. People have sensations to which they give no expression – pains which they conceal or dream sensations which they report to no one – and, if the sensations give rise to behaviour, the subject is aware of the sensation as a separate event from the behaviour to which it gives rise.

I emphasize my definition of the mental as that to which the subject has privileged access. There are many properties which we attribute to people, which we might sometimes call "mental" but which are not mental in my sense but are merely properties of public behaviour. When we say that someone is generous or irritable or a useful source of information, it may be that we are just saying something about the way they behave in public, not anything about the life of thought and feeling which lies behind such behaviour. We may naturally describe being irritable as a mental property, but it is not a mental property in my defined sense. My concern is to make the point that there are mental events in my sense, distinct from brain events. In making this point, I do not for one moment wish to deny that most of my mental events are caused by my brain events. An event in my brain (itself caused by an event in my tooth) caused my toothache; and another event in my brain (itself caused by the branch outside the window moving) caused my belief that the branch moved. But the point is that, just as ignition of petrol is distinct from the explosion which it subsequently causes, so the brain event is distinct from the pain or whatever which it causes. And, of course, there is causation in the other direction too: my purposes cause (unintentionally) the brain events which in turn cause the motion of my limbs (which I intend).

Humans, unlike inanimate things, have mental properties; they have a mental life. But there is more to humans than just having a mental life connected to a body. That mental life itself, I now argue, is the state of an immaterial substance, a soul, which is connected to the body. That humans consist of two connected substances – body and soul – is the view known as substance dualism. The alternative is to say that humans are just bodies (I am the same thing as what we loosely call my body). In that case, my mental properties, such as being in pain or having an after-image, would be properties of my body. Let us call this view about humans *substance monism* – the view that there are only substances of one kind, material substances. If monism were correct, then there would be nothing more to the history of the world than the succession of those events which involve material substances, their coming into existence or ceasing to exist and having properties and relations (physical or mental). But, I am now going to point out, if you knew all that, you would still not know one of the most important things of all – whether you or any other human continued over time to live a conscious life.

Let me illustrate this with the example of brain transplants. The brain consists of two hemispheres and a brain-stem. There is good evidence that humans can survive and behave as conscious beings if much of one hemisphere is destroyed. Now imagine my brain (hemispheres plus brain-stem) divided into two, and each half-brain taken out of my skull and transplanted into the empty skull of a body from which a brain has just been removed; and there to be added to each half-brain from some other brain (e.g. the brain of my identical twin) whatever other parts (e.g. more brain-stem) are necessary in order for the transplant to take and for there to be two living persons with lives of conscious experiences. Now I am very well aware that an operation of this delicacy is not at present practically possible and perhaps never will be possible for mere human scientists with mere human resources; but I cannot see that there are any insuperable theoretical difficulties standing in the way of such an operation. (Indeed that is a mild understatement – I fully expect it to be done one day.) We are, therefore, entitled to ask the further question – if this operation were done and we then had two living persons, both with lives of conscious experiences, which would be me? Probably both would to some extent behave like me and claim to be me and to remember having done what I did; for behaviour and speech depend, in large part, on brain-states, and there are very considerable overlaps between the "information" carried by the two hemispheres which gives rise to behaviour and speech. But both persons would not be me. For if they were both identical with me, they would be the same person as each other (if *a* is the same as *b*, and *b* is the same as *c*, then *a* is the same as *c*) and they are not. They now have different experiences and lead different lives. There remain three other possibilities: that the person with my right half-brain is me, or that the person with my left half-brain is me, or that neither is me. But we cannot be certain which holds. It follows that mere knowledge of what happens to brains or bodies or anything else material does not tell you what happens to persons.

It is tempting to say that it is a matter of arbitrary definition which of the three possibilities is correct. But this temptation must be resisted. There is a crucial factual issue here – which can be shown if we imagine that I have been captured by a mad surgeon who is about to perform the split-brain operation on me. He tells me (and I have every reason to believe him) that the person to be formed from my left half-brain is to have an enjoyable life and the person to be formed from my right half-brain is to be subjected to a life of torture. Whether my future life will be happy or very painful, or whether I shall survive an operation at all, are clearly factual questions. (Only someone under the grip of some very strong philosophical dogma would deny that.) Yet, as I await the transplant and know exactly what will happen to my brain, I am in no position to know the answer to the question – what will happen to me. Maybe neither future person will be me – it may be that cutting the brain-stem will destroy the original person once and for all, and that, although repairing the severed stem will create two new persons, neither of them will be me. Perhaps I will be the left half-brain person, or maybe it will be the right half-brain person who will be me. Even if one subsequent person resembles the earlier me more in character and memory claims than does the other, that one may not be me. Maybe I will survive the operation but be changed in character and have lost much of my memory as a result of it, in consequence of which the other subsequent person will resemble the earlier me more in his public behaviour than I will.

Reflection on this thought experiment shows that, however much we know about what has happened to my brain – we may know exactly what has happened to every atom in it – and to every other material part of me, we do not necessarily know what has happened to me. From that it follows that there must be more to me than the matter of which my body and brain are made, a further essential immaterial part whose continuing in existence makes the brain (and so body) to which it is connected my brain (and body), and to this something I give the traditional name of "soul." I am my soul plus whatever brain (and body) it is connected to. Normally my soul goes when my brain goes, but in unusual circumstances (such as when my brain is split) it is uncertain where it goes.

Take a slightly different example. I die of a brain haemorrhage which today's doctors cannot cure, but my relatives take my corpse and put it straight into a deep freeze in California. Shortly thereafter there is an earthquake as a result of which my frozen brain is split into many parts, a few of which get lost. However, fifty years later, when medical technology has improved, my descendants take the bits of my broken corpse, warm it up and mend it, replacing the missing parts from elsewhere. The body becomes the body of a living person who behaves somewhat like me and seems to remember quite a lot of my past life. Have I come to life again, or not? Maybe, maybe not. Again there is a truth here, about whether I have survived the haemorrhage as I wanted to, and yet a truth of which we cannot be sure, however much we know about the story of my brain. Hence, my survival consists in the continuing of something else, which I call my soul, linked to my previous body; and I survive in this new body if and only if that soul is connected with it. And note that the extra truth is not a truth about what kind of mental life is connected to the brain. It is not a truth about mental properties, about what thoughts and feelings and purposes the revived person has. Rather, the extra truth, the truth about whether I have survived, is a truth about WHO – that is, which substance – those properties are instantiated in. And, since mere knowledge of what has happened to every material substance does not tell me that, it must be a truth about an immaterial substance. So long as I continue to have thoughts and feelings and purposes, I have survived any operation – whatever happens to any material parts of me. So my soul is the essential part of me – its survival constitutes my survival; and thoughts, feelings, and so on belong to me in virtue of belonging to my soul. The soul is the essential part of the human person.

Dualism is not a popular philosophical position today, but I find these arguments (of an entirely non-theological kind) in its favour inescapable. You have left something all-important out of the history of the world if you tell just the story of which physical events were succeeded by which other physical events. How people thought and felt is all-important. And equally important is who had those thoughts and feelings – when did one person cease to exist and another come into being.

Now certainly, as I have written, we normally know the answers to these questions. I do not wish to question any of our common-sense judgements about when someone is conscious, and who that person is. Our observation of bodies normally tells us when persons are the same and what they are feeling. Of course, if a baby screams when prodded with a needle, it is in pain. But it is not so obvious, when a human-looking organism made in a factory or a creature from another planet is prodded with a needle and emits some sound, whether that is in pain. And, of course, the person with this body today who has not been subject to a brain operation and shares the same patterns of behaviour as the person with this body yesterday is the same person as the latter. But after humans, let alone creatures from some distant planet, have had massive brain operations, it is not at all clear whether we are dealing with the same person as before. What these examples bring out is that someone feeling pain is a different event from their being prodded by a needle, and this person being the same person as that is different from this body being the same body as that; even if normally an event of the latter kind goes with an event of the former kind. A full history of the world will tell the story of feelings as well as of brain events, and of persons (and so their essential immaterial parts, souls) as well as of bodies.

35

These arguments which show that humans have two parts – body and soul – will show that any creature which has a mental life will also have two parts. The same issues will arise for a chimpanzee or a cat as for a human. If some cat is to undergo a serious brain operation, the question arises whether the cat has reason to fear the bad experiences and look forward to the good experiences which the post-operation cat will have. That question cannot necessarily be answered merely by knowing what has happened to every molecule in the cat's brain. So we must postulate a cat-soul which is the essential part of the cat, and whose continuation makes for the continuation of the cat. Only when we come to animals without thought or feeling does such a question not arise, and then there is no need to postulate an immaterial part of the animal. Certainly human souls have different capacities from the souls of higher animals (the former can have kinds of thought – thoughts about morality or logic – which the latter cannot have; and form kinds of purpose – e.g. to solve an equation – which the latter cannot.) But what my arguments show is that animals who have thought and feeling have as their essential part an immaterial soul.

Just as I do not wish to deny that brain events cause mental events (i.e. events in the soul, once it exists) and vice versa, so I do not necessarily wish to deny that events in the brain play a role in causing the existence of souls. At some stage of animal evolution, an animal brain became so complex that that caused the existence of a soul connected to it, and the continued development and operation of that brain sustained the existence of the soul; and, as evolution moves on, similar complexity causes similar souls. The connection between one soul and one brain which gets established is a causal one. It is events in this particular brain which cause events in this particular soul, and events in this particular soul which cause events in this particular brain; this is what the connection between this brain and this soul amounts to.

At which stage of the evolutionary process did animals first start to have souls and so a mental life? We do not know. But fairly clearly their behaviour shows that the mammals do have a mental life. My view is that all the vertebrates have a mental life, because they all have a brain similar to the human brain, which, we know, causes a mental life in us, and their behaviour, too, is best explained in terms of their having feelings and beliefs. Dogs and birds and fish all feel pain. But there is no reason at all to attribute a mental life to viruses and bacteria, nor in my view to ants and beetles. They do not have the kind of brain which we do, nor do we need to attribute feelings and beliefs to them in order to explain their behaviour. It follows that at some one particular moment in evolutionary history there appeared something utterly new – consciousness, a mental life, to be analysed in terms of souls having mental properties.

36

The reluctance of so many philosophers and scientists to admit that at a particular moment of evolutionary history there came into existence, connected to animal bodies, souls with mental properties seems to me to be due in part to the fact that, if such a thing happened, they are utterly lost for an explanation of how it came to happen. But it is highly irrational to say that something is not there, just because you cannot explain how it came to be there. We should accept the evident fact; and if we cannot explain it, we must just be humble and acknowledge that we are not omniscient. But I am going on to suggest that, although there cannot be an inanimate explanation, of the kind characteristic of the natural sciences, of the occurrence of souls and their mental life, the theist does have an explanation.

No scientific explanation

Since brain events cause mental events, and mental events cause brain events, scientists could perhaps establish a long list of such causal connections in humans, at any rate. The list would state that brain events of a certain kind cause blue images, and brain events of a different kind cause red images; brain events of one kind cause a belief that $36 \times 2 = 72$, and brain events of another kind cause a strong desire to drink tea; and that a purpose to eat cake together with a belief that cake is in the cupboard cause the brain events which cause leg movements in the direction of the cupboard. And so on. Also, just possibly, scientists could list which primitive brains give rise to consciousness – that is, to souls. The reason why I wrote "just possibly" is that our only grounds for believing that any other organism – whether some animal whose body was formed by normal sexual processes on earth, or some creature on another planet, or some machine made in a factory – is conscious is provided by the similarity of its behaviour and brain organization to ourselves. We do not have an independent check on whether it is conscious. And when the similarities are not strong – as between frogs, say, and human beings – it is in no way obvious whether the animal is conscious. But let us waive difficulties about how we could establish such things, and suppose that we have lists of causal connections between brain events and mental events, and lists of which kinds of primitive brain give rise to consciousness – that is, souls – in which subsequent brain events cause subsequent mental events, and mental events cause brain events.

So there are the phenomena. The problem is to explain them. Why does the formation of a brain of a complexity as great as or greater than that of a certain animal (perhaps an early vertebrate) give rise to consciousness – that is, to a soul with mental states? And why do brain events give rise to the particular mental events they do? Why does a brain event of this kind cause a blue image, and one of that kind cause a red image, and not vice versa? Why does eating chocolate cause the brain events which cause the taste we call chocolatey rather than the taste we call pineappley? A mere list of correlations would be like a list of sentences of a foreign language which translate sentences of English, without any grammar or word dictionary to explain why those sentences are correct translations. And, in the absence of a grammar and dictionary, you are in no position to translate any new sentence.

To provide an inanimate explanation of these phenomena we would need a scientific soul–body theory which satisfied the criteria described in Chapter 2 [of *Is There a God?*]. It would contain a few simple laws from which it would follow that this nerve or computer or other material network would give rise to a soul, and that one would not; that this brain event would cause a red image and that one a blue image; and that this brain event would cause the thought that Russia is a big country, and that one would cause the thought that every human has his own vocation. And so on. The theory would then enable us to predict which brain events of a new kind would give rise to which mental events of a new kind, and which new kinds of machine would have feelings and which not.

Now what makes a theory of mechanics able to explain a diverse set of mechanical phenomena is that the laws of mechanics all deal with the same sort of thing – material objects, their mass, shape, size, and position, and change of mass, shape, size, and position. And material objects differ from each other in respect of these properties in measurable ways (one has twice as much mass as another, or is three times as long as another). Because the properties are measurable, we can have general laws which relate two or more measured quantities in all bodies by a mathematical formula. We do not merely have to say that, when an object of this mass and this velocity collides with an object of that mass and that velocity, such and such results; and so on for innumerable different objects. We can have a general formula, a law saying that for every pair of material objects in collision the quantity of the sum of the mass of the first multiplied by its velocity plus the mass of the second multiplied by its velocity is always conserved. But that can hold only if mass can be measured on a scale – for example, of grams or pounds; and likewise with velocity.

Now a soul–body theory would deal with very different kinds of thing. The mass and velocity, and electrical and other physical properties, of material objects are utterly different from the mental (private) properties of thought and feeling which pertain to souls. Physical properties are measurable. So brain events differ from each other in the chemical elements involved in them (which in turn differ from each other in measurable ways) and the speed and direction of the transmission of electric charge. But thoughts do not differ from each other along measurable scales.

38

One thought does not have twice as much of some sort of meaning as another one. So there could not be a general formula showing the effects of variations in the properties of brain events on mental events, for the former differ in measurable respects and the latter do not. And what goes for thoughts, goes for mental events of other kinds. A desire for roast beef is not distinguished from a desire for chocolate by having twice as much of something. (Of course, the underlying causes of the one may have twice as much of something as the underlying causes of the other – but that is not the same.) So there could not be a general formula showing how certain variations in brain events produced changes of desires, only a list of which variations in the brain caused which changes of desire and since sensations, thoughts, and so on do not differ from other sensations and thoughts in measurable ways, even more obviously sensations do not differ from thoughts or purposes from beliefs in measurable ways; and so there cannot be an explanation deriving from some general formula of why this brain event was caused by a purpose and that one caused a belief, and another one caused a taste of chocolate. Not merely are the kinds of property possessed from time to time by material objects and by souls so different, but, even more obviously, material objects are totally different kinds of things from souls. Souls do not differ from each other or anything else in being made of more or less of some quantity of stuff. So, again, there could be no general formula correlating increase of brain complexity with the occurrence of a soul. Neural networks may become more and more compli-cated, but there could not be a formula of which it was a consequence that one degree of complexity would not and one just a little greater would give rise to a soul. Having a soul is all-or-nothing (a creature either has some feeling and awareness and so a soul, or no feeling or awareness and so no soul); it cannot be measured. For these reasons there could not be an explanation of soul–brain correlation, a soul–brain science; merely a long list of inexplicable causal connections.

But does not science always surprise us with new discoveries? The history of science is punctuated with many "reductions," of one whole branch of science to another apparently totally different, or "integration" of appar-ently very disparate sciences into a super-science. Thermodynamics dealing with heat was reduced to statistical mechanics dealing with velocities of large groups of particles of matter and collisions between them; the temper-ature of a gas proved to be the mean kinetic energy of its molecules. Optics was reduced to electromagnetism; light proved to be an electromagnetic wave. And the separate sciences of electricity and magnetism came together to form a super-science of electromagnetism. How is it that such great integrations can be achieved if my argument is correct that there cannot be a super-science which explains both mental events and brain events?

There is a crucial difference between these cases. Every earlier integration into a super-science, of sciences dealing with entities and properties apparently qualitatively very distinct, was achieved by saying that really some of these entities and properties were not as they appeared to be. A distinction was made between the underlying (not immediately observable) material entities and physical properties on the one hand, and the sensory properties to which they gave rise. Thermodynamics was initially concerned with the laws of temperature exchange; and temperature was supposed to be a property inherent in an object which you felt when you touched the object. The felt hotness of a hot body is indeed qualitatively distinct from particle velocities and collisions. The reduction to statistical mechanics was achieved by distinguishing between the underlying cause of the hotness (the motion of molecules) and the sensations which the motion of molecules causes in observers, and saying that really the former was what temperature was, the latter was just the effect of temperature on observers such as us. That done, temperature falls naturally within the scope of statistical mechanics – for molecules are particles; the entities and properties are not now of distinct kinds. Since the two sciences now dealt with entities and properties of the same (measurable) kind, reduction of one to the other now became a practical prospect. But the reduction was achieved at the price of separating off the felt hotness from its causes, and only explaining the latter.

All other "reductions" of one science to another and "integrations" of separate sciences dealing with apparently very disparate properties have been achieved by this device of denying that the apparent properties (such as the "secondary qualities" of colour, heat, sound, taste) with which one science dealt belonged to the physical world at all. It siphoned them off to the world of the mental. But then, when you come to face the problem of the mental events themselves, you cannot do this. If you are to explain the mental events themselves, you cannot distinguish between them and their underlying causes and only explain the latter. In fact, the enormous success of science in producing an integrated physico-chemistry has been achieved at the expense of separating off from the physical world colours, smells, and tastes, and regarding them as purely private sensory phenomena. What the evidence of the history of science shows is that the way to achieve integration of sciences is to ignore the mental. The physical world is governed by simple laws (i.e. material objects have the same simple powers and liabilities); the way to discover those laws is to ignore the mental. The very success of science in achieving its vast integrations in physics and chemistry is the very thing which has apparently ruled out any final success in integrating the world of the mind and the world of physics.

As we saw in Chapter 4 [of *Is There a God?*], the Darwinian theory of evolution by natural selection is able to provide an explanation of the evolution of human and animal bodies, though not, I argued, an ultimate explanation. But that Darwinian explanation would explain equally well the evolution of inanimate robots. Could not Darwinism also tell us something about how the bodies came to be connected with consciousness – that is, souls? Natural selection is a theory of elimination; it explains why so many of the variants thrown up by evolution were eliminated – they were not fitted for survival. But it does not explain why they were thrown up in the first place. In the case of physical variants (such as the length of the giraffe's neck), there is no doubt an adequate explanation in terms of a mutation (a random chemical change) producing a new gene with properties which cause the new variant to appear in accordance with the basic laws of chemistry. But our problem is to explain why some physical state caused the emergence of souls with such mental properties as beliefs, desires, purposes, thoughts, and sensations. Darwinism is of no use in solving this problem.

Darwinian theory might, however, be of use in solving one different problem, and certainly is of use in solving a third problem; but neither of these problems must be confused with the original problem. The first of these additional problems is why, having first appeared in evolutionary history, conscious animals survived. Darwinian theory might be able to show that conscious organisms have some advantage in the struggle for survival over non-conscious organisms programmed to react to their environment in similar ways. It is difficult to see what that could be, but maybe there is an advantage.

The second additional problem is one to which Darwinism can produce a clear, and to my mind fairly obviously correct, answer. That is this problem. Given the existence of mind–brain connections, and given that organisms with a mental life will be favoured in the struggle for survival, why are the brain events which cause and are caused by mental events connected with other bodily events and extra-bodily events in the way in which they are. Take beliefs. A brain event causes the belief that there is a table present. That brain event is caused by a nerve impulse along the optic nerve from the eye when a table image is formed in the eye by light rays arriving from a table. But an animal could have evolved in which the brain event which caused the table belief was caused by quite different events in the outside world. Why these particular connections between the brain and the outside world? The answer is evident: animals with beliefs are more likely to survive if their beliefs are largely true. False beliefs – for example, about the location of food or predators – will lead to rapid elimination in the struggle for food or to avoid predators. If you believe that there is no table present, when there is one, you will fall over it, and so on. Those in whom the brain states which give rise to beliefs are connected by causal chains to the outside world, in such a way that the causal chain is normally only activated by a state of affairs which causes the brain state which in turn causes the belief that the state of affairs holds, will normally hold true beliefs about the world and in consequence be more likely to survive. Similarly, given that I am going to have desires caused by brain events, there are evolutionary advantages in my having some under some circumstances rather than others under other circumstances – for example, desire for food when I am hungry rather than when I am satiated. The same kind of account can be given of why the brain events produced by purposes give rise to the movements of body purposed. If, when I tried to move my foot, my hand moved instead, predators would soon overtake me. But this correct explanation of why (given that brain events cause mental events) the brain is connected by nerves to the rest of the body in the way it is does not explain why brain events cause mental events, which is a quite different problem. And similarly for why mental events cause brain events.

So then, in summary, the evolution of the mental life of animals (i.e. animals having souls with certain mental events) involves:

(a) there existing certain physical–mental connections (certain physical events causing the existence of souls with certain mental properties, and conversely);
(b) there existing animals with brains whose states give rise to souls having an advantage in the struggle for survival;
(c) evolution selecting animals whose brains are "wired in" to their bodies in certain ways.

Darwinian mechanisms can explain (c), and possibly (b); but neither Darwinism nor any other science has much prospect of explaining (a). The origination of the most novel and striking features of animals (their conscious life of feeling, choice, and reason) seem to lie utterly beyond the range of science.

Yet there are these causal connections between soul and brain which do not seem to arise from the powers and liabilities of material objects of a kind that science can explain. There are causal connections between particular kinds of brain event and particular kinds of mental event; and causal connections between brain events and the very existence of souls.

I must however now qualify even the latter claim. It may well be that certain primitive brain states cause the existence of souls – as the foetal brain reaches a certain state of development it gives rise to a soul connected with it. But what it could not cause is – which soul is connected with it. It could not be the powers of this brain, of the molecules of this foetus arising from these genes, which cause it to be the case that *my* soul is connected to this brain and yours to that, rather than vice versa. It would be equally compatible with all the regularities between kinds of event (this kind of

42

brain organization and the existence of a kind of thing – a soul) that science could ever discover that you and I should have been connected to brains in the opposite way to the way in which we are connected. There simply is no possible scientific discovery which anyone could ever imagine which would explain why it happened this way rather than that way. Once the connection is made, we begin to become suited to the particular brain; connected to a male brain, I begin to have male thoughts. But that has no relevance to the question of why the "I" of unformed character was fitted to a male rather than to a female brain. Here science simply stops.

Theistic explanation

But theism can provide an explanation of these things. God, being omnipotent, is able to join souls to bodies. He can cause there to be the particular brain event–mental event connections which there are. He can do this by causing molecules when formed into brains to have powers to produce mental events in souls to which they are connected, and the liabilities to execute the purposes of such connected souls (new powers and liabilities not deriving from the ordinary ones which chemistry analyses). And he can make the souls in the first place and choose to which brain (and so body) each soul is to be connected when foetal brain events require a soul to be connected to the brain.

He has good reason to cause the existence of souls and join them to bodies, in the goodness of the existence of embodied animals and human beings who can have enjoyable sensations, satisfy their desires, have their beliefs about what the world is like, and form their own purposes in the light of these beliefs which make a difference to the world. This involves the existence of regular causal connections between mental events and brain events. We cannot make a difference to the world if, each time we try to move our leg, some different effect is caused in the brain and thereby in the body – one time the arm moves, one time we find ourselves sneezing, and so on. Likewise, if we are to discriminate between one object and another, they have to look (feel, etc.) different, and so there has to be a regular causal connection between the brain events caused by objects of each kind and the mental visual impressions of them. And, if we are to have the awesome power of reproduction, there have to be regular connections between our sexual acts, the foetus to which they give rise, and some soul or other linked to that foetus. God has reason to set up all these connections. He may also have a reason to join this soul to this particular body, but, if there is no reason for joining one soul to one body rather than to a different body, he has reason by a "mental toss up" to produce one-or-other connection – that is, to make it a chance matter which connection holds.

A perfectly good God will love creatures, and love creatures of varying natures – including creatures with narrow ranges of purposes and beliefs, such as rats and dogs. But he has a special reason for producing human beings. Human beings differ from the higher animals in the kinds of beliefs and purposes they have. For instance, we have moral beliefs, beliefs about the origin of our existence or fundamental theories of mathematics. We can reason from this to that, and our beliefs are consciously based on other beliefs (we come to have a particular belief about the Romans because we believe that a particular thing was found in Chichester). And our purposes are not just immediate purposes to get food or drink, but purposes to create complicated machines, build beautiful buildings, and purposes to change ourselves and each other – to form our characters so that we are naturally inclined to do this sort of action and not that.

Humans also, I believe, have free will – that is, our purposes are not fully determined by our brain states or anything else. It does seem to us that way, as we choose, that it is up to us how we choose. I should at this stage say something briefly about an objection to this which will occur to the reader. Is not the brain an ordinary material object in which normal scientific laws operate? How, then, can a human freely choose to move his arm or not, or perform any piece of public behaviour, without violating scientific laws? For the way a human moves his arm or does anything public is by bringing about a brain event (unintentionally) and thereby intentionally bringing about the public movement. So, if humans have free will, would they not then be able to prevent normal scientific laws operating in the brain? One answer to this is that quite obviously the brain is not an ordinary material object, since – unlike ordinary material objects – it gives rise to souls and their mental lives. Hence we would not necessarily expect it to be governed totally by the normal laws of physics which concern ordinary material objects. But a second answer is that, even if the brain is governed by the same laws as govern other material objects, that could still be compatible with humans having free will. This is because one of the two great theories of modern physics, Quantum Theory, shows that the physical world on the small scale is not fully deterministic. An element of unpredictability governs the behaviour of atoms, and the even smaller electrons, protons, and photons, and other fundamental particles out of which atoms are made. This unpredictability is not just a limit to human ability to predict effects, but, if Quantum Theory is true, a limit to the extent to which material objects have precise effects, a limit to the extent to which the physical world is deterministic. Exactly how an electron or photon will move is unpredictable, though we can often say that it is more probable that it will move along one path than along another path. Likewise atoms of one kind often "decay," turning into atoms of another kind. All that Quantum Theory can tell us is how probable it is that an atom of, say, radium will decay within a given time, not exactly when it will decay. But, while such unpredictability at the atomic level does not normally give rise to any significant unpredictability on the larger scale, it can do so. We could construct a machine which would ensure that, if some atom decayed within a certain time, a nuclear bomb would explode but otherwise it would not. Then we could not predict whether the bomb would explode or not. Now the brain is an intricate machine which also magnifies small changes, and it may well be like this: that the unpredictable small changes in the brain are the ones which cause our thought and observable behaviour. In that case, when humans form their purposes to think of this or that or behave in such and such a way, they thereby cause those small changes unpredictable by science which in turn cause the thought and behaviour. In this way, humans can exercise free will without their doing so involving any violation of the physical laws which govern the brain. These two answers suggest that there is no reason from physics for supposing that things are not as they seem to be with respect to free human choice.

So we humans have great possibilities for acquiring true and deep beliefs about the world and for moulding not just our environment on the large scale in complex ways, but also ourselves. In so many different ways we can choose between good and evil, and our choices make a big difference. A generous God has reason to create such beings.

The evidence deployed in this chapter suggests that the existence of souls and their connections to bodies are not due to the physical processes codified in natural laws. Some new powers have been given to foetal brains, and to the souls to which they are joined, powers which do not have a scientific explanation. The existence of God, a simple hypothesis which leads us with some probability to expect the phenomena discussed in the last chapter [of *Is There a God?*], also leads us to expect these phenomena. Hence they constitute further evidence for his existence. Although the powers of the brain and its liability to exercise these when it receives certain nerve impulses from the eye provide a full explanation of my having a blue image when I do, those powers are created and conserved by God, and so his action provides the ultimate explanation of the occurrence of the blue image. God's action also provides the ultimate explanation of there being a soul (and it being my soul rather than yours) which is joined to this body. It has been a common (though not universal) Christian doctrine that, while God operates through "secondary causes" (i.e. natural processes) to do much else in the world, he intervenes directly to create human souls and link them to bodies. I have gone beyond it to suggest that the same is true of the souls of the higher animals.

IB

THE PROBLEM OF INTERACTION

3

E.J. Lowe, "The Problem of Psychophysical Causation"

It is widely supposed that dualist theories of the mind–body relation face an intractable difficulty concerning psychophysical causation – even if it is not always agreed what, precisely, the nature of the difficulty is. Perhaps two main, if vague, areas of concern can be identified, one more serious than the other. The first is that dualism, in representing the mind as utterly distinct from and unlike anything physical, has a problem in rendering intelligible any kind of causal nexus between the two domains. But the proper response to this, first given by Hume, is to deny that we should expect *any* causal nexus to be "intelligible" in the sense in which dualism allegedly fails to represent psychophysical causation as being. One does not have to adopt a "Humean" theory of causation – the "regularity" or "constant conjunction" theory – to avail oneself of this response (and, incidentally, it doesn't presently concern me whether Hume himself was a "Humean" in this sense). All one has to draw from Hume is the idea that causal relations are not knowable *a priori*, like logico-mathematical relations. Anyway, I have no intention of discussing further this (to my mind) spurious aspect of the supposed problem that psychophysical causation poses for the dualist. The more serious area of concern is created by the suspicion that dualist views of the mind–body relation – and certainly those that are interactionist – are somehow at odds with the findings of modern physical science: not only physiology and neurology, but also, more fundamentally, physics itself.

But before exploring this area of concern, some remarks are in order concerning *dualism*: what exactly might be meant by that term, and why we should have any interest in exploring dualism's alleged difficulties. It is customary when introducing this topic to distinguish between "substance dualism" and "property dualism," and to treat the former – with Descartes

E.J. Lowe, "The Problem of Psychophysical Causation," *Australasian Journal of Philosophy*, 70(3) (1992): 263–76.

as its archetypal proponent – as the principal target of criticism. (I should stress that I am only concerned to discuss *interactionist* dualisms, not epiphenomenalist or parallelist theories, which avoid the problem of psychophysical causation only by denying – utterly implausibly – that such causation occurs and is a two-way affair.) *Substance dualism* is traditionally conceived as the view that mind and body are distinct and separable substances, the former unextended and conscious, the latter extended and non-conscious. *Property dualism* (attributed to Spinoza by some commentators) is then the view that mental and physical properties are quite distinct, but may none the less be properties of the same substantial particular – which by some accounts might be the brain (a physical substance).

But this familiar dichotomy is not an altogether satisfactory basis for classifying dualisms. For one thing, there are non-Cartesian dualisms which are classifiable as substance dualisms according to some accounts of the term "substance" – for instance, Strawson's dualism of persons and bodies (a view towards which I much incline), which treats persons as distinctive in being subjects of *both* psychological *and* physical predicates.[1] Secondly, "property dualism" as hitherto defined subsumes a variety of different positions, some but not all of which are fairly straightforwardly *physicalist* theories of mind – for a great deal turns on the bearing that one takes property dualism to have on the status of mental events and processes. An espousal of property dualism might only indicate a rejection of so-called "type–type" identity theories of mental events (and needn't even entail that, depending on one's theory of events and event-types). Certainly one can maintain a "token–token" identity theory of mental events – identifying individual mental events with individual physical events in the brain – while upholding property dualism.

Further needless discussion can however be avoided at this stage by observing that since (as I shall for the moment be assuming, at least) causation is a relation between individual events, if any form of dualism has a problem as regards psychophysical causation, it has one *only if* it represents individual mental events as being distinct from – non-identical with – individual physical events. I should stress that I say "only if," not "if." For it is possible to reject token identity between mental and physical events and yet still be a species of physicalist concerning the mind, and hence avoid the problem of psychophysical causation – for one may espouse some form of *supervenience* theory, whereby mental events supervene upon, but are not necessarily identical with, physical events. According to such a view – which holds, roughly, that there is never a mental difference without an underlying physical difference – mental events have no independent causal powers: for any causal difference they make to the train of physical (and other mental) events they do so in virtue of the difference made by the physical events upon which they supervene. In short, a dualist theory is faced by a problem over psychophysical causation if and only if it maintains that mental events have *independent causal powers* – that they make a difference to how the world goes over and above any difference made by physical events.

Now: why should we concern ourselves with the problems of any such form of dualism? Well, I have a personal concern because I believe that some such form of dualism is probably *true* – because I reject both token–token identity theories and supervenience theories of mental events and processes. I cannot go into my reasons now in any detail, beyond saying that I consider token–token theories to be of dubious intelligibility because I think that mental events and physical events have different and incompatible criteria of individuation and identity, while I regard supervenience theories as being inherently unamenable to empirical (much less *a priori*) support or confirmation.[2] One thing worth saying in this connection, however, concerns some of the philosophical arguments that are adduced in favour of identity and supervenience theories: very often these arguments effectively proceed from an assumption that *only* the physical can (ultimately) have causal powers – so that if mental events have causal powers they can do so only by virtue of being identical with, or supervening upon, physical events. But, fairly transparently, this is a form of argument that illicitly assumes precisely what it attempts to establish. Non-question-begging arguments for identity or supervenience theories are hard – indeed, I think impossible – to find.[3]

Let me give a simple example. It is sometimes urged that if a mental event M is to be regarded as the (or even *a*) cause of a physical event P, then since (as it is assumed) P will have a *wholly physical* causal explanation in terms of the occurrence of a set of prior physical events P_1 -P_n, the mental event M must either be identical with one of P_1-P_n (or with the "fusion" of two or more of these), or at least somehow "supervene" upon or be "realized" by one or more of P_1-P_n – for to deny this is to imply, quite implausibly, that P and indeed all other mentally caused physical events are systematically causally overdetermined. But the assumption that P has a "wholly physical" causal explanation precisely begs the question against the dualist who maintains that M is a non-physical event with independent causal powers.[4]

To be fair, however, charges of question-begging have to be handled delicately, and in the present case matters are perhaps more complicated than I have so far represented them as being. The claim that only the physical can have causal powers – or, at least, that only the physical can causally affect the physical – may be seen by many not just as some question-begging antidualist prejudice, but as a cornerstone of modern physical science. It is the principle that the physical world is a *causally closed system* – a principle which might be viewed as the metaphysical implication of the various conservation laws of physics: the laws of the conservation of energy and of linear and angular momentum. And these laws, surely, are not mere prejudices but, on the contrary, very high-level but none the less empirical generalizations discovered over the centuries by hard thought and backed by countless observations and experiments.

But now that we are going to take these complications seriously, we must see that we haven't yet reached the end of them. For one thing, we shall see shortly that the principle that the physical world is causally closed by no means follows from the conservation laws of physics alone, and that what has to be added to them to get that principle is by no means uncontroversial. For another thing, we can no longer afford to go on taking for granted what we mean by the words "physical" and "physics."[5] If either expression is partially defined in terms of the causal closure principle itself (as is sometimes effectively assumed), then the victory of the "physicalist" over the "dualist" will be an empty one. That is, if we insist that partly what we *mean* by describing an event as "physical" is that it can enter into causal relations with other "physical" events (where these include such paradigm physical events as, say, limb-movements), then mental events will inevitably qualify as "physical" if we accept the existence of psychophysical causation at all. But if, on the other hand, we *don't* write the causal closure principle into the very meaning of the word "physical," how *do* we demarcate the realm of the physical? (It won't do to say that the physical is the subject-matter of the current science of physics, for that is far too parochial; nor can we usefully appeal to some ideal "completed" physics of the distant future, about which we have no right to speculate.) However, if we have no principled and non-question-begging way of demarcating the realm of the physical, "physicalism" as a metaphysical position appears to be drained of all substance (as perhaps is "dualism" too, at least if it is defined partly in terms of opposition to physicalism).[6]

So are we in fact still left with a genuine *problem* for dualism concerning psychophysical causation? Well, perhaps, yes. If physics poses a serious threat to dualism, I think it does so in virtue of the possible clash of dualism with the conservation laws. (By "physics," here, I mean physics as it is currently formulated according to leading informed opinion.) Indeed, if we look to the history of dualist interactionism's supposed problems, we find in Leibniz's criticism of Descartes' theory of psychophysical causation precisely this focus on the apparent incompatibility of Descartes' account with the law of the conservation of momentum.[7]

Descartes – so the familiar story goes – thought that the mind exercised causal influence on the body by altering the direction of motion of animal spirits (a form of rarefied matter) in the pineal gland of the brain, these motions then being communicated purely mechanically to the extremities of the body through the flow of the animal spirits in the nerve filaments, giving rise to movements of the various limbs in accordance with the mind's desires. But Descartes was unaware that this process conflicts with the law of the conservation of momentum, partly because he lacked the modern concept of momentum as a vector (the product of mass and *velocity)* and was under the misapprehension that what had to be conserved was what he called *quantity of motion* (effectively, the product of mass and *speed,* a scalar quantity). That is, he failed to realize that even altering the *direction* of flow of the animal spirits, while leaving their *rate* of flow unaltered, would result in a change of momentum, a conserved quantity which could not be supplied from the non-physical mind but only from matter in motion (or at least by the operation of physical forces of some sort, even if one does not insist – as Descartes did – that these are all contact forces of a mechanical nature).

Now this analysis of Descartes' difficulty is essentially that provided by Leibniz – but we need not assume that Descartes would have agreed with this diagnosis had he lived to hear of it. For one thing, although it is true that Descartes himself believed in a principle of conservation of quantity of motion, it is not clear that he thought that this principle applied to cases of *psychophysical* interaction (as opposed to purely material interactions), and so not clear that he thought he needed to demonstrate the compatibility of his account of mental causation with this conservation law. By the same token, then, had Descartes lived to learn that his scalar law was mistaken and required to be replaced by the modern law of the conservation of linear momentum, it is conceivable that he would have taken the view that that law only reigns in the realm of inanimate matter – in short, that momentum simply is *not* conserved in mind–brain interactions, however perfectly it may be conserved in purely material interactions.

Nor would this have been as *ad hoc* a proposal as might initially be supposed – at least from a Cartesian point of view. For one thing, to the extent that the law of conservation of momentum is conceived of as an empirical generalization supported by observation (rather than as a regulative principle of experimental method, with a quasi *a priori* status), it must be remarked that the evidence in support of it to date has come exclusively from the observation of purely material interactions (a point which the physicalist, to be sure, is in no position to dispute!). Secondly, Descartes as a theist supposed that God, at least – an infinite mind – could create matter in motion (and hence momentum) *ex nihilo*, and yet clearly did not think of this as violating any natural law of Cartesian physics. So why should not finite minds likewise be conceived of as being capable of affecting the quantity of motion or momentum in existence without thereby contravening the physical conservation laws, appropriately construed as only applying unreservedly to purely material interactions?

However, if Descartes had taken this line of defence he would still have been open to a line of criticism the force of which was clear to Leibniz. This is that if, as is now being supposed, a law like that of the conservation of linear momentum is regarded as applying exceptionlessly only to purely material interactions, because the non-physical mind can create momentum *ex nihilo*, or conversely annihilate it, then it will prove impossible to state any simple, universal law governing the kinematic and dynamic behaviour of all material bodies – because of the ever-present possibility of the interference of mind. There will be no guarantee that there are any "purely material" interactions, much less that we shall be able to ascertain which they are. (Indeed, since *observation* is a mental activity, we won't be able to be sure that in observing a material interaction we don't render it "impure" – a suggestion which may remind one of some contemporary views of the role of the observer in quantum mechanics, but now made more general.)

Leibniz thought that the wisdom and goodness of God implied a world combining the greatest possible variety of particular matters of fact with the least possible number and complexity of general laws governing those matters of fact: and the Cartesian world just described would fail miserably on the latter score. Nor need we share Leibniz's theological perspective to feel the unsatisfactoriness of such a position. On criteria of simplicity and parsimony, such as are regularly appealed to in both scientific and metaphysical theory-construction, the Cartesian picture just sketched is an unattractively messy one. (But I should stress that this does not conclusively remove it from the field of competition: after all, in our own times continuous creation *ex nihilo*, in contravention of supposed conservation laws, has been proposed by Hoyle and others as a perfectly respectable scientific hypothesis, albeit one now out of favour for purely empirical reasons.)[8]

Suppose, now, that we accept this Leibnizian line of criticism of the dualist who is prepared to reject the universal applicability of the physical conservation laws in order to "make room" for an independent causal contribution from the mind in physical affairs. Does that leave no other strategy for the dualist interactionist – is he compelled to follow Leibniz's lead by opting for some form of parallelism in order to cling on to dualism? By no means. For an important point which has so far gone unnoticed is that classical particle mechanics – Newton's laws of motion, which form the basis of the conservation laws – *is not a deterministic theory*, surprising though that might superficially seem. This has been pointed out in an important paper by Richard Montague, and before him by Ernest Nagel, but it is really quite obvious on a little reflection.[9]

A simple example will illustrate the point. Suppose two worlds, w_a and w_b, in each of which a particle of mass m_1 is falling from rest at time t_1 and height h_1 towards the centre of the earth, which has mass m_2. In each world, suppose that energy and momentum are conserved. It is still perfectly possible for the two particles to differ in their positions and velocities at a subsequent time t_2. This is because those positions and velocities will depend on the value of g, the strength of the earth's gravitational field, and hence ultimately (given that we are assuming the earth's mass to be fixed at m_2) upon the value of the universal gravitational constant G. Each particle will gain in kinetic energy ($1/2 m_1 v^2$, where v is its velocity at time t_2) exactly what it loses in potential energy ($m_1 g(h_1 - h_2)$, where h_2 is its height at t_2). Also, the net momentum of the earth-particle system will remain unaltered (assuming the operation of no external forces), since the particle's gain of momentum in the downward direction ($m_1 v$) will be exactly compensated for by the earth's gain of momentum in the upward direction ($m_2 u$, say). But the crucial point is that by setting g (and G) at different values for worlds w_a and w_b, the value v of the particle's velocity at time t_2 can be made to vary as we please between those two worlds. Furthermore, we have been presupposing so far that only gravitational forces are in play – but of course there might be others, such as electro-magnetic forces, the strengths of which in the two worlds will depend ultimately on the value of the charge on the electron, which again may be supposed to differ between the two worlds (not to speak of the possibility that one of the worlds might contain forces not present at all in the other). In the terminology of Nagel and Montague, what has to be added to classical particle mechanics to transform it into a deterministic theory is a specification of the *force-function*, which will tell us what laws of force are in play and specify the values of the various constants which feature in those laws.

But how does all this bear upon the issue of dualist interactionism? Well, there are two ways in which a proponent of that view might exploit the points that have just been made. One strategy would be to propose the existence of distinctive *psychic forces* – forces supplementary to the familiar physical forces of gravitation and electromagnetism and so forth. (Contemporary wisdom has it that there are just four fundamental physical forces – the two just mentioned plus the so-called "strong" and "weak" nuclear forces: though the electromagnetic and "weak" nuclear force are now thought to be aspects of the same phenomenon, and attempts continue to "unify" all four forces.) Postulating laws of psychic force would just be one way of contributing to a specification of the force-function. Just as adding electromagnetic forces to a situation hitherto supposed only to involve gravitational forces makes a difference to the predicted kinematic

behaviour of (charged) material particles in that situation – without in any
way threatening a conflict with the conservation laws – so adding psychic
forces would have this effect.

But there is an obvious objection to this sort of proposal. It is that these
so-called "psychic" forces would have to be construed as being just a new
variety of *physical* force, and so would provide no comfort for the genuine
dualist. Why so? Well – or so I anticipate the answer to be – anything
which *can* exert a force on physical objects, that is, which can do work
on a physical system, is *ipso facto* something "physical" and the force it
exerts is consequently a "physical" one. The very definition of the "physical," one is tempted to say, is that it is something capable of *exerting force*,
or equivalently of *doing work* or *contributing energy* to a system. But this
answer should remind us at once of an idea we encountered earlier, that a
"physical" event is by definition one which can enter into causal relations
with other "physical" events: the problem with both suggestions is that they
threaten to render the self-styled physicalist's victory over dualism a purely
empty one. Suppose that the existence of the postulated "psychic" forces
was confirmed empirically, and suppose that the laws governing them
differed markedly from those governing the more familiar physical forces
(suppose, say, that there was absolutely no prospect of "unifying" the
psychic forces with any of the latter) – *would* it really be so obvious and
natural to classify them as just a new species of "physical" force? It simply
isn't clear what a decision of this sort ought to turn on, but I certainly don't
think that it can properly be made a mere matter of stipulative definition.
(I don't want to suggest that physicalists typically think that it *can*, only to
warn against the temptation to do so.) We have again struck one of the
chief obstacles to fruitful discussion of the dispute between physicalism
and dualism – the absence of any agreed and principled definition of the
"physical," which doesn't just beg the question one way or the other.

Even so, the dualist proposal now under consideration – the postulation
of "psychic" forces – has another serious drawback, to which I shall draw
attention shortly, after I have explained a second strategy which might be
exploited by a dualist who doesn't want to come into direct conflict with
the conservation laws while yet remaining an interactionist. According
to this second line of thought, the mind exerts causal influence on the body
not through the exercise of psychic (non-physical) *forces* of any sort, but
through influencing the values of the so-called "constants" which feature
in various *physical* force laws – for instance, by influencing (presumably
only locally and to a vanishingly small degree) the value of the universal
constant of gravitation G or the value of the charge on the electron.
Thus it would turn out that these so-called "constants" are strictly speaking
variables.

This is not in principle such a shocking or heretical idea. There are indeed cosmological theories – such as E.A. Milne's kinematic relativity – according to which the so-called "constant" of gravitation undergoes a secular increase, with the consequence that the sum of the universe's mass/energy increases with time.[10] It is true, then, that postulating variability in such constants is *in a sense* at odds with the classical principle of the conservation of energy, but not in the way that the earlier proposal made on Descartes' behalf was. For it is not now being suggested that the mind has a power of creating energy *ex nihilo* or conversely annihilating it. The latter proposal has a disagreeable air of hocus pocus about it, nor is it apparent how such a process could be conceived of as operating in a lawlike way. But the idea that what have hitherto been assumed to be constants of nature are in reality variables open to influence by mental operations is not obviously vulnerable to either of these objections. And it has the advantage over the alternative idea of "psychic" forces that it does not require us to think of the mind as being capable of contributing energy to, or absorbing it from, a physical system.

However, notwithstanding these advantages, this latest proposal still has a fundamental difficulty which also besets the idea of psychic forces, and indeed the "Cartesian" proposal mooted earlier. This is that all three theories seem to be inherently incapable of explaining why the mind's causal influence upon the material world has to be channelled through the brain: none of them can readily explain why telekinesis is not a ubiquitous phenomenon. Of course, it might be urged on behalf of all three that the mind – or the human mind, at least – can exert only a very weak influence on matter, an influence which has to be amplified by many orders of magnitude if it is to give rise to macroscopic effects such as limb-movements: and that the human body is precisely such an amplifier, partly having evolved to serve that very function. But then there still remains a puzzle as to why one mind should not be able to exploit the amplifying capacities of *another* mind's body, but only those of its own, and indeed why telepathy is not a ubiquitous phenomenon. All three theories, then – even the last one to be presented – have a quasi-magical aura by virtue of their apparent commitment to the possibility of mysteriously elusive psychic phenomena, such as telekinesis and telepathy. Of course, those who are convinced that such phenomena *do* occur will not regard what I have just said as a valid objection to any of those theories. But they still have to explain why the phenomena are so elusive, and that may not be at all easy.

Perhaps the fundamental problem with all three of the dualist interactionist proposals that we have been examining is one which they inherit from Descartes' own conception of the nature of mind–body interaction, according to which the mind exerts causal influence on the body by *setting matter in motion* (or at least by affecting the motion of matter). On one level, of course, this *must* be what the mind does, inasmuch as mental events and processes are ultimately causally responsible for the gross movements of our limbs that we make in performing (intentional) bodily actions, like walking or raising an arm. But Descartes, because his conception of physics was wholly mechanical, assumed that these gross movements of our limbs must be mediated by movements of *other* quantities of matter – the flow of animal spirits in the nerve filaments – so that at some stage in the process the mind would have to act *directly* upon matter to produce or alter motion in it: a stage which he famously located in the pineal gland, the "seat of the soul." But in fact one can espouse dualist interactionism without accepting this aspect of Descartes' position at all – especially as it is no longer appropriate to think of physics, in Cartesian style, as being just the science of mechanics. In supposing that the mind can causally influence the course of physical events, we need never suppose that it does so by (directly) affecting the state of motion of physical particles. Hence we need not ascribe to the mind some mysterious power of telekinesis, creating for ourselves the problem of explaining why this power can only be exercised on the brain (and not just any brain, but only one's own).

In what remains of this paper I want to sketch an altogether new picture of dualist interactionism, which will escape the difficulty that I have just identified.[11] Rather than ask how a mental event (conceived dualistically as non-physical) can directly cause a physical event in the brain (such as an alteration in the flow of animal spirits, or some modern variant thereof) thus initiating a causal chain leading thereafter through purely physical links to a movement in the limbs, it may be more profitable to begin from the other end – the limb-movement – and consider what happens when causal chains are traced backwards from this. It seems likely that as these causal chains are traced backwards through neural pathways leading to and into the brain, the chains will begin to display a tree-structure – quite possibly one exhibiting a "fractal" pattern (so that branches of the tree are smaller trees, the branches of which are still smaller trees, and so on indefinitely).[12] Moreover, trees emanating from different peripheral events (limb-movements and the like) will soon become inextricably intertwined. (I should stress that I am not talking about the neural pathways as such – though they will certainly also display branching: I am talking about causal chains of events occurring in those pathways.[13] Also, I am not assuming fully deterministic physical causation at all the nodes in the branching causal chains: we can suppose if we like – and as seems plausible on empirical grounds – that at least some of the physical causation is probabilistic, with antecedent events only fixing the chances of their effects at values between 0 and 1.)

Now, if that is a correct description of the topology of the causal chains involved in deliberative action, then the implication appears to be that it would just be quite wrong to imagine that the mind's role in action could be to *initiate* causal chains leading to peripheral events. For these causal chains – or rather trees, as we now see them to be – don't have "tips" which could provide the locus of the mind's interaction, nor are the trees which are traced back from different peripheral events distinguishable or separable once their branches have become inextricably intertwined.[14] In all this maze of neural events there are simply *none* of which we can say that *they* are the ones directly caused by some specific mental event which is ultimately responsible for a given peripheral event.

The picture, then, is as follows: I desire or will to raise my arm, and *as a result* my arm goes up – the movement being the terminus of a causal tree branching in a fractal pattern backwards into the maze of antecedent neural events. But though that causal tree *mediates* the causal relation between my desire or volition and the movement of my arm, it does not do so by virtue of my volition or desire initiating the "growth" of the tree from the "tips" down: for the tree has *no* tips, and certainly none that it can call exclusively its own.

But now it may be objected that if this is the picture we want to adopt of the causal antecedents of peripheral events, why do we need to invoke the mind at all, conceived dualistically? *Every* physical event in a causal tree has purely physical antecedent causes, precisely because there are no "tips." So haven't we conceded, in effect, that the body-cum-brain is a *causally closed physical system* (ignoring inputs from the physical environment, at least, which are not relevant to present considerations)? And in that case the mind (conceived dualistically) surely has no causal role to play: it is causally quite superfluous. But since it is just *false* that the mind is in fact causally superfluous (mental events *do* have physical effects), we have no option but to abandon dualism by identifying mental events with certain neural events (or at least saying that they supervene upon them).

No: the objection is mistaken. First of all, we can capitalize on the accepted fact that peripheral events (like limb-movements) have clearly identifiable mental causes – desires or volitions or intentions or whatever you like to call them. This particular limb-movement – my arm's going up just now – had a quite specific mental cause: my particular desire or volition just now to raise that very arm at that moment. But, as we have seen, on the physical side there is plausibly *no* clearly individuable neural event or set of neural events which can similarly be identified as the cause of the limb-movement – and hence nothing on the physical side which constitutes a suitable candidate for identity with the desire or volition (or even a suitable candidate for "realizing" that desire or volition, as a supervenience theorist might have it). The *physical* causes of different peripheral events become inextricably interwoven beyond a certain point – unlike the *mental* causes, which accordingly cannot be identified with the physical causes since the latter can't be individuated in a way which will allow us to put them into one-to-one relation with the mental causes (and the same applies, *mutatis mutandis*, for a "realization" account). Incidentally, let us not be sidetracked here by worries about the propriety of ever speaking of "the" cause of a given event – worries motivated by the familiar suggestion that one person's "cause" is another person's "background condition."[15] It suffices to point out that individual desires or volitions have an indisputable salience in the causal explanation of deliberative action which is not mirrored by any of the neural events individuable on the physical side.

Very well, the physicalist may reply, then this just shows that we were mistaken after all to accept the common-sense view that distinctly individuable mental causes – particular desires or volitions – really exist: we should espouse some version of eliminative materialism, whereby the categories of "folk psychology" have no place in a scientific account of the aetiology of human behaviour.[16] But if that is the extreme to which physicalism is driven, then so much the worse for physicalism, say I – the boot now begins to look as though it is on the dualist's foot. For I don't need to rehearse here all the difficulties which beset eliminative materialism.

But it still remains for the dualist to explain how mental causes can fail to be superfluous, given the picture sketched earlier of the causal antecedents of peripheral events. My proposed solution to this problem is as follows. As we have seen, when a peripheral event E (such as a limb-movement) has a distinct mental cause M (such as a particular volition or desire), it is not the case that M is the direct (that is, unmediated) cause of *any* physical event in the causal tree of neural events terminating in E: every event in that tree has, as its immediate causes, other wholly physical events – which is why we can in a sense allow that a principle of physical causal closure is satisfied and discern no threat to the physical conservation laws. Even so, it seems to me, we can still insist that M is genuinely causally efficacious in the production of E because M is responsible for (is, in the circumstances, necessary and sufficient for) the very fact that there exists a causal tree of neural events culminating in E. I am *not*, to repeat, saying that M is the direct cause of each or any member of the particular maze of neural events which happens to converge upon E, but rather that it is causally responsible for the fact that *there exists a maze at all with that particular convergence characteristic.*[17] For this fact, it seems to me, is *not* causally explicable purely by reference to physical events antecedent to E.

From a purely physical perspective, the convergence upon E looks like (indeed, I should say *is*) a quite remarkable and inexplicable coincidence –

rather like rings on the surface of a pond miraculously converging upon a central point, instead of spreading out from a disturbance there towards the pond's edges. (Or – to continue the tree metaphor – it is like supposing that a tree might grow from the tips of its branches down to its trunk, instead of *vice versa*.) And, of course, what makes the case of deliberative action importantly different from that of *actual* pond disturbances is that rings in ponds *never do* display convergence patterns but only ones of divergence, whereas in deliberative action convergence is the norm. From the purely physical point of view, thus, such convergence in the action case makes it look like a time-reversed process involving backward causation. But that can't be what is really going on, of course: and that is why it is not only legitimate but highly plausible to assign a distinctive causal role to an antecedent mental event M – an event which, like a desire or volition, has the later peripheral event E as its object. And here I mean "object" in a dual sense: E is the *intentional* object of M – in that M is a volition or desire that *that particular event E* occur – and E is also the objective or *goal* of the agent's endeavour. Thus the intentionality – in both senses of the word – of volition or desire is quite crucial to its capacity to play the causal role here required of it.

I should emphasize that the foregoing proposal is not compatible with a supervenience theory of mental states, for its implication is that mental states like volitions or desires have genuinely independent causal powers – that they make a difference to how the world goes over and above any difference made by physical events. I might add that if this view of mental causation is correct, it may help to explain – as previously mentioned dualist accounts apparently could not – why a particular mind is incapable of exercising its influence on physical objects other than its own brain and body: for causal networks of physical events susceptible to the sort of convergence now being discussed are quite probably only to be found within unified nervous systems, with patterns of convergence in different nervous systems being idiosyncratic and highly dependent upon the individual historical development of those systems.

If one still feels uneasy, even so, about the causal role which is now being assigned to mental events like desires or volitions, then perhaps a theological parallel will be of some help (though I don't mean to suggest that the parallel is an exact one). It is a familiar enough point that even in a deterministic physical universe with an infinite past a distinctive causal role can still be assigned to God: not, indeed, as a "prime mover" or temporally first cause, for *ex hypothesi* in such a system every physical event has wholly physical antecedent causes which are necessary and sufficient for its occurrence. But – as Leibniz made us aware – God can still be invoked to explain why *this* universe was actualized rather than any of the infinitely many other possible universes equally well exhibiting determinism with an infinite past: for, of course, there can be any amount of difference between all these universes in respect of both particular matters of fact and general laws (even if there are certain very high-level conservation principles which they all obey). The point of these remarks is to impress upon us that there can be more to explaining a pattern of events than is explained by specifying the immediate causes of each event in the pattern. And that "more," I suggest, is precisely what minds can characteristically contribute to the causal explanation of physical phenomena. Minds – whether infinite or merely finite – can explain some of the otherwise inexplicable patterns in nature. For it is of the essence of intelligence to seek patterns and to attempt to impose them upon otherwise chaotic phenomena.

An objection that I anticipate here is that the history of science already reveals to us ways in which order can emerge out of chaos without any need to appeal to the intervention of mind, however attractive such an appeal might pretheoretically have been. The classic example is provided by the evolution of animal life-forms, which are no longer explained by appeal to divine providence but rather in terms of the "blind" mechanisms of random variation and natural selection. But to carry this strategy over to the case of deliberative action itself – in which of all cases appeal to the intervention of mind is surely *not* out of place – is effectively to commit oneself to some form of eliminative materialism, denying any genuine causal role (and hence even genuine existence) to mental states like volitions or desires. Thus suppose it is suggested, say, that modern "chaos theory" could in principle explain why a particular maze of neural events should converge upon a specific peripheral event E, in a case of what we would pretheoretically describe as intentional action.[18] Then that is in effect to deny that the agent's *volition* or *desire* for E to occur could after all have a genuine causal role to play in the genesis of E. For a "chaos theory" explanation of the convergence upon E would precisely *deny* that E had a highly salient and virtually sure-fire singular cause, such as a volition or desire is conceived to be with respect to the peripheral event that is its object.

To be sure, evolutionary theory and chaos theory *can* explain how a wide variety of forms and patterns – from wing-feathers to weather-fronts – may emerge out of apparently random sets of events.[19] But such explanations are *rivals* to explanations in terms of mental or intentional causation if directed at the same explananda, and hence are not representable as ways of showing how the latter kind of causation might be implemented in physical systems. I should add, however, that I see not the slightest reason to suppose that chaos theory, or some evolution-inspired theory of neural functioning, *could* in fact provide an alternative – much less a superior – explanation of (what we would have to cease calling) deliberative action to that which is provided by appeal to intentional mental states like volition or desire.[20] So, in sum, the alternative to my dualist approach that is now being canvassed is neither particularly promising on its own terms nor acceptable in principle to any but a committed eliminativist. And, finally, I should in any case stress that my main aim in this paper has not been to argue conclusively that dualism must be *true*, but only to show that it *can* handle the problem of psychophysical causation, and consequently that it remains a viable competitor in the field of rival theories of the mind–body relationship.[21]

Notes

1 See P.F. Strawson, *Individuals: An Essay in Descriptive Metaphysics* (London: Methuen, 1959), ch. 3.

2 On token–token identity theories, see further my *Kinds of Being: A Study of Individuation, Identity and the Logic of Sortal Terms* (Oxford: Blackwell, 1989), pp. 113–114, 132–133. On supervenience theories, see further my "Substance and Selfhood," *Philosophy* 66 (1991), pp. 81–99, esp. pp. 93–94.

3 Cf. T. Crane, "Why Indeed? Papineau on Supervenience," *Analysis* 51 (1981), pp. 32–37.

4 See further my "Against an Argument for Token Identity," *Mind* 90 (1991), pp. 120–121.

5 See further Crane, *op. cit.*, and also T. Crane and D.H. Mellor, "There is No Question of Physicalism," *Mind* 99 (1990), pp. 185–206.

6 I myself do not offer a definition of the physical in this paper, but since no positive thesis of mine hinges on the provision of one, this is excusable. I am content to characterize dualism as the view that mental events and processes are neither identical with nor supervenient upon brain events and processes, and to assume that the latter must qualify as "physical" by any criterion.

7 The next few paragraphs owe much to R.S. Woolhouse, "Leibniz's Reaction to Cartesian Interactionism," *Proceedings of the Aristotelian Society* 86 (1985/86), pp. 69–82 and D. Garber, "Mind, Body, and the Laws of Nature in Descartes and Leibniz," *Midwest Studies in Philosophy* 8 (1983), pp. 105–133.

8 See H. Bondi, *Cosmology*, 2nd edn (Cambridge: Cambridge University Press, 1961), ch. 12.

9 See R. Montague, "Deterministic Theories," in his *Formal Philosophy* (New Haven: Yale University Press, 1974) and E. Nagel, *The Structure of Science* (London: Routledge, 1961), ch. 7.

10 See Bondi, *op. cit.*, ch. 11 and E.A. Milne, *Modern Cosmology and the Christian Idea of God* (Oxford: Clarendon Press, 1952), ch. 6.

11 I must stress that what follows *is* only a sketch of an alternative approach for dualists to explore: a fully-fledged theory along the lines to be proposed would require a great deal more work, not least of an empirical nature.

12 There is indeed empirical evidence that the pattern of brain activity which characteristically precedes voluntary movement is (until very shortly before the movement) non-specific, widely distributed over the cortex, and built up gradually: for details, see K.R. Popper and J.C. Eccles, *The Self and its Brain:*

An Argument for Interactionism (Berlin: Springer, 1977), pp. 282ff, 293f. I might remark that I am not wholly sympathetic to Eccles' own interactionist theory, though some features of his approach accord with mine.

13 That neural structures themselves exhibit a fractal geometry is well attested: see further A.L. Goldberger *et al.*, "Chaos and Fractals in Human Physiology," *Scientific American* 262 (1990), pp. 34–41.

14 I am not suggesting that the trees lack "tips" because the fractal branching proceeds literally *ad infinitum*, with each pathway constituting an infinite series of causally related events the totality of which occurs within a finite period of time – an idea reminiscent of one invoked by Lukasiewicz in attempted refutation of determinism: see J. Lukasiewicz, *Aristotle's Syllogistic from the Standpoint of Modern Formal Logic*, 2nd edn (Oxford: Clarendon Press, 1957), pp. 207–208. For although such a scheme is mathematically possible, it seems unlikely from a physical point of view. Rather, the trees lack "tips" because the fractal branching proceeding from any one peripheral event eventually merges seamlessly into the prior causal history of the whole brain, fusing with the branching of other trees. Incidentally, empirical confirmation of my claim that the mind does not *initiate* causal chains of neural events leading to peripheral events is provided by Libet's finding that conscious awareness of the will to act occurs some 350 msec *after* the onset of the pattern of brain activity ("readiness-potential") which characteristically precedes voluntary movement, though still some 200 msec before the movement itself occurs: see B. Libet, "Unconscious Cerebral Initiative and the Role of Conscious Will in Voluntary Action," *Behavioral and Brain Sciences* 8 (1985), pp. 529–566.

15 See further J.L. Mackie, *The Cement of the Universe: A Study of Causation* (Oxford: Clarendon Press, 1974), pp. 34ff.

16 See, e.g., P.M. Churchland, *A Neurocomputational Perspective: The Nature of Mind and the Structure of Science* (Cambridge, Mass.: MIT Press, 1989), ch. 1. For forceful criticism, see L.R. Baker, *Saving Belief: A Critique of Physicalism* (Princeton: Princeton University Press, 1987), ch. 7.

17 This commits me to holding that events can stand in causal relations to *facts*, and not just to other events, contrary to the assumption that I have been working with until now: but I am happy to accept the commitment. On the distinction between event causation and fact causation, see further J. Bennett, *Events and their Names* (Oxford: Clarendon Press, 1988), pp. 21ff. Incidentally, don't ask me *how* the mind can do what I am now proposing that it does, if what you want is an answer which will render its mode of operation "intelligible" in the sense discussed at the beginning of the paper.

18 For a general and not unduly technical account of chaos theory, see J.P. Crutchfield *et al.*, "Chaos," *Scientific American* 255 (1986), pp. 38–49.

19 It appears that chaos theory has an important role to play in explaining certain patterns of behaviour in the autonomic nervous system, such as the normal heartbeat: see Goldberger *et al.*, *op. cit.* But such bodily activity is, of course, precisely *not* deliberative.

20 For one recent evolution-inspired theory of brain function, see G.M. Edelman, *Neural Darwinism: The Theory of Neuronal Group Selection* (Oxford: Oxford University Press, 1989).

21 I am grateful to colleagues and students in Durham for their reactions to an earlier version of this paper, and to members of the editorial panel for helpful comments on the penultimate draft.

4

Jaegwon Kim, "Lonely Souls: Causality and Substance Dualism"*

I. The problem

We commonly think that we, as persons, have both a mental and a bodily dimension – or, if you prefer, mental aspects and material aspects. Something like this dualism of personhood, I believe, is common lore shared across most cultures and religious traditions, although such beliefs are not always articulated in the form of an explicit set of doctrines as in some established religions. It is often part of this "folk dualism" that we are able to survive bodily deaths, as "pure spirits," and retain all or most of the spiritual aspects of ourselves after our bodies are gone.

Spirits and souls as conceived in popular lore seem to have physical properties as well, if only vestigially physical ones, and are not what Descartes and other philosophical dualists would call souls or minds – wholly immaterial and nonphysical substances outside physical space with no physical properties whatever. For example, souls are commonly said to *leave* the body when a person dies and *rise upward* toward heaven, indicating that they are thought to have, and are able to change, locations in physical space. And they can be heard and seen, we are told, by people endowed with special virtues and in especially propitious mental states. Souls are sometimes pictured as balls of bright light, causing the air to stir barely perceptibly as they move and even emitting some unearthly sounds. Perhaps, they are composed of pure immaterial Cartesian souls and some

* Thanks to David Armstrong, Jerry Katz, Noah Latham, Barry Loewer, Eugene Mills, Timothy O'Connor, Alvin Plantinga, and Ernest Sosa for helpful comments and suggestions. This paper is descended from a paper first presented at a conference on mind–body dualism at the University of Notre Dame in March 1998.

Jaegwon Kim, "Lonely Souls: Causality and Substance Dualism" (slightly modified), in Kevin Corcoran (ed.), *Soul, Body and Survival: Essays on the Metaphysics of Human Persons* (Cornell University Press, Ithaca, 2001), pp. 30–43.

rare, strange matter unknown to science. As is well known, Descartes thought of persons in a similar way – the difference is that for Descartes a person is a combination, or "union" as he called it, of an immaterial soul and a human body composed of ordinary matter, not some weird and ethereal stuff.

But does this conception of a person, as something made up of two radically diverse components, a body and an immaterial soul, make sense, whether the body is made up of ordinary matter or some mysterious ethereal stuff? One contention of this paper is that there is reason to think that such a conception of a person is ultimately unintelligible. My arguments will be principally based on considerations of causation – specifically, I will try to undermine the idea that immaterial souls can causally interact with material bodies, thereby forming a "union" with them. If I am right, it is an idea that we cannot make intelligible. In fact, it will be seen that much of the interest of my discussion, such as it is, concerns issues about mental causation and, more generally, causation itself, and, if the general drift of my arguments is correct, it will cast serious doubts on the usefulness and viability of the very notion of immaterial substance. My claim about the Cartesian "two-component" conception of persons will fall out as a corollary of what I have to say about mind–body causation under substance dualism.

II. Descartes and mental causation

Conventional wisdom has it that the downfall of Cartesian mind–body dualism was due to its inability to account for mental causation. In particular, as has often been noted, his radical dualism of mental and material substances was thought to be inconsistent with the possibility of causal transactions between them. Princess Elizabeth of Bohemia famously asked Descartes to explain "how man's soul, being only a thinking substance, can determine animal spirits so as to cause voluntary action."[1] According to one commentator, Richard A. Watson, the perceived inconsistency between the radical duality of minds and bodies and their causal interaction was not only a major theoretical flaw in Cartesianism but also the historical cause of its demise.[2]

The reason standardly offered for the supposed incoherence of Cartesian interactionist dualism is that it is difficult to conceive how two substances with such radically diverse natures, one in space–time with mass, inertia, and the like and the other lacking wholly in material properties and not even located in physical space, could stand in causal relations to each other. Apparently, various principles about causation, such as that cause and effect

66

must show a certain degree of "mutual affinity" or "essential likeness," or that there can be no "greater reality" in an effect than there is in its cause, seem to have played a role. Anthony Kenny, for example, writes: "On Descartes' principles it is difficult to see how an unextended thinking substance can cause motion in an extended unthinking substance and how the extended unthinking substance can cause sensations in the unextended thinking substance. The properties of the two kinds of substance seem to place them in such diverse categories that it is impossible for them to interact."[3] That is pretty much all that Kenny has to say about Descartes's troubles with mind–body causation – and, as far as I know, that is pretty much all we get from Descartes's critics and commentators. But as an argument this is incomplete and unsatisfying. As it stands, it is not much of an argument – it hardly gets started; rather, it only expresses a vague dissatisfaction of the sort that ought to prompt us to look for a real argument. Why is it incoherent to think that there can be causal relations between "diverse substances"? Why is it "impossible," as Kenny puts it, for things with diverse natures to enter into causal relations with one another? Just what sorts of diverseness make trouble and why?

It has not been an easy matter to pin down exactly what is wrong with positing causal relations between substances with diverse natures and explain in concrete terms what it is about the natures of mental and material substances that make them unfit to enter into causal relations with each other. And there have been commentators who have defended Descartes against the Kenny-style charge of incoherence. Louis Loeb is one of them.[4] Loeb's defense rests on his claim that Descartes was a proto-Humean about causation – namely that, for Descartes, causality amounted to nothing more than brute regularity, or "constant conjunction," and there can be no a priori metaphysical constraint, such as resemblance or mutual affinity, on what events can be causally joined with what other events. Loeb quotes from Descartes:

> There is no reason to be surprised that certain motions of the heart should be naturally connected in this way with certain thoughts, which they in no way resemble. The soul's natural capacity for union with a body brings with it the possibility of an association between thoughts and bodily motions or conditions so that when the same conditions recur in the body they impel the soul to the same thought; and conversely when the same thought recurs, it disposes the body to return to the same conditions.[5]

On Loeb's view, then, the fact that soul and body are of such diverse natures was, for Descartes, no barrier at all for their entering into the most intimate

JAEGWON KIM

of causal relations, to form a "union" that is a person. Taking Loeb's word
for it that Descartes was indeed a proto-Humean on the nature of causation, his point seems to me sufficient as a response to the kind of vaguely
worded and inchoate objection of the sort that Kenny and many others have
advanced. But does the constant conjunction view of causation really help
save Descartes? I don't think it does, and the reason, I think, is simple to
see and also instructive.

Suppose that two persons, Smith and Jones, are "psychophysically
synchronized," as it were, in such a way that each time Smith's mind wills
to raise his hand so does Jones's, and vice versa, and every time they will
to raise their hands, their hands rise. There is a constant conjunction
between Smith's mind's willing to raise a hand and Smith's hand's rising,
and, similarly, between Jones's mind's willing to raise a hand and Jones's
hand's going up. If you are a pure constant conjunctionist about causation,
this would suffice for saying that a given instance of Smith's willing to raise
a hand is a cause of the subsequent rising of his hand, and similarly in the
case of Jones. But there is a problem here. For we see that instances of
Smith's mind's willing to raise a hand are constantly conjoined not only
with his hand's rising but *also with Jones's hand's rising*, and, similarly,
instances of Jones's mind's willing to raise a hand are constantly conjoined
with Smith's hand's rising. So why is it not the case that Smith's volition
causes Jones's hand to go up, and that Jones's volition causes Smith's
hand to go up?

If, however, you believe in the idea of "causal necessity" and think that
constant conjunction, if it is to support a causal relation, must hold with
necessity in some form, you have a prima facie answer: the constant and
regular conjunction between Smith's mind's willing to raise a hand and
Jones's hand going up is only coincidental, carrying no force of necessity.
And this is perhaps manifest in the fact that there are no counterfactual
dependencies between these events: for example, it is not true that if
Smith had not willed that a hand should rise, Jones's hand would not have
gone up.

But it won't do to say that after all Smith wills *his* hand to rise and that's
why his willing causes his hand, not Jones's hand, to rise. It isn't clear what
this reply can accomplish, but it begs the question on hand. The reason is
that, according to the standard interpretation of Descartes, what makes
Smith's hand Smith's, not Jones's – that is, what makes Smith's body the
body with which Smith's mind is "united" – is the fact that there is specially
intimate and direct causal commerce between the two. To say that this is
the body with which this mind is united is to say that this body is the only
material thing that this mind can *directly* affect – that is, without other
bodies serving as causal intermediaries – and that all changes this mind can

68

cause in other bodies are caused by changes in this body. This is *my* body, and this is *my* arm, because it is something that I can move without moving any other body. I can raise *your* arm only by grabbing it with my hand and pulling it up.[6] And something similar must obtain in the direction of body-to-mind causation as well. The "union" of a mind and a body that Descartes speaks of, therefore, presupposes mental causation. Whether or not this interpretation of Descartes is historically correct, a causal account of "ownership" seems the most natural option for substance dualists, and I do not know of noncausal alternatives that make any real sense.

I have heard some people say that we could simply take the concept of the mind's "union" with a body as a primitive, and that it is simply a brute and unexplainable fact, perhaps divinely ordained, that this mind and this body are integrated into a proper union that is a person. But I find such an approach unhelpful. For it seems to concede that the notion of "union" of minds and bodies, and hence the notion of a person, are unintelligible. If God chose to unite my body with my mind, just what is it that he did? I am not asking *why* he chose to unite this particular mind with this partic- ular body, or *why* he decided to engage in such activities as uniting minds and bodies at all, or *whether* he, or anyone else, could have powers to do things like that. If God united my mind and my body there must be a rela- tionship R such that a mind stands in relation R to a body if and only if that mind and that body constitute a unitary person. Unless we know what R is, we do not know what God did. Again, we are not asking *how* God managed to establish R between a mind and a body – as far as we are concerned, that can remain a mystery forever. We only want to know *what* God did.

III. Causation and the "pairing" problem

The difficulty we have seen with Loeb's interpretation of Descartes as a Humean in matters of causation, I believe, points to a more fundamental difficulty in the idea that mental substances, outside physical space, can enter into causal relations with objects in physical space, a difficulty that is not resolved when, as above, some sort of "necessary connection" is invoked as a constituent of causal relations. What is perhaps more surprising, the very same difficulty besets the idea that such nonspatial mental substances can enter into any sort of causal relations, whether with material things or with other mental substances.

Let us begin with a simple example of physical causation: two rifles, A and B, are simultaneously fired, and this results in the simultaneous death of two persons, Andy and Buddy. What makes it the case that the firing of rifle A caused Andy's death and the firing of rifle B caused Buddy's death, and not the other way around? What are the principles that underlie the correct and incorrect *pairings* of cause and effect in a situation like this? We can call this "the causal pairing problem," or "the pairing problem" for short.[7]

Two possible ways for handling this problem come to mind.

1. We can trace a continuous causal chain from the firing of rifle A to Andy's death, and another such chain from the firing of B to Buddy's death. (Indeed, we can, with a high-speed camera, trace the bullet's path from rifle A to Andy, etc.) No causal chain exists from the firing of A to Buddy's death, or from the firing of B to Andy's death.

2. We look for a "pairing relation," R, that holds between A's firing and Andy's death and between B's firing and Buddy's death, but not between A's firing and Buddy's death or B's firing and Andy's death. In this particular case, when the two rifles were fired, rifle A, not rifle B, was located at a certain distance from Andy and pointed in his direction, and similarly with rifle B and Buddy. It is these *spatial relations* (distance, orientation, etc.) that help pair the firing of A with Andy's death and the firing of B with Buddy's death. Spatial relations seem to serve as the "pairing relations" in this case, and perhaps for all cases of physical causation involving distinct objects.

The two methods may be related, but let us set aside this question for now.

Let us now turn to a situation involving nonphysical Cartesian souls as causal agents. There are two souls, A and B, and they perform a certain mental action, as a result of which a change occurs in material substance M. We may suppose that mental actions of the kind involved generally cause physical changes of the sort that happened in M, and, moreover, that in the present case it is soul A's action, not soul B's, that caused the change in M. Surely, such a possibility must exist. But ask: What relation might perform the job of pairing soul A's action with the change in M, a relation that is absent in the case of soul B's action and the change in M? Evidently, no spatial relations can be invoked to answer this question, for souls are not in space and are not able to bear spatial relations to material things. Soul A cannot be any "nearer" to material object M, or more appropriately "oriented" with respect to it, than soul B is. Is there anything that can do for souls what space, or the network of spatial relations, does for material things?

Now consider the possibility of causality within a purely mental world – a world inhabited only by Cartesian souls. Soul A acts in a certain way at time *t* and so does soul B at the same time. This is followed by certain changes in two other souls, A* and B*. Suppose that actions of A and B are causes of the changes in A* and B*. But which cause caused which effect? If we want a solution that is analogous to case 2 above for rifle firings and dyings, what we need is a pairing relation R such that R holds for A and A* and for B and B*, but not for A and B* or for B and A*. Since the entities are immaterial souls outside physical space, R cannot be a spatial, or any other kind of physical, relation. The radical non-spatiality of mental substances rules out the possibility of invoking any spatial relationship for the cause–effect pairing.

Evidently, then, the pairing relation R must be some kind of psychological relation. But what could that be? Could R be some kind of intentional relation, such as thinking of, picking out, and referring? Perhaps, soul A gazes at soul A* and B*, and then picks out A*, and causes a change in it. But how do we understand these relations like gazing at and picking out? What is it for A to pick out A* rather than B*? To pick out something outside us, we must be in a certain epistemic relationship with it; we must perceive it somehow and be able to distinguish it from other things around it – that is, perceptually identify it. Take perception: What is it for me to perceive this tree, not another tree that is hidden behind it and that is qualitatively indistinguishable from it? The only credible answer is that the tree I perceive is the one that is causing my perceptual experience as of a tree, and that I do not see the hidden tree because it bears no causal relation to my perceptual experience.[8] Ultimately, these intentional relations must be explained on the basis of causal relations (this is not to say that they are entirely reducible to causality), and I do not believe we can explain what it is for soul A to pick out soul A* rather than B* except by positing some kind of causal relation that holds for A and A* but not for A and B*. If this is right, invoking intentional relations to do causal pairings begs the question: we need causal relations to understand intentional relations. Even if intentional relations were free of causal involvements, that would not in itself show that they would suffice as pairing relations. In addition, they must satisfy certain structural requirements; this will become clear below.

We are not necessarily supposing that one single R will suffice for all causal relations between two mental substances. But if the physical case is any guide, we seem to be in need of a certain kind of "space," not physical space of course, but some kind of a nonphysical coordinate system that gives every mental substance and every event involving a mental substance a *unique location* (at a time), and which yields for each pair of mental entities a determinate relationship defined by their locations. Such a system of "mental space" could provide us with a basis for a solution to the pairing problem, and enable us to make sense of causal relations between nonspatial mental entities. But I don't think that we have the foggiest idea what

71

such a framework might look like or what psychological relations might generate such a structure.

What about using the notion of causal chain to connect the souls in the cause–effect relationships? Can there be a causal chain between soul A's action and the change in soul A*, and between soul B's action and the change in soul B*? But do we have an understanding of such purely mental causal chains? What could such chains be like outside physical space? Hume required that a cause–effect pair of events that are spatiotemporally separated be connected by a causal chain of *spatially contiguous* events. It is difficult to imagine what kind of causal chain might be inserted between events involving two mental substances. Presumably we have to place a third soul, C, between soul A and soul A*, such that A's action causes a change in C which in turn causes the change in A*. But what could "between" mean here? What is it for an immaterial and nonspatial thing to be "between" two other immaterial and nonspatial things? In the physical case it is physical space that gives a sense to betweenness. In the mental case, what would serve the role that space serves in the physical case?

One might say: For C to be "between" A and A* in a sense relevant to present purposes is for A's action to cause a change in C and for this change to cause a change in A*. That is, betweenness is to be taken simply as causal betweenness. This of course is the idea of a causal chain, but it is clear that this idea does not give us an independent handle on the pairing problem. The reason is simple: it begs the question. Our original question was: How do we pair soul A's action with a change in soul A*? Now we have two pairing problems instead of one: First, we need to pair soul A's action with a change in a third soul, C, and then pair this change in C with the change in A*. This means that methods 1 and 2 above are not really independent. The very idea of a causal chain makes sense only if an appropriate notion of causation is already on hand, and this requires a prior solution to the pairing problem. This means that method 2 is the only thing we have.

We are, therefore, back with 2 – that is, with the question of what psychological relations might serve the role that spatial relations serve in the case of physical causation. The problem here is independent of the Humean constant conjunction view of causation, and therefore independent of the difficulty we raised for Loeb's defense of Descartes. For suppose that there is a "necessary," counterfactual sustaining, regularity connecting properties F and G of immaterial mental substances. A mental substance, A has F at t, and at t^*, an instant later, two mental substances, B and C, acquire property G. I think we would like the following to be a possible situation: A's having F at t causes B to have G at t^*, but it does not cause C to have G at t^*. If so, there must be an intelligible account of why A acts on B but not on C, and such an account must be grounded in a certain relation, a "pairing relation," holding for A and B but not for A and C. What conceivable psychological or intentional relation, or system of such relations, could serve this purpose? I don't have a clue.

If these reflections are not entirely wrongheaded, our idea of causation requires that the causally connected items be situated in a spacelike framework. It has been widely believed, as we noted, that Cartesian dualism of two substances runs into insurmountable difficulties in explaining the possibility of causal relations across the two domains, mental-to-physical and physical-to-mental – especially the former. But what our considerations show is that there is an even deeper difficulty – substantival dualism is faced with difficulties even in explaining how mental-to-mental causation is possible, how two distinct Cartesian souls could be in causal commerce with each other. Perhaps Leibniz was wise to renounce all causal relations between individual substances, or monads – although I have no idea as to his actual reasons for this view. A purely Cartesian world seems like a pretty lonely place, inhabited by immaterial souls each of which is an island unto itself, totally isolated from all other souls. Even the actual world, if we are immaterial souls, would be a lonely place for us; each of us, as an immaterial entity, would be entirely cut off from anything else, whether physical or nonphysical, in our surroundings. Can you imagine an existence that is more solitary than an immaterial self?

IV. Causation and space

The fact, assuming this to be a fact, that the causal pairing problem for physical causation is solved only by invoking spatial relations tells us, I believe, something important about physical causation and the physical domain. By locating each and every physical item – object and event – in an all-encompassing coordinate system, this framework imposes a determinate relation on every pair of items in the physical domain. Causal structure of the physical domain, or our ability to impose a causal structure on it, presupposes this space–time framework. Causal relations must be selective and discriminating, in the sense that there can be two objects with identical intrinsic properties such that a third object causally acts on one of them but not the other (this can be stated for events as well), and, similarly, that there can be two intrinsically indiscernible objects such that one of them, but not the other, causally acts on a third object. If so, there must be a principled way of distinguishing the two intrinsically indiscernible objects in such causal situations, and it seems that spatial relations provide us with the principal means for doing this. Although this isn't the place to enter into detailed discussion, spatial relations have the right sorts of properties; for example, causal influences generally diminish as distance in space increases, and various sorts of barriers can be set up in the right places in space to prevent or impede propagation of causal influences (though perhaps not gravity!). In general, causal relations between physical objects or events depend crucially on their spatiotemporal relations to each other; just think of the point of establishing alibis – "I wasn't there," if true, is sufficient for "I didn't do it." And the temporal order alone will not be sufficient to provide us with such a basis. We need a full space–time framework for this purpose. It wasn't for nothing, after all, that Hume included "contiguity" in space and time, as well as constant conjunction, among his conditions for causal relations. From our present perspective, the contiguity condition can be seen as Hume's response to the pairing problem.

If this is right, it gives us one plausible way of vindicating the critics of Descartes who, as we saw, argued that the radically diverse natures of mental and material substances preclude causal relations between them. It is of the essence of material substances that they have determinate positions in the space–time framework and that there is a determinate spatiotemporal relationship between each pair of them. Descartes of course talked of extendedness in space as the essence of matter, but we can broadly construe this to include other spatial properties and relations for material substances. Now consider the mental side: as I take it, the Cartesian doctrine has it that it is part of the souls' essential nature that they are outside the spatial order and lack all spatial properties, though they do belong to the temporal order. And it is this essential nonspatiality that makes trouble for their participation in causal structures. What is interesting is that it isn't just mind-to-body causation but also mind-to-mind causation that is put in jeopardy.

We have already seen how difficulties arise for mind-to-body and mind-to-mind causation. Unsurprisingly, body-to-mind causation fares no better. Let's quickly run through this: Consider a physical object causally acting on a mental substance, causing it to have property F at time t. Suppose that there is another mental substance that comes to have F at t, but not as a causal result of the physical object's action. How might the pairing problem be solved in this case? To solve it, we need to identify a relation R that holds between the physical object and the mental substance it causally affects but which does not hold between the physical object and the second mental substance. The only relation that can do this for physical objects is the spatial relation, but the very essence of a mental substance excludes it from any and all spatial relations. Moreover, given the fact that we could not devise a system of pairing relations for the domain of mental substances, it seems out of the question that we could generate a system that would work across the divide between the mental and material realms. If this is true, not even epiphenomenalism is an option for the substance dualist.

I am not claiming that these considerations are what motivated the anti-Cartesian argument that mind–body causal interaction is incoherent given the radically diverse natures of minds and bodies, or the absence of similarity or affinity between them. I am only suggesting that this may be one way to flesh out the critics' worries and show that there is a real and concrete basis for these worries. Causal interaction is precluded between mental and material substances because of their diverse essential natures – more specifically, because of the essential spatiality of bodies and the essential non-spatiality of minds. Causality requires a pairing relation, and this diversity between minds and bodies does not permit such relations connecting minds and bodies. What the critics perhaps didn't see was the possibility that essentially the same difficulty bedevils causal relations *within* the realm of the minds as well.

V.   Can we locate souls in space?

These reflections might lead one to wonder whether it would help the cause of substance dualism if mental substances were at least given spatial locations, not as extended substances like material bodies but as extensionless geometric points. After all, Descartes spoke of the pineal gland as "the seat" of the soul, and it is easy to find passages in his writings that seem to give souls positions in space, although this probably was not part of his official doctrine. And most people who believe in souls, philosophers included, appear to think that our souls are in our bodies at least – my soul in my body, your soul in your body, and so on. But I would hazard the guess that this conviction is closely associated with the idea that my soul is in direct causal contact with my body and your soul with your body. The pineal gland is the seat of the soul for Descartes, as I take it, only because it is where unmediated mind–body causal interaction takes place. If all this is right, this confirms my speculation that mind–body causation generates pressure to somehow bring minds into space, which, for Descartes, is exclusively the realm of the matter.

In any case, putting souls into physical space may create more problems than it solves. For one thing, we need a principled way of locating each soul at a particular point in space. It is difficult to imagine how this can be done (why can't we locate all the souls in the world in one place, say in this empty coffee mug on my desk, like the many angels on the head of a pin?). It would obviously beg the question to locate my soul where my body, or brain, is on the ground that my soul and my body are in direct causal interaction with each other. Second, if locating souls in space is to help with the pairing problem, it must be the case that no more than one soul can occupy any given spatial point; for otherwise spatial relations would not suffice to uniquely identify each soul in relation to other souls in space. This is analogous to the so-called principle of "impenetrability of matter," a principle whose point can be taken as the claim that space provides us with a criterion of individuation for material things. According to it, material objects occupying exactly the same spatial region are one and the same. What we need is a similar principle for souls, that is, a principle of "impenetrability of souls": Two distinct souls cannot occupy exactly the same point in space. But if souls are subject to spatial exclusion, in addition to the fact that the exercise of their causal powers is constrained by spatial relations, why aren't souls just material objects, albeit of a very special and strange kind? Moreover, there is a prior question: Why should we think that a principle of spatial exclusion applies to immaterial souls? To solve the pairing problem for souls by placing them in space requires such a principle, but that's not a reason for thinking that the principle holds; we cannot wish it into being – we need independent reasons and evidence.

Moreover, if a soul, all of it, is at a geometric point, it is puzzling how it could have enough structure to account for all the marvelous causal work it is supposed to perform and explain the differences between souls in regard to their causal powers. You may say: A soul's causal powers arise from its mental structure, and mental structure doesn't take up space. But what is mental structure? What are its parts and how are the parts configured in a structure? If a soul's mental structure is to account for its distinctive causal powers, then, given the pairing problem and the essentiality of spatial relations for causation, it is unclear how wholly nonspatial mental structure could give an explanation of a soul's causal powers. To go on: If souls exclude each other for spatial occupancy, do souls exclude material bodies as well? If not, why not? It may be that one's dualist commitments dictate certain answers to these questions. But that would hardly show they are the "true" answers. We shouldn't do philosophy by first deciding what conclusions we want to prove, or what aims we want to realize, and then posit convenient entities and premises to get us where we want to go. When we think of the myriad problems and puzzles that arise from locating souls in physical space, it is difficult to escape the impression that whatever answers that might be offered would likely look ad hoc and fail to convince.

I have tried to explore considerations that seem to show that the causal relation indeed exerts a strong, perhaps irresistible, pressure toward a degree of homogeneity over its domain, and, moreover, that the kind of homogeneity it requires probably includes, at a minimum, spatiotemporality, which arguably entails physicality. The more we think about causation, the clearer becomes our realization that the possibility of causation between distinct objects depends on a shared spacelike coordinate system in which these objects are located, a scheme that individuates objects by their "locations". Are there such schemes other than the scheme of physical space? I don't believe we know of any. This alone makes trouble for serious substance dualisms and dualist conceptions of personhood – unless, like Leibniz, you are prepared to give up causal relations substances altogether. Malebranche denied causal relations between all finite substances, reserving causal powers exclusively for God, the only genuine causal agent that there is. It is perhaps not surprising that among the dualists of his time, Descartes was the only major philosopher who chose to include minds as an integral part of the causal structure of the world. In defense of Descartes, we can ask: What would be the point of having souls as immaterial substances if they turn out to have no causal powers, not even powers to be affected by things around them? Before we castigate Descartes for his possibly unworkable metaphysics, we should applaud him for showing a healthy respect for common sense in his defense of mental causation and his insistence on making sense of our intuitive dualistic conception of what it is to be a person.

Notes

1 Margaret Wilson, ed., *The Essential Descartes* (New York: New American Library, 1969), 373.
2 Richard A. Watson, *The Downfall of Cartesianism 1673–1712* (The Hague: Martinus Nijhoff, 1966).
3 Anthony Kenny, *Descartes* (New York: Random House, 1968), 222–23.
4 Louis E. Loeb, *From Descartes to Hume* (Ithaca: Cornell University Press, 1981). See 134–49.
5 Anthony Kenny, trans. and ed., *Descartes' Philosophical Letters* (Oxford: Oxford University Press, 1963), 210. I am rather dubious as to whether this passage supports Loeb's Humean interpretation of Descartes, for Descartes is using here causal verbs, "impel" and "dispose," to describe the regularities. But Loeb may well be right, and I am not in a position to challenge him on this point.
6 Does this exclude telekinesis? Yes. This probably is the main reason why there is something a priori strange about telekinesis. If telekinesis were a widespread everyday phenomenon, that might very well undermine the idea that each of us has a distinct body.
7 I first discussed this problem in "Causation, Nomic Subsumption, and the Concept of Event," *Journal of Philosophy* 70 (1973): 217–36. I was prompted to reflect on the issues involved here by John Foster's "Psychophysical Causal Relations," *American Philosophical Quarterly* 5 (1968): 64–70.
8 This of course is the causal theory of perception. See H.P. Grice, "The Causal Theory of Perception," *Proceedings of the Aristotelian Society*, supp. vol. 35 (1961).

IC

IDEALISM

5

Howard Robinson, "The General Form of the Argument for Berkeleian Idealism"

My objective in this essay is to outline the argument required to establish Berkeleian idealism. At some points I shall sketch the argument briefly, at others I shall argue in greater depth. My aim in presenting a survey containing hard argument at some crucial places is to show that the overall endeavour of defending idealism is more plausible than it is generally believed to be.

I. The problem

A defender of Berkeleian idealism must justify two propositions. He must prove (1) that the ordered nature of our experience both requires and is susceptible to explanation by reference to something other than experience itself. He has to show (2) that the postulation of a non-human spiritual agent or agents provides a better account of the structure of experience than the postulation of a mind-independent physical world.

These propositions can be further broken down. There are various grounds for claiming that experience requires explanation. The simplest, and Berkeley's own, is that the very existence of ideas of sense requires explaining "since it is repugnant that they should subsist by themselves."[1] As we do not produce our own sensations, there must be an external cause. Hume notoriously denied that nothing could come into existence without a cause, and I can see no way to disprove this.[2] If one accepts that Hume is not demonstrably wrong, then it is necessary to point to some particular feature of experience other than its mere existence which puts it in need of explanation. The natural feature to select is its orderedness – the fact that

Howard Robinson, "The General Form of the Argument for Berkeleian Idealism," in John Foster and Howard Robinson (eds), *Essays on Berkeley: A Tercentennial Celebration* (Clarendon Press, Oxford, 1985), pp. 163–86.

our sensations are so regular in their contents that we can interpret them as being of a stable physical environment.

Furthermore, arguing that experience *requires* explanation is not the same as showing that it is susceptible to it, for it could be the case either that (i) experience called for an explanation, but that nothing would count as an explanation of it, so that its nature was necessarily mysterious and improbable or that (ii) the nature of experience did not require an explanation – there was no reason not to treat it as a brute fact – yet it might have an explanation (i.e. a cause) in fact. I know of no philosopher who adopts the former view, but it is a prima facie conceivable position. Someone who held both that the order of experience was a priori improbable but that there could not be such a thing as causal power or necessity might hold that experience both called for, and could not receive, a causal explanation. Someone who disagreed with Hume about a priori probabilities but agreed with him on causation might think himself to be in this position. (ii) is the position of someone who holds, with Hume, that there are no a priori probabilities and hence that the ordering of experience does not stand in need of an explanation, and, hence, that a sceptical phenomenalism is all that reason justifies; but believes also that there might in fact be an external cause of experience. Whether one chose to believe in such a cause would be a matter of taste or instinct – perhaps determined by "natural belief." Someone in this position who chose to explain experience by the direct action of God would be a sort of Berkeleian idealist, but would not be holding that his theistic idealism was positively supported by reason. A more likely position under (ii) is that of a naturalistic Humean who would allow instinct to lead him to believe in an external physical world, though reason in no way supports the conclusion. A hard-line Humean position would be that experience neither requires nor is susceptible to explanation and that any object of instinctual belief located beyond experience could not figure as an explanation or cause of experience: if it be present there, it is an epiphenomenon with regard to the physical world and its postulation serves only to satisfy our impulse to believe. An orthodox Berkeleian, on the other hand, must hold both that experience requires and that it is susceptible to explanation.

The argument for (2) involves both discrediting the postulation of a mind-independent physical world and giving credibility to the belief that some non-human mind or minds are responsible for our experience. Typically, most of the argument is devoted to the former task, and, this done, it is usually assumed to be enough to argue that a will could be efficacious in bringing about the phenomena. Like most other writers I, too, shall concentrate on how to discredit the postulation of a mind-independent physical world.

Although (2) is, logically, the second task, usually one aspect of it is given priority over (1). My account of what a Berkeleian has to do would probably have seemed more familiar if I had broken it down into three stages. The first would have been the refutation of the naïve realist theory of perception, followed by (1) and (2) as given above. This is wrong for two reasons. First, if the order in experience requires no explanation then we would have no reason to believe that the objects of our experience or anything lying behind them existed when we were not perceiving them. (Which means, in the case of things lying behind experience – i.e. of any represented, but not directly perceived reality – we would have no reason to believe in its existence at all.) Thus, even if naïve realism were true and the immediate objects of sense were physical, we would have no reason to believe they existed when not perceived unless there were something inherently improbable in those objects existing only at the times we perceived them. Rationally, it would be mere speculation to suggest that they existed otherwise. Secondly, the refutation of naïve realism is really part of the process of discrediting belief in the physical world and hence belongs with (2). From an idealist standpoint, the significance of refuting naïve realism is not only that it generates epistemological difficulties for belief in a mind-independent physical world, but that it is the first stage in an argument which is meant to prove that we can form no positive conception of the fundamental properties of the matter of such a world. Its purpose is to show that the sensible qualities of which we are aware are mind-dependent and hence to put difficulties in the way of attributing them to anything independent of mind. By contrast, if naïve realism were possible then it would seem that there was no difficulty attributing a sufficiency of properties to matter, for we could attribute the primary and secondary qualities of sense to it.

If I am right in describing the Berkeleian's task as that of proving (1) and (2), it follows that his opponents are, first, the sceptic and, second, the devotee of mind-independent matter. The arguments against the sceptic are sometimes passed over briefly, because the idealist's dialectical opponent is usually, nowadays, a physical realist and so both parties have an interest in playing down the sceptical arguments. An idealist, however, has less right than most to dismiss counter-intuitive positions. I shall try, therefore, to take seriously the sceptical opinion that the organized structure of our experience is something which requires no explanation.

II. Scepticism concerning a priori probabilities

Our experience is sufficiently highly structured for us to be able to interpret it as experience of a fairly stable physical world. The phenomena are pretty highly and reliably ordered. Our natural response to this is to assume that experience has a cause: it doesn't just happen in this ordered way by accident. Berkeley himself takes it for granted that, given that we do not cause our own sensations, some other agent must be responsible, but this assumption is rationally justified only if it is rational to accept the principle that it is objectively improbable that such order would occur by accident – that is, without something explaining (presumably by causing) it. I shall call this the principle that Order Requires Explanation. In applying this principle to our experience we are presuming that it is an a priori principle; we do not learn a posteriori that the order in the phenomena has a cause, for we have reason to believe that experience has a cause only if we take its orderedness as being evidence for such an hypothesis. The Humean tradition rejects the application of a priori probabilities to empirical questions. On the other hand, belief in such an application is as difficult to doubt as it has been to justify. Common sense argues that if there are no causal constraints on a succession of events then those events should not exhibit clear and distinctive regularities. We assume that, in the absence of causal influence, all possibilities are equally likely and that no striking regularities should emerge. The sceptical rebuttal of this common sense assumption is well known.[3] The sceptic argues that a highly ordered sequence is, a priori, no less probable than any other. Taking the example of throws of a die, a succession of ten throws of six is no more improbable than a succession of any other numbers, including apparently random ones; e.g. 2, 4, 1, 4, 6, 3, 3, 2, 5, 1. This is because at each throw each number has a chance of one in six, so a sequence of sixes and the random series each have a probability of $\frac{1}{6} \times \frac{1}{6} \times \frac{1}{6} \ldots$ for each throw; that is, of $1^{10}/6^{10}$. It follows from this that an apparently random sequence of experiences would have just the same improbability as an ordered sequence. A priori probabilities merely state how many possibilities there are and assign a probability to each of one over the total.

Although this argument often fails to carry conviction, it has proved difficult to refute. Indeed most non-sceptical philosophers, especially ones not expert in probability theory – are tempted to follow the strategy of the Scottish minister preaching on the problem of evil ("Brethren, this is a very difficult problem, which we must look squarely in the face, and pass on"). Their intuition that order requires explanation remains undimmed, though they abandon the task of justifying it. I, too, am tempted by such involuntary modesty and what I have to say is extremely tentative.

Perhaps one can solve the problem by switching attention from the probability of particular series to the probability of types of series. What we are interested in is the probability of a series which is *so structured that a conscious subject is able to discern manageable recurrent regularities.*

There are obviously many more series of logically possible experiences that do not fit this requirement than ones that do. What we are interested in is the probability of a series *qua* member of such a class. As there are many more series which do not fit this requirement than ones that do, a priori it is improbable that one fitting the requirement would occur by chance. A standard reply to this is that we can always invent a class for any given series which makes it improbable in this way. Thus supposing the series 2, 4, 1, 4 etc. actually occurred, we could say that it belonged to the class containing it alone, or a class containing it and another equally undistinguished series, and argue that it was a priori improbable that a member of such a class should occur. It is essential to my suggested approach that it be true and important that such classes do not pick out a genuine kind of series, but are only classes connected by enumeration. Assuming (as I shall) that there is a difference between genuine kinds, whose members are really similar, and artificial classes, then classes of the arbitrary sort are just irrelevant to questions concerning whether a particular *kind* of series is probable or not. It is natural to suspect that the introduction of kinds of series in preference to individual series as bearers of probability is jerrymandering. Why aren't the probabilities of individual series relevant too? I think the answer to this might lie in the fact that probabilities are comparative and an improbability is only salient if it shows an event to be improbable relative to the other options. All series taken as individuals are equiprobable, so the outcome would not have been less improbable if a different series had occurred. From the perspective of genuine kinds of series this is not so, and on this basis series can be differentiated.

I leave this issue with no confidence that I have advanced it. Even if I have not, this is no comfort to the realist, and the Berkeleian can still fall back on the strong intuition that there must be *some* explanation of order, though the intuition is not yet justified. Popper rejects solipsism on the grounds that he is sure that he could not have produced the music of Bach; to establish the principle that manifest order is not self-explanatory we need only add to Popper's modesty a conviction that the music of Bach did not write itself.[4]

III.   Berkeley's credibility gap

Given that it can be shown that it is rational to believe that the order in experience requires an explanation, we have to decide what is the best explanation. The most obvious hypothesis is that it is explained by the activity of a mind-independent physical world. This is the most obvious explanation because it spontaneously seems to us that it is an independent physical world we experience. Notice that I do not say that it spontaneously seems to us that it is such a world which *explains* our experience, but that it spontaneously seems to us that we experience a mind-independent physical world. No doubt it follows from the latter that the physical world does explain our experience and no doubt only a moment's reflection is needed to see this, but it is important that what we believe spontaneously is not some explanatory theory which could be common to both direct and representative realism, but is direct realism itself. This is directly relevant to how one should weigh the relative merits of the arguments for idealism and for physical realism.

When it comes to evaluating Berkeley's idealism, even rational thinkers are often openly not disposed to proportion their belief to the evidence or the force of the arguments. Boswell's remarks are typical: "to me it is not conceivable how Berkeley can be answered from pure reasonings"; "though we are satisfied his doctrine is not true, it is impossible to refute it."[5] Berkeley's audience, philosophers or intelligent laymen, have their consciences tried because they are conscious both of the power of the argument and of their unwillingness to accept the conclusion however powerful the argument may seem. The question is whether this common refusal to follow the argument where it appears to lead is a genuinely disreputable stubbornness, or a manly determination to stand four-square on common sense. I shall argue that it is the former and my principal ally in so arguing is Hume. Hume correctly diagnosed the source of the resistance to Berkeley and showed it to be unreasonable. Not all Berkeley's opponents accept his arguments whilst rejecting his conclusions. Many reject the arguments too. The danger of bad faith comes principally at the point where the arguments purporting to refute naïve realism are accepted, but the idealist response to this situation is ruled out of court. That is, the prejudice against Berkeley shows itself in those who, following the refutation of naïve realism, are determined to hang on to a representative realism, however obscure, rather than adopt idealism, because they believe a priori that any form of physical realism is more plausible than idealism. Hume sees through this prejudice and argues that "[representative realism] has no primary recommendation either to reason or the imagination, but acquires all its influence on the imagination from the former [i.e. naïve realism]."[6]

In other words, the seemingly overwhelming intuitive priority of realism entirely draws its force from our feeling that the immediate objects of our awareness are mind-independent physical objects. This is the sole origin of the psychological power of realism. Once one is persuaded that these immediate objects are not mind-independent, then the intuitive priority we give to realism has entirely lost its rationale. It is bad faith to pretend that representative realism answers to the intuitions which make realism psychologically compelling, because to get to the representative level we have already discounted as false the substance of that intuition, which was that the immediate objects of awareness are mind-independent. This is surely one matter on which Hume's sceptical argument rings true. Once naïve realism is refuted, the explanation of the nature of the physical world is entirely open and no one type of account starts with any greater legitimate claims on our credence than any other.

Against this it might be argued that a theory which makes out the origin of our experience to be rather like the world which naïve realism posits is inherently more plausible than a theory which makes the origin of our experience very different from what we had supposed. Now such a theory is likely to go some way towards satisfying our psychological urge towards realism, but that does not mean that it answers to the intuitive ground or rationale of that urge. To see this, suppose that all our experience seemed to have subjective immediate objects, so that we were no more naturally inclined to think of our visual, tactile, or auditory sense-data as external than we are to think it of our pains. Suppose, further, that we were nevertheless still prone to look for an explanation of our experience and of why it fitted into such useful patterns. In these circumstances a representative physical realist explanation would not commend itself intuitively any more than the alternatives. Indeed, we would probably be inclined to doubt whether the notion of something rather like these phenomena yet outside the mind really made sense, just as we think it obvious that nothing outside the mind could resemble pains or other bodily sensations. It is surely not plausible to claim that representative realism is made genuinely more plausible by its fitting a *mistaken* understanding of our experience (namely our inclination to take the immediate objects of our experience as independent of mind) when, if we were not prone to make that mistake, it would seem especially implausible amongst the accounts of the origin of experience.

IV.   The refutation of naïve realism

In the *Third Dialogue* Philonous says,

> I do not pretend to be a setter-up of *new notions*. My endeavours tend only to unite and place in a clearer light that truth, which was before shared between the vulgar and the philosophers: the former being of opinion, that *those things they immediately perceive are the real things*; and the latter, that *the things immediately perceived, are ideas which exist only in the mind*. Which two notions put together, do in effect constitute the substance of what I advance.[7]

In the present section I am concerned with Berkeley's defence of the philosophic refutation of that naïve realism which takes the immediate objects of sense to be extra-mental. In section V I shall defend the vulgar view that the realm of immediate experience is the physical world.

As well as his a priori arguments against all forms of extra-mentality, Berkeley has some conceptual arguments specifically against naïve realism. They roughly follow the line of thought that what we perceive are ideas, and such ideas are sensations and that it is "plainly repugnant" that sensations should exist independently of sense.[8] But in addition to these rather dubious arguments he also employs both the argument from illusion and the causal argument.[9] Although he employs this last argument only in the First Dialogue, I wish to take it up because it is the best prospect for refuting naïve realism. Pitcher states Berkeley's version of the causal argument as follows:

Let us suppose for the moment that there really are, surrounding us, physical objects that exist independently of my mind, and that have colors, emit sounds, and so on. The question then arises: how can anyone perceive the supposed properties of these supposed distant objects? The answer must be that the properties start, or anyway contribute to, a causal chain of events that includes the stimulation of the perceiver's relevant sense organs and, later, of his brain. The brain stimulation, finally, produces in the perceiver's soul sensations of red, C-sharp, or whatever – i.e., ideas of sense. The properties that a person directly perceives, then – i.e., what we have called perceptual properties – are, in every case, nothing but ideas of sense.[10]

At first sight it might seem odd for Berkeley to use such an argument. Tipton claims that it is not available to an idealist because it depends on the physical realism of the scientists:

Locke could take for granted the scientific explanation of perception because he believed that neurophysiological processes played a causal role in the production of data. Not so with Berkeley. Berkeley is quite clear on the point that any physiological apparatus which we suppose plays a causal role in the production of ideas will itself consist of ideas and thus be incapable of playing the causal role.[11]

This criticism is mistaken. Russell said that naïve realism led to science and that science refutes naïve realism.[12] *If sound*, the causal argument shows that the discoveries of science are inconsistent with naïve realism, and I doubt whether any naïve realist would wish to be committed to denying the accounts of the causal mechanisms of perception which science discovers. Hence the argument is a legitimate *reductio*. Berkeley's idealist reinterpretation of what it is for there to be a mechanism of perception is on the same footing as his reinterpretation of any other micro-physical explanation. It simply reinterprets the view that the neural process caused the experience, saying instead that in those circumstances under which someone observing S's brain would have certain experiences, which we treat as perceptions of, for example, the visual cortex, S himself will invariably be having visual experience.

Pitcher's objection to the causal argument is a familiar one, namely that it confuses the false claim that the stimulation of the brain produces an object of awareness with the correct claim that it produces a state or act of awareness of something.[13] This objection will be unsound if it is the case that a state or act of awareness must invariably possess an internal object, for then production of the state or act carries with it the production of an object. I shall argue that this is the case.

First, it is a necessary truth that without an object in some sense there cannot be an experience, for any experience must be *of* something. Second, in the case of pure hallucination the object of the experience must be something generated internally by the brain, and not an external thing, for there is no appropriate external thing involved. So if we can show that what is true of hallucinations must also be true of normal perception the causal argument is vindicated. What we require to achieve this generalization is the truth of the following two propositions:

(1) It is theoretically possible by activating some brain process which is involved in a particular type of perception to cause a hallucination which exactly resembles that perception in its subjective character.

(2) It is necessary to give the same account of both hallucinating and perceptual experiences *when they have the same neural cause.* Thus, it is not, for example, plausible to say that the hallucinatory experience involves a mental image or sense-datum, but that the perception does not, if the two experiences have the same proximate – i.e. neural – cause.

Together they entail that perceptual processes in the brain produce some subjective experiential content – that is some object of awareness which cannot be identified with any feature of the external world. This is contrary to any form of naïve or direct realism, which requires that, in ordinary perception, features of the external world constitute the only objects or contents of experience. It is irrelevant for present purposes whether the subjective experiential content be construed as sense-data, qualia, intentional objects, or modes of sensing (though I think the first two options represent the most plausible accounts). What matters is that there is some sort of "veil of perception" dividing us from the mind-independent world.

Of these two propositions, the second is the more controversial. Indeed, (1) seems to be generally accepted and for present purposes I shall assume that it is uncontroversial and concentrate on (2).

A perceptual realist will probably decide to concede (1), accepting that the appropriate brain process is sufficient to produce a given subjective type of experience however it itself is brought about; whether, that is, it is activated in the course of perception, or artificially. To prevent the refutation of naïve realism he therefore denies proposition (2). He denies that the brain process produces more than a bare act of awareness in the case of normal perception, whilst allowing that the same process produces an internal object when artificial stimulation produces a hallucination. "I agree," he might say, "that being in a certain brain state is a sufficient internal causal condition for having an experience of a certain subjective type, but I believe that we must give a separate account of hallucinatory or artificial experiences from that which we give of normal experiences. When the brain process is induced artificially, the subject has a hallucination, and he 'sees' or 'has' images of physical objects, but when the objects are the causes of the brain state in the normal way, then he sees them themselves directly." Someone who argues in this way is adopting what Hinton calls *the disjunctive analysis* of experience: that is, he is claiming that two radically different states constitute subjectively similar experiential states, as between perception and hallucination. There would, of course, be nothing strange in such a theory, if we had not stipulated that both experiences have the same immediate neural cause. This is what makes it seem strange to say that the experiences which result from this one type of cause can be of intrinsically different types.

The disjunctive theory has achieved something of a vogue, but its two most recent exponents, Snowdon and McDowell, ignore the difficulties posed for the theory by allowing that perception and hallucination might have the same immediate cause.[14] Pitcher and Hinton, however, take note of the case where hallucination and perception operate through precisely the same brain state and see the need to defend the view that nevertheless the products of that brain state are essentially different in the two cases.[15]

The general principle lying behind (2) could be put in the form of the slogan "Same proximate cause, same immediate effect." Call this slogan "S." Pitcher accepts S, but in a form which would not sustain (2). He says, "this principle S although it may be true for every cause-and-effect pair, is not true for them *under every description*."[16]

The idea is that though the immediate effects of a certain brain state may always involve "seeming to see something red," and thus in that respect always be of the same type, they may also be of different types in that sometimes the immediate effect will fall under the description "hallucinating something red" and sometimes under the description "seeing something red." The general principle that immediate effects of the same type of proximate cause need not be of identical type under all descriptions is quite sound. For example, if someone strikes identical nails into identical walls with identical hammers with identical force the effect in one might be describable as "the picture's being hung" and in the other as "the gas pipe's being severed," each description applying to only one of the effects. The description common to both effects will concern a nail moving a certain distance into a wall. However, it is plainly not arbitrary what the common description is. If it were sufficient for the satisfaction of S simply that there be *some* common description then it would become vacuous. Suppose that, despite the qualitative identity of hammers, nails, walls, and force of blow, in one case the nail penetrated one inch, in the other two inches. This would involve an infringement of S, for the same cause would have had relevantly different effects, but nevertheless the effects are identical under some descriptions; e.g. the description "a nail's penetrating a wall." It is often said that any two things are similar in some respect: if this is true, then any effects of some one type of cause will be identical under some description or other. To save S from vacuity it is therefore essential to say something about the descriptions under which the events must be similar: some restrictions must be imposed. Intuitively, it is not difficult to do this. The different descriptions which applied to the nail applied in virtue of features of the situation more remote from the causal event – the hammer blow – than was its immediate effect, the nail's movement. They relate either to context – e.g. the presence of the picture – or to further effects – e.g. the nail's piercing the pipe. Intuitively, S applies to the most specific and immediate characterization of the effect. Thus the communality of a generic description such as "entering the wall" will not satisfy S if one nail entered by one inch, the other by two: nor will it do that both hammerings had the remote or mediate effect of hanging a picture if each did so by moving the nail a different distance. The former situation parallels what Pitcher says about the mental state caused by the brain process. He says that the same brain state will always cause a "seeming to see something red" but that sometimes it will do this by causing a genuine seeing and sometimes by causing a hallucination, where these two states are quite different. We do not in fact have a genuine case of S where the effects brought under the same description are analysed as having relevantly different structures or component elements. A sense-datum theorist, for example, has no problem with this, for he says that the same brain state causes something – a having of a sense-datum – by which it causes either seeing or hallucinating and which common element is a part of both larger effects, each depending also on further circumstances. But on the disjunctive analysis seeing and hallucinating are not to be analysed into a shared element plus differing extra features.

It seems, then, that when one realizes the need to apply S to certain sorts of effect, Pitcher's argument will not work. Hinton does what is required and simply denies S. He says that it rests on "dubious and arbitrary general and metaphysical beliefs ... about effects of causes."[17] He presents an explicitly disjunctive analysis of such generic concepts as "experience" or "seeming to see." Such expressions are taken as referring not to something common to both perception and hallucination but generically to a disjunction of them both. Thus he deals with the final outcome of the causal process as follows:

The impulse reaches certain specified structures, and then what? My continuation was, "– and then one perceives a flash of light or has the illusion of doing so, as the case may be, according to the nature of the initial stimulus."[18]

He is quite aware of the motives that gave rise to belief in S:

But it is natural to make some such retort as this, that what then happens cannot depend on the initial stimulus; what happens next must be the same, whether the initial stimulus was light striking the retina, or an electric current passing through the retina, or whatever it was.[19]

But he rejects this "natural retort" on the grounds cited above, namely that it rests on arbitrary and dubious metaphysical beliefs. Hinton holds that S is a sound principle when applied to causal laws that relate physical or public events, but that it is mere prejudice to extend it to psychophysical connections (or, for that matter, to mental–mental ones). His argument is that we know that S applies to physical laws because we can in these cases identify the effect independently of identifying the cause – this is part of the publicity of physical events – and have thereby been able to establish empirically the truth of S in these contexts. But we cannot do this for mental effects; for example, it follows *ex hypothesi* that one cannot tell the type of hallucination that we are considering from a perception without knowing the causal ancestry of the experience: the experience itself does not reveal which it is. Therefore we are not compelled to apply S in the mental case, for we have not identified the nature of the effect independently of the causal context and verified that S applies.[20] However, this is an adequate argument only if there are no general considerations in favour of S – only if, that is, S relies upon empirical proof in each type of context.

First, we can concede that one is under no compulsion to accept S, if by compulsion one means logical necessity. Second, we can concede that S is more incontrovertibly established in purely physical contexts. However, it seems that there are good reasons for extending it to psychophysical contexts and indeed for adopting it as a perfectly general principle. The reason for applying it in psychophysical contexts is that if one does not do so one is saddled with two bizarre mysteries. First, there would be the problem of trying to understand how a brain process could alter its causal properties in response to its own remote causes. It would be as if the brain knew that when it was being activated artificially it needed to provide subjective content for the experience, whereas when activated normally it knew that the external world would perform that task for it! Second and consequently, there is another problem, namely that unless S applies to psychophysical connections the existence of hallucinations becomes a mystery. Given that Hinton is conceding that hallucinations could be produced by stimulating just those brain states involved in perception (i.e. he concedes (1)) how are we to make sense of why this should be so if it is not by thinking of these as cases in which the state is activated and performs its normal function – i.e. has its normal upshot – in an abnormal context? Otherwise the production of hallucinations in this sort of way would seem to cast the brain state in a role something like that of a Cartesian demon, producing an effect specialized solely to the context of deception. This would be a strange expedient to adopt in an attempt to save direct realism. In order to make sense of why it should be possible to produce hallucinations in the way specified in (1) we have to be able to make sense of the notion of "what the brain state does in both cases" – that is of a common element not itself analysable into Hinton's disjunction. Thus we face a choice between accepting the radical unintelligibility of why there should be hallucinations in these contexts or of accepting that S is applicable here.

It seems, therefore, that S is sound (*contra* Hinton) and sound in a strict enough sense (*contra* Pitcher) to justify (2), for the production of an internal object of experience is part of the brain state's immediate effect and failure to characterize it as "internal" would be to fail to describe it specifically. Hence Berkeley is right to believe that the causal argument refutes naïve realism.

V.   The refutation of representative realism

Once naïve realism is refuted the idealist can see his objective in sight. Naïve, common-sense realism can no longer be transformed into a philosophical position, and physical realism has lost any legitimate hold on our intuition.

At this point the modern idealist's argument must diverge from Berkeley's own in one important respect. Berkeley's argument against representative realism rests fundamentally on the impossibility of conceiving of unperceived objects. His arguments for this have a stronger and a weaker form. In the strong form he argues that the very notion of unperceived existence is unintelligible: the weaker version is specifically directed against Locke's theory and maintains that the existence of primary without secondary qualities is inconceivable.[21] The emphasis on what we can conceive is associated with an imagist theory of thought and together they generate a very restricted and nominalist theory of meaning. If such a theory is defensible at all, I know of no way of defending it. Nevertheless, the spirit of Berkeley's attack on representative realism can be disconnected from these doubtful arguments. Two genuinely Berkeleian thoughts can be used to generate arguments against a transcendental material realm beyond the veil of perception. First there is the thought that we can give no adequate content to our conception of such matter. Second is the conviction that our conception of the physical world is so tied to the manifest and discoverable structure of the world as we experience it that nothing transcendental and possibly remote from that structure could qualify as our world. We shall see that these lines of thought are mutually supporting. I shall begin by pursuing the first.

Apart from undermining the intuitive legitimacy of realism, the main significance of the refutation of naïve realism is that it makes it implausible to impute non-dispositional secondary qualities to matter itself. The arguments for this are too well known to need rehearsing here. This leaves us with the problem of trying to decide what properties matter is supposed to possess. Notoriously, the Cartesian idea that it is purely geometrical will not do for it leaves no distinction between matter and empty volumes: a filler for these volumes is required. Notoriously too, Locke's filler, solidity, will not do the job, for that quality collapses on examination into a composite of the dispositional-cum-relational property of impenetrability, and the secondary quality, hardness. What the physical realist requires is clearly put by Harré:

> Solidity is the alleged quality, the possession of which is responsible
> for the fact that two material things cannot occupy the same place at

the same time and is logically connected with impenetrability, the power to resist penetration, in that the possession of the former is supposed to account for the manifestation of the latter.[22]

Mackie appears to believe that this is possible. He says that our conception of solidity is "only the indirect and relative notion of it as the supposed or inferred ground of a power which is itself learned from its manifestation."[23]

We can presume here that Mackie intends "ground" to signify something stronger than contingent connection, otherwise the grounding of impenetrability would no more explain impenetrability than would colour if all impenetrable objects were coloured. I take it that Mackie is after something of the sort Harré describes. But how can there be a necessary connection between a dispositional and a categorical property? Such a connection can be made trivially by use of a "bridge concept." A puncture is by definition a double event consisting first of the breaching of a surface, then of the escape of a contained gas or liquid, but the existence of this concept does not explain the connection of the first event with the second. Similarly, calling something "solid" if it possessed quality Q in association with impenetrability, would not explain how the former grounded the latter. Mackie seems to be confused about what would constitute the prescribed sort of necessary connection. He says: "Modern physics will not use [solidity]; but electric charge is one feature which has come into physical theory to play a corresponding part, and mass (rest mass) is perhaps another."[24]

Electric charge is akin to concepts such as energy or field and is a dispositional or power concept. Mass, too, is either defined in, for our purposes, a question-begging way as a "quantity of matter" or simply records how objects behave in their interactions. Now some philosophers have claimed that the physical world consists essentially of relational properties – generally of active powers or fields. Hume's objection to conceiving bodies as volumes of impenetrability is still essentially the objection to such conceptions, namely that they are vacuous.[25] An object cannot simply be a spatially extended capacity to effect other spatially extended capacities to effect . . . An ontology of mutual influences is not an ontology at all unless the possessors of the influence possess more substantial features.

It might be objected that the claim that there could not be a categorical property which was logically connected with a power is an a priori prejudice, probably inspired by atomistic and empiricist assumptions: we cannot legislate a priori about what types of property there may be. But the objection to this sort of property is not based upon such an appeal to intuition.

It is trivially true that there is no property P the possession of which analytically entails the possession of a power Q, P not itself being explicitly a power. As the connection would not be nominal or analytic, it would have to be *de re* a posteriori. In fact two sorts of such connection are sometimes considered. The first is not properly a posteriori, but rather lives in the shadow cast by the "paradox of analysis." There are some truths which are not analytic in the sense of being trivially obvious or merely verbal, but which are still knowable a priori by conceptual analysis. Those physicalists who seek to prepare the way for identifying mental with physical properties by giving the former a topic neutral analysis see truths about mentality in this way. One way in which a necessary connection might be discovered between some non-power property and a power would be if a philosophical analysis uncovered an unobvious connection between them. I do not see how this method could lead to a solution in the present case, because I do not see how, once the non-power concept was fully analysed, if it revealed a power-entailing element, that could be other than contingently associated with its non-power aspect. Anyway, I know of no such analysis. The second and properly a posteriori necessary connection which is nowadays discerned between concepts would be some form of *de re* necessity. It is often said, for example, that a *de re* necessity links the property of being hot and that of possessing a high mean kinetic energy of its constitutive molecules. Such necessities, however, seem to be more a matter of verbal definition than is generally allowed. Even if we decide to annex the term "heat" to phenomena associated with mean kinetic energy and "mean kinetic energy" to behaviour which includes the normal phenomena of heat, it does not follow that there could not be phenomena in all other respects just like either of them yet lacking this connection. (Indeed, if Kripke is correct in his explanation of how such identities can be a posteriori, there must be such possibilities.)[26] Heat and mean kinetic energy, therefore, seem to be only "bridge concepts," like "puncture" and do not non-trivially explain the connection between the two sets of phenomena which belong paradigmatically to each. The same would apply to any attempt to explain impenetrability in terms of any underlying quality or structure.

The situation is, therefore, that the following three negative propositions concerning the nature of matter can be proved beyond reasonable doubt: (i) that matter does not possess non-dispositional secondary qualities; (ii) that matter does not possess any sort of primary quality which could logically ground its basic powers – e.g. its impenetrability; (iii) that matter cannot consist solely of spatially arranged powers or dispositions. As far as I can see this leaves only one possible conception, namely (iv) that matter possesses some unknown quality or qualities, conceived on analogy with a sensible quality such as colour. As we have shown that there cannot be an internal or necessary connection between an intrinsic quality of this sort and causal properties, the causal properties of matter must be dictated by laws or powers which are only contingently connected with the matter: that is, there is nothing about the intrinsic nature of the matter which determines what laws govern its conduct, nor to prevent its being governed by different laws at different times.

We have done all we can to develop the first Berkeleian thought, which was that we can give no adequate content to our concept of matter, and have forced the realist to (iv) in his defence. Against that we now bring to bear our second Berkeleian thought, which was that a transcendental world beyond the veil of perception would not be the physical world that we inhabit.

The picture of the physical-cum-empirical world which the present conception of matter, when combined with the refutation of naïve realism, requires might be called a "two-world" picture. There is the world of transcendental physical reality, which consists of objects possessing the unknown qualitative nature, and there is the common, collective, or intersubjective phenomenal "world," which is the world-as-experienced. The latter world is usually thought of as *representing* the former by *resembling* it, at least in structural or abstract ways. One thing which is meant by saying that the phenomenal world represents or resembles the transcendental physical world is that the scientific laws devised to apply to the former, if correct, also apply (at least approximately) to the latter. Physical science, though developed through our acquaintance with the world-as-experienced, aspires to describe the formal features of the world-in-itself. On the present theory of matter, however, there is no need for there to be such a match between the laws discovered by empirical science and those which govern the world in itself. The world-in-itself consists of the qualitative core contingently governed by certain laws. Amongst these laws are those which determine how the world will appear. In this way the transcendental physical world gives rise to the empirical world. But it is logically possible that there might be many different exclusive sets of laws which fix how the world should appear. It follows that, from how it appears we cannot infer how it works in itself. There is an uncertainty in our conception of how the transcendental world is which parallels that which is generally supposed to exist in our explanation of actions from beliefs and desires. It has been argued that different combinations of imputed beliefs and desires will explain the same action, and, as we have no independent way of fixing either parameter, the explanation is holistic and undecidable. Similarly, our experience is the product of (a) how the world-in-itself really works and (b) the laws transforming that into experience. *Ex hypothesi* we have no direct access to either of these things, for we experience the product, the intersubjective empirical world. Remember that the qualitative core of itself entails no particular laws, for the qualitative core intrinsically possesses no causal properties, not even of solidity. It is as if the transcendental world was in a code which is being interpreted by a machine to the internal working of which we can have no access. The messages that reach us are clear and consistent, but that is quite compatible with the original code being changed daily, so long as the principles on which the interpreting machine works also change. It follows that it is both epistemically and logically (or *metaphysically*, as some say in such contexts) possible that the transcendental world operates on laws quite different from those which a perfect science of the empirical world would generate. That it is logically (or metaphysically) possible follows from the fact that the intrinsic nature of the world (i.e. the unknown qualitative nature of its matter) entails nothing about the laws of its operation and hence provides no constraints on how it should operate and hence on whether its laws of operation should alter. (It is not reasonable to say that the identity of the transcendental world changes if its laws change, because the very same quality-bearing objects could come to be governed by different laws: if they are the same objects then it is the same world.) It is, therefore, not merely the case that we do not know whether the transcendental world follows the laws derivable from the empirical world, but that, even if it does, it is logically and metaphysically possible that it might cease to do so, without our being any the wiser.

This creates a problem for the physical realist. The physical realist's conception of the physical world has two components. The first is that the world is mind-independent; the second is that the physical world is what physical science investigates and hence its nomological structure is what physical science approximately uncovers. Both these are necessary truths for the physical realist. It is the former which distinguishes his position as realist, but the second condition is also essential, both (a) because it is a conceptual truth that the physical world is what physical science investigates, if it investigates anything real, and (b) because if mind-independence is severed from being the object of science then "physicality" comes to mean simply "non-mentality," and to have no positive content of its own. But the concept of physicality is not that thin. It combines both the idea of being "out there" with that of being investigable by us in certain ways. A world not accessible to certain sorts of investigation – paradigmatically those exhibited by physical science – is not the physical world. Once naïve realism is refuted these two conditions come apart, for the following reasons.

The representative realist holds that the transcendental world is the physical world. It is a necessary condition for the truth of this that the transcendental world have approximately the same nomological structure as a developed physical science would attribute to the physical world. An argument against physical realism might initially proceed:

(1) As I have shown it is possible that the transcendental world does not realize, even approximately, physical laws.

(2) It has already been established that realizing physical laws, at least approximately, is a necessary condition for being the physical world.

Therefore:

(3) It is possible that the transcendental world be not the physical world.

(4) Identities are necessary.

Therefore:

(5) The transcendental world is not the physical world.

The necessity of identities is essential to the argument. The representative realist's natural inclination will be to say that the transcendental world is the physical world provided that the transcendental world embodies scientific laws; if it does not then there is no physical world, however things may appear. This could be maintained consistently with the necessity of identities provided that the realization (or not) of scientific laws were an essential feature of a given transcendental world, so that if the actual transcendental world embodies physical laws, it then qualifies essentially as physical. But the contingent connection between laws and ultimate objects means that it is a contingent feature of a given transcendental world whether or not it realizes a given set of laws. Suppose that the transcendental world did realize physical laws and thus itself counted as physical, it might cease to realize them. The realist would then have to say that the physical world had ceased to exist, though the transcendental world, which had been the physical world, endured. Wiggins has, I think, shown that identity cannot work in this way, provided that the referring expression in question (in this case "the transcendental world" and "the physical world") pick out a substantial and complete object.[27] The transcendental world could be, then cease to be, the physical world only if being the physical world was a matter of playing a certain role, like being Lord Mayor, not a matter of being a particular thing or substance. But if we adopt this view of being physical, then it follows that what is physical (what "plays that role") is not essentially physical. First, this is not our normal (especially not our normal realist) conception of the physical world: and second it concedes to the non-realist that the physical world is a logically secondary product of the action of something not itself physical. Additionally, the representative realist's premiss that there is no physical world unless it is the transcendental world is not plausible. Suppose that initially the transcendental world realized physical laws, but then came not to do so, though the world remained unchanged from the viewpoint of all conscious beings within the natural or empirical realm. It seems wrong to say that the physical world would have ceased to exist just because the way it was sustained by the transcendental reality had changed. If that change were gradual, there would be no point at which it was natural to say that, unbeknownst to us, the physical world had ceased to exist. If this is accepted, then being the physical world is not just a role played by the transcendental world because the physical world can continue when the transcendental world ceases to play that role.[28]

In sum, my position is this: acceptance that if there is a physical world then that is what physical science investigates, and observation of the logical features of identity, together show that what lies behind the veil of perception cannot be the physical world. Naïve realism, Berkeleian style, is correct; the physical world is the world of experience, irrespective of what more distant reality sustains it. And the world of experience is essentially mind-dependent because given the falsehood of the physical realist version of naïve realism the immediate objects of experience are mind-dependent.

VI. The transcendental cause of experience

To complete the Berkeleian programme it is necessary to show that God is the transcendental reality which causes experience. The argument so far is neutral on this matter, being compatible with taking that reality to be, for example, a Kantian noumenal world. All that we have proved is that the transcendental cause of experience is not the physical world. What can be concluded, I think, is that, if one is a theist, then it is rational to assign God the Berkeleian role, because the only reason a theist resists this position is that he wishes God to create and use the physical world as an instrument, but we have proved that the phenomenal, not the transcendental world, is the physical world. To demonstrate the full conclusion it would probably be necessary to prove that only a mind can be an agent, hence nothing non-mental could cause our experience. Then it would be necessary to prove that there is just one such agent and he is God; or, perhaps, that God is the controlling principal among such agents. It would be disingenuous to suggest that lack of space is the only reason why I cannot prove this at present.

Notes

1 *Principles*, 146.
2 *A Treatise of Human Nature*, ed. J. Selby-Bigge (Clarendon Press, Oxford, 1888), Bk I, Pt. iii, Sect. 3, 78–82.

3 See, for example, A.J. Ayer, *Probability and Evidence* (Macmillan, London, 1972), 27–53.
4 Karl Popper, *Realism and the Aims of Science*, ed. W.W. Bartley III (Hutchinson, London, 1983), 83.
5 *Life of Johnson* (Oxford University Press, London, 1953), 333.
6 *A Treatise of Human Nature*, 211.
7 *Dialogues*, 262.
8 *Principles, 4.*
9 For use of both, see *Dialogues*, 178–91.
10 G. Pitcher, *Berkeley* (Routledge, London, 1977), 106–7.
11 I.C. Tipton, *Berkeley: the Philosophy of Immaterialism* (Methuen, London, 1974), 253.
12 B. Russell, *An Inquiry into Meaning and Truth* (George Allen and Unwin, London, 1940), 13.
13 *Berkeley*, 108.
14 P. Snowdon, "Perception, vision and causation," *P.A.S.* LXXXI (1980–1), 176–92. J. McDowell, "Criteria, defeasibility and knowledge," *Proc. Brit. Acad.* 1982 (Oxford University Press, London, 1983), 455–79.
15 G. Pitcher, *A Theory of Perception* (Princeton University Press, New Jersey, 1971), 54–7. J. Hinton, *Experiences* (Clarendon Press, Oxford, 1973), 75–93.
16 *A Theory of Perception*, 56–7.
17 *Experiences*, 75.
18 Ibid.
19 Ibid.
20 Ibid., 77–82.
21 Stronger version, *Principles*, 22–4; weaker version, *Principles*, 9–10.
22 R. Harré, *Principles of Scientific Thinking* (Macmillan, London, 1970), 305.
23 J.L. Mackie, *Problems from Locke* (Clarendon Press, Oxford, 1976), 25.
24 Ibid.
25 *Treatise* I. iv. 4, 228–30.
26 S. Kripke, *Naming and Necessity* (Blackwell, Oxford, 1980), 132 f.; excerpts from this work are reprinted as Chapter 7 in this volume.
27 D.R.P. Wiggins, in either *Identity and Spatio-Temporal Continuity* (Blackwell, Oxford. 1967), 1–25, or *Sameness and Substance* (Blackwell, Oxford, 1980), 15–44.
28 My argument for idealism is a much simplified version of one employed by John Foster in *The Case for Idealism* (Routledge, London, 1982), Part III. My argument and Foster's both involve the claim that a transcendental world could have an essentially different nomological organization from the one we attribute to the physical world. To reach the idealist conclusion, I am content to appeal to the intuition that a physical world must realize the laws uncovered by a complete physical science, from which it follows that a transcendental world, not essentially possessing that organization, is not physical. Foster's argument does not rest on such an appeal to intuition, because he proves that the possible differences in nomological organization between the transcendental world and the world as pictured in physical science include possible differences in the geometries of their spaces. It follows from this that the space of a transcendental world could not be physical space and hence, *a fortiori*, that such a world is not the physical world. It will not have escaped

some readers' notice that the claim that a transcendental world might fail to realize scientific law is challenged by Hilary Putnam in the final lecture of *Meaning and the Moral Sciences* (Routledge, London, 1980). It is not possible here to investigate the relationship between his form of anti-realism and the idealism for which I am arguing, except to say that they are entirely different.

QUESTIONS

1   At one point in his chapter, Zimmerman considers whether my being disembodied is "more conceivable" than my being identical with (a part of) my body. In which senses of "conceivable," if any, is this true? In these same senses, is conceivability a reliable guide to possibility, so that in this respect the dualist would have an edge over the materialist?

2   Consider the following parody of Swinburne's argument: "Suppose I have an axe – call it *A* – and I remove the head from the handle. *A*'s head goes on to a new handle, forming axe *B*, and *A*'s handle receives a new head, forming axe *C*. Now there clearly must be some fact of the matter about whether *A* survives this process, and if so, whether *A* is *B* or *C*. But we know all the relevant physical facts, and they don't answer these questions. So there must be an immaterial element to *A*, an 'axe soul.'" Clearly this argument should not persuade us. But where exactly does it go wrong? What feature(s) of persons would Swinburne point to in order to distinguish this argument from his own? Do these features really make a difference?

3   In his book *Subjects of Experience* (Cambridge: Cambridge University Press, 1996, pp. 82–83), Lowe uses a spider-web analogy to explain how dualist interaction is possible:

> consider again the spider and its movements. If we just observed the movements and took no notice of the web, we would observe no "gaps" in the movements – each movement would ensue from and be ensued by other movements continuously. So we might wonder how the web contributed anything at all to the movements: it didn't "initiate" any of them, all the "initiation" coming from the spider's limbs. The answer, of course, is that the web is what we might call an "enabling" or "facilitating" cause, rather than an "initiating" cause, of the spider's movements – it enables and constrains these movements to take place in certain directions rather than others. Now, so too might states of consciousness both facilitate and impose constraints upon patterns of neural events.

To what extent does this analogy illustrate how an immaterial mind can make a difference in a world in which every physical event is "initiated" only by a physical cause? Are there important differences between the

103

spider-web case and the mind–body case which might undermine the usefulness of the analogy?

4   Both idealism and materialism collapse the mind–body distinction, asserting that reality has a unified nature. Materialism says this nature is physical, while idealism says it is mental. But in the end is this merely an arbitrary decision on what to *call* the world's nature? Materialists call the one, unified world "physical," while idealists call it "mental," but is there really any substantive disagreement between the two? Put another way, can we give some positive content to the concepts *mental* and *physical* so that the two views are making distinct claims?

PART II

MATERIALISM

INTRODUCTION

The selections in Part I considered variations on the thesis of mind–body dualism. Dualism conceives mental processes as essentially "inner," reflected outwardly in behavior. I immediately apprehend my own conscious mental states, or have a capacity to become so aware by focusing my attention on the matter. I just know "straight away" that I am now having a visual experience representing a computer screen and auditory experience as of keys clicking; I am now believing that I am composing an essay and desiring to make substantial progress on it this day. But for the mental states of everyone else, even those standing directly in front of me, I must infer the presence of a directing mind from the behavior of their bodies. I cannot see or touch their non-physical minds (not even when their skulls are opened on an operating table). But I do see the effects of such minds in all manner of seemingly goal-directed behavior: walking, talking, reaching, gesturing, looking, smiling, and so on. In my own case, I recognize such outward behavior to flow from my intentions, beliefs, desires, and emotions. (I "perceive" both sides of the causal process.) In the case of others, I see only the effect side, and infer to a similar cause, a purposive mind. To be sure, if the dualist is right, I am not making these inferences in the way I infer the murderer from a series of clues – consciously and deliberately. I am aware of no such reflective inference upon encountering a person (or the person's bodily aspect). So if I am making something like an inference, it must be the sort that is immediate, automatic, and unconscious.

I. Behaviorism

One form of materialist reaction to this dualist picture of mentality is known as behaviorism. Behaviorism's repudiation of dualism is wholesale. It holds that the behavior which the dualist takes to indicate a hidden mental reality in fact constitutes mentality. To be a minded thing just is to engage, or be disposed to engage, in certain kinds of complex behavior. The "inner" realm of a distinctively mental kind of state or process is simply denied. I need not infer my neighbor's believing that there is water in the glass and desiring to drink some; her reaching for the glass in appropriate conditions constitutes her so believing and desiring.

Behaviorism has two central motivations. The philosophical motivation is to get around problems many see in dualism's account of our knowledge of minds other than our own and the related matter of how language involving mental terms works. The inference to the minds of others which dualism posits is shaky: from the single case (my own) of seeing a correlation between mental states and certain kinds of behavior, I must infer an indefinite number of such correlations in cases where I have direct evidence of only one of the correlates. That seems a hasty generalization. Consider further reference to mental states on the dualist's scheme. The term "pain" is intended to refer to a particular sort of phenomena typical of people who exhibit various kinds of "pain behavior" (writhing, moaning, etc.). For the dualist, I grasp its referent "from the inside" when I have a painful experience. I associate this type of experience with the term, so that when I say of other people that they are in pain, given their behavior, I am claiming that they are having this kind of experience. The puzzle here is to see how the term "pain" can become part of a public language. We all see other people apply the term under certain circumstances – e.g., when they themselves or others exhibit pain behavior. But (assuming dualism) we only directly verify the nature of its referent in our own case. What if the private experience that leads to pain behavior differs from person to person, in more or less dramatic ways? (In other words, what if that "hasty generalization" I spoke of above goes the way of many such generalizations, and is simply false?) How could I or anyone else ever tell? Now if the term "pain" is to mean anything – and surely it does – there must be a fairly determinate class of cases to which it applies, cases that ordinary language users reliably manage to identify. But if all they have to go on is pain behavior, and this is wholly distinct from pain itself, it is perhaps problematic how they manage to acquire this ability. (A deeply influential argument on this point is found in Wittgenstein 1953 – see his discussion of "the beetle in a box" in §293.) Contrariwise, if pain behavior under publicly identifiable circumstances constitutes being in pain, there is no such problem at all.

The second motivation for behaviorism is scientific. The subjective phenomena claimed by dualism, it is argued, are not amenable to study within an objective scientific framework. The methodological stricture that working psychologists should restrict their attention to evidence available from an impersonal, third-person point of view, such as behavior and associated bodily reactions, can easily slide into the ontological claim that there is nothing else to psychological phenomena outside a complex series of dispositions to behave in certain ways and the regular outworking of these dispositions in actual behavior.

INTRODUCTION

Behaviorism had a strong following in the early to mid-twentieth century. Its scientific champion was B.F. Skinner (1953). An important philosophical exponent of the position was Carl Hempel (1935). Hempel defined "logical behaviorism" as the thesis that the meaning of any psychological statement consists in its abbreviating certain physical stimulus–response patterns characteristic of humans (and in some cases, higher animals). He gave as an example a partial behaviorist analysis of the statement "Paul has a toothache":

- Paul weeps and makes gestures of such and such kinds.
- At the question "What is the matter?," Paul utters the words "I have a toothache."
- Closer examination reveals a decayed tooth with exposed pulp.
- Paul's blood pressure, digestive processes, and the speed of his reactions show such and such changes.
- Such and such processes occur in Paul's central nervous system.

Hempel acknowledges that we might add any number of further dispositions true of a person experiencing a toothache. The crucial point is that the behaviorist holds that all such dispositions can be stated in physical, non-psychological terms, since he holds that psychology is entirely reducible to the category of behavioral and bodily dispositions.

Enthusiasm for behaviorism has sharply waned, to the point that its main significance for understanding contemporary philosophical discussion of mind is as an important forerunner to a view known as functionalism, which is discussed below. Behaviorism's demise among philosophers resulted from two decisive criticisms (see also Chomsky 1959).

First, it appears unlikely that one could give a fully satisfactory behaviorist analysis of any psychological statement. The factors influencing what a person is apt to do under specified conditions are highly complex, including not only social and cultural norms, but other mental states (see e.g. Fodor 1968, p. 71). I may be disposed to reach for a peach on the table in front of me if I desire food, but only if I also believe that there is desirable food in front of me and that I am able to take it. Furthermore, it has to be true that I do not have a competing and more powerful desire, say, a desire to fast for religious reasons. We might try to reduce these psychological conditions on the truth of my desiring food by further behaviorist analyses of them. The problem, however, is that any such analyses, if plausible, are likely to end up referring back to the original item, the desire for food. (My belief that there is fruit in front of me will dispose me to reach for it, e.g. only if I desire to have food. I won't do so if I just had a large meal, or if I dislike peaches.) In this way, the analyses will turn out to be circular, and so we will not have succeeded in reducing individual psychological statements to purely physical and behavioral ones.

A second criticism of behaviorism points to the possibility of "super-actors" who train themselves to suppress any disposition to act on certain psychological states. Hilary Putnam (1965) describes a group of super-spartans who feel pain as we do but who never engage in pain behavior of any kind. They neither wince nor groan. If you ask them how they're feeling, they'll never admit to being in pain. While it would be extremely difficult, and perhaps impossible as a practical matter, for human beings to attain the status of super-spartans, it does not seem impossible that there should be super-spartans in some race or other of sentient beings. But the logical behaviorist cannot admit this possibility, since he holds that the meaning of psychological statements is exhausted by statements about what they are apt to do under various circumstances. Saying that Sparticus is in pain while not apt to express pain behavior under any objective circumstance is, by the behaviorist's lights, a contradiction. But since this "thought experiment" does not seem, pre-theoretically, to involve any contradiction, it counts as evidence for the untenability of the behaviorist analysis.

II. Mind–brain identity theory

A second materialist strategy takes there really to be psychological states beyond their expression in behavior. But rather than taking them as basic states wholly distinct from basic physical states, it identifies such states with states of the brain (or central nervous system more generally) – hence the label "mind–brain identity theory." A very influential elucidation and defense of the identity theory is given in Chapter 6 by J.J.C. Smart. Smart's point of departure is the observation that the mind–brain correlations of ordinary experience (head injuries adversely affect thinking ability) have led, in mature science, to much more specific correlations of brain state and psychological state types. We can well imagine that future science will be able to make these correlations even more exact and systematic. This gives rise to the materialist conjecture that the relationship is stronger than mere correlation and is, in fact, one of *identity*. There are not two states regularly co-occurring (in the philosopher's fanciful example, "C-fiber firing" and pain), but one, alternately described. Toothache experiences of the sort Paul is suffering from are just instances of a specific type of neural state, a type which it is the task of neuroscience to pick out.

Smart motivates acceptance of the identity theory even now (prior to our knowing the precise nature of the identities), on the grounds of ontological and theoretical simplicity. Everywhere else in the study of nature, he contends, we have made strides towards understanding phenomena involving large-scale objects (e.g. the biological life of organisms) as identical to the activity of a complex array of small-scale objects (those of chemistry and ultimately fundamental physics). Supposing that the mental lives of animals are the one exception to this rule is theoretically unattractive; it would involve "nomological danglers" – primitive psychological states related by fundamental natural laws to physical states involving billions of microscopic entities. If, instead, mental states are just complex physical states, then there is no need for basic laws beyond those of elementary physics. The virtue of theoretical economy makes this identity supposition irresistible, provided there are no insuperable obstacles to it similar to those faced by behaviorism.

Before considering objections to the identity theory, however, we need to express its central claim with greater care. By identity, we mean numerical identity: certain neural and psychological states are not just highly or even exactly similar, "they" are one and the same. But what do we mean by "states" here? Clearly, the identity theorist holds that, say, the occurrence of pain in Paul at 2 p.m. yesterday is just the firing of C-fibers in a particular pattern in his brain at that very time, and the occurrence of pain in Susan at 11 a.m. today is just the firing of C-fibers in a particular pattern in her brain at that very time. Note that here we are asserting the identity of particular pain and neural state instances or "tokens." But this is consistent with saying that the different instances of the type of pain are identical in each case to instances of very different neural types. That is, psychological–neural token identities are consistent with there being no psychological–neural type identities. Were an identity theorist to rest content with this, the theory would clearly be unsatisfying, for we would lack a physical understanding of what is common to instances of pain, which is to say we would lack a theory of pain. An identity theory, then, will assert something stronger than the existence of token identities. It will suppose that there are interesting type identities, such that any event which consists in a person's having a determinate sort of pain will be an event of some one determinate neural type. The property of painfulness (of a determinate sort) is just the neural property N for some N.

Our ordinary way of identifying occurrences of pain is totally unlike this, of course. The term "pain" does not mean anything like "C-fiber firing pattern 257." Smart argues that this is no evidence against the identity thesis, for we likewise don't mean by "lightning" an electrical discharge of a certain sort, but that is just what lightning is. Not all true identity claims are trivial, grounded solely in the meanings of terms. Confirming some of these requires empirical advance and theoretically grounded inference. Supposing continued scientific advance, the identity theorist anticipates a day when the identity of psychological and neural state types will be as well confirmed as that of lightning with electrical discharge in our own day.

A second, more powerful objection to the identity theory is that psychological states, at least many of them, such as pain, seem to have a distinctive character that we are immediately aware of in experiencing them. There is a quality of pain, goes the objection, that is simply not captured by any physical description. Smart responds to this by denying that there is any such quality to our experience that is immediately discerned, apart from study of the brain. He suggests instead that everything we should want to say about the nature of our experiences is captured within a "topic-neutral" analysis of reports we typically make about our experiences. ("Topic-neutral" in that the analysis is neutral as to whether the experience is irreducibly psychological, as the dualist believes, or is purely physical, as the identity theorist maintains.) Paul, e.g., might exclaim, "I am feeling a toothache!" Smart suggests that this should be analyzed thus: "something is going on in me that is like what is going on when there is decay in my tooth (with nerve intact) and I hold my jaw and wince." Or to switch to Smart's own example of experiencing an orangish-yellow afterimage: "Something is going on in me that is like what goes on when I am looking at an orangish-yellow color patch in good lighting conditions." That is, all that we immediately apprehend about our experiences is their similarity to other experiences which are classed by reference to *the external conditions of their typical occurrence*, rather than to their intrinsic qualities (which are neurophysiological).

Saul Kripke (Chapter 7) famously developed a third criticism of the identity theory which has persuaded a number of philosophers. He begins by focusing on the "modal status" that Smart assigns to the type–type identities he believes future science will discover. Many truths are merely contingent. The world might have differed in various ways, with the result that these propositions, which are actually true, would have been false. (Some of the ways the world might have differed are banal, such as my becoming a roofer rather than a philosopher; others are more fanciful, as with the worlds imagined in science fiction.) We may say that a set of propositions that is consistent and complete, in that it assigns "true" or "false" to every proposition whatever, without contradiction, describes a *possible world*. The range of possible worlds is surely vast, far beyond the limits of human imagination and duration. A contingent proposition is one that comes out as true in some possible worlds but false in others. Most truths that occupy our attention are like that, presumably. They happen to be true, but we can imagine a coherent scenario wherein they would be false. Some truths, however, are absolutely necessary – true in all the possible worlds. Which ones are those? For starters, truths of pure mathematics and logic. Imagine whatever differences you please in the laws and occupants of nature, and it will still be the case that $2 + 2 = 4$ and that any statement of the form "if A or B and *not-A*, then B" will be true.

Let us again use the fictitious *pain = C-fiber firing pattern 257* as a stand-in for whatever the actual identity is. Smart holds that this identity is merely contingent. As a matter of empirical fact, there is such an identity, but it might have been otherwise. It might have been that we were immaterial mental substances, so that states of pain would have been identical to states of such substances. This certainly seems possible, and so it would be a point against the identity theory if one had to suppose the identity to be a necessary one.

Now Kripke tries to give us a handle on discerning when identity statements are contingent and when they are necessary. Consider the following: George W. Bush is the US president in 2002. This is clearly contingent. In some possible worlds, Al Gore manages to squeak out a win in the hotly contested race; in others, Bush never opts to run in the first place; in still others, he does not exist, owing to a parachuting accident involving George Bush Sr at a young age, and so on. The source of the contingency, says Kripke, is the designator on the right-hand side of the statement. "US president in 2002" is a *non-rigid* designator, in that it refers to different persons who occupy the office of president in different possible scenarios. "George W. Bush" (and proper names in general), by contrast, rigidly designate the very same individual in all possibilities where he exists. (In possibilities where he does not exist, as in our final scenario, the name does not refer to anyone at all.) When we ask about the possibilities involving George W. Bush, we "hold fixed" the actual referent of that name, whatever the differences in him or his circumstances. We are asking about *that individual* who happens to go by the name "George W. Bush" and considering what might have been insofar as it involves him. Now that very individual might have had a different name; he might have been called "Walker G. Bush," for example. Still, where we – here in the one, actual world – consider the possibility in which he is so named, we use the designator "George W. Bush" to pick him out, even though he would not have been so designated had that possibility been actual. We use "George W. Bush" and other proper names rigidly when contemplating what might have been.

Many philosophers agree with the thrust of Kripke's position as described thus far. Note that it is at bottom a claim about language, about how certain designating terms work. Some are rigid and others are non-rigid. An identity thesis will be contingent only if at least one of the designators is non-rigid. If both rigidly pick out some one phenomena in all possible worlds, the identity claim will be necessary. This is true, for example, for the identity claim, "Samuel Clemens is Mark Twain." Since both designators are proper names and proper names designate rigidly, they refer to the same individual (the one who in actual fact wrote *Huckleberry Finn* under the Twain pseudonym) in all possible worlds or none at all. There is no possible world where Samuel Clemens exists but Mark Twain does not (though there are worlds where Samuel Clemens does not adopt the pseudonym Mark Twain).

Kripke then applies his machinery to Smart's thesis that *pain = C-fiber firing pattern 257* is contingently true. Kripke asks, if this is so, which of the two designators occurring within it are non-rigid? It cannot be *C-fiber firing pattern 257*, as this designates a natural kind and such terms seem to function exactly like proper names with respect to rigidity. (See the opening remarks of Kripke's third lecture.) But, likewise, it cannot be *pain*, as pain is not (as Smart seems to suppose) just a term for whatever happens to occupy the "pain role" of prompting the experiencer to avoid further tissue damage, and so on. Essential to pain is its phenomenal character, how it feels. Whatever C-fiber firings may happen to co-exist with pain in our world, the fundamental nature of pain is – well – its painfulness. Where that phenomenal quality is present, there is pain; where it is absent, regardless of there being a surrogate which occupies the pain role, pain is absent too.

Supposing we accept all this, what is the upshot? The identity theorist cannot suppose that there are merely contingent truths of psychological–neural identity. Any such truths must be absolutely necessary. But this, says Kripke, is implausible, as Smart himself seems to grasp in asserting the contingency thesis. For it seems possible that there is a world with pain that lacks C-fibers; indeed, it seems possible that there is pain in a world where all persons lack bodies altogether. So the identity theory itself is in trouble. (For more on Kripke's argument, see Hill 1997.)

Kripke's argument has persuaded some. Even more philosophers have been led to abandon the identity theory on the basis of a different sort of criticism, one that has ushered in a now-dominant form of materialism. In Chapter 11, Hilary Putnam invites us to reflect on the physical differences in organisms that we typically suppose experience pain. The physical substrate of pain in humans is quite different from that of mollusks, for example. And even among humans, there are anatomical differences among brains, which suggests differences in the specific neural-state types correlated with pain. There are even important changes within a single human brain over time. It is now known that in some cases in which a young person undergoes a moderate injury to the brain, certain psychological functions that once were associated with one region of his brain may, over time, migrate to another region. All of this, argues Putnam, suggests that pain is "multiply realizable" – that is to say, while it may be contingently true that all pain occurs in some complex physical structure or other, there may be a plurality of physical-state types that are capable of "realizing" pain. In us, pain may be realized in C-fiber firing patterns (though probably not restricted to a single such pattern). In mollusks, it is realized by a rather different sort of structure, given the general anatomical differences between the brains of mammals and mollusks. Realization is not identity as it is a many–one relation. So the identity theory is false.

III. Functionalism

If we accept the point about multiple realization of mental states, where does it lead? According to Putnam (and many others since, e.g. Shoemaker 1984), it leads to a functional understanding of mental states. Mental states are defined in terms of the role they play in a psychological system, whether human, mollusk, or artificial. Functionalists often appeal in this connection to computers: different sorts of hardware can carry out the same software. Computer scientists study computational processes in abstraction from the physical details of their mechanical–electrical implementation, or realization, in actual computers, which is the province of electrical engineers and others. Just so, in ordinary life, we describe the behavior of each other in the functional terms of "folk psychology" without knowing (or needing to know) the physico-chemical details of how our psychology is realized.

Note that the functionalist understanding is formally neutral on the dualism/materialism debate. That, says the functionalist, is an empirical question of hardware, and as such is irrelevant to the abstract functional character of our mental states themselves. Still, many functionalists are materialists who see in functionalism a way of respecting the intuitions often thought to favor dualism while still being materialists. Where Kripke (following a long line of dualists going back at least to Descartes) argues that it is at least possible that there might be pain in the absence of anything like human neurophysiology, the materialist functionalist can cheerfully agree. There might have been nonphysical realizers of pain, but, as it happens, there are not. (More modestly still, a functionalist might hold that all thinking beings of our immediate acquaintance are wholly realized in physical stuff, but allow that there may be supernatural beings such as God and angels whose psychology is realized in nonphysical stuff.) A given functionalist is a materialist, then, just in case he asserts, as an additional, independent thesis, that all mental states are in fact physically realized. (Functionalists need to say more about realization. Many will say that it implies mental–physical supervenience – roughly, that, as a matter of causal necessity, there is no psychological difference between thinkers without a corresponding physical difference.)

The point of agreement with the dualist is that the kind of physical stuff occupying the natural world is not essential to mentality as such; the functionalist goes on to add, in opposition to the dualist, that any nonphysical stuff there is or might have been, is not necessary either.

What, then, *is* necessary for there to be a minded thing, according to the functionalist? Mental concepts are functional concepts, like the concept of a carburetor. Something is a carburetor if it takes in air and gasoline, combines them appropriately, and feeds the result into a combustible engine. Carburetors vary in size, structure, and constituting material. These details matter to the ability of a carburetor to function in relation to a particular engine, but none is essential to a particular object's counting as a carburetor. For that, all that matters is that it is capable of playing the carburetor role in the particular environment in which it is placed. We might express this idea by saying that the requirements of a functional concept are all relational, rather than intrinsic. Switching back to the mental concept of pain, on a functionalist's under-standing, we can see that no physical state is *sufficient* for the state of being in pain, since there could have been something having the same intrinsic phys-ical state as Paul's experience of toothache, while failing to be in pain because it was "wired differently,"·such that the state played a role other than one of pain. That no specific physical state is *necessary* follows from the multiple realizability of pain. But, more strongly, if the realization possibilities for pain are very diverse (they do not even fall in a fairly limited range of physical state types), then intrinsic features of particular pains will be quite irrelevant to the study of pain as such. All that matters is that the intrinsic features be such as to have the right dispositional character in relation to the rest of the system and its environment.

Our speaking of the importance of dispositions to mental states will remind the reader of our discussion of behaviorism. The connection is not slight, as the functionalist position owes much to the earlier influence of behaviorism. Behaviorism views ascriptions of mental states as shorthand for asserting a set of conditional statements about what a person is apt to do in specific circum-stances. Functionalism also holds that it is essential to, e.g., desiring food, that one is disposed in certain ways in relation to certain conditions. However, it goes beyond this sort of claim in holding that mental states are internal states (logically distinct from behavioral dispositions) that mediate inputs and outputs to the system. A state of desiring food is a state that has certain typical causes and certain typical effects, both relative to specific background circum-stances. Furthermore, among the typical causes and effects defining a given type of mental state are other mental states. You cannot understand what a desire for food is without also understanding what beliefs about food are, for desires translate into action only when coupled with appropriate beliefs. We saw this point in a criticism of behaviorism. The functionalist accepts the point without difficulty, by giving a holistic definition of a whole network of possible psychological states. (For an account of how this goes, see Chapter 10.) Something need not have *all* the states to have any one of them, of course. But, says the functionalist, they must be disposed towards having other states under the right circumstance.

Where does the functionalist's blueprint come from? According to some, from "folk psychology." That is, from the tacit, commonly accepted general-izations of ordinary people about what causes certain desires and beliefs, how they interplay, and what they in turn tend to lead people to do in the right circumstance. It is as if human beings posited certain interconnected, inner states (and invented a corresponding language) to capture certain generaliza-tions about behavior. The generalizations hold up, at least for the most part. It is then the job of the "structural engineers" (the neuroscientists) to tell us

116

the details concerning the states that actually play the roles posited in our folk science. Other functionalists say that folk psychology merely got us off the ground in working towards the abstract functional understanding that will one day show up in an actual blueprint of human psychology. (This second approach is what Block in Chapter 12 calls "Psychofunctionalism," whereas the first is what he terms "Functionalism.") We may have made lots of mistakes, so empirical psychology is not beholden to folk generalizations. The very concept of desire or of belief may undergo subtle revision and other concepts may need to be invented to handle adequately the facts revealed through sophisticated investigation. And some of the factors that figure into the blueprint, while still abstracting from the physical realizers, may be a bit more specific to human hardwiring. So the resulting blueprint may not fully carry over to the psychology of nonhuman animals.

As noted earlier, Putnam construes functionalism as sharply opposed to the Identity Theory, and in this he is joined by Block. As they see it, functionalism posits states distinct from, though realized in, physical states, and these states play distinctive causal roles. However, other functionalists (Lewis, Chapter 10 and Armstrong 1968) see their functionalism as a version of the Identity Theory! The difference here turns on a subtle matter of definition. On Lewis–Armstrong functionalism, functional terms *specify* the physical states that occupy the functional role. When we refer to Paul's pain, we refer to the physical state that occupies the pain role. Since the type of physical state involved likely will not be identical to the type involved in mollusk pain, Lewis suggests that we understand it to be tacitly restricted to species-type: it is pain-in-humans that is identical to *C-fiber firing pattern 257*. So we have two interpretations of functionalism: functional-state and functional-specification. Block (1980a) argues for the former, on the grounds that only it can give an answer to the question, what makes all pains to be pain? It can do so because it posits a distinctive, albeit highly abstract, state that is common to all beings in pain, whether human or not. Lewis argues for the specification construal on the grounds that pains are supposed to cause things. Since the physical realizers of pain clearly cause those very effects, if we suppose that pains are distinct from their realizers, we would have to (absurdly) double-count our causes.

A critic of functionalism will see in this dispute the makings of a dilemma for the doctrine: if (with Block) we say that pains are distinct states from their physical realizations, it will be difficult to make sense of mental causation. (See Kim's Chapter 8, along with Block himself in Block 1990). If instead (with Lewis) we say that psychological language is just a convenient, inspecific way of picking out complex physical states, we must swallow the implausibility of holding that there is no real unity corresponding to the various applications of a psychological term, so that, e.g., pains do not cause pain behavior in

117

virtue of their being pains. (Lewis's retreat to species-specific pain-neural identities will not do the job. As already noted, there are likely to be important
variations among neural correlates of pain, even within a species. And pain-
in-Paul-at-time-*t* is not the sort of state that will figure into an interesting
psychological generalization.)

In conclusion, it is apparent that, recent conceptual innovations notwithstanding, the viability of materialism, no less than that of dualism, is still not
beyond question. Which is to say, the fundamental nature of mind persists as
one of the enduring problems of philosophy.

FURTHER READING

Armstrong, D. (1968) *A Materialist Theory of Mind*, New York: Humanities Press.
Block, N. (1980a) "Introduction: What is Functionalism?," in Block 1980b.
—— (ed.) (1980b) *Readings in Philosophy of Psychology, Vol. 1*, Cambridge, Mass.:
    Harvard University Press.
—— (1990) "Can the Mind Change the World?," in G. Boolos (ed.), *Meaning and
    Method*, Cambridge: Cambridge University Press.
Chomsky, N. (1959) "A Review of B.F. Skinner's *Verbal Behavior*," in Block 1980b.
Davidson, D. (1980) "Mental Events," in *Essays on Actions and Events*, Oxford: Oxford
    University Press.
Fodor, J. (1968) *Psychological Explanation*, New York: Random House.
—— (1974) "Special Sciences, or the Disunity of Science as a Working Hypothesis,"
    Synthese 28: 97–115.
Hempel, C. (1935) "The Logical Analysis of Psychology," reprinted in Block 1980b.
Hill, C. (1991) *Sensations: A Defense of Type Materialism*, Cambridge: Cambridge
    University Press.
—— (1997) "Imaginability, Conceivability, Possibility and the Mind–Body Problem,"
    Philosophical Studies 87: 61–85.
Kim, J. (1996) *Philosophy of Mind*, Boulder, Colo.: Westview Press.
Macdonald, C. (1989) *Mind–Body Identity Theories*, London: Routledge.
Putnam, H. (1965) "Brains and Behavior," reprinted in Block 1980b.
Shoemaker, S. (1984) *Identity, Cause, and Mind*, Cambridge: Cambridge University
    Press.
Skinner, B.F. (1953) "Selections from *Science and Human Behavior*," reprinted in Block
    1980b.
Wittgenstein, L. (1953) *Philosophical Investigations*, trans. G.E.M. Anscombe, New
    York: The Macmillan Company.

IIA

THE IDENTITY THEORY

6

J.J.C. Smart, "Sensations and Brain Processes"

This paper[1] takes its departure from arguments to be found in U.T. Place's "Is Consciousness a Brain Process?"[2] I have had the benefit of discussing Place's thesis in a good many universities in the United States and Australia, and I hope that the present paper answers objections to his thesis which Place has not considered and that it presents his thesis in a more nearly unobjectionable form. This paper is meant also to supplement the paper "The 'Mental' and the 'Physical,'" by H. Feigl,[3] which in part argues for a similar thesis to Place's.

Suppose that I report that I have at this moment a roundish, blurry-edged after-image which is yellowish towards its edge and is orange towards its center. What is it that I am reporting? One answer to this question might be that I am not reporting anything, that when I say that it looks to me as though there is a roundish yellowy-orange patch of light on the wall I am expressing some sort of *temptation*, the temptation to say that there *is* a roundish yellowy-orange patch on the wall (though I may know that there is not such a patch on the wall). This is perhaps Wittgenstein's view in the *Philosophical Investigations* (see §§ 367, 370). Similarly, when I "report" a pain, I am not really reporting anything (or, if you like, I am reporting in a queer sense of "reporting"), but am doing a sophisticated sort of wince. (See § 244: "The verbal expression of pain replaces crying and does not describe it." Nor does it describe anything else?).[4] I prefer most of the time to discuss an after-image rather than a pain, because the word "pain" brings in something which is irrelevant to my purpose: the notion of "distress." I think that "he is in pain" entails "he is in distress," that is, that he is in a certain agitation-condition.[5] Similarly, to say "I am in pain" may be to do more than "replace pain behavior": it may be partly to report something,

J.J.C. Smart, "Sensations and Brain Processes," in V.C. Chappell (ed.) *The Philosophy of Mind* (Dover Publications, New York, 1981), pp. 160–72.

though this something is quite nonmysterious, being an agitation-condition, and so susceptible of behavioristic analysis. The suggestion I wish if possible to avoid is a different one, namely that "I am in pain" is a genuine report, and that what it reports is an irreducibly psychical something. And similarly the suggestion I wish to resist is also that to say "I have a yellowish-orange after-image" is to report something irreducibly psychical.

Why do I wish to resist this suggestion? Mainly because of Occam's razor. It seems to me that science is increasingly giving us a viewpoint whereby organisms are able to be seen as physicochemical mechanisms:[6] it seems that even the behavior of man himself will one day be explicable in mechanistic terms. There does seem to be, so far as science is concerned, nothing in the world but increasingly complex arrangements of physical constituents. All except for one place: in consciousness. That is, for a full description of what is going on in a man you would have to mention not only the physical processes in his tissues, glands, nervous system, and so forth, but also his states of consciousness: his visual, auditory, and tactual sensations, his aches and pains. That these should be *correlated* with brain processes does not help, for to say that they are *correlated* is to say that they are something "over and above." You cannot correlate something with itself. You correlate footprints with burglars, but not Bill Sikes the burglar with Bill Sikes the burglar. So sensations, states of consciousness, do seem to be the one sort of thing left outside the physicalist picture, and for various reasons I just cannot believe that this can be so. That everything should be explicable in terms of physics (together of course with descriptions of the ways in which the parts are put together – roughly, biology is to physics as radio-engineering is to electromagnetism) except the occurrence of sensations seems to me to be frankly unbelievable. Such sensations would be "nomological danglers," to use Feigl's expression.[7] It is not often realized how odd would be the laws whereby these nomological danglers would dangle. It is sometimes asked, "Why can't there be psychophysical laws which are of a novel sort, just as the laws of electricity and magnetism were novelties from the standpoint of Newtonian mechanics?" Certainly we are pretty sure in the future to come across new ultimate laws of a novel type, but I expect them to relate simple constituents: for example, whatever ultimate particles are then in vogue. I cannot believe that ultimate laws of nature could relate simple constituents to configurations consisting of perhaps billions of neurons (and goodness knows how many billion billions of ultimate particles) all put together for all the world as though their main purpose in life was to be a negative feedback mechanism of a complicated sort. Such ultimate laws would be like nothing so far known in science. They have a queer "smell" to them. I am just unable to believe in the nomological danglers themselves, or in the laws whereby they would dangle.

If any philosophical arguments seemed to compel us to believe in such things, I would suspect a catch in the argument. In any case it is the object of this paper to show that there are no philosophical arguments which compel us to be dualists.

The above is largely a confession of faith, but it explains why I find Wittgenstein's position (as I construe it) so congenial. For on this view there are, in a sense, no sensations. A man is a vast arrangement of physical particles, but there are not, over and above this, sensations or states of consciousness. There are just behavioral facts about this vast mechanism, such as that it expresses a temptation (behavior disposition) to say "there is a yellowish-red patch on the wall" or that it goes through a sophisticated sort of wince, that is, says "I am in pain." Admittedly Wittgenstein says that though the sensation "is not a something," it is nevertheless "not a nothing either" (§ 304), but this need only mean that the word "ache" has a use. An ache is a thing, but only in the innocuous sense in which the plain man, in the first paragraph of Frege's *Foundations of Arithmetic*, answers the question "What is the number one?" by "a thing." It should be noted that when I assert that to say "I have a yellowish-orange after-image" is to express a temptation to assert the physical-object statement "There is a yellowish-orange patch on the wall," I mean that saying "I have a yellowish-orange after-image" is (partly) the exercise of the disposition[8] which is the temptation. It is not to *report* that I have the temptation, any more than is "I love you" normally a report that I love someone. Saying "I love you" is just part of the behavior which is the exercise of the disposition of loving someone.

Though for the reasons given above, I am very receptive to the above "expressive" account of sensation statements, I do not feel that it will quite do the trick. Maybe this is because I have not thought it out sufficiently, but it does seem to me as though, when a person says "I have an after-image," he *is* making a genuine report, and that when he says "I have a pain," he *is* doing more than "replace pain-behavior," and that "this more" is not just to say that he is in distress. I am not so sure, however, that to admit this is to admit that there are nonphysical correlates of brain processes. Why should not sensations just be brain processes of a certain sort? There are, of course, well-known (as well as lesser-known) philosophical objections to the view that reports of sensations are reports of brain-processes, but I shall try to argue that these arguments are by no means as cogent as is commonly thought to be the case.

Let me first try to state more accurately the thesis that sensations are brain-processes. It is not the thesis that, for example, "after-image" or "ache" means the same as "brain process of sort X" (where "X" is replaced by a description of a certain sort of brain process). It is that, in so far as

123

"after-image" or "ache" is a report of a process, it is a report of a process that *happens to be* a brain process. It follows that the thesis does not claim that sensation statements can be *translated* into statements about brain processes.[9] Nor does it claim that the logic of a sensation statement is the same as that of a brain-process statement. All it claims is that, in so far as a sensation statement is a report of something, that something is in fact a brain process. Sensations are nothing over and above brain processes. Nations are nothing "over and above" citizens, but this does not prevent the logic of nation statements being very different from the logic of citizen statements, nor does it ensure the translatability of nation statements into citizen statements. (I do not, however, wish to assert that the relation of sensation statements to brain-process statements is very like that of nation statements to citizen statements. Nations do not just *happen to be* nothing over and above citizens, for example. I bring in the "nations" example merely to make a negative point: that the fact that the logic of A-statements is different from that of B-statements does not ensure that A's are anything over and above B's.)

Remarks on identity

When I say that a sensation is a brain process or that lightning is an electric discharge, I am using "is" in the sense of strict identity. (Just as in the – in this case necessary – proposition "7 is identical with the smallest prime number greater than 5.") When I say that a sensation is a brain process or that lightning is an electric discharge I do not mean just that the sensation is somehow spatially or temporally continuous with the brain process or that the lightning is just spatially or temporally continuous with the discharge. When on the other hand I say that the successful general is the same person as the small boy who stole the apples I mean only that the successful general I see before me is a time slice[10] of the same four-dimensional object of which the small boy stealing apples is an earlier time slice. However, the four-dimensional object which has the general-I-see-before-me for its late time slice is identical in the strict sense with the four-dimensional object which has the small-boy-stealing-apples for an early time slice. I distinguish these two senses of "is identical with" because I wish to make it clear that the brain-process doctrine asserts identity in the *strict* sense.

I shall now discuss various possible objections to the view that the processes reported in sensation statements are in fact processes in the brain. Most of us have met some of these objections in our first year as philosophy students. All the more reason to take a good look at them. Others of the objections will be more recondite and subtle.

124

Objection 1. Any illiterate peasant can talk perfectly well about his after-images, or how things look or feel to him, or about his aches and pains, and yet he may know nothing whatever about neurophysiology. A man may, like Aristotle, believe that the brain is an organ for cooling the body without any impairment of his ability to make true statements about his sensations. Hence the things we are talking about when we describe our sensations cannot be processes in the brain.

Reply. You might as well say that a nation of slugabeds, who never saw the Morning Star or knew of its existence, or who had never thought of the expression "the Morning Star," but who used the expression "the Evening Star" perfectly well, could not use this expression to refer to the same entity as we refer to (and describe as) "the Morning Star."[11]

You may object that the Morning Star is in a sense not the very same thing as the Evening Star, but only something spatiotemporally continuous with it. That is, you may say that the Morning Star is not the Evening Star in the strict sense of "identity" that I distinguished earlier.

There is, however, a more plausible example. Consider lightning.[12] Modern physical science tells us that lightning is a certain kind of electrical discharge due to ionization of clouds of water vapor in the atmosphere. This, it is now believed, is what the true nature of lightning is. Note that there are not two things: a flash of lightning and an electrical discharge. There is one thing, a flash of lightning, which is described scientifically as an electrical discharge to the earth from a cloud of ionized water molecules. The case is not at all like that of explaining a footprint by reference to a burglar. We say that what lightning really is, what its true nature as revealed by science is, is an electrical discharge. (It is not the true nature of a footprint to be a burglar.)

To forestall irrelevant objections, I should like to make it clear that by "lightning" I mean the publicly observable physical object, lightning, not a visual sense-datum of lightning. I say that the publicly observable physical object lightning is in fact the electrical discharge, not just a correlate of it. The sense-datum, or rather the having of the sense-datum, the "look" of lightning, may well in my view be a correlate of the electrical discharge. For in my view it is a brain state *caused* by the lightning. But we should no more confuse sensations of lightning with lightning than we confuse sensations of a table with the table.

In short, the reply to Objection 1 is that there can be contingent statements of the form "A is identical with B," and a person may well know that something is an A without knowing that it is a B. An illiterate peasant might well be able to talk about his sensations without knowing about his brain processes, just as he can talk about lightning though he knows nothing of electricity.

Objection 2. It is only a contingent fact (if it is a fact) that when we have a certain kind of sensation there is a certain kind of process in our brain. Indeed it is possible, though perhaps in the highest degree unlikely, that our present physiological theories will be as out of date as the ancient theory connecting mental processes with goings on in the heart. It follows that when we report a sensation we are not reporting a brain-process.

Reply. The objection certainly proves that when we say "I have an after-image" we cannot *mean* something of the form "I have such and such a brain-process." But this does not show that what we report (having an after-image) is not *in fact* a brain process. "I see lightning" does not *mean* "I see an electrical discharge." Indeed, it is logically possible (though highly unlikely) that the electrical discharge account of lightning might one day be given up. Again, "I see the Evening Star" does not *mean* the same as "I see the Morning Star," and yet "The Evening Star and the Morning Star are one and the same thing" is a contingent proposition. Possibly Objection 2 derives some of its apparent strength from a "Fido"–Fido theory of meaning. If the meaning of an expression were what the expression named, then of course it *would* follow from the fact that "sensation" and "brain-process" have different meanings that they cannot name one and the same thing.

Objection 3.[13] Even if Objections 1 and 2 do not prove that sensations are something over and above brain-processes, they do prove that the qualities of sensations are something over and above the qualities of brain-processes. That is, it may be possible to get out of asserting the existence of irreducibly psychic processes, but not out of asserting the existence of irreducibly psychic *properties.* For suppose we identify the Morning Star with the Evening Star. Then there must be some properties which logically imply that of being the Morning Star, and quite distinct properties which entail that of being the Evening Star. Again, there must be some properties (for example, that of being a yellow flash) which are logically distinct from those in the physicalist story.

Indeed, it might be thought that the objection succeeds at one jump. For consider the property of "being a yellow flash." It might seem that this property lies inevitably outside the physicalist framework within which I am trying to work (either by "yellow" being an objective emergent property of physical objects, or else by being a power to produce yellow sense-data, where "yellow," in this second instantiation of the word, refers to a purely phenomenal or introspectible quality). I must therefore digress for a moment and indicate how I deal with secondary qualities. I shall concentrate on color.

First of all, let me introduce the concept of a normal percipient. One person is more a normal percipient than another if he can make color discriminations that the other cannot. For example, if A can pick a lettuce leaf out of a heap of cabbage leaves, whereas B cannot though he can pick a lettuce leaf out of a heap of beetroot leaves, then A is more normal than B. (I am assuming that A and B are not given time to distinguish the leaves by their slight difference in shape, and so forth.) From the concept of "more normal than" it is easy to see how we can introduce the concept of "normal." Of course, Eskimos may make the finest discriminations at the blue end of the spectrum, Hottentots at the red end. In this case the concept of a normal percipient is a slightly idealized one, rather like that of "the mean sun" in astronomical chronology. There is no need to go into such subtleties now. I say that "This is red" means something roughly like "A normal percipient would not easily pick this out of a clump of geranium petals though he would pick it out of a clump of lettuce leaves." Of course it does not exactly mean this: a person might know the meaning of "red" without knowing anything about geraniums, or even about normal percipients. But the point is that a person can be *trained* to say "This is red" of objects which would not easily be picked out of geranium petals by a normal percipient, and so on. (Note that even a color-blind person can reasonably assert that something is red, though of course he needs to use another human being, not just himself, as his "color meter.") This account of secondary qualities explains their unimportance in physics. For obviously the discriminations and lack of discriminations made by a very complex neurophysiological mechanism are hardly likely to correspond to simple and nonarbitrary distinctions in nature.

I therefore elucidate colors as powers, in Locke's sense, to evoke certain sorts of discriminatory responses in human beings. They are also, of course, powers to cause sensations in human beings (an account still nearer Locke's). But these sensations, I am arguing, are identifiable with brain processes.

Now how do I get over the objection that a sensation can be identified with a brain process only if it has some phenomenal property, not possessed by brain processes, whereby one-half of the identification may be, so to speak, pinned down?

Reply. My suggestion is as follows. When a person says, "I see a yellowish-orange after-image," he is saying something like this: "*There is something going on which is like what is going on when* I have my eyes open, am awake, and there is an orange illuminated in good light in front of me, that is, when I really see an orange." (And there is no reason why a person should not say the same thing when he is having a veridical sense-datum, so long as we construe "like" in the last sentence in such a sense that something can be like itself.) Notice that the italicized words, namely "there is something going on which is like what is going on when," are all quasi-logical or topic-neutral words. This explains why the ancient Greek peasant's reports about his sensations can be neutral between dualistic metaphysics or my materialistic metaphysics. It explains how sensations can be brain-processes and yet how a man who reports them need know nothing about brain-processes. For he reports them only very abstractly as "something going on which is like what is going on when . . . ." Similarly, a person may say "someone is in the room," thus reporting truly that the doctor is in the room, even though he has never heard of doctors. (There are not two people in the room: "someone" *and* the doctor.) This account of sensation statements also explains the singular elusiveness of "raw feels" – why no one seems to be able to pin any properties on them.[14] Raw feels, in my view, are colorless for the very same reason that *something* is colorless. This does not mean that sensations do not have plenty of properties, for if they are brain-processes they certainly have lots of neurological properties. It only means that in speaking of them as being like or unlike one another we need not know or mention these properties.

This, then, is how I would reply to Objection 3. The strength of my reply depends on the possibility of our being able to report that one thing is like another without being able to state the respect in which it is like. I do not see why this should not be so. If we think cybernetically about the nervous system we can envisage it as able to respond to certain likenesses of its internal processes without being able to do more. It would be easier to build a machine which would tell us, say on a punched tape, whether or not two objects were similar, than it would be to build a machine which would report wherein the similarities consisted.

Objection 4. The after-image is not in physical space. The brain-process is. So the after-image is not a brain-process.

Reply. This is an *ignoratio elenchi.* I am not arguing that the after-image is a brain-process, but that the experience of having an after-image is a brain-process. It is the *experience* which is reported in the introspective report. Similarly, if it is objected that the after-image is yellowy-orange, my reply is that it is the experience of seeing yellowy-orange that is being described, and this experience is not a yellowy-orange something. So to say that a brain-process cannot be yellowy-orange is not to say that a brain-process cannot in fact be the experience of having a yellowy-orange after-image. There is, in a sense, no such thing as an after-image or a sense-datum, though there is such a thing as the experience of having an image, and this experience is described indirectly in material object language, not in phenomenal language, for there is no such thing.[15] We describe the experience by saying, in effect, that it is like the experience we have when, for example, we really see a yellowy-orange patch on the wall. Trees and wallpaper can be green, but not the experience of seeing or imagining a tree or wallpaper. (Or if they are described as green or yellow this can only be in a derived sense.)

Objection 5. It would make sense to say of a molecular movement in the brain that it is swift or slow, straight or circular, but it makes no sense to say this of the experience of seeing something yellow.

Reply. So far we have not given sense to talk of experiences as swift or slow, straight or circular. But I am not claiming that "experience" and "brain-process" mean the same or even that they have the same logic. "Somebody" and "the doctor" do not have the same logic, but this does not lead us to suppose that talking about somebody telephoning is talking about someone over and above, say, the doctor. The ordinary man when he reports an experience is reporting that something is going on, but he leaves it open as to what sort of thing is going on, whether in a material solid medium or perhaps in some sort of gaseous medium, or even perhaps in some sort of nonspatial medium (if this makes sense). All that I am saying is that "experience" and "brain-process" may in fact refer to the same thing, and if so we may easily adopt a convention (which is not a change in our present rules for the use of experience words but an addition to them) whereby it would make sense to talk of an experience in terms appropriate to physical processes.

Objection 6. Sensations are private, brain processes are *public*. If I sincerely say, "I see a yellowish-orange after-image," and I am not making a verbal mistake, then I cannot be wrong. But I can be wrong about a brain-process. The scientist looking into my brain might be having an illusion. Moreover, it makes sense to say that two or more people are observing the same brain-process but not that two or more people are reporting the same inner experience.

Reply. This shows that the language of introspective reports has a different logic from the language of material processes. It is obvious that until the brain-process theory is much improved and widely accepted there will be no *criteria* for saying "Smith has an experience of such-and-such a sort" *except* Smith's introspective reports. So we have adopted a rule of language that (normally) what Smith says goes.

129

Objection 7. I can imagine myself turned to stone and yet having images, aches, pains, and so on.

Reply. I can imagine that the electrical theory of lightning is false, that lightning is some sort of purely optical phenomenon. I can imagine that lightning is not an electrical discharge. I can imagine that the Evening Star is not the Morning Star. But it is. All the objection shows is that "experience" and "brain-process" do not have the same meaning. It does not show that an experience is not in fact a brain process.

This objection is perhaps much the same as one which can be summed up by the slogan: "What can be composed of nothing cannot be composed of anything."[16] The argument goes as follows: on the brain-process thesis the identity between the brain-process and the experience is a contingent one. So it is logically possible that there should be no brain-process, and no process of any other sort either (no heart process, no kidney process, no liver process). There would be the experience but no "corresponding" physiological process with which we might be able to identify it empirically.

I suspect that the objector is thinking of the experience as a ghostly entity. So it is composed of something, not of nothing, after all. On his view it is composed of ghost stuff, and on mine it is composed of brain stuff. Perhaps the counter-reply will be[17] that the experience is simple and uncompounded, and so it is not composed of anything after all. This seems to be a quibble, for, if it were taken seriously, the remark "What can be composed of nothing cannot be composed of anything" could be recast as an a priori argument against Democritus and atomism and for Descartes and infinite divisibility. And it seems odd that a question of this sort could be settled a priori. We must therefore construe the word "composed" in a very weak sense, which would allow us to say that even an indivisible atom is composed of something (namely, itself). The dualist cannot really say that an experience can be composed of nothing. For he holds that experiences are something over and above material processes, that is, that they are a sort of ghost stuff. (Or perhaps ripples in an underlying ghost stuff.) I say that the dualist's hypothesis is a perfectly intelligible one. But I say that experiences are not to be identified with ghost stuff but with brain stuff. This is another hypothesis, and in my view a very plausible one. The present argument cannot knock it down a priori.

Objection 8. The "beetle in the box" objection (see Wittgenstein, *Philosophical Investigations,* § 293). How could descriptions of experiences, if these are genuine reports, get a foothold in language? For any rule of language must have public criteria for its correct application.

Reply. The change from describing how things are to describing how we feel is just a change from uninhibitedly saying "this is so" to saying "this looks so." That is, when the naïve person might be tempted to say, "There is a patch of light on the wall which moves whenever I move my eyes" or "A pin is being stuck into me," we have learned how to resist this temptation and say "It *looks as though* there is a patch of light on the wallpaper" or "It *feels as though* someone were sticking a pin into me." The introspective account tells us about the individual's state of consciousness in the same way as does "I see a patch of light" or "I feel a pin being stuck into me": it differs from the corresponding perception statement in so far as it withdraws any claim about what is actually going on in the external world. From the point of view of the psychologist, the change from talking about the environment to talking about one's perceptual sensations is simply a matter of disinhibiting certain reactions. These are reactions which one normally suppresses because one has learned that in the prevailing circumstances they are unlikely to provide a good indication of the state of the environment.[18] To say that something looks green to me is simply to say that my experience is like the experience I get when I see something that really is green. In my reply to Objection 3, I pointed out the extreme openness or generality of statements which report experiences. This explains why there is no language of private qualities. (Just as "someone," unlike "the doctor," is a colorless word.)[19]

If it is asked what is the difference between those brain processes which, in my view, are experiences and those brain processes which are not, I can only reply that it is at present unknown. I have been tempted to conjecture that the difference may in part be that between perception and reception (in D.M. MacKay's terminology) and that the type of brain process which is an experience might be identifiable with MacKay's active "matching response."[20] This, however, cannot be the whole story, because sometimes I can perceive something unconsciously, as when I take a handkerchief out of a drawer without being aware that I am doing so. But at the very least, we can classify the brain processes which are experiences as those brain processes which are, or might have been, causal conditions of those pieces of verbal behavior which we call reports of immediate experience.

I have now considered a number of objections to the brain-process thesis. I wish now to conclude with some remarks on the logical status of the thesis itself. U.T. Place seems to hold that it is a straight-out scientific hypothesis.[21] If so, he is partly right and partly wrong. If the issue is between (say) a brain-process thesis and a heart thesis, or a liver thesis, or a kidney thesis, then the issue is a purely empirical one, and the verdict is overwhelmingly in favor of the brain. The right sorts of things don't go on in the heart, liver, or kidney, nor do these organs possess the right sort of complexity of structure. On the other hand, if the issue is between a brain-or-liver-or-kidney thesis (that is, some form of materialism) on the one hand and epiphenomenalism on the other hand, then the issue is not an empirical one. For there is no conceivable experiment which could decide between materialism and epiphenomenalism. This latter issue is not like the average straight-out empirical issue in science, but like the issue between the nineteenth-century English naturalist Philip Gosse[22] and the orthodox geologists and paleontologists of his day. According to Gosse, the earth was created about 4000 B.C. exactly as described in *Genesis,* with twisted rock strata, "evidence" of erosion, and so forth, and all sorts of fossils, all in their appropriate strata, just as if the usual evolutionist story had been true. Clearly this theory is in a sense irrefutable: no evidence can possibly tell against it. Let us ignore the theological setting in which Philip Gosse's hypothesis had been placed, thus ruling out objections of a theological kind, such as "what a queer God who would go to such elaborate lengths to deceive us." Let us suppose that it is held that the universe just *began* in 4004 B.C. with the initial conditions just everywhere as they were in 4004 B.C., and in particular that our own planet began with sediment in the rivers, eroded cliffs, fossils in the rocks, and so on. No scientist would ever entertain this as a serious hypothesis, consistent though it is with all possible evidence. The hypothesis offends against the principles of parsimony and simplicity. There would be far too many brute and inexplicable facts. Why are pterodactyl bones just as they are? No explanation in terms of the evolution of pterodactyls from earlier forms of life would any longer be possible. We would have millions of facts about the world as it was, in 4004 B.C. that just have to be *accepted.*

The issue between the brain-process theory and epiphenomenalism seems to be of the above sort. (Assuming that a behavioristic reduction of introspective reports is not possible.) If it be agreed that there are no cogent philosophical arguments which force us into accepting dualism, and if the brain process theory and dualism are equally consistent with the facts, then the principles of parsimony and simplicity seem to me to decide overwhelmingly in favor of the brain-process theory. As I pointed out earlier, dualism involves a large number of irreducible psychophysical laws (whereby the "nomological danglers" dangle) of a queer sort, that just have to be taken on trust, and are just as difficult to swallow as the irreducible facts about the paleontology of the earth with which we are faced on Philip Gosse's theory.

"Postscript (1995)"

Though I mostly agree with what I said in "Sensations and Brain Processes" there are some minor changes and some elucidations that I should like to make.

Experiences (havings of sensations and images) seemed to be particularly recalcitrant to the behaviouristic approach of Gilbert Ryle, which I had previously espoused. When I wrote the article in question I still thought that beliefs and desires could be elucidated wholly in terms of hypothetical propositions about behaviour. I soon got persuaded by D.M. Armstrong that we should identify beliefs and desires with mental *states* which are contingently identified with brain states. I would have eventually come anyway to such a view because of my general realism and worries about the semantics of the contrary to fact conditionals that play an essential part in a behaviouristic analysis. Beliefs and desires raise questions about intentionality. I can desire a unicorn but there are no unicorns to be desired. This is very odd. I cannot kick a football without there being a football to be kicked. Also I cannot kick a football without kicking some particular football. I can desire a bicycle but no particular one: any decent one will do. So "desire" does not work like "kick." The best way to deal with this seems to be Quine's: say something like "believes-true S" and "desires-true S" where S is a sentence. The sentence serves to individuate a mental state (brain state). Or I could use a predicate in the case of "I desire a unicorn": "I desire-true of myself 'possesses a unicorn.'" (Unicorns may not exist but the predicate "possesses a unicorn" does. I shall not attempt here to defend this account against various objections that might come to mind.)

Another place in which I was too behaviouristic was in my account of colours. I would now identify the yellow colour of a lemon with a state

J.J.C. Smart, "Postscript (1995)" (originally titled "Postscript"), in Paul K. Moser and J.D. Trout (eds), *Contemporary Materialism: A Reader* (Routledge, London, 1995), pp. 104–6.

of the surface of the lemon. It is a state (described "topic-neutrally" as between physicalist and non-physicalist accounts) contingently identified with a physical state, admittedly a highly disjunctive and idiosyncratic state, of no interest presumably to (say) Alpha Centaurians who had very different visual systems, but a physical state nevertheless. Still, this physical state is identified by the discriminatory reactions of normal human percipients in normal light (e.g. cloudy Scottish daylight). See "On Some Criticisms of a Physicalist Theory of Colours" in my *Essays Metaphysical and Moral* (Oxford: Basil Blackwell, 1987).

It has widely been supposed that the identity theory has been outmoded by "functionalism." This is the theory that mental entities are functionally described in terms of their inputs (stimuli) and outputs (behaviour). Thus a kidney might be described not anatomically but (say) as an organ that regulated water flow and cleaned body fluids of poisons. Then we could go on contingently to identify a kidney with a certain shaped piece of anatomy. Or at least in the case of humans and related mammals. Similarly a functionalist might deny that brain states in you and me need to be at all similar, so long as the functions are the same. Now it seems to me that the difference between identity theory and functionalism has been greatly exaggerated. My topic-neutral formula "What is going on in me is like what goes on in me when . . ." is very like a functionalist description, though it asserts (what the functionalist at least would not deny) that the experience of toothache, say, is not something abstract, like a function, but is something *going on.* (So plausibly a brain process.)

The functionalist need not take sides on whether your brain process when you have a pain is similar or not to mine. It is not an all or nothing matter between the functionalist and me. I would expect some similarity. I would expect even more similarity between my present and past brain processes. Perhaps less between mine and a sheep's, but some all the same. Even if we were to make an electronic robot that could feel pain I would expect a similarity at least of an abstract sort (e.g. of wave form) between my brain process and the electronic one. So it is not an all or nothing issue. The same would apply to the distinction between so-called type–type identity theories and so-called token–token ones. A token–token identity theorist holds only that any individual experience is identical with some individual brain process, whereas a type–type theorist would hold that all experiences of a certain sort are identical with brain processes of a certain sort. If asked whether I was a type–type identity theorist I would say "Yes and no," depending on how abstract you allowed the similarities to be.

When we are aware of our inner experiences we are aware of patterns of similarity and difference between them. References to such patterns are "topic-neutral" and so also are descriptions in terms of topic-neutral words such as being intermittent or waxing and waning. I need to contend that we can be aware of salient similarities and differences without being able to say in what respects these similarities subsist, but this contention seems to me to be plausible. (See my article "Materialism," *Journal of Philosophy* LX (1963), 651–62.) Brain processes answer to these topic-neutral descriptions but also have neurophysiological descriptions of which we are unaware. Nevertheless if a sensation is identical with a brain process it must have all the properties of the brain process. (I would no longer speak of the need for a convention as I did in the reply to Objection 6. The thing just follows from the logic of identity.)

Why then does it seem intuitive to us that a sensation has "spooky," non-physical, properties? D.M. Armstrong has suggested in his article "The Headless Woman Illusion and the Defence of Materialism" (*Analysis* XXIX (1968), 48–9) that the trouble comes from confusing "I am not aware of my present experience as being neurophysiological" with the stronger "I am aware of my present experience as non-neurophysiological." The former is true and the latter is false: the true one is compatible with my experience in fact being neurophysiological.

I am now disposed to think of the identity theory as a straight-out scientific hypothesis (as U.T. Place did). In the final two paragraphs of my article I was being too empiricist. Ockham's Razor and considerations of simplicity are perfectly good scientific principles for deciding between hypotheses which are equally favoured by the empirical evidence. Of course philosophical clarification is needed also, but that is common in theoretical science too.

Notes

1 This is a very slightly revised version of a paper which was first published in the *Philosophical Review*, LXVIII (1959), 141–56. Since that date there have been criticisms of my paper by J.T. Stevenson, *Philosophical Review*, LXIX (1960), 505–10, to which I have replied in *Philosophical Review*, LXX (1961), 406–7, and by G. Pitcher and by W.D. Joske, *Australasian Journal of Philosophy*, XXXVIII (1960), 150–60, to which I have replied in the same volume of that journal, pp. 252–54.

2 *British Journal of Psychology*, XLVII (1956), 44–50; page references are to the reprint in V.C. Chappell (ed.), *The Philosophy of Mind* (New York: Dover Publications, 1981, pp. 101–9).

3 *Minnesota Studies in the Philosophy of Science*, Vol. II (Minneapolis: University of Minnesota Press, 1958), pp. 370–497.

4 Some philosophers of my acquaintance, who have the advantage over me in having known Wittgenstein, would say that this interpretation of him is too behavioristic. However, it seems to me a very natural interpretation of his printed words, and whether or not it is Wittgenstein's real view it is certainly

an interesting and important one. I wish to consider it here as a possible rival both to the "brain-process" thesis and to straight-out old-fashioned dualism.

5 See Ryle, *The Concept of Mind* (London: Hutchinson's University Library, 1949), p. 93.

6 On this point see Paul Oppenheim and Hilary Putnam, "Unity of Science as a Working Hypothesis," in *Minnesota Studies in the Philosophy* of *Science*, Vol. II (Minneapolis: University of Minnesota Press, 1958), pp. 3–36.

7 Feigl, *op. cit.*, p. 428. Feigl uses the expression "nomological danglers" for the laws whereby the entities dangle: I have used the expression to refer to the dangling entities themselves.

8 Wittgenstein did not like the word "disposition." I am using it to put in a nutshell (and perhaps inaccurately) the view which I am attributing to Wittgenstein. I should like to repeat that I do not wish to claim that my interpretation of Wittgenstein is correct. Some of those who knew him do not interpret him in this way. It is merely a view which I find myself extracting from his printed words and which I think is important and worth discussing for its own sake.

9 See Place, *op. cit.*, p. 102, and Feigl, *op. cit.*, p. 390, near top.

10 See J.H. Woodger, *Theory Construction*, International Encyclopedia of Unified Science, II, No. 5 (Chicago: University of Chicago Press, 1939), 38. I here permit myself to speak loosely. For warnings against possible ways of going wrong with this sort of talk, see my note "Spatialising Time," *Mind*, LXIV (1955), 239–41.

11 Cf. Feigl, *op. cit.*, p. 439.

12 See Place, *op. cit.*, p. 106; also Feigl, *op cit.*, p. 438.

13 I think this objection was first put to me by Professor Max Black. I think it is the most subtle of any of those I have considered, and the one which I am least confident of having satisfactorily met.

14 See B.A. Farrell, "Experience," *Mind*, LIX (1950), 170–98; reprinted in Chappell, *op. cit.*, pp. 23–48; see especially p. 27.

15 Dr J.R. Smythies claims that a sense-datum language could be taught independently of the material object language ("A Note on the Fallacy of the 'Phenomenological Fallacy,'" *British Journal of Psychology*, XLVIII [1957], 141–44). I am not so sure of this: there must be some public criteria for a person having got a rule wrong before we can teach him the rule. I suppose someone might *accidentally* learn color words by Dr Smythies' procedure. I am not, of course, denying that we can learn a sense-datum language in the sense that we can learn to report our experience. Nor would Place deny it.

16 I owe this objection to Dr C.B. Martin. I gather that he no longer wishes to maintain this objection, at any rate in its present form.

17 Martin did not make this reply, but one of his students did.

18 I owe this point to Place, in correspondence.

19 The "beetle in the box" objection is, *if it is sound*, an objection to *any* view, and in particular the Cartesian one, that introspective reports are genuine reports. So it is no objection to a weaker thesis that I would be concerned to uphold, namely, that if introspective reports of "experiences" are genuinely reports, then the things they are reports of are in fact brain processes.

20 See his article "Towards an Information-Flow Model of Human Behaviour," *British Journal of Psychology*, XLVII (1956), 30–43.

21 *Op. cit.* For a further discussion of this, in reply to the original version of the present paper, see Place's note "Materialism as a Scientific Hypothesis," *Philosophical Review*, LXIX (1960), 101–4.
22 See the entertaining account of Gosse's book *Omphalos* by Martin Gardner in *Fads and Fallacies in the Name of Science*, 2nd edn (New York: Dover, 1957), pp. 124–27.

7

Saul A. Kripke, "Naming and Necessity"

Lecture I: January 20, 1970

. . .

This table is composed of molecules. Might it not have been composed of molecules? Certainly it was a scientific discovery of great moment that it was composed of molecules (or atoms). But could anything be this very object and not be composed of molecules? Certainly there is some feeling that the answer to that must be "no." At any rate, it's hard to imagine under what circumstances you would have this very object and find that it is not composed of molecules. A quite different question is whether it is in fact composed of molecules in the actual world and how we know this. (I will go into more detail about these questions about essence later on.)

I wish at this point to introduce something which I need in the methodology of discussing the theory of names that I'm talking about. We need the notion of "identity across possible worlds" as it's usually and, as I think, somewhat misleadingly called,[1] to explicate one distinction that I want to make now. What's the difference between asking whether it's necessary that 9 is greater than 7 or whether it's necessary that the number of planets is greater than 7? Why does one show anything more about essence than the other? The answer to this might be intuitively "Well, look, the number of planets might have been different from what it in fact is. It doesn't make any sense, though, to say that nine might have been different from what it in fact is." Let's use some terms quasi-technically. Let's call something a *rigid designator* if in every possible world it designates the same object, a *nonrigid* or *accidental designator* if that is not the case. Of course we don't require that the objects exist in all possible worlds. Certainly Nixon might not have existed if his parents had not gotten married, in the normal

Saul A. Kripke, *Naming and Necessity* (excerpts) (Harvard University Press, Cambridge, Mass., 1980), pp. 47–50, 75–6, 97–100, 127–32, 139–55.

course of things. When we think of a property as essential to an object we usually mean that it is true of that object in any case where it would have existed. A rigid designator of a necessary existent can be called *strongly rigid*.

One of the intuitive theses I will maintain in these talks is that *names* are rigid designators. Certainly they seem to satisfy the intuitive test mentioned above: although someone other than the U.S. President in 1970 might have been the U.S. President in 1970 (e.g., Humphrey might have), no one other than Nixon might have been Nixon. In the same way, a designator rigidly designates a certain object if it designates that object wherever the object exists; if, in addition, the object is a necessary existent, the designator can be called *strongly rigid*. For example, "the President of the U.S. in 1970" designates a certain man, Nixon; but someone else (e.g., Humphrey) might have been the President in 1970, and Nixon might not have; so this designator is not rigid.

In these lectures, I will argue, intuitively, that proper names are rigid designators, for although the man (Nixon) might not have been the President, it is not the case that he might not have been Nixon (though he might not have been *called* "Nixon"). Those who have argued that to make sense of the notion of rigid designator, we must antecedently make sense of "criteria of transworld identity" have precisely reversed the cart and the horse; it is *because* we can refer (rigidly) to Nixon, and stipulate that we are speaking of what might have happened to *him* (under certain circumstances), that "transworld identifications" are unproblematic in such cases.[2]

The tendency to demand purely qualitative descriptions of counterfactual situations has many sources. One, perhaps, is the confusion of the epistemological and the metaphysical, between a prioricity and necessity. If someone identifies necessity with a prioricity, and thinks that objects are named by means of uniquely identifying properties, he may think that it is the properties used to identify the object which, being known about it *a priori*, must be used to identify it in all possible worlds, to find out which object is Nixon. As against this, I repeat: (1) Generally, things aren't "found out" about a counterfactual situation, they are stipulated; (2) possible worlds need not be given purely qualitatively, as if we were looking at them through a telescope. And we will see shortly that the properties an object has in every counterfactual world have nothing to do with properties used to identify it in the actual world.[3]

. . .

Lecture II: January 22, 1970

. . .

Similarly, even if we define what a meter is by reference to the standard meter stick, it will be a contingent truth and not a necessary one that that particular stick is one meter long. If it had been stretched, it would have been longer than one meter. And that is because we use the term "one meter" rigidly to designate a certain length. Even though we fix what length we are designating by an accidental property of that length, just as in the case of the name of the man we may pick the man out by an accidental property of the man, still we use the name to designate that man or that length in all possible worlds. The property we use need not be one which is regarded in any way as necessary or essential. In the case of a yard, the original way this length was picked out was, I think, the distance when the arm of King Henry I of England was outstretched from the tip of his finger to his nose. If this was the length of a yard, it nevertheless will not be a necessary truth that the distance between the tip of his finger and his nose should be a yard. Maybe an accident might have happened to foreshorten his arm; that would be possible. And the reason that it's not a necessary truth is not that there ought be other criteria in a "cluster concept" of yard-hood. Even a man who strictly uses King Henry's arm as his one standard of length can say, counterfactually, that if certain things had happened to the King, the exact distance between the end of one of his fingers and his nose would not have been exactly a yard. He need not be using a cluster as long as he uses the term "yard" to pick out a certain fixed reference to be that length in all possible worlds.

. . .

I think the next topic I shall want to talk about is that of statements of identity. Are these necessary or contingent? The matter has been in some dispute in recent philosophy. First, everyone agrees that descriptions can be used to make contingent identity statements. If it is true that the man who invented bifocals was the first Postmaster General of the United States – that these were one and the same – it's contingently true. That is, it might have been the case that one man invented bifocals and another was the first Postmaster General of the United States. So certainly when you make identity statements using descriptions – when you say "the x such that φx and the x such that ψx are one and the same" – that can be a contingent fact. But philosophers have been interested also in the question of identity statements between names. When we say "Hesperus is Phosphorus" or "Cicero is Tully," is what we are saying necessary or contingent? Further, they've been interested in another type of identity statement, which comes

140

from scientific theory. We identify, for example, light with electromagnetic radiation between certain limits of wavelengths, or with a stream of photons. We identify heat with the motion of molecules; sound with a certain sort of wave disturbance in the air; and so on. Concerning such statements the following thesis is commonly held. First, that these are obviously contingent identities: we've found out that light is a stream of photons, but of course it might not have been a stream of photons. Heat is in fact the motion of molecules; we found that out, but heat might not have been the motion of molecules. Secondly, many philosophers feel damned lucky that these examples are around. Now, why? These philosophers, whose views are expounded in a vast literature, hold to a thesis called "the identity thesis" with respect to some psychological concepts. They think, say, that pain is just a certain material state of the brain or of the body, or what have you – say the stimulation of C-fibers. (It doesn't matter what.) Some people have then objected, "Well, look, there's perhaps a *correlation* between pain and these states of the body; but this must just be a contingent correlation between two different things, because it was an empirical discovery that this correlation ever held. Therefore, by 'pain' we must mean something different from this state of the body or brain; and, therefore, they must be two different things."

Then it's said, "Ah, but you see, this is wrong! Everyone knows that there can be contingent identities." First, as in the bifocals and Postmaster General case, which I have mentioned before. Second, in the case, believed closer to the present paradigm, of theoretical identifications, such as light and a stream of photons, or water and a certain compound of hydrogen and oxygen. These are all contingent identities. They might have been false. It's no surprise, therefore, that it can be true as a matter of contingent fact and not of any necessity that feeling pain, or seeing red, is just a certain state of the human body. Such psychophysical identifications can be contingent facts just as the other identities are contingent facts. And of course there are widespread motivations – ideological, or just not wanting to have the "nomological dangler" of mysterious connections not accounted for by the laws of physics, one to one correlations between two different kinds of thing, material states, and things of an entirely different kind, which lead people to want to believe this thesis.

I guess the main thing I'll talk about first is identity statements between names. But I hold the following about the general case. First, that characteristic theoretical identifications like "Heat is the motion of molecules," are not contingent truths but necessary truths, and here of course I don't mean just physically necessary, but necessary in the highest degree – whatever that means. (Physical necessity, *might* turn out to be necessity in the highest degree. But that's a question which I don't wish to prejudge. At least for this sort of example, it might be that when something's physically necessary, it always is necessary *tout court*.) Second, that the way in which these have turned out to be necessary truths does not seem to me to be a way in which the mind–brain identities could turn out to be either necessary or contingently true. So this analogy has to go. It's hard to see what to put in its place. It's hard to see therefore how to avoid concluding that the two are actually different.

. . .

Lecture III: January 29, 1970

. . .

According to the view I advocate, then, terms for natural kinds are much closer to proper names than is ordinarily supposed. The old term "common name" is thus quite appropriate for predicates marking out species or natural kinds, such as "cow" or "tiger." My considerations apply also, however, to certain mass terms for natural kinds, such as "gold," "water," and the like. It is interesting to compare my views to those of Mill. Mill counts both predicates like "cow," definite descriptions, and proper names as names. He says of "singular" names that they are connotative if they are definite descriptions but non-connotative if they are proper names. On the other hand, Mill says that *all* "general" names are connotative; such a predicate as "human being" is defined as the conjunction of certain properties which give necessary and sufficient conditions for humanity – rationality, animality, and certain physical features.[4] The modern logical tradition, as represented by Frege and Russell, seems to hold that Mill was wrong about singular names, but right about general names. More recent philosophy has followed suit, except that, in the case of both proper names and natural kind terms, it often replaces the notion of defining properties by that of a cluster of properties, only some of which need to be satisfied in each particular case. My own view, on the other hand, regards Mill as more-or-less right about "singular" names, but wrong about "general" names. *Perhaps* some "general" names ("foolish," "fat," "yellow") express properties.[5] In a significant sense, such general names as "cow" and "tiger" do not, unless *being a cow* counts trivially as a property. Certainly "cow" and "tiger" are *not* short for the conjunction of properties a dictionary would take to define them, as Mill thought. Whether science can discover empirically that certain properties are *necessary* of cows, or of tigers, is another question, which I answer affirmatively.

Let's consider how this applies to the types of identity statements expressing scientific discoveries that I talked about before – say, that water is H_2O. It certainly represents a discovery that water is H_2O. We identified water originally by its characteristic feel, appearance and perhaps taste, (though the taste may usually be due to the impurities). If there were a substance, even actually, which had a completely different atomic structure from that of water, but resembled water in these respects, would we say that some water wasn't H_2O? I think not. We would say instead that just as there is a fool's gold there could be a fool's water; a substance which, though having the properties by which we originally identified water, would not in fact be water. And this, I think, applies not only to the actual world but even when we talk about counterfactual situations. If there had been a substance, which was a fool's water, it would then be fool's water and not water. On the other hand if this substance can take another form – such as the polywater allegedly discovered in the Soviet Union, with very different identifying marks from that of what we now call water – it is a form of water because it is the same substance, even though it doesn't have the appearances by which we originally identified water.

Let's consider the statement "Light is a stream of photons" or "Heat is the motion of molecules." By referring to light, of course, I mean something which we have some of in this room. When I refer to heat, I refer not to an internal sensation that someone may have, but to an external phenomenon which we perceive through the sense of feeling; it produces a characteristic sensation which we call the sensation of heat. Heat *is* the motion of molecules. We have also discovered that increasing heat corresponds to increasing motion of molecules, or, strictly speaking, increasing average kinetic energy of molecules. So temperature is identified with mean molecular kinetic energy. However I won't talk about temperature because there is the question of how the actual scale is to be set. It might just be set in terms of the mean molecular kinetic energy.[6] But what represents an interesting phenomenological discovery is that when it's hotter the molecules are moving faster. We have also discovered about light that light is a stream of photons; alternatively it is a form of electromagnetic radiation. Originally we identified light by the characteristic internal visual impressions it can produce in us, that make us able to see. Heat, on the other hand, we originally identified by the characteristic effect on one aspect of our nerve endings or our sense of touch.

Imagine a situation in which human beings were blind or their eyes didn't work. They were unaffected by light. Would that have been a situation in which light did not exist? It seems to me that it would not. It would have been a situation in which our eyes were not sensitive to light. Some creatures may have eyes not sensitive to light. Among such creatures are unfortunately some people, of course; they are called "blind." Even if all people had had awful vestigial growths and just couldn't see a thing, the light might have been around; but it would not have been able to affect people's eyes in the proper way. So it seems to me that such a situation would be a situation in which there was light, but people could not see it. So, though we may identify light by the characteristic visual impressions it produces in us, this seems to be a good example of fixing a reference. We fix what light is by the fact that it is whatever, out in the world, affects our eyes in a certain way. But now, talking about counterfactual situations in which, let's say, people were blind, we would not then say that since, in such situations, nothing could affect their eyes, light would not exist; rather we would say that that would be a situation in which light – the thing we have identified as that which in fact enables us to see – existed but did not manage to help us see due to some defect in us.

Perhaps we can imagine that, by some miracle, sound waves somehow enabled some creature to see. I mean, they gave him visual impressions just as we have, maybe exactly the same color sense. We can also imagine the same creature to be completely *insensitive* to light (photons). Who knows what subtle undreamt of possibilities there may be? Would we say that in such a possible world, it was sound which was light, that these wave motions in the air were light? It seems to me that, given our concept of light, we should describe the situation differently. It would be a situation in which certain creatures, maybe even those who were called "people" and inhabited this planet, were sensitive not to light but to sound waves, sensitive to them in exactly the same way that we are sensitive to light. If this is so, once we have found out what light is, when we talk about other possible worlds we are talking about *this* phenomenon in the world, and not using "light" as a phrase *synonymous* with "whatever gives us the visual impression – whatever helps us to see"; for there might have been light and it not helped us to see; and even something else might have helped us to see. The way we identified light *fixed a reference*.

And similarly for other such phrases, such as "heat." Here heat is something which we have identified (and fixed the reference of its name) by its giving a certain sensation, which we call "the sensation of heat." We don't have a special name for this sensation other than as a sensation of heat. It's interesting that the language is this way. Whereas you might suppose it, from what I am saying, to have been the other way. At any rate, we identify heat and are able to sense it by the fact that it produces in us a sensation of heat. It might here be so important to the concept that its reference is fixed in this way, that if someone else detects heat by some sort of instrument, but is unable to feel it, we might want to say, if we like, that the concept of heat is not the same even though the referent is the same.

Nevertheless, the term "heat" doesn't *mean* "whatever gives people these sensations." For first, people might not have been sensitive to heat, and yet the heat still have existed in the external world. Secondly, let us suppose that somehow light rays, because of some difference in their nerve endings, *did* give them these sensations. It would not then be heat but light which gave people the sensation which we call the sensation of heat.

Can we then imagine a possible world in which heat was not molecular motion? We can imagine, of course, having discovered that it was not. It seems to me that any case which someone will think of, which he thinks at first is a case in which heat – contrary to what is actually the case – would have been something other than molecular motion, would actually be a case in which some creatures with different nerve endings from ours inhabit this planet (maybe even we, if it's a contingent fact about us that we have this particular neural structure), and in which these creatures were sensitive to that something else, say light, in such a way that they felt the same thing that we feel when we feel heat. But this is not a situation in which, say, light would have been heat, or even in which a stream of photons would have been heat, but a situation in which a stream of photons would have produced the characteristic sensations which *we* call "sensations of heat."

Similarly for many other such identifications, say, that lightning is electricity. Flashes of lightning are flashes of electricity. Lightning is an electrical discharge. We can imagine, of course, I suppose, other ways in which the sky might be illuminated at night with the same sort of flash without any electrical discharge being present. Here too, I am inclined to say, when we imagine this, we imagine something with all the visual appearances of lightning but which is not, in fact, lightning. One could be told: this appeared to be lightning but it was not. I suppose this might even happen now. Someone might, by a clever sort of apparatus, produce some phenomenon in the sky which would fool people into thinking that there was lightning even though in fact no lightning was present. And you wouldn't say that that phenomenon, because it looks like lightning, was in fact lightning. It was a different phenomenon from lightning, which is the phenomenon of an electrical discharge; and this is not lightning but just something that deceives us into thinking that there is lightning.

. . .

Usually, when a proper name is passed from link to link, the way the reference of the name is fixed is of little importance to us. It matters not at all that different speakers may fix the reference of the name in different ways, provided that they give it the same referent. The situation is probably not very different for species names, though the temptation to think that the metallurgist has a different concept of gold from the man who has never seen any may be somewhat greater. The interesting fact is that the way the reference is fixed seems overwhelmingly important to us in the case of sensed phenomena: a blind man who uses the term "light," even though he uses it as a rigid designator for the very same phenomenon as we, seems to us to have lost a great deal, perhaps enough for us to declare that he has a different concept. ("Concept" here is used non-technically!) The fact that we identify light in a certain way seems to us to be *crucial*, even though it is not necessary; the intimate connection may create an *illusion* of necessity. I think that this observation, together with the remarks on property-identity above, may well be essential to an understanding of the traditional disputes over primary and secondary qualities.[7]

Let us return to the question of theoretical identification. Theoretical identities, according to the conception I advocate, are generally identities involving two rigid designators and therefore are examples of the necessary *a posteriori*. Now in spite of the arguments I gave before for the distinction between necessary and *a priori* truth, the notion of *a posteriori* necessary truth may still be somewhat puzzling. Someone may well be inclined to argue as follows: "You have admitted that heat might have turned out not to have been molecular motion, and that gold might have turned out not to have been the element with the atomic number 79. For that matter, you also have acknowledged that Elizabeth II might have turned out not to be the daughter of George VI, or even to originate in the particular sperm and egg we had thought, and this table might have turned out to be made from ice made from water from the Thames. I gather that Hesperus might have turned out not to be Phosphorus. What then can you mean when you say that such eventualities are impossible? If Hesperus might have *turned out* not to be Phosphorus, then Hesperus might not have *been* Phosphorus. And similarly for the other cases: if the world could have *turned out* otherwise, it could have *been* otherwise. To deny this fact is to deny the self-evident modal principle that what is entailed by a possibility must itself be possible. Nor can you evade the difficulty by declaring the 'might have' of 'might have turned out otherwise' to be merely epistemic, in the way that 'Fermat's Last Theorem might turn out to be true and might turn out to be false' merely expresses our present ignorance, and 'Arithmetic might have turned out to be complete' signals our former ignorance. In these mathematical cases, we may have been ignorant, but it was in fact mathematically impossible for the answer to turn out other than it did. Not so in your favorite cases of essence and of identity between two rigid designators: it really is logically possible that gold should have turned out to be a compound, and this table might really have turned out not to be made of wood, let alone of a given particular block of wood. The contrast with the mathematical case could not be greater and would not be alleviated even if, as you suggest, there may be mathematical truths which it is impossible to know a *priori*."

Perhaps anyone who has caught the spirit of my previous remarks can give my answer himself, but there is a clarification of my previous discussion which is relevant here. The objector is correct when he argues that if I hold that this table could not have been made of ice, then I must also hold that it could not have turned out to be made of ice; *it could have turned out that P* entails that P could have been the case. What, then, does the intuition that the table might have turned out to have been made of ice or of anything else, that it might even have turned out not to be made of molecules, amount to? I think that it means simply that there might have been *a table* looking and feeling just like this one and placed in this very position in the room, which was in fact made of ice. In other words, I (or some conscious being) could have been *qualitatively in the same epistemic situation* that in fact obtains, I could have the same sensory evidence that I in fact have, about *a table* which was made of ice. The situation is thus akin to the one which inspired the counterpart theorists; when I speak of the possibility of the table turning out to be made of various things, I am speaking loosely. *This* table itself could not have had an origin different from the one it in fact had, but in a situation qualitatively identical to this one with respect to all the evidence I had in advance, the room could have contained *a table made of ice* in place of this one. Something like counterpart theory is thus applicable to the situation, but it applies only because we are *not* interested in what might have been true of *this particular* table, but in what might or might not be true of *a table* given certain evidence. It is precisely because it is *not* true that this table might have been made of ice from the Thames that we must turn here to qualitative descriptions and counterparts. To apply these notions to genuine *de re* modalities is, from the present standpoint, perverse.

The general answer to the objector can be stated, then, as follows: Any necessary truth, whether *a priori* or *a posteriori*, could not have turned out otherwise. In the case of some necessary *a posteriori* truths, however, we can say that under appropriate qualitatively identical evidential situations, an appropriate corresponding qualitative statement might have been false. The loose and inaccurate statement that gold might have turned out to be a compound should be replaced (roughly) by the statement that it is logically possible that there should have been a compound with all the properties originally known to hold of gold. The inaccurate statement that Hesperus might have turned out not to be Phosphorus should be replaced by the true contingency mentioned earlier in these lectures: two distinct bodies might have occupied, in the morning and the evening, respectively, the very positions actually occupied by Hesperus-Phosphorus-Venus.[8] The reason the example of Fermat's Last Theorem gives a different impression is that here no analogue suggests itself, except for the extremely general statement that, in the absence of proof or disproof, it is possible for *a mathematical conjecture* to be either true or false.

147

I have not given any general paradigm for the appropriate corresponding qualitative contingent statement. Since we are concerned with how things might have turned out otherwise, our general paradigm is to redescribe both the prior evidence and the statement qualitatively and claim that they are only contingently related. In the case of identities, using two rigid designators, such as the Hesperus–Phosphorus case above, there is a simpler paradigm which is often usable to at least approximately the same effect. Let "R_1" and "R_2" be the two rigid designators which flank the identity sign. Then "$R_1 = R_2$" is necessary if true. The references of "R_1" and "R_2," respectively, may well be fixed by nonrigid designators "D_1" and "D_2," in the Hesperus and Phosphorus cases these have the form "the heavenly body in such-and-such position in the sky in the evening (morning)." Then although "$R_1 = R_2$" is necessary, "$D_1 = D_2$" may well be contingent, and this is often what leads to the erroneous view that "$R_1 = R_2$" might have turned out otherwise.

I finally turn to an all too cursory discussion of the application of the foregoing considerations to the identity thesis. Identity theorists have been concerned with several distinct types of identifications: of a person with his body, of a particular sensation (or event or state of having the sensation) with a particular brain state (Jones's pain at 06:00 was his C-fiber stimulation at that time), and of *types* of mental states with the corresponding *types* of physical states (pain is the stimulation of C-fibers). Each of these, and other types of identifications in the literature, present analytical problems, rightly raised by Cartesian critics, which cannot be avoided by a simple appeal to an alleged confusion of synonymy with identity. I should mention that there is of course no obvious bar, at least (I say cautiously) none which should occur to any intelligent thinker on a first reflection just before bedtime, to advocacy of some identity theses while doubting or denying others. For example, some philosophers have accepted the identity of particular sensations with particular brain states while denying the possibility of identities between mental and physical *types*.[9] I will concern myself primarily with the type–type identities, and the philosophers in question will thus be immune to much of the discussion; but I will mention the other kinds of identities briefly.

Descartes, and others following him, argued that a person or mind is distinct from his body, since the mind could exist without the body. He might equally well have argued the same conclusion from the premise that the body could have existed without the mind.[10] Now the one response which I regard as plainly inadmissible is the response which cheerfully accepts the Cartesian premise while denying the Cartesian conclusion. Let "Descartes" be a name, or rigid designator, of a certain person, and let "B" be a rigid designator of his body. Then if Descartes were indeed identical to B, the supposed identity, being an identity between two rigid designators, would be necessary, and Descartes could not exist without B and B could not exist without Descartes. The case is not at all comparable to the alleged analogue, the identity of the first Postmaster General with the inventor of bifocals. True, this identity obtains despite the fact that there could have been a first Postmaster General even though bifocals had never been invented. The reason is that "the inventor of bifocals" is not a rigid designator; a world in which no one invented bifocals is not *ipso facto* a world in which Franklin did not exist. The alleged analogy therefore collapses; a philosopher who wishes to refute the Cartesian conclusion must refute the Cartesian premise, and the latter task is not trivial.

Let "A" name a particular pain sensation, and let "B" name the corresponding brain state, or the brain state some identity theorist wishes to identify with A. *Prima facie*, it would seem that it is at least logically possible that B should have existed (Jones's brain could have been in exactly that state at the time in question) without Jones feeling any pain at all, and thus without the presence of A. Once again, the identity theorist cannot admit the possibility cheerfully and proceed from there; consistency, and the principle of the necessity of identities using rigid designators, disallows any such course. If A and B were identical, the identity would have to be necessary. The difficulty can hardly be evaded by arguing that although B could not exist without A, *being a pain* is merely a contingent property of A, and that therefore the presence of B without pain does not imply the presence of B without A. Can any case of essence be more obvious than the fact that *being a pain* is a necessary property of each pain? The identity theorist who wishes to adopt the strategy in question must even argue that *being a sensation* is a contingent property of A, for *prima facie* it would seem logically possible that B could exist without any sensation with which it might plausibly be identified. Consider a particular pain, or other sensation, that you once had. Do you find it at all plausible that *that very sensation* could have existed without being a sensation, the way a certain inventor (Franklin) could have existed without being an inventor?

I mention this strategy because it seems to me to be adopted by a large number of identity theorists. These theorists, believing as they do that the supposed identity of a brain state with the corresponding mental state is to be analyzed on the paradigm of the contingent identity of Benjamin Franklin with the inventor of bifocals, realize that just as his contingent activity made Benjamin Franklin into the inventor of bifocals, so some contingent property of the brain state must make it into a pain. Generally they wish this property to be one statable in physical or at least "topic-neutral" language, so that the materialist cannot be accused of positing irreducible non-physical properties. A typical view is that *being a pain*, as

149

a property of a physical state, is to be analyzed in terms of the "causal role" of the state,[11] in terms of the characteristic stimuli (e.g., pinpricks) which cause it and the characteristic behavior it causes. I will not go into the details of such analyses, even though I usually find them faulty on specific grounds in addition to the general modal considerations I argue here. All I need to observe here is that the "causal role" of the physical state is regarded by the theorists in question as a contingent property of the state, and thus it is supposed to be a contingent property of the state that it is a mental state at all, let alone that it is something as specific as a pain. To repeat, this notion seems to me self-evidently absurd. It amounts to the view that the *very pain I now have* could have existed without being a mental state at all.

I have not discussed the converse problem, which is closer to the original Cartesian consideration – namely, that just as it seems that the brain state could have existed without any pain, so it seems that the pain could have existed without the corresponding brain state. Note that *being a brain state* is evidently an essential property of B (the brain state). Indeed, even more is true: not only being a brain state, but even being a brain state of a specific type is an essential property of B. The configuration of brain cells whose presence at a given time constitutes the presence of B at that time is essential to B, and in its absence B would not have existed. Thus someone who wishes to claim that the brain state and the pain are identical must argue that the pain A could not have existed without a quite specific type of configuration of molecules. If $A = B$, then the identity of A with B is necessary, and any essential property of one must be an essential property of the other. Someone who wishes to maintain an identity thesis cannot simply *accept* the Cartesian intuitions that A can exist without B, that B can exist without A, that the correlative presence of anything with mental properties is merely contingent to B, and that the correlative presence of any specific physical properties is merely contingent to A. He must explain these intuitions away, showing how they are illusory. This task may not be impossible; we have seen above how some things which appear to be contingent turn out, on closer examination, to be necessary. The task, however, is obviously not child's play, and we shall see below how difficult it is.

The final kind of identity, the one which I said would get the closest attention, is the type–type sort of identity exemplified by the identification of pain with the stimulation of C-fibers. These identifications are supposed to be analogous with such scientific type–type identifications as the identity of heat with molecular motion, of water with hydrogen hydroxide, and the like. Let us consider, as an example, the analogy supposed to hold between the materialist identification and that of heat with molecular motion; both identifications identify two types of phenomena. The usual view holds that

the identification of heat with molecular motion and of pain with the stimulation of C-fibers are both contingent. We have seen above that since "heat"
and "molecular motion" are both rigid designators, the identification of the
phenomena they name is necessary. What about "pain" and "C-fiber stimulation"? It should be clear from the previous discussion that "pain" is a
rigid designator of the type, or phenomenon, it designates: if something is
a pain it is essentially so, and it seems absurd to suppose that pain could
have been some phenomenon other than the one it is. The same holds for
the term "C-fiber stimulation," provided that "C-fibers" is a rigid designator, as I will suppose here. (The supposition is somewhat risky, since I
know virtually nothing about C-fibers, except that the stimulation of them
is said to be correlated with pain.[12] The point is unimportant; if "C-fibers"
is not a rigid designator, simply replace it by one which is, or suppose it
used as a rigid designator in the present context.) Thus the identity of pain
with the stimulation of C-fibers, if true, must be *necessary.*

So far the analogy between the identification of heat with molecular
motion and pain with the stimulation of C-fibers has not failed; it has
merely turned out to be the opposite of what is usually thought – both, if
true, must be necessary. This means that the identity theorist is committed
to the view that there could not be a C-fiber stimulation which was not a
pain nor a pain which was not a C-fiber stimulation. These consequences
are certainly surprising and counterintuitive, but let us not dismiss the identity theorist too quickly. Can he perhaps show that the apparent possibility
of pain not having turned out to be C-fiber stimulation, or of there being
an instance of one of the phenomena which is not an instance of the other,
is an illusion of the same sort as the illusion that water might not have been
hydrogen hydroxide, or that heat might not have been molecular motion?
If so, he will have rebutted the Cartesian, not, as in the conventional
analysis, by accepting his premise while exposing the fallacy of his argument, but rather by the reverse – while the Cartesian argument, given its
premise of the contingency of the identification, is granted to yield its
conclusion, the premise is to be exposed as superficially plausible but false.

Now I do not think it likely that the identity theorist will succeed in such
an endeavor. I want to argue that, at least, the case cannot be interpreted
as analogous to that of scientific identification of the usual sort, as exemplified by the identity of heat and molecular motion. What was the strategy
used above to handle the apparent contingency of certain cases of the necessary *a posteriori*? The strategy was to argue that although the statement
itself is necessary, someone could, *qualitatively* speaking, be in the same
epistemic situation as the original, and in such a situation a *qualitatively*
analogous statement could be false. In the case of identities between two
rigid designators, the strategy can be approximated by a simpler one:

Consider how the references of the designators are determined; if these coincide only contingently, it is this fact which gives the original statement its illusion of contingency. In the case of heat and molecular motion, the way these two paradigms work out is simple. When someone says, inaccurately, that heat might have turned out not to be molecular motion, what is true in what he says is that someone could have sensed a phenomenon in the same way we sense heat, that is, feels it by means of its production of the sensation we call "the sensation of heat" (call it "S"), even though that phenomenon was not molecular motion. He means, additionally, that the planet might have been inhabited by creatures who did not get S when they were in the presence of molecular motion, though perhaps getting it in the presence of something else. Such creatures would be, in some qualitative sense, in the same epistemic situation as we are, they could use a rigid designator for the phenomenon that causes sensation S in them (the rigid designator could even be "heat"), yet it would not be molecular motion (and therefore not heat!), which was causing the sensation.

Now can something be said analogously to explain away the feeling that the identity of pain and the stimulation of C-fibers, if it is a scientific discovery, could have turned out otherwise? I do not see that such an analogy is possible. In the case of the apparent possibility that molecular motion might have existed in the absence of heat, what seemed really possible is that molecular motion should have existed without being *felt as heat*, that is, it might have existed without producing the sensation S, the sensation of heat. In the appropriate sentient beings is it analogously possible that a stimulation of C-fibers should have existed without being felt as pain? If this is possible, then the stimulation of C-fibers can itself exist without pain, since for it to exist without being *felt as pain* is for it to exist without there *being any* pain. Such a situation would be in flat out contradiction with the supposed necessary identity of pain and the corresponding physical state, and the analogue holds for any physical state which might be identified with a corresponding mental state. The trouble is that the identity theorist does not hold that the physical state merely *produces* the mental state, rather he wishes the two to be identical and thus *a fortiori* necessarily co-occurrent. In the case of molecular motion and heat there is something, namely, the sensation of heat, which is an intermediary between the external phenomenon and the observer. In the mental–physical case no such intermediary is possible, since here the physical phenomenon is supposed to be identical with the internal phenomenon itself. Someone can be in the same epistemic situation as he would be if there were heat, even in the absence of heat, simply by feeling the sensation of heat, and even in the presence of heat, he can have the same evidence as he would have in the absence of heat simply by lacking the sensation S. No such possibility

152

exists in the case of pain and other mental phenomena. To be in the same epistemic situation that would obtain if one had a pain *is* to have a pain; to be in the same epistemic situation that would obtain in the absence of a pain *is* not to have a pain. The apparent contingency of the connection between the mental state and the corresponding brain state thus cannot be explained by some sort of qualitative analogue as in the case of heat.

We have just analyzed the situation in terms of the notion of qualitatively identical epistemic situation. The trouble is that the notion of an epistemic situation qualitatively identical to one in which the observer had a sensation *S* simply *is* one in which the observer had that sensation. The same point can be made in terms of the notion of what picks out the reference of a rigid designator. In the case of the identity of heat with molecular motion the important consideration was that although "heat" is a rigid designator, the reference of that designator was determined by an accidental property of the referent, namely the property of producing in us the sensation *S*. It is thus possible that a phenomenon should have been rigidly designated in the same way as a phenomenon of heat, with its reference also picked out by means of the sensation *S*, without that phenomenon being heat and therefore without its being molecular motion. Pain, on the other hand, is not picked out by one of its accidental properties; rather it is picked out by the property of being pain itself, by its immediate phenomenological quality. Thus pain, unlike heat, is not only rigidly designated by "pain" but the reference of the designator is determined by an essential property of the referent. Thus it is not possible to say that although pain is necessarily identical with a certain physical state, a certain phenomenon can be picked out in the same way we pick out pain without being correlated with that physical state. If any phenomenon is picked out in exactly the same way that we pick out pain, then that phenomenon *is* pain.

Perhaps the same point can be made more vivid without such specific reference to the technical apparatus in these lectures. Suppose we imagine God creating the world; what does He need to do to make the identity of heat and molecular motion obtain? Here it would seem that all He needs to do is to create the heat, that is, the molecular motion itself. If the air molecules on this earth are sufficiently agitated, if there is a burning fire, then the earth will be hot even if there are no observers to see it. God created light (and thus created streams of photons, according to present scientific doctrine) before He created human and animal observers; and the same presumably holds for heat. How then does it appear to us that the identity of molecular motion with heat is a substantive scientific fact, that the mere creation of molecular motion still leaves God with the additional task of making molecular motion into heat? This feeling is indeed illusory, but what *is* a substantive task for the Deity is the task of making molecular motion felt as heat. To do this He must create some sentient beings to insure that the molecular motion produces the sensation S in them. Only after he has done this will there be beings who can learn that the sentence "Heat is the motion of molecules" expresses an *a posteriori* truth in precisely the same way that we do.

What about the case of the stimulation of C-fibers? To create this phenomenon, it would seem that God need only create beings with C-fibers capable of the appropriate type of physical stimulation; whether the beings are conscious or not is irrelevant here. It would seem, though, that to make the C-fiber stimulation correspond to pain, or be felt as pain, God must do something in addition to the mere creation of the C-fiber stimulation; He must let the creatures feel the C-fiber stimulation as *pain,* and not as a tickle, or as warmth, or as nothing, as apparently would also have been within His powers. If these things in fact are within His powers, the relation between the pain God creates and the stimulation of C-fibers cannot be identity. For if so, the stimulation could exist without the pain; and since "pain" and "C-fiber stimulation" are rigid, this fact implies that the relation between the two phenomena is not that of identity. God had to do some work, in addition to making the man himself, to make a certain man be the inventor of bifocals; the man could well exist without inventing any such thing. The same cannot be said for pain; if the phenomenon exists at all, no further work should be required to make it into pain.

In sum, the correspondence between a brain state and a mental state seems to have a certain obvious element of contingency. We have seen that identity is not a relation which can hold contingently between objects. Therefore, if the identity thesis were correct, the element of contingency would not lie in the relation between the mental and physical states. It cannot lie, as in the case of heat and molecular motion, in the relation between the phenomenon (= heat = molecular motion) and the way it is felt or appears (sensation S), since in the case of mental phenomena there is no "appearance" beyond the mental phenomenon itself.

Here I have been emphasizing the possibility, or apparent possibility, of a physical state without the corresponding mental state. The reverse possibility, the mental state (pain) without the physical state (C-fiber stimulation) also presents problems for the identity theorists which cannot be resolved by appeal to the analogy of heat and molecular motion.

I have discussed similar problems more briefly for views equating the self with the body, and particular mental events with particular physical events, without discussing possible countermoves in the same detail as in the type–type case. Suffice it to say that I suspect that the considerations given indicate that the theorist who wishes to identify various particular mental and physical events will have to face problems fairly similar to those of the type–type theorist; he too will be unable to appeal to the standard alleged analogues.

That the usual moves and analogies are not available to solve the problems of the identity theorist is, of course, no proof that no moves are available. I certainly cannot discuss all the possibilities here. I suspect, however, that the present considerations tell heavily against the usual forms of materialism. Materialism, I think, must hold that a physical description of the world is a *complete* description of it, that any mental facts are "ontologically dependent" on physical facts in the straightforward sense of following from them by necessity. No identity theorist seems to me to have made a convincing argument against the intuitive view that this is not the case.[13]

Notes

1 Misleadingly, because the phrase suggests that there is a special problem of "transworld identification," that we cannot trivially stipulate whom or what we are talking about when we imagine another possible world. The term "possible world" may also mislead; perhaps it suggests the "foreign country" picture. I have sometimes used "counterfactual situation" in the text; Michael Slote has suggested that "possible state (or history) of the world" might be less misleading than "possible world." It is better still, to avoid confusion, not to say, "In some possible world, Humphrey would have won" but rather, simply, "Humphrey might have won." The apparatus of possible words has (I hope) been very useful as far as the set-theoretic model-theory of quantified modal logic is concerned, but has encouraged philosophical pseudo-problems and misleading pictures.

2 Of course I don't imply that language contains a name for every object. Demonstratives can be used as rigid designators, and free variables can be used as rigid designators of unspecified objects. Of course when we specify a counterfactual situation, we do not describe the whole possible world, but only the portion which interests us.

3 See Lecture I, p. 53 (on Nixon), and Lecture II, pp. 74–7 [of the Harvard University Press edition of *Naming and Necessity*].

4 Mill, *A System of Logic*.

5 I am not going to give any criterion for what I mean by a "pure property," or Fregean intension. It is hard to find unquestionable examples of what is meant. Yellowness certainly expresses a manifest physical property of an object and, relative to the discussion of gold above, can be regarded as a property in the required sense. Actually, however, it is not without a certain referential element of its own, for on the present view yellowness is picked out and rigidly designated as that external physical property of the object which we sense by means of the *visual impression of yellowness.* It does in this respect resemble the natural kind terms. The phenomenological quality of the sensation itself, on the other hand, can be regarded as a *quale* in some pure sense. Perhaps I am rather vague about these questions, but further precision seems unnecessary here.

6 Of course, there is the question of the relation of the statistical mechanical notion of temperature to, for example, the thermodynamic notion. I wish to leave such questions aside in this discussion.

7 To understand this dispute, it is especially important to realize that yellowness is not a dispositional property, although it is related to a disposition. Many philosophers for want of any other theory of the meaning of the term "yellow," have been inclined to regard it as expressing a dispositional property. At the same time, I suspect many have been bothered by the "gut feeling" that yellowness is a manifest property, just as much "right out there" as hardness or spherical shape. The proper account, on the present conception is, of course, that the reference of "yellowness" is fixed by the description "that (manifest) property of objects which causes them, under normal circumstances, to be seen as yellow (i.e., to be sensed by certain visual impressions)"; "yellow," of course, does not *mean* "tends to produce such and such a sensation"; if we had had different neural structures, if atmospheric conditions had been different, if we had been blind, and so on, then yellow objects would have done no such thing. If one tries to revise the definition of "yellow" to be, "tends to produce such and such visual impressions under circumstances *C*," then one will find that the specification of the circumstances *C* either circularly involves yellowness or plainly makes the alleged definition into a scientific discovery rather than a synonymy. If we take the "fixes a reference" view, then it is up to the physical scientist to identify the property so marked out in any more fundamental physical terms that he wishes.

   Some philosophers have argued that such terms as "sensation of yellow," "sensation of heat," "sensation of pain," and the like, could not be in the language unless they were identifiable in terms of external observable phenomena, such as heat, yellowness, and associated human behavior. I think that this question is independent of any view argued in the text.

8 Some of the statements I myself make above may be loose and inaccurate in this sense. If I say, "Gold *might* turn out not to be an element," I speak correctly; "might" here is *epistemic* and expresses the fact that the evidence does not justify *a priori* (Cartesian) certainty that gold is an element. I am also strictly correct when I say that the elementhood of gold was discovered *a posteriori*. If I say, "Gold *might have* turned out not to be an element," I seem to mean this metaphysically and my statement is subject to the correction noted in the text.

9 Thomas Nagel and Donald Davidson are notable examples. Their views are very interesting, and I wish I could discuss them in further detail. It is doubtful that such philosophers wish to call themselves "materialists." Davidson, in particular, bases his case for his version of the identity theory on the supposed *impossibility* of correlating psychological properties with physical ones.

   The argument against token–token identification in the text *does* apply to these views.

10 Of course, the body *does* exist without the mind and presumably without the person, when the body is a corpse. This consideration, if accepted, would already show that a person and his body are distinct. (See David Wiggins, "On Being at the Same Place at the Same Time," *Philosophical Review*, Vol. 77 (1968), pp. 90–5.) Similarly, it can be argued that a statue is not the hunk of matter of which it is composed. In the latter case, however, one might say

instead that the former is "nothing over and above" the latter; and the same device might be tried for the relation of the person and the body. The difficulties in the text would not then arise in the same form, but analogous difficulties would appear. A theory that a person is nothing over and above his body in the way that a statue is nothing over and above the matter of which it is composed, would have to hold that (necessarily) a person exists if and only if his body exists and has a certain additional physical organization. Such a thesis would be subject to modal difficulties similar to those besetting the ordinary identity thesis, and the same would apply to suggested analogues replacing the identification of mental states with physical states. A further discussion of this matter must be left for another place. Another view which I will not discuss, although I have little tendency to accept it and am not even certain that it has been set out with genuine clarity, is the so-called functional state view of psychological concepts.

11 For example, David Armstrong, *A Materialist Theory of the Mind*, London and New York, 1968 – see the discussion review by Thomas Nagel, *Philosophical Review* 79 (1970), pp. 394–403; and David Lewis, "An Argument for the Identity Theory," *The Journal of Philosophy*, pp. 17–25.

12 I have been surprised to find that at least one able listener took my use of such terms as "correlated with," "corresponding to," and the like as already begging the question against the identity thesis. The identity thesis, so he said, is not the thesis that pains and brain states are correlated, but rather that they are identical. Thus my entire discussion presupposes the anti-materialist position that I set out to prove. Although I was surprised to hear an objection which concedes so little intelligence to the argument, I have tried especially to avoid the term "correlated" which seems to give rise to the objection. Nevertheless, to obviate misunderstanding, I shall explain my usage. Assuming, at least *arguendo*, that scientific discoveries have turned out so as not to refute materialism from the beginning, both the dualist and the identity theorist agree that there is a correlation or correspondence between mental states and physical states. The dualist holds that the "correlation" relation in question is irreflexive; the identity theorist holds that it is simply a special case of the identity relation. Such terms as "correlation" and "correspondence" can be used neutrally without prejudging which side is correct.

13 Having expressed these doubts about the identity theory in the text, I should emphasize two things: first, identity theorists have presented positive arguments for their view, which I certainly have not answered here. Some of these arguments seem to me to be weak or based on ideological prejudices, but others strike me as highly compelling arguments which I am at present unable to answer convincingly. Second, rejection of the identity thesis does not imply acceptance of Cartesian dualism. In fact, my view above that a person could not have come from a different sperm and egg from the ones from which he actually originated implicitly suggests a rejection of the Cartesian picture. If we had a clear idea of the soul or the mind as an independent, susbsistent, spiritual entity, why should it have to have any necessary connection with particular material objects such as a particular sperm or a particular egg? A convinced dualist may think that my views on sperms and eggs beg the question against Descartes. I would tend to argue the other way; the fact that it is hard to imagine me coming from a sperm and egg different from my actual

origins seems to me to indicate that we have no such clear conception of a soul or self. In any event, Descartes' notion seems to have been rendered dubious ever since Hume's critique of the notion of a Cartesian self. I regard the mind–body problem as wide open and extremely confusing.

8

Jaegwon Kim, "Multiple Realization and the Metaphysics of Reduction"*

I. Introduction

It is part of today's conventional wisdom in philosophy of mind that psychological states are "multiply realizable," and are in fact so realized, in a variety of structures and organisms. We are constantly reminded that any mental state, say pain, is capable of "realization," "instantiation," or "implementation" in widely diverse neural-biological structures in humans, felines, reptiles, mollusks, and perhaps other organisms further removed from us. Sometimes we are asked to contemplate the possibility that extraterrestrial creatures with a biochemistry radically different from the earthlings' or even electro-mechanical devices, can "realize the same psychology" that characterizes humans. This claim, to be called hereafter "the Multiple Realization Thesis" ("MR,"[1] for short), is widely accepted by philosophers, especially those who are inclined to favor the functionalist line on mentality. I will not here dispute the truth of MR, although what I will say may prompt a reassessment of the considerations that have led to its nearly universal acceptance.

And there is an influential and virtually uncontested view about the philosophical significance of MR. This is the belief that MR refutes psychophysical reductionism once and for all. In particular, the classic psychoneural identity theory of Feigl and Smart, the so-called "type physicalism,"

* This paper is descended from an unpublished paper, "The Disunity of Psychology as a Working Hypothesis?," which was circulated in the early 1980s. I am indebted to the following persons, among others, for helpful comments: Fred Feldman, Hilary Kornblith, Barry Loewer, Brian McLaughlin, Joe Mendola, Marcelo Sabates, and James Van Cleve.

Jaegwon Kim, "Multiple Realization and the Metaphysics of Reduction," in *Supervenience and Mind* (Cambridge University Press, Cambridge, 1993), pp. 309–35.

is standardly thought to have been definitively dispatched by MR to the heap of obsolete philosophical theories of mind. At any rate, it is this claim, that MR proves the physical irreducibility of the mental, that will be the starting point of my discussion.

Evidently, the current popularity of antireductionist physicalism is owed, for the most part, to the influence of the MR-based antireductionist argument originally developed by Hilary Putnam and elaborated further by Jerry Fodor[2] – rather more so than to the "anomalist" argument associated with Donald Davidson.[3] For example, in their elegant paper on non-reductive physicalism,[4] Geoffrey Hellman and Frank Thompson motivate their project in the following way:

> Traditionally, physicalism has taken the form of reductionism – roughly, that all scientific terms can be given explicit definitions in physical terms. Of late there has been growing awareness, however, that reductionism is an unreasonably strong claim.

But why is reductionism "unreasonably strong"? In a footnote Hellman and Thompson explain, citing Fodor's "Special Sciences":

> Doubts have arisen especially in connection with functional explanation in the higher-level sciences (psychology, linguistics, social theory etc.). Functional predicates may be physically realizable in heterogeneous ways, so as to elude physical definition.

And Ernest LePore and Barry Loewer tell us this:[5]

> It is practically received wisdom among philosophers of mind that psychological properties (including content properties) are not identical to neurophysiological or other physical properties. The relationship between psychological and neurophysiological properties is that the latter *realize* the former. Furthermore, a single psychological property might (in the sense of conceptual possibility) be realized by a large number, perhaps an infinitely many, of different physical properties and even by non-physical properties.

They then go on to sketch the reason why MR, on their view, leads to the rejection of mind–body reduction:[6]

> If there are infinitely many physical (and perhaps nonphysical) properties which can realize F then F will not be reducible to a basic physical property. Even if F can only be realized by finitely many

160

basic physical properties it might not be reducible to a basic physical property since the disjunction of these properties might not itself be a basic physical property (i.e., occur in a fundamental physical law). We will understand "multiple realizability" as involving such irreducibility.

This antireductionist reading of MR continues to this day; in a recent paper, Ned Block writes:[7]

> Whatever the merits of physiological reductionism, it is not available to the cognitive science point of view assumed here. According to cognitive science, the essence of the mental is computational, and any computational state is "multiply realizable" by physiological or electronic states that are not identical with one another, and so content cannot be identified with any one of them.

Considerations of these sorts have succeeded in persuading a large majority of philosophers of mind[8] to reject reductionism and type physicalism. The upshot of all this has been impressive: MR has not only ushered in "non-reductive physicalism" as the new orthodoxy on the mind–body problem, but in the process has put the very word "reductionism" in disrepute, making reductionisms of all stripes an easy target of disdain and curt dismissals.

I believe a reappraisal of MR is overdue. There is something right and instructive in the antireductionist claim based on MR and the basic argument in its support, but I believe that we have failed to follow out the implications of MR far enough, and have as a result failed to appreciate its full significance. One specific point that I will argue is this: the popular view that psychology constitutes an *autonomous special science*, a doctrine heavily promoted in the wake of the MR-inspired antireductionist dialectic, may in fact be inconsistent with the real implications of MR. Our discussion will show that MR, when combined with certain plausible metaphysical and methodological assumptions, leads to some surprising conclusions about the status of the mental and the nature of psychology as a science. I hope it will become clear that the fate of type physicalism is not among the more interesting consequences of MR.

II. Multiple realization

It was Putnam, in a paper published in 1967,[9] who first injected MR into debates on the mind–body problem. According to him, the classic reductive theories of mind presupposed the following naive picture of how psychological kinds (properties, event and state types, etc.) are correlated with physical kinds:

> For each psychological kind M there is a unique physical (presumably, neurobiological) kind P that is *nomologically coextensive* with it (i.e., as a matter of law, any system instantiates M at t iff that system instantiates P at t).

(We may call this "the Correlation Thesis.") So take pain: the Correlation Thesis has it that pain as an event kind has a neural substrate, perhaps as yet not fully and precisely identified, that, as a matter of law, always co-occurs with it in all pain-capable organisms and structures. Here there is no mention of species or types of organisms or structures: the neural correlate of pain is invariant across biological species and structure types. In his 1967 paper, Putnam pointed out something that, in retrospect, seems all too obvious:[10]

> Consider what the brain-state theorist has to do to make good his claims. He has to specify a physical-chemical state such that *any* organism (not just a mammal) is in pain if and only if (a) it possesses a brain of a suitable physical-chemical structure; and (b) its brain is in that physical-chemical state. This means that the physical-chemical state in question must be a possible state of a mammalian brain, a reptilian brain, a mollusc's brain (octopuses are mollusca, and certainly feel pain), etc. At the same time, it must not be a possible brain of any physically possible creature that cannot feel pain.

Putnam went on to argue that the Correlation Thesis was *empirically false.* Later writers, however, have stressed the multiple realizability of the mental as a *conceptual* point: it is an a priori, conceptual fact about psychological properties that they are "second-order" physical properties, and that their specification does not include constraints on the manner of their physical implementation.[11] Many proponents of the functionalist account of psychological terms and properties hold such a view.

Thus, on the new, improved picture, the relationship between psychological and physical kinds is something like this: there is no single neural kind N that "realizes" pain, across all types of organisms or physical systems; rather, there is a multiplicity of neural-physical kinds, N_h, N_r, N_m, ... such that N_h realizes pain in humans, N_r realizes pain in reptiles, N_m realizes pain in Martians, etc. Perhaps, biological species as standardly understood are too broad to yield unique physical-biological realization bases; the neural basis of pain could perhaps change even in a single organism over time. But the main point is clear: any system capable of psychological states (that is, any system that "has a psychology") falls under some structure type T such that systems with structure T share the same physical base for each mental state or kind that they are capable of instantiating (we should regard this as relativized with respect to time to allow for the possibility that an individual may fall under different structure types at different times). Thus physical realization bases for mental states must be relativized to species or, better, physical structure types. We thus have the following thesis:

> If anything has mental property M at time t, there is some physical structure type T and physical property P such that it is a system of type T at t and has P at t, and it holds as a matter of law that all systems of type T have M at a time just in case they have P at the same time.

We may call this "the Structure-Restricted Correlation Thesis" (or "the Restricted Correlation Thesis" for short).

It may have been noticed that neither this nor the correlation thesis speaks of "realization."[12] The talk of "realization" is not metaphysically neutral: the idea that mental properties are "realized" or "implemented" by physical properties carries with it a certain ontological picture of mental properties as derivative and dependent. There is the suggestion that when we look at concrete reality there is nothing over and above instantiations of physical properties and relations, and that the instantiation on a given occasion of an appropriate physical property in the right contextual (often causal) setting simply *counts as*, or *constitutes*, an instantiation of a mental property on that occasion. An idea like this is evident in the functionalist conception of a mental property as *extrinsically* characterized in terms of its "causal role," where what fills this role is a physical (or, at any rate, nonmental) property (the latter property will then be said to "realize" the mental property in question). The same idea can be seen in the related functionalist proposal to construe a mental property as a "second-order property" consisting in the having of a physical property satisfying certain extrinsic specifications. We will recur to this topic later; however, we should note that someone who accepts either of the two correlation theses need not espouse the "realization" idiom. That is, it is prima facie a coherent position to think of mental properties as "first-order properties" in their own right, characterized by their intrinsic natures (e.g., phenomenal feel), which, as it happens, turn out to have nomological correlates in neural properties. (In fact, anyone interested in defending a serious dualist position on the mental should eschew the realization talk altogether and consider mental properties as first-order properties on a par with physical properties.) The main point of MR that is relevant to the antireductionist argument it has generated is just this: *mental properties do not have nomically coextensive physical properties, when the latter are appropriately individuated.* It may be that properties that are candidates for reduction must be thought of as being realized, or implemented, by properties in the prospective reduction base;[13] that is, if we think of certain properties as having their own intrinsic characterizations that are entirely independent of another set of properties, there is no hope of *reducing* the former to the latter. But this point needs to be argued, and will, in any case, not play a role in what follows.

Assume that property M is realized by property P. How are M and P related to each other and, in particular, how do they covary with each other? LePore and Loewer say this:[14]

> The usual conception is that e's being P realizes e's being F iff e is P and there is a strong connection of some sort between P and F. We propose to understand this connection as a necessary connection which is *explanatory*. The existence of an explanatory connection between two properties is stronger than the claim that $P \rightarrow F$ is physically necessary since not every physically necessary connection is explanatory.

Thus, LePore and Loewer require only that the realization base of M be *sufficient* for M, not both necessary and sufficient. This presumably is in response to MR: if pain is multiply realized in three ways as above, each of N_h, N_r, and N_m will be sufficient for pain, and none necessary for it. This I believe is not a correct response, however; the correct response is not to weaken the joint necessity and sufficiency of the physical base, but rather to *relativize* it, as in the Restricted Correlation Thesis, with respect to species or structure types. For suppose we are designing a physical system that will instantiate a certain psychology, and let $M_1, \ldots, M_n$ be the psychological properties required by this psychology. The design process must involve the specification of an n-tuple of physical properties, $P_1, \ldots, P_n$, all of them instantiable by the system, such that for each i, P_i constitutes a *necessary and sufficient* condition *in this system* (and others of relevantly similar physical structure), not merely a sufficient one, for the occurrence of M_i. (Each such n-tuple of physical properties can be called a "physical realization" of the psychology in question.[15]) That is, for each psychological state we must design into the system a nomologically coextensive physical state. We must do this *if we are to control both the occurrence and nonoccurrence of the psychological states involved*, and control of this kind is necessary if we are to ensure that the physical device will properly instantiate the psychology. (This is especially clear if we think of building a computer; computer analogies loom large in our thoughts about "realization.")

But isn't it possible for multiple realization to occur "locally" as well? That is, we may want to avail ourselves of the flexibility of allowing a psychological state, or function, to be instantiated by alternative mechanisms within a single system. This means that P_i can be a *disjunction* of physical properties; thus, M_i is instantiated in the system in question at a time if and only if at least one of the disjuncts of P_i is instantiated at that time. The upshot of all this is that LePore and Loewer's condition that $P \rightarrow M$ holds as a matter of law needs to be upgraded to the condition that, *relative to the species or structure type in question (and allowing P to be disjunctive)*, $P \leftrightarrow M$ holds as a matter of law.[16]

For simplicity let us suppose that pain is realized in three ways as above, by N_h in humans, N_r in reptiles, and N_m in Martians. The finitude assumption is not essential to any of my arguments: if the list is not finite, we will have an infinite disjunction rather than a finite one (alternatively, we can talk in terms of "sets" of such properties instead of their disjunctions). If the list is "open-ended," that's all right, too; it will not affect the metaphysics of the situation. We allowed above the possibility of a realization base of a psychological property itself being disjunctive; to get the discussion going, though, we will assume that these Ns, the three imagined physical realization bases of pain, are not themselves disjunctive or, at any rate, that their status as properties is not in dispute. The propriety and significance of "disjunctive properties" is precisely one of the principal issues we will be dealing with below, and it will make little difference just at what stage this issue is faced.

III. Disjunctive properties and Fodor's argument

An obvious initial response to the MR-based argument against reducibility is "the disjunction move": Why not take the disjunction, $N_h \vee N_r \vee N_m$, as the single physical substrate of pain? In his 1967 paper, Putnam considers such a move but dismisses it out of hand: "Granted, in such a case the brain-state theorist can save himself by *ad hoc* assumptions (e.g. defining the disjunction of two states to be a single 'physical-chemical state'), but this does not have to be taken seriously."[17] Putnam gives no hint as to why he thinks the disjunction strategy does not merit serious consideration.

If there is something deeply wrong with disjunctions of the sort involved here, that surely isn't obvious; we need to go beyond a sense of unease with such disjunctions and develop an intelligible rationale for banning them. Here is where Fodor steps in, for he appears to have an argument for disallowing disjunctions. As I see it, Fodor's argument in "Special Sciences" depends crucially on the following two assumptions:

(1) To reduce a special-science theory T_M to physical theory T_P, each "kind" in T_M (presumably, represented by a basic predicate of T_M) must have a nomologically coextensive "kind" in T_P;
(2) A disjunction of heterogeneous kinds is not itself a kind.

Point (1) is apparently prompted by the derivational model of inter-theoretic reduction due to Ernest Nagel:[18] the reduction of T_2 to T_1 consists in the derivation of laws of T_2 from the laws of T_1, in conjunction with "bridge" laws or principles connecting T_2-terms with T_1-terms. Although this characterization does not in general require that each T_2-term be cor-related with a *coextensive* T_1-term, the natural thought is that the existence of T_1-coextensions for T_2-terms would in effect give us definitions of T_2-terms in T_1-terms, enabling us to rewrite T_2-laws exclusively in the vocabulary of T_1; we could then derive these rewrites of T_2-laws from the laws of T_1 (if they cannot be so derived, we can add them as additional T_1-laws – assuming both theories to be true).

Another thought that again leads us to look for T_1-coextensions for T_2-terms is this: for genuine reduction, the bridge laws must be construed as *property identities*, not mere *property correlations* – namely, we must be in a position to identify the property expressed by a given T_2-term (say, water-solubility) with a property expressed by a term in the reduction base (say, having a certain molecular structure). This of course requires that each T_2-term have a nomic (or otherwise suitably modalized) coextension in the vocabulary of the reduction base. To put it another way, ontologi-cally significant reduction requires the reduction of higher-level *properties*, and this in turn requires (unless one takes an eliminativist stance) that they be identified with complexes of lower-level properties. Identity of properties of course requires, at a minimum, an appropriately modalized coextensivity.[19]

So assume M is a psychological kind, and let us agree that to reduce M, or to reduce the psychological theory containing M, we need a physical coextension, P, for M. But why should we suppose that P must be a physical "kind"? But what is a "kind," anyway? Fodor explains this notion in terms of *law*, saying that a given predicate P is a "kind predicate" of a science just in case the science contains a law with P as its antecedent or conse-quent.[20] There are various problems with Fodor's characterization, but we don't need to take its exact wording seriously; the main idea is that kinds, or kind predicates, of a science are those that figure in the laws of that science.

To return to our question, why should "bridge laws" connect kinds to kinds, in this special sense of "kind"? To say that bridge laws are "laws" and that, by definition, only kind predicates can occur in laws is not much of an answer. For that only invites the further question why "bridge laws" ought to be "laws" – what would be lacking in a reductive derivation if bridge laws were replaced by "bridge principles" which do not necessarily connect kinds to kinds.[21] But what of the consideration that these principles must represent property identities? Does this force on us the requirement that each reduced kind must find a coextensive kind in the reduction base? No; for it isn't obvious why it isn't perfectly proper to reduce kinds by identifying them with properties expressed by non-kind (disjunctive) predicates in the reduction base.

There is the following possible argument for insisting on kinds: if M is identified with non-kind Q (or M is reduced via a biconditional bridge principle "$M \leftrightarrow Q$," where Q is a non-kind), M could no longer figure in special science laws; e.g., the law, "$M \rightarrow R$," would in effect reduce to "$Q \rightarrow R$," and therefore lose its status as a law on account of containing Q, a non-kind.

I think this is a plausible response – at least, the beginning of one. As it stands, though, it smacks of circularity: "$Q \rightarrow R$" is not a law because a non-kind, Q, occurs in it, and Q is a non-kind because it cannot occur in a law and "$Q \rightarrow R$," in particular, is not a law. What we need is an *independent* reason for the claim that the sort of Q we are dealing with under MR, namely a badly heterogeneous disjunction, is unsuited for laws.

This means that point (1) really reduces to point (2) above. For, given Fodor's notion of a kind, (2) comes to this: disjunctions of heterogeneous kinds are unfit for laws. What we now need is an *argument* for this claim; to dismiss such disjunctions as "wildly disjunctive" or "heterogeneous and unsystematic" is to label a problem, not to offer a diagnosis of it.[22] In the sections to follow, I hope to take some steps toward such a diagnosis and draw some implications which I believe are significant for the status of mentality.

IV. Jade, jadeite, and nephrite

Let me begin with an analogy that will guide us in our thinking about multiply realizable kinds.

Consider *jade*: we are told that jade, as it turns out, is not a mineral kind, contrary to what was once believed; rather, jade comprises two distinct minerals with dissimilar molecular structures, *jadeite* and *nephrite*. Consider the following generalization:

(L) Jade is green

We may have thought, before the discovery of the dual nature of jade, that (L) was a law, a law about jade; and we may have thought, with reason, that (L) had been strongly confirmed by all the millions of jade samples that had been observed to be green (and none that had been observed not to be green). We now know better: (L) is really a conjunction of these two laws:

(L₁) Jadeite is green
(L₂) Nephrite is green

But (L) itself might still be a law as well; is that possible? It has the standard basic form of a law, and it apparently has the power to support counterfactuals: if anything were jade – that is, if anything were a sample of jadeite or of nephrite – then, in either case, it would follow, by law, that it was green. No problem here.

But there is another standard mark of lawlikeness that is often cited, and this is "projectibility," the ability to be confirmed by observation of "positive instances." Any generalized conditional of the form "All Fs are G" can be confirmed by the *exhaustion* of the class of Fs – that is, by eliminating all of its potential falsifiers. It is in this sense that we can verify such generalizations as "All the coins in my pockets are copper" and "Everyone in this room is either first-born or an only child." Lawlike generalizations, however, are thought to have the following further property: observation of positive instances, Fs that are G, can strengthen our credence in the next F's being G. It is this kind of instance-to-instance accretion of confirmation that is supposed to be the hallmark of lawlikeness; it is what explains the possibility of confirming a generalization about an indefinitely large class of items on the basis of a finite number of favorable observations. This rough characterization of projectibility should suffice for our purposes.

Does (L), "Jade is green," pass the projectibility test? Here we seem to have a problem.[23] For we can imagine this: on re-examining the records of past observations, we find, to our dismay, that all the positive instances of (L), that is, all the millions of observed samples of green jade, turn out to have been samples of jadeite, and none of nephrite! If this should happen, we clearly would not, and should not, continue to think of (L) as well confirmed. All we have is evidence strongly confirming (L₁), and none having anything to do with (L₂). (L) is merely a conjunction of two laws, one well confirmed and the other with its epistemic status wholly up in the air. But all the millions of green jadeite samples *are* positive instances of (L): they satisfy both the antecedent and the consequent of (L). As we have just seen, however, (L) is not confirmed by them, at least not in the standard way we expect. And the reason, I suggest, is that jade is a true disjunctive kind, a disjunction of two heterogeneous nomic kinds which, however, is not itself a nomic kind.[24]

That disjunction is implicated in this failure of projectibility can be seen in the following way: inductive projection of generalizations like (L) with disjunctive antecedents would sanction a cheap, and illegitimate, confirmation procedure. For assume that "All *F*s are *G*" is a law that has been confirmed by the observation of appropriately numerous positive instances, things that are both *F* and *G*. But these are also positive instances of the generalization "All things that are *F or H* are G," for any *H* you please. So, if you in general permit projection of generalizations with a disjunctive antecedent, this latter generalization will also be well confirmed. But "All things that are *F or H* are G" logically implies "All *H*s are G." Any statement implied by a well-confirmed statement must itself be well confirmed.[25] So "All *H*s are G" is well confirmed – in fact, it is confirmed by the observation of *F*s that are *G*s!

One might protest: "Look, the very same strategy can be applied to something that is a genuine law. We can think of any nomic kind – say, being an emerald – as a disjunction, being an African emerald or a non-African emerald. This would make 'All emeralds are green' a conjunction of two laws, 'All African emeralds are green' and 'All non-African emeralds are green.' But surely this doesn't show there is anything wrong with the lawlikeness of 'All emeralds are green.'" Our reply is obvious: the disjunction, "being an African emerald or non-African emerald," does not denote some heterogeneously disjunctive, nonnomic kind; it denotes a perfectly well-behaved nomic kind, that of being an emerald! There is nothing wrong with disjunctive predicates as such; the trouble arises when the kinds denoted by the disjoined predicates are heterogeneous, "wildly disjunctive," so that instances falling under them do not show the kind of "similarity," or unity, that we expect of instances falling under a single kind.

The phenomenon under discussion, therefore, is related to the simple maxim sometimes claimed to underlie inductive inference: "similar things behave in similar ways," "same cause, same effect," and so on. The source of the trouble we saw with instantial confirmation of "All jade is green" is the fact, or belief, that samples of jadeite and samples of nephrite do not exhibit an appropriate "similarity" with respect to each other to warrant inductive projections from the observed samples of jadeite to unobserved samples of nephrite. But similarity of the required sort presumably holds for African emeralds and non-African emeralds – at least, that is what we believe, and that is what makes the "disjunctive kind," being an African emerald or a non-African emerald, a single nomic kind. More generally, the phenomenon is related to the point often made about disjunctive properties: disjunctive properties, unlike conjunctive properties, do not guarantee similarity for instances falling under them. And similarity, it is said, is the core of our idea of a property. If that is your idea of a property, you will believe that there are no such things as disjunctive properties (or "negative properties"). More precisely, though, we should remember that properties are not inherently disjunctive or conjunctive any more than classes are inherently unions or intersections, and that any property can be expressed by a disjunctive predicate. Properties of course can be conjunctions, or disjunctions, of other properties. The point about disjunctive properties is best put as a closure condition on properties: the class of properties is not closed under disjunction (presumably, nor under negation). Thus, there may well be properties P and Q such that P or Q is also a property; but its being so doesn't follow from the mere fact that P and Q are properties.[26]

V. Jade and pain

Let us now return to pain and its multiple realization bases, N_h, N_r, and N_m. I believe the situation here is instructively parallel to the case of jade in relation to jadeite and nephrite. It seems that we think of jadeite and nephrite as distinct kinds (and of jade not as a kind) because they are different chemical kinds. But why is their being distinct as chemical kinds relevant here? Because many important properties of minerals, we think, are supervenient on, and explainable in terms of, their microstructure, and chemical kinds constitute a microstructural taxonomy that is explanatorily rich and powerful. Microstructure is important, in short, because macrophysical properties of substances are determined by microstructure. These ideas make up our "metaphysics" of microdetermination for properties of minerals and other substances, a background of partly empirical and partly metaphysical assumptions that regulate our inductive and explanatory practices.

The parallel metaphysical underpinnings for pain, and other mental states in general, are, first, the belief, expressed by the Restricted Correlation Thesis, that pain, or any other mental state, occurs in a system when, and only when, appropriate physical conditions are present in the system, and, second, the corollary belief that significant properties of mental states, in particular nomic relationships amongst them, are due to, and explainable in terms of, the properties and causal-nomic connections among their physical "substrates." I will call the conjunction of these two beliefs "the Physical Realization Thesis."[27] Whether or not the microexplanation of the sort indicated in the second half of the thesis amounts to a "reduction" is a question we will take up later. Apart from this question, though, the Physical Realization Thesis is widely accepted by philosophers who talk of "physical realization," and this includes most functionalists; it is all but explicit in LePore and Loewer, for example, and in Fodor.[28]

Define a property, N, by disjoining N_h, N_r, and N_m; that is, N has a disjunctive definition, $N_h \vee N_r \vee N_m$. If we assume, with those who endorse the MR-based antireductionist argument, that N_h, N_r, and N_m are a heterogeneous lot, we cannot make the heterogeneity go away merely by introducing a simpler expression, "N"; if there is a problem with certain disjunctive properties, it is not a *linguistic* problem about the form of expressions used to refer to them.

Now, we put the following question to Fodor and like-minded philosophers: If pain is nomically equivalent to N, the property claimed to be wildly disjunctive and obviously nonnomic, *why isn't pain itself equally heterogeneous and nonnomic as a kind?* Why isn't pain's relationship to its realization bases, N_h, N_r, and N_m, analogous to jade's relationship to jadeite and nephrite? If jade turns out to be nonnomic on account of its dual "realizations" in distinct microstructures, why doesn't the same fate befall pain? After all, the group of actual and nomologically possible realizations of pain, as they are described by the MR enthusiasts with such imagination, is far more motley than the two chemical kinds comprising jade.

I believe we should insist on answers to these questions from those functionalists who view mental properties as "second-order" properties, i.e., properties that consist in having a property with a certain functional specification.[29] Thus, pain is said to be a second-order property in that it is the *property of having some property with a certain specification* in terms of its typical causes and effects and its relation to other mental properties; call this "specification H." The point of MR, on this view, is that there is more than one property that meets specification H – in fact, an open-ended set of such properties, it will be said. But pain itself, it is argued, is a more abstract but well-behaved property at a higher level, namely the property of having one of these properties meeting specification H. It should be clear why a position like this is vulnerable to the questions that have been raised. For the property of having property P is exactly identical with P, and the property of having *one* of the properties, $P_1 P_2, \ldots, P_n$, is exactly identical with the disjunctive property, $P_1 \vee P_2 \vee \ldots \vee P_n$. On the assumption that N_h, N_r, and N_m are all the properties satisfying specification H, the property of having a property with H, namely pain, is none other than the property of having either N_h or N_r or N_m[30] – namely, the *disjunctive* property, $N_h \vee N_r \vee N_m$! We cannot hide the disjunctive character of pain behind the second-order *expression*, "the property of having a property with specification H." Thus, on the construal of mental properties as second-order properties, mental properties will in general turn out to be disjunctions of their physical realization bases. It is difficult to see how one could have it both ways – that is, to castigate $N_h \vee N_r \vee N_m$ as unacceptably disjunctive while insisting on the integrity of pain as a scientific kind.

Moreover, when we think about making projections over pain, very much the same worry should arise about their propriety as did for jade. Consider a possible law: "Sharp pains administered at random intervals cause anxiety reactions." Suppose this generalization has been well confirmed for humans. Should we expect *on that basis* that it will hold also for Martians whose psychology is implemented (we assume) by a vastly different physical mechanism? Not if we accept the Physical Realization Thesis, fundamental to functionalism, that psychological regularities hold, to the extent that they do, in virtue of the causal-nomological regularities at the physical implementation level. The reason the law is true for humans is due to the way the human brain is "wired"; the Martians have a brain with a different wiring plan, and we certainly should not expect the regularity to hold for them just because it does for humans.[31] "Pains cause anxiety reactions" may turn out to possess no more unity as a scientific law than does "Jade is green."

Suppose that in spite of all this Fodor insists on defending pain as a nomic kind. It isn't clear that that would be a viable strategy. For he would then owe us an explanation of why the "wildly disjunctive" N, which after all is equivalent to pain, is not a nomic kind. If a predicate is nomically equivalent to a well-behaved predicate, why isn't that enough to show that it, too, is well behaved, and expresses a well-behaved property? To say, as Fodor does,[32] that "it is a law that . . ." is "intensional" and does not permit substitution of equivalent expressions ("equivalent" in various appropriate senses) is merely to locate a potential problem, not to resolve it.

Thus, the nomicity of pain may lead to the nomicity of N; but this isn't very interesting. For given the Physical Realization Thesis, and the priority of the physical implicit in it, our earlier line of argument, leading from the nonnomicity of N to the nonnomicity of pain, is more compelling. We must, I think, take seriously the reasoning leading to the conclusion that pain, and other mental states, might turn out to be nonnomic. If this turns out to be the case, it puts in serious jeopardy Fodor's contention that its physical irreducibility renders psychology an autonomous special science. If pain fails to be nomic, it is not the sort of property in terms of which laws can be formulated; and "pain" is not a predicate that can enter into a scientific theory that seeks to formulate causal laws and causal explanations. And the same goes for all multiply realizable psychological kinds – which, according to MR, means *all* psychological kinds. There are no scientific theories of jade, and we don't need any; if you insist on having one, you can help yourself to the *conjunction* of the theory of jadeite and the theory of nephrite. In the same way, there will be theories about human pains (instances of N_h), reptilian pains (instances of N_r), and so on; but there will be no unified, integrated theory encompassing all pains in all pain-capable organisms, only a conjunction of pain theories for appropriately individuated biological species and physical structure types. Scientific psychology, like the theory of jade, gives way to a conjunction of structure-specific theories. If this is right, the correct conclusion to be drawn from the MR-inspired antireductionist argument is not the claim that psychology is an irreducible and autonomous science, but something that contradicts it, namely that it cannot be a science with a unified subject matter. This is the picture that is beginning to emerge from MR when combined with the Physical Realization Thesis.

These reflections have been prompted by the analogy with the case of jade; it is a strong and instructive analogy, I think, and suggests the possibility of a general argument. In the following section I will develop a direct argument, with explicit premises and assumptions.

VI. Causal powers and mental kinds

One crucial premise we need for a direct argument is a constraint on concept formation, or kind individuation, in science that has been around for many years; it has lately been resurrected by Fodor in connection with content externalism.[33] A precise statement of the constraint may be difficult and controversial, but its main idea can be put as follows:

> [Principle of Causal Individuation of Kinds] Kinds in science are individuated on the basis of causal powers; that is, objects and events fall under a kind, or share in a property, insofar as they have similar causal powers.

I believe this is a plausible principle, and it is, in any case, widely accepted.

We can see that this principle enables us to give a specific interpretation to the claim that N_h, N_r, and N_m are *heterogeneous* as kinds: the claim must mean that they are *heterogeneous as causal powers* – that is, they are diverse as causal powers and enter into diverse causal laws. This must mean, given the Physical Realization Thesis, that pain itself can show no more unity as a causal power than the disjunction, $N_h \vee N_r \vee N_m$. This becomes especially clear if we set forth the following principle, which arguably is implied by the Physical Realization Thesis (but we need not make an issue of this here):

> [The Causal Inheritance Principle] If mental property M is realized in a system at t in virtue of physical realization base P, the causal powers of *this instance of M* are identical with the causal powers of P.[34]

It is important to bear in mind that this principle only concerns the causal powers of *individual instances of M;* it does not identify the causal powers of mental property M *in general* with the causal powers of some physical property P; such identification is precluded by the multiple physical realizability of M.

Why should we accept this principle? Let us just note that to deny it would be to accept *emergent* causal powers: causal powers that magically emerge at a higher level and of which there is no accounting in terms of lower-level properties and their causal powers and nomic connections. This leads to the notorious problem of "downward causation" and the attendant violation of the causal closure of the physical domain.[35] I believe that a serious physicalist would find these consequences intolerable.

It is clear that the Causal Inheritance Principle, in conjunction with the Physical Realization Thesis, has the consequence that mental kinds cannot satisfy the Causal Individuation Principle, and this effectively rules out mental kinds as scientific kinds. The reasoning is simple: instances of M that are realized by the same physical base must be grouped under one kind, since *ex hypothesi* the physical base is a causal kind; and instances of M with different realization bases must be grouped under distinct kinds, since, again *ex hypothesi*, these realization bases are distinct as causal kinds. Given that mental kinds are realized by diverse physical causal kinds, therefore, it follows that mental kinds are not causal kinds, and hence are disqualified as proper scientific kinds. Each mental kind is sundered into as many kinds as there are physical realization bases for it, and psychology as a science with disciplinary unity turns out to be an impossible project.

What is the relationship between this argument and the argument adumbrated in our reflections based on the jade analogy? At first blush, the two arguments might seem unrelated: the earlier argument depended chiefly on epistemological considerations, considerations on inductive projectibility of certain predicates, whereas the crucial premise of the second argument is the Causal Individuation Principle, a broadly metaphysical and methodological principle about science. I think, though, that the two arguments are closely related, and the key to seeing the relationship is this: causal powers involve laws, and laws are regularities that are projectible. Thus, if pain (or jade) is not a kind over which inductive projections can be made, it cannot enter into laws, and therefore cannot qualify as a causal kind; and this disqualifies it as a scientific kind. If this is right, the jade-inspired reflections provide a possible rationale for the Causal Individuation Principle. Fleshing out this rough chain of reasoning in precise terms, however, goes beyond what I can attempt in this paper.

VII.   The status of psychology: local reductions

Our conclusion at this point, therefore, is this: If MR is true, psychological kinds are not scientific kinds. What does this imply about the status of psychology as a science? Do our considerations show that psychology is a pseudo-science like astrology and alchemy? Of course not. The crucial difference, from the metaphysical point of view, is that psychology has physical realizations, but alchemy does not. To have a physical realization is to be physically grounded and explainable in terms of the processes at an underlying level. In fact, if each of the psychological kinds posited in a psychological theory has a physical realization for a fixed species, the theory can be "locally reduced" to the physical theory of that species, in the following sense. Let S be the species involved; for each law L_M of psychological theory T_M, $S \to L_M$ (the proposition that L_M holds for members of S) is the "S-restricted" version of L_M; and $S \to T_M$ is the S-restricted version of T_M, the set of all S-restricted laws of T_M. We can then say that T_M is "locally reduced" for species S to an underlying theory, T_P, just in case $S \to T_M$ is reduced to T_P. And the latter obtains just in case each S-restricted law of T_M, $S \to L_M$,[36] is derivable from the laws of the reducing theory T_P, taken together with bridge laws. What bridge laws suffice to guarantee the derivation? Obviously, an array of S-restricted bridge laws of the form, $S \to (M_i \leftrightarrow P_i)$, for each mental kind M_i. Just as unrestricted psychophysical bridge laws can underwrite a "global" or "uniform" reduction of psychology, species- or structure-restricted bridge laws sanction its "local" reduction.

If the same psychological theory is true of humans, reptiles, and Martians, the psychological kinds posited by that theory must have realizations in human, reptilian, and Martian physiologies. This implies that the theory is locally reducible in three ways, for humans, reptiles, and Martians. If the dependence of the mental on the physical means anything, it must mean that the regularities posited by this common psychology must have divergent physical explanations for the three species. The very idea of physical realization involves the possibility of physically explaining psychological properties and regularities, and the supposition of multiple such realizations, namely MR, involves a commitment to the possibility of multiple explanatory reductions of psychology.[37] The important moral of MR we need to keep in mind is this: *if psychological properties are multiply realized, so is psychology itself*. If physical realizations of psychological properties are a "wildly heterogeneous" and "unsystematic" lot, psychological theory itself must be realized by an equally heterogeneous and unsystematic lot of physical theories.

I am inclined to think that multiple local reductions, rather than global reductions, are the rule, even in areas in which we standardly suppose

175

reductions are possible. I will now deal with a possible objection to the idea of local reduction, at least as it is applied to psychology. The objection goes like this: given what we know about the differences among members of a single species, even species are too wide to yield determinate realization bases for psychological states, and given what we know about the phenomena of maturation and development, brain injuries, and the like, the physical bases of mentality may change even for a single individual. This throws into serious doubt, continues the objection, the availability of species-restricted bridge laws needed for local reductions.

The point of this objection may well be correct as a matter of empirical fact. Two points can be made in reply, however. First, neurophysiological research goes on because there is a shared, and probably well-grounded, belief among the workers that there are not huge individual differences within a species in the way psychological kinds are realized. Conspecifics must show important physical-physiological similarities, and there probably is good reason for thinking that they share physical realization bases to a sufficient degree to make search for species-wide neural substrates for mental states feasible and rewarding. Researchers in this area evidently aim for neurobiological explanations of psychological capacities and processes that are generalizable over all or most ("normal") members of a given species.

Second, even if there are huge individual differences among conspecifics as to how their psychology is realized, that does not touch the metaphysical point: as long as you believe in the Physical Realization Thesis, you must believe that every organism or system with mentality falls under a physical structure type such that its mental states are realized by determinate physical states of organisms with that structure. It may be that these structures are so finely individuated and so few *actual* individuals fall under them that research into the neural bases of mental states in these structures is no longer worthwhile, theoretically or practically. What we need to recognize here is that the scientific possibility of, say, human psychology, is a contingent fact (assuming it is a fact); it depends on the fortunate fact that individual humans do not show huge physiological-biological differences that are psychologically relevant. But if they did, that would not change the metaphysics of the situation one bit; it would remain true that the psychology of each of us was determined by, and locally reducible to, his neurobiology.

Realistically, there are going to be psychological differences among individual humans: it is a commonsense platitude that no two persons are exactly alike – either physically or psychologically. And individual differences may be manifested not only in particular psychological facts but in psychological regularities. If we believe in the Physical Realization Thesis, we must believe that our psychological differences are rooted in, and explainable by, our physical differences, just as we expect our psychological similarities to be so explainable. Humans probably are less alike among themselves than, say, tokens of a Chevrolet model.[38] And psychological laws for humans, at a certain level of specificity, must be expected to be statistical in character, not deterministic – or, if you prefer, "ceteris paribus laws" rather than "strict laws." But this is nothing peculiar to psychology; these remarks surely apply to human physiology and anatomy as much as human psychology. In any case, none of this affects the metaphysical point being argued here concerning microdetermination and microreductive explanation.

VIII. Metaphysical implications

But does local reduction have any interesting philosophical significance, especially in regard to the status of mental properties? If a psychological property has been multiply locally reduced, does that mean that the property itself has been reduced? Ned Block has raised just such a point, arguing that species-restricted reductionism (or species-restricted type physicalism) "sidesteps the main metaphysical question: 'What is common to the pains of dogs and people (and all other species) in virtue of which they are pains?'"[39]

Pereboom and Kornblith elaborate on Block's point as follows:

> ... even if there is a single type of physical state that normally realizes pain in each type of organism, or in each structure type, this does not show that pain, *as a type of mental state*, is reducible to physical states. Reduction, in the present debate, must be understood as reduction of types, since the primary object of reductive strategies is explanations and theories, and explanations and theories quantify over types.... The suggestion that there are species-specific reductions of pain results in the claim that pains in different species have nothing in common. But this is just a form of eliminativism.[40]

There are several related but separable issues raised here. But first we should ask: Must all pains have "something in common" in virtue of which they are pains?

According to the phenomenological conception of pain, all pains do have something in common: they all *hurt*. But as I take it, those who hold this view of pain would reject any reductionist program, independently of the issues presently on hand. Even if there were a species-invariant uniform bridge law correlating pains with a single physical substrate across all species and structures, they would claim that the correlation holds as a brute, unexplainable matter of fact, and that pain as a qualitative event, a "raw feel," would remain irreducibly distinct from its neural substrate. Many emergentists apparently held a view of this kind.

I presume that Block, and Pereboom and Kornblith, are speaking not from a phenomenological viewpoint of this kind but from a broadly functionalist one. But from a functionalist perspective, it is by no means clear how we should understand the question "What do all pains have in common in virtue of which they are all pains?" Why should all pains have "something in common"? As I understand it, at the core of the functionalist program is the attempt to explain the meanings of mental terms *relationally*, in terms of inputs, outputs, and connections with other mental states. And on the view, discussed briefly earlier, that mental properties are second-order properties, pain is the property of having a property with a certain functional specification H (in terms of inputs, outputs, etc.). This yields a short answer to Block's question: what all pains have in common is the pattern of connections as specified by H. The local reductionist is entitled to that answer as much as the functionalist is. Compare two pains, an instance of N_h and one of N_m; what they have in common is that each is an instance of a property that realizes pain – that is, they exhibit the same pattern of connections among input, output, and other internal states, namely the pattern specified by H.

But some will say: "But H is only an *extrinsic* characterization; what do these instances of pain have in common that is *intrinsic* to them?" The local reductionist must grant that on his view there is nothing intrinsic that all pains have in common in virtue of which they are pains (assuming that N_h, N_r, and N_m "have nothing intrinsic in common"). But that is also precisely the consequence of the functionalist view. That, one might say, is the whole point of functionalism: the functionalist, especially one who believes in MR, would not, and should not, look for something common to all pains over and above H (the heart of functionalism, we might say, is the belief that mental states have no "intrinsic essence").

But there is a further question raised by Block *et al.*: What happens to properties that have been locally reduced? Are they still with us, distinct and separate from the underlying physical-biological properties? Granted: human pain is reduced to N_h, Martian pain to N_m, and so forth, but what of *pain itself*? It remains unreduced. Are we still stuck with the dualism of mental and physical properties?

I will sketch two possible ways of meeting this challenge. First, recall my earlier remarks about the functionalist conception of mental properties as second-order properties: pain is *the property of having a property with specification H*, and, given that N_h, N_r, and N_m are the properties meeting H, pain turns out to be the disjunctive property, $N_h \lor N_r \lor N_m$. If you hold the second-order property view of mental properties, pain has been reduced to, and survives as, this disjunctive physical kind. Quite apart from considerations of local reduction, the very conception of pain you hold commits you to the conclusion that pain is a disjunctive kind, and if you accept any form of respectable physicalism (in particular, the Physical Realization Thesis), it is a disjunctive *physical* kind. And even if you don't accept the view of mental properties as second-order properties, as long as you are comfortable with disjunctive kinds and properties, you can, in the aftermath of local reduction, identify pain with the disjunction of its realization bases. On this approach, then, you have another, more direct, answer to Block's question: what all pains have in common is that they all fall under the disjunctive kind, $N_h \vee N_r \vee N_m$.

If you are averse to disjunctive kinds, there is another more radical, and in some ways more satisfying, approach. The starting point of this approach is the frank acknowledgement that MR leads to the conclusion that pain as a property or kind must go. Local reduction after all is reduction, and to be reduced is to be eliminated as an *independent* entity. You might say: global reduction is different in that it is also *conservative* – if pain is globally reduced to physical property P, pain survives as P. But it is also true that, under local reduction, pain survives as N_h in humans, as N_r in reptiles, and so on. It must be admitted, however, that pain as a kind does not survive multiple local reduction. But is this so bad?

Let us return to jade once again. Is jade a *kind*? We know it is not a mineral kind; but is it any kind of a kind? That of course depends on what we mean by "kind." There are certain shared criteria, largely based on observable macroproperties of mineral samples (e.g., hardness, color, etc.), that determine whether something is a sample of jade, or whether the predicate "is jade" is correctly applicable to it. What all samples of jade have in common is just these observable macrophysical properties that define the applicability of the predicate "is jade." In this sense, speakers of English who have "jade" in their repertoire associate the same *concept* with "jade"; and we can recognize the existence of the concept of jade and at the same time acknowledge that the concept does not pick out, or answer to, a property or kind in the natural world.

I think we can say something similar about pain and "pain": there are shared criteria for the application of the predicate "pain" or "is in pain," and these criteria may well be for the most part functionalist ones. These criteria generate for us a *concept of pain*, a concept whose clarity and determinacy depend, we may assume, on certain characteristics (such as explicitness, coherence, and completeness) of the criteria governing the application of "pain." But the concept of pain, on this construal, need not pick out an objective kind any more than the concept of jade does.

179

All this presupposes a distinction between concepts and properties (or kinds). Do we have such a distinction? I believe we do. Roughly, concepts are in the same ball park as predicates, meanings (perhaps, something like Fregean *Sinnen*), ideas, and the like; Putnam has suggested that concepts be identified with "synonymy classes of predicates,"[41] and that comes close enough to what I have in mind. Properties and relations, on the other hand, are "out there in the world"; they are features and characteristics of things and events in the world. They include fundamental physical magnitudes and quantities, like mass, energy, size, and shape, and are part of the causal structure of the world. The property of being water is arguably identical with the property of being H_2O, but evidently the concept of water is distinct from the concept of H_2O (Socrates had the former but not the latter). Most of us would agree that ethical predicates are meaningful, and that we have the concepts of "good," "right," etc.; however, it is a debatable issue, and has lately been much debated, whether there are such properties as goodness and rightness.[42] If you find that most of these remarks make sense, you understand the concept–property distinction that I have in mind. Admittedly, this is all a little vague and programmatic, and we clearly need a better articulated theory of properties and concepts; but the distinction is there, supported by an impressively systematic set of intuitions and philosophical requirements.[43]

But is this second approach a form of mental eliminativism? In a sense it is: as I said, on this approach no properties in the world answer to general, species-unrestricted mental concepts. But remember: there still are pains, and we sometimes are in pain, just as there still are samples of jade. We must also keep in mind that the present approach is not, in its ontological implications, a form of the standard mental eliminativism currently on the scene.[44] Without elaborating on what the differences are, let us just note a few important points. First, the present view does not take away species-restricted mental properties, e.g., human pain, Martian pain, canine pain, and the rest, although it takes away "pain as such." Second, while the standard eliminativism consigns mentality to the same ontological limbo to which phlogiston, witches, and magnetic effluvia have been dispatched, the position I have been sketching views it on a par with jade, tables, and adding machines. To see jade as a non-kind is not to question the existence of jade, or the legitimacy and utility of the concept of jade. Tables do not constitute a scientific kind; there are no laws about tables as such, and being a table is not a causal-explanatory kind. But that must be sharply distinguished from the false claim that there are no tables. The same goes for pains. These points suggest the following difference in regard to the status of psychology: the present view allows, and in fact encourages, "species-specific psychologies," but the standard eliminativism would do away with all things psychological – species-specific psychologies as well as global psychology.

To summarize, then, the two metaphysical schemes I have sketched offer these choices: either we allow disjunctive kinds and construe pain and other mental properties as such kinds, or else we must acknowledge that our general mental terms and concepts do not pick out properties and kinds in the world (we may call this "mental property irrealism"). I should add that I am not interested in promoting either disjunctive kinds or mental irrealism, a troubling set of choices to most of us. Rather, my main interest has been to follow out the consequences of MR and try to come to terms with them within a reasonable metaphysical scheme.

I have already commented on the status of psychology as a science under MR. As I argued, MR seriously compromises the disciplinary unity and autonomy of psychology as a science. But that does not have to be taken as a negative message. In particular, the claim does not imply that a scientific study of psychological phenomena is not possible or useful; on the contrary, MR says that psychological processes have a foundation in the biological and physical processes and regularities, and it opens the possibility of enlightening explanations of psychological processes at a more basic level. It is only that at a deeper level, psychology becomes sundered by being multiply locally reduced. However, species-specific psychologies, e.g., human psychology, Martian psychology, etc., can all flourish as scientific theories. Psychology remains *scientific*, though perhaps not a *science*. If you insist on having a global psychology valid for all species and structures, you can help yourself to that, too; but you must think of it as a *conjunction* of species-restricted psychologies and be careful, above all, with your inductions.

Notes

1 On occasion, "MR" will refer to the *phenomenon* of multiple realization rather than the *claim* that such a phenomenon exists; there should be no danger of confusion.
2 Jerry Fodor, "Special Sciences, or the Disunity of Sciences as a Working Hypothesis" (hereafter, "Special Sciences"), *Synthese* 28 (1974): 97–115; reprinted in *Representations* (Cambridge: MIT Press, 1981), and as the introductory chapter in Fodor, *The Language of Thought* (New York: Crowell, 1975).
3 Donald Davidson, "Mental Events," reprinted in *Essays on Actions and Events* (Oxford: Oxford University Press, 1980).
4 "Physicalism: Ontology, Determination, and Reduction," *Journal of Philosophy* 72 (1975): 551–64. The two quotations below are from p. 551.
5 "More on Making Mind Matter," *Philosophical Topics* 17 (1989): 175–92. The quotation is from p. 179.
6 "More on Making Mind Matter," p. 180.

7 In "Can the Mind Change the World?," in *Meaning and Method: Essays in Honor of Hilary Putnam*, ed. George Boolos (Cambridge: Cambridge University Press, 1990), p. 146.

8 They include Richard Boyd, "Materialism Without Reductionism: What Physicalism Does Not Entail," in Block, *Readings in Philosophy of Psychology*, vol. 1; Block, in "Introduction: What is Functionalism," in his anthology just cited, pp. 178–79; John Post, *The Faces of Existence* (Ithaca: Cornell University Press, 1987); Derk Pereboom and Hilary Kornblith, "The Metaphysics of Irreducibility," *Philosophical Studies* 63 (1991): 125–45. One philosopher who is not impressed by the received view of MR is David Lewis; see his "Review of Putnam," in Block, *Readings in Philosophy of Psychology*, vol 1.

9 Hilary Putnam, "Psychological Predicates," in W.H. Capitan and D.D. Merrill, eds., *Art, Mind, and Religion* (Pittsburgh: University of Pittsburgh, 1967); reprinted with a new title, "The Nature of Mental States," in Ned Block, ed., *Readings in Philosophy of Psychology*, vol. 1 (Cambridge: Harvard University Press, 1980), and as Chapter 11 in this volume.

10 "The Nature of Mental States," pp. 216–17 (in this volume).

11 Thus, Post says, "Functional and intentional states are defined without regard to their physical or other realizations," *The Faces of Existence*, p. 161. Also compare the earlier quotation from Block.

12 As far as I know, the term "realization" was first used in something like its present sense by Hilary Putnam in "Minds and Machines," in Sydney Hook, ed., *Dimensions of Mind* (New York: New York University Press, 1960).

13 On this point see Robert Van Gulick, "Nonreductive Materialism and Intertheoretic Constraints," in *Emergence or Reduction?*, ed. Ansgar Beckermann, Hans Flohr, and Jaegwon Kim (Berlin: De Gruyter, 1992).

14 "More on Making Mind Matter," p. 179.

15 Cf. Hartry Field, "Mental Representation," in Block, *Readings in Philosophy of Psychology* (Cambridge: Harvard University Press, 1981), vol. 2.

16 What of LePore and Loewer's condition (ii), the requirement that the realization basis "explain" the realized property? Something like this explanatory relation may well be entailed by the realization relation; however, I do not believe it should be part of the definition of "realization"; that such an explanatory relation holds should be a consequence of the realization relation, not constitutive of it.

17 "The Nature of Mental States," p. 217 (in this volume).

18 *The Structure of Science* (New York: Harcourt, Brace & World, 1961), chap. 11.

19 My remarks here and in the preceding paragraph assume that the higher-level theory requires no "correction" in relation to the base theory. With appropriate caveats and qualifications, they should apply to models of reduction that allow such corrections, or models that only require the deduction of a suitable analogue, or "image," in the reduction base – as long as the departures are not so extreme as to warrant talk of replacement or elimination rather than reduction. Cf. Patricia Churchland, *Neurophilosophy* (Cambridge: MIT Press, 1986), chap. 7.

20 See "Special Sciences," pp. 132–33 (in *Representations*).

21 Fodor appears to assume that the requirement that bridge laws must connect "kinds" to "kinds" is part of the classic positivist conception of reduction. I don't believe there is any warrant for this assumption, however.

22 See Pereboom and Kornblith, "The Metaphysics of Irreducibility," in which it is suggested that laws with disjunctive predicates are not "explanatory." I think, though, that this suggestion is not fully developed there.

23 The points to follow concerning disjunctive predicates were developed about a decade ago; however, I have just come across some related and, in some respects similar, points in David Owens's interesting paper "Disjunctive Laws," *Analysis* 49 (1989): 197–202. See also William Seager, "Disjunctive Laws and Supervenience," *Analysis* 51 (1991): 93–98.

24 This can be taken to define one useful sense of kind heterogeneity: two kinds are heterogeneous with respect to each other just in case their disjunction is not a kind.

25 Note: this doesn't say that for any e, if e is "positive evidence" for h and h logically implies j, then e is positive evidence for j. About the latter principle there is some dispute; see Carl G. Hempel, "Studies in the Logic of Confirmation," reprinted in Hempel, *Aspects of Scientific Explanation* (New York: The Free Press, 1965), especially pp. 30–35; Rudolf Carnap, *Logical Foundations of Probability* (Chicago: University of Chicago Press, 1950), pp. 471–76.

26 On issues concerning properties, kinds, similarity, and lawlikeness, see W.V. Quine, "Natural Kinds," in *Ontological Relativity and Other Essays* (New York: Columbia University Press, 1969); David Lewis, "New Work for a Theory of Universals," *Australasian Journal of Philosophy* 61 (1983): 347–77; D.M. Armstrong, *Universals* (Boulder, Colo.: Westview Press, 1989).

27 This term is a little misleading since the two subtheses have been stated without the term "realization" and may be acceptable to those who would reject the "realization" idiom in connection with the mental. I use the term since we are chiefly addressing philosophers (mainly functionalists) who construe the psychophysical relation in terms of realization, rather than, say, emergence or brute correlation.

28 See "Special Sciences," and "Making Mind Matter More," *Philosophical Topics* 17 (1989): 59–79.

29 See, e.g., Block, "Can the Mind Change the World?," p. 155.

30 We might keep in mind the close relationship between disjunction and the existential quantifier standardly noted in logic textbooks.

31 It may be a complicated affair to formulate this argument within certain functionalist schemes; if, for example, mental properties are functionally defined by Ramseyfying a total psychological theory, it will turn out that humans and Martians cannot share any psychological state unless the same total psychology (including the putative law in question) is true (or held to be true) for both.

32 "Special Sciences," p. 140 (in *Representations*).

33 See, e.g., Carl G. Hempel, *Fundamentals of Concept Formation in Empirical Science* (Chicago: University of Chicago Press, 1952); W.V. Quine, "Natural Kinds." Fodor gives it an explicit statement in *Psychosemantics* (Cambridge: MIT Press, 1988), chap. 2. A principle like this is often invoked in the current externalism/internalism debate about content; most principal participants in this debate seem to accept it.

34 A principle like this is sometimes put in terms of "supervenience" and "supervenience base" rather than "realization" and "realization base." See my "Epiphenomenal and Supervenient Causation," Essay 6 of *Supervenience and Mind* (Cambridge: Cambridge University Press, 1993). Fodor appears to accept just such a principle of supervenient causation for mental properties in chap. 2 of his *Psychosemantics.* In "The Metaphysics of Irreducibility" Pereboom and Kornblith appear to reject it.

35 For more details see my " 'Downward Causation' in Emergentism and Non-reductive Physicalism," in *Emergence or Reduction?*, ed. Beckermann, Flohr, and Kim, and "The Nonreductivist's Troubles with Mental Causation," Essay 17 of *Supervenience and Mind.*

36 Or an appropriately corrected version thereof (this qualification applies to the bridge laws as well).

37 In "Special Sciences" and "Making Mind Matter More" Fodor appears to accept the local reducibility of psychology and other special sciences. But he uses the terminology of local *explanation*, rather than reduction, of psychological regularities in terms of underlying microstructure. I think this is because his preoccupation with Nagelian uniform reduction prevents him from seeing that this is a form of inter-theoretic reduction if anything is.

38 Compare J.J.C. Smart's instructive analogy between biological organisms and superheterodyne radios, in *Philosophy and Scientific Realism* (London: Routledge & Kegan Paul, 1963), pp. 56–57. Smart's conception of the relation between physics and the special sciences, such as biology and psychology, is similar in some respects to the position I am defending here.

39 "Introduction: What is Functionalism?," in *Readings in Philosophy of Psychology*, pp. 178–79.

40 In their "The Metaphysics of Irreducibility." See also Ronald Endicott, "On Physical Multiple Realization," *Pacific Philosophical Quarterly* 70 (1989): 212–24. In personal correspondence Earl Conee and Joe Mendola have raised similar points. There is a useful discussion of various metaphysical issues relating to MR in Cynthia Macdonald, *Mind–Body Identity Theories* (London and New York: Routledge, 1989).

41 In "The Nature of Mental States."

42 I of course have in mind the controversy concerning moral realism; see essays in Geoffrey Sayre-McCord, ed., *Essays on Moral Realism* (Ithaca: Cornell University Press, 1988).

43 On concepts and properties, see, e.g., Hilary Putnam, "On Properties," in *Mathematics, Matter and Method* (Cambridge: Cambridge University Press, 1975); Mark Wilson, "Predicate Meets Property," *Philosophical Review* 91 (1982): 549–90, especially section III.

44 Such as the versions favored by W.V. Quine, Stephen Stich, and Paul Churchland.

9

Arnold Zuboff, "The Story of a Brain"

I

Once upon a time, a kind young man who enjoyed many friends and great wealth learned that a horrible rot was overtaking all of his body but his nervous system. He loved life; he loved having experiences. Therefore he was intensely interested when scientist friends of amazing abilities proposed the following:

"We shall take the brain from your poor rotting body and keep it healthy in a special nutrient bath. We shall have it connected to a machine that is capable of inducing in it any pattern at all of neural firings and is therein capable of bringing about for you any sort of total experience that it is possible for the activity of your nervous system to cause or to be."

The reason for this last disjunction of the verbs *to cause* and *to be* was that, although all these scientists were convinced of a general theory that they called "the neural theory of experience," they disagreed on the specific formulation of this theory. They all knew of countless instances in which it was just obvious that the state of the brain, the pattern of its activity, somehow had made for a man's experiencing this rather than that. It seemed reasonable to them all that ultimately what decisively controlled any particular experience of a man – controlled whether it existed and what it was like – was the state of his nervous system and more specifically that of those areas of the brain that careful research had discovered to be involved in the various aspects of consciousness. This conviction was what had prompted their proposal to their young friend. That they disagreed about whether an experience simply consisted in or else was caused by neural activity was irrelevant to their belief that as long as their friend's

Arnold Zuboff, "The Story of a Brain," in Douglas R. Hofstadter and Daniel C. Dennett (eds), *The Mind's I: Fantasies and Reflections on Self and Soul* (Bantam Books, New York, 1981), pp. 202–12.

ARNOLD ZUBOFF

brain was alive and functioning under their control, they could keep him having his beloved experience indefinitely, just as though he were walking about and getting himself into the various situations that would in a more natural way have stimulated each of those patterns of neural firings that they would bring about artificially. If he were actually to have gazed through a hole in a snow-covered frozen pond, for instance, the physical reality there would have caused him to experience what Thoreau described: "the quiet parlor of the fishes, pervaded by a softened light as through a window of ground glass, with its bright sanded floor the same as in summer." The brain lying in its bath, stripped of its body and far from the pond, if it were made to behave precisely as it naturally would under such pond-hole circumstances, would have for the young man that very same experience.

Well, the young man agreed with the concept and looked forward to its execution. And a mere month after he had first heard the thing proposed to him, his brain was floating in the warm nutrient bath. His scientist friends kept busy researching, by means of paid subjects, which patterns of neuron firings were like the natural neural responses to very pleasant situations; and, through the use of a complex electrode machine, they kept inducing only these neural activities in their dear friend's brain.

Then there was trouble. One night the watchman had been drinking, and, tipsily wandering into the room where the bath lay, he careened forward so his right arm entered the bath and actually split the poor brain into its two hemispheres.

The brain's scientist friends were very upset the next morning. They had been all ready to feed into the brain a marvelous new batch of experiences whose neural patterns they had just recently discovered.

"If we let our friend's brain mend after bringing the parted hemispheres together," said Fred, "we must wait a good two months before it will be healed well enough so that we can get the fun of feeding him these new experiences. Of course, he won't know about the waiting; but we sure will! And unfortunately, as we all know, two separated halves of a brain can't entertain the same neural patterns that they can when they're together. For all those impulses which cross from one hemisphere to another during a whole-brain experience just can't make it across the gap that has been opened between them."

The end of this speech gave someone else an idea. Why not do the following? Develop tiny electrochemical wires whose ends could be fitted to the synapses of neurons to receive or discharge their neural impulses. These wires could then be strung from each neuron whose connection had been broken in the split to that neuron of the other hemisphere to which it had formerly been connected. "In this way," finished Bert, the proposer of this idea, "all those impulses that were supposed to cross over from one hemisphere to the other could do just that – carried over the wires."

This suggestion was greeted with enthusiasm, since the construction of the wire system, it was felt, could easily be completed within a week. But one grave fellow named Cassander had worries. "We all agree that our friend has been having the experiences we've tried to give him. That is, we all accept in some form or other the neural theory of experience. Now, according to this theory as we all accept it, it is quite permissible to alter as one likes the context of a functioning brain, just so long as one maintains the pattern of its activity. We might look at what we're saying this way. There are various conditions that make for the usual having of an experience – an experience, for instance, like that pond-hole experience we believe we gave our friend three weeks ago. Usually these conditions are the brain being in an actual body on an actual pond stimulated to such neural activity as we did indeed give our friend. We gave our friend the neural activity without those other conditions of its context, because our friend has no body and because we believe that what is essential and decisive for the existence and character of an experience anyway is not such context but rather only the neural activity that it can stimulate. The contextual conditions, we believe, are truly inessential to the bare fact of a man having an experience – even if they *are* essential conditions in the normal having of that experience. If one has the wherewithal, as we do, to get around the normal necessity of these external conditions of an experience of a pond hole, then such conditions are no longer necessary. And this demonstrates that within our concept of experience they never were necessary in principle to the bare fact of having the experience.

"Now, what you men are proposing to do with these wires amounts to regarding as inessential just one more normal condition of our friend's having his experience. That is, you are saying something like what I just said about the context of neural activity – but *you're* saying it about the condition of the *proximity* of the hemispheres of the brain to one another. You're saying that the two hemispheres being attached to one another in the whole-brain experiences may be necessary to the coming about of those experiences in the usual case, but if one can get around a breach of this proximity in some, indeed, *un*usual case, as you fellows would with your wires, there'd still be brought about just the same bare fact of the same experience being had! You're saying that proximity isn't a necessary condition to this bare fact of an experience. But isn't it possible that even reproducing precisely the whole-brain neural patterns in a sundered brain would, to the contrary, *not* constitute the bringing about of the whole-brain experience? Couldn't proximity be not just something to get around in creating a particular whole-brain experience but somehow an absolute condition and principle of the having of a whole-brain experience?"

Cassander got little sympathy for his worries. Typical replies ran something like this: "Would the damn hemispheres *know* they were connected by wires instead of attached in the usual way? That is, would the fact get encoded in any of the brain structures responsible for speech, thought or any other feature of awareness? How could this fact about how his brain looks to external observers concern our dear friend in his pleasures at all – any more than being a naked brain sitting in a warm nutrient bath does? As long as the neural activity in the hemispheres – together *or* apart – matches precisely that which would have been the activity in the hemispheres lumped together in the head of a person walking around having fun, then the person himself is having that fun. Why, if we hooked up a mouth to these brain parts, he'd be telling us it about his fun." In reply to such answers, which were getting shorter and angrier, Cassander could only mutter about the possible disruption of some experiential field "or some such."

But after the men had been working on the wires for a while someone else came up with an objection to their project that *did* stop them. He pointed out that it took practically no time for an impulse from one hemisphere to enter into the other when a brain was together and functioning normally. But the travel of these impulses over wires must impose a tiny increase on the time taken in such crossovers. Since the impulses in the rest of the brain in each hemisphere would be taking their normal time, wouldn't the overall pattern get garbled, operating as if there were a slow-down in only one region? Certainly it would be impossible to get precisely the normal sort of pattern going – you'd have something strange, disturbed.

When this successful objection was raised, a man with very little training in physics suggested that somehow the wire be replaced by radio signals. This could be done by outfitting the raw face – of the split – of each hemisphere with an "impulse cartridge" that would be capable of sending any pattern of impulses into the hitherto exposed and unconnected neurons of that hemisphere, as well as of receiving from those neurons any pattern of impulses that that hemisphere might be trying to communicate to the other hemisphere. Then each cartridge could be plugged into a special radio transmitter and receiver. When a cartridge received an impulse from a neuron in one hemisphere intended for a neuron of the other, the impulse could then be radioed over and properly administered by the other cartridge. The fellow who suggested this even mused that then each half of the brain could be kept in a separate bath and yet the whole still be engaged in a single whole-brain experience.

The advantage of this system over the wires, this fellow thought, resided in the "fact" that radio waves take no time, unlike impulses in wires, to travel from one place to another. He was quickly disabused of this idea. No, the radio system still suffered from the time-gap obstacle.

But all this talk of impulse cartridges inspired Bert. "Look, we could feed each impulse cartridge with the same pattern of impulses it would have been receiving by radio but do so by such a method as to require no radio or wire transmission. All we need do is fix to each cartridge not a radio transmitter and receiver but an 'impulse programmer,' the sort of gadget that would play through whatever program of impulses you have previously given it. The great thing about this is that there is no longer any need for the impulse pattern going into one hemisphere to be *actually caused*, in part, by the pattern coming from the other. Therefore there need not be any wait for the transmission. The programmed cartridges can be so correlated with the rest of our stimulation of neural patterns that all of the timing can be just as it would have been if the hemispheres were together. And, yes, then it will be easy to fix each hemisphere in a separate bath – perhaps one in the laboratory here and one in the laboratory across town, so that we may employ the facilities of each laboratory in working with merely half a brain. This will make everything easier. And we can then bring in more people; there are many who've been bothering us to let them join our project."

But now Cassander was even more worried. "We have already disregarded the condition of proximity. Now we are about to abandon yet another condition of usual experience – that of actual causal connection. Granted you can be clever enough to get around what is usually quite necessary to an experience coming about. So now, with your programming, it will no longer be necessary for impulses in one half of the brain actually to be a cause of the completion of the whole-brain pattern in the other hemisphere in order for the whole-brain pattern to come about. But is the result still the bare fact of the whole-brain experience or have you, in removing this condition, removed an absolute principle of, an essential condition for, a whole-brain experience really being had?"

The answers to this were much as they had been to the other. How did the neural activity *know* whether a radio-controlled or programmed impulse cartridge fed it? How could this fact, so totally external to them, register with the neural structures underlying thought, speech, and every other item of awareness? Certainly it could not register mechanically. Wasn't the result then precisely the same with tape as with wire except that now the time-gap problem had been overcome? And wouldn't a properly hooked-up mouth even report the experiences as nicely after the taped as after the wired assistance with crossing impulses?

The next innovation came soon enough – when the question was raised about whether it was at all important, since each hemisphere was now working separately, to synchronize the two causally unconnected playings of the impulse patterns of the hemispheres. Now that each hemisphere would in effect receive all the impulses that in a given experience it would have received from the other hemisphere – and receive them in such a way as would work perfectly with the timing of the rest of its impulses – and since this fine effect could be achieved in either hemisphere quite independent of its having yet been achieved in the other, there seemed no reason for retaining what Cassander sadly pointed to as the "condition of synchronization." Men were heard to say, "How does either hemisphere *know*, how could it register when the other goes off, in the time of the external observer, anyway? For each hemisphere what more can we say than that it is just precisely as if the other had gone off with it the right way? What is there to worry about if at one lab they run through one half of a pattern one day and at the other lab they supply the other hemisphere with its half of the pattern another day? The pattern gets run through fine. The experience comes about. With the brain parts hooked up properly to a mouth, our friend could even report his experience."

There was also some discussion about whether to maintain what Cassander called "topology" – that is, whether to keep the two hemispheres in the general spatial relation of facing each other. Here too Cassander's warnings were ignored.

II

Ten centuries later the famous project was still engrossing men. But men now filled the galaxy and their technology was tremendous. Among them were billions who wanted the thrill and responsibility of participating in the "Great Experience Feed." Of course, behind this desire lay the continuing belief that what men were doing in programming impulses still amounted to making a man have all sorts of experiences.

But in order to accommodate all those who now wished to participate in the project, what Cassander had called the "conditions" of the experiencing had, to the superficial glance, changed enormously. (Actually, they were in a sense more conservative than they had been when we last saw them, because, as I shall explain later, something like "synchronization" had been restored.) Just as earlier each hemisphere of the brain had rested in its bath, now *each individual neuron* rested in one of its own. Since there were billions of neurons, each of the billions of men could involve himself with the proud task of manning a neuron bath.

To understand this situation properly, one must go back again ten centuries, to what had occurred as more and more men had expressed a desire for a part of the project. First it was agreed that if a whole-brain experience could come about with the brain split and yet the two halves programmed as I have described, the same experience could come about if each hemisphere too were carefully divided and each piece treated just as each of the two hemispheres had been. Thus each of four pieces of brain could now be given not only its own bath but a whole lab – allowing many more people to participate. There naturally seemed nothing to stop further and further divisions of the thing, until finally, ten centuries later, there was this situation – a man on each neuron, each man responsible for an impulse cartridge that was fixed to both ends of that neuron – transmitting and receiving an impulse whenever it was programmed do so.

Meanwhile there had been other Cassanders. After a while none of these suggested keeping the condition of proximity, since this would have so infuriated all his fellows who desired to have a piece of the brain. But it *was* pointed out by such Cassanders that the original topology of the brain, that is, the relative position and directional attitude of each neuron, could be maintained even while the brain was spread apart; and also it was urged by them that the neurons continue to be programmed to fire with the same chronology – the same temporal pattern – that their firings would have displayed when together in the brain.

But the suggestion about topology always brought a derisive response. A sample: "How should each of the neurons *know*, how should it register on a single neuron, where it is in relation to the others? In the usual case of an experience it is indeed necessary for the neurons, in order at all to get firing in that pattern that is or causes the experience, to be next to each other, actually causing the firing of one another, in a certain spatial relation to one another – but the original necessity of all these conditions is overcome by our techniques. For example, they are not necessary to the *bare fact* of the coming about of the experience that we are now causing to be had by the ancient gentleman whose neuron this is before me. And if we should bring these neurons together into a hookup with a mouth, then he would tell you of the experience personally."

Now as for the second part of the Cassanderish suggestion, the reader might suppose that after each successive partitioning of the brain, synchronization of the parts would have been consistently disregarded, so that eventually it would have been thought not to matter when each individual neuron was to be fired in relation to the firings of the other neurons – just as earlier the condition had been disregarded when there were only two hemispheres to be fired. But somehow, perhaps because disregarding the timing and order of individual neuron firings would have reduced the art of programming to absurdity, the condition of order and timing had crept back, but without the Cassanderish reflectiveness. "Right" temporal order of firings is now merely *assumed* as somehow essential to bringing about a given experience by all those men standing before their baths and *waiting* for each properly programmed impulse to come to its neuron.

But now, ten centuries after the great project's birth, the world of these smug billions was about to explode. Two thinkers were responsible.

One of these, named Spoilar, had noticed one day that the neuron in his charge was getting a bit the worse for wear. Like any other man with a neuron in that state, he merely obtained another fresh one just like it and so replaced the particular one that had gotten worn – tossing the old one away. Thus he, like all the others, had violated the Cassanderish condition of "neural identity" – a condition never taken very seriously even by Cassanders. It was realized that in the case of an ordinary brain the cellular metabolism was always replacing all the particular matter of any neuron with other particular matter, forming precisely the same kind of neuron. What this man had done was really no more than a speeding-up of this process. Besides, what if, as some Cassanders had implausibly argued, replacing one neuron by another just like it somehow resulted, when it was eventually done to all the neurons, in a new identity for the experiencer? There still would be *an* experiencer having the same experience every time the same patterns of firings were realized (and what it would mean to say he was a different experiencer was not clear at all, even to the Cassanders). So any shift in neural identity did not seem destructive of the fact of an experience coming about.

This fellow Spoilar, after he had replaced the neuron, resumed his waiting to watch his own neuron fire as part of an experience scheduled several hours later. Suddenly, he heard a great crash and a great curse. Some fool had fallen against another man's bath, and it had broken totally on the floor when it fell. Well, this man whose bath had fallen would just have to miss out on any experiences his neuron was to have been part of until the bath and neuron could be replaced. And Spoilar knew that the poor man had had one coming up soon.

The fellow whose bath had just broken walked up to Spoilar. He said, "Look, I've done favors for you. I'm going to have to miss the impulse coming up in five minutes – that experience will have to manage with one less neuron firing. But maybe you'd let me man yours coming up later. I just hate to miss all the thrills coming up today!"

Spoilar thought about the man's plea. Suddenly, a strange thought hit him. "Wasn't the neuron you manned the same sort as mine?"

"Yes."

"Well, look. I've just replaced my neuron with another like it, as we all do occasionally. Why don't we take my entire bath over to the old position of yours? Then won't it still be the same experience brought about in five minutes that it would have been with the old neuron if we fire this then, since this one is just like the old one? Surely the *bath's* identity means nothing. Anyway, then we can bring the bath back here and I can use the neuron for the experience it is scheduled to be used for later on. Wait a minute! We both believe the condition of topology is baloney. So why need we move the bath at all? Leave it here; fire it for yours; and then I'll fire it for mine. Both experiences must still come about. Wait a minute again! Then all we need do is fire this one neuron here in place of all the firings of all neurons just like it! Then there need be only one neuron of each type firing again and again and again to bring about all these experiences! But how would the neurons *know* even that they were repeating an impulse when they fired again and again? How would they *know* the relative order of their firings? Then we could have one neuron of each sort firing once and that would provide the physical realization of all patterns of impulses (a conclusion that would have been arrived at merely by consistently disregarding the necessity of synchronization in the progress from parted hemispheres to parted neurons). And couldn't these neurons simply be any of those naturally firing in any head? So what are we all doing here?"

Then an even more desperate thought hit him, which he expressed thus: "But if all possible neural experience will be brought about simply in the firing once of one of each type of neuron, how can any experiencer believe that he is connected to anything more than this bare minimum of physical reality through the fact of his having *any* of his experiences? And so all this talk of heads and neurons in them, which is supposedly based on the true discovery of physical realities, is undermined entirely. There may be a true system of physical reality, but if it involves all this physiology we have been hoodwinked into believing, it provides so cheaply for so much experience that we can never know what is an actual experience of *it*, the physical reality. And so belief in such a system undermines itself. That is, unless it's tempered with Cassanderish principles."

The other thinker, coincidentally also named Spoilar, came to the same conclusion somewhat differently. He enjoyed stringing neurons. Once he got his own neuron, the one he was responsible for, in the middle of a long chain of like neurons and then recalled he was supposed to have it hooked up to the cartridge for a firing. Not wanting to destroy the chain, he simply hooked the two end neurons of the chain to the two poles of the impulse cartridge and adjusted the timing of the cartridge so that the impulse, traveling now through this whole chain, would reach his neuron at just the right time. Then he noticed that here a neuron, unlike one in usual experience, was quite comfortably participating in two patterns of firings at once – the chain's, which happened to have proximity and causal connection, and the programmed experience for which it had fired. After this Spoilar went about ridiculing "the condition of neural context." He'd say, "Boy, I could hook my neuron up with all those in your head, and if I could get it to fire just at the right time, I could get it into one of these programmed experiences as fine as if it were in my bath, on my cartridge."

Well, one day there was trouble. Some men who had not been allowed to join the project had come at night and so tampered with the baths that many of the neurons in Spoilar's vicinity had simply died. Standing before his own dead neuron, staring at the vast misery around him, he thought about how the day's first experience must turn out for the experiencer when so many neuron firings were to be missing from their physical realization. But as he looked about he suddenly took note of something else. Nearly everyone was stooping to inspect some damaged equipment just under his bath. Suddenly it seemed significant to Spoilar that next to every bath there was a head, each with its own billions of neurons of all sorts, with perhaps millions of each sort firing at any given moment. Proximity didn't matter. But then at any given moment of a particular pattern's being fired through the baths all the requisite activity was already going on anyway in the heads of the operators – in even *one* of those heads, where a loose sort of proximity condition was fulfilled too! Each head was bath and cartridge enough for any spread-brain's realization: "But," thought Spoilar, "the same kind of physical realization must exist for every experience of every brain – since all brains are spreadable. And that includes mine. But then all my beliefs are based on thoughts and experiences that might exist only as some such floating cloud. They are all suspect – including those that had convinced me of all this physiology in the first place. Unless Cassander is right, to some extent, then physiology reduces to absurdity. It undermines itself."

Such thinking killed the great project and with it the spread-brain. Men turned to other weird activities and to new conclusions about the nature of experience. But what these were is another story.

IIB

FUNCTIONALISM

10

David Lewis, "Reduction of Mind"*

I am a realist and a reductive materialist about mind. I hold that mental states are contingently identical to physical – in particular, neural – states. My position is very like the "Australian materialism" of Place, Smart, and especially Armstrong. Like Smart and Armstrong, I am an ex-Rylean, and I retain some part of the Rylean legacy. In view of how the term is contested, I do not know whether I am a "functionalist."

My reductionism about mind begins as part of an *a priori* reductionism about everything. This world, or any possible world, consists of things which instantiate fundamental properties and which, in pairs or triples or . . . , instantiate fundamental relations. Few properties are fundamental: the property of being a club or a tub or a pub, for instance, is an unnatural gerrymander, a condition satisfied by miscellaneous things in miscellaneous ways. A fundamental, or "perfectly natural," property is the extreme opposite. Its instances share exactly some aspect of their intrinsic nature. Likewise for relations.[1] I hold, as an *a priori* principle, that every contingent truth must be made true, somehow, by the pattern of coinstantiation of fundamental properties and relations. The whole truth about the world, including the mental part of the world, supervenes on this pattern. If two possible worlds were exactly isomorphic in their patterns of coinstantiation of fundamental properties and relations, they would thereby be exactly alike *simpliciter*.[2]

It is a task of physics to provide an inventory of all the fundamental properties and relations that occur in the world. (That's because it is also a task of physics to discover the fundamental laws of nature, and only the

* Thanks to the Boyce Gibson Memorial Library and the philosophy department of Birkbeck College; and to the editor, Ned Block, Alex Byrne, Mark Crimmins, Allen Hazen, Ned Hall, Elijah Millgram, Thomas Nagel, and especially Frank Jackson.

David Lewis, "Reduction of Mind" (excerpts), in Samuel Guttenplan (ed.), *A Companion to the Philosophy of Mind* (Blackwell, Oxford, 1994), pp. 412–21.

fundamental properties and relations may appear in the fundamental laws.[3]) We have no *a priori* guarantee of it, but we may reasonably think that present-day physics already goes a long way toward a complete and correct inventory. Remember that the physical nature of ordinary matter under mild conditions is very well understood.[4] And we may reasonably hope that future physics can finish the job in the same distinctive style. We may think, for instance, that mass and charge are among the fundamental properties; and that whatever fundamental properties remain as yet undiscovered are likewise instantiated by very small things that come in very large classes of exact duplicates. We may further think that the very same fundamental properties and relations, governed by the very same laws, occur in the living and the dead parts of the world, and in the sentient and the insentient parts, and in the clever and the stupid parts. In short: if we optimistically extrapolate the triumph of physics hitherto, we may provisionally accept that all fundamental properties and relations that actually occur are physical. This is the thesis of materialism.

(It was so named when the best physics of the day was the physics of matter alone. Now our best physics acknowledges other bearers of fundamental properties: parts of pervasive fields, parts of causally active spacetime. But it would be pedantry to change the name on that account, and disown our intellectual ancestors. Or worse, it would be a tacky marketing ploy, akin to British Rail's decree that second class passengers shall now be called "standard class customers.")

If materialism is true, as I believe it is, then the *a priori* supervenience of everything upon the pattern of coinstantiation of *fundamental* properties and relations yields an *a posteriori* supervenience of everything upon the pattern of coinstantiation of fundamental *physical* properties and relations. Materialist supervenience should be a contingent matter. To make it so, we supply a restriction that makes reference to actuality. Thus: if two worlds were physically isomorphic, and if no fundamental properties or relations alien to actuality occurred in either world, then these worlds would be exactly alike *simpliciter*. Disregarding alien worlds, the whole truth supervenes upon the physical truth. In particular, the whole mental truth supervenes. So here we have the common core of all materialist theories of the mind.[5]

A materialist who stops here has already said enough to come under formidable attack. An especially well-focused version of the attack comes from Frank Jackson.[6] Mary, confined in a room where all she can see is black or white, studies the physics of colour and colour vision and colour experience (and any other physics you might think relevant) until she knows it all. Then she herself sees colour for the first time, and at last she knows what it's like to see colour. What is this knowledge that Mary has gained?

It may seem that she has eliminated some possibilities left open by all her previous knowledge; she has distinguished the actual world from other possible worlds that are exactly like it in all relevant physical respects. But if materialist supervenience is true, this cannot be what has happened.

Materialists have said many things about what does happen in such a case. I myself, following Nemirow, call it a case of know-how: Mary gains new imaginative abilities.[7] Others have said that Mary gains new relations of acquaintance, or new means of mental representation; or that the change in her is just that she has now seen colour. These suggestions need not be taken as rival alternatives. And much ink has been spent on the question whether these various happenings could in any sense be called the gaining of "new knowledge," "new belief," or "new information." But for a materialist, the heart of the matter is not what *does* happen but what *doesn't*: Mary does not distinguish the actual world from other worlds that are its physical duplicates but not its duplicates *simpliciter*.

Imagine a grid of a million tiny spots – pixels – each of which can be made light or dark. When some are light and some are dark, they form a picture, replete with interesting intrinsic gestalt properties. The case evokes reductionist comments. Yes, the picture really does exist. Yes, it really does have those gestalt properties. However, the picture and the properties reduce to the arrangement of light and dark pixels. They are nothing over and above the pixels. They make nothing true that is not made true already by the pixels. They could go unmentioned in an inventory of what there is without thereby rendering that inventory incomplete. And so on.

Such comments seem to me obviously tight. The picture reduces to the pixels. And that is because the picture supervenes on the pixels: there could be no difference in the picture and its properties without some difference in the arrangement of light and dark pixels. Further, the supervenience is asymmetric: not just any difference in the pixels would matter to the gestalt properties of the picture. And it is supervenience of the large upon the small and many. In such a case, say I, supervenience is reduction. And the materialist supervenience of mind and all else upon the arrangement of atoms in the void – or whatever replaces atoms in the void in true physics – is another such case.

Yet thousands say that what's good about stating materialism in terms of supervenience is that this avoids reductionism! There's no hope of settling this disagreement by appeal to some uncontested definition of the term "reductionism." Because the term *is* contested, and the aim of some contestants is to see to it that whatever position they may hold, "reductionism" shall be the name for something else.

At any rate, materialist supervenience means that for anything mental, there are physical conditions that would be sufficient for its presence, and physical conditions that would be sufficient for its absence. (These conditions will include conditions saying that certain inventories are complete: an electron has only so-and-so quantum numbers, for instance, and it responds only to such-and-such forces. But it's fair to call such a condition "physical," since it answers a kind of question that physics does indeed address.) And no matter how the world may be, provided it is free of fundamental properties or relations alien to actuality, a condition of the one sort or the other will obtain. For all we know so far, the conditions associated with a given mental item might be complicated and miscellaneous – even infinitely complicated and miscellaneous. But so long as we limit ourselves just to the question of how this mental item can find a place in the world of fundamental physics, it is irrelevant how complicated and miscellaneous the conditions might be.

It may seem unsatisfactory that physical conditions should always settle whether the mental item is present or absent. For mightn't that sometimes be a vague question with no determinate answer? A short reply to this objection from vagueness is that if it did show that the mental was irreducible to fundamental physics despite supervenience, it would likewise show that boiling was irreducible to fundamental physics – which is absurd. For it is a vague matter just where simmering leaves off and boiling begins.

A longer reply has three parts. (1) If the physical settles the mental insofar as anything does, we still have materialist supervenience. Part of what it means for two physically isomorphic worlds to be just alike mentally is that any mental indeterminacy in one is exactly matched by mental indeterminacy in the other. (2) Whenever it is a vague question whether some simplistic mental classification applies, it will be determinate that some more subtle classification applies. What's determinate may be not that you do love him or that you don't, but rather that you're in a certain equivocal state of mind that defies easy description. (3) If all indeterminacy is a matter of semantic indecision,[8] then there is no indeterminacy in the things themselves. How could we conjure up some irreducible mental item just by failing to decide exactly which reducible item we're referring to?

It may seem that when supervenience guarantees that there are physical conditions sufficient for the presence or absence of a given mental item, the sufficiency is of the wrong sort. The implication is necessary but not *a priori*. You might want to say, for instance, that black-and-white Mary really did gain new knowledge when she first saw colour; although what she learned followed necessarily from all the physics she knew beforehand, she had remained ignorant because it didn't follow *a priori*.

A short reply to this objection from necessity *a posteriori* is that if it did show that the mental was irreducible to fundamental physics, it would

200

likewise show that boiling was irreducible to fundamental physics – which is absurd. For the identity between boiling and a certain process described in fundamental physical terms is necessary *a posteriori* if anything is.

. . .

If we limit ourselves to the question how mind finds a place in the world of physics, our work is done. Materialist supervenience offers a full answer. But if we expand our interests a little, we'll see that among the supervenient features of the world, mind must be very exceptional. There are countless such features. In our little toy example of the picture and the pixels, the supervenient properties number 2 to the power: 2 to the millionth power. In the case of materialist supervenience, the number will be far greater. The infinite cardinal beth-3 is a conservative estimate. The vast majority of supervenient features of the world are given only by miscellaneously infinite disjunctions of infinitely complex physical conditions. Therefore they are beyond our power to detect, to name, or to think about one at a time. Mental features of the world, however, are not at all beyond our ken. Finite assemblies of particles – us – can track them. Therefore there must be some sort of simplicity to them. Maybe it will be a subtle sort of simplicity, visible only if you look in just the right way. (Think of the Mandelbrot set: its overwhelming complexity, its short and simple recipe.) But somehow it must be there. Revealing this simplicity is a job for conceptual analysis.

Arbiters of fashion proclaim that analysis is out of date. Yet without it, I see no possible way to establish that any feature of the world does or does not deserve a name drawn from our traditional mental vocabulary. We should repudiate not analysis itself, but only some simplistic goals for it. We should allow for semantic indecision: any interesting analysandum is likely to turn out vague and ambiguous. Often the best that any one analysis can do is to fall safely within the range of indecision. And we should allow for semantic satisficing: analysis may reveal what it would take to deserve a name perfectly, but imperfect deservers of the name may yet deserve it well enough. (And sometimes the perfect case may be impossible.) If so, there is bound to be semantic indecision about how well is well enough.

I offer not analyses, but a recipe for analyses. We have a very extensive shared understanding of how we work mentally. Think of it as a theory: folk psychology. It is common knowledge among us; but it is tacit, as our grammatical knowledge is. We can tell which particular predictions and explanations conform to its principles, but we cannot expound those principles systematically.[9] Folk psychology is a powerful instrument of prediction. We are capable of all sorts of behaviour that would seem bizarre and unintelligible, and this is exactly the behaviour that folk psychology predicts, rightly, will seldom occur. (But we take a special interest in questions that lie beyond the predictive power of folk psychology; wherefore ingrates may fairly complain of a lack of *interesting* predictions!) Folk psychology has evolved through thousands of years of close observation of one another. It is not the last word in psychology, but we should be confident that so far as it goes – and it does go far – it is largely right.

Folk psychology concerns the causal relations of mental states, perceptual stimuli, and behavioural responses. It says how mental states, singly or in combination, are apt for causing behaviour; and it says how mental states are apt to change under the impact of perceptual stimuli and other mental states. Thus it associates with each mental state a typical causal role. Now we have our recipe for analyses. Suppose we've managed to elicit all the tacitly known general principles of folk psychology. Whenever M is a folk-psychological name for a mental state, folk psychology will say that state M typically occupies a certain causal role: call this the M-role. Then we analyse M as meaning "the state that typically occupies the M-role." Folk psychology implicitly defines the term M, and we have only to make that definition explicit.

Since the causal roles of mental states involve other mental states, we might fear circularity. The remedy is due in its essentials to Ramsey.[10] Suppose, for instance, that folk psychology had only three names for mental states: L, M, N. We associate with this triplet of names a complex causal role for a triplet of states, including causal relations within the triplet: call this the LMN-role. Folk psychology says that the states L, M, N jointly occupy the LMN-role. That implies that M occupies the derivative role: coming second in a triplet of states that jointly occupy the LMN-role. Taking this as our M-role, we proceed as before. Say that the names L, M, N are *interdefined*. The defining of all three via the LMN-role is a package deal.

We might fear circularity for another reason. The causal roles of mental states involve responses to perceptual stimuli. But the relevant feature of the stimulus will often be some secondary quality – for instance, a colour. We cannot replace the secondary quality with a specification of the stimulus in purely physical terms, on pain of going beyond what is known to folk psychology. But if we analyse the secondary quality in terms of the distinctive mental states its presence is apt to evoke, we close a definitional circle. So we should take interdefinition further. Let folk psychology include folk psychophysics. This will say, for instance, that the pair of a certain colour and the corresponding sensation jointly occupy a complex causal role that consists in part, but only in part, of the former being apt to cause the latter. Now we have a derivative role associated with the name of the colour, and another associated with the name of the sensation: the role of coming first or coming second, respectively, in a pair that jointly occupies this complex role.

We might worry also about the behaviour that mental states are apt for causing. Often we describe behaviour in a mentally loaded way: as action. To say that you kicked the ball to your teammate is to describe your behaviour. But such a description presupposes a great deal about how your behaviour was meant to serve your desires according to your beliefs; and also about the presence of the ball and the playing surface and the other player, and about the social facts that unite players into teams. More threat of circularity? More need for interdefinition? I don't know how such further interdefinition would work; and anyway, it would be well to call a halt before folk psychology expands into a folk theory of the entire *Lebenswelt*!

Describing the behaviour in purely physical terms – the angle of the knee, the velocity of the foot – would get rid of those presuppositions. But, just as in the case of the stimuli, it would go beyond what is known to folk psychology. Further, these descriptions would never fit the behaviour of space aliens not of humanoid shape; and yet we should not dismiss out of hand the speculation that folk psychology might apply to aliens as well as to ourselves.

Fortunately there is a third way to describe behaviour. When you kicked the ball, your body moved in such a way that *if* you had been on a flat surface in Earth-normal gravity with a suitably placed ball in front of you and a suitably placed teammate some distance away, *then* the impact of your foot upon the ball would have propelled the ball onto a trajectory bringing it within the teammate's reach. That description is available to the folk. They wouldn't give it spontaneously, but they can recognize it as correct. It presupposes nothing about your mental states, not even that you have any; nothing about whether the ball and the playing field and the gravity and the teammate are really there; nothing about your humanoid shape, except that you have some sort of foot. It could just as well describe the behaviour of a mindless mechanical contraption, in the shape of a space alien (with a foot), thrashing about in free fall.

(I don't say that we should really use these "if – then" descriptions of behaviour. Rather, my point is that their availability shows how to unload the presuppositions from our ordinary descriptions.)

If M means "the state that typically occupies the M-role" and if that role is only imperfectly occupied, what are we to do? – Satisfice: let the name M go to a state that deserves it imperfectly. And if nothing comes anywhere near occupying the M-role? – Then the name M has no referent. The boundary between the cases is vague. To take an example from a different term-introducing theory, I suppose it to be indeterminate whether "dephlogisticated air" refers to oxygen or to nothing. But folk psychology is in far better shape than phlogiston theory, despite scare stories to the contrary. We can happily grant that there are no perfect deservers of folk-psychological names, but we shouldn't doubt that there are states that deserve those names well enough.

What to do if the M-role, or the LMN-role, turns out to be doubly occupied? I used to think that in this case too the name M had no referent.[11] But now I think it might be better, sometimes or always, to say that the name turns out to be ambiguous in reference. That follows the lead of Field; and it is consistent with, though not required by, the treatment of Carnap.[12] Note that we face the same choice with phrases like "the moon of Mars"; and in that case too I'd now lean toward ambiguity of reference rather than lack of it.

My recipe for analyses, like Rylean analytic behaviourism, posits analytic truths that constrain the causal relations of mental states to behaviour. (We have no necessary connections between distinct existences, of course; the necessity is verbal. The state itself could have failed to occupy its causal role, but would thereby have failed to deserve its mental name.) But the constraints are weak enough to be credible. Because the state that typically occupies a role need not occupy it invariably, and also because a state may deserve a name well enough in virtue of a role that it occupies imperfectly, we are safe from the behaviourist's bugbears. We have a place for the resolute deceiver, disposed come what may to behave as if his mental states were other than they really are. We have a place for the total and incurable paralytic with a rich mental life and no behavioural dispositions whatever. We even have a place for a madman whose mental states are causally related to behaviour and stimuli and one another in a totally haywire fashion.[13] And yet not anything goes. At some point – and just where that point comes is a matter of semantic indecision – weird tales of mental states that habitually offend against the principles of folk psychology stop making sense; because at some point the offending states lose all claim to their folk-psychological names. To that extent, analytic behaviourism was right. To quote my closest ally in these matters, ". . . outward physical behaviour and tendencies to behave do in some way enter into our ordinary concept of mind. Whatever theory of mind is true, it has a debt to pay, and a peace to be made, with behaviourism."[14]

When we describe mental state M as the occupant of the M-role, that is what Smart calls a topic-neutral description.[15] It says nothing about what sort of state it is that occupies the role. It might be a non-physical or a physical state, and if it is physical it might be a state of neural activity in the brain, or a pattern of currents and charges on a silicon chip, or the jangling of an enormous assemblage of beer cans. What state occupies the M-role and thereby deserves the name M is an *a posteriori* matter. But if materialist supervenience is true, and every feature of the world supervenes upon fundamental physics, then the occupant of the role is some physical state or other – because there's nothing else for it to be. We know enough to rule out the chip and the cans, and to support the hypothesis that what occupies the role is some pattern of neural activity. When we know more, we shall know what pattern of neural activity it is. Then we shall have the premises of an argument for psychophysical identification:[16]

mental state M = the occupant of the M-role (by analysis),
physical state P = the occupant of the M-role (by science),
therefore $M = P$.

That's how conceptual analysis can reveal the simple formula – or anyway, the much less than infinitely complicated formula – whereby, when we know enough, we can pick out a mental feature of the world from all the countless other features of the world that likewise supervene on fundamental physics.

The causal-role analyses would still hold even if materialist supervenience failed. They might even still yield psychophysical identifications. Even if we lived in a spook-infested world, it might be physical states that occupied the causal roles (in us, if not in the spooks) and thereby deserved the folk-psychological names. Or it might be non-physical states that occupied the roles. Then, if we knew enough parapsychology, we would have the premises of an argument for psycho-*non*physical identification.

When our argument delivers an identification $M = P$, the identity is contingent. How so? – All identity is self-identity, and nothing could possibly have failed to be self-identical. But that is not required. It's contingent, and it can only be known *a posteriori*, which physical (or other) states occupy which causal roles. So if M means "the occupant of the M-role" it's contingent which state is the referent of M; it's contingent whether some one state is the common referent of M and P; so it's contingent whether $M = P$ is true.

Kripke vigorously intuits that some names for mental states, in particular "pain," are rigid designators: that is, it's not contingent what their referents are.[17] I myself intuit no such thing, so the non-rigidity imputed by causal-role analyses troubles me not at all.

Here is an argument that "pain" is not a rigid designator. Think of some occasion when you were in severe pain, unmistakable and unignorable. All will agree, except for some philosophers and faith healers, that there is a state that actually occupies the pain role (or near enough); that it is called "pain"; and that you were in it on that occasion. For now, I assume nothing about the nature of this state, or about how it deserves its name. Now consider an unactualized situation in which it is some different state that occupies the pain role in place of the actual occupant; and in which you were in that different state; and which is otherwise as much like the actual situation as possible. Can you distinguish the actual situation from this unactualized alternative? I say not, or not without laborious investigation. But if "pain" is a rigid designator, then the alternative situation is one in which you were not in pain, so you could distinguish the two very easily. So "pain" is not a rigid designator.

Philosophical arguments are never incontrovertible – well, hardly ever. Their purpose is to help expound a position, not to coerce agreement. In this case, the controverter might say that if the actual occupant of the pain role is not a physical state, but rather is a special sort of non-physical state, then indeed you can distinguish the two situations. He might join me in saying that this would not be so if the actual occupant of the role were a physical state – else neurophysiology would be easier than it is – and take this together with intuitions of rigidity to yield a *reductio* against materialism. Myself, I don't see how the physical or non-physical nature of the actual occupant of the role has anything to do with whether the two situations can be distinguished. Talk of "phenomenal character" and the like doesn't help. Either it is loaded with question-begging philosophical doctrine, or else it just reiterates the undisputed fact that pain is a kind of experience.[18]

If there is variation across worlds with respect to which states occupy the folk-psychological roles and deserve the folk-psychological names (and if this variation doesn't always require differences in the laws of nature, as presumably it doesn't) then also there can be variations within a single world. For possibility obeys a principle of recombination: roughly, any possible kind of thing can coexist with any other.[19] For all we know, there may be variation even within this world. Maybe there are space aliens, and maybe there will soon be artificial intelligences, in whom the folk-psychological roles are occupied (or near enough) by states very different from any states of a human nervous system. Presumably, at least some folk-psychological roles are occupied in at least some animals, and maybe there is variation across species. There might even be variation within humanity. It depends on the extent to which we are hard-wired, and on the extent of genetic variation in our wiring.

We should beware, however, of finding spurious variation by overlooking common descriptions. Imagine two mechanical calculators that are just alike in design. When they add columns of numbers, the amount carried goes into a register, and the register used for this purpose is selected by throwing a switch. Don't say that the carry-seventeen role is occupied in one machine by a state of register *A* and in the other by a state of register *B*. Say instead that in both machines alike the role is occupied by a state of the register selected by the switch. (Equivalently, by a state of a part of the calculator large enough to include the switch and both registers.) If there is a kind of thinking that some of us do in the left side of the brain and others do in the right side, that might be a parallel case.

If M means "the occupant of the M-role" and there is variation in what occupies the M-role, then our psychophysical identities need to be restricted: not plain $M = P$, but M-in-$K = P$, where K is a kind within which P occupies the M-role. Human pain might be one thing, Martian pain might be something else.[20] As with contingency, which is variation across worlds, so likewise with variation in a single world: the variability in no way infects the identity relation, but rather concerns the reference of the mental name.

The threat of variation has led many to retreat from "type–type" to "token–token" identity. They will not say that $M = P$, where M and P are names for a state that can be common to different things at different times – that is, for a property had by things at times. But they will say that $m = p$, where m and p are mental and physical names for a particular, unrepeatable event. Token–token identities are all very well, in their derivative way, but the flight from type–type identities was quite unnecessary. For our restricted identities, of the form M-in-$K = P$, are still type–type.

But don't we at least have a choice? Couldn't our causal role analyses be recast in terms of the causal roles of tokens, and if they were, would they not then yield token–token identities? After all, the only way for a type to occupy a causal role is through the causes and effects of its tokens. The effects of pain are the effects of pain-events. – I think, following Jackson, Pargetter, and Prior, that this recasting of the analyses would not be easy.[21] There are more causal relations than one. Besides causing, there is preventing. It too may figure in folk-psychological causal roles; for instance, pain tends to prevent undivided attention to anything else. Prevention cannot straightforwardly be treated as a causal relation of tokens, because the prevented tokens do not exist – not in this world, anyway. It is better taken as a relation of types.

If a retreat had been needed, a better retreat would have been to "subtype–subtype" identity. Let MK name the conjunctive property of being in state M and being of kind K; and likewise for PK. Do we really want psychophysical identities of the form $MK = PK$? – Close, but I think not quite right. For one thing, M-in-K is not the same thing as MK. The former but not the latter can occur also in something that isn't of kind K. For another thing, it is P itself, not PK, that occupies the M-role in things of kind K.

Non-rigidity means that M is different states in different possible cases; variation would mean that M was different states in different actual cases. But don't we think that there is *one* property of being in the state M – one property that is common to all, actual or possible, of whatever kind, who can truly be said to be in state M? – There is. It is the property such that, for any possible X, X has it just in case X is in the state that occupies the M-role for X's kind at X's world.[22] The gerund "being in M" can be taken, at least on one good disambiguation, as a rigid designator of this property. However, this property is not the occupant of the M-role. It cannot occupy that or any other causal role because it is excessively disjunctive, and therefore no events are essentially havings of it.[23] To admit it as causally efficacious would lead to absurd double-counting of causes. It would be like saying that the meat fried in Footscray cooked because it had the property of being either fried in Footscray or boiled in Bundoora – only worse, because the disjunction would be much longer and more miscellaneous.

Since the highly disjunctive property of being in M does not occupy the M-role, I say it cannot be the referent of M. Many disagree. They would like it if M turned out to be a rigid designator of a property common to all who are in M. So the property I call "being in M," they call simply M; and the property that I call M, the occupant of the M-role, they call "the realisation of M." They have made the wrong choice, since it is absurd to deny that M itself is causally efficacious. Still, their mistake is superficial. They have the right properties in mind, even if they give them the wrong names.

It is unfortunate that this superficial question has sometimes been taken to mark the boundary of "functionalism." Sometimes so and sometimes not – and that's why I have no idea whether I am a functionalist.

Those who take "pain" to be a rigid designator of the highly disjunctive property will need to controvert my argument that "pain" is not rigid, and they will not wish to claim that one can distinguish situations in which the pain-role is differently occupied. Instead, they should controvert the first step, and deny that the actual occupant of the pain-role is called "pain." I call that denial a *reductio*.

. . .

Notes

1   See David Lewis, "New Work for a Theory of Universals," *Australasian Journal of Philosophy* 61 (1983), pp. 343–377; and David Lewis, *On the Plurality of Worlds* (Blackwell, 1986), pp. 59–69.
2   See David Lewis, "Critical Notice of D.M. Armstrong, *A Combinatorial Theory of Possibility*," *Australasian Journal of Philosophy* 70 (1992), pp. 211–224.
3   Lewis, "New Work for a Theory of Universals," pp. 365–370.
4   Gerald Feinberg, "Physics and the Thales Problem," *Journal of Philosophy* 66 (1966), pp. 5–13.
5   Lewis, "New Work for a Theory of Universals," pp. 361–365.

6 Frank Jackson, "Epiphenomenal Qualia," *Philosophical Quarterly* 32 (1982), pp. 127–136.

7 Laurence Nemirow, "Physicalism and the Cognitive Role of Acquaintance" and David Lewis, "What Experience Teaches," both in *Mind and Cognition: A Reader*, ed. by W.G. Lycan (Blackwell, 1990); the latter is reprinted in this volume as Chapter 23.

8 Lewis, *On the Plurality of Worlds*, pp. 212–213.

9 *Pace* David Lewis, "Psychophysical and Theoretical Identifications," *Australasian Journal of Philosophy* 50 (1972), pp. 249–258, eliciting the general principles of folk psychology is no mere matter of gathering platitudes.

10 F.P. Ramsey, "Theories" in Ramsey, *The Foundations of Mathematics* (Routledge & Kegan Paul, 1931), pp. 212–236; Rudolf Carnap, "Replies and Expositions" in *The Philosophy of Rudolf Carnap*, ed. by P.A. Schilpp (Cambridge University Press, 1963), pp. 958–966. See also David Lewis, "How to Define Theoretical Terms," *Journal of Philosophy* 67 (1970), pp. 427–446, reprinted in Lewis, *Philosophical Papers,* Vol. 1 (Oxford University Press, 1983); and Lewis, "Psychophysical and Theoretical Identifications."

11 David Lewis, "How to Define Theoretical Terms" and "Psychophysical and Theoretical Identifications."

12 Hartry Field, "Theory Change and the Indeterminacy of Reference," *Journal of Philosophy* 70 (1973), pp. 462–481; Carnap *loc. cit.*

13 David Lewis, "Mad Pain and Martian Pain," in *Readings in Philosophy of Psychology*, Vol. 1, ed. by N. Block (Harvard University Press, 1980), reprinted with postscript in Lewis, *Philosophical Papers*, Vol. 1 (Oxford University Press, 1983).

14 D.M. Armstrong, *A Materialist Theory of Mind* (Routledge & Kegan Paul, 1968), p. 68.

15 J.J.C. Smart, "Sensations and Brain Processes," *Philosophical Review*, 68 (1959), pp. 141–156; reprinted as Chapter 6 in this volume.

16 See David Lewis, "An Argument for the Identity Theory," *Journal of Philosophy* 63 (1966), pp. 17–25, reprinted with additions in Lewis, *Philosophical Papers*, Vol. 1 (Oxford University Press, 1983); and Lewis, "Psychophysical and Theoretical Identifications." See Armstrong, *A Materialist Theory of the Mind*, for an independent and simultaneous presentation of the same position, with a much fuller discussion of what the definitive causal roles might be.

17 Saul Kripke, *Naming and Necessity* (Blackwell, 1980), pp. 147–148; excerpts from this work are reprinted as Chapter 7 in this volume.

18 The controverter just imagined would agree with the discussion in Kripke, *Naming and Necessity*, pp. 144–155. But I don't mean to suggest that Kripke would agree with him. At any rate, the words I have put in his mouth are not Kripke's.

19 Lewis, *On the Plurality of Worlds*, pp. 86–92.

20 Lewis, "Mad Pain and Martian Pain."

21 Frank Jackson, Robert Pargetter, and Elizabeth Prior, "Functionalism and Type–type Identity Theories," *Philosophical Studies* 42 (1982), pp. 209–225.

22 In "How to Define Theoretical Terms" I called it the "diagonalized sense" of *M*.

23 David Lewis, "Events" in Lewis, *Philosophical Papers*, Vol. 2 (Oxford University Press, 1986).

11

Hilary Putnam, "The Nature of Mental States"

The typical concerns of the Philosopher of Mind might be represented by three questions: (1) How do we know that other people have pains? (2) Are pains brain states? (3) What is the analysis of the concept *pain*? I do not wish to discuss questions (1) and (3) in this chapter. I shall say something about question (2).[1]

I.   Identity questions

"Is pain a brain state?"(Or, "Is the property of having a pain at time *t* a brain state?")[2] It is impossible to discuss this question sensibly without saying something about the peculiar rules which have grown up in the course of the development of "analytical philosophy" – rules which, far from leading to an end to all conceptual confusions, themselves represent considerable conceptual confusion. These rules – which are, of course, implicit rather than explicit in the practice of most analytical philosophers – are (1) that a statement of the form "being *A* is being *B*" (e.g. "being in pain is being in a certain brain state") can be *correct* only if it follows, in some sense, from the meaning of the terms *A* and *B*; and (2) that a statement of the form "being *A* is being *B*" can be philosophically *informative* only if it is in some sense reductive (e.g. "being in pain is having a certain unpleasant sensation" is not philosophically informative; "being in pain is having a certain behaviour disposition" is, if true, philosophically informative). These rules are excellent rules if we still believe that the program of reductive analysis (in the style of the 1930s) can be carried out; if we

Hilary Putnam, "The Nature of Mental States," in *Mind, Language, and Reality: Philosophical Papers*, Vol. 2 (Cambridge University Press, Cambridge, 1975), pp. 429–40.

don't, then they turn analytical philosophy into a mug's game, at least so far as "is" questions are concerned.

In this paper I shall use the term "property" as a blanket term for such things as being in pain, being in a particular brain state, having a particular behavior disposition, and also for magnitudes such as temperature, etc. – i.e. for things which can naturally be represented by one-or-more-place predicates or functors. I shall use the term "concept" for things which can be identified with synonymy-classes of expressions. Thus the concept *temperature* can be identified (I maintain) with the synonymy-class of the word "temperature."[3] (This is like saying that the number 2 can be identified with the class of all pairs. This is quite a different statement from the peculiar statement that 2 *is* the class of all pairs. I do not maintain that concepts *are* synonymy-classes, whatever that might mean, but that they can be identified with synonymy-classes, for the purpose of formalization of the relevant discourse.)

The question "What is the concept *temperature*?" is a very "funny" one. One might take it to mean "What is temperature? Please take my question as a conceptual one." In that case an answer might be (pretend for a moment "heat" and "temperature" are synonyms) "temperature is heat," or even "the concept of temperature is the same concept as the concept of heat." Or one might take it to mean "What are *concepts*, really? For example, what is 'the concept of temperature'?" In that case heaven knows what an "answer" would be. (Perhaps it would be the statement that concepts *can be identified with* synonymy-classes.)

Of course, the question "What is the property temperature?" is also "funny." And one way of interpreting it is to take it as a question about the concept of temperature. But this is not the way a physicist would take it.

The effect of saying that the property P_1 can be identical with the property P_2 only if the terms P_1, P_2 are in some suitable sense "synonyms" is, to all intents and purposes, to collapse the two notions of "property" and "concept" into a single notion. The view that concepts (intensions) *are* the same as properties has been explicitly advocated by Carnap (e.g. in *Meaning and Necessity*). This seems an unfortunate view, since "temperature is mean molecular kinetic energy" appears to be a perfectly good example of a true statement of identity of properties, whereas "the concept of temperature is the same concept as a concept of mean molecular kinetic energy" is simply false.

Many philosophers believe that the statement "pain is a brain state" violates some rules or norms of English. But the arguments offered are hardly convincing. For example, if the fact that I can know that I am in pain without knowing that I am in brain state S shows that pain cannot be brain state S, then, by exactly the same argument, the fact that I can know

211

that the stove is hot without knowing that the mean molecular kinetic energy is high (or even that molecules exist) shows that it is *false* that temperature is mean molecular kintetic energy, physics to the contrary. In fact, all that immediately follows from the fact that I can know that I am in pain without knowing that I am in brain state S is that the concept of pain is not the same concept as the concept of being in brain state S. But either pain, or the state of being in pain, or some pain, or some pain state, might still be brain state S. After all, the concept of temperature is not the same concept as the concept of mean molecular kinetic energy. But temperature is mean molecular kinetic energy.

Some philosophers maintain that both "pain is a brain state" and "pain states are brain states" are unintelligible. The answer is to explain to these philosophers, as well as we can, given the vagueness of all scientific methodology, what sorts of considerations lead one to make an empirical reduction (i.e. to say such things as "water is H_2O," "light is electromagnetic radiation," "temperature is mean molecular kinetic energy"). If, without giving reasons, he still maintains in the face of such examples that one cannot imagine parallel circumstances for the use of "pains are brain states" (or, perhaps, "pain states are brain states") one has grounds to regard him as perverse.

Some philosophers maintain that "P_1 is P_2" is something that can be true, when the "is" involved is the "is" of empirical reduction, only when the properties P_1 and P_2 are (a) associated with a spatio-temporal region; and (b) the region is one and the same in both cases. Thus "temperature is mean molecular kinetic energy" is an admissible empirical reduction, since the temperature and the molecular energy are associated with the same space–time region, but "having a pain in my arm is being in a brain state" is not, since the spatial regions involved are different.

This argument does not appear very strong. Surely no one is going to be deterred from saying that mirror images are light reflected from an object and then from the surface of a mirror by the fact that an image can be "located" three feet *behind* the mirror! (Moreover, one can always find *some* common property of the reductions one is willing to allow – e.g. temperature is mean molecular kinetic energy – which is not a property of some one identification one wishes to disallow. This is not very impressive unless one has an argument to show that the very purposes of such identification depend upon the common property in question.)

Again, other philosophers have contended that all the predictions that can be derived from the conjunction of neurophysiological laws with such statements as "pain states are such-and-such brain states" can equally well be derived from the conjunction of the same neurophysiological laws with "being in pain is correlated with such-and-such brain states," and hence (*sic!*) there can be no methodological grounds for saying that pains (or pain states) *are* brain states, as opposed to saying that they are *correlated* (invariantly) with brain states. This argument, too, would show that light is only correlated with electromagnetic radiation. The mistake is in ignoring the fact that, although the theories in question may indeed lead to the same predictions, they open and exclude different *questions*. "Light is invariantly correlated with electromagnetic radiation" would leave open the questions "What is the light then, if it isn't the same as the electromagnetic radiation?" and "What makes the light accompany the electromagnetic radiation?" – questions which are excluded by saying that the light *is* the electromagnetic radiation. Similarly, the purpose of saying that pains are brain states is precisely to exclude from empirical meaningfulness the questions "What is the pain, then, if it isn't the same as the brain state?" and "What makes the pain accompany the brain state?" If there are grounds to suggest that these questions represent, so to speak, the wrong way to look at the matter, then those grounds are grounds for a theoretical identification of pains with brain states.

If all arguments to the contrary are unconvincing, shall we then conclude that it is meaningful (and perhaps true) to say either that pains are brain states or that pain states are brain states?

(1) It is perfectly meaningful (violates no "rule of English," involves no "extension of usage") to say "pains are brain states."

(2) It is not meaningful (involves a "changing of meaning" or an extension of usage," etc.) to say "pains are brain states."

My own position is not expressed by either (1) or (2). It seems to me that the notions "change of meaning" and "extension of usage" are simply so ill defined that one cannot in fact say *either* (1) or (2). I see no reason to believe that either the linguist, or the man-on-the-street, or the philosopher possesses today a notion of "change of meaning" applicable to such cases as the one we have been discussing. The *job* for which the notion of change of meaning was developed in the history of the language was just a *much* cruder job than this one.

But, if we don't assert either (1) or (2) – in other words, if we regard the "change of meaning" issue as a pseudo-issue in this case – then how are we to discuss the question with which we started? "Is pain a brain state?"

The answer is to allow statements of the form "pain is *A*," where "pain" and "*A*" are in no sense synonyms, and to see whether any such statement can be found which might be acceptable on empirical and methodological grounds. This is what we shall now proceed to do.

213

II.   Is pain a brain state?

We shall discuss "Is pain a brain state?" then. And we have agreed to waive the "change of meaning" issue.

Since I am discussing not what the concept of pain comes to, but what pain is, in a sense of "is" which requires empirical theory-construction (or, at least, empirical speculation), I shall not apologize for advancing an empirical hypothesis. Indeed, my strategy will be to argue that pain is *not* a brain state, not on *a priori* grounds, but on the grounds that another hypothesis is more plausible. The detailed development and verification of my hypothesis would be just as Utopian a task as the detailed development and verification of the brain-state hypothesis. But the putting-forward, not of detailed and scientifically "finished" hypotheses, but of schemata for hypotheses, has long been a function of philosophy. I shall, in short, argue that pain is not a brain state, in the sense of a physical-chemical state of the brain (or even the whole nervous system), but another *kind* of state entirely. I propose the hypothesis that pain, or the state of being in pain, is a functional state of a whole organism.

To explain this it is necessary to introduce some technical notions. In previous papers I have explained the notion of a Turing Machine and discussed the use of this notion as a model for an organism. The notion of a Probabilistic Automaton is defined similarly to a Turing Machine, except that the transitions between "states" are allowed to be with various probabilities rather than being "deterministic." (Of course, a Turing Machine is simply a special kind of Probabilistic Automaton, one with transition probabilities 0, 1). I shall assume the notion of a Probabilistic Automaton has been generalized to allow for "sensory inputs" and "motor outputs" – that is, the Machine Table specifies, for every possible combination of a "state" and a complete set of "sensory inputs," an "instruction" which determines the probability of the next "state," and also the probabilities of the "motor outputs." (This replaces the idea of the Machine as printing on a tape.) I shall also assume that the physical realization of the sense organs responsible for the various inputs, and of the motor organs, is specified, but that the "states" and the "inputs" themselves are, as usual, specified only "implicitly" – i.e. by the set of transition probabilities given by the Machine Table.

Since an empirically given system can simultaneously be a "physical realization" of many different Probabilistic Automata, I introduce the notion of a *Description* of a system. A Description of S where S is a system, is any true statement to the effect that S possesses distinct states $S_1, S_2 \ldots S_n$ which are related to one another and to the motor outputs and sensory inputs by the transition probabilities given in such-and-such a Machine Table.

The Machine Table mentioned in the Description will then be called the Functional Organization of S relative to that Description, and the S_i such that S is in state S_i at a given time will be called the Total State of S (at the time) relative to that Description. It should be noted that knowing the Total State of a system relative to a Description involves knowing a good deal about how the system is likely to "behave," given various combinations of sensory inputs, but does *not* involve knowing the physical realization of the S_i as, e.g. physical-chemical states of the brain. The S_i, to repeat, are specified only *implicitly* by the Description – i.e. specified *only* by the set of transition probabilities given in the Machine Table.

The hypothesis that "being in pain is a functional state of the organism" may now be spelled out more exactly as follows:

(1) All organisms capable of feeling pain are Probabilistic Automata.

(2) Every organism capable of feeling pain possesses at least one Description of a certain kind (i.e. being capable of feeling pain *is* possessing an appropriate kind of Functional Organization).

(3) No organism capable of feeling pain possesses a decomposition into parts which separately possess Descriptions of the kind referred to in (2).

(4) For every Description of the kind referred to in (2), there exists a subset of the sensory inputs such that an organism with that Description is in pain when and only when some of its sensory inputs are in that subset.

This hypothesis is admittedly vague, though surely no vaguer than the brain-state hypothesis in its present form. For example, one would like to know more about the kind of Functional Organization that an organism must have to be capable of feeling pain, and more about the marks that distinguish the subset of the sensory inputs referred to in (4). With respect to the first question, one can probably say that the Functional Organization must include something that resembles a "preference function," or at least a preference partial ordering and something that resembles an "inductive logic" (i.e. the Machine must be able to "learn from experience"). (The meaning of these conditions, for Automata models, is discussed in "The Mental Life of Some Machines.") In addition, it seems natural to require that the Machine possess "pain sensors," i.e. sensory organs which normally signal damage to the Machine's body, or dangerous temperatures, pressures, etc., which transmit a special subset of the inputs, the subset referred to in (4). Finally, and with respect to the second question, we would want to require at least that the inputs in the distinguished subset have a high disvalue on the Machine's preference function or ordering (further conditions are discussed in "The Mental Life of Some Machines"). The purpose of condition (3) is to rule out such "organisms" (if they can count as such) as swarms of bees as single pain-feelers. The condition (1) is, obviously, redundant, and is only introduced for expository reasons. (It is, in fact, empty, since everything is a Probabilistic Automaton under *some* Description.)

I contend, in passing, that this hypothesis, in spite of its admitted vagueness, is far *less* vague than the "physical-chemical state" hypothesis is today, and far more susceptible to investigation of both a mathematical and an empirical kind. Indeed, to investigate this hypothesis is just to attempt to produce "mechanical" models of organisms – and isn't this, in a sense, just what psychology is about? The difficult step, of course, will be to pass from models to *specific* organisms to a *normal form* for the psychological description of organisms – for this is what is required to make (2) and (4) precise. But this too seems to be an inevitable part of the program of psychology.

I shall now compare the hypothesis just advanced with (a) the hypothesis that pain is a brain state, and (b) the hypothesis that pain is a behavior disposition.

III.   Functional state versus brain state

It may, perhaps, be asked if I am not somewhat unfair in taking the brain-state theorist to be talking about *physical-chemical* states of the brain. But (a) these are the only sorts of states ever mentioned by brain-state theorists. (b) The brain-state theorist usually mentions (with a certain pride, slightly reminiscent of the Village Atheist) the incompatibility of his hypothesis with all forms of dualism and mentalism. This is natural if physical-chemical states of the brain are what is at issue. However, functional states of whole systems are something quite different. In particular, the functional-state hypothesis is *not* incompatible with dualism! Although it goes without saying that the hypothesis is "mechanistic" in its inspiration, it is a slightly remarkable fact that a system consisting of a body and a "soul," if such things there be, can perfectly well be a Probabilistic Automaton. (c) One argument advanced by Smart is that the brain-state theory assumes only "physical" properties, and Smart finds "non-physical" properties unintelligible. The Total States and the "inputs" defined above are, of course, neither mental nor physical *per se*, and I cannot imagine a functionalist advancing this argument. (d) If the brain-state theorist does mean (or at least allow) states other than physical-chemical states, then his hypothesis is completely empty, at least until he specifies *what* sort of "states" he *does* mean.

Taking the brain-state hypothesis in this way, then, what reasons are there to prefer the functional-state hypothesis over the brain-state hypothesis? Consider what the brain-state theorist has to do to make good his claims. He has to specify a physical-chemical state such that *any* organism (not just a mammal) is in pain if and only if (a) it possesses a brain of a suitable physical-chemical structure; and (b) its brain is in that physical-chemical state. This means that the physical-chemical state in question must be a possible state of a mammalian brain, a reptilian brain, a mollusc's brain (octopuses are mollusca, and certainly feel pain), etc. At the same time, it must *not* be a possible (physically possible) state of the brain of any physically possible creature that cannot feel pain. Even if such a state can be found, it must be nomologically certain that it will also be a state of the brain of any extraterrestrial life that may be found that will be capable of feeling pain before we can even entertain the supposition that it may *be* pain.

It is not altogether impossible that such a state will be found. Even though octopus and mammal are examples of parallel (rather than sequential) evolution, for example, virtually identical structures (physically speaking) have evolved in the eye of the octopus and in the eye of the mammal, notwithstanding the fact that this organ has evolved from different kinds of cells in the two cases. Thus it is at least possible that parallel evolution, all over the universe, might *always* lead to one and the same physical "correlate" of pain. But this is certainly an ambitious hypothesis.

Finally, the hypothesis becomes still more ambitious when we realize that the brain-state theorist is not just saying that *pain* is a brain state; he is, of course, concerned to maintain that *every* psychological state is a brain state. Thus if we can find even one psychological predicate which can clearly be applied to both a mammal and an octopus (say "hungry"), but whose physical-chemical "correlate" is different in the two cases, the brain-state theory has collapsed. It seems to me overwhelmingly probable that we can do this. Granted, in such a case the brain-state theorist can save himself by *ad hoc* assumptions (e.g. defining the disjunction of two states to be a single "physical-chemical state"), but this does not have to be taken seriously.

Turning now to the considerations *for* the functional-state theory, let us begin with the fact that we identify organisms as in pain, or hungry, or angry, or in heat, etc., on the basis of their *behavior*. But it is a truism that similarities in the behavior of two systems are at least a reason to suspect similarities in the functional organization of the two systems, and a much *weaker* reason to suspect similarities in the actual physical details. Moreover, we expect the various psychological states – at least the basic ones, such as hunger, thirst, aggression, etc. – to have more or less similar "transition probabilities" (within wide and ill defined limits, to be sure) with each other and with behavior in the case of different species, because this is an artifact of the way in which we identify these states. Thus, we would not count an animal as *thirsty* if its "unsatiated" behavior did not seem to be directed toward drinking and was not followed by "satiation for liquid." Thus any animal that we count as capable of these various states will at least *seem* to have a certain rough kind of functional organization. And, as already remarked, if the program of finding psychological laws that are not species-specific – i.e. of finding a normal form for psychological theories of different species – ever succeeds, then it will bring in its wake a delineation of the kind of functional organization that is necessary and sufficient for a given psychological state, as well as a precise definition of the notion "psychological state." In contrast, the brain-state theorist has to hope for the eventual development of neuro-physiological laws that are species-independent, which seems much less reasonable than the hope that psychological laws (of a sufficiently general kind) may be species-independent, or, still weaker, that a species-independent *form* can be found in which psychological laws can be written.

IV. Functional state versus behavior-disposition

The theory that being in pain is neither a brain state nor a functional state but a behavior disposition has one apparent advantage: it appears to agree with the way in which we verify that organisms are in pain. We do not in practice know anything about the brain state of an animal when we say that it is in pain; and we possess little if any knowledge of its functional organization, except in a crude intuitive way. In fact, however, this "advantage" is no advantage at all: for, although statements about how we verify that x is A may have a good deal to do with what the concept of being A comes to, they have precious little to do with what the property A *is*. To argue on the ground just mentioned that pain is neither a brain state nor a functional state is like arguing that heat is not mean molecular kinetic energy from the fact that ordinary people do not (they think) ascertain the mean molecular kinetic energy of something when they verify that it is hot or cold. It is not necessary that they should; what is necessary is that the marks that they take as indications of heat should in fact be explained by the mean molecular kinetic energy. And, similarly, it is necessary to our hypothesis that the marks that are taken as behavioral indications of pain should be explained by the fact that the organism is a functional state of the appropriate kind, but not that speakers should *know* that this is so.

The difficulties with "behavior disposition" accounts are so well known that I shall do little more than recall them here. The difficulty – it appears to be more than a "difficulty," in fact – of specifying the required behavior disposition except as "the disposition of X to behave as if X were in *pain*," is the chief one, of course. In contrast, we *can* specify the functional state with which we propose to identify pain, at least roughly, without using the notion of pain. Namely, the functional state we have in mind is the state of receiving sensory inputs which play a certain role in the Functional Organization of the organism. This role is characterized, at least partially, by the fact that the sense organs responsible for the inputs in question are organs whose function is to detect damage to the body, or dangerous extremes of temperature, pressure, etc., and by the fact that the "inputs" themselves, whatever their physical realization, represent a condition that the organism assigns a high disvalue to. As I stressed in "The Mental Life of Some Machines" this does *not* mean that the Machine will always *avoid* being in the condition in question ("pain"); it only means that the condition will be avoided unless not avoiding it is necessary to the attainment of some more highly valued goal. Since the behavior of the Machine (in this case, an organism) will depend not merely on the sensory inputs, but also on the Total State (i.e. on other values, beliefs, etc.), it seems hopeless to make any general statement about how an organism in such a condition *must* behave; but this does not mean that we must abandon hope of characterizing the condition. Indeed, we have just characterized it.[4]

Not only does the behavior-disposition theory seem hopelessly vague; if the "behavior" referred to is peripheral behavior, and the relevant stimuli are peripheral stimuli (e.g. we do not say anything about what the organism will do if its brain is operated upon), then the theory seems clearly false. For example, two animals with all motor nerves cut will have the same actual and potential "behavior" (namely, none to speak of); but if one has cut pain fibers and the other has uncut pain fibers, then one will feel pain and the other won't. Again, if one person has cut pain fibers, and another suppresses all pain responses deliberately due to some strong compulsion, then the actual and potential peripheral behavior may be the same, but one will feel pain and the other won't. (Some philosophers maintain that this last case is conceptually impossible, but the only evidence for this appears to be that *they* can't, or don't want to, conceive of it.)[5] If, instead of pain, we take some sensation the "bodily expression" of which is easier to suppress – say, a slight coolness in one's left little finger – the case becomes even clearer.

Finally, even if there *were* some behavior disposition invariantly correlated with pain (species-independently!), and specifiable without using the term "pain," it would still be more plausible to identify being in pain with some state whose presence *explains* this behavior disposition – the brain state or functional state – than with the behavior disposition itself. Such considerations of plausibility may be somewhat subjective; but if other things *were* equal (of course, they aren't) why shouldn't we allow considerations of plausibility to play the deciding role?

V. Methodological considerations

So far we have considered only what might be called the "empirical" reasons for saying that being in pain is a functional state, rather than a brain state or a behavior disposition; namely, that it seems more likely that the functional state we described is invariantly "correlated" with pain, species-independently, than that there is either a physical-chemical state of the brain (must an organism have a *brain* to feel pain? perhaps some ganglia will do) or a behavior disposition so correlated. If this is correct, then it follows that the identification we proposed is at least a candidate for consideration. What of methodological considerations?

The methodological considerations are roughly similar in all cases of reduction, so no surprises need be expected here. First, identification of psychological states with functional states means that the laws of psychology can be derived from statements of the form "such-and-such organisms have such-and-such Descriptions" together with the identification statements ("being in pain is such-and-such a functional state," etc.). Secondly, the presence of the functional state (i.e. of inputs which play the role we have described in the Functional Organization of the organism) is not merely "correlated with" but actually explains the pain behavior on the part of the organism. Thirdly, the identification serves to exclude questions which (if a naturalistic view is correct) represent an altogether wrong way of looking at the matter, e.g. "What *is* pain if it isn't either the brain state or the functional state?" and "What causes the pain to be always accompanied by this sort of functional state?" In short, the identification is to be tentatively accepted as a theory which leads to both fruitful predictions and to fruitful *questions*, and which serves to discourage fruitless and empirically senseless questions, where by "empirically senseless" I mean "senseless" not merely from the standpoint of verification, but from the standpoint of what there in fact *is*.

Notes

1   I have discussed these and related topics in "Brains and Behavior," "Minds and Machines," and "The Mental Life of Some Machines," reprinted as chapters 16, 18, and 20, respectively, in *Mind, Language, and Reality: Philosophical Papers*, Vol. 2 (Cambridge: Cambridge University Press, 1975).
2   In this paper I wish to avoid the vexed question of the relation between *pains* and *pain states*. I only remark in passing that one common argument *against* identification of these two – namely, that a pain can be in one's arm but a state (of the organism) cannot be in one's arm – is easily seen to be fallacious.
3   There are some well-known remarks by Alonzo Church on this topic. Those remarks do not bear (as might at first be supposed) on the identification of

concepts with synonymy-classes as such, but rather support the view that (in formal semantics) it is necessary to retain Frege's distinction between the normal and the "oblique" use of expressions. That is, even if we say that the concept of temperature *is* the synonymy-class of the word "temperature," we must not thereby be led into the error of supposing that "the concept of temperature" is synonymous with "the synonymy-class of the word 'temperature'" – for then "the concept of temperature" and "der Begriff der Temperatur" would not be synonymous, which they are. Rather, we must say that the concept of "temperature" *refers to* the synonymy-class of the word "temperature" (on this particular reconstruction); but that class is *identified* not as "the synonymy class to which such-and-such a word belongs," but in another way (e.g. as the synonymy-class whose members have such-and-such a characteristic use).

4   In "The Mental Life of Some Machines" a further, and somewhat independent, characteristic of the pain inputs is discussed in terms of Automata models – namely the spontaneity of the inclination to withdraw the injured part, etc. This raises the question, which is discussed in that chapter, of giving a functional analysis of the notion of a spontaneous inclination, Of course, still further characteristics come readily to mind – for example, that feelings of pain are (or seem to be) *located* in the parts of the body.

5   Cf. the discussion of "super-spartans" in "Brains and Behavior."

12

Ned Block, "Troubles with Functionalism"

. . .

1.2   Homunculi-headed robots

In this section I shall describe a class of devices that embarrass all versions of functionalism in that they indicate functionalism is guilty of liberalism – classifying systems that lack mentality as having mentality.

Consider the simple version of machine functionalism already described. It says that each system having mental states is described by at least one Turing-machine table of a certain kind, and each mental state of the system is identical to one of the machine-table states specified by the machine table. I shall consider inputs and outputs to be specified by descriptions of neural impulses in sense organs and motor-output neurons. This assumption should not be regarded as restricting what will be said to Psycho-functionalism rather than Functionalism. As already mentioned, every version of functionalism assumes *some* specification of inputs and outputs. A Functionalist specification would do as well for the purposes of what follows.

Imagine a body externally like a human body, say yours, but internally quite different. The neurons from sensory organs are connected to a bank of lights in a hollow cavity in the head. A set of buttons connects to the motor-output neurons. Inside the cavity resides a group of little men. Each has a very simple task: to implement a "square" of a reasonably adequate machine table that describes you. On one wall is a bulletin board on which is posted a state card, i.e., a card that bears a symbol designating one of the states specified in the machine table. Here is what the little men do:

Ned Block, "Troubles with Functionalism" (excerpts), in C. Wade Savage (ed.), *Minnesota Studies in Philosophy of Science*, 9: *Perception and Cognition: Issues in the Foundations of Psychology* (University of Minnesota Press, Minneapolis, 1978), pp. 277–81, 285–93, 321–2.

Suppose the posted card has a "G" on it. This alerts the little men who implement G squares – "G-men" they call themselves. Suppose the light representing input I_{17} goes on. One of the G-men has the following as his sole task: when the card reads "G" and the I_{17} light goes on, he presses output button O_{191} and changes the state card to "M." This G-man is called upon to exercise his task only rarely. In spite of the low level of intelligence required of each little man, the system as a whole manages to simulate you because the functional organization they have been trained to realize is yours. A Turing machine can be represented as a finite set of quadruples (or quintuples, if the output is divided into two parts) – current state, current input; next state, next output. Each little man has the task corresponding to a single quadruple. Through the efforts of the little men, the system realizes the same (reasonably adequate) machine table as you do and is thus functionally equivalent to you.

I shall describe a version of the homunculi-headed simulation, which is more clearly nomologically possible. How many homunculi are required? Perhaps a billion are enough; after all, there are only about a billion neurons in the brain.

Suppose we convert the government of China to functionalism, and we convince its officials that it would enormously enhance their international prestige to realize a human mind for an hour. We provide each of the billion people in China (I chose China because it has a billion inhabitants) with a specially designed two-way radio that connects them in the appropriate way to other persons and to the artificial body mentioned in the previous example. We replace the little men with a radio transmitter and receiver connected to the input and output neurons. Instead of a bulletin board, we arrange to have letters displayed on a series of satellites placed so that they can be seen from anywhere in China. Surely such a system is not physically impossible. It could be functionally equivalent to you for a short time, say an hour.

"But," you may object, "how could something be functionally equivalent to me for *an hour*? Doesn't my functional organization determine, say, how I would react to doing nothing for a week but reading *Reader's Digest*?" Remember that a machine table specifies a set of conditionals of the form: if the machine is in S_i and receives input I_j, it emits output O_k and goes into S_l. Any system that has a set of inputs, outputs, and states related in the way described realizes that machine table, even if it exists for only an instant. For the hour the Chinese system is "on," it *does* have a set of inputs, outputs, and states of which such conditionals are true. Whatever the initial state, the system will respond in whatever way the machine table directs. This is how *any* computer realizes the machine table it realizes.

Of course, there are signals the system would respond to that you would not respond to, e.g., massive radio interference or a flood of the Yangtze River. Such events might cause a malfunction, scotching the simulation, just as a bomb in a computer can make it fail to realize the machine table it was built to realize. But just as the computer *without* the bomb *can* realize the machine table, the system consisting of the people and artificial body can realize the machine table so long as there are no catastrophic interferences, e.g., floods, etc.

"But," someone may object, "there is a difference between a bomb in a computer and a bomb in the Chinese system, for in the case of the latter (unlike the former), inputs as specified in the machine table can be the cause of the malfunction. Unusual neural activity in the sense organs of residents of Chungking Province caused by a bomb or by a flood of the Yangtze can cause the system to go haywire."

Reply: the person who says what system he or she is talking about gets to say what counts as inputs and outputs. I count as inputs and outputs only neural activity in the artificial body connected by radio to the people of China. Neural signals in the people of Chungking count no more as inputs to this system than input tape jammed by a saboteur between the relay contacts in the innards of a computer count as an input to the computer.

Of course, the object consisting of the people of China + the artificial body has *other* Turing machine descriptions under which neural signals in the inhabitants of Chungking *would* count as inputs. Such a new system (i.e., the object under such a new Turing-machine description) would not be functionally equivalent to you. Likewise, any commercial computer can be redescribed in a way that allows tape jammed into its innards to count as inputs. In describing an object as a Turing machine, one draws a line between the inside and the outside. (If we count only neural impulses as inputs and outputs, we draw that line inside the body; if we count only peripheral stimulations as inputs and only bodily movements as outputs, we draw that line at the skin.) In describing the Chinese system as a Turing machine, I have drawn the line in such a way that it satisfies a certain type of functional description – one that you *also* satisfy, and one that, according to functionalism, justifies attributions of mentality. Functionalism does not claim that every mental system has a machine table of a sort that justifies attributions of mentality with respect to *every* specification of inputs and outputs, but rather, only with respect to *some* specification.

Objection: The Chinese system would work too slowly. The kind of events and processes with which we normally have contact would pass by far too quickly for the system to detect them. Thus, we would be unable to converse with it, play bridge with it, etc.[1]

Reply: It is hard to see why the system's time scale should matter. What reason is there to believe that *your* mental operations could not be very much slowed down, yet remain mental operations? Is it really contradictory or nonsensical to suppose we could meet a race of intelligent beings with whom we could communicate only by devices such as time-lapse photography. When we observe these creatures, they seem almost inanimate. But when we view the time-lapse movies, we see them conversing with one another. Indeed, we find they are saying that the only way they can make any sense of us is by viewing movies greatly slowed down. To take time scale as all important seems crudely behavioristic. Further, even if the time-scale objection is right, I can elude it by retreating to the point that a homunculus-head that works in normal time is *metaphysically* possible, even if not nomologically possible. Metaphysical possibility is all my argument requires (see Section 1.3).[2]

What makes the homunculi-headed system (count the two systems as variants of a single system) just described a prima facie counter-example to (machine) functionalism is that there is prima facie doubt whether it has any mental states at all – especially whether it has what philosophers have variously called "qualitative states," "raw feels," or "immediate phenomenological qualities." (You ask: What is it that philosophers have called qualitative states? I answer, only half in jest: As Louis Armstrong said when asked what jazz is, "If you got to ask, you ain't never gonna get to know.") In Nagel's terms (1974), there is a prima facie doubt whether there is anything which it is like to be the homunculi-headed system.

. . .

1.3 What kind of possibility does the absent qualia argument appeal to?

According to functionalism, each mental state, e.g., Q, is identical to a functional state, e.g., S_q. The Absent Qualia Argument argues that there is a possible system that has S_q but whose possession of Q is subject to prima facie doubt, and thus there is prima facie doubt that $Q = S_q$. What notion of possibility does the Absent Qualia Argument appeal to? And what is the basis for the assumption that if $Q = S_q$ it is not possible for something to have S_q without Q?

Let us take the notion of possibility to be nomological possibility. And let us restrict our attention to identity statements of the form $\ulcorner \alpha = \beta \urcorner$, where α and β are rigid designators. It is hard to conceive of a mildly plausible criterion of identity for properties (or for types of states) that allows both that F = G *and* that it is nomologically possible for something to have

225

or be in F but not in G. As Kripke (1980) has shown, true identities are necessarily true. Thus, if F = G there is no possible world and hence no nomologically possible world in which F ≠ G; hence, there is no nomologically possible world in which something is in (or has) F but is not in (or lacks) G.

I conclude that on the nomological reading of "possible," the Absent Qualia Argument is valid. Further, if the Chinese system described earlier is nomologically possible, and if there is prima facie doubt about its qualia, the argument is sound. However, even if such a homunculi-headed simulation is not nomologically possible, it is surely metaphysically possible. Therefore, assuming there is prima facie doubt about the qualia of the homunculi-headed simulations, understanding "possible" as "metaphysically possible" ensures the soundness of the Absent Qualia Argument, while retaining validity. Kripke has shown that true identities are metaphysically necessary. Thus, if $Q = S_q$ then (assuming "Q" and "S_q" are rigid designators) it is necessary that $Q = S_q$. And it is necessary that something has Q just in case it has S_q. Since there is a possible object (a homunculi-headed simulation) that has S_q but whose possession of Q is subject to prima facie doubt, there is prima facie doubt about whether $Q = S_q$.

Kripke's arguments against materialism (based on his principle that identities are necessary) are subject to a number of difficulties. If the Absent Qualia Argument is forced to rely on Kripke's principle (i.e., if homunculi-headed simulations are not nomologically possible), is the Absent Qualia Argument subject to the same difficulties as Kripke's argument against materialism? In the remainder of this section I shall argue that none of the serious difficulties that beset Kripke's arguments against materialism besets the Absent Qualia Argument.

Kripke argues (against an opponent who says pain is stimulation of c-fibers) that we can conceive of a possible world in which c-fiber stimulation occurs in the absence of pain and that we can also conceive of a possible world in which pain occurs in the absence of c-fiber stimulation. So far, so good: but how do we judge the truth of claims to conceive of such possible worlds? (Notice that I am using "conceive" such that if anyone can conceive of a possible world in which such and such obtains, then there is such a possible world. "Imagine" has no such implication.) Kripke provides us with a way of ruling out false conceivability claims. Suppose someone, call him "Epistemagine," claims he can conceive of a world which contains heat but no corresponding molecular agitation. Kripke argues that what Epistemagine is really imagining is being in the epistemic situation we would have been in had we discovered that heat phenomena (e.g., our sensation of heat) were caused by something other than molecular agitation, say, y-radiation. Thus, what Epistemagine is really conceiving is a

Again, I do not inherit Kripke's difficulties. Nothing in the Absent Qualia Argument dictates anything controversial about the essential qualitativeness of any particular qualitative or functional state.

1.4   What if I turned out to have little men in my head?

Before I go any further, I shall briefly discuss a difficulty for my claim that there is prima facie doubt about the qualia of homunculi-headed realizations of human functional organization. It might be objected, "What if *you* turned out to be one?" Let us suppose that, to my surprise, X-rays reveal that inside my head are thousands of tiny, trained fleas, each of which has been taught (perhaps by a joint subcommittee of the American Philosophical Association and the American Psychological Association empowered to investigate absent qualia) to implement a square in the appropriate machine table.

Now there is a crucial issue relevant to this difficulty which philosophers are far from agreeing on (and about which I confess I cannot make up my mind): Do I know on the basis of my "privileged access" that I do not have utterly absent qualia, no matter what turns out to be inside my head? Do I know there is something it is like to be me, even if I am a flea head? Fortunately, my vacillation on this issue is of no consequence, for either answer is compatible with the Absent Qualia Argument's assumption that there is doubt about the qualia of homunculi-headed folks.

Suppose the answer is no. It is not the case that I know there is something it is like to be me even if I am a flea head. Then I should admit that my qualia would be in (prima facie) doubt if (God forbid) I turned out to have fleas in my head. Likewise for the qualia of all the other homunculi-headed folk. So far, so good.

Suppose, on the other hand, that my privileged access does give me knowledge that I have qualia. No matter what turns out to be inside my head, my states have qualitative content. There is something it is like to be me. Then if I turn out to have fleas in my head, at least one homunculi-head turns out to have qualia. But this would not challenge my claim that the qualia of homunculi-infested simulations is in doubt. Since I do, in fact, have qualia, supposing I have fleas inside my head is supposing someone with fleas inside his head has qualia. But this supposition that a homunculi-head has qualia is just the sort of supposition my position doubts. Using such an example to argue against my position is like twitting a man who doubts there is a God by asking what he would say if he turned out to *be* God. Both arguments against the doubter beg the question against the doubter by hypothesizing a situation which the doubter admits is logically possible, but doubts is *actual*. A doubt that there is a God entails a doubt that I am God. Similarly, (given that I do have qualia) a doubt that flea heads have qualia entails a doubt that I am a flea head.

1.5   Putnam's proposal

One way functionalists can try to deal with the problem posed by the homunculi-headed counterexamples is by the ad hoc device of stipulating them away. For example, a functionalist might stipulate that two systems cannot be functionally equivalent if one contains parts with functional organizations characteristic of sentient beings and the other does not. In his article hypothesizing that pain is a functional state, Putnam stipulated that "no organism capable of feeling pain possesses a decomposition into parts which separately possess Descriptions" (as the sort of Turing machine which can be in the functional state Putnam identifies with pain). The purpose of this condition is "to rule out such 'organisms' (if they count as such) as swarms of bees as single pain feelers" (Putnam, 1975, pp. 434–9; [pp. 215–16 in this volume).

One way of filling out Putnam's requirement would be: a pain feeling organism cannot possess a decomposition into parts *all* of which have a functional organization characteristic of sentient beings. But this would not rule out my homunculi-headed example, since it has nonsentient parts, such as the mechanical body and sense organs. It will not do to go to the opposite extreme and require that *no* proper parts be sentient. Otherwise pregnant women and people with sentient parasites will fail to count as pain-feeling organisms. What seems to be important to examples like the homunculi-headed simulation I have described is that the sentient beings *play a crucial role* in giving the thing its functional organization. This suggests a version of Putnam's proposal which requires that a pain-feeling organism has a certain functional organization and that it has no parts which (1) themselves possess that sort of functional organization and also (2) play a crucial role in giving the whole system its functional organization.

Although this proposal involves the vague notion "crucial role," it is precise enough for us to see it will not do. Suppose there is a part of the universe that contains matter quite different from ours, matter that is infinitely divisible. In this part of the universe, there are intelligent creatures of many sizes, even humanlike creatures much smaller than our elementary particles. In an intergalactic expedition, these people discover the existence of our type of matter. For reasons known only to them, they decide to devote the next few hundred years to creating out of their matter substances with the chemical and physical characteristics (except at the subelementary particle level) of our elements. They build hordes of space ships of different varieties about the sizes of our electrons, protons, and other elementary particles, and fly the ships in such a way as to mimic the behavior of these elementary particles. The ships also contain generators to produce the type of radiation elementary particles give off. Each ship has a staff of experts on the nature of our elementary particles. They do this to produce huge (by our standards) masses of substances with the chemical and physical characteristics of oxygen, carbon, etc. Shortly after they accomplish this, you go off on an expedition to that part of the universe, and discover the "oxygen," "carbon," etc. Unaware of its real nature, you set up a colony, using these "elements" to grow plants for food, provide "air" to breathe, etc. Since one's molecules are constantly being exchanged with the environment, you and other colonizers come (in a period of a few years) to be composed mainly of the "matter" made of the tiny people in space ships. Would you be any less capable of feeling pain, thinking, etc. just because the matter of which you are composed contains (and depends on for its characteristics) beings who themselves have a functional organization characteristic of sentient creatures? I think not. The basic electrochemical mechanisms by which the synapse operates are now fairly well understood. As far as is known, changes that do not affect these electrochemical mechanisms do not affect the operation of the brain, and do not affect mentality. The electrochemical mechanisms in your synapses would be unaffected by the change in your matter.[3]

It is interesting to compare the elementary-particle-people example with the homunculi-headed examples the chapter started with. A natural first guess about the source of our intuition that the initially described homunculi-headed simulations lack mentality is that they have *too much* internal mental structure. The little men may be sometimes bored, sometimes excited. We may even imagine that they deliberate about the best way to realize the given functional organization and make changes intended to give them more leisure time. But the example of the elementary-particle people just described suggests this first guess is wrong. What seems important is *how* the mentality of the parts contributes to the functioning of the whole.

There is one very noticeable difference between the elementary-particle-people example and the earlier homunculus examples. In the former, the change in you as you become homunculus-infested is not one that makes any difference to your psychological processing (i.e., information processing) or neurological processing but only to your microphysics. No techniques proper to human psychology or neurophysiology would reveal any difference in you. However, the homunculi-headed simulations described in the beginning of the chapter are not things to which neurophysiological theories true of us apply, and *if they are construed as Functional* (rather than Psychofunctional) simulations, they need not be things to which

psychological (information-processing) theories true of us apply. This difference suggests that our intuitions are in part controlled by the not unreasonable view that our mental states depend on our having the psychology
and/or neurophysiology we have. So something that differs markedly from
us in both regards (recall that it is a Functional rather than Psychofunctional
simulation) should not be assumed to have mentality just on the ground that
it is Functionally equivalent to us.[4]

. . .

Notes

1   This point has been raised with me by persons too numerous to mention.
2   One potential difficulty for Functionalism is provided by the possibility that
    one person may have two radically different Functional descriptions of the sort
    that justify attribution of mentality. In such a case, Functionalists might have
    to ascribe two radically different systems of belief, desire, etc., to the same
    person, or suppose that there is no fact of the matter about what the person's
    propositional attitudes are. Undoubtedly, Functionalists differ greatly on what
    they make of this possibility, and the differences reflect positions on such
    issues as indeterminacy of translation.
3   Since there is a difference between the role of the little people in producing
    your functional organization in the situation just described and the role of the
    homunculi in the homunculi-headed simulations this chapter began with,
    presumably Putnam's condition could be reformulated to rule out the latter
    without ruling out the former. But this would be a most ad hoc maneuver.
    Further, there are other counterexamples which suggest that a successful
    reformulation is likely to remain elusive.
        Careful observation of persons who have had the nerve bundle connecting the
    two halves of the brain (the *corpus callosum)* severed to prevent the spread of
    epilepsy, suggest that each half of the brain has the functional organization
    of a sentient being. The same is suggested by the observation that persons
    who have had one hemisphere removed or anesthetized remain sentient beings.
    It was once thought that the right hemisphere had no linguistic capacity, but it
    is now known that the adult right hemisphere has the vocabulary of a 14-year-
    old and the syntax of a 5-year-old (*Psychology Today*, 12/75, p. 121). Now the
    functional organization of each hemisphere is different from the other and from
    that of a whole human. For one thing, in addition to inputs from the sense
    organs and outputs to motor neurons, each hemisphere has many input and
    output connections to the other hemisphere. Nonetheless, each hemisphere
    may have the functional organization of a sentient being. Perhaps Martians
    have many more input and output organs than we do. Then each half brain
    could be functionally like a whole Martian brain. If each of our hemispheres has
    the functional organization of a sentient being, then a Putnamian proposal
    would rule us out (except for those of us who have had hemispherectomies) as
    pain-feeling organisms.
        Further, it could turn out that other parts of the body have a functional
    organization similar to that of some sentient being. For example, perhaps indi-

vidual neurons have the same functional organization as some species of insect.

(The argument of the last two paragraphs depends on a version of functionalism that construes inputs and outputs as neural impulses. Otherwise, individual neurons could not have the same functional organization as insects. It would be harder to think of such examples if, for instance, inputs were taken to be irradiation of sense organs or the presence of perceivable objects in the "range" of the sense organs.)

4   A further indication that our intuitions are in part governed by the neurophysiological and psychological differences between us and the original homunculi-headed simulation (construed as a Functional simulation) is that intuition seems to founder on an intermediate case: a device that simulates you by having a billion little men each of whom simulates one of your neurons. It would be like you in psychological mechanisms, but not in neurological mechanisms, except at a very abstract level of description.

There are a number of differences between the original homunculi-heads and the elementary-particle-people example. The little elementary-particle people were not described as knowing your functional organization or trying to simulate it, but in the original example, the little men have *as their aim* simulating your functional organization. Perhaps when we know a certain functional organization is intentionally produced, we are thereby inclined to regard the thing's being functionally equivalent to a human as a misleading fact. One could test this by changing the elementary-particle-people example so that the little people have the aim of simulating your functional organization by simulating elementary particles; this change seems to me to make little intuitive difference.

There are obvious differences between the two types of examples. It is *you* in the elementary case and the change is *gradual*; these elements seem obviously misleading. But they can be eliminated without changing the force of the example much. Imagine, for example, that your spouse's parents went on the expedition and that your spouse has been made of the elementary-particle-people since birth.

References

Boyd, R. (1980) "Materialism Without Reductionism: What Physicalism Does Not Entail," in N. Block (ed.), *Readings in Philosophy of Psychology*, Vol. 1 (Cambridge, Mass.: Harvard University Press), pp. 67–106.

Feldman, F. (1973) "Kripke's Argument Against Materialism," *Philosophical Studies* 24: 416–419.

Kripke, S. (1980) *Naming and Necessity* (Cambridge, Mass.: Harvard University Press). Excerpts from this work are reprinted as Chapter 7 in this volume.

Nagel, T. (1974) "What Is It Like to Be a Bat?," *Philosophical Review* 83: 435–450.

Putnam H. (1975) "The Nature of Mental States," in *Mind, Language, and Reality: Philosophical Papers*, Vol. 2 (Cambridge: Cambridge University Press), pp. 429–440. Reprinted as Chapter 11 in this volume.

13

David J. Chalmers, "Absent Qualia, Fading Qualia, Dancing Qualia"

I.   The principle of organizational invariance

It is widely accepted that conscious experience has a physical basis. That is, the properties of experience (phenomenal properties, or qualia) systematically depend on physical properties according to some lawful relation. There are two key questions about this relation. The first concerns the strength of the laws: are they logically or metaphysically necessary, so that consciousness is nothing "over and above" the physical, or are they merely contingent laws like the law of gravity? This question is the basis for debates over physicalism and property dualism. The second question concerns the shape of the laws: precisely how do phenomenal properties depend on physical properties? What sort of physical properties enter into the laws' antecedents, for instance; consequently, what sort of physical systems can give rise to conscious experience? It is this second question that I address in this paper.

To put the issue differently, even once it is accepted that experience arises from physical systems, the question remains open: in virtue of what sort of physical properties does conscious experience arise? Properties that brains can possess will presumably be among them, but it is far from clear just what the relevant properties are. Some have suggested biochemical properties; some have suggested quantum-mechanical properties; many have professed uncertainty. A natural suggestion is that when experience arises from a physical system, it does so in virtue of the system's *functional organization*. On this view, the chemical and indeed the quantum substrates of the brain are not directly relevant to the existence of consciousness,

David J. Chalmers, "Absent Qualia, Fading Qualia, Dancing Qualia," in Thomas Metzinger (ed.), *Conscious Experience* (Schoeningh-Verlag, Paderborn, 1995), pp. 309–28.

although they may be indirectly relevant. What is central is rather the brain's abstract causal organization, an organization that might be realized in many different physical substrates.

In this paper I defend this view. Specifically, I defend a principle of *organizational invariance*, holding that experience is invariant across systems with the same fine-grained functional organization. More precisely, the principle states that given any system that has conscious experiences, then any system that has the same functional organization at a fine enough grain will have qualitatively identical conscious experiences. A full specification of a system's fine-grained functional organization will fully determine any conscious experiences that arise.

To clarify this, we must first clarify the notion of functional organization. This is best understood as the *abstract pattern of causal interaction* between the components of a system, and perhaps between these components and external inputs and outputs. A functional organization is determined by specifying (1) a number of abstract components, (2) for each component, a number of different possible states, and (3) a system of dependency relations, specifying how the states of each component depends on the previous states of all components and on inputs to the system, and how outputs from the system depend on previous component states. Beyond specifying their number and their dependency relations, the nature of the components and the states is left unspecified.

A physical system *realizes* a given functional organization when the system can be divided into an appropriate number of physical components each with the appropriate number of possible states, such that the causal dependency relations between the components of the system, inputs, and outputs precisely reflect the dependency relations given in the specification of the functional organization. A given functional organization can be realized by diverse physical systems. For example, the organization realized by the brain at the neural level might in principle be realized by a silicon system.

A physical system has functional organization at many different levels, depending on how finely we individuate its parts and on how finely we divide the states of those parts. At a coarse level, for instance, it is likely that the two hemispheres of the brain can be seen as realizing a simple two-component organization, if we choose appropriate interdependent states of the hemispheres. It is generally more useful to view cognitive systems at a finer level, however. For our purposes I will always focus on a level of organization fine enough to determine the behavioural capacities and dispositions of a cognitive system. This is the role of the "fine enough grain" clause in the statement of the organizational invariance principle; the level of organization relevant to the application of the principle is one fine enough to determine a system's behavioral dispositions. In the brain, it is likely that the neural level suffices, although a coarser level might also work. For the purposes of illustration I will generally focus on the neural level of organization of the brain, but the arguments generalize.

Strictly speaking, for the purposes of the invariance principle we must require that for two systems to share their functional organization, they must be in corresponding states at the time in question; if not for this requirement, my sleeping twin might count as sharing my organization, but he certainly does not share my experiences. When two systems share their organization at a fine enough grain (including the requirement that they be in corresponding states), I will say that they are *functionally isomorphic* systems, or that they are *functional isomorphs*. The invariance principle holds that any functional isomorph of a conscious system has experiences that are qualitatively identical to those of the original system.

II. Absent qualia and inverted qualia

The principle of organizational invariance is far from universally accepted. Some have thought it likely that for a system to be conscious it must have the right sort of biochemical makeup; if so, a metallic robot or a silicon-based computer could never have experiences, no matter what its causal organization. Others have conceded that a robot or a computer might be conscious if it were organized appropriately, but have held that it might nevertheless have experiences quite different from the kind that we have. These two sorts of objections are often known as the *absent qualia* and *inverted qualia* objections to broadly functionalist theories of consciousness.

Arguments for the absent qualia objection usually consist in the description of a system that realizes whatever functional organization might be specified, but that is so outlandish that it is natural to suppose that it lacks conscious experience. For example, Block (1980) points out that the functional organization of the brain might be instantiated by the population of China, if they were organized appropriately, and argues that it is bizarre to suppose that this would somehow give rise to a group mind. In a similar way, John Searle (1980) notes that a given organization might be realized by "a sequence of water-pipes, or a set of wind-machines" but argues that these systems would not be conscious.

Arguments for the inverted qualia objection are often illustrated by considerations about experiences of colour. According to this line of argument (taken by Shoemaker 1982 and Horgan 1984, among others), it is possible that a system might make precisely the same colour discriminations that I do, but that when confronted by red objects it has the kind of experience that I have when confronted by blue objects. Further, it is argued that this might happen even when the systems are functionally isomorphic. If this argument succeeds, then even if the appropriate functional organization suffices for the existence of conscious experiences, it does not determine their specific nature. Instead, the specific nature of experiences must be dependent on non-organizational properties, such as specific neurophysiological properties.

Sometimes these arguments are intended as arguments for "possibility" only in some weak sense, such as logical or metaphysical possibility. These less ambitious forms of the arguments are the most likely to be successful. It seems difficult to deny that the absent qualia and inverted qualia scenarios are at least intelligible. With the aid of certain assumptions about possibility, this intelligibility can be extended into an argument for the logical and perhaps the metaphysical possibility of the scenarios. If successful, even these less ambitious arguments would suffice to refute some strong versions of functionalism, such as analytic functionalism and the view that phenomenal properties are identical to functional properties.

In the present paper I am not concerned with the logical or metaphysical possibility of these scenarios, however, but rather with their *empirical* (or natural, or nomological) possibility. The mere logical or metaphysical possibility of absent qualia is compatible with the claim that in the actual world, whenever the appropriate functional organization is realized, conscious experience is present. By analogy: many have judged it logically possible that a *physical* replica of a conscious system might lack conscious experience, while not wishing to deny that in the actual world, any such replica will be conscious. It is the claim about empirical possibility that is relevant to settling the issue at hand, which concerns a possible lawful relation between organization and experience. Mere intelligibility does not bear on this, any more than the intelligibility of a world without relativity can falsify Einstein's theory.

On the question of empirical possibility, the success of the absent qualia and inverted qualia arguments is unclear. To be sure, many have found it *counter-intuitive* that the population of China might give rise to conscious experience if organized appropriately. The natural reply, however, is that it seems equally counter-intuitive that a mass of 10^{11} appropriately organized neurons should give rise to consciousness, and yet it happens. Intuition is unreliable as a guide to empirical possibility, especially where a phenomenon as perplexing as conscious experience is concerned. If a brain can do the job of enabling conscious experience, it is far from obvious why an appropriately organized population, or indeed an appropriate organized set of water-pipes, could not.

The debate over absent and inverted qualia tends to produce a stand-off, then. Both proponents and opponents claim intuitions in support of their positions, but there are few grounds on which to settle the debate between them. Both positions seem to be epistemic possibilities, and due to the notorious difficulties in collecting experimental evidence about conscious experience, things might seem likely to stay that way.

I believe that the stand-off can be broken, and in this paper I will offer considerations that offer strong support to the principle of organizational invariance, suggesting that absent qualia and inverted qualia are empirically impossible. These arguments involve thought-experiments about gradual neural replacement, and take the form of a *reductio*. The first thought-experiment demonstrates that if absent qualia are possible, then a phenomenon involving what I will call *fading qualia* is possible; but I will argue that we have good reason to believe that fading qualia are impossible. The second argument has broader scope and is more powerful, demonstrating that if absent qualia *or* inverted qualia are possible, then a phenomenon involving what I will call *dancing qualia* is possible; but I will argue that we have even better reason to believe that dancing qualia are impossible. If the arguments succeed, we have good reason to believe that absent and inverted qualia are impossible, and that the principle of organizational invariance is true.

These arguments do not constitute conclusive *proof* of the principle of organizational invariance. Such proof is generally not available in the domain of conscious experience, where for familiar reasons one cannot even disprove the hypothesis that there is only one conscious being. But even in the absence of proof, we can bring to bear arguments for the plausibility and implausibility of different possibilities, and not all possibilities end up equal. I use these thought-experiments as a *plausibility argument* for the principle of organizational invariance, by showing that the alternatives have implausible consequences. If an opponent wishes to hold on to the possibility of absent or inverted qualia she can still do so, but the thought-experiments show that the cost is higher than one might have expected.

Perhaps it is useful to see these thought-experiments as playing a role analogous to that played by the "Schrödinger's cat" thought-experiment in the interpretation of quantum mechanics. Schrödinger's thought-experiment does not deliver a decisive verdict in favor of one interpretation or another, but it brings out various plausibilities and implausibilities in the interpretations, and it is something that every interpretation must ultimately come to grips with. In a similar way, any theory of consciousness must ultimately come to grips with the fading and dancing qualia scenarios, and some will handle them better than others. In this way, the virtues and drawbacks of various theories are clarified.

III. Fading qualia

The first scenario that I will present is relatively familiar,[1] but it is important to analyse it correctly, and it is a necessary preliminary to the more powerful second argument. In this thought-experiment, we assume for the purposes of *reductio* that absent qualia are empirically possible. It follows that there can be a system with the same functional organization as a conscious system (such as me), but which lacks conscious experience entirely due to some difference in non-organizational properties. Without loss of generality, suppose that this is because the system is made of silicon chips rather than neurons. Call this functional isomorph Robot. The causal patterns in Robot's processing system are the same as mine, but there is nothing it is like to be Robot.

Given this scenario, we can construct a series of cases intermediate between me and Robot such that there is only a very small change at each step and such that functional organization is preserved throughout. We can imagine, for instance, replacing a certain number of my neurons by silicon chips. In the first such case, only a single neuron is replaced. Its replacement is a silicon chip that performs precisely the same local function as the neuron. We can imagine that it is equipped with tiny transducers that take in electrical signals and chemical ions and transforms these into a digital signal upon which the chip computes, with the result converted into the appropriate electrical and chemical outputs. As long as the chip has the right input/output function, the replacement will make no difference to the functional organization of the system.

In the second case, we replace two neighboring neurons with silicon chips. This is just as in the previous case, but once both neurons are replaced we can eliminate the intermediary, dispensing with the awkward transducers and effectors that mediate the connection between the chips and replacing it with a standard digital connection. Later cases proceed in a similar fashion, with larger and larger groups of neighboring neurons replaced by silicon chips. Within these groups, biochemical mechanisms have been dispensed with entirely, except at the periphery. In the final case, every neuron in the system has been replaced by a chip, and there are no biochemical mechanisms playing an essential role. (I abstract away here from detailed issues concerning whether, for instance, glial cells play a non-trivial role; if they do, they will be components of the appropriate functional organization, and will be replaced also.)

We can imagine that throughout, the internal system is connected to a body, is sensitive to bodily inputs, and produces motor movements in an appropriate way via transducers and effectors. Each system in the sequence will be functionally isomorphic to me at a fine enough grain to share my behavioral dispositions. But while the system at one end of the spectrum is me, the system at the other end is essentially a copy of Robot.

To fix imagery, imagine that as the first system I am having rich conscious experiences. Perhaps I am at a basketball game, surrounded by shouting fans, with all sorts of brightly-colored clothes in my environment, smelling the delicious aroma of junk food and perhaps suffering from a throbbing headache. Let us focus in particular on the bright red and yellow experiences I have when I watch the players' uniforms. ("Red experience" should be taken as shorthand for "colour experience of the kind I usually have when presented with red objects," and so on throughout.) The final system, Robot, is in the same situation, processing the same inputs and producing similar behaviour, but by hypothesis is experiencing nothing at all.

The question arises: *What is it like to be the systems in between?* For those systems intermediate between me and Robot, what, if anything, are they experiencing? As we move along the spectrum of cases, how does conscious experience vary? Presumably the very early cases have experiences much like mine, and the very late cases have little or no experience, but what of the cases in the middle?

Given that Robot, at the far end of the spectrum, is not conscious, it seems that one of two things must happen along the way. Either consciousness gradually fades over the series of cases, before eventually disappearing, or somewhere along the way consciousness suddenly blinks out, although the preceding case had rich conscious experiences. Call the first possibility *fading qualia* and the second *suddenly disappearing qualia*.

On the second hypothesis, the replacement of a single neuron could be responsible for the vanishing of an entire field of conscious experience. If so, we could switch back and forth between a neuron and its silicon replacement, with a field of experience blinking in and out of existence on demand. This seems antecedently implausible, if not entirely bizarre. If suddenly disappearing qualia were possible, there would be brute discontinuities in the laws of nature unlike those we find anywhere else.[2] Any specific point for qualia suddenly to disappear (50 per cent neural? 25 per cent?) would be quite arbitrary. We might even run the experiment at a finer grain within the neuron, so that ultimately the replacement of a few molecules produces a sudden disappearance of experience. As always in these matters, the hypothesis cannot be disproved, but its antecedent plausibility is very low.

This leaves the first hypothesis, fading qualia. To get a fix on this hypothesis, consider a system halfway along the spectrum between me and Robot, after consciousness has degraded considerably but before it has gone altogether. Call this system Joe. What is it like to be Joe? Joe, of course, is functionally isomorphic to me. He *says* all the same things about his experiences as I do about mine. At the basketball game, he exclaims about the vivid bright red and yellow uniforms of the basketball players. By hypothesis, though, Joe is not having bright red and yellow experiences at all. Instead, perhaps he is experiencing tepid pink and murky brown. Perhaps he is having the faintest of red and yellow experiences. Perhaps his experiences have darkened almost to black. There are various conceivable ways in which red experiences might gradually transmute to no experience, and probably more ways that we cannot conceive. But presumably in each of these transmutation scenarios, experiences stop being *bright* before they vanish (otherwise we are left with the problem of suddenly disappearing qualia). Similarly, there is presumably a point at which subtle distinctions in my experience are no longer present in an intermediate system's experience; if we are to suppose that all the distinctions in my experience are present right up until a moment when they simultaneously vanish, we are left with another version of suddenly disappearing qualia.

For specificity, then, let us imagine that Joe experiences faded pink where I see bright red, with many distinctions between shades of my experience no longer present in shades of his experience. Where I am having loud noise experiences, perhaps Joe is experiencing only a distant rumble. Not everything is so bad for Joe: where I have a throbbing headache, he only has the mildest twinge.

The crucial point here is that Joe is systematically *wrong* about everything that he is experiencing. He certainly *says* that he is having bright red and yellow experiences, but he is merely experiencing tepid pink. If you ask him, he will claim to be experiencing all sorts of subtly different shades of red, but in fact many of these are quite homogeneous in his experience. He may even complain about the noise, when his auditory experience is really very mild. Worse, on a functional construal of judgment, Joe will even *judge* that he has all these complex experiences that he in fact lacks. In short, Joe is utterly out of touch with his conscious experience, and is incapable of getting in touch.

There is a significant implausibility here. This is a being whose rational processes are functioning and who is in fact *conscious*, but who is completely wrong about his own conscious experiences. Perhaps in the extreme case, when all is dark inside, it is reasonable to suppose that a system could be so misguided in its claims and judgments – after all, in a sense there is nobody in there to be wrong. But in the intermediate case, this is much less plausible. In every case with which we are familiar, conscious beings are generally capable of forming accurate judgments about their experience, in the absence of distraction and irrationality. For a sentient, rational being that is suffering from no functional pathology to be so systematically out of touch with its experiences would imply a strong dissociation between consciousness and cognition. We have little reason to believe that consciousness is such an ill-behaved phenomenon, and good reason to believe otherwise.

To be sure, fading qualia may be *logically* possible. Arguably, there is no contradiction in the notion of a system that is so wrong about its experiences. But logical possibility and empirical possibility are different things. One of the most salient empirical facts about conscious experience is that when a conscious being with the appropriate conceptual sophistication has experiences, it is at least capable of forming reasonable judgments about those experiences. Perhaps there are some cases where judgment is impaired due to a malfunction in rational processes, but this is not such a case. Joe's processes are *functioning* as well as mine – by hypothesis, he is functionally isomorphic. It is just that he happens to be completely misguided about his experience.

There are everyday cases in which qualia fade, of course. Think of what happens when one is dropping off to sleep; or think of moving back along the evolutionary chain from people to trilobites. In each case, as we move along a spectrum of cases, conscious experience gradually fades away. But in each of these cases, the fading is accompanied by a corresponding change in *functioning*. When I become drowsy, I do not believe that I am wide awake and having intense experiences (unless perhaps I start to dream, in which case I very likely *am* having intense experiences). The lack of richness in a dog's experience of colour accompanies a corresponding lack of discriminatory power in a dog's visual mechanisms. These cases are quite unlike the case under consideration, in which experience fades while functioning stays constant. Joe's mechanisms can still discriminate subtly different wavelengths of light, and he certainly judges that such discriminations are reflected in his experience, but we are to believe that his experience does not reflect these discriminations at all.

Searle (1992) discusses a thought-experiment like this one, and suggests the following possibility:

> as the silicon is progressively implanted into your dwindling brain, you find that the area of your conscious experience is shrinking, but that this shows no effect on your external behavior. You find, to your total amazement, that you are indeed losing control of your external behavior. You find, for example, that when the doctors test your vision, you hear them say, "We are holding up a red object in front of you; please tell us what you see." You want to cry out, "I can't see anything. I'm going totally blind." But you hear your voice saying in a way that is completely out of your control, "I see a red object in front of me." If we carry the thought-experiment out to the limit,

we get a much more depressing result than last time. We imagine that your conscious experience slowly shrinks to nothing, while your externally observable behavior remains the same (pp. 66–7).

Here, Searle embraces the possibility of fading qualia, but suggests that such a system need not be systematically mistaken in its beliefs about its experience. The system might have true beliefs about its experience, but beliefs that are impotent to affect its behaviour.[3]

It seems that this possibility can be ruled out, however. There is simply no room in the system for any new beliefs to be formed. Unless one is a dualist of a very strong variety, beliefs must be reflected in the functioning of a system – *perhaps* not in behaviour, but at least in some process. But this system is identical to the original system (me) at a fine grain. There is no room for new beliefs like "I can't see anything," new desires like the desire to cry out, and other new cognitive states such as amazement. Nothing in the physical system can correspond to that amazement. There is no room for it in the neurons, which after all are identical to a subset of the neurons supporting the usual beliefs; and Searle is surely not suggesting that the silicon replacement is itself supporting the new beliefs! Failing a remarkable, magical interaction effect between neurons and silicon – and one that does not manifest itself anywhere in processing, as organization is preserved throughout – such new beliefs will not arise.

While it might just seem plausible that an organization-preserving change from neurons to silicon might twist a few experiences from red to blue, a change in beliefs from "Nice basketball game" to "I seem to be stuck in a bad horror movie!" is of a different order of magnitude. If such a major change in cognitive contents were not mirrored in a change in functional organization, cognition would float free of internal functioning like a disembodied mind. If the contents of cognitive states supervened on physical states at all, they could do so only by the most arbitrary and capricious of rules (if this organization in neurons, then "pretty colours!"; if this organization in silicon, then "Alas!").

It follows that the possibility of fading qualia requires either a bizarre relationship between belief contents and physical states, or the possibility of beings that are massively mistaken about their own conscious experiences despite being fully rational. Both of these hypotheses are significantly less plausible than the hypothesis that rational conscious beings are generally correct in their judgments about their experiences. A much more reasonable hypothesis is therefore that when neurons are replaced, qualia do not fade at all. A system like Joe, in practice, will have conscious experiences just as rich as mine. If so, then our original assumption was wrong, and the original isomorph, Robot, has conscious experiences.

This thought-experiment can be straightforwardly extended to other sorts of functional isomorphs, including isomorphs that differ in shape, size, and physical makeup. All we need do is construct a sequence of inter-mediate cases, each with the same functional organization. In each case the conclusion is the same. If such a system is not conscious, then there exists an intermediate system that is conscious, has faded experiences, and is completely wrong about its experiences. Unless we are prepared to accept this massive dissociation between consciousness and cognition, the original system must have been conscious after all.

We can even extend the reasoning straightforwardly to the case of an appropriately-organized population: we simply need to imagine neurons replaced one-by-one with tiny homunculi, ending up with a network of homunculi that is essentially equivalent to the population controlling a robot. (If one objects to tiny homunculi, they can be external and of normal size, as long as they are equipped with appropriate radio connections to the body when necessary.) Precisely the same considerations about intermediate cases arise. One can also imagine going from a multiple-homunculi case to a single-homunculus case, yielding something like Searle's "Chinese room" example. We need only suppose that the homunculi gradually "double up" on their tasks, leaving written records of the state of each component, until only a single homunculus does all the work. If the causal organization of the original system is preserved, even if it is only among a system of marks on paper, then the same arguments suggest that the system will have experi-ences. (Of course, we should not expect the homunculus itself to have the experiences; it is merely acting as a sort of causal facilitator.)

If absent qualia are possible, then fading qualia are possible. But I have argued above that it is very unlikely that fading qualia are possible. It follows that it is very unlikely that absent qualia are possible.

Some might object that these thought-experiments are the stuff of science fiction rather than the stuff of reality, and point out that this sort of neural replacement would be quite impossible in practice. But although it might be technologically impossible, there is no reason to believe that the neural replacement scenario should contravene the laws of nature. We already have prosthetic arms and legs. Prosthetic eyes lie within the foreseeable future, and a prosthetic neuron seems entirely possible in principle. Even if it were impossible for some technical reason (perhaps there would not be enough room for a silicon replacement to do its work?), it is unclear what bearing this technical fact would have on the principled force of the thought-experiment. There will surely be *some* systems between which gradual replacement is possible: will the objector hold that the invariance principle holds for those systems, but no other? If so, the situation seems quite arbitrary; if not, then there must be a deeper objection available.

Others might object that no silicon replacement could perform even the local function of a neuron, perhaps because neural function is uncomputable. There is little evidence for this, but it should be noted that even if it is true, it does not affect the argument for the invariance principle. If silicon really could not even duplicate the *function* of a neural system, then a functional isomorph made of silicon would be impossible, and the assessment of silicon systems would simply be irrelevant to the invariance principle. To evaluate the truth of the principle, it is only functionally isomorphic systems that are relevant.

Another objection notes that there are actual cases in which subjects are seriously mistaken about their experiences. For example, in cases of blindness denial, subjects believe that they are having visual experiences when they likely have none. In these cases, however, we are no longer dealing with fully rational systems. In systems whose belief-formation mechanisms are impaired, anything goes. Such systems might believe that they are Napoleon, or that the moon is pink. My "faded" isomorph Joe, by contrast, is a fully rational system, whose cognitive mechanisms are functioning just as well as mine. In conversation, he seems perfectly sensible. We cannot point to any unusually poor inferential connections between his beliefs, or any systematic psychiatric disorder that is leading his thought processes to be biased toward faulty reasoning. Joe is an eminently thoughtful, reasonable person, who exhibits none of the confabulatory symptoms of those with blindness denial. The cases are therefore disanalogous. The plausible claim is not that no system can be massively mistaken about its experiences, but that no rational system whose cognitive mechanisms are unimpaired can be so mistaken. Joe is certainly a rational system whose mechanisms are working as well as mine, so the argument is unaffected.

Some object that this argument has the form of a Sorites or "slippery-slope" argument, and observe that these arguments are notoriously suspect. Using a Sorites argument, we can "show" that even a grain of sand is a heap; after all, a million grains of sand form a heap, and if we take a single grain away from a heap we still have a heap. This objection is based on a superficial reading of the thought-experiment, however. Sorites arguments gain their force by ignoring the fact that some apparent dichotomy is in fact a continuum; there are all sorts of vague cases between heaps and non-heaps, for instance. The fading qualia argument, by contrast, explicitly accepts the possibility of a continuum, but argues that intermediate cases are impossible for independent reasons. The argument is therefore not a Sorites argument.

Ultimately, the only tenable way for an opponent of organizational invariance to respond to this argument is to bite the bullet and accept the possibility of fading qualia, and the consequent possibility that a rational conscious system might be massively mistaken about its experience, or perhaps to bite another bullet and accept suddenly disappearing qualia and the associated brute discontinuities. These positions seem much less plausible than the alternative, other things being equal, but they are the only way to avoid it. But there is worse to come: the argument to follow provides an even more powerful case against the possibility of absent qualia, so opponents of organizational invariance cannot rest easily.

IV. Dancing qualia

If the fading qualia argument succeeds, it establishes that functional isomorphs of a conscious system will have conscious experience, but it does not establish that isomorphs have the *same* sort of conscious experience. The preceding argument has no bearing on the possibility of inverted qualia. For all that has gone before, where I am having a red experience, my silicon functional isomorph might be having a blue experience, or some other kind of experience that is quite foreign to me.

One might think that the fading qualia argument could be directly adapted to provide an argument against the possibility of inverted qualia, but that strategy fails. If I have a red experience and my functional isomorph has a blue experience, there is no immediate problem with the idea of intermediate cases with intermediate experiences. These systems might be simply suffering from milder cases of qualia inversion, and are no more problematic than the extreme case. These systems will not be systematically wrong about their experiences. Where they claim to experience distinctions, they may really be experiencing distinctions; where they claim to be having intense experiences, they may still be having intense experiences. To be sure, the experiences they call "red" differ from those I call "red" but this is already an accepted feature of the usual inversion case. The difference between these cases and the fading qualia cases is that these cases preserve the *structure* of experience throughout, so that their existence implies no implausible dissociation between experience and cognition.

Nevertheless, a good argument against the possibility of inverted qualia can be found in the vicinity. Once again, for the purposes of *reductio*, assume that inverted qualia are empirically possible. Then there can be two functionally isomorphic systems that are having different experiences. Suppose for the sake of illustration that these systems are me, having a red experience, and my silicon isomorph, having a blue experience (there is a small caveat about generality, which I discuss below).

As before, we construct a series of cases intermediate between me and my isomorph. Here, the argument takes a different turn. We need not worry about the *way* in which experiences change as we move along the series.

246

All that matters is that there must be two points A and B in this series, such that no more than one-tenth of the system is replaced between A and B, and such that A and B have significantly different experiences. To see that this must be the case, we need only consider the points at which 10 per cent, 20 per cent, and so on up to 90 per cent of the brain has been replaced. Red and blue are sufficiently different experiences that some neighboring pairs here *must* be significantly different (that is, different enough that the difference would be noticeable if they were experienced by the same person); there is no way to get from red to blue by ten non-noticeable jumps.

There must therefore be two systems that differ in at most one-tenth of their internal makeup, but that have significantly different experiences. For the purposes of illustration, let these systems be me and Bill. Where I have a red experience, Bill has a slightly different experience. We may as well suppose that Bill has a blue experience; perhaps his experience will be more similar to mine than that, but that makes no difference to the argument. The two systems also differ in that where there are neurons in some small region of my brain, there are silicon chips in Bill's brain. This substitution of a silicon circuit for a neural circuit is the only physical difference between me and Bill.

The crucial step in the thought-experiment is to take a silicon circuit just like Bill's and install it in my head as a *backup circuit*. This circuit will be functionally isomorphic to a circuit already present in my head. We equip the circuit with transducers and effectors so that it can interact with the rest of my brain, but we do not hook it up directly. Instead, we install a *switch* that can switch directly between the neural and silicon circuits. Upon flipping the switch, the neural circuit becomes irrelevant and the silicon circuit takes over. We can imagine that the switch controls the points of interface where the relevant circuit affects the rest of the brain. When it is switched, the connections from the neural circuit are pushed out of the way, and the silicon circuit's effectors are attached. (We might imagine that the transducers for both circuits are attached the entire time, so that the state of both circuits evolves appropriately, but so that only one circuit at a time plays a role in processing. We could also run a similar experiment where both transducers and effectors are disconnected, to ensure that the backup circuit is entirely isolated from the rest of the system. This would change a few details, but the moral would be the same.)

Immediately after flipping the switch, processing that was once performed by the neural circuit is now performed by the silicon circuit. The flow of control within the system has been redirected. However, my functional organization is exactly the same as it would have been if we had not flipped the switch. The only relevant difference between the two cases is the physical makeup of one circuit within the system. There is also a difference in the physical makeup of another "dangling" circuit, but this is irrelevant to functional organization, as it plays no role in affecting other components of the system and directing behaviour.

What happens to my experience when we flip the switch? Before installing the circuit, I was experiencing red. After we install it but before we flip the switch, I will presumably still be experiencing red, as the only difference is the addition of a circuit that is not involved in processing in any way; for all the relevance it has to my processing, I might as well have eaten it. *After* flipping the switch, however, I am more or less the same system as Bill. The only difference between Bill and me now is that I have a causally irrelevant neural circuit dangling from the system (we might even imagine that the circuit is destroyed when the switch is flipped). Bill, by hypothesis, was enjoying a blue experience. After the switch, then, I will have a blue experience too.

What will happen, then, is that my experience will change "before my eyes." Where I was once experiencing red, I will now experience blue. All of a sudden, I will have a *blue* experience of the apple on my desk. We can even imagine flipping the switch back and forth a number of times, so that the red and blue experiences "dance" before my eyes.

This might seem reasonable at first – it is a strangely appealing image – but something very odd is going on here. My experiences are switching from red to blue, but *I do not notice any change.* Even as we flip the switch a number of times and my qualia dance back and forth, I will simply go about my business, not noticing anything unusual. My functional organization remains normal throughout. In particular, my functional organization after flipping the switch evolves just as it would have if the switch had not been flipped. There is no special difference in my behavioural dispositions. I am not suddenly disposed to say "Hmm! Something strange is going on!" There is no room for a sudden start, for an exclamation, or even for a distraction of attention. My cognitive organization is just as it usually is, and in particular is precisely as it would have been had the switch not been flipped.

Certainly, on any functional construal of judgment, it is clear that I do not make any novel judgments due to the flip. Even if one were to dispute a functional account of judgment, it is is extremely implausible that a simple organization-preserving replacement of a neural circuit by a silicon circuit could be responsible for the addition of significant new judgments such as "My qualia just flipped." As in the case of fading qualia, there is simply no room for such a change to take place, unless it is in an accompanying Cartesian disembodied mind.

We are therefore led once more into a *reductio ad absurdum.* It seems entirely implausible to suppose that my experiences could change in such a significant way, even with me paying full attention, without my being able to notice the change. It would suggest once again an extreme dissociation between consciousness and cognition. If this kind of thing could happen, then psychology and phenomenology would be radically out of step, much further out of step than even the fading qualia scenario would imply.

This "dancing qualia" scenario may be logically possible (although the case is so extreme that it seems *only just* logically possible), but that does not mean we should take it seriously as an empirical possibility, any more than we should take seriously the possibility that the world was created five minutes ago. As an empirical hypothesis, it is far more plausible that when one's experiences change significantly, then as long as one is rational and paying attention, one should be able to notice the change. If not, then consciousness and cognition are tied together by only the most slender of threads.

Indeed, if we are to suppose that dancing qualia are empirically possible, we are led to a worrying thought: they might be *actual*, and happening to us all the time. The physiological properties of our functional mechanisms are constantly changing. The functional properties of the mechanisms are reasonably robust; one would expect that this robustness would be ensured by evolution. But there is no adaptive reason for the non-functional properties to stay constant. From moment to moment there will certainly be changes in low-level molecular properties. Properties such as position, atomic makeup, and so on can change while functional role is preserved, and such change is almost certainly going on constantly.

If we allow that qualia are dependent not just on functional organization but on implementational details, it may well be that *our* qualia are in fact dancing before our eyes all the time. There seems to be no principled reason why a change from neurons to silicon should make a difference while a change in neural realization should not; the only place to draw a *principled* line is at the functional level. The reason why we doubt that such dancing is taking place in our own cases is that we accept the following principle: when one's experiences change significantly, one can notice the change. If we were to accept the possibility of dancing qualia in the original case, we would be discarding this principle, and it would no longer be available as a defense against skepticism even in the more usual cases.

It is not out of the question that we could actually perform such an experiment. Of course the practical difficulties would be immense, but at least in principle, one could install such a circuit in me and *I* could see what happened, and report it to the world. But of course there is no point performing the experiment: we know what the result will be. I will report that my experience stayed the same throughout, a constant shade of red, and that I noticed nothing untoward. I will become even more convinced than I was before that qualia are determined by functional organization. Of course this will not be a *proof*, but it will be hard seriously to dispute the evidence.

I conclude that by far the most plausible hypothesis is that replacement of neurons while preserving functional organization will preserve qualia, and that experience is wholly determined by functional organization.

The argument leaves open a few small loopholes, but none of the loopholes leads to an attractive position. For example, while the dancing qualia scenario is straightforwardly extendible to most functional isomorphs, there are a couple of exceptions involving speed and history. If an isomorph is much faster or slower than the original system, we cannot simply substitute a circuit from one system into the other and expect everything to function normally. We can still perform the experiment on a slowed-down or speeded-up version of the system in question, however, so at most we have left open the possibility that a change in speed might invert qualia. A similar loophole is left open for physical isomorphs that differ in their *history*: perhaps if I was born in the southern hemisphere I experience green, whereas a physical twin born in the north would experience red. History cannot be varied in a dancing qualia scenario (although it can be varied in a fading qualia scenario), so the argument does not bear on the hypothesis that qualia supervene on the past.

But neither of these hypotheses were very plausible in the first place. It is reasonable that history should affect our qualia by affecting our physical structure, but the history-dependence required above would be much stronger: there would in effect be a "nonlocal" effect of distal history on present qualia, unmediated by anything in physical structure or nearby in space and time. As for speed, it would seem quite arbitrary that a change in speed would invert qualia when nothing else could. The hypotheses here are coherent, but there is little reason to embrace them.

Another small caveat is that the argument does not refute the possibility of a very mild spectrum inversion. Between dark red and a slightly darker red, for instance, there may be nine intermediate shades such that no two neighboring shades are distinguishable. In such a case the dancing qualia scenario is not a problem; if the system notices no difference on flipping the switch, that is just what we might expect.

Of course, there is nothing special about the figure of one-tenth as the amount of difference between two neighboring systems. But we cannot make the figure too high. If we made it as high as one half, we would run into problems with personal identity: it might reasonably be suggested that upon flipping the switch, we are creating a new person, and it would not be a problem that the new person noticed no change. Perhaps we might go as high as one-fifth or one-quarter without such problems; but that would still allow the possibility of very mild inversions, the kind that could be composed of four or five unnoticeable changes. We can reduce the impact of this worry, however, by noting that it is very unlikely that experience depends equally on all areas of the brain. If colour experience depends largely on a small area of the visual cortex, say, then we could perform any qualia inversion in one fell swoop while only replacing a small portion of the system, and the argument would succeed against even the mildest noticeable qualia inversion.

In any case, the possibility of a mild under-determination of experience by organization is an unthreatening one. If we wished, we could accept it, noting that any differences between isomorphs would be so slight as to be uninteresting. More likely, we can note that this would seem an odd and unlikely way for the world to be. It would seem reasonable that experiences should be invertible across the board, or not invertible at all, but why should the world be such that a small inversion is possible but nothing more? This would seem quite arbitrary. We cannot rule it out, but it is not a hypothesis with much antecedent plausibility.

In a similar way, the argument leaves open the loophole that *unattended* qualia might be invertible. If we are not attending to the fringes of our visual field, for example, a qualia inversion might take place there without our noticing. But to exploit this loophole would leave one in the unattractive position that qualia are organizationally invariant when they are central enough in one's attention, but dependent on other features when they are not. (Presumably an inverted green experience on the fringe will flip back to red when one attends to it?) Such an asymmetric position would be theoretically unsatisfying in the extreme.

It should be noted that the dancing qualia argument works just as well against the possibility of absent qualia as against that of inverted qualia. If absent qualia are possible, then on the path to absent qualia we can find two slightly different systems whose experience differs significantly, and we can install a backup circuit in the same way. As before, the hypothesis implies that switching will cause my qualia to dance before my eyes, from vivid to tepid and back, without my ever noticing any change. This is implausible for the same reasons as before, so we have good reason to believe that absent qualia are impossible.

Overall, the dancing qualia argument seems to make an even more convincing case against absent qualia than the fading qualia argument does, although both have a role to play. Where an opponent might bite the bullet and accept the possibility of fading qualia, dancing qualia are an order of magnitude more difficult to accept. The very immediacy of the switch makes a significant difference, as does the fact that the subject cannot notice something so striking and dynamic. The possibility of fading qualia would imply that some systems are out of touch with their conscious experience, but dancing qualia would establish a much stranger gap.

V. Nonreductive functionalism

To summarize: we have established that if absent qualia are possible, then fading qualia are possible; if inverted qualia are possible, then dancing qualia are possible; and if absent qualia are possible, then dancing qualia are possible. But it is implausible that fading qualia are possible, and it is extremely implausible that dancing qualia are possible. It is therefore extremely implausible that absent qualia and inverted qualia are possible. It follows that we have good reason to believe that the principle of organizational invariance is true, and that functional organization fully determines conscious experience.

It should be noted that these arguments do not establish functionalism in the strongest sense, as they establish at best that absent and inverted qualia are empirically (naturally, nomologically) impossible. There are two reasons why the arguments cannot be extended into an argument for logical or metaphysical impossibility. First, both fading qualia and dancing qualia seem to be intelligible hypotheses, even if they are very implausible. Some might dispute their logical possibility, perhaps holding that it is constitutive of qualia that subjects can notice differences between them. This conceptual intuition would be controversial, but in any case, even if we were to accept the logical impossibility of fading and dancing qualia, there is a second reason why these arguments do not establish the logical or metaphysical determination of conscious experience by functional organization.

To see this second reason, note that the arguments take as an *empirical* premise certain facts about the distribution of functional organization in physical systems: that I have conscious experiences of a certain kind, or that some biological systems do. If we established the logical impossibility of fading and dancing qualia, this might establish the logical necessity of the *conditional*: if one system with fine-grained functional organization F has a certain sort of conscious experiences, then any system with organization F has those experiences. But we cannot establish the logical necessity of the conclusion without establishing the logical necessity of the premise, and the premise is itself empirical. On the face of it, it is difficult to see why it should be logically necessary that *brains* with certain physical properties give rise to conscious experience. Perhaps the most tenable way to argue for this necessity is via a form of analytic functionalism; but in the context of using the fading and dancing qualia arguments to *establish* this sort of functionalism, this strategy would be circular. It follows that the fading and dancing qualia arguments are of little use in arguing for the logical and metaphysical impossibility of absent and inverted qualia.

The arguments therefore fail to establish a strong form of functionalism upon which functional organization is *constitutive* of conscious experience; but they succeed in establishing a weaker form, on which functional organization *suffices* for conscious experience with natural necessity. We can call this view *nonreductive functionalism*, as it holds that conscious experience is determined by functional organization without necessarily being reducible to functional organization. As things stand, the view is just as compatible with certain forms of property dualism about experience as with certain forms of physicalism. Whether the view should be strengthened into a reductive version of functionalism is a matter that the fading and dancing qualia arguments leave open.

In any case, the conclusion is a strong one. It tells us that systems that duplicate our functional organization will be conscious even if they are made of silicon, constructed out of water-pipes, or instantiated in an entire population. The arguments in this paper can thus be seen as offering support to some of the ambitions of artificial intelligence. The arguments also make progress in constraining the principles in virtue of which consciousness depends on the physical. If successful, they show that biochemical and other non-organizational properties are at best indirectly relevant to the instantiation of experience, relevant only insofar as they play a role in determining functional organization.

The principle of organizational invariance is not the last word in constructing a theory of conscious experience. There are many unanswered questions: we would like to know just what sort of organization gives rise to experience, and what sort of experience a given organization gives rise to. Further, the principle is not cast at the right level to be a truly *fundamental* theory of consciousness; eventually, we would like to construct a fundamental theory that has the principle as a consequence. In the meantime, the principle acts as a strong constraint on an ultimate theory.

Notes

1 Neural replacement scenarios along the lines discussed in this section are discussed by Pylyshyn (1980), Savitt (1982), Cuda (1985) and Searle (1992), among others.

2 One might argue that there are situations in nonlinear dynamics in which one magnitude depends sensitively on another, with large changes in the first arising from small changes in the second. But in these cases the dependence is nevertheless continuous, so there will be intermediate cases in which the dependent magnitude takes on intermediate values; the analogy therefore leads to fading qualia, below. And in any case, the sensitive dependence in

these cases generally arise from the compound effects of a number of more basic gradual dependencies. In all fundamental laws known to date, the dependence of one magnitude on another is continuous in this fashion, and there is no way to compound continuity into discontinuity. Suddenly disappearing qualia, in contrast to nonlinear dynamics, would therefore require brute discontinuities in fundamental laws.

3   Searle also raises the possibility that upon silicon replacement, the system might be slowly reduced to paralysis, or have its functioning otherwise impaired. Such a scenario is irrelevant to the truth of the invariance principle, however, which applies only to systems with the appropriate functional organization. If a silicon system does not duplicate the organization of the original system, the principle does not even come into play.

References

Block, N. (1980) Troubles with functionalism. In N. Block (ed.), *Readings in the Philosophy of Psychology*, Vol. I. Cambridge, Mass.: MIT Press, pp. 268–305. Excerpts from this work are reprinted as Chapter 12 in this volume.

Cuda, T. (1985) Against neural chauvinism. *Philosophical Studies*, 48, 111–27.

Horgan, T. (1984) Functionalism, qualia, and the inverted spectrum. *Philosophy and Phenomenological Research*, 44, 453–69.

Pylyshyn, Z. (1980) The "causal power" of machines. *Behavioral and Brain Sciences*, 3, 442–4.

Savitt, S. (1982) Searle's demon and the brain simulator reply. *Behavioral and Brain Sciences*, 5, 342–3.

Searle, J.R. (1980) Minds, brains, and programs. *Behavioral and Brain Sciences*, 3, 417–57. Reprinted as Chapter 16 in this volume.

Searle, J.R. (1992) *The Rediscovery of the Mind*. Cambridge, Mass.: MIT Press.

Shoemaker, S. (1982) The inverted spectrum. *Journal of Philosophy*, 79, 357–81.

QUESTIONS

1　The dispute between Smart and Kripke hinges in part on whether it is plausible to suppose that for every mental state there is a physical state of the brain with which it is identical. Try to characterize the difference between claims of mental–physical *token* identity and *type* identity. How are type-identity claims significantly stronger assertions than token-identity claims?

2　Kripke's thesis about rigid and non-rigid designators is a claim about language. Yet from this he draws an anti-materialist conclusion about the nature of mental states. What *else* does Kripke claim (beyond the points about designators) to bridge the gap from language to the nature of mind?

3　Explain Kim's "Causal Inheritance Principle." What conclusion concerning mental states does he draw from this principle (in conjunction with the thesis that mental states are all physically realized)?

4　Functionalism defines kinds of mental states in part in terms of each other. (For example, beliefs are characterized in part in terms of their causal relations to desires.) Lewis says there is nothing objectionably circular about this procedure. Explain his reasoning. Is he right?

5　Block introduces a "nation of China" thought-experiment in which the citizens of China engage in behavior (using radio signals) that instantiates the abstract "functional program" of human psychology. Why does he draw the conclusion that functionalism is implausible? Compare this "conceivability argument" with the Cartesian argument discussed in Chapter 1. Do the arguments depend on the same kind of conceivability? Is one argument stronger than the other?

PART III

MIND AND
REPRESENTATION

INTRODUCTION

The selections in Parts I and II of this volume are concerned with the nature of mind, in particular with the relation between the mental and the physical. The selections in Parts III and IV never depart from these general metaphysical issues, which are always at least in the background. But the following chapters are focused on two particular features of the mind, features that, though utterly central to our mental lives, have proven to be especially mysterious. Part III is about intentionality, Part IV about consciousness.

I. The puzzle of intentionality

One of the mind's most impressive and useful capacities is its ability to represent, to have states that are about something. The nineteenth-century philosopher and psychologist Franz Brentano called this feature, known as intentionality, the "mark of the mental" – it's what distinguishes the mental from the non-mental. (Descartes, by contrast, took consciousness to be the mark of the mental.) Yet intentionality is at the same time an extraordinary, almost magical power. Consider the following:

- Intentionality is selective. There are a vast (perhaps infinite) number of objects in our universe, yet a thought about Socrates, for example, is able to refer to just one of these. And of all the facts there are, a belief that, say, plants need sunlight to grow picks out just one.
- Intentionality can reach across space and time. A thought about Socrates refers to a person who existed in Greece about 2,400 years ago. One can also think about what is future, such as the next United States presidential election. Even more impressive is how intentionality can reach outside space and time. If Platonists are right about the nature of numbers, then a thought about the number two, for example, manages to pick out something non-spatiotemporal.

- Intentionality is apparently not even confined to the realm of existence. One can think about the Easter Bunny or Hamlet, even though there are no such beings. There are texts and pictures about them, of course, but we seem to be able to think, not just about the texts and pictures, but about the bunny and the man themselves.
- Finally, and perhaps most importantly, even when intentional states do refer, they can misrepresent what they refer to. One can mistakenly believe that Aristotle was Socrates' teacher, or misperceive a distant person as one's friend.

Now when we focus on words and other intentional artifacts, such feats may not seem particularly remarkable. After all, that the word "Socrates" picks out a person who lived 2,400 years ago is explained relatively easily: *we* bestow meaning on it. Thinking of the historical Socrates, we collectively decide to use the word to refer to him. And even if the social mechanisms underlying conventional word meaning are more complicated than this, the central point here is that the intentionality of words is derived: words inherit their intentional powers from our minds. It is because we can already think about Socrates that the word refers to him. But mental states, unlike words, have *original* intentionality (Haugeland 1997). A thought can somehow, without the aid of an external mind, be about Socrates. And it is with respect to *original* intentionality that the feats listed above are especially remarkable.

Original intentionality is sometimes presented as especially problematic for materialists. How could anything physical be, in itself, about something else? How could it have such powers? These questions should trouble the materialist, but it is worth noting that it is just as mysterious how any state of an immaterial substance (e.g. a Cartesian mind) could have original intentionality. Aboutness just doesn't seem to be able to find a foothold in any part of the world, physical or otherwise. An instructive analogy here is provided by moral properties. Philosophers have puzzled over how the world in itself could contain features such as rightness and wrongness. Moral properties just do not seem to be in the world in the way that the properties of, say, mass and shape are. In response to this puzzle, some philosophers have argued that moral properties are in fact merely projected by us on to external objects and events. No mind-independent object or event is right or wrong in itself. But while a projectivist theory may be workable for moral properties, it looks hopeless for explaining original intentionality, for projection is itself an act that requires intentionality. We must be able to think about the external world before we project anything on to it. It seems we have no choice but to admit that original intentionality is a real, non-projected feature of the world. But again, this is the puzzle: how could anything have this quality of aboutness?

II. Naturalizing intentionality

The puzzle of original intentionality (hereafter just "intentionality") has inspired a number of rival philosophical positions. The first and most popular tries to naturalize intentionality, to show that it is, in spite of its remarkable powers, reducible to philosophically and scientifically respectable (i.e. non-intentional) features of the world. A second option is to take intentionality to be real but irreducible, existing alongside charge, mass, and the like as basic properties. And third, one might take the puzzle of intentionality – along with a perceived failure of naturalist projects – to show that there is no intentionality; the phenomenon just does not exist.

The first of these options, the naturalist project, has been the focus of much recent philosophical attention (for a survey, see Cummins 1989). The naturalist's goal is to show that intentionality, while real, is reducible to the non-intentional, to features that are comfortably located in the worldview of modern science. And a promising candidate to fill this role is causality (see e.g. Stampe 1977). While causality does not on the face of it have all the marks of intentionality listed earlier, it does have some of the most crucial: it is selective, it can reach across space, and it can reach through time. The hope is that causality can be the main ingredient in a naturalist theory of intentionality (or if not causality as such, some closely related notion such as counterfactual or nomological dependence).

Causality takes center-stage in the naturalist project of Chapter 14. Fodor begins with what he calls the Crude Causal Theory: a symbol denotes its causes. Suppose that whenever you are presented with a horse, this causes you (or your brain) to go into a certain physical state S, one that meets the functional/computational requirements for being a mental symbol. Since horses cause S (in you), S refers to horses. In this way, S's aboutness is reduced to the naturalistically respectable relation of causality.

While the Crude Causal Theory may be on the right track, it has a number of obstacles to overcome. On the face of it, it cannot account for our ability to think about what is causally isolated from us, such as objects and properties that are future, abstract, or non-existent. But Fodor focuses on a more basic problem: the Crude Causal Theory leaves no room for misrepresentation. An effect is never "mistaken" about its cause: it simply has the cause it does. Yet our minds are sometimes mistaken about what they represent: one can hallucinate, misperceive, make faulty inferences, and so on. How can misrepresentation be reduced to what seems to be an infallible relation? Suppose, for example, that though S is caused by horses, it is also occasionally caused by (distant) cows. What is needed is some way to favor horses over cows so that S really represents just the former causes and not the latter. Fodor calls this the "disjunction problem" because it looks as if the Crude Causal

Theory is forced into saying that S never misrepresents at all, but is merely an infallible symbol of *horse or cow*, the disjunction of its causes.

Fodor's solution is to abandon the Crude Causal Theory in favor of a more complex (but still naturalistic) account. While S is caused by both horses and cows, there's a clear sense in which it is caused by cows only because it is already caused by horses. That is, if horses did not cause S, distant cows (which resemble horses) wouldn't either. In this way, the causal route from cows to the symbol is dependent or parasitic on the route from horses. But the dependence is asymmetric because the reverse doesn't hold: even if distant cows did not look like horses, even if they did not cause S, this symbol would still be caused by horses. Fodor hopes to account for misrepresentation using such asymmetric dependence. Out of all the objects and properties that cause S, the symbol "favors" those on which the rest are asymmetrically dependent. And so when the symbol is caused by a dependent object, misrepresentation results. (For more on Fodor's project, see Fodor 1990 and Loewer and Rey 1991.)

In Chapter 15, naturalist Fred Dretske is also concerned with the problem of misrepresentation, and causal dependence (or relations akin to it) play a role in his view: they capture the relation of what he calls *indication*. Certain kinds of spots indicate measles, for example, and this is because there is a causal/nomic dependence between measles and spots. But indication by itself cannot be all there is to intentionality, which has a particularly normative character. Embedded in intentionality, that is, is the notion of what a representation *should* indicate. Only given such normativity is misrepresentation possible, and the puzzle for Dretske, as a naturalist, is finding such normativity in the natural world. While causal accounts may be able to explain what it is for some state in your brain to indicate horses, in virtue of what could it be true that this state is supposed to indicate horses?

Dretske finds the required normativity in natural functions. Just as the heart has the natural function of circulating blood, so various states of our brains have the functions of indicating particular objects or properties. Importantly, these states do not acquire their functions from an external agent. (This would mean abandoning the naturalist project, since to assign a function to something involves, at a minimum, thinking about it.) Natural functions are, rather, present by the non-intentional processes of nature itself. An organ such as the heart may acquire a natural function from our evolutionary history, but how can some internal state S of your brain acquire the function of indicating, say, horses? Dretske's central idea is that S, which already indicates horses, acquires the function of doing so by coming to cause movements of my body that are, in the presence of horses, successful in meeting my desires. (This is only a sketch; for details, see Dretske 1988, Chapter 4.)

In Chapter 16, John Searle tries to throw some cold water on the naturalist program. Searle's explicit target is what he calls Strong AI (Strong Artificial

Intelligence), the view that any system running an appropriate computer program is, by virtue of that alone, intelligent. Yet it is clear that Searle is concerned not just with intelligence, but with intentionality generally, and that his target is not just Strong AI, but any naturalist attempt to reduce intentionality to something more fundamental. At the center of Searle's paper is his much-discussed Chinese Room thought-experiment: Searle imagines himself inside a room, manipulating marked pieces of paper according to a complex set of instructions. By following the instructions, he is unwittingly running a computer program in which he is simulating one side of a conversation in Chinese (the pieces of paper are marked with Chinese characters). Nevertheless, in spite of running this program – which can be made as complex as one likes – Searle himself does not understand Chinese. To him, the pieces of paper he is manipulating are just so many meaningless squiggles. Running a computer program, then, is not sufficient for understanding Chinese. And the conclusion is meant to generalize: no program can by itself bestow understanding – original intentionality – on a system. (For responses to the Chinese Room, see the 1980 issue of *Behavioral and Brain Sciences* in which Searle's paper originally appeared, and Preston and Bishop 2002.)

Searle grants that an appropriately programmed computer will at least have what he elsewhere calls "as if" intentionality. The states of the system will mean something to someone else, e.g. the Chinese-speaking programmers. But such a system cannot have (at least not merely in virtue of running a program) original intentionality, what Searle calls "intrinsic" intentionality. The symbols a computer manipulates do not mean anything to the computer itself. And against causal theorists such as Fodor, Searle argues that such meaning would not arise even if causal connections were established between the states of the system and the outside world (see his response to the "Robot Reply"). What, then, would bestow original intentionality on a system? Here Searle provides few details. His view seems to be that while intentionality is a physical phenomenon caused by processes in the brain, it is not reducible to any such processes, but instead is a basic, unanalyzable feature of the world (see also Searle 1984, 1992).

III. The propositional attitudes

Intentional mental states include thoughts, mental images, and perceptual experiences. But philosophers have paid special attention to the class of intentional states Bertrand Russell called "propositional attitudes," states that have propositions as their objects. (A proposition is what a declarative sentence expresses. So, for example, "It's raining" and "Está lloviendo" are sentences from different languages, yet they express the same proposition. It is useful to think of propositions as *facts*, though strictly speaking, only *true* propositions are facts.)

Propositional attitudes include believing (I believe *that Pluto is not really a planet*), hoping (I hope *that this milk is still fresh*), wishing (I wish *that I were Superman*), and others. But of all the propositional attitudes, one has received quite a lot of attention from philosophers: belief (for a recent study, see Crimmins 1992). Why? First, there's reason to think that belief is the fundamental propositional attitude, in the sense that all of the others pre-suppose it. So, for example, if I hope that this milk is fresh, I must also believe (among other things) that this is milk. And if I wish that I were Superman, I must also have certain beliefs about Superman's qualities. A second reason to focus on belief is that it is a central component of knowledge, which is tradi-tionally defined as justified true belief. Given the fundamental philosophical importance of knowledge, it is not surprising that belief would come under special scrutiny. And third, belief plays an indispensable role in explaining behavior. What one (rationally) does is a direct function of what one believes.

Fodor, Dretske, and Searle, in spite of their disagreements, are all realists about belief and intentional states generally. A belief for the realist is a concrete mental particular, one with propositional content and an appropriate set of causal powers. (Realism is sometimes called the Representational Theory of Mind (RTM). A particularly strong version of RTM is endorsed by Fodor, who thinks that beliefs are literally internal sentences in a "language of thought," sentences that play a certain computational role in one's mental life.) Realism is challenged, in one way or another, by Davidson, Dennett, and Churchland, the authors of Chapters 17–19.

Davidson's chapter draws on elements of his philosophy of language, which can be a bit daunting. (Those interested in digging deeper should start with Evnine 1991 before taking on Davidson 1984.) Here Davidson is primarily concerned to demonstrate a connection between belief (or thought) and language. In particular, he argues that it is impossible to have beliefs unless one can interpret the language of another. One immediate and striking conse-quence of this thesis is that non-linguistic animals cannot have beliefs. (See also Chapter 25 for more skepticism about animal minds.) But why think the thesis is true? Davidson's main argument comes at the end of his chapter and may be reconstructed as follows: (1) A creature must be able to interpret the language of another – must "be a member of a speech community" – in order to have the concept of belief. (2) A creature cannot have beliefs without having the concept of belief. Therefore, (3) a creature must be able to interpret the language of another in order to have beliefs. The bulk of Davidson's chapter is spent setting the stage for premise (1), and it is here where his challenge to intentional realism emerges.

For Davidson, attributing a belief to others and understanding their linguistic utterances are inextricably bound together in the process of inter-pretation. When confronted with another person – call her Mary – all we can observe are the manifestations of her behavioral dispositions, where such manifestations include, importantly, Mary's utterances. To know what such utterances mean, we must know, at a minimum, what beliefs they are intended to express. Yet our primary behavioral data for attributing beliefs to Mary is what she says. We can break into this circle only by adopting the "Principle of Charity," only by assuming that Mary is rational and has by and large true beliefs. Given this assumption, we can appeal to what is true (by our own lights, at least) to attribute beliefs to Mary, and thereby to interpret her utterances. This is not to say, however, that belief-attributions are prior to and independent of how we assign meanings to utterances, for it is only by interpreting what Mary says that we can attribute *fine-grained* beliefs to her – the belief that, say, there is a cat in the bushes, not the belief that Dave's favorite pet is in the bushes, even though this latter proposition also is true. It is because of this feature of fine-grainedness, of "semantic opacity," that premise (1) must be true, that having the concept of belief requires being able to understand the interpretation of language (see also Heil 1992, Chapter 6).

What are we to say, however, when the Principle of Charity, combined with a person's behavioral dispositions, still leaves open a number of rival belief attributions? An interpretationist, it seems, must say that there is no fact of the matter about what Mary really believes in such cases, and in this sense interpretationism is opposed to realism. As a way of making this clearer, it may be useful at this point to introduce the notion of a *truthmaker* (see Armstrong forthcoming). The truthmaker for a sentence (alternatively, a proposition) is what makes the sentence true. So, for example, "There are mice" has many truthmakers: each of the world's mice; "I am hungry" has a particular state, my hunger, as a truthmaker, and so on. Now consider a realist and an interpretationist who both take the belief-ascription, "Mary believes that Roberts is late," to be true. What is the truthmaker for such a claim? According to the realist, the ascription is made true by a concrete particular in Mary's mind, a state (a) with the content that Roberts is late and (b) which plays the appropriate causal role in Mary's mental life. According to the interpretationist, by contrast, what makes the ascription true is Mary's behavioral dispositions plus an interpretive scheme imposed, in accordance with the Principle of Charity, on to this system of dispositions. In this way an interpretive scheme is literally part of what grounds the truth of the belief-ascription. The interpretationist, then, seems to be committed to a kind of intentional relativism, according to which a person never believes something *simpliciter*, but believes it, if at all, only relative to this or that interpretive scheme. In opposition to this, a realist will insist that interpretive schemes enter only into our knowledge of what Mary believes, not into the fact of believing itself.

In Chapter 18, Daniel Dennett also defends a view in the interpretationist tradition. For Dennett, ascribing beliefs and other intentional states to a system

– a human being, artifact, or what have you – is a matter of adopting a certain kind of predictive stance towards it, the *intentional stance*. To adopt the intentional stance, one assumes the system in question is rational and has beliefs and desires appropriate to its situation. If such a stance is successful in predicting the system's behavior in a wide and diverse range of circumstances, the system is ipso facto a believer. What it is to have beliefs and the like is to be a system whose behavior can be successfully predicted from the intentional stance. In this sense, Dennett rejects intentional realism, at least in its extreme forms: a belief ascription is made true merely by the patterns of behavior that make the intentional stance useful. Yet Dennett insists that he is a realist of sorts. The behavioral patterns in question are objectively there, independent of what anyone might think about them. And furthermore, Dennett grants that it is empirically likely there are in our heads the sorts of concrete representations that realists postulate. Yet Dennett claims that what makes these internal states beliefs is the role they play in making the intentional stance toward Mary successful. Whether, and it what sense, any of this makes Dennett a realist is a matter of continuing debate (see e.g. Ross *et al.* 2000).

While Davidson and Dennett, in their own ways, reject intentional realism, they at least grant that ascriptions of beliefs and other intentional states are true. But in Chapter 19, Paul Churchland argues that there is good empirical evidence to think that such ascriptions are just flat false. Belief and related intentional concepts are part of a vast theory we use for explaining and predicting human behavior, a theory Churchland and others have called folk psychology. And like any theory, folk psychology is open to empirical investigation and, perhaps, refutation. While fans of folk psychology tout the explanatory power of folk-psychological concepts, Churchland points to their explanatory failures. Concepts such as belief and desire, argues Churchland, have proved to be too crude in explaining complex mental phenomena such as mental illness, creative imagination, the psychological functions of sleep, and the ability to perform complex motor tasks, such as catching a fly ball. Furthermore, it has become increasingly unlikely that folk psychology will be able to integrate with the advancing sciences of the brain. In all likelihood, the concepts of belief and desire will eventually be eliminated and replaced by the more sophisticated, explanatorily powerful concepts of neuroscience (see also Churchland 1989).

Eliminativism has provoked a number of responses from defenders of folk psychology (e.g. Horgan and Woodward 1985 and Lycan forthcoming). One simple response is to say that eliminativism is at odds with the introspective knowledge we have of our own mental states, knowledge normally thought to be quite secure. (Such a line might also, by the way, be pressed against interpretationists. I know from the first-person perspective that there is a fact about what I believe that is not relative to any interpretive scheme.) The introspective strategy is pursued by, for example, John Searle. To eliminativists who say that beliefs and desires are merely theoretical entities postulated to explain behavior, Searle replies:

> we do not *postulate* beliefs and desires to account for anything. We simply experience conscious beliefs and desires. Think about real-life examples. It is a hot day and you are driving a pickup truck in the desert outside of Phoenix. No air conditioning. You can't remember when you were so thirsty, and you want a cold beer so bad you could scream. Now where is the "postulation" of a desire? Conscious desires are experienced. They are no more postulated than conscious pains (Searle 1992, p. 59).

One question this raises is whether cognitive states such as beliefs and desires are, like pains, consciously experienced. In Searle's example, is it literally the desire for a beer that you experience, or is it merely the qualitative states associated with thirst (e.g. the experience of a dry throat)? And second, an eliminativist such as Churchland will insist that even introspection is theory laden: facts about our own mental lives are not, as Searle would have it, available to us unmediated. Just as our judgments about the external world are colored by the concepts we bring to sensory experience, so our judgments about our own mental lives are colored by the concepts of folk psychology, a theory which may, according to Churchland, end up being false. In any case, the introspective response to eliminativism raises an important methodological question: can the mind be primarily studied from the first-person perspective, or should it, like other objects of scientific inquiry, be studied using only objective, third-person methods? This question will be particularly relevant in Part IV.

FURTHER READING

Armstrong, D.M. (forthcoming) *Truth and Truthmakers*.

Churchland, P.S. (1989) *Neurophilosophy: Toward a Unified Science of Mind–brain*, Cambridge: Mass.: MIT Press.

Crimmins, M. (1992) *Talk About Beliefs*, Cambridge, Mass.: MIT Press.

Cummins, R. (1989) *Meaning and Mental Representation*, Cambridge, Mass.: MIT Press.

Davidson, D. (1984) *Inquiries into Truth and Interpretation*, Oxford: Clarendon Press.

Dretske, F. (1988) *Explaining Behavior: Reasons in a World of Causes*, Cambridge, Mass.: MIT Press.

Evnine, S. (1991) *Donald Davidson*, Stanford: Stanford University Press.

Fodor, J. (1990) *A Theory of Content and Other Essays*, Cambridge, Mass.: MIT Press.

Haugeland, J. (1997) "What is Mind Design?," in J. Haugeland (ed.), *Mind Design II*, Cambridge, Mass.: MIT Press.

PART III: MIND AND REPRESENTATION

Heil, J. (1992) *The Nature of True Minds*, Cambridge: Cambridge University Press.

Horgan, T. and Woodward, J. (1985) "Folk Psychology is Here to Stay," *Philosophical Review* 94: 197–225.

Loewer, B. and Rey G. (eds) (1991) *Meaning in Mind: Fodor and His Critics*, Oxford: Blackwell.

Lycan, W. (forthcoming) "A Particularly Compelling Refutation of Eliminative Materialism," in D.M. Johnson (ed.), *Mind as Scientific Object: Between Brain and Culture*, Oxford: Oxford University Press.

Preston, J. and Bishop, M. (2002) *Views Into the Chinese Room: New Essays on Searle and Artificial Intelligence*, Oxford: Oxford University Press.

Ross, D., Brook, A., and Thompson, D. (eds) (2000) *Dennett's Philosophy: A Comprehensive Assessment*, Cambridge, Mass.: MIT Press.

Searle, J. (1984) *Minds, Brains, and Science*, Cambridge, Mass.: Harvard University Press.

—— (1992) *The Rediscovery of the Mind*, Cambridge, Mass.: MIT Press.

Stampe, D.W. (1977) "Toward a Causal Theory of Linguistic Representation," in P.A. French *et al.* (eds), *Midwest Studies in Philosophy, Vol. 2*, Minneapolis: University of Minnesota Press.

IIIA

INTENTIONALITY

14

Jerry A. Fodor, "Meaning and the World Order"

Introduction

I suppose that sooner or later the physicists will complete the catalogue they've been compiling of the ultimate and irreducible properties of things. When they do, the likes of *spin*, *charm*, and *charge* will perhaps appear upon their list. But *aboutness* surely won't; intentionality simply doesn't go that deep. It's hard to see, in face of this consideration, how one can be a Realist about intentionality without also being, to some extent or other, a Reductionist. If the semantic and the intentional are real properties of things, it must be in virtue of their identity with (or maybe of their supervenience on?) properties that are themselves *neither* intentional *nor* semantic. If aboutness is real, it must be really something else.

And, indeed, the deepest motivation for intentional irrealism derives not from such relatively technical worries about individualism and holism as we've been considering, but rather from a certain ontological intuition: that there is no place for intentional categories in a physicalistic view of the world; that the intentional can't be *naturalized*. It is time that we should face this issue. What is it, then, for a physical system to have intentional states?[1]

Let's, to begin with, try to get clear on just *where* the naturalization problem arises in the sort of account of propositional attitudes that I've been pushing. I've assumed that what most needs to be explained about the attitudes is that they have conditions of semantic evaluation; such facts as that beliefs have truth conditions, for example. Now, according to my story, you generate conditions for the semantic evaluation of an attitude by *fixing a context* for the tokenings of certain symbols; symbols which jointly

Jerry Fodor, "Meaning and the World Order," Chapter 4 of *Psychosemantics* (MIT Press, Cambridge, Mass., 1988), pp. 97–127, 163–5.

constitute a system of mental representations. (The reader will recall that RTM [the Representational Theory of Mind] is operative, and that RTM identifies token attitudes with relations between organisms and the token mental representations that they entertain.) So, then, what is it to fix a context for a system of mental representations?

Well, whatever else you have to do, you must at least specify an interpretation for items in the primitive nonlogical vocabulary of the language to which the symbols belong.[2] For example, you fix a context for tokenings of the (Mentalese) expression "this is water" by specifying – inter alia – that in the context in question the symbol "water" expresses the property H_2O, or the property XYZ, or whatever. Granting an interpretation of the primitive nonlogical vocabulary, the business of generating conditions of evaluation for derived formulas can proceed by means which, though certainly not unproblematic, are at least familiar; viz., by the construction of a truth definition. In short: Given RTM, the intentionality of the attitudes reduces to the content of mental representations. Given a truth definition, the content of mental representations is determined by the interpretation of their primitive nonlogical vocabulary. So it's the interpretation of the primitive nonlogical vocabulary of Mentalese that's at the bottom of the pile according to the present view. Correspondingly, we would have largely solved the naturalization problem for a propositional-attitude psychology if we were able to say, in nonintentional and nonsemantic idiom, what it is for a primitive symbol of Mentalese to have a certain interpretation in a certain context.

Alas, I don't know how to carry out this program. But I see no principled reason why it can't be carried out; I even imagine that we might make a little progress within the foreseeable future. In particular, I think it's plausible that the interpretation of (primitive, nonlogical; from now on I'll omit these qualifiers) Mentalese symbols is determined by certain of their causal relations. For example, what makes it the case that (the Mentalese symbol) "water" expresses the property H_2O is that tokens of that symbol stand in certain causal relations to water samples. Presumably if tokens of "water" have a different interpretation on Twin-Earth (or, equivalently, if Twin-Earth counts as a *different context* for tokens of "water"; or, equivalently, if tokens of "water" are type-distinct from tokens of "water2"; or, equivalently, if Mentalese2 counts as a different language from Mentalese), that is all because it's XYZ that bears to "water2" tokens the sort of causal relations that H_2O bears to tokens of "water."

So the causal story goes. I think it points a promising route to the naturalization of such semantics as RTM requires. At a minimum, I think that some of the standard objections to that sort of story can be met; that's what I propose to argue in the following.

Here, then, are the ground rules. I want a *naturalized* theory of meaning; a theory that articulates, in nonsemantic and nonintentional terms, sufficient conditions for one bit of the world to *be about* (to express, represent, or be true of) another bit. I don't care – not just now at least – whether this theory holds for *all* symbols or for all things that represent. Maybe the occurrence of smoke expresses the proximity of fire; maybe the number of tree rings expresses the age of the tree; maybe the English predicate "is red" expresses the property of being red; maybe the thermostat represents the temperature of the ambient air (see note 1). It's OK with me if any or all of this is so; but I'm not particularly anxious that the theory that naturalizes the semantic properties of mental representations should work for smoke, tree rings, or English words. On the contrary, I'm prepared that it should turn out that smoke and tree rings represent only relative to our interests in predicting fires and ascertaining the ages of trees, that thermostats represent only relative to our interest in keeping the room warm, and that English words represent only relative to our intention to use them to communicate our thoughts. I'm prepared, that is, that only mental states (hence, according to RTM, only mental representations) should turn out to have semantic properties *in the first instance*; hence, that a naturalized semantics should apply, strictu dictu, to mental representations only.

But it had better apply to them.

The Crude Causal Theory

Let's start with the most rudimentary sort of example: the case where a predicative expression ("horse," as it might be) is said of, or thought of, an object of predication (a horse, as it might be). Let the Crude Causal Theory of Content be the following: In such cases the symbol tokenings denote their causes, and the symbol types express the property whose instantiations reliably cause their tokenings. So, in the paradigm case, my utterance of "horse" says *of* a horse that it *is* one.

"Reliable causation" requires that the causal dependence of the tokening of the symbol upon the instancing of the corresponding property be counterfactual supporting: either instances of the property actually do cause tokenings of the symbol, or instances of the property *would* cause tokenings of the symbol *were they to occur*, or both. I suppose that it is necessary and sufficient for such reliable causation that there be a nomological – lawful – relation between certain (higher-order) properties of events; in the present case, between the property of being an instance of the property *horse* and the property of being a tokening of the symbol "horse." The intuition that underlies the Crude Causal Theory is that the semantic interpretations of mental symbols are determined by, and only by, such nomological relations.

273

You can see straight off why the Crude Causal Theory has a much better chance of working for mental representations than it does for (e.g.) English words. CCT wants the tokening of a symbol to depend upon the instantiation of the property it expresses. But whether an English word gets tokened (e.g., uttered) depends not just on what it means but also upon the motivations, linguistic competences, and communicative intentions of English speakers. Giving voice to an utterance, unlike entertaining a thought, is typically a voluntary act.

So, for example, suppose Smith notices that Mary's hair is on fire – and hence, perforce, thinks: *Mary's hair is on fire,* thereby tokening the Mentalese expression whose truth condition is that Mary's hair is on fire. Whether he then chooses to *say* "Mary's hair is on fire," thereby tokening the English expression whose truth condition is that Mary's hair is on fire, depends on whether he thinks that Mary (or some other suitably situated auditor) would be interested to know that Mary's hair is on fire. Paul Grice has made us all aware how complex these sorts of pragmatic determinants of speech acts can become.

In short, the causal dependence of tokenings of mental representations upon semantically relevant situations in the world is typically more reliable than the causal dependence of tokenings of English expressions upon semantically relevant situations in the world. That's because the chains that connect tokenings of mental representations to their semantically relevant causes are typically *shorter than* (indeed, are typically links in) the chains that connect tokenings of English sentences to their semantically relevant causes. This is the principal reason why it is mental representations, and not the formulas of any natural language, that are the natural candidates for being the primitive bearers of semantic properties. If, however, mental representations are the bearers of semantic properties in the first instance, then it is the semantic properties of mental representations that are, in the first instance, apt for naturalization. CCT and RTM are made for one another.

Which is not, of course, to say that the Crude Causal Theory will work for mental representations; only that it's unlikely to work for anything else. CCT has – I admit it – lots of problems. I want to argue, however, that some of what look to be its worst problems have natural and appealing solutions. This makes me hopeful that maybe, someday, some refinement of the Crude Causal Theory might actually be made to work. Maybe.

The Crude Causal Theory says, in effect, that a symbol expresses a property if it's nomologically necessary that *all* and *only* instances of the property cause tokenings of the symbol. There are problems with the "all" part (since not all horses actually do cause "horse" tokenings) and there are problems with the "only" part (cows sometimes cause "horse" tokenings; e.g., when they are mistaken for horses). The main business of this chapter will be the consideration of these problems; in reverse order.

So here is what I am going to do. I shall start by assuming – contrary to fact, of course – that *all* horses cause "horses," and I'll show you why a causal theory doesn't need to require that *only* horses do consonant with "horse" meaning HORSE. Having thus fixed the "only" clause, I'll then go back and fix the "all" clause. We will then have a Slightly Less Crude Causal Theory; one that requires neither that all horses cause "horses" nor that only horses do, but that nevertheless claims that it's in virtue of the causal connections between horses and "horses" that "horse" means what it does. This Slightly Less Crude Causal Theory I shall then commend to your kind consideration.

Error in the Crude Causal Theory

An embarrassment: It seems that, according to CCT, there can be no such thing as *misrepresentation*. Suppose, for example, that tokenings of the symbol "A" are nomologically dependent upon instantiations of the property A; viz., upon A's. Then, according to the theory, the tokens of the symbol denote A's (since tokens denote their causes) and they represent them *as* A's (since symbols express the property whose instantiations cause them to be tokened). But symbol tokenings that represent A's as A's are ipso facto veridical. So it seems that the condition for an "A"-token meaning A is identical to the condition for such a token being true. How, then, do you get *un*veridical "A" tokens into the causal picture?

This may not look awfully worrying so far, since it invites the following obvious reply: "*Sometimes* 'A' tokens are caused by A's (and thus represent their causes as A's, and are thus veridical); but other times 'A' tokens are caused by B's where, as we may suppose, whatever is B is *not* A. Well, since 'A' tokens express the property of being A, 'A' tokens that are caused by B's represent B's as A's and are ipso facto not veridical. 'A' tokens that are caused by B's are ipso facto misrepresentations of their causes. *That's* how misrepresentation gets into the causal picture."

But though that answer sounds all right, CCT can't make it stick. Since there are B-caused tokenings of "A," it follows that the causal dependence of "A"s upon A's is imperfect; A's are sufficient for the causation of "A"s, *but so too are B's*. If, however, symbols express the properties whose instantiations reliably cause them, it looks as though what "A" must express is not the property of *being A* (or the property of *being B*) but rather the *disjunctive property of being (A v B)*. But if "A" expresses the property *(A v B)*, then B-caused "A" tokenings are veridical after all. They're not misrepresentations since, of course, B's *are A v B*. But if B-caused "A" tokenings are true of their causes, then we don't yet have a theory of misrepresentation.

That's what I'll call the "disjunction problem." We can put it that a viable causal theory of content has to acknowledge *two* kinds of cases where there are disjoint causally sufficient conditions for the tokenings of a symbol: the case where the content of the symbol is disjunctive ("A" expresses the property of *being (A v B)*) and the case where the content of the symbol is *not* disjunctive and some of the tokenings are false ("A" expresses the property of *being A*, and B-caused "A" tokenings misrepresent). The present problem with the Crude Causal Theory is that it's unable to distinguish between these cases; it always assigns disjunctive content to symbols whose causally sufficient conditions are themselves disjoint.

The disjunction problem is extremely robust; so far as I know, it arises in one or another guise for every causal theory of content that has thus far been proposed. Accordingly, there are various ideas for circumventing it in the literature in which such theories are espoused. None of these proposals has been very satisfactory, however; and the rumor has gotten around that the problem that causal theories have with misrepresentation is perhaps intrinsic and ineliminable (see, for example, Matthews, 1984). I'm about to try and scotch that rumor. First, however, let's look at the remedies currently on offer.

Dretske's solution

Fred Dretske's important book *Knowledge and the Flow of Information* was largely responsible for the present widespread enthusiasm for causal theories of content, so his treatment of misrepresentation bears careful consideration.[3] For Dretske, the cardinal semantic relation is the one that holds between two events when one of them (the tokening of a symbol, as it might be) *transmits information about* the other. Here is how he proposes to construe misrepresentation in that theoretical context:

> In the learning situation special care is taken to see that incoming signals have an intensity, a strength, sufficient unto delivering the required piece of information *to* the learning subject. . . . Such precautions are taken in the learning situation . . . in order to ensure that an internal structure is developed with . . . the information that *s* is *F*. . . . But once we have meaning, once the subject has articulated a structure that is selectively sensitive to information about the *F*-ness of things, instances of this structure, tokens of this type, can be triggered by signals that *lack* the appropriate piece of information. . . . We [thus] have a case of misrepresentation – a token of a structure with a false content. We have, in a word, meaning without truth (Dretske, 1981, pp. 194–195; emphases Dretske's).

All you need to know to understand this well enough for present purposes is that Dretske's notion of information is fundamentally that of counterfactual-supporting correlation: events of type "A" carry information about events of type A to the extent that the latter sort of events are reliably causally responsible for events of the former sort. (There is, in fact, rather more than this to Dretske's official account of information; but none of the rest is essential to his treatment of the problem of false content.)

So information reduces to a certain sort of correlation. And the problem is this: Correlations can be better or worse – more or less reliable – but there is no sense to the notion of a *mis*correlation, so there appears to be nothing for Dretske to make a theory of misinformation out of. His solution is to enforce a strict distinction between what happens in the learning period and what happens thereafter. The correlation that the learning period establishes determines what "A" events represent, and it's the teacher's function to ensure that this correlation reliably connects "A" tokens to A's. It may be, however, that *after* the learning period "A" tokens are brought about by something *other than* A's (by B's, for example); if so, then these are, as I'll sometimes say, "wild" tokenings, and their content is false.

I think this move is ingenious but hopeless. Just for starters, the distinction between what happens in the learning period and what happens thereafter surely isn't principled; there is no time after which one's use of a symbol stops being merely shaped and starts to be, as it were, in earnest. (Perhaps idealization will bear some of the burden here, but it's hard to believe that it could yield a notion of *learning period* sufficiently rigorous to underwrite the distinction between truth and falsity; which is, after all, exactly what's at issue.) Moreover, if Dretske insists upon the learning-period gambit, he thereby limits the applicability of his notion of misrepresentation to *learned* symbols. This is bad for me because it leaves no way for innate information to be false; and it's bad for Dretske because it implies a dichotomy between *natural* representation (smoke and fire; rings in the tree and the age of the tree) and the intentionality of mental states. Dretske is explicit that he wants a naturalized semantics to apply in the same way to such cases.

But the real problem about Dretske's gambit is internal. Consider a trainee who comes to produce "A" tokens in A circumstances during the learning period. And suppose that the teacher does his job and ensures that *only* A's elicit "A" tokenings in the course of training. Well, time passes, a whistle blows (or whatever), and the learning period comes to an end. At some time later still, the erstwhile trainee encounters an instance of B and produces an "A" in causal consequence thereof. The idea is, of course, that this B-elicited tokening of "A" is ipso facto wild and, since it happened after the training ended, it has the (false) content *that A*.

But this won't work; it ignores counterfactuals that are clearly relevant to determining *which* symbol-to-world correlation the training has brought about. Imagine, in particular, what *would have* happened if an instance of B *had* occurred during the training period. Presumably what would have happened is this: it would have caused a tokening of "A." After all, B's are supposed to be sufficient to cause "A" tokenings *after* training; that's the very supposition upon which Dretske's treatment of wild "A" tokenings rests. So we can also assume – indeed, we can stipulate – that if a B had occurred *during* training, it too would have brought about an "A." But that means, of course, that if you take account of the relevant counterfactuals, then the correlation that training established is (not between instances of A and tokenings of "A" but) between instances of *A v B* and tokenings of "A." [Equivalently, what the training established was (not a nomological dependence of "A"s on A's but) a nomological dependence of A's on *(A v B)*s.] So we have the old problem back again. If "A"s are correlated with *(A v B)*s, then the content of a tokening of "A" is *that A v B.* So a B-caused "A" tokening isn't false. So we're still in want of a way out of the disjunction problem.

The teleological solution

A suggestion that crops up in several recent papers about causation and content (see Stampe, 1977; and also a paper of mine, Fodor, 1990) goes like this:

We suppose that there's a causal path from A's to "A"s and a causal path from B's to "A"s, and our problem is to find some difference between B-caused "A"s and A-caused "A"s in virtue of which the former but not the latter misrepresent. Well, perhaps the two paths differ in their *counterfactual* properties. In particular, though A's and B's both cause "A"s as a matter of fact, perhaps we can assume that only A's *would* cause "A"s in – as one says – "optimal circumstances." We could then hold that a *symbol expresses its "optimal" property*; viz., the property that would causally control its tokening in optimal circumstances. Correspondingly, when the tokening of a symbol is causally controlled by properties other than its optimal property, the tokens that eventuate are ipso facto wild.

Now, I'm supposing that this story about "optimal circumstances" is proposed as part of a naturalized semantics for mental representations. In which case it is, of course, essential that it be possible to say what the optimal circumstances for tokening a mental representation are *in terms that are not themselves either semantical or intentional.* (It wouldn't do, for example, to identify the optimal circumstances for tokening a symbol as those in which the tokens are *true*; that would be to assume precisely the sort of semantical notions that the theory is supposed to naturalize.) Well, the suggestion – to put it in a nutshell – is that appeals to *optimality* should be buttressed by appeals to *teleology*: optimal circumstances are the ones in which the mechanisms that mediate symbol tokenings are functioning "as they are supposed to." In the case of mental representations, these would be paradigmatically circumstances where *the mechanisms of belief fixation* are functioning as they are supposed to.

The reference to "mechanisms of belief fixation" perhaps makes this look circular, but it's not. At least not so far. Remember that we're assuming a functional theory of *believing* (though not, of course, a functional theory of *believing that P*; see chapter 3 [of Fodor, 1998]). On this assumption, having a belief is just being in a state with a certain causal role, so – in principle at least – we can pick out the belief states of an organism without resort to semantical or intentional vocabulary. But then it follows that we can pick out the organism's mechanisms of belief *fixation* without recourse to semantical or intentional vocabulary: the mechanisms of belief fixation are, of course, the ones whose operations eventuate in the organism's having beliefs.

So, then: The teleology of the cognitive mechanisms determines the optimal conditions for belief fixation, and the optimal conditions for belief fixation determine the content of beliefs. So the story goes.

I'm not sure that this teleology/optimality account is false, but I do find it thoroughly unsatisfying. The story has it that only A's cause "A"s in optimal circumstances; hence, that when the mechanisms of belief fixation are operating properly the beliefs they fix are true. But how do we know – or rather, why should we believe – that the mechanisms of belief fixation *are* designed always to deliver truths? Suppose some of these mechanisms are designed to *repress* truths; truths, for example, the acknowledgment of which would be unbearable.[4] Clearly we can't define "optimal circumstances" in terms of the teleology of *those* mechanisms; not if we're to define truth *conditions* as the ones that are satisfied when a symbol is caused in optimal circumstances. But there's no obvious way to weed mechanisms of repression out of the definition of optimality unless we can independently identify them *as* mechanisms of repression; viz., as mechanisms tending to the fixation of beliefs that are false.

To put this objection in slightly other words: The teleology story perhaps strikes one as plausible in that it understands one normative notion – truth – in terms of another normative notion – optimality. But this appearance of fit is spurious; there is no guarantee that the kind of optimality that teleology reconstructs has much to do with the kind of optimality that the explication of "truth" requires. When mechanisms of repression are working "optimally" – when they're working "as they're supposed to" – what they deliver are likely to be *falsehoods*.

Or again: There's no obvious reason why conditions that are optimal for the tokening of one sort of mental symbol need be optimal for the tokening of other sorts. Perhaps the optimal conditions for fixing beliefs about very large objects (you do best from the middle distance) are different from the optimal conditions for fixing beliefs about very small ones (you do best from quite close up); perhaps the conditions that are optimal for fixing beliefs about sounds (you do best with your eyes closed) are different from the optimal conditions for fixing beliefs about sights (you do best with your eyes open). But this raises the possibility that if we're to say which conditions are optimal for the fixation of a belief, we'll have to know what the content of the belief is – what it's a belief *about*. Our explication of content would then require a notion of optimality whose explication in turn requires a notion of content, and the resulting pile would clearly be unstable.

As I say, I'm uncertain whether these sorts of objections to the optimality/ teleology story can be met; but I propose to delay having to meet them as long as I can. In particular, I think maybe we can get a theory of error without relying on notions of optimality or teleology; and if we can, we should. All else being equal, the less Pop-Darwinism the better, surely.

How to solve the disjunction problem

We need a way to break the symmetry between A-caused "A" tokenings (which are, by hypothesis, true) and B-caused "A" tokenings (which are, by hypothesis, false). In particular, we need a difference between A-caused "A" tokenings and B-caused "A" tokenings that can be expressed in terms of nonintentional and nonsemantic properties of causal relations; for nonintentional and nonsemantic properties of causal relations are all that the Crude Causal Theory of Content has to play with. My suggestion is that the teleological story was on the right track in appealing to the *counterfactual* properties of the causal relations between A's and "A"s, on the one hand, and B's and "A"s, on the other. Only the teleological story got hold of the wrong counterfactual properties.

It's an old observation – as old as Plato, I suppose – that falsehoods are *ontologically dependent* on truths in a way that truths are not ontologically dependent on falsehoods. The mechanisms that deliver falsehoods are somehow *parasitic on* the ones that deliver truths. In consequence, you can only have false beliefs about what you can have true beliefs about (whereas you can have, true beliefs about anything that you can have beliefs about at all). So the intuition goes, and I think that there is something to it. What's more, I think that it points the way out of the disjunction problem.

Consider the following situation: I see a cow which, stupidly, I misidentify. I take it, say, to be a horse. So taking it causes me to effect the tokening of a symbol; viz., I say "horse." Here we have all the ingredients of the disjunction problem (set up, as it happens, for a token of English rather than a token of Mentalese; but none of the following turns on that). So, on the one hand, we want it to be that my utterance of "horse" means *horse* in virtue of the causal relation between (some) "horse" tokenings and horses; and, on the other hand, we *don't* want it to be that my utterance of "horse" means *cow* in virtue of the causal relation between (some) "horse" tokenings and cows. But if the causal relations are the same, and if causation makes representation, how can the semantic connections not be the same too? What we want is the situation in Figure 14.1 (where the dashed line stands for the representation relation and the other lines stand for causal relations); but how are we to get what we want?

Answer: As previously remarked, the causal relations aren't identical in their counterfactual properties. In particular, misidentifying a cow as a horse wouldn't have led me to say "horse" *except that there was independently a semantic relation between "horse" tokenings and horses*. But for the fact that the word "horse" expresses the property of *being a horse* (i.e., but for the fact that one calls *horses* "horses") it would not have been *that* word that taking a cow to be a horse would have caused me to utter. Whereas, by contrast, since "horse" does mean *horse,* the fact that horses cause me to say "horse" does not depend upon there being a semantic – or, indeed, any – connection between "horse" tokenings and cows.

From a semantic point of view, mistakes have to be *accidents*: if cows aren't in the extension of "horse," then cows being called horses can't be *required* for "horse" to mean what it does. By contrast, however, if "horse" didn't mean what it does, being mistaken for a horse wouldn't ever get a cow called "horse." Put the two together and we have it that the possibility of saying "that's a horse" falsely presupposes the existence of a *semantic setup* for saying it truly, but not vice versa.[5] Put it in terms of CCT, and we have it that the fact that cows cause one to say "horse" depends on the fact that horses do; but the fact that horses cause one to say "horse" does *not* depend on the fact that cows do.

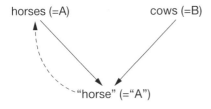

Figure 14.1

JERRY A. FODOR

So, the causal connection between cows and "horse" tokenings is, as I shall say, *asymmetrically dependent* upon the causal connection between horses and "horse" tokenings. So now we have a necessary condition for a B-caused "A" token to be wild: B-caused "A" tokenings are wild only if they are asymmetrically dependent upon non-B-caused "A" tokenings.[6]

What we've got so far is, in effect, a theory that understands wildness in terms of an empirical dependence among causal relations. Since all the notions employed are naturalistic, as per prior specifications, we could stop here. Alternatively, we can press the analysis further by reconstructing the notion of an empirical dependence in the familiar way, viz., by reference to subjunctives: If B-caused "A" tokenings are wild – if they falsely represent B's as A's – then there *would be* a causal route from A's to "A" even if there *were no* causal route from B's to "A"s; but there would be no causal route from B's to "A"s if there were no causal route from A's to "A"s.

Suppose that a counterfactual is true in a world iff its consequent is true in "nearby" possible worlds in which its antecedent is true. (One possible world is "near" another if, by and large, the laws that hold in the first also hold in the second. See Lewis, 1973.) So "if I were smart I would be rich" is true here because I'm rich in the nearby possible worlds in which I'm smart. Then we can spell out the proposed condition on wild tokens as follows. In a world where B-caused "A" tokens are wild (and express the property *A*), the nomic relations among properties have to be such that

1. A's cause "A"s.
2. "A" tokens are *not* caused by B's in nearby worlds in which A's *don't* cause "A"s.
3. A's cause "A"s in nearby worlds in which B's don't cause "A"s.

Caveat: These conditions are supposed to apply with – as it were – synchronic force. For imagine a case where someone learns "horse" entirely from noninstances. For example, from ostensions of cows, all of which happen to look a lot like horses. No doubt, once "horse" has been mastered, wild (cow-caused) "horse" tokens would depend upon tame (horse-caused) "horse" tokenings, exactly as required. But the dependence isn't, in this case, asymmetric, since the speaker's current disposition to apply "horse" to horses is a historical consequence of his previous disposition to apply it to cows. *Had he not previously applied "horse" to cows, he would not now apply "horse" to horses.*[7] So it looks like we've got error *without* asymmetric dependence, contrary to the condition previously endorsed. But this is OK, since, as just remarked, the sort of asymmetrical dependence that's necessary for wildness is *synchronic*; and in the case imagined, my present disposition to apply "horse" to horses does *not* depend on any corresponding *current* disposition to apply it to cows. We get the asymmetric dependence back when we respect the tenses, to put it in a nutshell.

As things stand thus far, I'm assuming only that the asymmetric dependence of B-caused "A" tokenings on A-caused "A" tokenings is *necessary* for B-caused "A" tokens to be wild. I emphasize this point because, on the one hand, it's more obvious that asymmetric dependence is necessary for wildness than that it's sufficient; and, on the other, mere necessity will do for the purpose at hand.[8]

The purpose at hand, remember, is solving the disjunction problem; and *you don't get the asymmetric dependence of B-caused "A" tokenings on A-caused "A" tokenings in the case where "A" means A v B.* Suppose the form of words "blue or green" means *blue or green*; then the fact that you use "blue or green" (rather than "blue") of a blue thing depends on the fact that you use it of green things; and the fact that you use "blue or green" (rather than "green") of a green thing depends on the fact that you use it of blue things. In short, in the case of disjunctive predicates, what you get is *symmetrical* dependence. Asymmetric dependence thus does what it's supposed to do if it's necessary for wildness; viz., it distinguishes wildness from disjunction.

I'm inclined, however, to think that asymmetric dependence is both necessary *and* sufficient for wildness. I don't think there could be, as it were, *adventitious* asymmetric dependence: worlds in which "A" means *B v C*, but it *just happens* that there's a law that C's don't cause "A"s unless B's do (and no law that B's don't cause "A"s unless C's do).

At a minimum, to suppose that there could be adventitious asymmetric dependence begs the question against causal theories of content. A causal theorist has to rule out this possibility *whatever* he says about error. For consider: according to the causal theory, a symbol expresses a property only if the instantiation of the property is nomologically sufficient for the tokening of the symbol. In particular, if "A" expresses the property *B v C*, then the instantiation of *B v C* has to be nomologically sufficient for the tokening of "A." But C's *do* instantiate the property *B v C*. So it can't be that "A" means *B v C* in a world where C's don't cause "A"s. A causal theorist can acknowledge only one kind of world in which X's don't cause "X"s; viz., the kind of world in which "X" doesn't mean X.[9]

Time to sum up

We began with the Very Crude idea that "A" means A iff all and only A's cause "A"s. Neither the all part nor the only part being defensible as stated, we decided to start by whittling away at the latter. This clause can now be replaced as follows: "A" means A iff all A's cause "A"s and "A" tokenings that are caused by non-A's are wild.

Wildness then gets defined by reference to asymmetric dependence: B-caused "A" tokenings are wild only if B-caused "A" tokenings are *asymmetrically* dependent on the causation of "A" tokenings by non-B's.

Correspondingly, B-caused "A" tokenings express the (disjunctive) property *A v B* only if B-caused "A" tokenings are *symmetrically* dependent on A-caused "A" tokenings.

And just to round things off: Ambiguity – viz., the case where "A" means A *and* "A" means B – requires symmetrical independence; A's cause "A"s in nearby worlds where B's don't, and B's cause "A"s in nearby worlds where "A"s don't.

A brief aside before we turn to other business. The treatment of error I've proposed is, in a certain sense, purely formal. It invokes a dependence among relations, and it is *compatible* with assuming that the relations among which this dependence holds are causal (that's why it's a help to CCT). But strictly speaking, it doesn't *require* that assumption. On the contrary, it looks like *any* theory of error will have to provide for the asymmetric dependence of false tokenings upon true ones. To that extent, the story I've been telling may be of use to you even if you don't care for causal theories of content and even if you're out of sympathy with the naturalization program. (I'm indebted for this point to Peter Slezak.)

So far, so good; but at best this far is only part way. The Crude Causal Theory (Pocket Version) says that "A"s express the property *A* iff *all A*'s and *only A*'s reliably cause "A"s. And, as I remarked earlier on, there are troubles with both clauses: it's not true that only horses cause "horse" tokenings (sometimes cows do); and it's not true that all horses cause "horse" tokenings (many horses live and die quite undenoted). Well, it may be that the problems about the "only" clause are merely technical and that fancy footwork along the lines just reviewed will save it: instead of saying "only A's cause 'A's" we can say "only A's are such that 'A's depend upon them asymmetrically." But the problems about the "all" clause are, in my view, very deep. It's here that the plausibility of a serious causal theory of content will be tested. And here I can offer no more than a sketch.

Toward a Slightly Less Crude Causal Theory of Content

The idea was that my Mentalese symbol "horse" expresses the property of being a horse only if *all* instantiations of the property cause the symbol to be tokened in my belief box. But that's preposterous on the face of it. What about Ancient Athenian horses? What about horses on Alpha Centauri? What about fortieth-century horses? What about horses in Peking (where,

unlike many horses, I have never been)? I am prepared to assume that "A"s
do express *A* if all A's cause "A"s; for if that's not true, then the causal
covariance approach to content is playing in entirely the wrong ball park.
But even if it is true, it's not much comfort, since not all A's do cause "A"s,
as previously noted. What we need is a *plausible* sufficient condition for
"A" expressing *A*; a condition such that it's plausible that, in at least some
cases, "A"s express *A because that condition is satisfied*.

One is, perhaps, inclined to put one's faith in counterfactuals; Pekingese
(Antique Greek; Alpha Centaurian; Post-Modern ... etc.) horses *would
cause (/would have caused)* corresponding "Horse" tokenings if .... And
here's the rub, because we don't know which counterfactuals to appeal to.
The viability of the Causal Theory depends on its being able to specify
(in naturalistic vocabulary, hence in nonsemantic and nonintentional
vocabulary) circumstances such that (a) in those circumstances, "horse"s
covary with horses; i.e., instantiations of *horse* would cause "horse" to be
tokened in my belief box (i.e., would cause me to believe *Here's a horse!*)
were the circumstances to obtain; and (b) "horse" expresses the property
horse (in my ideolect of Mentalese) in virtue of the truth of (a). Just which
circumstances are those, pray?

This is, as I say, a very hard problem. And there's worse; horses aren't
the half of it. Suppose that there *are* circumstances under which horse
instantiations are, as it were, guaranteed to stuff tokens of the (Mentalese)
expression "horse" down one's throat (more precisely, to stuff them into
one's belief box). What about expressions like "proton" or "is a segment
of curved space–time"? If the Causal Theory is going to work at all, it's got
to work for the so-called "theoretical vocabulary" too. But if protons qua
protons affect the content of one's belief box, they must do so via a complicated chain of intermediate causes, and some of the links of this chain must
be inferences that one draws from the physical theories that one believes.
And of course, neither "inference" and "belief" – which are intentional
notions – nor "theory" – which is a semantical notion – are at the disposal
of a naturalistic treatment of meaning.

Still, it's an ill wind and all that. If reflection on the semantics of soi-
disant theoretical terms makes the prospects for a causal theory of content
look glum, reflection on the semantics of soi-disant observation terms
makes them look appreciably better.[10] To wit:

The "psychophysical" basis

There *are* circumstances in which beliefs about observables do seem to force
themselves upon one in something like the way that the Crude Causal
Theory requires. For example: Paint the wall red, turn the lights up, point

your face toward the wall, and open your eyes. The thought "red there" will occur to you; just try it and see if it doesn't. To put it another way (to put it in a way that assumes RTM): If (enough of the) wall is (bright enough) red, and if you're close (enough) to the wall, and if your eyes are pointed toward the wall and your visual system is functioning, then the Mentalese equivalent of "red there" will get stuffed into your belief box *willy-nilly.*

It goes without saying that not *every* instantiation of *red* affects the contents of your belief box. Think of all the reds in China. But what we've got is just as good for the purposes at hand: there are circumstances such that red instantiations control "red" tokenings whenever those circumstances obtain; and it's plausible that "red" expresses the property *red* in virtue of the fact that red instantiations cause "red" tokenings in those circumstances; *and the circumstances are nonsemantically, nonteleologically, and nonintentionally specifiable.*

In fact, they're *psychophysically* specifiable. Psychophysics is precisely in the business of telling us how much of the wall has to be painted red (more strictly speaking, what angle the retinal image of the red part of the wall has to subtend), and how red it has to be painted, and how close to the wall one has to be, and how bright the lights have to be, and so forth ... such that if it's that much red, and that bright, and you're that close ... then you'll think "red" if your eyes are pointed toward the wall and your visual system is intact. To a close first approximation (caveats to follow), psychophysics is the science that tells us how the content of an organism's belief box varies with the values of certain physical parameters in its local environment. And it does so in nonintentional, nonsemantical vocabulary: in the vocabulary of wavelengths, candlepowers, retinal·irradiations, and the like.

Of course, not all the organism's concepts are under the sort of local causal control that psychophysics talks about; for example, the theoretical concept PROTON patently isn't; and we'll see later why middle-sized-object concepts like HORSE aren't either. (Equivalently, not all properties are such that their instances exert the relevant sort of local control on the contents of the belief box; for example, the property of *being a proton* doesn't, and neither does the property of *being a horse*). Still, psychophysics does what it does, and ingratitude is a vice. For the concepts and properties that it applies to, psychophysics is just what the causal theory ordered. The Crude Causal Theory, together with psychophysics, provides a plausible sufficient condition for certain symbols to express certain properties: viz., that tokenings of those symbols are connected to instantiations of the properties they express *by psychophysical law.*

This isn't everything, but it isn't nothing either. You can imagine a whole mental life constituted by beliefs about observables – equivalently, given

RTM, a system of mental representations whose nonlogical vocabulary consists exhaustively of observation terms. Perhaps, indeed, the mental life of some animals is rather like this. For such a mind, the Crude Causal Theory, as psychophysically emended, would approximate a complete solution to the naturalization problem. This ought to bother you if your view is that there are principled – metaphysical – reasons why there can't be plausible, naturalistic, sufficient conditions for intentionality.

A couple of caveats: It doesn't, to begin with, matter to this line of thought that the observational theory distinction isn't epistemologically or ontologically principled; for, in fact, I'm not wanting to do any epistemological or ontological work with it. All that matters is that there are concepts (Mentalese terms) whose tokenings are determined by psychophysical law; and that these concepts are plausibly viewed as expressing the properties upon which their tokening is thus lawfully contingent; and that the psychophysical conditions for the tokenings of these concepts can be expressed in nonintentional and nonsemantical vocabulary.

It also doesn't matter that the tokenings in question be, strictly speaking, "in the belief box"; i.e., it's not required that we view psychophysics as enunciating sufficient conditions for the fixation of *belief*. It will do, for our purposes, if psychophysics enunciates sufficient conditions for the fixation of *appearances*.

The point is that belief fixation is a *conservative* process. You may stare at what looks to be a paradigm case of red wall, and something you know – some part of the cognitive background – may nevertheless convince you that the wall isn't red after all (where "after all" means quite literally "appearances to the contrary notwithstanding"). Belief fixation is about what happens *on balance*. Psychophysics can't do anything about this; it can't guarantee that you'll *believe* "red there," only that "red there" will occur to you.[11] But a guaranteed correlation between instances of red and tokenings of "red there" in the occurs-to-me box will do perfectly nicely for the purposes of semantic naturalization; all semantics wants is *some* sort of nomologically sufficient conditions for instances of *red* to cause psychologically active tokenings of "red." On this view, the theory of belief fixation strictly so called belongs not to semanticists but to cognitive psychologists, among whose goals it is to say what determines which of the things that occur to you you actually come to believe (how information flows from the occurs-to-me box to the belief box, if you like that way of putting it).

Well, where do you go from here? The psychophysical cases are close to ideal from the point of view of a causal theory; they're the ones for which it appears most clearly possible to enumerate the conditions in which (reliable, causal) correlation makes content. So a rational research strategy would be to try to work outward from these cases – somehow to extend an analogous treatment to apparently less tractable examples such as HORSE or PROTON. There's a variety of proposals around that are plausibly viewed as variants of this strategy; the idea that the semantics of observation terms is somehow at the core of the theory of meaning is, after all, pretty traditional among philosophers.

Reduction

For example, it would be extremely convenient if one could talk oneself into a reductionist account of the relation between observation terms and the rest of the nonlogical vocabulary of Mentalese: perhaps something to the effect that any Mentalese formula that can express an intentional content at all is equivalent to some Mentalese formula all of whose nonlogical vocabulary is observational. It would be convenient to believe this because if it were true, the naturalization problem would be largely solved. Psychophysics would be all the theory of mind/world interaction that the semantics of Mentalese requires.

This sort of solution has, of course, a long and respectable history in the tradition of classical Empiricism. In effect, you reduce all concepts to sensory concepts, which are in turn assumed to be connected to their instances by some such "natural" (viz., putatively nonintentional and nonsemantic) relation as resemblance or causation. This is an appealing idea, one which effectively expresses the intuition that the semantics of observation terms is unproblematic in ways that the semantics of the theoretical vocabulary is not.

But of course it won't do. PROTON and HORSE aren't the concepts of a set of actual or possible experiences. (Nor, mutatis mutandis, are the concepts WATER and WATER2; if they were, they'd be the *same* concept.)[12] Or, to put the same point in terms that are congenial to the causal theory: We need a story about how PROTON connects causally with instantiations of the property of *being a proton*. And our trouble is that *being a proton* is not a property in the domain of psychophysical law.

Psychophysics gives us a naturalization of a certain set of concepts; the reductionist strategy was to show that all other concepts are logical constructions out of these. But there's another alternative to consider. Perhaps we've underestimated the number of concepts that can be treated as psychophysical. Perhaps that treatment can be extended, if not to PROTON, then at least to an indefinite variety of concepts that subtend "middle-sized" objects. Here is how it might go.

Psychophysical imperialism

Psychophysics purports to specify what one might call an "optimal" point of view with respect to red things; viz., a viewpoint with the peculiar property that any intact observer who occupies it *must* – nomologically must; must in point of psychophysical law – have "red there" occur to him. Well then, why can't a suitably extended psychophysics do as much for HORSE? Of course there are instantiations of *horse* (horses in Peking and so forth) that don't affect the contents of one's belief box; arguably, however, that's only because one doesn't occupy a psychophysically optimal viewpoint with respect to those instantiations. For, plant a horse right there in the foreground, turn the lights up, point the observer horsewards, *rub his nose in horse*, to put the proposal as crudely as possible . . . and surely the thought "horse there" will indeed occur to him. The suggestion is that horses *must* cause "horse" tokenings whenever there is an observer on the spot; and that we can rely on psychophysics to tell us exactly what being on the spot consists in. So, all that's required for a guaranteed correlation between horses and "horses" is what they call in Europe *being there!* (God's omniscience, according to this view, is largely implicit in His omnipresence. Notes toward a truly *naturalized* theology.)

It's not, then, just for RED, but also for HORSE and CLOCK-TOWER and many, many other such concepts, that psychophysics provides just what a naturalized semantics needs: circumstances in which instances of a property are guaranteed to cause tokens of the symbol that expresses it. This is a proposal rather in the spirit of an eighteenth-century commonplace about how to draw the distinction between perception and thought: Whereas thought is somehow voluntary – so that one can, in Reflection, conjure up the Idea of a horse at will – percepts simply intrude themselves. You *can't but* entertain the Idea HORSE when you're presented with a horse close up. But then, perhaps the fact that horses force "horses" upon one in psychophysically optimal circumstances is *all there is* to "horse" expressing *horse*. Just as the fact that red things force "red" upon one in psychophysically optimal circumstances is arguably all there is to "red" expressing *red*.

I think that this is all rather pleasing. It is, for example, the grain of sense in the Gibsonian idea that there are "ecologically" sufficient conditions for perceptual achievements. (See also Fodor, 1990, where something of this sort is argued for, though not in quite the present terms.) But it doesn't work; HORSE won't do as a psychophysical concept. Here's why:

Psychophysics can guarantee circumstances in which you'll see a horse and, presumably, have the appropriate horsy experiences. It can't, however, guarantee the *intentional content* of the mental state that you're in in those circumstances. That's because it can't guarantee that when you see the horse you'll see it *as* a horse. Roughly, seeing a horse as a horse requires applying the concept HORSE to what you see. And of course, intact observers qua intact observers *don't have to have* the concept HORSE. So then, it's perfectly nomologically possible to be in a psychophysically optimal relation to a horse and yet not have the thought *here's a horse* occur to one.

You can now see why Darwinian/teleological apparatus does no good for the purposes at hand. Suppose you *could* get a teleological notion of optimal conditions as – e.g. – the ones that obtain when the cognitive mechanisms are behaving as the forces of selection intended them to. Even so, you still couldn't infer from (a) the presence of a horse and (b) the optimality of the conditions that (c) "horse" will get tokened. For: there is no Darwinian guarantee that a properly functioning intentional system ipso facto has the concept HORSE (to say nothing of the concept PROTON). And what you don't have, you can't token.

It is, by the way, easy to miss all this if you think of perceiving as just the entertaining of a mental image; that is, as imaging rather than judging. For that sort of treatment leaves the question of the intentional content of the percept wide open. The present point, put in those terms, is that psychophysics can guarantee circumstances in which you'll have a horse image, but not circumstances in which you'll take what you're having to be an image of a horse. Compare Hume, who I'm inclined to think got this wrong for once.

Let's go back to RED. There are, of course, cases where one sees red things but fails to see them *as* red: you're too far away to make out colors; the illumination is bad ... and so forth. But what makes RED special – what makes it a "psychophysical concept" within the meaning of the act – is that the difference between merely seeing something red and succeeding in seeing it *as* red vanishes when the observer's point of view is psychophysically optimal. You can't – or so I claim – see something red under psychophysically optimal viewing conditions and *not* see it as red. That is, perhaps, the hard core of truth that underlies the traditional doctrine of the "theory neutrality" of observation: qua intact observers, we do have some concepts that we token willy-nilly under circumstances about which psychophysicists can tell us the whole story. Perceptual applications of such concepts are, in that sense, independent of – not mediated by – the perceiver's background of cognitive commitments. But most of our concepts – even ones like HORSE; certainly ones like PROTON – just aren't like that. There are no *psychophysically* specifiable circumstances in which it is nomologically necessary that one sees horses as such.

The box score seems to be as follows: Psychophysics naturalizes the semantics of a certain – relatively quite small – set of mental representations; viz., those for which the distinction between seeing and seeing as vanishes in psychophysically optimal circumstances. These representations have the peculiarity that sufficient conditions for their tokenings can be specified in entirely "external" terms; when one's psychophysical situation is optimal, the world, as it were, reaches in and stuffs them into one's belief box. But it isn't true that these concepts provide a reduction base for the rest of Mentalese; and it isn't true that this psychophysical model can be extended, in any obvious way, to concepts like HORSE whose tokenings – even in psychophysically optimal circumstances – are characteristically inferentially mediated. (To say nothing of PROTON, for whose tokenings the notion of psychophysically optimal circumstances is thus far undefined, since, of course, protons are very small and you can't see them even with the lights turned up.) So what now?

A demure foundationalism

Here's what we want: we want circumstances such that (1) they are naturalistically specifiable; (2) horses (/protons) reliably cause "horses" (/"protons") in those circumstances; (3) it's plausible that "horse" (/"proton") expresses *horse (/proton)* because it's the case that (2). We really do need to know at least roughly what such circumstances might be like, on pain of having the metaphysical worry that – excepting psychophysical concepts – *we have no idea at all* what a naturalized semantics would be like for the nonlogical vocabulary of Mentalese.

Here is how I propose to proceed: first I'll tell you a sketch of a story about (2) and (3), but I'll tell the story in a question-begging vocabulary; viz., in a vocabulary that flouts (1). Then I'll say a little about how it might be possible to tell the same story sketch, only naturalistically. Then I'll ask you to try very, very hard to believe that some day the naturalistic version of this story sketch might actually be filled in, thereby solving the naturalization problem.

The story is, I admit, sort of old-fashioned, since, roughly, it connects having concepts with having experiences and knowing meanings with knowing what would count as evidence. Whenever I tell this story to Granny, she grins and rocks and says "I told you so."

The question-begging version

Horse isn't a psychophysical property (see above); but instantiations of *horse* are, very often, causally responsible for instantiations of what *are* psychophysical properties. It is, for example, because Dobbin is a horse that Dobbin has that horsy look.[13] And it's entirely plausible that having that horsy look reduces to having some or other (maybe quite disjunctive) bundle of psychophysical properties (though, of course, *being a horse* doesn't).

Proton is a little different, because there isn't a look (taste, smell, etc.) that being a proton is typically causally responsible for a thing's having. Protons are, as previously remarked, too small to see. But I think the principle is very much the same. It turns out that it's possible to construct environments in which instantiations of *proton* do have characteristic psychophysical consequences. These are called "experimental" environments; they involve the deployment of "instruments of observation"; and they are, more often than not, very expensive to build. The reason they're so expensive is that because protons are very small, the observable effects of instantiating *proton* at a particular position in spacetime tend to be fairly negligible compared to the causal contributions of other sources of variance. It therefore requires great delicacy to ensure that a given psychophysical effect really is specific to the instantiation of *proton*. But, as I say, it turns out to be possible to do so – to an acceptable level of reliability – assuming you're prepared to pay for it.

We're trying to imagine a kind of connection between horses (or protons) in the world and "horse"s (or "proton"s) in the belief box such that it's plausibly because that connection obtains that "horse" means *horse* (and "proton" means *proton*). The Crude Causal Theory says that this connection ought to be a species of causally reliable covariation. Aside from that, all we know so far is that the covariation can't be mediated by brute psychophysical law because neither HORSE nor PROTON is a psychophysical concept.

On the other hand, there's no reason why instantiations of psychophysical properties shouldn't be *links in a causal chain* that reliably connects horses and protons with "horse"s and "proton"s respectively. This is a hopeful suggestion, because, as we've seen, there are (presumably naturalistically specifiable) circumstances in which instantiations of psychophysical properties are reliably caused by – indeed, are specific to – instantiations of nonpsychophysical properties such as *horse* and *proton*; and, as we've also seen, there are (naturalistically specifiable) circumstances in which instantiations of psychophysical properties reliably causally control what's in the belief box.

So far, everything is OK: physics – including the physics of the experimental environment – guarantees a reliable causal covariation between instantiations of *proton* and the psychophysical properties of the photographic plate, or the cloud chamber, or the voltmeter, or whatever apparatus you're using to detect protons (if physics didn't guarantee this correlation, what you're using wouldn't count as a proton detector). And psychophysics guarantees a reliable causal covariation between the observable properties of the apparatus and the tokening of concepts in the belief box (if psycho-physics didn't guarantee this correlation, these properties of the apparatus wouldn't count as observable). And "reliably causally covaries with" is, I suppose, fairly transitive; transitive enough for the purposes at hand.

Remember that what we wanted for semantics was naturalistically specifiable conditions under which instantiations of *proton* are guaranteed to affect what's in the belief box, our problem being that, patently, not all instances of *proton* succeed in doing so. Well, we can now have what we wanted: for semantical purposes, we require only that instances of *proton* affect the belief box if[14] (a) they take place in an "experimental environment," i.e., *they are causally responsible for the instantiation of psychophysical properties*; and (b) the experimental environment is viewed by an observer who is in an optimal psychophysical position with respect to that environment. (So instances of *proton* that leave traces on photographic plates that are never examined are ipso facto *not* required to affect the contents of any belief boxes.) Notice that so far we haven't even cheated. Because physics connects protons with the look of the photographic plate and psychophysics connects the look of the photographic plate with what's in the belief box, we can specify the conditions under which instances of *proton* are required to affect tokens in the belief box nonsemantically and nonintentionally.

This is *much* better than the Crude Causal Theory, since we no longer require that *all* instantiations of *proton* (mutatis mutandis, *horse*) need to affect the belief box in order that "proton" should express *proton* (mutatis mutandis, in order that "horse" should express *horse*). In fact, in the case of *proton* (though not, perhaps, in the case of *horse*) the number of instances that have been causally responsible for semantically relevant tokenings of representations in belief boxes is infinitesimally small; vastly, astronomically, unimaginably more protons go undetected than not. On the present view, this is quite compatible with there being mental representations that mean *proton*. Fine so far.

But still no good over all. We've got something into the belief box for which instantiations of *proton* are causally responsible; but it's the wrong thing. It's not a token of the concept PROTON; rather, it's a token of some (probably complex) *psychophysical* concept, some concept whose tokening is lawfully connected with the look of the photographic plate. This is clear from the way that the counterfactuals go. Suppose what happens in the experimental environment is that instances of *proton* turn photographic plates red. Then what we're guaranteed gets into the belief box of an observer whose situation with respect to the plate is psychophysically optimal is a symbol whose tokens are reliably correlated with instantiations of *red whether or not* the instantiations of *red* are causally dependent on instances of *proton*. I.e., it's the same symbol that gets tokened in the belief boxes of observers whose situations are psychophysically optimal with respect to ripe tomatoes.

Something needs to be done about this. Here is where the cheating starts.

It's clear enough what story one *wants* to tell: Some people – physicists, for example – *know about* the causal relation between, on the one hand, instantiations of *proton* and, on the other, the redness of photographic plates that are exposed in appropriate experimental environments. Such people are thus in a position to draw the relevant inferences from the look of the plate to the presence of the particle. So, for these people, there is the required correlation between "proton" in the belief box and protons in the world, mediated – as we've seen – by "automatic" tokenings of psychophysical concepts, but also by theoretical inferences that draw upon the cognitive background for their premises. Alas, this sort of correlation does a naturalized semantics no good at all, because to specify the conditions in which the required connections between protons and "protons" will obtain you have to talk about states like *knowing physical theories* and processes like *drawing inferences from what one knows*. Utterly anathema, it goes without saying.

Well, but perhaps not *utterly* anathema, on second thought. What we need is some process that will put a token of "proton" into the belief box whenever a proton in the world is causally responsible (via physical and psychophysical law) for a token of "red" being in the belief box. Now, what in fact normally performs this function is a theoretically based inference: the observer holds a theory that implies that red plates signal protons, and he applies what he knows to infer the presence of the proton from the color of the plate. When the theory is true, the inferences it mediates will indeed succeed in correlating instantiations of *proton* in the experimental environment with tokenings of "proton" in the belief box. True theories – when internalized – correlate the state of the head with the state of the world; that's exactly what's so nice about them.

But though protons typically exert causal control over "protons" via the activation of intentional mechanisms, a naturalistic semantics doesn't need to specify all that. All it needs is that the causal control should actually obtain, *however* it is mediated. The claim, to put it roughly but relatively intuitively, is that it's sufficient for "proton" to express *proton* if there's a reliable correlation between protons and "protons," effected by a mechanism whose response is specific to psychophysical traces for which protons are *in fact* causally responsible. And *that* claim *can* be made in non-intentional, nonsemantic vocabulary. It just was.

No doubt mechanisms that track nonobservables in the required way typically satisfy intentional characterizations (they're typically inferential) and semantic characterizations (they work because the inferences that they draw are sound). But that's OK because on the one hand, the semantic/intentional properties of such mechanisms are, as it were, only *contingently* conditions for their success in tracking protons; and, on the other, what's required for "proton" to express *proton* is only that the tracking actually be successful. For purposes of semantic naturalization, *it's the existence of a reliable mind/world correlation that counts, not the mechanisms by which that correlation is effected.*

So what's proposed is a sort of foundationalism. The semantics of observation concepts is indeed special: First, in that – given an intact observer – the nomologically sufficient and semantically relevant conditions for their tokenings are specifiable "purely externally"; viz., purely psychophysically. And second, in that all the other semantically relevant symbol/world linkages run via the tokening of observation concepts. "Horse" means *horse* if "horse" tokenings are reliably caused by tokenings of psychophysical concepts that are in turn caused by instantiations of psychophysical properties for which instantiations of *horse* are in fact causally responsible.[15] The causal chain runs from horses in the world to horsy looks in the world to psychophysical concepts in the belief box to "horse" in the belief box. "Horse" means *horse* because that chain is reliable.

All right, Granny, have it your way: in effect, the satisfaction of this condition for having a HORSE concept requires that you be able to have certain experiences; and that you be prepared to take your having of those experiences to be evidence for the presence of horses; and, indeed, that you can sometimes be *right* in taking your having of those experiences to be evidence of horses. Only do stop rocking; you make me nervous.

A number of points, all in a jumble and mostly in a concessive and ecumenical tone of voice:

First: There's a detectable family resemblance between the present doctrine and Quine's analysis – in *Word and Object* – of what it is to know a scientific theory like, for example, chemistry. Knowing chemistry, Quine says, is a matter of the associative "interanimation of sentences." It's a matter of having the right psychological connections between, on the one hand, sentences like "This is wet/tasteless/colorless" and sentences like "This is water"; and, on the other hand, between sentences like "This is water" and sentences like "This is H_2O." "Thus someone mixes the contents of two test tubes, observes a green tint, and says 'There was copper in it.' Here the sentence is elicited by a nonverbal stimulus, but the stimulus depends for its efficacy upon an earlier network of associations of words with words; viz., one's learning of chemical theory .... The intervening theory is composed of sentences associated with one another in multifarious ways not easily reconstructed even in conjecture" (Quine, 1960, p. 11).

Now that is, of course, *not* what it is to know chemistry; at a minimum, knowing chemistry is a matter of judging that certain propositions are true, and there is – as Kant decisively remarked – no way of reducing judging (as it might be, judging that if *P* then *Q*) to associating (as it might be, associating "*Q*" with "*P*").

Nevertheless, there may be a use for Quine's picture; it may be that Quine gives you everything you need to characterize the role of internalized theories in fixing the content of mental representations. Viz., all the internalized theory need do is "transfer activation" from observation sentences to theoretical sentences on the appropriate occasions; and all *that* requires is that the sentences involved form the right sort of associative network. So, to that extent, Quine's right: the part of the story about how internalized theories operate that's essential to their functioning in supporting semantically relevant conceptual world correlations can be told in the (nonintentional, nonsemantic) vocabulary of Associationism.[16]

In similar spirit: There is, in my view, almost nothing to be said for the idea that theories are "mere calculating devices" when it is proposed as a piece of philosophy of science. But it may be that that's precisely the story that you want to tell about how theories (more generally, bits of the cognitive background) function in fixing the semantics of mental representations.

The picture is that there's, as it were, a computer between the sensorium and the belief box, and that the tokening of certain psychophysical concepts eventuates in the computer's running through certain calculations that in turn lead to tokenings of "proton" (or of "horse," or whatever) on the appropriate occasions. De facto, these would normally be calculations that appeal, for premises, to internalized beliefs; and they would actually succeed in correlating "proton"s with protons only when these beliefs are true. But you don't need to mention any of that to say what it is about the computer's calculations that's relevant to fixing the semantics of "proton"; all *that* requires is that the computer output "proton" when its inputs are tokenings of psychophysical concepts for which protons are in fact causally responsible.

To put it in a nutshell: The *epistemological* properties of theories are, of course, sensitive to their intentional and semantic properties; what we want of our beliefs is that their *contents* should be *true*. But maybe only the *computational* properties of our theories matter to their role in fixing the meanings of mental representations; *for those purposes* our theories are just the formalism we use to calculate what to put in the belief box when.

Second: The condition I'm imagining is supposed to be *sufficient* but not *necessary* for "proton" meaning *proton*. For all I care, there may be other sorts of routes that would connect concepts to their instances in a semantically relevant way; for example, ones that *don't* depend on the existence of psychophysical laws. I emphasize this point because I don't trust Granny; give her an a priori connection between content and (what she calls) "the possibility of experience" and she's likely to try for antimetaphysical arguments in the familiar, Positivist vein (worse still, for philosophical constraints on the conceptual apparatus of science). Chaque à son rocker; I am *not* doing "critical philosophy." Rather, I'm arguing with a guy who says that there are a priori, metaphysical reasons for supposing that semantics can't be naturalized. A plausible, naturalistic, *sufficient* condition for "A"s meaning *A* is all I need to win the argument with him.

Third: Although the present condition for "proton" meaning *proton* is a lot more plausible than the Crude requirement that all protons cause "protons," it's still too strong to be *entirely* plausible; for example, it requires the tokening of "proton" in *all* environments in which psychophysical consequences for which protons are causally responsible are detected. But, of course, there may be correlations between protons and psychophysical traces that nobody knows about, correlations that our (current) physics doesn't specify; and such correlations are ipso facto unlikely to function as links in chains from protons to "protons." For instance: for all I know, I am right now registering psychophysical traces that are specific to protons. That my belief box is nevertheless innocent of a tokening of PROTON would not imply that I lack that concept. All that would follow is that my internalized physics is incomplete. Oh boy, is it ever!

But I don't propose to linger over this sort of worry. It seems to me that we're now playing in the right ball park and the rest is arguably just fine tuning. Perhaps what we want to say is sufficient for "proton" meaning *proton* is that there be *at least one* kind of environment in which there are psychophysical traces of protons which, when detected, cause the tokening of "proton" in the belief box. Or perhaps, slightly more interesting, the right thing to say is that there should be *a fair number* of such kinds of environments, thereby allowing the concept HAVING THE CONCEPT PROTON to exhibit the sort of vagueness of boundary characteristic of most of the notions that the special sciences employ (cf. RIVER, TORNADO, FEUDAL SOCIETY, FEMALE, and the like).

Fourth: Precisely because the present proposal requires only that there be the right kind of correlation between protons and "protons," we're allowing the fixation of meaning by radically false theories. On this view, somebody who believes really crazy things – that protons are alive, as it might be – could still have the concept PROTON. He would do so if his crazy theory happens to have the property of reliably connecting "protons" with protons via their psychophysical traces. For reasons given in chapter 3 [of Fodor, 1988] I regard this as a virtue; people *can* have radically false theories and really crazy views, consonant with our understanding perfectly well, thank you, which false views they have and what radically crazy things it is that they believe. Berkeley thought that chairs are *mental,* for Heaven's sake! Which are we to say he lacked, the concept MENTAL or the concept CHAIR?

A consequence of the present view is that although theories mediate symbol/world connections, still Meaning Holism is not thereby implied. That's because the *content* of a theory does *not* determine the meanings of the terms whose connections to the world the theory mediates. What determines their meanings is *which things in the world the theory connects them to.* The unit of meaning is not the theory; it's the world/symbol correlation *however mediated.*

Let me tell you – by way of making the spirit of the proposal clear – a story about what was wrong with Verificationism. Verificationism was the idea that the meaning of an expression could be identified with whatever route connects the use of the expression to its denotation. So, for example, there's something that connects our use of the word "star" to stars; a causal chain that starts with light leaving stars, passing – maybe – through telescopes, falling on our retinas, and eventuating in utterances of "star" (mutatis mutandis, with tokenings of "star" in the belief box). The Verificationist idea was that it's *that sort of thing* that constitutes the meaning of "star."

Now, there is something right about this – namely, that tokenings of the verification procedures for "star" must have stars on one end and "stars" on the other; it's true a priori that when they work, verification procedures connect terms with their denotations. If they didn't, they wouldn't *be* verification procedures.

But there is something wrong with it too. Namely, that verification procedures connect terms with their denotations *in too many ways.* Think of the routes along which stars can get connected to tokenings of "star": via just looking; via looking at reflections in a puddle; via inference from astronomical theory; via inference from astrological theory; via inference from what somebody happened to say; via paintings of stars in a museum; via just thinking about stars . . . etc. The point is that "star" isn't umpteen ways ambiguous; these different routes *do not determine correspondingly different semantic values for "star."* On the contrary, what determines the semantic value of "star" is precisely what all these routes have *in common*; viz., the fact that they connect "stars" with stars. The moral is that *the route doesn't matter (much)*; what makes "star" mean *star* is *that* the two are connected, not *how* the two are connected. It's the covariance that counts.

Similarly for concepts, of course. It may be that my concept of water is, from time to time, connected to water via my concept of cat: I believe that water is what cats like; I find that my cat likes this stuff; I infer that this stuff is water. But it's not being connected to water via CAT that makes my concept of water a water concept. What makes it a water concept is that its tokenings covary with water instances – under appropriate circumstances – by whatever route the covariance may be achieved. That theories mediate the semantically relevant concept-to-world connections does *not* imply Meaning Holism. For we get meaning by *quantifying over* the routes from a symbol to its denotation.

Summary

Just a word to recapitulate the architecture of the discussion that we've been pursuing. We started with the Crude idea that a plausible sufficient condition for "A"s to express A is that it's nomologically necessary that (1) every instance of A causes a token of "A"; and (2) only instances of A cause tokens of "A."

The Slightly Less Crude Causal Theory of Content offers the following two friendly amendments: for (2) read: "If non-A's cause 'A's, then their doing so is asymmetrically dependent upon A's causing 'A's." For (1) read: "All instances of A's cause 'A's when (i) the A's are causally responsible for psychophysical traces to which (ii) the organism stands in a psychophysically optimal relation."

What's claimed for SLCCTC is that it does what metaphysical skeptics about intentionality doubt *can* be done: it provides a sufficient condition for one part of the world to be semantically related to another part (specifically, for a certain mental representation to express a certain property); it does so in nonintentional, nonsemantical, nonteleological, and, in general, non-question-begging vocabulary; and it's reasonably plausible – it isn't crazy to suppose that at least some mental symbols have the content that they do because they stand in the sort of relation to the world that SLCCTC prescribes.

I do, however, admit to two checks still outstanding. I've helped myself to the notion of an intact organism; and I've helped myself to the notion of one event being the cause of another. I have therefore to claim that, whatever the right unpacking of these concepts may be, it doesn't smuggle in intentional/semantic notions (perhaps, in the latter case, via the – alleged; Granny and I don't believe it for a minute – "interest relativity" of explanation).

Obligation noted. On the other hand, there is nothing in this line of thought to comfort a skeptic; for if INTACT ORGANISM and THE CAUSE OF AN EVENT are indeed covertly intentional/semantic, then it looks as though belief/desire psychology isn't, after all, the only science whose practice presupposes that intentional/semantic categories are metaphysically kosher. That the organism is (relevantly) intact is part of the background idealization of practically all biological theorizing; and (so I believe) we need to distinguish between the cause of an event and its causally necessary conditions *whenever* we do the kind of science that's concerned with the explanation of particular happenings (cf. the formation of the great Siberian Crater, the extinction of the dinosaur, and the like).

So if INTACT ORGANISM and THE CAUSE are indeed intentional/semantic, then there is nothing special about belief/desire psychology after all. The availability of intentional apparatus would then be quite widely presupposed in the special sciences, so its deployment by psychologists for the explanation of behavior would require no special justification. In which case, I've just wasted a lot of time that I could have put in sailing.

Ah well!

Notes

1 Notice that this is *not* the same question as: "What is it for a physical system to be an 'intentional system'?" Intentional systems have, by definition, propositional attitudes: beliefs, as it might be. And being a belief requires (not just having an intentional object but) having the right sort of functional role. I'm leaving it open that a good reconstruction of intentionality might recognize things that have intentional states but no propositional attitudes; hence, things that have intentional states but are not intentional systems. For example, it doesn't seem to me to count against a theory of intentionality if it entails that the curvature of the bimetalic strip in a thermostat represents the temperature of the ambient air. By contrast, a theory that entails that thermostats are intentional systems — that they have beliefs and desires – would thereby refute itself.

2 No doubt, some questions are begged by assuming that the totality of an organism's mental representations does constitute a language. In particular, I'm taking it for granted that Mentalese has a combinatorial semantics. The arguments for assuming this are set out in the Appendix [of Fodor, 1988].

3 Skinner and Quine had, of course, proposed causal accounts of meaning in the '50s. But they assumed the psychological framework of conditioning theory; and Skinner, at least, seems not to have understood the central importance of combinatorial structure in language. Chomsky took critical note of both these flaws, with results that were enormously liberating for both linguistics and psychology. But the impact on semantics was, perhaps, more equivocal; in particular, philosophical interest in causal accounts of meaning was among the casualties of Chomsky's attack and it has only recently begun to recover.

It is, therefore, worth emphasizing that a causal theory of meaning need not assume a behavioristic psychology; and that there is no contradiction between a combinatorial semantics and a causal solution to the naturalization problem. It seems, in retrospect, that the Chomsky landslide may after all have buried something valuable.

4 Any case where false beliefs have greater survival value than the corresponding true ones would, of course, do just as well as repression to point this moral. See Stich, 1983, where this sort of argument against teleological semantics is pressed; plausibly, in my view.

5 This isn't supposed to be a Paradigm Case Argument: it's perfectly possible to say "that's a unicorn" falsely even though there aren't any unicorns and no one ever says "that's a unicorn" truly. But even here the possibility of making false predications depends upon the semantical setup being available for making true ones, if only the world would cooperate by providing some unicorns to make them *of*.

Perhaps what CCT should say about unicorns is that they *would* be nomically sufficient for "unicorn"-tokenings if there were any. (There can, of course, be a nomic connection between properties *one* or more of which is de facto uninstantiated.) On the other hand, I suppose that treatment would require unicorns to be at least *nomologically possible*; so Heaven only knows what a causal theory ought to say if they're not. For that matter, Heaven only knows what a causal theory ought to say about *any* symbol which expresses a property that can't be instantiated; perhaps that such a symbol can't be primitive.

6 It needs to be borne in mind, however, that this construal of asymmetric dependence, formulated in terms of causal connections between B's and "A"s (between, say, cows and "horses"), is short for a more precise version formulated in terms of nomic dependences between higher-order properties (between, say, the property of being an instantiation of *cow* and the property of being a tokening of "horse"). So, the parade version goes like this:

B-caused "A" tokens are wild only if the nomic dependence of instantiations of the property of being an "A" tokening upon instantiations of the property of being a B tokening is itself dependent upon the nomic dependence of the property of being an "A" tokening upon instantiations of some property other than B.

You can see why I prefer to work with the undress version. Still, the difference between the formulations sometimes matters. One reason why it does is made clear by a puzzle that I owe to Scott Weinstein. Consider:

(*i*)   Small horses cause "horses."
(*ii*) Horses cause "horses."
(*iii*) (*i*) depends on (*ii*) (small horses wouldn't cause "horses" unless horses did).
(*iv*) (*ii*) is not dependent on (*i*) (horses would cause "horses" even if small horses didn't; even if, for example, there were only large horses).
(*v*)   So small-horse-caused "horse" tokenings are asymmetrically dependent on horse-caused horse tokenings; so small-horse-caused "horse" tokenings are wild.

This seems to show that asymmetric dependence can't be sufficient for wildness even if it's necessary. One avoids the conclusion, however, by noting that (*Pi*), the parade version of (*i*),

(*Pi*) "Horse" tokenings are nomically dependent on the instantiation of small horse.

301

is false; the counterfactual-supporting connection is between "horse" token-ings and *horse* instantiation, not between "horse" tokenings and *small horse* instantiation. Notice how the subjunctives go: this (recently denoted) small horse would have caused a "horse" tokening *even if it had been larger*; to a first approximation, horses cause "horse" tokenings regardless of their size.

7 I'm indebted for this case to Georges Rey, Barry Loewer, and Ron McClamrock.
8 To deny that it's *even* necessary, you must accept the following as a possible case: We apply "horse" to cows, and we would continue to do so even if we didn't apply "horse" to horses; yet "horse" means horse, and applications of "horse" to cows are ipso facto false.

This doesn't look like a possible case to me. What on earth would *make* "horse" mean *horse* in such a case? What would stop it from meaning *cow*?
9 A number of people have suggested to me that the extensions of concepts with prototype structure would exhibit a sort of asymmetric dependence: the non-prototypic members wouldn't be in the extension unless the prototypic ones were, but the prototypic ones would be in even if the others weren't.

But I think this is wrong. Sparrows are prototypical birds. But suppose they turned out to be reptiles, hence not birds at all (in the way that whales turned out to be mammals, hence not fish at all). It wouldn't follow that we would stop calling penguins and parrots "birds"; that would depend on whether they turned out to be reptiles too. You don't destroy a category by showing that its prototype is incoherent (in the way that you *do* destroy a category by showing that its *definition* is incoherent).

This suggests what's independently plausible; viz., that prototype structure has nothing much to do with *meaning*. (What then *does* it have to do with? Well might one wonder.)
10 Terminology in this area is a bit unstable. What I'm calling "observation" vocabulary (and what often does get called that in epistemological theorizing) is more or less the same as what gets called "sensory" vocabulary in traditional philosophical psychology. The intuition that there is an important distinction in this area is wider spread than consensus on what to call it or how to draw it.
11 Even the claim that there are circumstances under which psychophysics guar-antees the contents of the occurs-to-me box is a little less drastic than it may seem at first: In the sort of psychology I'm assuming, an organism need not be conscious of the thoughts that occur to it. On the other hand, it's a good deal more than vacuous, since, given functionalism, what's in the occurs-to-me box (or any other box, for that matter) is ipso facto guaranteed to modify the flow of mental processing actually or potentially.
12 It is, however, perfectly possible to imagine creatures for which WATER is a psychophysical concept; creatures that have transducers for H_2O so that, in particular, their sensory mechanisms respond differently to samples of water than they do to samples of XYZ. If we were creatures, Putnam would have had to choose a different example.

This by way of emphasizing that if "observation concept" means "psychophysical concept," then which concepts *are* observational can't be determined a priori.
13 This means more than "Dobbin's being a horse is *causally necessary* for Dobbin's having that horsy look"; but I don't know how much more. I take it,

however, that it's OK for an astronomer to say "a meteor was the cause of the Great Siberian Crater," knowing that he means more by this than "no meteor, no crater." Well, if he can help himself to "the cause" without further analysis, so can I. I propose to.

It is *simply unreasonable* to require that a solution to the naturalization problem for semantics should also provide an account of causal explanation. Semantics is respectable if it can make do with the same metaphysical apparatus that the rest of the empirical sciences require; it doesn't *also* have to incorporate a theory of that apparatus.

14 More precisely, what's required is of the form: It's nomologically necessary that protons affect the belief box if .... We want the modal operator to insure against vacuous or accidental satisfactions of the conditional.

15 And, of course, the causation of "horse"s by nonhorses has to be asymmetrically dependent upon the causation of "horse"s by horses, as per the first half of this chapter.

16 At this level of psychological unsophistication, intertranslation between the association story and the belief-box story is trivial and not worth the bother of spelling out. I emphasize, however, that I am *not*, by any conceivable stretch of the imagination, endorsing an associative theory of the mind. My point is just that the role of internalized theories *in fixing the semantic contents of concepts* is so merely mechanical that even an Associationist can reconstruct it.

References

Dretske, F. (1981) *Knowledge and the Flow of Information*, Cambridge, Mass.: MIT Press.

Fodor, J. (1988) *Psychosemantics*, Cambridge, Mass.: MIT Press.

—— (1990) "Psychosemantics or: Where Do Truth Conditions Come From?," in W.G. Lycan (ed.), *Mind and Cognition*, Oxford: Blackwell, pp. 312–337.

Lewis, D. (1973) *Counterfactuals*, Oxford: Blackwell.

Matthews, R. (1984) "Troubles with Representationalism," *Social Research* 51: 1065–1097.

Quine, W.V. (1960) *Word and Object*, Cambridge: Mass.: MIT Press.

Stampe, D. (1977) "Towards a Causal Theory of Linguistic Representation," in P. French *et al.* (eds.), *Midwest Studies in Philosophy*, vol. 2, Minneapolis: University of Minnesota Press, pp. 42–63.

Stich, S. (1983) *From Folk Psychology to Cognitive Science*, Cambridge, Mass.: MIT Press.

15

Fred Dretske, "Representational Systems"

. . .

3.1 Conventional systems of representation: Type I

By a representational system (RS) I shall mean any system whose function it is to indicate how things stand with respect to some other object, condition, or magnitude. If RS's function is to indicate whether O is in condition A or B, for instance, and the way RS performs this function (*when* it performs it) is by occupying one of two possible states, a (indicating that O is A) and b (indicating that O is B), then a and b are the expressive elements of RS and *what they represent* (about O) is *that* it is A (in the case of a) and *that* it is B (in the case of b).

Depending on the kind of function involved, and on the way a system manages to carry out this function (the way it manages to *indicate*), representational systems can be variously classified. What follows is one possible classification. My chief interest is in *natural* representations (systems of Type III), but the special properties of such systems are best understood by comparing and contrasting them with their conventional (to varying degrees) cousins. So I begin with conventional systems of representation.

Let this dime on the table be Oscar Robertson, let this nickel (heads uppermost) be Kareem Abdul-Jabbar, and let this nickel (tails uppermost) be the opposing center. These pieces of popcorn are the other players, and this glass is the basket. With this bit of stage setting I can now, by moving coins and popcorn around on the table, represent the positions and movements of these players. I can use these objects to describe a basketball play I once witnessed.

Fred Dretske, "Representational Systems" (excerpt), Chapter 3 of *Explaining Behavior: Reasons in a World of Causes* (MIT Press, Cambridge, Mass., 1988), pp. 52–77.

If memory fails me, I may end up misrepresenting things. I may move pieces of popcorn here when the players went there. The coins and the popcorn have been assigned a temporary function, the function of *indicating* (by *their* positions and movement) the relative positions and movements of certain players during a particular game. But these elements, the coins and the popcorn, obviously enjoy no intrinsic power to do what they have been assigned the function of doing – *indicating* the positions and the movements of various players in a game long since over. Whatever success they enjoy in the performance of their job obviously derives *from me*, from my memory of the game being represented and my skill in translating that knowledge into the chosen idiom. The popcorn and the coins indicate, and in this sense perform their assigned function, only insofar as *I* am a reliable conduit for information about the situation being represented and a reliable and well-intentioned manipulator of the expressive medium.

The coins and the popcorn do their job, then, only insofar as some *other* indicator system is functioning satisfactorily, only insofar as there is something in the manipulator of these symbols (in this case, something *in me*) that indicates how things stood on the basketball court at the time in question. If I am ignorant of what Oscar and Kareem did with the ball, the coins and the popcorn are unable to perform the function they have been assigned – unable to indicate, by their various positions and movements, what took place on the court that day. This is merely to acknowledge that these objects are, considered by themselves, representationally lifeless. They are merely my representational instruments.

The elements of Type I systems have no *intrinsic* powers of representation – no power that is not derived from us, their creators and users.[1] Both their function (what they, when suitably deployed, are *supposed* to indicate) and their power to perform that function (their success in indicating what it is their function to indicate) are derived from another source: human agents with communicative purposes. Many familiar RSs are like this: maps, diagrams, certain road signs (of the informational variety), prearranged signals, musical notation, gestures, codes, and (to some degree, at least) natural language. I call the representational elements of such systems *symbols*. Symbols are, either explicitly or implicitly, *assigned* indicator functions, functions that they have no intrinsic power to perform. *We* give them their functions, and *we* (when it suits our purposes) see to it that they are *used* in accordance with this function. Such representational systems are, in this sense, *doubly* conventional: *we* give them a job to do, and then *we* do it for them.

3.2 Natural signs and information

In contrast with the relationship between popcorn and professional basket-ball players, we don't have to *let* tracks in the snow, bird songs, fingerprints, and cloud formations stand for the things we take them to indicate. There is a sense in which, whether we like it or not, these tracks, prints, songs, and formations indicate what they do quite independent of us, of how we exploit them for investigative purposes, and of whether we even recognize their significance at all. These are what are sometimes called *natural signs*: events and conditions that derive their indicative powers, not (as in the case of symbols) from us, from our *use* of them to indicate, but from the way they are objectively related to the conditions they signify.

To understand conventional systems of representation of Type II and the way they differ from RSs of Type I, it is important to understand the dif-ference between symbols and signs. In systems of Type II, natural signs are *used* in a way that exploits their *natural* meaning, their *unconventional* powers of indication, for representational, and partly conventional, pur-poses. This makes systems of Type II a curious blend of the conventional and the natural. It is the purpose of this section to say something useful about signs and their meaning in preparation for the description of repre-sentational systems of Type II. This, in turn, will prepare the way for our discussion of the representational systems that are of real interest to this project: natural systems of representation.

Although a great deal of intelligent thought and purpose went into the design and manufacture of an ordinary bathroom scale, once the scale has been finished and placed into use there is nothing conventional, purposeful, or intelligent about its operation. This device indicates what it does without any cooperation or help from either its maker or its user. All you do is get *on* it. It then gives you the bad news. Somebody put the numbers on the dial, of course, and did so with certain intentions and purposes; but this is merely a convenience, something that (to use fashionable jargon) makes it user-friendly. It has nothing to do with what the instrument indicates. A clock doesn't stop keeping time if the numerals are removed from its face. The symbols on a clock or on a bathroom scale merely make it easier for us to *tell* what the pointer positions *mean*. They do not change what these pointer positions indicate.

The same is true of any measuring instrument. As long as an instrument is connected properly and functioning normally, it behaves in accordance with electrical and mechanical laws whose validity is quite independent of its creator's or its user's purposes or knowledge. Furthermore, these laws, by determining whether and (if so) how the pointer positions are correlated with weights, times, pressures, and speeds, determine what these pointer positions indicate about weights, times, pressures, and speeds.

Some people think that all indication is indication *for* or *to* someone. Gauge readings and naturally occurring signs (e.g., tracks in the snow) do not indicate anything if there is no one *to whom* or *for whom* they do this. Gauge readings are like trees falling in the forest: if no one is around to hear, there is no sound; if no one peeks at the scale, it doesn't indicate anything about anyone's weight. Tracks in the snow, fingerprints on a gun, and melting ice do not indicate anything about the animals in the woods, the person who touched the gun, or the temperature *unless* someone observes the tracks, the prints, or the melting ice and makes an appropriate inference. If no one knows that quail, and *only* quail, make tracks of *that* kind, then, despite this regularity, the tracks do not indicate that there are (or were) quail in the woods.

This view, I submit, is merely a special version of the more general and even more implausible idea that nothing is true unless it is true for someone, unless someone knows (or at least believes) it. I do not intend to quarrel about this matter. I shall simply assume that if one mistakes a perfectly reliable and properly functioning boiler-pressure gauge for something else, thinks it is broken, completely ignores it, or never even sees it – if, in other words, the registration of this gauge does not indicate what the boiler pressure is *to anyone* – it nonetheless still indicates what the boiler pressure is. It just doesn't indicate it *to* anyone. And, for the same reason, if, for superstitious reasons, everyone takes the color of the wooly caterpillar's fur as an indication or sign of a cold winter, everyone is simply wrong. That isn't what it means. Taking something to be so, taking it to be not so, or not taking it to be either does not make it so, does not make it not so, and does not make it neither. And this holds for what things indicate as well as for where things are and what they are doing.

I have occasionally used the verb "mean" as a synonym for "indicate." Let me explain. Paul Grice (1957) distinguished what he called a natural sense from a non-natural sense of the word "meaning." The natural sense of "meaning" is virtually identical to that of "indicate," and that is how I shall normally use the word. The 24 rings in a tree stump, the so-called growth rings, mean (indicate) that the tree is 24 years old. A ringing bell – a ringing *door*bell – means (indicates) that someone is at the door. A scar on a twig, easily identified as a leaf scar, means, in this natural sense, that a leaf grew there. As Grice observes, nothing can mean that P in the *natural* sense of meaning if P is not the case. This distinguishes it from non-natural meaning, where something (e.g., a statement) can mean that P without P's being the case. A person can *say*, and *mean*, that a quail was here without a quail's having been here. But the tracks in the snow cannot mean (in this natural sense of "meaning") that a quail was here unless, in fact, a quail *was* here. If the tracks were left by a pheasant, then the tracks might, depending on how distinctive they are, mean that a pheasant was here. But they certainly do not mean that a quail was here, and the fact that a Boy Scout *takes* them to mean that cannot *make* them mean that.

Furthermore, even if P does obtain, the indicator or sign does not mean (indicate) that P is the case unless the requisite *dependency* exists between the sign and P. Even if the tracks in the snow *were* left by a quail, the tracks may not mean or indicate that this is so. If pheasants, also in the woods, leave the very same kind of tracks, then the tracks, though made by a quail, do not indicate that it was a quail that made them. A picture of a person, taken from the back at a great distance, does not indicate *who* the picture is a picture of if other people look the same from that angle and distance.

If a fuel gauge is broken (stuck, say, at "half full"), it *never* indicates anything about the gasoline in the tank. Even if the tank *is* half full, and even if the driver, unaware of the broken gauge, comes to believe (correctly, as it turns out) that the tank is half full, the reading is not a sign – does not mean or indicate – that the tank is half full. Broken clocks are *never* right, not even twice a day, if being right requires them to *indicate* the correct time of day.

When there is any chance of confusing this use of the word "meaning" with what Grice calls non-natural meaning – the kind of meaning associated with language, the kind of meaning that is (I shall later argue) closer to what it is the *function* of something to mean (naturally) or indicate – I shall either combine the word "meaning" with the word "natural" or use it together with its synonym "indicate." The word "represent" is sometimes used in a way that I am using "indicate" and "mean" (naturally). Since I wish to reserve the idea of representation for something that is closer to genuine meaning, the kind of meaning (Grice's non-natural meaning) in which something can mean that P *without* P's being the case, I will *never* use the words "represent" and "indicate" interchangeably. As I am using these words, there can be no *mis*indication, only misrepresentation.

The power of signs to mean or indicate something derives from the way they are related to what they indicate or mean. The red spots all over Tommy's face mean that he has the measles, not simply because he *has* the measles, but because people without the measles don't have spots of that kind. In most cases the underlying relations are causal or lawful in character. There is, then, a lawful dependency between the indica*tor* and the indica*ted*, a dependency that we normally express by conditionals in the subjunctive mood: if Tommy didn't have the measles, he wouldn't have those red spots all over his face. Sometimes, however, the dependency between a natural sign and its meaning derives, at least in part, from other sources. It is partly the fact, presumably not itself a physical law, that animals do not regularly depress doorbuttons while foraging for food that makes a ringing doorbell *mean* that some *person* is at the door. If squirrels changed their habits (because, say, doorbuttons were made out of nuts), then a ringing doorbell would no longer mean what it now does. But as things *now* stand, we can say that the bell would not be ringing unless someone was at the door. It therefore indicates or means that someone is at the door. But this subjunctively expressed dependency between the ringing bell and someone's presence at the door, though not a coincidence, is not grounded in natural law either. There are surely no laws of nature that prevent small animals from pressing, or randomly falling meteorites from hitting, doorbuttons. There certainly is nothing in the laws of physics that prevents an occasional short circuit in the electrical wiring, something that might cause the bell to ring when no one was at the door. Normally, though, these things don't happen. At least they have never happened to *me*. And this is no lucky coincidence, no freaky piece of good fortune. It isn't like getting a long run of heads while flipping a (fair) coin. Chance correlations between two variables, no matter how prolonged, are not enough. In order for one thing to indicate something about another, the dependencies must be genuine. There must actually be some condition, lawful or otherwise, that *explains* the persistence of the correlation. This is the difference between a lucky run of heads obtained with a fair coin and the not-at-all-lucky run of rings when someone has been at my door, a difference that enables my bell (but not coin flips) to indicate something about the correlated condition. This, of course, is a fact about *my* house, *my* neighborhood, and *my* doorbell wiring. If your house or neighborhood is different, maybe the ringing of *your* doorbell means something different.[2]

In many cases of biological interest, a sign – some internal indicator on which an animal relies to locate and identify, say, food – will only have this kind of local validity. It will, that is, be a reliable indicator only *in* the animal's natural habitat or in conditions that approximate that habitat. Flies, for instance, when given a choice between nutritionally worthless sugar fructose and some nutritive substance like sorbitol, will invariably choose the nutritionally worthless substance and starve to death. Surprising? Not really. Under *natural* conditions (Grier 1984, p. 536) the substances that stimulate the receptors *are* nutritional. Under natural conditions, in a fly's normal habitat, then, receptor activity indicates a nutritional substance. Furthermore, the correlation between receptor activity and nutritional value of its activator is no accident. There is something that explains it. Flies would not have developed (or maintained without modification) such a receptor system in environments where such a correlation did not exist. The same is true of me and my doorbell. I would not keep a doorbell system that did not convey the desired information, that did not (because of pesky squirrels, say) indicate what it was installed to indicate. I would, as I assume the flies (over many generations) would, get a more discriminating detector.

I have elsewhere (1981, 1983), under the rubric *information*, tried to say something more systematic about the idea of an objective, mind-independent, indicator relation. Aside from the above brief remarks tracing the idea of natural meaning to the objective relations of dependency between a natural sign and its meaning, between the indicator and what it indicates, I will not here attempt to recapitulate that earlier analysis. Nor will I presuppose the details. Sufficient unto present purposes is the assumption – an altogether plausible assumption, I hope – that there is something *in* nature (not merely in the minds that struggle to comprehend nature), some objective, observer-independent fact or set of facts, that forms the basis of one thing's meaning or indicating something about another.[3] In what follows I shall occasionally, partly as a terminological convenience but also partly to exhibit the deep connections between representational systems and information-processing models of human cognition, advert to the idea of information. Talking about information is yet a third way of talking about the fundamentally important relation of indication or natural meaning. So, for example, if S (sign, signal), by being a, indicates or means that O is A, then S (or, more precisely, S's being a) carries the information that O is A. What an event or condition (whether we think of it as a signal or not is irrelevant) indicates or means about another situation is the information it carries about that other situation.

3.3   Conventional systems of representation: Type II

In systems of Type II, natural signs take the place of symbols as the representational elements. A sign is given the job of doing what it (suitably deployed) can already do.

It should be remembered that what a system *represents* is *not* what its (expressive) elements indicate or mean. It is what these elements have the *function* of indicating or meaning. It is important to keep this point in mind, since the natural signs used in systems of Type II typically indicate a great many things. Normally, though, they are used to represent only *one* of these conditions – a condition which we, for whatever reason, take a special interest in and give the function of indicating. If a full tank of gas means (because of the weight of the gas) that there is a large downward force on the bolts holding the tank to the car's frame, then the fuel gauge indicates a large downward force on these bolts whenever it indicates a full tank of gas. In addition, electrically operated fuel gauges indicate not only the amount of fuel left in the tank but also the amount of electrical current flowing in the wires connecting the gauge to the tank, the amount of torque on the armature to which the pointer is affixed, and the magnitude of the magnetic field surrounding this armature. Given the way these gauges operate, they cannot indicate (i.e., have their behavior depend on) the amount of fuel in the tank without indicating (exhibiting at least the same degree of dependency on) these related conditions.

Nevertheless, we take one of these indicated conditions to be what the gauge *represents*, one of these correlated conditions to define what *kind* of gauge it is. It is, or so we say, a *fuel* gauge, not a galvanometer recording potential differences between points in the automobile's electrical wiring (though that, in a sense, is precisely what it is). Since we are interested in the amount of gasoline in the tank, not (except derivatively) in these correlated conditions, we *assign* the gauge the function of indicating the amount of gasoline in the tank. We *give* it the job of delivering *this* piece of information, calibrate and label it accordingly, and ignore the collateral pieces of information it necessarily supplies in the process. Since what an instrument or gauge represents is what it is *supposed* to indicate, what it has the *function* of indicating, and since *we* determine these functions, *we* determine what the gauge represents. If, by jacking up the fuel tank, I remove the force on the bolts securing the tank to the car frame, the fuel gauge, though still indicating the amount of fuel in the tank, no longer indicates the amount of force on these bolts. But, under these unusual conditions, the gauge does not *misrepresent* the force on these bolts the way it could, and the way gauges sometimes *do*, misrepresent the amount of fuel in the tank. The reason it doesn't is because the gauge, even when things are operating normally, does not *represent* (though it does *indicate*) the magnitude of this force. Its *representational* efforts – and therefore its representational failures, its misrepresentations – are limited to what it has the *function* of indicating. And since the gauge does not have the function of indicating the force on these bolts, it does not misrepresent this force when it fails to indicate it. Though it is hard to imagine why we would do this, we could *give* the gauge this function. Were we to do so, then, under the unusual conditions described above, when we removed the force on these bolts by jacking up the tank, the gauge would misrepresent the force on the bolts.

It is for this reason that what the gauge represents is *partly* conventional, *partly* a matter of what we say it represents. In contrast with the case of Type I systems, however, this dependence on us, our interests and purposes, is only partial. The reason it is only partial is because the indicator functions assigned an instrument are limited to what the instrument *can* indicate, to what its various states and conditions depend on. You can't assign a rectal thermometer the job of indicating the Dow-Jones Industrial Average.[4] The height of the mercury doesn't depend on these economic conditions. The mercury and the market fluctuate independently. Trying to use a thermometer in this way is like assigning a rock the job of washing dishes.[5] My son can be given this job (even if he never does it) because he, unlike the rock, *can* wash dishes. The functions we assign to instruments are similarly restricted to what the instruments *can* do, or, if Wright (1973) is correct, what (in the case of artifacts) we *think* they can do. This makes the functions of systems of Type II restricted in a way that those of Type I systems are not restricted. It is this fact, together with the fact that once a device has been given such a function it performs without any help from us, that makes such systems only *partly* conventional.

The conventional, interest-relative, and purpose-dependent character of systems of Type II is especially obvious when our interests and purposes change. An altimeter represents altitude until we remove it from the aircraft for testing on the ground. It then "becomes" an aneroid barometer, representing not altitude but air pressure – something it *always* indicated, of course, but something in which we weren't interested (except insofar as it depended on, and hence served as an accurate indicator of, altitude) when flying the plane. Calibration is a process in which one's interests and purposes undergo a temporary change. *Now*, during calibration, one uses the needle's position as an indicator, not of the quantity the instrument is usually used to measure, but of the instrument's own internal condition – whether, for example, its batteries are getting weak, or whether it needs adjustment, repair, or alignment. With RSs of Type II we can, and sometimes do, change the magnitude being represented (not merely the scale for measuring a given magnitude) merely by consulting a different set of numbers on the face of the instrument. A change in the way we *use* the instrument is enough to change its function and, hence, what it represents.

One way of thinking about the difference between Type I and Type II representational systems is that in systems of Type I the function, as it were, comes first. The representational elements are given a function and then, if things go right, are *used* in conformity with this function – *used* to indicate what, relative to this function, they are supposed to indicate. I first give the dime, *its* position and movements, the function of indicating the position and movements of Oscar Robertson. Then I manipulate the dime in accordance with this assigned function. I, in virtue of my knowledge and manipulative skills, see to it that it indicates what I have assigned it the function of indicating. Not only the coin's *job* but also its *performance* of that job derives, therefore, wholly from me, the creator and user of the representational system. RSs of Type I are, then, *manifestations* or *displays* of the representational talents of their users in much the same way that a TV monitor is a *display* of the information-processing capabilities of the machinery lying behind it. With systems of Type II, however, things are different. The power of their elements to indicate comes first; their function comes second. They acquire or are assigned the function of doing one of the things they are already doing or, if not *already* doing, already *capable* of doing once harnessed in the right way. Their ability to perform their function does *not*, as in the case of systems of Type I, depend on us, on a user-system already in possession of the required indicator skills. The status of these elements as indicators is therefore *intrinsic*. What is extrinsic, and therefore still conventional, still relative to the interests and purposes of its users, is the determination of which among the various things they can already do it is their function to do.

3.4   Natural systems of representation

A natural system of representation is not only one in which the elements, like the elements of Type II systems, have a power to indicate that is independent of the interests, purposes, and capacities of any other system, but also one in which, in contrast with systems of Type II, the functions determining what these signs *represent* are also independent of such extrinsic factors. Natural systems of representation, systems of Type III, are ones which have *their own* intrinsic indicator functions, functions that derive from the way the indicators are developed and used *by the system of which they are a part*. In contrast with systems of Type I and II, these functions are not assigned. They do not depend on the way *others* may use or regard the indicator elements.

Whatever one might think about the possibility of intrinsic functions, the type of functions that define Type III systems (a contentious point to which I will return in a moment), it is clear that what I have been calling natural signs – events, conditions, and structures that somehow indicate how things stand elsewhere in the world – are essential to every animal's biological heritage. Without such internal indicators, an organism has no way to negotiate its way through its environment, no way to avoid predators, find food, locate mates, and do the things it has to do to survive and propagate. This, indeed, is what sense perception is all about. An animal's senses (at least the so-called exteroceptors) are merely the diverse ways nature has devised for making what happens inside an animal depend, in some indicator-relevant way, on what happens outside. If the firing of a particular neuron in a female cricket's brain did not indicate the distinctive chirp of a conspecific male, there would be nothing to guide the female in its efforts to find a mate (Huber and Thorson 1985). The *place*, *misplace*, and *displace* neural units in the rat's brain (O'Keefe 1976), units that guide the animal in its movements through its environment, are merely internal indicators of place, of alterations in place, and of movement through a place. Such is the stuff of which cognitive maps are made, part of the normal endowment for even such lowly organisms as ants and wasps (Gallistel 1980).

The firing of neural cells in the visual cortex, by indicating the presence and orientation of a certain energy gradient on the surface of the photoreceptors, indicates the whereabouts and the orientation of "edges" in the optical input and therefore indicates something about the surfaces in the environment from which light is being reflected. The activity of these cells, not to mention comparable activity by other cells in a wide variety of sensory systems, is as much a natural sign or indicator as are the more familiar events we commonly think of as signs – the autumnal change in maple leaves, growth rings in a tree, and tracks in the snow.

We are accustomed to hearing about biological functions for various bodily organs. The heart, the kidneys, and the pituitary gland, we are told, have functions – things they are, in this sense, *supposed to do*. The fact that these organs are supposed to do these things, the fact that they have these functions, is quite independent of what *we* think they are supposed to do. Biologists *discovered* these functions, they didn't invent or assign them. We cannot, by agreeing among ourselves, *change* the functions of these organs in the way that I can change, merely by making an appropriate announcement, what the coins and the popcorn in my basketball game stand for. The same seems true for sensory systems, those organs by means of which highly sensitive and continuous dependencies are maintained between external, public events and internal, neural processes. Can there be a serious question about whether, in the same sense in which it is the heart's function to pump the blood, it is, say, the task or function of the noctuid moth's auditory system to detect the whereabouts and movements of its archenemy, the bat?

Some marine bacteria have internal magnets, magnetosomes, that function like compass needles, aligning themselves (and, as a result, the bacterium) parallel to the Earth's magnetic field (Blakemore and Frankel 1981). Since the magnetic lines incline downward (toward geomagnetic north) in the northern hemisphere, bacteria in the northern hemisphere, oriented by their internal magnetosomes, propel themselves toward geomagnetic north. Since these organisms are capable of living only in the absence of oxygen, and since movement toward geomagnetic north will take northern bacteria away from the oxygen-rich and therefore toxic surface water and toward the comparatively oxygen-free sediment at the bottom, it is not unreasonable to speculate, as Blakemore and Frankel do, that *the function* of this primitive sensory system is to indicate the whereabouts of benign (i.e., anaerobic) environments.[6]

Philosophers may disagree about how best to analyze the attribution of function to the organs, processes, and behaviors of animals and plants (see, for example, Nagel 1961, Wright 1973, Boorse 1976, and Cummins 1975, all conveniently collected in Sober 1984), but that some of these things *have* functions – functions, like those of the bacterium's magnetic sense or the moth's auditory sense, to be *discovered* (not invented or assigned) – seems evident not only from a common-sense standpoint but also from the practice, if not the explicit avowals, of biologists and botanists.

This is, nevertheless, a controversial topic, at least among philosophers (see, e.g., Dennett 1987), and I do not wish to rest a case for a *philosophical* thesis on what seems evident to common sense or what is taken for granted by biologists. So for the moment I take the biological examples as more or less (depending on your point of view) plausible illustrations of intrinsic functions – plausible examples, therefore, of sensory systems that, by having such functions, qualify as *natural* systems of representation. As we shall see later (Chapter 4 [of *Explaining Behavior*]), the case for representational systems of Type III will rest on quite different sorts of functions: those that are derived, not from the evolution of the species, but from the development of the individual. Nevertheless, it is useful to think, if only for illustrative purposes, about the way certain indicator systems developed, in the evolutionary history of a species, to serve the biological needs of its members. It should be understood, though, that my use of such examples is merely an expository convenience. The *argument* that there are functions of the kind required for Type III systems, hence an argument for the *existence* of Type III systems, systems with a natural power of representation, remains to be made.

3.5   Intentionality: misrepresentation[7]

Philosophers have long regarded intentionality as a mark of the mental. One important dimension of intentionality is the capacity to misrepresent, the power (in the case of the so-called propositional attitudes) to *say* or *mean* that P when P is not the case. The purpose of this section is to describe how systems of representation, as these have now been characterized, possess this capacity and, hence, exhibit some marks of the mental. Two other important dimensions of intentionality will be discussed in the following section.

Before we begin, it is perhaps worth noting that, since systems of Types I and II derive their representational powers, including their power to misrepresent, from systems (typically humans) that already have the full range of intentional states and attitudes (knowledge, purpose, desire, etc.), *their* display of intentional characteristics is not surprising. As we shall see, the traces of intentionality exhibited by such systems are merely *reflections* of the minds, *our* minds, that assign them the properties, in particular the functions, from which they derive their status as representations. This is not so, however, for systems of Type III. If there are such systems, *their* intentionality will not be a thing of our making. They will have what Haugeland (1981) calls *original* intentionality and Searle (1980) calls *intrinsic* intentionality.

The first aspect of intentionality to be described is the capacity some systems have to represent something as being so when it is not so – the power of *misrepresentation*. It may be thought odd to accent the negative in this way, odd to focus on a system's ability to get things wrong – on its vices, as it were, instead of its virtues. There is, though, nothing backward about this approach. The ability to correctly represent how things stand elsewhere in the world *is* the ability of primary value, of course, but this value adheres to representations only insofar as the representation in question is the sort of thing that *can* get things wrong. In the game of representation, the game of "saying" how things stand elsewhere in the world, telling the truth isn't a virtue if you *cannot* lie. I have already said that indication, as I am using this word, and as Grice used the idea of natural meaning, describes a relation that cannot fail to hold between an indicator and what it indicates. There can be no *mis*indication. If the gas tank is empty, the gauge *cannot*, in this sense of the word, indicate that it is full. This is not to say that someone might not *take* the gauge as indicating a full tank. It is only to say that the gauge does not, in fact, indicate a full tank. Since indicators cannot, in this sense, fail to indicate, they do not possess the capacity of interest: the power to get things wrong. *They* don't get things wrong. *We* get things wrong by (sometimes) misreading the signs, by *taking* them to indicate something they don't. What we are after is the power of a system to say, mean, or represent (or, indeed, *take*) things as *P whether or not P is the case*. That is the power of words, of beliefs, of thought – the power that *minds* have – and that, therefore, is the power we are seeking in representational systems. Whatever *word* we use to describe the relation of interest (representation? meaning?), it is the power to misrepresent, the capacity to get things wrong, to say things that are not true, that helps *define* the relation of interest. *That* is why it is important to stress a system's capacity for misrepresentation. For only if a system has this capacity does it have, in its power to get things right, something approximating *meaning*. That is why the capacity to misrepresent is an important aspect of intentionality and why it figures so large in the philosophy of mind and the philosophy of language.

For this reason it is important to remember that not every indicator, not even those that occur *in* plants and animals, is a representation. It is essential that it be the indicator's *function* – natural (for systems of Type III) or otherwise (for systems of Type II) – to indicate what it indicates. The width of growth rings in trees growing in semi-arid regions is a sensitive rain gauge, an accurate indication of the amount of rainfall in the year corresponding to the ring. This does not mean, however, that these rings *represent* the amount of rainfall in each year. For that to be the case, it would be necessary that it be the function of these rings to indicate, by their width, the amount of rain in the year corresponding to each ring.[8] This, to say the least, is implausible – unless, of course, we start thinking of the rings as an RS of Type II. We, or botanists, might *use* these rings to learn about past climatic conditions. Should this happen in some regular, systematic way, the rings might take on some of the properties of an instrument or gauge (for the people who use them this way). Insofar as these rings start *functioning* in the information-gathering activities of botanists as a sign of past rainfall, they may, over time, and in the botanical community, acquire an indicator function and thereby assume a genuine representational (of Type II) status. At least they might do so *for* the botanists who use them this way. But this is clearly not an RS of Type III. Though there is something in the tree, the width of the fourteenth ring, that indicates the amount of rainfall fourteen years ago, it is implausible to suppose it is the ring's function to indicate this. The variable width of the rings is merely the effect of variable rainfall. The distension of an animal's stomach is, likewise, an indicator of the amount of food the animal has eaten and (for this reason, perhaps) an indicator of the amount of food available in its environment. But this is surely not the function of a distended stomach.

This point is important if we are to understand the way RSs manage to misrepresent things. The capacity for misrepresentation is easy enough to understand in systems of Type I. For here the power of the elements to misrepresent depends on *our* willingness and skill in manipulating them in accordance with the (indicator) functions we have assigned them. Since I am responsible for what the coins and the popcorn in my basketball game stand for, since I assigned them their indicator function, and since I am responsible for manipulating them in accordance with this function, the arrangement of coins and popcorn can be made to misrepresent whatever I, deliberately or out of ignorance, make them misrepresent. Their misrepresentations are really *my* misrepresentations.

Misrepresentation in systems of Type II is not quite so simple an affair, but, once again, its occurrence ultimately traces to whoever or whatever assigns the functions that determine the system's representational efforts. Since there is no such thing as a *mis*indication, no such thing as a natural sign's meaning that something is so when it is not so, the only way a system of natural signs can misrepresent anything is if the signs that serve as its representational elements fail to indicate something they are *supposed* to indicate. And what they are *supposed* to indicate is what *we*, for purposes of our own, and independent of a sign's success in carrying out its mission on particular occasions, *regard* them as having (or give them) the job of doing. Without *us* there are no standards for measuring failure, nothing the system fails to do that it is supposed to do. Although the actual failures aren't *our* failures, the standards (functions) that make them failures are our standards. Putting chilled alcohol in a glass cylinder doesn't generate a misrepresentation unless somebody calibrates the glass, hangs it on the wall, and calls it a thermometer.

Only when we reach RSs of Type III – only when the functions defining what a system is supposed to indicate are intrinsic functions – do we find a *source*, not merely a reflection, of intentionality. Only here do we have systems sufficiently self-contained in their representational efforts to serve, in this one respect at least, as models of thought, belief, and judgment.

A system could have acquired the *function* of indicating that something was F without, in the present circumstances, or any longer, or perhaps *ever*, being able to indicate that something is F. This is obvious in the case of a Type II RS, where, by careless assembly, a device can fail to do what it was designed to do. As we all know, some shiny new appliances don't work the way they are supposed to work. They *never* do what it is their function to do. When what they are supposed to do is indicate, such devices are doomed to a life of misrepresentation. Others leave the factory in good condition but later wear out and no longer retain the power to indicate what it is their function to indicate. Still others, though they don't wear out, are used in circumstances that curtail their ability to indicate what they were designed to indicate. A compass is no good in a mineshaft, and a thermometer isn't much good in the sun. In order to do what they are supposed to do, care has to be taken that such instruments are used when and where they can do their job.

The same is true of RSs of Type III. Suppose a primitive sensory ability evolves in a species because of what it is capable of telling its possessors about some critical environmental condition F. Let us assume, for the sake of the example, that the manner in which this indicator developed, the way it was (because of its critical role in delivering needed information) favored by the forces of selection, allows us to say that this indicator has the function of indicating F. Through some reproductive accident, an individual member of this species (call him Inverto) inherits his F-detector in defective (let us suppose inverted) condition. Poor Inverto has an RS that always misrepresents his surroundings: it represents things as being F when they are not, and vice versa.[9] Unless he is fortunate enough to be preserved in some artificial way – unless, that is, he is removed from a habitat in which the detection of Fs is critical – Inverto will not long survive. He emerged defective from the factory and will soon be discarded. On the other hand,

318

his cousins, though emerging from the factory in good condition, may simply wear out. As old age approaches, their RSs deteriorate, progressively losing their ability to indicate when and where there is an *F*. They retain their function, of course, but they lose the capacity to perform that function. Misrepresentation becomes more and more frequent until, inevitably, they share Inverto's fate.

And, finally, we have the analogue, in a Type III system, of an instrument used in disabling circumstances – the compass in a mineshaft, for instance. Consider a sensitive biological detector that, upon removal from the habitat in which it developed, flourished, and faithfully serviced its possessor's biological needs, is put into circumstances in which it is no longer capable of indicating what it is supposed to indicate. We earlier considered bacteria that relied on internal detectors (magnetosomes) of magnetic north in order to reach oxygen-free environments. Put a northern bacterium into the southern hemisphere and it will quickly destroy itself by swimming in the wrong direction. If we suppose (we needn't; see footnote 6) that it is the function of these internal detectors to indicate the whereabouts of anaerobic conditions, then misrepresentation occurs – in this case with fatal consequences.

Put a frog in a laboratory where carefully produced shadows simulate edible bugs. In these unnatural circumstances the frog's neural detectors – those that have, for good reason, been called "bug detectors" – will no longer indicate the presence or the location of bugs. They will no longer indicate this (even when they are, by chance, caused to fire by real edible bugs) because their activity no longer *depends* in the requisite way on the presence of edible bugs. Taking a frog into the laboratory is like taking a compass down a mineshaft: things no longer work the way they are supposed to work. Indicators stop indicating. If we suppose, then, that it is the function of the frog's neural detectors to indicate the presence of edible bugs, then, in the laboratory, shadows are misrepresented *as* edible bugs. The frog has an analogue of a false belief.[10] Occasionally, when an edible bug flies by, the frog will correctly represent it as an edible bug, but this is dumb luck. The frog has the analogue of a true belief, a correct representation, but no *knowledge*, no *reliable* representation. Taking a compass down a mineshaft will not change what it "says" (namely, that whichever way the needle points is geomagnetic north), but it will change the reliability, and (often enough) the truth, of what it says. Likewise, taking a frog into the laboratory will not change what it "thinks," but it will change the number of times it *truly* thinks what it thinks.

All this is conditional on assumptions about what it is the *function* of an indicator to indicate. Upon realizing that a typical fuel gauge in an automobile cannot distinguish between gasoline and water in the tank, one could insist that it is the gauge's function to register not how much gasoline is left in the tank but how much *liquid* is left in the tank. It is our job, the job of those who use the gauge, to see to it that the liquid is gasoline. If this is indeed how the function of the gauge is understood, then, of course, the gauge does *not* misrepresent anything when there is water in the tank; it correctly represents the tank as half full of liquid. And a similar possibility exists for the frog. If the function of the neural detectors on which the frog depends to find food is merely that of informing the frog of the whereabouts of small moving dark spots, then the frog is *not* misrepresenting its surroundings when, in the laboratory, it starves to death while flicking at shadows. For the internal representation triggering this response is perfectly accurate. It indicates what it is supposed to indicate: the presence and whereabouts of small, moving dark spots. The shadows *are* small moving dark spots, so nothing is being misrepresented.

Misrepresentation depends on two things: the *condition* of the world being represented and the *way* that world is represented. The latter, as we have seen, is determined, not by what a system indicates about the world, but by what it has the function of indicating about the world. And as long as there remains this indeterminacy of function, there is no clear sense in which misrepresentation occurs. Without a determinate function, one can, as it were, always exonerate an RS of error, and thus eliminate the occurrence of misrepresentation, by changing what it is *supposed* to be indicating, by changing what it is its function to indicate. It is this indeterminacy that Dennett (1987) dramatizes in his arguments against the idea of *original* or *intrinsic* intentionality.

What this shows is that the occurrence of misrepresentation depends on there being some principled, nonarbitrary way of saying what the indicator function of a system is. In systems of Types I and II there is no special problem because *we* are the source of the functions. We can, collectively as it were, eliminate this indeterminacy of function by agreeing among ourselves or by taking the designer's and the manufacturer's word as to what the device is supposed to do. If a watch is really a calendar watch, as advertised, then it is *supposed* to indicate the date. It "says" today is the fourth day of the month. It isn't. So it is misrepresenting the date. Case closed.

The case is not so easily closed in systems of Type III. It can only be successfully closed when internal indicators are harnessed to a control mechanism. Only by *using* an indicator in the production of movements whose successful outcome depends on *what is being indicated* can this functional indeterminacy be overcome, or so I shall argue in chapter 4 [of *Explaining Behavior*].

3.6 Intentionality: reference and sense

If an RS has the function of indicating that *s* is *F*, then I shall refer to the proposition expressed by the sentence "*s* is *F*" as the *content* of the representation. There are always two questions that one can ask about representational contents. One can ask, first, about its reference – the object, person, or condition the representation is a representation *of*. Second, one can ask about the way what is represented is represented. What does the representation say or indicate (or, when failure occurs, what is it *supposed* to say or indicate) about what it represents? The second question is a question about what I shall call the sense or meaning of the representational content. Every representational content has both a sense and a reference, or, as I shall sometimes put it, a topic and a comment – what it says (the comment) and what it says it about (the topic). These two aspects of representational systems capture two additional strands of intentionality: the *aboutness* or *reference* of an intentional state and (when the intentional state has a propositional content) the *intensionality* (spelled with an "s") of sentential expressions of that content.

Nelson Goodman (1976) distinguished between pictures *of* black horses and what he called black-horse pictures. This is basically my distinction between topic and comment. Black-horse pictures represent the black horses they are pictures of *as* black horses. Imagine a black horse photographed at a great distance in bad light with the camera slightly out of focus. The horse appears as a blurry spot in the distance. This *is* a picture of a black horse, but not what Goodman calls a black-horse picture. When invited to see pictures of your friend's black horse, you expect to see, not only pictures of a black horse, but black-horse pictures – pictures in which the denotation, topic, or reference of the picture is *identifiably* a black horse – or, if not a *black* horse, then at least a horse or an animal of some sort.

Not all representations are pictorial. Many representations are not expected, even under optimal conditions, to *resemble* the objects they represent. Language is a case in point, but even in the case of Type II RSs it is clear that ringing doorbells do not resemble depressed doorbuttons (or people at the door) and that fuel gauges (at least the old-fashioned kind) do not resemble tanks full of gasoline. And if, as seems likely, there is in a wolf's skull some neural representation of the wounded caribou it so relentlessly follows (ignoring the hundreds of healthy animals nearby), this representation of the caribou's condition, position, and movements does not actually resemble, in the way a photograph or a documentary film might resemble, a terrified caribou. A picture, though, is only one kind of representation, a representation in which information about the referent is carried by means of elements that visually resemble the items they represent.

A nonpictorial representation, however, exhibits the same dimensions. It has a reference and a meaning, a topic and a comment. My fuel gauge is not only a representation *of* an empty gasoline tank; it is also (when things are working right) an empty-tank representation. That the tank is empty is what it indicates, the information it carries, the comment it makes, about that topic. My gas tank is also very rusty, but the gauge does not comment on this feature of its topic.

The wolf's internal representation of a sick caribou may or may not be a sick-and-fleeing-caribou representation, but it certainly is a representation *of* a sick, fleeing caribou. *How* the neural machinery represents *what* it represents is, to some degree, a matter of speculation, a matter of divining what the patterns of neural activity in the wolf's brain indicate about the caribou and (since we are talking about *representations*) what, if anything, it is the function of these sensory-cognitive elements to indicate about prey. Does the wolf really represent caribou *as* caribou? Sick and lame caribou *as* sick and lame? If it turns out (it doesn't) that the wolf cannot distinguish a caribou from a moose, the answer to the first question is surely No. Perhaps the wolf merely represents caribou as large animals of some sort. Or merely as food. But the point is that unless the wolf has some means of representing comparatively defenseless caribou – a way of commenting on these creatures that is, for practical wolfish purposes, extensionally equivalent to *being a (comparatively) defenseless caribou* – its relentless and unerring pursuit of comparatively defenseless caribou is an absolute mystery, like the flawless performance of an automatic door opener that has nothing in it to signal (indicate) the approach of a person or an object. There has to be something in there that "tells" the door opener what it needs to know in order for it to do what it does – to open the door *when* someone approaches. The same is true of the wolf.

Our ordinary descriptions of what animals (including people) see, hear, smell, feel, know, believe, recognize, and remember reflect the distinction between a representation's topic and its comment. This, I think, lends support to the idea that a cognitive system *is* a representational system of some kind, presumably a system of Type III. We say, for example, that Clyde can see a black horse in the distance without (for various reasons having to do either with the great distance, the camouflage, the lighting, or the fact that Clyde forgot his glasses) its *looking like* a black horse to Clyde, without its presenting (as some philosophers like to put it) *a black-horse appearance.* Clyde doesn't know what it is, but he thinks it might be the brown cow he has been looking for. In talking this way, and it is a common way of talking, we describe what Clyde's representation is a representation *of* (a black horse) and say how he represents it (as a brown cow). In Goodman's language, Clyde has a brown-cow representation of a black horse. At other times perhaps all we can say about how Clyde represents the black horse is as *something* in the distance. This may be the only comment Clyde's representational system is making about that topic. This isn't much different from a cheap scale's representing a 3.17-pound roast as weighing somewhere between 3 and 4 pounds. It is a rough comment on a perfectly determinate topic.

Compare Clyde's perceptual relationship to the black horse with a fuel gauge's relation to a full tank of gasoline. When things are working properly, the gauge carries information about the tank: the information that it is full. Since it is the gauge's assigned function to deliver this information, it represents the tank as full. It does not, however, carry information about *which* tank is full. Normally, of course, an automobile comes equipped with only one gasoline tank. The gauge is connected to *it*. There is no reason to comment on which topic (which tank) the gauge is making a remark about, since there is only one topic on which to comment and everybody knows this. Suppose, however, there were several auxiliary tanks, with some mechanism letting the gauge systematically access different tanks. Or suppose we were to connect (by radio control, say) Clyde's gauge to *my* tank. In this case the representation would have a different referent, a different topic, but the *same* comment. The gauge would "say" not that Clyde's tank was full but that *my* tank was full. The fact that it was saying this, rather than something else, would not be evident from the representation itself, of course. But neither is it evident from Clyde's representation of the black horse that it is, indeed, a representation of a black horse. To know this one needs to know, just as in the case of the gauge, to what Clyde is connected in the appropriate way. Examining the representation itself won't tell you what condition in the world satisfies it, what condition would (were it to obtain) make the representation an accurate representation. For this one has to look at the wiring. In Clyde's case, there being no wires connecting him to the black horse, you have to look at the connections that *do* establish which topic his representation is a representation of. In the case of vision, that connection is pretty clearly, in most normal cases, whatever it is *from which* the light (entering Clyde's eyes) is reflected.[11]

The job of gauges and instruments is to carry information about the items (tanks, circuits, shafts, etc.) to which they are connected, not information about which item it is to which they are connected. So it is with pictures and most other forms of representation. Perceptual beliefs of a certain sort – what philosophers call *de re* beliefs (e.g., *that* is moving) – are often as silent as gauges about what it is they represent, about what topic it is on which they comment, about their *reference*. Clyde can see a black horse in the distance, thereby getting information about a black horse (say, that it is near a barn), without getting the information that it is a black

horse – without, in other words, seeing *what* it is. Just as a gauge represents the gas level in my tank without representing it as the amount of gas
in *my* tank, Clyde can have a belief about (a representation *of*) my horse
without believing that it is (without representing it *as*) my (or even *a*) horse.

A great many representational contents are of this *de re* variety. There
is a representation *of* the tank as being half full, *of* an animal as being lame
or sick, *of* a doorbutton as being depressed, *of* a cat as being up a tree (or
of a cat and *of* a tree as the one being up the other). These are called *de re*
contents because the things (*re*) about which a comment is made is determined by nonrepresentational means, by means other than *how* that item
is represented. That this is a picture, a photographic representation, *of* Sue
Ellen, *not* her twin sister Ellen Sue, is not evident – indeed (given that they
are identical twins) not discoverable – from the representation itself, from
the *way* she is represented. One has to know who was standing in front of
the camera to know who it is a picture of, and this fact cannot be learned
(given the twin sister) from the picture itself. If causal theories are right (see,
e.g., Stampe 1977), the reference of such representations will be determined
by causal relations: that object, condition, or situation which is, as Sue Ellen
was, causally responsible for the properties possessed by the representation
(e.g., the color and distribution of pigment on the photographic paper).

Though most representations of Type II have a *de re* character, there are
ready examples of comparatively simple systems having a *de dicto* content,
a content whose reference is determined by *how* it is represented. Imagine
a detector whose function it is to keep track of things as they pass it on an
assembly line and to record each thing's color and ordinal position. At the
time it is registering the color (red) and the position (fourth) of *delta*, it can
be said that this mechanism provides a *de re* representation *of delta* as red
and as the fourth item to pass by. The reference is *delta* because that is the
item on the assembly line that the detector is currently monitoring (to which
it is causally connected), and the meaning or sense is given by the expression "is red and number four" because that is what the detector indicates,
and has the function of indicating, about the items it is presently scanning.
At a later time, though, a time when the apparatus is no longer directly
recording facts about delta, its representation of the fourth item as red
changes its character. Its reference to delta, its representation *of* delta, now
occurs via its description of delta as the fourth item. At this later time,
delta's color is relevant to the determination of the correctness of the representation *only insofar* as *delta* was the fourth item on the assembly line. If
it wasn't, then even if *delta was* the item the detector registered (incorrectly)
as the fourth item, *delta*'s color is irrelevant to the correctness of the representation. It is *the fourth item*, not *delta*, that has to be red in order for
this (later) representation to be correct. Compare my belief, one day later,

that the fourth person to enter the room was wearing a funny hat. If I retain in memory no other description capable of picking out who I believe to have been wearing a funny hat (as is the case with our imagined detector), then this later belief, unlike the original belief, is a belief about *whoever* was the fourth person to enter the room. I may never have seen, never have been causally connected to, the person who makes this belief true.

One can go further in this direction of separating the reference of a representation from the object that is causally responsible for the representation by equipping an RS with projectional resources, with some means of extrapolating or interpolating indicated patterns. Something like this would obviously be useful in a representation-driven control system that had a "need to act" in the absence of firm information. Imagine our detector, once again, given the function of simultaneously monitoring items on *several* assembly lines, recording the color and the ordinal value of each, and, on the basis of this information, making appropriate adjustments in some sorting mechanism. Think of it as an overworked device for weeding out rotten (nonred) apples. Since "attention" paid to one line requires ignoring the others, the device must "guess" about items it fails to "observe," or else a switching mechanism can be introduced that allows the detector to withdraw continuous attention from a line that exhibits a sufficiently long sequence of red apples. A "safe" line will be sampled intermittently, at a frequency of sampling determined by the line's past safety record. The detector "keeps an eye on" the lines that have poor performance records, and "infers" that the apples on good lines are OK. If things are working reasonably well, this device produces a printed record containing representations of apples it has never inspected. This device has the function of indicating something about objects to which it is *never* causally related.

It is not hard to imagine nature providing animals with similar cognitive resources. Donald Griffin (1984), drawing on the work of J.L. Gould (1979, 1982), describes the way honeybees perform a comparable piece of extrapolation. Honeybees were offered a dish of sugar water at the entrance of their hive. The dish was then moved a short distance away, and the bees managed to find it. This was continued until, when the feeder was more than 100 or 200 meters from the hive, the bees began waiting for the dish beyond the spot where it had last been left, at what would be the next logical stopping place (20 to 30 meters from the last location). The bees, Griffin observes, "seem to have realized that this splendid new food source moves and that to find it again they should fly farther out from home" (pp. 206–207). The benefits of such extrapolative mechanisms are obvious. Aside from the search technique of the bees, an animal without beliefs (whether we call them anticipations, expectations, or fears) about *the next* A will not survive long in an environment where the next A can be dangerous.

Much more can, and should, be said about the reference or topic of a representation. But it is time to turn to its sense or meaning, *how* it represents what it represents, the comment it makes on that topic. All systems of representation, whatever type they happen to be, are what I shall call *property specific.* By this I mean that a system can represent something (call it *s*) as having the property F without representing it as having the property G even though everything having the first property has the second, even though every F *is* G. Even if the predicate expressions "F" and "G" are *coextensional* (correctly apply to exactly the same things), this doesn't guarantee that an RS will represent *s* as F just because it represents *s* as G (or vice versa). These extensionally equivalent expressions give expression to quite different representational contents. This is a very important fact about representational systems. It gives their content a fine-grainedness that is characteristic of intentional systems. It makes verbal expressions of their content *intensional* rather than *extensional.* It is this feature, together with the system's capacity for misrepresentation and the reference or aboutness of its elements, that many philosophers regard as the essence of the mental.

Representational contents exhibit this peculiar fine-grainedness because even when properties F and G are so intimately related that nothing can indicate that something is F without indicating that it (or some related item) is G, it can be the device's *function* to indicate one without its being its function to indicate the other.[12] Nothing can indicate that *x* is red unless it thereby indicates that *x* is colored, but it can be a device's function to indicate the color of objects (e.g. that they are red) without its being its function to indicate that they are colored.

The specificity of functions to particular properties, even when these properties are related in ways (e.g., by logical or nomological relations) that prevent one's being indicated without the other's being indicated, is easy to illustrate with assigned functions, functions *we* give to instruments and detectors. For here the assignment of functions merely reflects *our* special interest in one property rather than the other. If we are, for whatever reason, interested in the number of angles in a polygon and not in the number of sides, then we can give a detector (or a *word*) the function of indicating the one without giving it the function of indicating the other even though the detector (or word) cannot successfully indicate that something is, say, a triangle without thereby indicating that it has three sides. We can make something into a voltmeter (something having the function of indicating voltage differences) without thereby giving it the function of indicating the amount of current flowing even if, because of constant resistance, these two quantities covary in some lawful way.

Though this phenomenon is easier to illustrate for Type I and Type II systems, it can easily occur, or can easily be imagined to occur, in systems of Type III. Dolphins, we are told, can recognize the shapes of objects placed in their pool from a distance of 50 feet. Apparently there is something in the dolphin, no doubt something involving its sensitive sonar apparatus, that indicates the *shapes* of objects in the water. But a dolphin that can infallibly identify, detect, recognize, or discriminate (use whatever cognitive verb you think appropriate here) cylinders from this distance should *not* be credited with the ability to identify, detect, recognize, or discriminate, say, *red* objects from this distance just because all (and only) the cylinders are red. If the fact that all (and only) the cylinders are red is a coincidence, of course, then something can indicate that X is a cylinder without indicating that X is red. This follows from the fact that an indicator could exhibit the requisite *dependence* on the shape of X without exhibiting any dependence on the color of X. But even if we suppose the connection between color and shape to be more intimate; we can, because of the different relevance of these properties to the well-being of an animal, imagine a detector having the function of indicating the shape of things without having the function of indicating their color.[13]

3.7 Summary

The elements of a representational system, then, have a content or a meaning, a content or meaning defined by what it is their function to indicate. This meaning or content is a species of what Grice called non-natural meaning. These meanings display many of the intentional properties of genuine thought and belief. If, then, there are systems of Type III, and these are located in the heads of some animals, then there is, in the heads of some animals (1) something that is *about* various parts of this world, even those parts of the world with which the animal has never been in direct perceptual contact; (2) something capable of representing and, just as important, *misrepresenting* those parts of the world it is about; and (3) something that has, thereby, a *content* or *meaning* (not itself in the head, of course) that is individuated in something like the way we individuate thoughts and beliefs.

Notes

1 That is, no intrinsic power to indicate *what it is their (assigned) function to indicate*. They may, of course, indicate something *else* in a way that is not dependent on us. For instance, the coins, being metal, indicate (by their volume) the temperature. They *could*, therefore, be used as crude thermometers. But, according to the story I am telling, this isn't their (assigned) function. If it was, then we would be talking about an RS of Type II.

2 Fodor (1987b) mentions an interesting illustration of this phenomenon discussed by David Marr and his associates: an algorithm (in the perceptual system) for computing three-dimensional form from two-dimensional rotation. The algorithm is not strictly valid, since there are worlds in which it reaches *false* three-dimensional conclusions from *true* two-dimensional premises – worlds in which spatial rotations are not rigid. Nevertheless, the algorithm is truth-preserving in the circumstances in which it is in fact employed – viz., *here*, in our world. Add to this the fact that the perceptual mechanisms that exploit this algorithm were evolved *here*, in *this* world, and we have a biological example of a uniformity – not lawful, but not fortuitous either – that enables sensory "premises" about two-dimensional rotations (that is, premises describing the two-dimensional transformations of the retinal image) to indicate something about the three-dimensional world we live in.

3 This is not to say that descriptions of what something means or indicates are always free of subjective factors. We often describe what something means or indicates in a way that reflects what we already *know* about the possibilities. If there are only two switches controlling a light, the light indicates that one of the two switches is closed. Knowing, however, that *this switch* (one of the two) *isn't* closed, I take the light's being on as an indication that *the other switch* is closed. In this case, the light (is said) to indicate something that it would not indicate unless I, the speaker, *knew* something about other possibilities.

In this sense the meanings we ascribe to signs is relative. It is relative to what the speaker already knows about possible alternatives. This, however, doesn't mean that natural meaning is *subjective*. A person's weight isn't subjective just because it is relative, just because people weigh less on the moon than they do on earth. If nobody knew anything, things would still indicate other things. They just wouldn't indicate the specific sort of thing (e.g., the other switch is closed) we now describe them as indicating.

4 Not, at least, as an RS of Type II. One could, however, use it as an RS of Type I. Just as I used coins and popcorn to represent basketball players, and the positions and movements of the players, there is nothing preventing one from *using* a rectal thermometer in a similar fashion to represent the Dow-Jones average.

5 For those who want to quarrel about this issue, I could, I suppose, assign a rock the job of doing my dishes if I mistook it for my son, just as I could assign a thermometer the job of indicating fluctuations in the stock market if I mistook it for something else. I do not, however, think a rock could actually *have* this function. Nor do I think a simple instrument could *have* the function of indicating something it could not indicate. This is not to say that the thermometer could not be incorporated into a more complex system that *could* indicate, and therefore could have the function of indicating, something about the stock market. But, by the same token, I could also make the rock part of a machine (pulleys, etc.) that *could* do (and, therefore, could have the function of doing) my dishes.

6 There may be some disagreement about how best to describe the function of this primitive sensory system. Does it have the function of indicating the location, direction, or whereabouts of anaerobic conditions? Or does it, perhaps, have the function of indicating the Earth's magnetic polarity (which in turn indicates the direction of anaerobic conditions)? In Dretske (1986) I described this as an "indeterminacy" of function. As long as this indeterminacy exists,

there is, of course, an associated indeterminacy in what the system represents. I return to this point later.

7 The material in this section is based on Dretske (1986). That work, and in fact this entire chapter, was heavily influenced by the important work of Stampe (1975, 1977), Millikan (1984, 1986), Enc (1979, 1982), and Fodor (1984, 1987a). Also see Papineau (1984).

8 Fodor (1984) makes this point against Stampe's (1977) idea that the rings in a tree *represent*, in the relevant sense, the tree's age. See Stampe (1986) for a reply.

9 An artificial approximation of this situation occurred when R.W. Sperry (1956) and his associates rotated, by surgical means, the eyeball of a newt by 180°. The vision of the animal was permanently reversed. As Sperry describes it: "When a piece of bait was held above the newt's head it would begin digging into the pebbles and sand on the bottom of the aquarium. When the lure was presented in front of its head, it would turn around and start searching in the rear."

It should be noted that one doesn't disable an indicator *merely* by reversing the code – letting *b* (formerly indicating *B)* indicate *A* and *a* (formerly indicating *A*) indicate *B*. As long as this reversal is systematic, the change is merely a change in the way information is being coded, not a change in the information being coded. But though *A* and *B* are still being indicated (by *b* and *a* respectively), they are, after the inversion, no longer being accurately *represented* unless there is a corresponding change (inversion) in the way the representational elements (*a* and *b*) function in the rest of the system. This is what did not happen with the newt. It still got the information it needed, but as a result of the coding change it misrepresented the conditions in its environment.

10 But not a real false belief, because, as we shall see in the next chapter [of *Explaining Behavior*], beliefs are *more* than internal representations. They are internal representations that help explain the behavior of the system of which they are a part.

11 Here I suppress difficult problems in the philosophy of perception, problems about the correct analysis of the perceptual object. Any responsible discussion of these topics would take me too far afield.

12 See Enc (1982) for further illustrations of this. Enc argues, convincingly to my mind, that we can distinguish between the representation of logically *equivalent* situations by appealing to (among other things) the functions of a system.

13 Taylor (1964, p. 150) notes that an experimenter can condition an animal to respond to red objects without conditioning it to respond to objects that differ in color from the experimenter's tie (which is green). He takes this to be a problem for how the property to which behavior is conditioned is selected. It should be clear that I think the answer to Taylor's problem lies, at least in part, in an adequate theory of representation, one that can distinguish between the representation of *X* as red and *X* as not green.

References

Blakemore, R.P. and Frankel, R.B. (1981) "Magnetic Navigation in Bacteria," *Scientific American* 245: 6.

Boorse, C. (1976) "Wright on Functions," *Philosophical Review* 85: 70–86.

Cummins, R. (1975) "Functional Analysis," *Journal of Philosophy* 72: 741–765.

Dennett, D. (1987) "Evolution, Error, and Intentionality," in *The Intentional Stance*, Cambridge, Mass.: MIT Press.

Dretske, F. (1981) *Knowledge and the Flow of Information*, Cambridge, Mass.: MIT Press.

—— (1983) "Précis of *Knowledge and the Flow of Information*," *Behavioral and Brain Sciences* 6: 55–63.

—— (1986) "Misrepresentation," in R. Bogdan (ed.) *Belief*, Oxford: Oxford University Press.

Enc, B. (1979) "Function Attributions and Functional Explanations," *Philosophy of Science* 46: 343–365.

—— (1982) "Intentional States of Mechanical Devices," *Mind* 91: 161–182.

Fodor, J. (1984) "Semantics, Wisconsin Style," *Synthese* 59: 1—20.

—— (1987a) *Psychosemantics*, Cambridge, Mass.: MIT Press.

—— (1987b) "A Situated Grandmother," *Mind and Language* 2: 64–81.

Gallistel, C.R. (1980) *The Organization of Action: A New Synthesis*, Hillsdale, N.J.: Erlbaum.

Goodman, N. (1976) *Languages of Art*, Indianapolis: Hackett.

Gould, J.L. (1979) "Do Honeybees Know What They Are Doing?," *Natural History* 88: 66–75.

—— (1982) *Ethology: The Mechanisms and Evolution of Behavior*, New York: Norton.

Grice, P. (1957) "Meaning," *Philosophical Review* 66: 377–388.

Grier, J.W. (1984) *Biology of Animal Behavior*, St Louis: Mosby.

Griffin, D.R. (1984) *Animal Thinking*, Cambridge, Mass.: Harvard University Press.

Haugeland, J. (1981) "Semantic Engines: An Introduction to Mind Design," in J. Haugeland (ed.) *Mind Design*, Cambridge, Mass.: MIT Press.

Huber, F. and Thorson, J. (1985) "Cricket Auditory Communication," *Scientific American* 253, 6: 60–68.

Millikan, R.G. (1984) *Language, Thought, and Other Biological Categories: New Foundations for Realism*, Cambridge, Mass.: MIT Press.

—— (1986) "Thoughts Without Laws: Cognitive Science With Content," *Philosophical Review* 95: 47–80.

Nagel, E. (1961) *The Structure of Science*, Indianapolis: Hackett.

O'Keefe, J. (1976) "Place Units in the Hippocampus of Freely Moving Rat," *Experimental Neurology* 51: 78–109.

Papineau, D. (1984) "Representation and Explanation," *Philosophy of Science* 51: 550–572.

Searle, J. (1980) "Minds, Brains, and Programs," *Behavioral and Brain Sciences* 3: 417–457. Reprinted as Chapter 16 in this volume.

Sober, E. (ed.) (1984) *Conceptual Issues in Evolutionary Biology*, Cambridge, Mass.: MIT Press.

Sperry, R.W. (1956) "The Eye and the Brain," in R. Held (ed.) *Perception: Mechanisms and Models*, San Francisco: Freeman.

Stampe, D. (1975) "Show and Tell," in B. Freed *et al.* (eds) *Forms of Representation*, Amsterdam: North-Holland.

—— (1977) "Toward a Causal Theory of Linguistic Representation," in P. French *et al.* (eds) *Midwest Studies in Philosophy*, Vol. 2, Minneapolis: University of Minnesota Press.

—— (1986) "Verification and a Causal Account of Meaning," *Synthese* 69: 107–137.

Taylor, C. (1964) *The Explanation of Behavior*, London: Routledge and Kegan Paul.

Wright, L. (1973) "Functions," *Philosophical Review* 82: 139–168.

16

John R. Searle, "Minds, Brains, and Programs"

What psychological and philosophical significance should we attach to recent efforts at computer simulations of human cognitive capacities? In answering this question I find it useful to distinguish what I will call "strong" AI from "weak" or "cautious" AI. According to weak AI, the principal value of the computer in the study of the mind is that it gives us a very powerful tool. For example, it enables us to formulate and test hypotheses in a more rigorous and precise fashion than before. But according to strong AI the computer is not merely a tool in the study of the mind; rather, the appropriately programmed computer really is a mind in the sense that computers given the right programs can be literally said to *understand* and have other cognitive states. And, according to strong AI, because the programmed computer has cognitive states, the programs are not mere tools that enable us to test psychological explanations; rather, the programs are themselves the explanations. I have no objection to the claims of weak AI, at least as far as this article is concerned. My discussion here will be directed to the claims I have defined as strong AI, specifically the claim that the appropriately programmed computer literally has cognitive states and that the programs thereby explain human cognition. When I refer to AI, it is the strong version as expressed by these two claims which I have in mind.

I will consider the work of Roger Schank and his colleagues at Yale (see, for instance, Schank and Abelson 1977), because I am more familiar with it than I am with any similar claims, and because it provides a clear example of the sort of work I wish to examine. But nothing that follows depends upon the details of Schank's programs. The same arguments would apply to Winograd's (1973) SHRDLU, Weizenbaum's (1965) ELIZA, and indeed, any Turing-machine simulation of human mental phenomena.

John R. Searle, "Minds, Brains, and Programs," *Behavioral and Brain Sciences* 3(3) (1980): 417–24.

Briefly, and leaving out the various details, one can describe Schank's program as follows: the aim of the program is to simulate the human ability to understand stories. It is characteristic of the abilities of human beings to understand stories that they can answer questions about the story, even though the information they give was not explicitly stated in the story. Thus, for example, suppose you are given the following story: "A man went into a restaurant and ordered a hamburger. When the hamburger arrived, it was burned to a crisp, and the man stormed out of the restaurant angrily without paying for the hamburger or leaving a tip." Now, if you are given the question "Did the man eat the hamburger?," you will presumably answer, "No, he did not." Similarly if you are given the following story: "A man went into a restaurant and ordered a hamburger; when the hamburger came, he was very pleased with it; and as he left the restaurant he gave the waitress a large tip before paying his bill," and you are asked the question "Did the man eat the hamburger?," you will presumably answer, "Yes, he ate the hamburger."

Now Schank's machines can similarly answer questions about restaurants in this fashion. In order to do so, they have a "representation" of the sort of information that human beings have about restaurants which enables them to answer such questions as those above, given these sorts of stories. When the machine is given the story and then asked the question, the machine will print out answers of the sort that we would expect human beings to give if told similar stories. Partisans of strong AI claim that in this question-and-answer sequence, not only is the machine simulating a human ability but also:

(a) The machine can literally be said to *understand* the story and provide answers to questions; and
(b) What the machine and its program do *explains* the human ability to understand the story and answer questions about it.

Claims (a) and (b) seem to me totally unsupported by Schank's work, as I will attempt to show in what follows.[1]

A way to test any theory of mind is to ask oneself what it would be like if one's own mind actually worked on the principles that the theory says all minds work on. Let us apply this test to the Schank program with the following *Gedankenexperiment*. Suppose that I am locked in a room and suppose that I'm given a large batch of Chinese writing. Suppose furthermore, as is indeed the case, that I know no Chinese either written or spoken, and that I'm not even confident that I could recognize Chinese writing as Chinese writing distinct from, say, Japanese writing or meaningless squiggles. Now suppose further that, after this first batch of Chinese writing,

333

I am given a second batch of Chinese script together with a set of rules for correlating the second batch with the first batch. The rules are in English and I understand these rules as well as any other native speaker of English. They enable me to correlate one set of formal symbols with another set of formal symbols, and all that "formal" means here is that I can identify the symbols entirely by their shapes. Now suppose also that I am given a third batch of Chinese symbols together with some instructions, again in English, that enable me to correlate elements of this third batch with the first two batches, and these rules instruct me how I am to give back certain Chinese symbols with certain sorts of shapes in response to certain sorts of shapes given me in the third batch.

Unknown to me, the people who are giving me all of these symbols call the first batch a "script," they call the second batch a "story," and they call the third batch "questions." Furthermore, they call the symbols I give them back in response to the third batch "answers to the questions," and the set of rules in English that they gave me they call "the program." To complicate the story a little bit, imagine that these people also give me stories in English which I understand, and they then ask me questions in English about these stories, and I give them back answers in English. Suppose also that after a while I get so good at following the instructions for manipulating the Chinese symbols and the programmers get so good at writing the programs that from the external point of view – that is, from the point of view of somebody outside the room in which I am locked – my answers to the questions are indistinguishable from those of native Chinese speakers. Nobody looking at my answers can tell that I don't speak a word of Chinese. Let us also suppose that my answers to the English questions are, as they no doubt would be, indistinguishable from those of other native English speakers, for the simple reason that I am a native speaker of English. From the external point of view, from the point of view of someone reading my "answers," the answers to the Chinese questions and the English questions are equally good. But in the Chinese case, unlike the English case, I produce the answers by manipulating uninterpreted formal symbols. As far as the Chinese is concerned, I simply behave like a computer; I perform computational operations on formally specified elements. For the purposes of the Chinese, I am simply an instantiation of the computer program.

Now the claims made by strong AI are that the programmed computer understands the stories and that the program in some sense explains human understanding. But we are now in a position to examine these claims in light of our thought experiment.

(a) As regards the first claim, it seems to me obvious in the example that I do not understand a word of the Chinese stories. I have inputs and outputs that are indistinguishable from those of the native Chinese speaker, and

I can have any formal program you like, but I still understand nothing. Schank's computer, for the same reasons, understands nothing of any stories, whether in Chinese, English, or whatever, since in the Chinese case the computer is me; and in cases where the computer is not me, the computer has nothing more than I have in the case where I understand nothing.

(b) As regards the second claim – that the program explains human understanding – we can see that the computer and its program do not provide sufficient conditions of understanding, since the computer and the program are functioning and there is no understanding. But does it even provide a necessary condition or a significant contribution to understanding? One of the claims made by the supporters of strong AI is this: when I understand a story in English, what I am doing is exactly the same – or perhaps more of the same – as what I was doing in the case of manipulating the Chinese symbols. It is simply more formal symbol manipulation which distinguishes the case in English, where I do understand, from the case in Chinese, where I don't. I have not demonstrated that this claim is false, but it would certainly appear an incredible claim in the example.

Such plausibility as the claim has derives from the supposition that we can construct a program that will have the same inputs and outputs as native speakers, and in addition we assume that speakers have some level of description where they are also instantiations of a program. On the basis of these two assumptions, we assume that even if Schank's program isn't the whole story about understanding, maybe it is part of the story. That is, I suppose, an empirical possibility, but not the slightest reason has so far been given to suppose it is true, since what is suggested – though certainly not demonstrated – by the example is that the computer program is irrelevant to my understanding of the story. In the Chinese case I have everything that artificial intelligence can put into me by way of a program, and I understand nothing; in the English case I understand everything, and there is so far no reason at all to suppose that my understanding has anything to do with computer programs – that is, with computational operations on purely formally specified elements.

As long as the program is defined in terms of computational operations on purely formally-defined elements, what the example suggests is that these by themselves have no interesting connection with understanding. They are certainly not sufficient conditions, and not the slightest reason has been given to suppose that they are necessary conditions or even that they make a significant contribution to understanding. Notice that the force of the argument is not simply that different machines can have the same input and output while operating on different formal principles – that is not the point at all – but rather that whatever purely formal principles you put into the computer will not be sufficient for understanding, since a human will be able to follow the formal principles without understanding anything, and no reason has been offered to suppose they are necessary or even contributory, since no reason has been given to suppose that when I understand English, I am operating with any formal program at all.

What is it, then, that I have in the case of the English sentences which I do not have in the case of the Chinese sentences? The obvious answer is that I know what the former mean but haven't the faintest idea what the latter mean. In what does this consist, and why couldn't we give it to a machine, whatever it is? Why couldn't the machine be given whatever it is about me that makes it the case that I know what English sentences mean? I will return to these questions after developing my example a little more.

I have had occasions to present this example to several workers in artificial intelligence and, interestingly, they do not seem to agree on what the proper reply to it is. I get a surprising variety of replies, and in what follows I will consider the most common of these (specified along with their geographical origins). First I want to block out some common misunderstandings about "understanding." In many of these discussions one finds fancy footwork about the word "understanding." My critics point out that there are different degrees of understanding, that "understands" is not a simple two-place predicate, that there are even different kinds and levels of understanding, and often the law of the excluded middle doesn't even apply in a straightforward way to statements of the form "x understands y," that in many cases it is a matter for decision and not a simple matter of fact whether x understands y. And so on.

To all these points I want to say: "Of course, of course." But they have nothing to do with the points at issue. There are clear cases where "understands" applies and clear cases where it does not apply; and such cases are all I need for this argument.[2] I understand stories in English; to a lesser degree I can understand stories in French; to a still lesser degree, stories in German; and in Chinese, not at all. My car and my adding machine, on the other hand, understand nothing; they are not in that line of business.

We often attribute "understanding" and other cognitive predicates by metaphor and analogy to cars, adding machines, and other artifacts; but nothing is proved by such attributions. We say, "The door *knows* when to open because of its photoelectric cell," "The adding machine *knows how* (*understands how*, is *able*) to do addition and subtraction but not division," and "The thermostat *perceives* changes in the temperature." The reason we make these attributions is interesting and has to do with the fact that in artifacts we extend our own intentionality;[3] our tools are extensions of our purposes, and so we find it natural to make metaphorical attributions of intentionality to them. But I take it no philosophical ice is cut by such examples. The sense in which an automatic door "understands instructions" from its photoelectric cell is not at all the sense in which I understand English.

If the sense in which Schank's programmed computers understand stories were supposed to be the metaphorical sense in which the door understands, and not the sense in which I understand English, the issue would not be worth discussing. Newell and Simon write that the sense of "understanding" they claim for computers is exactly the same as for human beings. I like the straightforwardness of this claim, and it is the sort of claim I will be considering. I will argue that, in that literal sense, the programmed computer understands what the car and the adding machine understand: exactly nothing. The computer's understanding is not just (as in the case of my understanding of German) partial or incomplete; it is zero.

Now to the replies.

I THE SYSTEMS REPLY (Berkeley): While it is true that the individual person who is locked in the room does not understand the story, the fact is that he is merely part of a whole system and the system does understand the story. The person has a large ledger in front of him in which are written the rules, he has a lot of scratch paper and pencils for doing calculations, he has "data banks" of sets of Chinese symbols. Now, understanding is not being ascribed to the mere individual; rather it is being ascribed to this whole system of which he is a part.

My response to the systems theory is simple. Let the individual internalize all of these elements of the system. He memorizes the rules in the ledger and the data banks of Chinese symbols, and he does all the calculations in his head. The individual then incorporates the entire system. There isn't anything at all to the system which he does not encompass. We can even get rid of the room and suppose he works outdoors. All the same, he understands nothing of the Chinese, and a fortiori neither does the system, because there isn't anything in the system which isn't in him. If he doesn't understand, then there is no way the system could understand because the system is just a part of him.

Actually I feel somewhat embarrassed even to give this answer to the systems theory because the theory seems to me so implausible to start with. The idea is that while a person doesn't understand Chinese, somehow the *conjunction* of that person and some bits of paper might understand Chinese. It is not easy for me to imagine how someone who was not in the grip of an ideology would find the idea at all plausible. Still, I think many people who are committed to the ideology of strong AI will in the end be inclined to say something very much like this; so let us pursue it a bit further.

According to one version of this view, while the man in the internalized systems example doesn't understand Chinese in the sense that a native Chinese speaker does (because, for example, he doesn't know that the story refers to restaurants and hamburgers, and so on), still "the man as formal symbol manipulation system" *really does understand Chinese.* The subsystem of the man which is the formal symbol manipulation system for Chinese should not be confused with the subsystem for English.

So there are really two subsystems in the man; one understands English, the other Chinese, and "it's just that the two systems have little to do with each other." But, I want to reply, not only do they have little to do with each other, they are not even remotely alike. The subsystem that understands English (assuming we allow ourselves to talk in this jargon of "subsystems" for a moment) knows that the stories are about restaurants and eating hamburgers, and the like; he knows that he is being asked questions about restaurants and that he is answering questions as best he can by making various inferences from the content of the story, and so on. But the Chinese system knows none of this; whereas the English subsystem knows that "hamburgers" refers to hamburgers, the Chinese subsystem knows only that "squiggle-squiggle" is followed by "squoggle-squoggle." All he knows is that various formal symbols are being introduced at one end and are manipulated according to rules written in English, and that other symbols are going out at the other end.

The whole point of the original example was to argue that such symbol manipulation by itself couldn't be sufficient for understanding Chinese in any literal sense because the man could write "squoggle-squoggle" after "squiggle-squiggle" without understanding anything in Chinese. And it doesn't meet that argument to postulate subsystems within the man, because the subsystems are no better off than the man was in the first place; they still don't have anything even remotely like what the English-speaking man (or subsystem) has. Indeed, in the case as described, the Chinese subsystem is simply a part of the English subsystem, a part that engages in meaningless symbol manipulation according to the rules of English.

Let us ask ourselves what is supposed to motivate the systems reply in the first place – that is, what *independent* grounds are there supposed to be for saying that the agent must have a subsystem within him that literally understands stories in Chinese? As far as I can tell, the only grounds are that in the example I have the same input and output as native Chinese speakers, and a program that goes from one to the other. But the point of the example has been to show that that couldn't be sufficient for understanding, in the sense in which I understand stories in English, because a person, hence the set of systems that go to make up a person, could have

338

the right combination of input, output, and program and still not understand anything in the relevant literal sense in which I understand English.

The only motivation for saying there *must* be a subsystem in me that understands Chinese is that I have a program and I can pass the Turing test: I can fool native Chinese speakers (see Turing 1950). But precisely one of the points at issue is the adequacy of the Turing test. The example shows that there could be two "systems," both of which pass the Turing test, but only one of which understands; and it is no argument against this point to say that, since they both pass the Turing test, they must both understand, since this claim fails to meet the argument that the system in me which understands English has a great deal more than the system which merely processes Chinese. In short the systems reply simply begs the question by insisting without argument that the system must understand Chinese.

Furthermore, the systems reply would appear to lead to consequences that are independently absurd. If we are to conclude that there must be cognition in me on the grounds that I have a certain sort of input and output and a program in between, then it looks as though all sorts of noncognitive subsystems are going to turn out to be cognitive. For example, my stomach has a level of description where it does information processing, and it instantiates any number of computer programs, but I take it we do not want to say that it has any understanding. Yet if we accept the systems reply, it is hard to see how we can avoid saying that stomach, heart, liver, and so on, are all understanding subsystems, since there is no principled way to distinguish the motivation for saying the Chinese subsystem understands from saying that the stomach understands. (It is, by the way, not an answer to this point to say that the Chinese system has information as input and output and the stomach has food and food products as input and output, since from the point of view of the agent, from my point of view, there is no information in either the food or the Chinese; the Chinese is just so many meaningless squiggles. The information in the Chinese case is solely in the eyes of the programmers and the interpreters, and there is nothing to prevent them from treating the input and output of my digestive organs as information if they so desire.)

This last point bears on some independent problems in strong AI, and it is worth digressing for a moment to explain it. If strong AI is to be a branch of psychology, it must be able to distinguish systems which are genuinely mental from those which are not. It must be able to distinguish the principles on which the mind works from those on which nonmental systems work; otherwise it will offer us no explanations of what is specifically mental about the mental. And the mental/nonmental distinction cannot be just in the eye of the beholder – it must be intrinsic to the systems.

For otherwise it would be up to any beholder to treat people as nonmental and, for instance, hurricanes as mental, if he likes.

But quite often in the AI literature the distinction is blurred in ways which would in the long run prove disastrous to the claim that AI is a cognitive inquiry. McCarthy, for example, writes: "Machines as simple as thermostats can be said to have beliefs, and having beliefs seems to be a characteristic of most machines capable of problem solving performance" (1979). Anyone who thinks strong AI has a chance as a theory of the mind ought to ponder the implications of that remark. We are asked to accept it as a discovery of strong AI that the hunk of metal on the wall which we use to regulate the temperature has beliefs in exactly the same sense that we, our spouses, and our children have beliefs, and furthermore that "most" of the other machines in the room – telephone, tape recorder, adding machine, electric light switch, and so on – also have beliefs in this literal sense. It is not the aim of this article to argue against McCarthy's point, so I will simply assert the following without argument. The study of the mind starts with such facts as that humans have beliefs and thermostats, telephones, and adding machines don't. If you get a theory that denies this point, you have produced a counter-example to the theory, and the theory is false.

One gets the impression that people in AI who write this sort of thing think they can get away with it because they don't really take it seriously and they don't think anyone else will either. I propose, for a moment at least, to take it seriously. Think hard for one minute about what would be necessary to establish that that hunk of metal on the wall over there has real beliefs, beliefs with direction of fit, propositional content, and conditions of satisfaction; beliefs that have the possibility of being strong beliefs or weak beliefs; nervous, anxious or secure beliefs; dogmatic, rational, or superstitious beliefs; blind faiths or hesitant cogitations; any kind of beliefs. The thermostat is not a candidate. Neither are stomach, liver, adding machine, or telephone. However, since we are taking the idea seriously, notice that its truth would be fatal to the claim of strong AI to be a science of the mind, for now the mind is everywhere. What we wanted to know is what distinguishes the mind from thermostats, livers, and the rest. And if McCarthy were right, strong AI wouldn't have a hope of telling us that.

II THE ROBOT REPLY (Yale): Suppose we wrote a different kind of program from Schank's program. Suppose we put a computer inside a robot, and this computer would not just take in formal symbols as input and give out formal symbols as output, but rather it would actually operate the robot in such a way that the robot does something very much like perceiving, walking, moving about, hammering nails, eating, drinking – anything you like. The robot would, for example, have a television camera attached to it that enabled it to see, it would have arms and legs that enabled it to act, and all of this would be controlled by its computer brain. Such a robot would, unlike Schank's computer, have genuine understanding and other mental states.

The first thing to notice about the robot reply is that it tacitly concedes that cognition is not solely a matter of formal symbol manipulation, since this reply adds a set of causal relations with the outside world. But the answer to the robot reply is that the addition of such "perceptual" and "motor" capacities adds nothing by way of understanding, in particular, or intentionality in general, to Schank's original program. To see this, notice that the same thought experiment applies to the robot case. Suppose that, instead of the computer inside the robot, you put me inside the room and you give me again, as in the original Chinese case, more Chinese symbols with more instructions in English for matching Chinese symbols to Chinese symbols and feeding back Chinese symbols to the outside.

Now suppose also that, unknown to me, some of the Chinese symbols that come to me come from a television camera attached to the robot, and other Chinese symbols that I am giving out serve to make the motors inside the robot move the robot's legs or arms. It is important to emphasize that all I am doing is manipulating formal symbols; I know none of these other facts. I am receiving "information" from the robot's "perceptual" apparatus, and I am giving out "instructions" to its motor apparatus without knowing either of these facts. I am the robot's homunculus, but unlike the traditional homunculus, I don't know what's going on. I don't understand anything except the rules for symbol manipulation. Now in this case I want to say that the robot has no intentional states at all; it is simply moving about as a result of its electrical wiring and its program. And furthermore, by instantiating the program, I have no intentional states of the relevant type. All I do is follow formal instructions about manipulating formal symbols.

III THE BRAIN-SIMULATOR REPLY (Berkeley and MIT): Suppose we design a program that doesn't represent information that we have about the world, such as the information in Schank's scripts, but simulates the actual sequence of neuron firings at the synapses of the brain of a native Chinese speaker when he understands stories in Chinese and gives answers to them. The machine takes in Chinese stories and questions about them as input, it simulates the formal structure of actual Chinese brains in processing these stories, and it gives out Chinese answers as outputs. We can even imagine that the machine operates not with a single serial program but with a whole set of programs operating in parallel, in the manner that actual human brains presumably operate when they process natural language. Now surely in such a case we would have to say that the machine understood the stories; and if we refuse to say that, wouldn't we also have to deny that native Chinese speakers understood the stories? At the level of the synapses what would or could be different about the program of the computer and the program of the Chinese brain?

Before addressing this reply, I want to digress to note that it is an odd reply for any partisan of artificial intelligence (functionalism, and so on) to make. I thought the whole idea of strong artificial intelligence is that we don't need to know how the brain works to know how the mind works. The basic hypothesis, or so I had supposed, was that there is a level of mental operations that consists in computational processes over formal elements which constitute the essence of the mental, and can be realized in all sorts of different brain processes in the same way that any computer program can be realized in different computer hardware. On the assumptions of strong AI, the mind is to the brain as the program is to the hardware, and thus we can understand the mind without doing neurophysiology. If we had to know how the brain worked in order to do AI, we wouldn't bother with AI.

However, even getting this close to the operation of the brain is still not sufficient to produce understanding. To see that this is so, imagine that instead of a monolingual man in a room shuffling symbols we have the man operate an elaborate set of water pipes with valves connecting them. When the man receives the Chinese symbols he looks up in the program, written in English, which valves he has to turn on and off. Each water connection corresponds to a synapse in the Chinese brain, and the whole system is rigged up so that after doing all the right firings – that is, after turning on all the right faucets – the Chinese answers pop out at the output end of the series of pipes.

Now where is the understanding in this system? It takes Chinese as input, it simulates the formal structure of the synapses of the Chinese brain, and it gives Chinese as output. But the man certainly doesn't understand Chinese, and neither do the water pipes. And if we are tempted to adopt what I think is the absurd view that somehow the *conjunction* of man *and* water pipes understands, remember that in principle the man can internalize the formal structure of the water pipes and do all the "neuron firings" in his imagination. The problem with the brain simulator is that it is simulating the wrong things about the brain. As long as it simulates only the formal structure of the sequence of neuron firings at the synapses, it won't have simulated what matters about the brain: its ability to produce intentional states. And that the formal properties are not sufficient for the causal properties is shown by the water pipe example. We can have all the formal properties carved off from the relevant neurobiological causal properties.

IV THE COMBINATION REPLY (Berkeley and Stanford): While each of the previous three replies might not be completely convincing by itself as a refutation of the Chinese room counter-example, if you take all three together they are collectively much more convincing and even decisive. Imagine a robot with a brain-shaped computer lodged in its cranial cavity; imagine the computer programmed with all the synapses of a human brain; imagine that the whole behavior of the robot is indistinguishable from human behavior; and now think of the whole thing as a unified system and not just as a computer with inputs and outputs. Surely in such a case we would have to ascribe intentionality to the system.

I entirely agree that in such a case we would find it rational and indeed irresistible to accept the hypothesis that the robot had intentionality, as long as we knew nothing more about it. Indeed, besides appearance and behavior, the other elements of the combination are really irrelevant. If we could build a robot whose behavior was indistinguishable over a large range from human behavior, we would attribute intentionality to it, pending some reason not to. We wouldn't need to know in advance that its computer brain was a formal analogue of the human brain.

But I really don't see that this is any help to the claims of strong AI, and here is why. According to strong AI, instantiating a formal program with the right input and output is a sufficient condition of, indeed is constitutive of, intentionality. As Newell (1980) puts it, the essence of the mental is the operation of a physical symbol system. But the attributions of intentionality that we make to the robot in this example have nothing to do with formal programs. They are simply based on the assumption that if the robot looks and behaves sufficiently like us, we would suppose, until proven otherwise, that it must have mental states like ours, which cause and are expressed by its behavior, and it must have an inner mechanism capable of producing such mental states. If we knew independently how to account for its behavior without such assumptions, we would not attribute intentionality to it, especially if we knew it had a formal program. And this is the point of my earlier response to the robot reply.

Suppose we knew that the robot's behavior was entirely accounted for by the fact that a man inside it was receiving uninterpreted formal symbols from the robot's sensory receptors and sending out uninterpreted formal symbols to its motor mechanisms, and the man was doing this symbol manipulation in accordance with a bunch of rules. Furthermore, suppose the man knows none of these facts about the robot; all he knows is which operations to perform on which meaningless symbols. In such a case we would regard the robot as an ingenious mechanical dummy. The hypothesis that the dummy has a mind would now be unwarranted and unnecessary; for there is now no longer any reason to ascribe intentionality to the robot or to the system of which it is a part (except of course for the man's intentionality in manipulating the symbols). The formal symbol manipulations go on, the input and output are correctly matched, but the only real locus of intentionality is the man, and he doesn't know any of the relevant intentional states; he doesn't, for example, *see* what comes into the robot's eyes, he doesn't *intend* to move the robot's arm, and he doesn't *understand* any of the remarks made to or by the robot. Nor, for the reasons stated earlier, does the system of which man and robot are a part.

To see the point, contrast this case with cases where we find it completely natural to ascribe intentionality to members of certain other primate species, such as apes and monkeys, and to domestic animals, such as dogs. The reasons we find it natural are, roughly, two: we can't make sense of the animal's behavior without the ascription of intentionality, and we can see that the beasts are made of stuff similar to our own – an eye, a nose, its skin, and so on. Given the coherence of the animal's behavior and the assumption of the same causal stuff underlying it, we assume both that the animal must have mental states underlying its behavior, and that the mental states must be produced by mechanisms made out of the stuff that is like our stuff. We would certainly make similar assumptions about the robot unless we had some reason not to; but as soon as we knew that the behavior was the result of a formal program, and that the actual causal properties of the physical substance were irrelevant, we would abandon the assumption of intentionality.

There are two other responses to my example which come up frequently (and so are worth discussing) but really miss the point:

V **THE OTHER-MINDS REPLY** (Yale): How do you know that other people understand Chinese or anything else? Only by their behavior. Now the computer can pass the behavior tests as well as they can (in principle), so if you are going to attribute cognition to other people, you must in principle also attribute it to computers.

The objection is worth only a short reply. The problem in this discussion is not about how I know that other people have cognitive states, but rather what it is that I am attributing to them when I attribute cognitive states to them. The thrust of the argument is that it couldn't be just computational processes and their output because there can be computational processes and their output without the cognitive state. It is no answer to this argument to feign anesthesia. In "cognitive sciences" one presupposes the reality and knowability of the mental in the same way that in physical sciences one has to presuppose the reality and knowability of physical objects.

VI THE MANY-MANSIONS REPLY (Berkeley): Your whole argument presupposes that AI is only about analogue and digital computers. But that just happens to be the present state of technology. Whatever these causal processes are that you say are essential for intentionality (assuming you are right), eventually we will be able to build devices that have these causal processes, and that will be artificial intelligence. So your arguments are in no way directed at the ability of artificial intelligence to produce and explain cognition.

I have no objection to this reply except to say that it in effect trivializes the project of strong artificial intelligence by redefining it as whatever artificially produces and explains cognition. The interest of the original claim made on behalf of artificial intelligence is that it was a precise, well defined thesis: mental processes are computational processes over formally defined elements. I have been concerned to challenge that thesis. If the claim is redefined so that it is no longer that thesis, my objections no longer apply, because there is no longer a testable hypothesis for them to apply to.

Let us now return to the questions I promised I would try to answer. Granted that in my original example I understand the English and I do not understand the Chinese, and granted therefore that the machine doesn't understand either English or Chinese, still there must be something about me that makes it the case that I understand English, and a corresponding something lacking in me which makes it the case that I fail to understand Chinese. Now why couldn't we give the former something, whatever it is, to a machine?

I see no reason in principle why we couldn't give a machine the capacity to understand English or Chinese, since in an important sense our bodies with our brains are precisely such machines. But I do see very strong arguments for saying that we could not give such a thing to a machine where

345

the operation of the machine is defined solely in terms of computational processes over formally defined elements – that is, where the operation of the machine is defined as an instantiation of a computer program. It is not because I am the instantiation of a computer program that I am able to understand English and have other forms of intentionality. (I am, I suppose, the instantiation of any number of computer programs.) Rather, as far as we know, it is because I am a certain sort of organism with a certain biological (that is, chemical and physical) structure, and this structure under certain conditions is causally capable of producing perception, action, understanding, learning, and other intentional phenomena. And part of the point of the present argument is that only something that had those causal powers could have that intentionality. Perhaps other physical and chemical processes could produce exactly these effects; perhaps, for example, Martians also have intentionality, but their brains are made of different stuff. That is an empirical question, rather like the question whether photosynthesis can be done by something with a chemistry different from that of chlorophyll.

But the main point of the present argument is that no purely formal model will ever be by itself sufficient for intentionality, because the formal properties are not by themselves constitutive of intentionality, and they have by themselves no causal powers except the power, when instantiated, to produce the next state of the formalism when the machine is running. And any other causal properties which particular realizations of the formal model have are irrelevant to the formal model, because we can always put the same formal model in a different realization where those causal properties are obviously absent. Even if by some miracle Chinese speakers exactly realize Schank's program, we can put the same program in English speakers, water pipes, or computers, none of which understand Chinese, the program notwithstanding.

What matters about brain operation is not the formal shadow cast by the sequence of synapses but rather the actual properties of the sequences. All arguments for the strong version of artificial intelligence that I have seen insist on drawing an outline around the shadows cast by cognition and then claiming that the shadows are the real thing.

By way of concluding I want to state some of the general philosophical points implicit in the argument. For clarity I will try to do it in a question-and-answer fashion, and I begin with that old chestnut:

• Could a machine think?

The answer is, obviously: Yes. We are precisely such machines.

• Yes, but could an artifact, a man-made machine, think?

Assuming it is possible to produce artificially a machine with a nervous system, neurons with axons and dendrites, and all the rest of it, sufficiently like ours, again the answer to the question seems to be obviously: Yes. If you can exactly duplicate the causes, you can duplicate the effects. And indeed it might be possible to produce consciousness, intentionality, and all the rest of it, using chemical principles different from those human beings use. It is, as I said, an empirical question.

• OK, but could a digital computer think?

If by "digital computer" we mean anything at all which has a level of description where it can correctly be described as the instantiation of a computer program, then, since we are the instantiations of any number of computer programs and we can think, again the answer is, of course: Yes.

• But could something think, understand, and so on, *solely by virtue of* being a computer with the right sort of program? Could instantiating a program, the right program of course, by itself be a sufficient condition for understanding?

This I think is the right question to ask, though it is usually confused with one or more of the earlier questions, and the answer to it is: No.

• Why not?

Because the formal symbol manipulations by themselves don't have any intentionality. They are meaningless – they aren't even *symbol* manipulations, since the "symbols" don't symbolize anything. In the linguistic jargon, they have only a syntax but no semantics. Such intentionality as computers appear to have is solely in the minds of those who program them and those who use them, those who send in the input and who interpret the output.

The aim of the Chinese room example was to try to show this by showing that, as soon as we put something into the system which really does have intentionality, a man, and we program the man with the formal program, you can see that the formal program carries no additional intentionality. It adds nothing, for example, to a man's ability to understand Chinese.

Precisely that feature of AI which seemed so appealing – the distinction between the program and the realization – proves fatal to the claim that simulation could be duplication. The distinction between the program and

347

its realization in the hardware seems to be parallel to the distinction between the level of mental operations and the level of brain operations. And if we could describe the level of mental operations as a formal program, it seems we could describe what was essential about the mind without doing either introspective psychology or neurophysiology of the brain. But the equation "Mind is to brain as program is to hardware" breaks down at several points, among them the following three.

First, the distinction between program and realization has the consequence that the same program could have all sorts of crazy realizations which have no form of intentionality. Weizenbaum (1976), for example, shows in detail how to construct a computer using a roll of toilet paper and a pile of small stones. Similarly, the Chinese story-understanding program can be programmed into a sequence of water pipes, a set of wind machines, or a monolingual English speaker – none of which thereby acquires an understanding of Chinese. Stones, toilet paper, wind, and water pipes are the wrong kind of stuff to have intentionality in the first place (only something that has the same causal powers as brains can have intentionality), and, though the English speaker has the right kind of stuff for intentionality, you can easily see that he doesn't get any extra intentionality by memorizing the program, since memorizing it won't teach him Chinese.

Second, the program is purely formal, but the intentional states are not in that way formal. They are defined in terms of their content, not their form. The belief that it is raining, for example, if defined not as a certain formal shape, but as a certain mental content, with conditions of satisfaction, a direction of fit, and so on (see Searle 1979). Indeed, the belief as such hasn't even got a formal shape in this syntactical sense, since one and the same belief can be given an indefinite number of different syntactical expressions in different linguistic systems.

Third, as I mentioned before, mental states and events are a product of the operation of the brain, but the program is not in that way a product of the computer.

- Well if programs are in no way constitutive of mental processes, then why have so many people believed the converse? That at least needs some explanation.

I don't know the answer to that. The idea that computer simulations could be the real thing ought to have seemed suspicious in the first place, because the computer isn't confined to simulating mental operations, by any means. No one supposes that computer simulations of a five-alarm fire will burn the neighborhood down, or that a computer simulation of a rainstorm will leave us all drenched. Why on earth would anyone suppose that a computer simulation of understanding actually understood anything? It is sometimes said that it would be frightfully hard to get computers to feel pain or fall in love, but love and pain are neither harder nor easier than cognition or anything else. For simulation, all you need is the right input and output and a program in the middle that transforms the former into the latter. That is all the computer has for anything it does. To confuse simulation with duplication is the same mistake, whether it is pain, love, cognition, fires, or rainstorms.

Still, there are several reasons why AI must have seemed, and to many people perhaps still does seem, in some way to reproduce and thereby explain mental phenomena. And I believe we will not succeed in removing these illusions until we have fully exposed the reasons that give rise to them.

First, and perhaps most important, is a confusion about the notion of "information processing." Many people in cognitive science believe that the human brain with its mind does something called "information processing," and, analogously, the computer with its program does information processing; but fires and rainstorms, on the other hand, don't do information processing at all. Thus, though the computer can simulate the formal features of any process whatever, it stands in a special relation to the mind and brain because, when the computer is properly programmed, ideally with the same program as the brain, the information processing is identical in the two cases, and this information processing is really the essence of the mental.

But the trouble with this argument is that it rests on an ambiguity in the notion of "information." In the sense in which people "process information" when they reflect, say, on problems in arithmetic or when they read and answer questions about stories, the programmed computer does not do "information processing." Rather, what it does is manipulate formal symbols. The fact that the programmer and the interpreter of the computer output use the symbols to stand for objects in the world is totally beyond the scope of the computer. The computer, to repeat, has a syntax but no semantics. Thus if you type into the computer "2 plus 2 equals?" it will type out "4." But it has no idea that "4" means 4, or that it means anything at all. And the point is not that it lacks some second-order information about the interpretation of its first-order symbols, but rather that its first-order symbols don't have any interpretations as far as the computer is concerned. All the computer has is more symbols.

The introduction of the notion of "information processing" therefore produces a dilemma. Either we construe the notion of "information processing" in such a way that it implies intentionality as part of the process, or we don't. If the former, then the programmed computer does not do information processing, it only manipulates formal symbols. If the latter, then, although the computer does information processing, it is only in the sense in which adding machines, typewriters, stomachs, thermostats, rainstorms, and hurricanes do information processing – namely, in the sense that there is a level of description at which we can describe them as taking information in at one end, transforming it, and producing information as output. But in this case it is up to outside observers to interpret the input and output as information in the ordinary sense. And no similarity is established between the computer and the brain in terms of any similarity of information processing in either of the two cases.

Secondly, in much of AI there is a residual behaviorism or operationalism. Since appropriately programmed computers can have input/output patterns similar to human beings, we are tempted to postulate mental states in the computer similar to human mental states. But once we see that it is both conceptually and empirically possible for a system to have human capacities in some realm without having any intentionality at all, we should be able to overcome this impulse. My desk adding machine has calculating capacities but no intentionality; and in this paper I have tried to show that a system could have input and output capabilities which duplicated those of a native Chinese speaker and still not understand Chinese, regardless of how it was programmed. The Turing test is typical of the tradition in being unashamedly behavioristic and operationalistic, and I believe that if AI workers totally repudiated behaviorism and operationalism, much of the confusion between simulation and duplication would be eliminated.

Third, this residual operationalism is joined to a residual form of dualism; indeed, strong AI only makes sense given the dualistic assumption that where the mind is concerned the brain doesn't matter. In strong AI (and in functionalism, as well) what matters are programs, and programs are independent of their realization in machines; indeed, as far as AI is concerned, the same program could be realized by an electronic machine, a Cartesian mental substance, or a Hegelian world spirit. The single most surprising discovery that I have made in discussing these issues is that many AI workers are shocked by my idea that actual human mental phenomena might be dependent on actual physical-chemical properties of actual human brains. But I should not have been surprised; for unless you accept some form of dualism, the strong AI project hasn't got a chance.

The project is to reproduce and explain the mental by designing programs; but unless the mind is not only conceptually but empirically independent of the brain, you cannot carry out the project, for the program is completely independent of any realization. Unless you believe that the mind is separable from the brain both conceptually and empirically – dualism in a strong form – you cannot hope to reproduce the mental by writing and running programs, since programs must be independent of brains or any other particular forms of instantiation. If mental operations consist of computational operations on formal symbols, it follows that they have no interesting connection with the brain, and the only connection would be that the brain just happens to be one of the indefinitely many types of machines capable of instantiating the program. This form of dualism is not the traditional Cartesian variety that claims there are two sorts of *substances*, but it is Cartesian in the sense that it insists that what is specifically mental about the mind has no intrinsic connection with the actual properties of the brain. This underlying dualism is masked from us by the fact that AI literature contains frequent fulminations against "dualism." What the authors seem to be unaware of is that their position presupposes a strong version of dualism.

- Could a machine think?

My own view is that *only* a machine could think, and indeed only very special kinds of machines, namely brains and machines that had the *same causal powers* as brains. And that is the main reason why strong AI has had little to tell us about thinking: it has nothing to tell us about machines. By its own definition it is about programs, and programs are not machines. Whatever else intentionality is, it is a biological phenomenon, and it is likely to be as causally dependent on the specific biochemistry of its origins as are lactation, photosynthesis, or any biological phenomena. No one would suppose that we could produce milk and sugar by running a computer simulation of the formal sequences in lactation and photosynthesis; but where the mind is concerned, many people are willing to believe in such a miracle, because of a deep and abiding dualism: the mind, they suppose, is a matter of formal processes and is independent of specific material causes in a way that milk and sugar are not.

In defense of this dualism, the hope is often expressed that the brain is a digital computer. (Early computers, by the way, were often called "electronic brains.") But that is no help. Of course the brain is a digital computer. Since everything is a digital computer, brains are too. The point is that the brain's causal capacity to produce intentionality cannot consist in its instantiating a computer program, since for any program you like it is possible for something to instantiate that program and still not have any mental states. Whatever it is that the brain does to produce intentionality it cannot consist in instantiating a program, since no program by itself is sufficient for intentionality.

Acknowledgments

I am indebted to a rather large number of people for discussion of these matters and for their patient attempts to overcome my ignorance of artificial intelligence. I would especially like to thank Ned Block, Hubert Dreyfus, John Haugeland, Roger Schank, Robert Wilensky, and Terry Winograd.

Notes

1   I am not saying, of course, that Schank himself is committed to these claims.
2   Also, "understanding" implies both the possession of mental (intentional) states and the truth (validity, success) of these states. For the purposes of this discussion, we are concerned only with the possession of the states.
3   Intentionality is by definition that feature of certain mental states by which they are directed at or are about objects and states of affairs in the world. Thus, beliefs, desires, and intentions are intentional states; undirected forms of anxiety and depression are not. (For further discussion, see Searle 1979).

References

McCarthy, J. (1979) "Ascribing Mental Qualities to Machines," in M. Ringle (ed.) *Philosophical Perspectives on Artificial Intelligence*, Atlantic Highlands, N.J.: Humanities Press.

Newell, A. (1980) "Physical Symbol Systems," *Cognitive Science* 4: 135–183.

Schank, R.C. and Abelson, R.P. (1977) *Scripts, Plans, Goals and Understanding*, Hillsdale, N.J.: Lawrence Erlbaum Associates.

Searle, J.R. (1979) "What Is an Intentional State?," *Mind* 88: 72–94.

Turing, A.M. (1950) "Computing Machinery and Intelligence," *Mind* 59: 433–460.

Weizenbaum, J. (1965) "Eliza – A Computer Program for the Study of Natural Language Communication between Man and Machine," *Communications of the Association for Computing Machinery* 9: 36–45.

—— (1976) *Computer Power and Human Reason*, San Francisco: W.H. Freeman.

Winograd, T. (1973) "A Procedural Model of Language Understanding," in R. Schank and K. Colby (eds) *Computer Models of Thought and Language*, San Francisco: W.H. Freeman.

IIIB

PROPOSITIONAL ATTITUDES
AND ELIMINATIVISM

17

Donald Davidson, "Thought and Talk"

What is the connection between thought and language? The dependence of speaking on thinking is evident, for to speak is to express thoughts. This dependence is manifest in endless further ways. Someone who utters the sentence "The candle is out" as a sentence of English must intend to utter words that are true if and only if an indicated candle is out at the time of utterance, and he must believe that by making the sounds he does he is uttering words that are true only under those circumstances. These intentions and beliefs are not apt to be dwelt on by the fluent speaker. But though they may not normally command attention, their absence would be enough to show he was not speaking English, and the absence of any analogous thoughts would show he was not speaking at all.

The issue is on the other side: can there be thought without speech? A first and natural reaction is that there can be. There is the familiar, irksome experience of not being able to find the words to express one's ideas. On occasion one may decide that the editorial writer has put a point better than one could oneself. And there is Norman Malcolm's dog who, having chased a squirrel into the woods, barks up the wrong tree. It is hard not to credit the dog with the belief that the squirrel is in that tree.

A definite, if feebler, intuition tilts the other way. It is possible to wonder whether the speaker who can't find the right words has a clear idea. Attributions of intentions and beliefs to dogs smack of anthropomorphism. A primitive behaviourism, baffled by the privacy of unspoken thoughts, may take comfort in the view that thinking is really "talking to oneself" – silent speech.

Beneath the surface of these opposed tendencies run strong, if turgid, currents, which may help to explain why philosophers have, for the most

Donald Davidson, "Thought and Talk," in Samuel Guttenplan (ed.), *Mind and Language: Wolfson College Lectures 1974* (Oxford University Press, Oxford, 1975), pp. 7–23.

part, preferred taking a stand on the issue to producing an argument. Whatever the reason, the question of the relationship between thought and speech seems seldom to have been asked for its own sake. The usual assumption is that one or the other, speech or thought, is by comparison easy to understand, and therefore the more obscure one (whichever that is) may be illuminated by analysing or explaining it in terms of the other.

The assumption is, I think, false: neither language nor thinking can be fully explained in terms of the other, and neither has conceptual priority. The two are, indeed, linked, in the sense that each requires the other in order to be understood; but the linkage is not so complete that either suffices, even when reasonably reinforced, to explicate the other. To make good this claim what is chiefly needed is to show how thought depends on speech, and this is the thesis I want to refine, and then to argue for.

We attribute a thought to a creature whenever we assertively employ a positive sentence the main verb of which is psychological – in English, "believes," "knows," "hopes," "desires," "thinks," "fears," "is interested" are examples – followed by a sentence and preceded by the name or description of the creature. (A "that" may optionally or necessarily follow the verb.) Some such sentences attribute states, others report events or processes: "believes," "thinks," and "wants" report states, while "came to believe," "forgot," "concluded," "noticed," "is proving" report events or processes. Sentences that can be used to attribute a thought exhibit what is often called, or analysed as, semantic intensionality, which means that the attribution may be changed from true to false, or false to true, by substitutions in the contained sentences that would not alter the truth value of that sentence in isolation.

I do not take for granted that if a creature has a thought, then we can, with resources of the kind just sketched, correctly attribute that thought to him. But thoughts so attributable at least constitute a good sample of the totality.

It is doubtful whether the various sorts of thought can be reduced to one, or even to a few: desire, knowledge, belief, fear, interest, to name some important cases, are probably logically independent to the extent that none can be defined using the others, even along with such further notions as truth and cause. Nevertheless, belief is central to all kinds of thought. If someone is glad that, or notices that, or remembers that, or knows that, the gun is loaded, then he must believe that the gun is loaded. Even to wonder whether the gun is loaded, or to speculate on the possibility that the gun is loaded, requires the belief, for example, that a gun is a weapon, that it is a more or less enduring physical object, and so on. There are good reasons for not insisting on any particular list of beliefs that are needed if a creature is to wonder whether a gun is loaded. Nevertheless, it is necessary that there be endless interlocked beliefs. The system of such beliefs identifies a thought by locating it in a logical and epistemic space.

Having a thought requires that there be a background of beliefs, but having a particular thought does not depend on the state of belief with respect to that very thought. If I consider going to a certain concert, I know I will be put to a degree of trouble and expense, and I have more complicated beliefs about the enjoyment I will experience. I will enjoy hearing Beethoven's *Grosse Fuge*, say, but only provided the performance achieves a reasonable standard, and I am able to remain attentive. I have the thought of going to the concert, but until I decide whether to go, I have no fixed belief that I will go; until that time, I merely entertain the thought.

We may say, summarizing the last two paragraphs, that a thought is defined by a system of beliefs, but is itself autonomous with respect to belief.

We usually think that having a language consists largely in being able to speak, but in what follows speaking will play only an indirect part. What is essential to my argument is the idea of an interpreter, someone who understands the utterances of another. The considerations to be put forward imply, I think, that a speaker must himself be an interpreter of others, but I shall not try to demonstrate that an interpreter must be a speaker, though there may be good reason to hold this. Perhaps it is worth pointing out that the notion of a language, or of two people speaking the same language does not seem to be needed here. Two speakers could interpret each other's utterances without there being, in any ordinary sense, a common language. (I do not want to deny that in other contexts the notion of a shared language may be very important.)

The chief thesis of this paper is that a creature cannot have thoughts unless it is an interpreter of the speech of another. This thesis does not imply the possibility of reduction, behaviouristic or otherwise, of thoughts to speech; indeed the thesis imputes no priority to language, epistemological or conceptual. The claim also falls short of similar claims in that it allows that there may be thoughts for which the speaker cannot find words, or for which there are no words.

Someone who can interpret an utterance of the English sentence "The gun is loaded" must have many beliefs, and these beliefs must be much like the beliefs someone must have if he entertains the thought that the gun is loaded. The interpreter must, we may suppose, believe that a gun is a weapon, and that it is a more or less enduring physical object. There is probably no definite list of things that must be believed by someone who understands the sentence "The gun is loaded," but it is necessary that there be endless interlocked beliefs.

An interpreter knows the conditions under which utterances of sentences are true, and often knows that if certain sentences are true, others must be.

For example, an interpreter of English knows that if "The gun is loaded and the door is locked" is true, then "The door is locked" is true. The sentences of a language have a location in the logical space created by the pattern of such relationships. Obviously the pattern of relations between sentences is very much like the pattern of relations between thoughts. This fact has encouraged the view that it is redundant to take both patterns as basic. If thoughts are primary, a language seems to serve no purpose but to express or convey thoughts; while if we take speech as primary, it is tempting to analyse thoughts as speech dispositions: as Sellars puts it, ". . . thinking at the distinctly human level . . . is essentially verbal activity."[1] But clearly the parallel between the structure of thoughts and the structure of sentences provides no argument for the primacy of either, and only a presumption in favour of their interdependence.

We have been talking freely of thoughts, beliefs, meanings, and interpretations; or rather, freely using sentences that contain these words. But of course it is not clear what entities, or sorts of entities, there must be to make systematic sense of such sentences. However, talk apparently of thoughts and sayings does belong to a familiar mode of explanation of human behaviour and must be considered an organized department of common sense that may as well be called a theory. One way of examining the relation between thought and language is by inspecting the theory implicit in this sort of explanation.

Part of the theory deals with the teleological explanation of action. We wonder why a man raises his arm; an explanation might be that he wanted to attract the attention of a friend. This explanation would fail if the arm-raiser didn't believe that by raising his arm he would attract the attention of his friend, so the complete explanation of his raising his arm, or at any rate a more complete explanation, is that he wanted to attract the attention of his friend *and* believed that by raising his arm he would attract his friend's attention. Explanation of this familiar kind has some features worth emphasizing. It explains what is relatively apparent – an arm-raising – by appeal to factors that are far more problematical: desires and beliefs. But if we were to ask for evidence that the explanation is correct, this evidence would in the end consist of more data concerning the sort of event being explained, namely further behaviour which is explained by the postulated beliefs and desires. Adverting to beliefs and desires to explain action is therefore a way of fitting an action into a pattern of behaviour made coherent by the theory. This does not mean, of course, that beliefs are nothing but patterns of behaviour, or that the relevant patterns can be defined without using the concepts of belief and desire. Nevertheless, there is a clear sense in which attributions of belief and desire, and hence teleological explanations of belief and desire, are supervenient on behaviour more broadly described.

A characteristic of teleological explanation not shared by explanation generally is the way in which it appeals to the concept of *reason*. The belief and desire that explain an action must be such that anyone who had that belief and desire would have a reason to act in that way. What's more, the descriptions we provide of desire and belief must, in teleological explanation, exhibit the rationality of the action in the light of the content of the belief and the object of the desire.

The cogency of a teleological explanation rests, as remarked, on its ability to discover a coherent pattern in the behaviour of an agent. Coherence here includes the idea of rationality both in the sense that the action to be explained must be reasonable in the light of the assigned desires and beliefs, but also in the sense that the assigned desires and beliefs must fit with one another. The methodological presumption of rationality does not make it impossible to attribute irrational thoughts and actions to an agent, but it does impose a burden on such attributions. We weaken the intelligibility of attributions of thoughts of any kind to the extent that we fail to uncover a consistent pattern of beliefs and, finally, of actions, for it is only against a background of such a pattern that we can identify thoughts. If we see a man pulling on both ends of a piece of string, we may decide he is fighting against himself, that he wants to move the string in incompatible directions. Such an explanation would require elaborate backing. No problem arises if the explanation is that he wants to break the string.

From the point of view of someone giving teleological explanations of the actions of another, it clearly makes no sense to assign priority either to desires or to beliefs. Both are essential to the explanation of behaviour, and neither is more directly open to observation than the other. This creates a problem, for it means that behaviour, which is the main evidential basis for attributions of belief and desire, is reckoned the result of two forces less open to public observation. Thus where one constellation of beliefs and desires will rationalize an action, it is always possible to find a quite different constellation that will do as well. Even a generous sample of actions threatens to leave open an unacceptably large number of alternative explanations.

Fortunately a more refined theory is available, one still firmly based on common sense: the theory of preference, or decision-making, under uncertainty. The theory was first made precise by Frank Ramsey, though he viewed it as a matter of providing a foundation for the concept of probability rather than as a piece of philosophical psychology.[2] Ramsey's theory works by quantifying strength of preference and degree of belief in such a way as to make sense of the natural idea that in choosing a course of action we consider not only how desirable various outcomes are, but also how apt available courses of action are to produce those outcomes. The theory does not assume that we can judge degrees of belief or make numerical comparisons of value directly. Rather it postulates a reasonable pattern of preferences between courses of action, and shows how to construct a system of quantified beliefs and desires to explain the choices. Given the idealized conditions postulated by the theory, Ramsey's method makes it possible to identify the relevant beliefs and desires uniquely. Instead of talking of postulation, we might put the matter this way: to the extent that we can see the actions of an agent as falling into a consistent (rational) pattern of a certain sort, we can explain those actions in terms of a system of quantified beliefs and desires.

We shall come back to decision theory presently; now it is time to turn to the question of how speech is interpreted. The immediate aim of a theory of interpretation is to give the meaning of an arbitrary utterance by a member of a language community. Central to interpretation, I have argued, is a theory of truth that satisfies Tarski's Convention T (modified in certain ways to apply to a natural language). Such a theory yields, for every utterance of every sentence of the language, a theorem of the form: "An utterance of sentence s by a speaker x at time t is true if and only if —." Here "s" is to be replaced by a description of a sentence, and the blank by a statement of the conditions under which an utterance of the sentence is true relative to the parameters of speaker and time. In order to interpret a particular utterance it is neither necessary nor sufficient to know the entire theory: it is enough to know what the theory says the truth conditions are for the utterance, and to know that those conditions are entailed by a theory of the required sort. On the other hand, to belong to a speech community – to be an interpreter of the speech of others – one does need to know much of a whole theory, in effect, and to know that it is a theory of the right kind.[3]

A theory of interpretation, like a theory of action, allows us to redescribe certain events in a revealing way. Just as a theory of action can answer the question of what an agent is doing when he has raised his arm by redescribing the act as one of trying to catch his friend's attention, so a method of interpretation can lead to redescribing the utterance of certain sounds as an act of saying that snow is white. At this point, however, the analogy breaks down. For decision theory can also explain actions, while it is not at all clear how a theory of interpretation can explain a speaker's uttering the words "Snow is white." But this is, after all, to be expected, for uttering words is an action, and so must draw for its teleological explanation on beliefs and desires. Interpretation is not irrelevant to the teleological explanation of speech, since to explain why someone said something we need to know, among other things, his own interpretation of what he said, that is, what he believes his words mean in the circumstances under which he speaks. Naturally this will involve some of his beliefs about how others will interpret his words.

The interlocking of the theory of action with interpretation will emerge in another way if we ask how a method of interpretation is tested. In the end, the answer must be that it helps bring order into our understanding of behaviour. But at an intermediary stage, we can see that the attitude of *holding true* or *accepting as true*, as directed towards sentences, must play a central role in giving form to a theory. On the one hand, most uses of language tell us directly, or shed light on the question, whether a speaker holds a sentence to be true. If a speaker's purpose is to give information, or to make an honest assertion, then normally the speaker believes he is uttering a sentence true under the circumstances. If he utters a command, we may usually take this as showing that he holds a certain sentence (closely related to the sentence uttered) to be false; similarly for many cases of deceit. When a question is asked, it generally indicates that the questioner does not know whether a certain sentence is true; and so on. In order to infer from such evidence that a speaker holds a sentence true we need to know much about his desires and beliefs, but we do not have to know what his words mean.

On the other hand, knowledge of the circumstances under which someone holds sentences true is central to interpretation. We saw in the case of thoughts that although most thoughts are not beliefs, it is the pattern of belief that allows us to identify any thought; analogously, in the case of language, although most utterances are not concerned with truth, it is the pattern of sentences held true that gives sentences their meaning.

The attitude of holding a sentence to be true (under specified conditions) relates belief and interpretation in a fundamental way. We can know that a speaker holds a sentence to be true without knowing what he means by it or what belief it expresses for him. But if we know he holds the sentence true *and* we know how to interpret it, then we can make a correct attribution of belief. Symmetrically, if we know what belief a sentence held true expresses, we know how to interpret it. The methodological problem of interpretation is to see how, given the sentences a man accepts as true under given circumstances, to work out what his beliefs are and what his words mean. The situation is again similar to the situation in decision theory where, given a man's preferences between alternative courses of action, we can discern both his beliefs and his desires. Of course it should not be thought that a theory of interpretation will stand alone, for as we noticed, there is no chance of telling when a sentence is held true without being able to attribute desires and being able to describe actions as having complex intentions. This observation does not deprive the theory of interpretation of interest, but assigns it a place within a more comprehensive theory of action and thought.[4]

It is still unclear whether interpretation is required for a theory of action, which is the question we set ourselves to answer. What is certain is that all the standard ways of testing theories of decision or preference under uncertainty rely on the use of language. It is relatively simple to eliminate the necessity for verbal responses on the part of the subject: he can be taken to have expressed a preference by taking action, by moving directly to achieve his end, rather than by saying what he wants. But this cannot settle the question of what he has chosen. A man who takes an apple rather than a pear when offered both may be expressing a preference for what is on his left rather than his right, what is red rather than yellow, what is seen first, or judged more expensive. Repeated tests may make some readings of his actions more plausible than others, but the problem will remain how to tell what he judges to be a repetition of the same alternative. Tests that involve uncertain events – choices between gambles – are even harder to present without using words. The psychologist, sceptical of his ability to be certain how a subject is interpreting his instructions, must add a theory of verbal interpretation to the theory to be tested. If we think of all choices as revealing a preference that one sentence rather than another be true, the resulting total theory should provide an interpretation of sentences, and at the same time assign beliefs and desires, both of the latter conceived as relating the agent to sentences or utterances. This composite theory would explain all behaviour, verbal and otherwise.

All this strongly suggests that the attribution of desires and beliefs (and other thoughts) must go hand in hand with the interpretation of speech, that neither the theory of decision nor of interpretation can be successfully developed without the other. But it remains to say, in more convincing detail, why the attribution of thought depends on the interpretation of speech. The general, and not very informative, reason is that without speech we cannot make the fine distinctions between thoughts that are essential to the explanations we can sometimes confidently supply. Our manner of attributing attitudes ensures that all the expressive power of language can be used to make such distinctions. One can believe that Scott is not the author of *Waverley* while not doubting that Scott is Scott; one can want to be the discoverer of a creature with a heart without wanting to be the discoverer of a creature with a kidney. One can intend to bite into the apple in the hand without intending to bite into the only apple with a worm in it; and so forth. The intensionality we make so much of in the attribution of thoughts is very hard to make much of when speech is not present. The dog, we say, knows that its master is home. But does it know that Mr Smith (who is his master), or that the president of the bank (who is that same master), is home? We have no real idea how to settle, or make sense of, these questions. It is much harder to say, when speech is not present, how to distinguish universal thoughts from conjunctions of thoughts, or how to attribute conditional thoughts, or thoughts with, so to speak, mixed quantification ("He hopes that everyone is loved by someone").

These considerations will probably be less persuasive to dog lovers than to others, but in any case they do not constitute an argument. At best what we have shown, or claimed, is that unless there is behaviour that can be interpreted as speech, the evidence will not be adequate to justify the fine distinctions we are used to making in the attribution of thoughts. If we persist in attributing desires, beliefs, or other attitudes under these conditions, our attributions and consequent explanations of actions will be seriously underdetermined in that many alternative systems of attribution, many alternative explanations, will be equally justified by the available data. Perhaps this is all we can say against the attribution of thoughts to dumb creatures; but I do not think so.

Before going on I want to consider a possible objection to the general line I have been pursuing. Suppose we grant, the objector says, that very complex behaviour not observed in infants and elephants is necessary if we are to find application for the full apparatus available for the attribution of thoughts. Still, it may be said, the sketch of how interpretation works does not show that this complexity must be viewed as connected with language. The reason is that the sketch makes too much depend on the special attitude of being thought true. The most direct evidence for the existence of this attitude is honest assertion. But then it would seem that we could treat as speech the behaviour of creatures that never did anything with language except make honest assertions. Some philosophers do dream of such dreary tribes; but would we be right to say they had a language? What has been lost to view is what may be called *the autonomy of meaning*. Once a sentence is understood, an utterance of it may be used to serve almost any extra-linguistic purpose. An instrument that could be put to only one use would lack autonomy of meaning; this amounts to saying it should not be counted as a language. So the complexity of behaviour needed to give full scope to attributions of thought need not, after all, be exactly the same complexity that allows, or requires, interpretation as a language.

I agree with the hypothetical objector that autonomy of meaning is essential to language; indeed it is largely this that explains why linguistic meaning cannot be defined or analysed on the basis of extra-linguistic intentions and beliefs. But the objector fails to distinguish between a language that *could* be used for only one purpose and one that *is* used for only one purpose. An instrument that could be used for only one purpose would not be language. But honest assertion alone might yield a theory of interpretation, and so a language that, though capable of more, might never be put to further uses. (As a practical matter, the event is unthinkable. Someone who knows under what conditions his sentences are socially true cannot fail to grasp, and avail himself of, the possibilities in dishonest assertion – or in joking, story-telling, goading, exaggerating, insulting, and all the rest of the jolly crew.)

A method of interpretation tells us that for speakers of English an utterance of "It is raining" by a speaker x at time t is true if and only if it is raining (near x) at t. To be armed with this information, and to know that others know it, is to know what an utterance means independently of knowing the purposes that prompted it. The autonomy of meaning also helps to explain how it is possible, by the use of language, to attribute thoughts. Suppose someone utters assertively the sentence "Snow is white." Knowing the conditions under which such an utterance is true I can add, if I please, "I believe that too," thus attributing a belief to myself. In this case we may both have asserted that snow is white, but sameness of force is not necessary to the self-attribution. The other may say with a sneer, expressing disbelief, "Snow is white" – and I may again attribute a belief to myself by saying, "But *I* believe that." It can work as well in another way: if I can take advantage of an utterance of someone else's to attribute a belief to myself, I can use an utterance of my own to attribute a belief to someone else. First I utter a sentence, perhaps "Snow is white," and then I add "He believes that." The first utterance may or may not be an assertion; in any case, it does not attribute a belief to anyone (though if it is an assertion, then I do *represent* myself as believing that snow is white). But if my remark "He believes that" is an assertion, I have attributed a belief to someone else. Finally, there is no bar to my attributing a belief to myself by saying first, "Snow is white" and then adding, "I believe that."

In all these examples, I take the word "that" to refer demonstratively to an utterance, whether it is an utterance by the speaker of the "that" or by another speaker. The "that" cannot refer to a sentence, both because, as Church has pointed out in similar cases, the reference would then have to be relativized to a language, since a sentence may have different meanings in different languages;[5] but also, and more obviously, because the same sentence may have different truth values in the same language.

What demonstrative reference to utterances does in the sort of case just considered it can do as well when the surface structure is altered to something like "I believe that snow is white" or "He believes that snow is white." In these instances also I think we should view the "that" as a demonstrative, now referring ahead to an utterance on the verge of production. Thus the logical form of standard attributions of attitude is that of two utterances paratactically joined. There is no connective, though the first utterance contains a reference to the second. (Similar remarks go, of course, for inscriptions of sentences.)

I have discussed this analysis of verbal attributions of attitude elsewhere, and there is no need to repeat the arguments and explanations here.[6] It is an analysis with its own difficulties, especially when it comes to analysing quantification into the contained sentence, but I think these difficulties can be overcome while preserving the appealing features of the idea. Here I want to stress a point that connects the paratactic analysis of attribution of attitude with our present theme. The proposed analysis directly relates the autonomous feature of meaning with our ability to describe and attribute thoughts, since it is only because the interpretation of a sentence is independent of its use that the utterance of a sentence can serve in the description of the attitudes of others. If my analysis is right, we can dispense with the unlikely (but common) view that a sentence bracketed into a "that"-clause needs an entirely different interpretation from the one that works for it in other contexts. Since sentences are not names or descriptions in ordinary contexts, we can in particular reject the assumption that the attitudes have objects such as propositions which "that"-clauses might be held to name or describe. There should be no temptation to call the utterance to which reference is made according to the paratactic analysis the object of the attributed attitude.

Here a facile solution to our problem about the relation between thoughts and speech suggests itself. One way to view the paratactic analysis, a way proposed by Quine in *Word and Object*, is this: when a speaker attributes an attitude to a person, what he does is ape or mimic an actual or possible speech act of that person.[7] Indirect discourse is the best example, and assertion is another good one. Suppose I say, "Herodotus asserted that the Nile rises in the Mountains of the Moon." My second utterance – my just past utterance of "The Nile rises in the Mountains of the Moon" – must, if my attribution to Herodotus is correct, bear a certain relationship to an utterance of Herodotus': it must, in some appropriate sense, be a translation of it. Since, assuming still that the attribution is correct, Herodotus and I are *samesayers*, my utterance mimicked his. Not with respect to force, of course, since I didn't assert anything about the Nile. The sameness is with respect to the content of our utterances. If we turn to other attitudes, the situation is more complicated, for there is typically no utterance to ape. If I affirm "Jones believes that snow is white," my utterance of "Snow is white" may have no actual utterance of Jones's to imitate. Still, we could take the line that what I affirm is that Jones would be honestly speaking his mind were he to utter a sentence translating mine. Given some delicate assumptions about the conditions under which such a subjunctive conditional is true, we could conclude that only someone with a language could have a thought, since to have a thought would be to have a disposition to utter certain sentences with appropriate force under given circumstances.

We could take this line, but unfortunately there seems no clear reason why we have to. We set out to find an argument to show that only creatures with speech have thoughts. What has just been outlined is not an argument, but a proposal, and a proposal we need not accept. The paratactic analysis of the logical form of attributions of attitude can get along without the mimic-theory of utterance. When I say, "Jones believes that snow is white" I describe Jones's state of mind directly: it is indeed the state of mind someone is in who could honestly assert "Snow is white" if he spoke English, but that may be a state a languageless creature could also be in.

In order to make my final main point, I must return to an aspect of interpretation so far neglected. I remarked that the attitude of holding true, directed to sentences under specified circumstances, is the basis for interpretation, but I did not say how it can serve this function. The difficulty, it will be remembered, is that a sentence is held true because of two factors: what the holder takes the sentence to mean, and what he believes. In order to sort things out, what is needed is a method for holding one factor steady while the other is studied.

Membership in a language community depends on the ability to interpret the utterances of members of the group, and a method is at hand if one has, and knows one has, a theory which provides truth conditions, more or less in Tarski's style, for all sentences (relativized, as always, to time and speaker). The theory is correct as long as it entails, by finitely stated means, theorems of the familiar form: " 'It is raining' is true for a speaker x at time t if and only if it is raining (near x) at t." The evidential basis for such a theory concerns sentences held true, facts like the following: " 'It is raining' is held true by Smith at 8 a.m. on 26 August and it did rain near Smith at that time." It would be possible to generate a correct theory simply by considering sentences to be true when held true, provided (1) there was a theory which satisfied the formal constraints and was consistent in this way with the evidence, and (2) all speakers held a sentence to be true just when that sentence was true – provided, that is, all beliefs, at least as far as they could be expressed, were correct.

But of course it cannot be assumed that speakers never have false beliefs. Error is what gives belief its point. We can, however, take it as given that *most* beliefs are correct. The reason for this is that a belief is identified by its location in a pattern of beliefs; it is this pattern that determines the subject matter of the belief, what the belief is about. Before some object in, or aspect of, the world can become part of the subject matter of a belief (true or false) there must be endless true beliefs about the subject matter. False beliefs tend to undermine the identification of the subject matter; to undermine, therefore, the validity of a description of the belief as being about that subject. And so, in turn, false beliefs undermine the claim that a connected belief is false. To take an example, how clear are we that the ancients – some ancients – believed that the earth was flat? *This* earth? Well, this earth of ours is part of the solar system, a system partly identified by the fact that it is a gaggle of large, cool, solid bodies circling around a very large, hot star. If someone believes *none* of this about the earth, is it certain that it is the earth that he is thinking about? An answer is not called for. The point is made if this kind of consideration of related beliefs can shake one's confidence that the ancients believed the earth was flat. It isn't that any one false belief necessarily destroys our ability to identify further beliefs, but that the intelligibility of such identifications must depend on a background of largely unmentioned and unquestioned true beliefs. To put it another way: the more things a believer is right about, the sharper his errors are. Too much mistake simply blurs the focus.

What makes interpretation possible, then, is the fact that we can dismiss *a priori* the chance of massive error. A theory of interpretation cannot be correct that makes a man assent to very many false sentences: it must generally be the case that a sentence is true when a speaker holds it to be. So far as it goes, it is in favour of a method of interpretation that it counts a sentence true just when speakers hold it to be true. But of course, the speaker may be wrong, and so may the interpreter. So in the end what must be counted in favour of a method of interpretation is that it puts the interpreter in general agreement with the speaker: according to the method, the speaker holds a sentence true under specified conditions, and these conditions obtain, in the opinion of the interpreter, just when the speaker holds the sentence to be true.

No simple theory can put a speaker and interpreter in perfect agreement, and so a workable theory must from time to time assume error on the part of one or the other. The basic methodological precept is, therefore, that a good theory of interpretation maximizes agreement. Or, given that sentences are infinite in number, and given further considerations to come, a better word might be *optimize*.

Some disagreements are more destructive of understanding than others, and a sophisticated theory must naturally take this into account. Disagreement about theoretical matters may (in some cases) be more tolerable than disagreement about what is more evident; disagreement about how things look or appear is less tolerable than disagreement about how they are; disagreement about the truth of attributions of certain attitudes to a speaker by that same speaker may not be tolerable at all, or barely. It is impossible to simplify the considerations that are relevant, for everything we know or believe about the way evidence supports belief can be put to work in deciding where the theory can best allow error, and what errors are least destructive of understanding. The methodology of interpretation is, in this respect, nothing but epistemology seen in the mirror of meaning.

The interpreter who assumes his method can be made to work for a language community will strive for a theory that optimizes agreement throughout the community. Since easy communication has survival value, he may expect usage within a community to favour simple common theories of interpretation.

If this account of radical interpretation is right, at least in broad outline, then we should acknowledge that the concepts of objective truth, and of error, necessarily emerge in the context of interpretation. The distinction between a sentence being held true and being in fact true is essential to the existence of an interpersonal system of communication, and when in individual cases there is a difference, it must be counted as error. Since the attitude of holding true is the same, whether the sentence is true or not, it corresponds directly to belief. The concept of belief thus stands ready to take up the slack between objective truth and the held true, and we come to understand it just in this connection.

We have the idea of belief only from the role of belief in the interpretation of language, for as a private attitude it is not intelligible except as an adjustment to the public norm provided by language. It follows that a creature must be a member of a speech community if it is to have the concept of belief. And given the dependence of other attitudes on belief, we can say more generally that only a creature that can interpret speech can have the concept of a thought.

Can a creature have a belief if it does not have the concept of belief? It seems to me it cannot, and for this reason. Someone cannot have a belief unless he understands the possibility of being mistaken, and this requires grasping the contrast between truth and error – true belief and false belief. But this contrast, I have argued, can emerge only in the context of interpretation, which alone forces us to the idea of an objective, public truth.

It is often wrongly thought that the semantical concept of truth is redundant, that there is no difference between asserting that a sentence s is true, and using s to make an assertion. What may be right is a redundancy theory of belief, that to believe that p is not to be distinguished from the belief that p is true. This notion of truth is not the semantical notion: language is not directly in the picture. But it is only just out of the picture; it is part of the frame. For the notion of a true belief depends on the notion of a true utterance, and this in turn there cannot be without shared language. As Ulysses was made to put it by a member of our speech community:

... no man is the lord of anything,
Though in and of him there be much consisting,

Till he communicate his parts to others;
Nor doth he of himself know them for aught
Till he behold them formed in th'applause
Where they're extended.

(*Troilus and Cressida*, III. iii. 115–20)

Notes

1   Wilfrid Sellars, "Conceptual Change," in *Conceptual Change*, ed. G. Pearce and P. Maynard, Dordrecht, 1973, p. 82.
2   Frank Ramsey, "Truth and Probability," in *Foundations of Mathematics and Other Essays*, ed. R.B. Braithwaite, London, 1931.
3   There is further discussion of these issues in my "Radical Interpretation," *Dialectica* (Vol. 27, Nos. 3–4, 1973).
4   The interlocking of decision theory and radical interpretation is explored also in my "Psychology as Philosophy," in *Philosophy of Psychology*, ed. S.C. Brown, London, 1974, pp. 41–52; and in my "Belief and the Basis of Meaning," *Synthese* (vol. 27, 1974, pp. 309–24).
5   Alonzo Church, "On Carnap's Analysis of Statements of Assertion and Belief," *Analysis* (X, 1950, pp. 97–9).
6   See "On Saying That," in *Words and Objections: Essays on the Work of W.V. Quine*, eds D. Davidson and J. Hintikka, Dordrecht, 1969, pp. 158–74.
7   W.V. Quine, *Word and Object*, Cambridge, Mass., 1960, p. 219.

18

Daniel C. Dennett, "True Believers: The Intentional Strategy and Why It Works"

Death speaks

There was a merchant in Baghdad who sent his servant to market to buy provisions and in a little while the servant came back, white and trembling, and said, Master, just now when I was in the market-place I was jostled by a woman in the crowd and when I turned I saw it was Death that jostled me. She looked at me and made a threatening gesture; now, lend me your horse, and I will ride away from this city and avoid my fate. I will go to Samarra and there Death will not find me. The merchant lent him his horse, and the servant mounted it, and he dug his spurs in its flanks and as fast as the horse could gallop he went. Then the merchant went down to the market-place and he saw me standing in the crowd, and he came to me and said, why did you make a threatening gesture to my servant when you saw him this morning? That was not a threatening gesture, I said, it was only a start of surprise. I was astonished to see him in Baghdad, for I had an appointment with him tonight in Samarra.

W. Somerset Maugham

In the social sciences, talk about *belief* is ubiquitous. Since social scientists are typically self-conscious about their methods, there is also a lot of talk about *talk about belief*. And since belief is a genuinely curious and perplexing phenomenon, showing many different faces to the world, there is abundant controversy. Sometimes belief attribution appears to be a dark, risky, and imponderable business – especially when exotic, and more particularly religious or superstitious, beliefs are in the limelight. These are

Daniel C. Dennett, "True Believers: The Intentional Strategy and Why It Works," in *The International Stance* (MIT Press, Cambridge, Mass., 1987), pp. 13–35.

not the only troublesome cases; we also court argument and skepticism when we attribute beliefs to nonhuman animals, or to infants, or to computers or robots. Or when the beliefs we feel constrained to attribute to an apparently healthy, adult member of our own society are contradictory, or even just wildly false. A biologist colleague of mine was once called on the telephone by a man in a bar who wanted him to settle a bet. The man asked: "Are rabbits birds?" "No" said the biologist. "Damn!" said the man as he hung up. Now could he *really* have believed that rabbits were birds? Could anyone really and truly be attributed that belief? Perhaps, but it would take a bit of a story to bring us to accept it.

In all of these cases belief attribution appears beset with subjectivity, infected with cultural relativism, prone to "indeterminacy of radical translation" – clearly an enterprise demanding special talents: the art of phenomenological analysis, hermeneutics, empathy, *Verstehen*, and all that. On other occasions, normal occasions, when familiar beliefs are the topic, belief attribution looks as easy as speaking prose and as objective and reliable as counting beans in a dish. Particularly when these straightforward cases are before us, it is quite plausible to suppose that in principle (if not yet in practice) it would be possible to confirm these simple, objective belief attributions by *finding something inside the believer's head* – by finding the beliefs themselves, in effect. "Look," someone might say, "You either believe there's milk in the fridge or you don't believe there's milk in the fridge" (you might have no opinion, in the latter case). But if you do believe this, that's a perfectly objective fact about you, and it must come down in the end to your brain's being in some particular physical state. If we knew more about physiological psychology, we could in principle determine the facts about your brain state and thereby determine whether or not you believe there is milk in the fridge, even if you were determined to be silent or disingenuous on the topic. In principle, on this view physiological psychology could trump the results – or non-results – of any "black box" method in the social sciences that divines beliefs (and other mental features) by behavioral, cultural, social, historical, *external* criteria.

These differing reflections congeal into two opposing views on the nature of belief attribution, and hence on the nature of belief. The latter, a variety of *realism*, likens the question of whether a person has a particular belief to the question of whether a person is infected with a particular virus – a perfectly objective internal matter of fact about which an observer can often make educated guesses of great reliability. The former, which we could call *interpretationism* if we absolutely had to give it a name, likens the question of whether a person has a particular belief to the question of whether a person is immoral, or has style, or talent, or would make a good wife. Faced with such questions, we preface our answers with "well, it all depends on what you're interested in," or make some similar acknowledgment of the relativity of the issue. "It's a matter of interpretation," we say. These two opposing views, so baldly stated, do not fairly represent any serious theorists' positions, but they do express views that are typically seen as mutually exclusive and exhaustive; the theorist must be friendly with one and only one of these themes.

I think this is a mistake. My thesis will be that while belief is a perfectly objective phenomenon (that apparently makes me a realist), it can be discerned only from the point of view of one who adopts a certain *predictive strategy*, and its existence can be confirmed only by an assessment of the success of that strategy (that apparently makes me an interpretationist).

First I will describe the strategy, which I call the intentional strategy or adopting the intentional stance. To a first approximation, the intentional strategy consists of treating the object whose behavior you want to predict as a rational agent with beliefs and desires and other mental stages exhibiting what Brentano and others call *intentionality*. The strategy has often been described before, but I shall try to put this very familiar material in a new light by showing *how* it works and by showing *how well* it works.

Then I will argue that any object – or as I shall say, any *system* – whose behavior is well predicted by this strategy is in the fullest sense of the word a believer. *What it is* to be a true believer is to be an *intentional system*, a system whose behavior is reliably and voluminously predictable via the intentional strategy. I have argued for this position before (Dennett 1978, chapters 1 and 14; 1987, chapter 3), and my arguments have so far garnered few converts and many presumed counterexamples. I shall try again here, harder, and shall also deal with several compelling objections.

The intentional strategy and how it works

There are many strategies, some good, some bad. Here is a strategy, for instance, for predicting the future behavior of a person: determine the date and hour of the person's birth and then feed this modest datum into one or another astrological algorithm for generating predictions of the person's prospects. This strategy is deplorably popular. Its popularity is deplorable only because we have such good reasons for believing that it does not work *(pace* Feyerabend 1978). When astrological predictions come true this is sheer luck, or the result of such vagueness or ambiguity in the prophecy that almost any eventuality can be construed to confirm it. But suppose the astrological strategy did in fact work well on some people. We could call those people *astrological systems* – systems whose behavior was, as a matter of fact, predictable by the astrological strategy. If there were such people, such

372

astrological systems, we would be more interested than most of us in fact are in *how the astrological strategy works* – that is, we would be interested in the rules, principles, or methods of astrology. We could find out how the strategy works by asking astrologers, reading their books, and observing them in action. But we would also be curious about *why* it worked. We might find that astrologers had no useful opinions about this latter question – they either had no theory of why it worked or their theories were pure hokum. Having a good strategy is one thing; knowing why it works is another.

So far as we know, however, the class of astrological systems is empty, so the astrological strategy is of interest only as a social curiosity. Other strategies have better credentials. Consider the physical strategy, or physical stance; if you want to predict the behavior of a system, determine its physical constitution (perhaps all the way down to the microphysical level) and the physical nature of the impingements upon it, and use your knowledge of the laws of physics to predict the outcome for any input. This is the grand and impractical strategy of Laplace for predicting the entire future of everything in the universe, but it has more modest, local, actually usable versions. The chemist or physicist in the laboratory can use this strategy to predict the behavior of exotic materials, but equally the cook in the kitchen can predict the effect of leaving the pot on the burner too long. The strategy is not always practically available, but that it will always work *in principle* is a dogma of the physical sciences. (I ignore the minor complications raised by the subatomic indeterminacies of quantum physics.)

Sometimes, in any event, it is more effective to switch from the physical stance to what I call the design stance, where one ignores the actual (possibly messy) details of the physical constitution of an object, and, on the assumption that it has a certain design, predicts that it will behave *as it is designed to behave* under various circumstances. For instance, most users of computers have not the foggiest idea what physical principles are responsible for the computer's highly reliable, and hence predictable, behavior. But if they have a good idea of what the computer is designed to do (a description of its operation at any one of the many possible levels of abstraction), they can predict its behavior with great accuracy and reliability, subject to disconfirmation only in cases of physical malfunction. Less dramatically, almost anyone can predict when an alarm clock will sound on the basis of the most casual inspection of its exterior. One does not know or care to know whether it is spring wound, battery driven, sunlight powered, made of brass wheels and jewel bearings or silicon chips – one just assumes that it is designed so that the alarm will sound when it is set to sound, and it is set to sound where it appears to be set to sound, and the clock will keep on running until that time and beyond, and is designed to run more or less accurately, and so forth. For more accurate and detailed design stance predictions of the alarm clock, one must descend to a less abstract level of description of its design; for instance, to the level at which gears are described, but their material is not specified.

Only the designed behavior of a system is predictable from the design stance, of course. If you want to predict the behavior of an alarm clock when it is pumped full of liquid helium, revert to the physical stance. Not just artifacts but also many biological objects (plants and animals, kidneys and hearts, stamens and pistils) behave in ways that can be predicted from the design stance. They are not just physical systems but designed systems.

Sometimes even the design stance is practically inaccessible, and then there is yet another stance or strategy one can adopt: the intentional stance. Here is how it works: first you decide to treat the object whose behavior is to be predicted as a rational agent; then you figure out what beliefs that agent ought to have, given its place in the world and its purpose. Then you figure out what desires it ought to have, on the same considerations, and finally you predict that this rational agent will act to further its goals in the light of its beliefs. A little practical reasoning from the chosen set of beliefs and desires will in many – but not all – instances yield a decision about what the agent ought to do; that is what you predict the agent *will* do.

The strategy becomes clearer with a little elaboration. Consider first how we go about populating each other's heads with beliefs. A few truisms: sheltered people tend to be ignorant; if you expose someone to something he comes to know all about it. In general, it seems, we come to believe all the truths about the parts of the world around us we are put in a position to learn about. Exposure to *x*, that is, sensory confrontation with *x* over some suitable period of time, is the *normally sufficient* condition for knowing (or having true beliefs) about *x*. As we say, we come to *know all about* the things around us. Such exposure is only *normally* sufficient for knowledge, but this is not the large escape hatch it might appear; our threshold for accepting abnormal ignorance in the face of exposure is quite high. "I didn't know the gun was loaded," said by one who was observed to be present, sighted, and awake during the loading, meets with a variety of utter skepticism that only the most outlandish supporting tale could overwhelm.

Of course we do not come to learn or remember all the truths our sensory histories avail us. In spite of the phrase "know all about," what we come to know, normally, are only all the *relevant* truths our sensory histories avail us. I do not typically come to know the ratio of spectacle-wearing people to trousered people in a room I inhabit, though if this interested me, it would be readily learnable. It is not just that some facts about my environment are below my thresholds of discrimination or beyond the integration and holding power of my memory (such as the height in inches of all the people present), but that many perfectly detectable, graspable, memorable facts are of no interest to me and hence do not come to be believed by me. So one rule for attributing beliefs in the intentional strategy is this: attribute as beliefs all the truths relevant to the system's interests (or desires) that the system's experience to date has made available. This rule leads to attributing somewhat too much – since we all are somewhat forgetful, even of important things. It also fails to capture the false beliefs we are all known to have. But the attribution of false belief, *any* false belief, requires a special genealogy, which will be seen to consist in the main in true beliefs. Two paradigm cases: *S* believes (falsely) that *p*, because *S* believes (truly) that Jones told him that *p*, that Jones is pretty clever, that Jones did not intend to deceive him, . . . etc. Second case: *S* believes (falsely) that there is a snake on the barstool, because *S* believes (truly) that he seems to see a snake on the barstool, is himself sitting in a bar not a yard from the barstool he sees, and so forth. The falsehood has to start somewhere; the seed may be sown in hallucination, illusion, a normal variety of simple misperception, memory deterioration, or deliberate fraud, for instance, but the false beliefs that are reaped grow in a culture medium of true beliefs.

Then there are the arcane and sophisticated beliefs, true and false, that are so often at the focus of attention in discussions of belief attribution. They do not arise directly, goodness knows, from exposure to mundane things and events, but their attribution requires tracing out a lineage of mainly good argument or reasoning from the bulk of beliefs already attributed. An implication of the intentional strategy, then, is that true believers mainly believe truths. If anyone could devise an agreed-upon method of individuating and counting beliefs (which I doubt very much), we would see that all but the smallest portion (say, less than ten percent) of a person's beliefs were attributable under our first rule.[1]

Note that this rule is a derived rule, an elaboration and further specification of the fundamental rule: attribute those beliefs the system *ought to have*. Note also that the rule interacts with the attribution of desires. How do we attribute the desires (preferences, goals, interests) on whose basis we will shape the list of beliefs? We attribute the desires the system *ought to have*. That is the fundamental rule. It dictates, on a first pass, that we attribute the familiar list of highest, or most basic, desires to people: survival, absence of pain, food, comfort, procreation, entertainment. Citing any one of these desires typically terminates the "Why?" game of reason giving. One is not supposed to need an ulterior motive for desiring comfort or pleasure or the prolongation of one's existence. Derived rules of desire attribution interact with belief attributions. Trivially, we have the rule: attribute desires for those things a system believes to be good for it. Somewhat more informatively, attribute desires for those things a system believes to be best means to other ends it desires. The attribution of bizarre and detrimental desires thus requires, like the attribution of false beliefs, special stories.

The interaction between belief and desire becomes trickier when we consider what desires we attribute on the basis of verbal behavior. The capacity to *express* desires in language opens the floodgates of desire attribution. "I want a two-egg mushroom omelette, some French bread and butter, and a half bottle of lightly chilled white Burgundy." How could one begin to attribute a desire for anything so specific in the absence of such verbal declaration? How, indeed, could a creature come to *contract* such a specific desire without the aid of language? Language *enables* us to formulate highly specific desires, but it also *forces* us on occasion to commit ourselves to desires altogether more stringent in their conditions of satisfaction than anything we would otherwise have any reason to endeavor to satisfy. Since in order to get what you want you often have to say what you want, and since you often cannot say what you want without saying something more specific than you antecedently mean, you often end up giving others evidence – the very best of evidence, your unextorted word – that you desire things or states of affairs far more particular than would satisfy you – or better, than would have satisfied you, for once you have declared, being a man of your word, you acquire an interest in satisfying exactly the desire you declared and no other.

"I'd like some baked beans, please."

"Yes sir. How many?"

You might well object to having such a specification of desire demanded of you, but in fact we are all socialized to accede to similar requirements in daily life – to the point of not noticing it, and certainly not feeling oppressed by it. I dwell on this because it has a parallel in the realm of belief, where our linguistic environment is forever forcing us to give – or concede – precise verbal expression to convictions that lack the hard edges verbalization endows them with (see Dennett 1969, pp. 184–85, and Dennett 1978, chapter 16). By concentrating on the *results* of this social force, while ignoring its distorting effect, one can easily be misled into thinking that it is *obvious* that beliefs and desires are rather like sentences stored in the head. Being language-using creatures, it is inevitable that we should often come to believe that some particular, actually formulated, spelled and punctuated sentence *is true*, and that on other occasions we should come to want such a sentence to *come true*, but these are special cases of belief and desire and as such may not be reliable models for the whole domain.

That is enough, on this occasion, about the principles of belief and desire attribution to be found in the intentional strategy. What about the rationality one attributes to an intentional system? One starts with the ideal of perfect rationality and revises downward as circumstances dictate. That is, one starts with the assumption that people believe all the implications of their beliefs and believe no contradictory pairs of beliefs. This does not create a practical problem of clutter (infinitely many implications, for instance), for one is interested only in ensuring that the system one is predicting is rational enough to get to the particular implications that are relevant to its behavioral predicament of the moment. Instances of irrationality, or of finitely powerful capacities of inferences, raise particularly knotty problems of interpretation, which I will set aside on this occasion (see Dennett 1987, chapter 4, and Cherniak 1986).

For I want to turn from the description of the strategy to the question of its use. Do people actually use this strategy? Yes, all the time. There may someday be other strategies for attributing belief and desire and for predicting behavior, but this is the only one we all know now. And when does it work? It works with people almost all the time. Why would it *not* be a good idea to allow individual Oxford colleges to create and grant academic degrees whenever they saw fit? The answer is a long story, but very easy to generate. And there would be widespread agreement about the major points. We have no difficulty thinking of the reasons people would then have for acting in such ways as to give others reasons for acting in such ways as to give others reasons for ... creating a circumstance we would not want. Our use of the intentional strategy is so habitual and effortless that the role it plays in shaping our expectations about people is easily overlooked. The strategy also works on most other mammals most of the time. For instance, you can use it to design better traps to catch those mammals, by reasoning about what the creature knows or believes about various things, what it prefers, what it wants to avoid. The strategy works on birds, and on fish, and on reptiles, and on insects and spiders, and even on such lowly and unenterprising creatures as clams (once a clam believes there is danger about, it will not relax its grip on its closed shell until it is convinced that the danger has passed). It also works on some artifacts: the chess-playing computer will not take your knight because it knows that there is a line of ensuing play that would lead to losing its rook, and it does not want that to happen. More modestly, the thermostat will turn off the boiler as soon as it comes to believe the room has reached the desired temperature.

The strategy even works for plants. In a locale with late spring storms, you should plant apple varieties that are particularly *cautious* about *concluding* that it is spring – which is when they *want* to blossom, of course. It even works for such inanimate and apparently undesigned phenomena as lightning. An electrician once explained to me how he worked out how to protect my underground water pump from lightning damage: lightning, he said, always wants to find the best way to ground, but sometimes it gets tricked into taking second-best paths. You can protect the pump by making another, better path more *obvious* to the lightning.

True believers as intentional systems

Now clearly this is a motley assortment of "serious" belief attributions, dubious belief attributions, pedagogically useful metaphors, *façons de parler,* and, perhaps worse, outright frauds. The next task would seem to be distinguishing those intentional systems that *really* have beliefs and desires from those we may find it handy to treat *as if* they had beliefs and desires. But that would be a Sisyphean labor, or else would be terminated by fiat. A better understanding of the phenomenon of belief begins with the observation that even in the worst of these cases, even when we are surest that the strategy works *for the wrong reasons,* it is nevertheless true that it does work, at least a little bit. This is an interesting fact, which distinguishes this class of objects, the class of *intentional systems,* from the class of objects for which the strategy never works. But is this so? Does our definition of an intentional system exclude any objects at all? For instance, it seems the lectern in this lecture room can be construed as an intentional system, fully rational, believing that it is currently located at the center of the civilized world (as some of you may also think), and desiring above all else to remain at that center. What should such a rational agent so equipped with belief and desire do? Stay put, clearly, which is just what the lectern does. I predict the lectern's behavior, accurately, from the intentional stance, so is it an intentional system? If it is, anything at all is.

What should disqualify the lectern? For one thing, the strategy does not recommend itself in this case, for we get no predictive power from it that we did not antecedently have. We already knew what the lectern was going to do – namely nothing – and tailored the beliefs and desires to fit in a quite unprincipled way. In the case of people or animals or computers, however, the situation is different. In these cases often the only strategy that is at all practical is the intentional strategy; it gives us predictive power we can get by no other method. But, it will be urged, this is no difference in nature, but merely a difference that reflects upon our limited capacities as scientists. The Laplacean omniscient physicist could predict the behavior of a computer – or of a live human body, assuming it to be ultimately governed by the laws of physics – without any need for the risky, short-cut methods of either the design or intentional strategies. For people of limited mechanical aptitude, the intentional interpretation of a simple thermostat is a handy and largely innocuous crutch, but the engineers among us can quite fully grasp its internal operation without the aid of this anthropomorphizing. It may be true that the cleverest engineers find it practically impossible to maintain a clear conception of more complex systems, such as a time-sharing computer system or remote-controlled space probe, without lapsing into an intentional stance (and viewing these devices as asking and telling, trying and avoiding, wanting and believing), but this is just a more advanced case of human epistemic frailty. We would not want to classify these artifacts with the true believers – ourselves – on such variable and parochial grounds, would we? Would it not be intolerable to hold that some artifact or creature or person was a believer from the point of view of one observer, but not a believer at all from the point of view of another, cleverer observer? That would be a particularly radical version of interpretationism, and some have thought I espoused it in urging that belief be viewed in terms of the success of the intentional strategy. I must confess that my presentation of the view has sometimes invited that reading, but I now want to discourage it. The decision to adopt the intentional stance is free, but the facts about the success or failure of the stance, were one to adopt it, are perfectly objective.

Once the intentional strategy is in place, it is an extraordinarily powerful tool in prediction – a fact that is largely concealed by our typical concentration on the cases in which it yields dubious or unreliable results. Consider, for instance, predicting moves in a chess game. What makes chess an interesting game, one can see, is the unpredictability of one's opponent's moves, except in those cases where moves are "forced" – where there is *clearly* one best move – typically the least of the available evils. But this unpredictability is put in context when one recognizes that in the typical chess situation there are very many perfectly legal and hence available moves, but only a few – perhaps half a dozen – with anything to be said for them, and hence only a few high-probability moves according to the intentional strategy. Even when the intentional strategy fails to distinguish a single move with a highest probability, it can dramatically reduce the number of live options.

The same feature is apparent when the intentional strategy is applied to "real world" cases. It is notoriously unable to predict the exact purchase and sell decisions of stock traders, for instance, or the exact sequence of words a politician will utter when making a scheduled speech, but one's confidence can be very high indeed about slightly less specific predictions: that the particular trader *will not buy utilities today*, or that the politician *will side with the unions against his party*, for example. This inability to predict fine-grained descriptions of actions, looked at another way, is a source of strength for the intentional strategy, for it is this neutrality with regard to details of implementation that permits one to exploit the

DANIEL C. DENNETT

intentional strategy in complex cases, for instance, in *chaining predictions* (see Dennett 1978). Suppose the US Secretary of State were to announce he was a paid agent of the KGB. What an unparalleled event! How unpredictable its consequences! Yet in fact we can predict dozens of not terribly interesting but perfectly salient consequences, and consequences of consequences. The President would confer with the rest of the Cabinet, which would support his decision to relieve the Secretary of State of his duties pending the results of various investigations, psychiatric and political, and all this would be reported at a news conference to people who would write stories that would be commented upon in editorials that would be read by people who would write letters to the editors, and so forth. None of that is daring prognostication, but note that it describes an arc of causation in space–time that could not be predicted under *any* description by any imaginable practical extension of physics or biology.

The power of the intentional strategy can be seen even more sharply with the aid of an objection first raised by Robert Nozick some years ago. Suppose, he suggested, some beings of vastly superior intelligence – from Mars, let us say – were to descend upon us, and suppose that we were to them as simple thermostats are to clever engineers. Suppose, that is, that they did not *need* the intentional stance – or even the design stance – to predict our behavior in all its detail. They can be supposed to be Laplacean super-physicists, capable of comprehending the activity on Wall Street, for instance, at the microphysical level. Where we see brokers and buildings and sell orders and bids, they see vast congeries of subatomic particles milling about – and they are such good physicists that they can predict days in advance what ink marks will appear each day on the paper tape labeled "Closing Dow Jones Industrial Average." They can predict the individual behaviors of all the various moving bodies they observe without ever treating any of them as intentional systems. Would we be right then to say that from *their* point of view we really were not believers at all (any more than a simple thermostat is)? If so, then our status as believers is nothing objective, but rather something in the eye of the beholder – provided the beholder shares our intellectual limitations.

Our imagined Martians might be able to predict the future of the human race by Laplacean methods, but if they did not also see us as intentional systems, they would be missing something perfectly objective: the *patterns* in human behavior that are describable from the intentional stance, and only from that stance, and that support generalizations and predictions. Take a particular instance in which the Martians observe a stockbroker deciding to place an order for 500 shares of General Motors. They predict the exact motions of his fingers as he dials the phone and the exact vibrations of his vocal cords as he intones his order. But if the Martians do not

see that indefinitely many *different* patterns of finger motions and vocal
cord vibrations – even the motions of indefinitely many different individuals
– could have been substituted for the actual particulars without perturbing
the subsequent operation of the market, then they have failed to see a real
pattern in the world they are observing. Just as there are indefinitely many
ways of *being a spark plug* – and one has not understood what an internal
combustion engine is unless one realizes that a variety of different devices
can be screwed into these sockets without affecting the performance of
the engine – so there are indefinitely many ways of *ordering 500 shares
of General Motors*, and there are societal sockets in which one of these
ways will produce just about the same effect as any other. There are also,
societal pivot points, as it were, where which way people go depends on
whether they *believe that p, or desire A*, and does not depend on any of
the other infinitely many ways they may be alike or different.

Suppose, pursuing our Martian fantasy a little further, that one of the
Martians were to engage in a predicting contest with an Earthling. The
Earthling and the Martian observe (and observe each other observing)
a particular bit of local physical transaction. From the Earthling's point of
view, this is what is observed. The telephone rings in Mrs Gardner's kitchen.
She answers, and this is what she says: "Oh, hello dear. You're coming home
early? Within the hour? And bringing the boss to dinner? Pick up a bottle
of wine on the way home, then, and drive carefully." On the basis of this
observation, our Earthling predicts that a large metallic vehicle with rubber
tires will come to a stop in the drive within one hour, disgorging two human
beings, one of whom will be holding a paper bag containing a bottle
containing an alcoholic fluid. The prediction is a bit risky, perhaps, but a
good bet on all counts. The Martian makes the same prediction, but has to
avail himself of much more information about an extraordinary number of
interactions of which, so far as he can tell, the Earthling is entirely ignorant. For instance, the deceleration of the vehicle at intersection A, five miles
from the house, without which there would have been a collision with
another vehicle – whose collision course had been laboriously calculated
over some hundreds of meters by the Martian. The Earthling's performance
would look like magic! How did the Earthling know that the human being
who got out of the car and got the bottle in the shop would get back in?
The coming true of the Earthling's prediction, after all the vagaries, intersections, and branches in the paths charted by the Martian, would seem to
anyone bereft of the intentional strategy as marvelous and inexplicable as
the fatalistic inevitability of the appointment in Samarra. Fatalists – for
instance, astrologers – believe that there is a pattern in human affairs that
is inexorable, that will impose itself *come what may*, that is, no matter how
the victims scheme and second-guess, no matter how they twist and turn in

their chains. These fatalists are wrong, but they are *almost* right. There *are* patterns in human affairs that impose themselves, not quite inexorably but with great vigor, absorbing physical perturbations and variations that might as well be considered random; these are the patterns that we characterize in terms of the beliefs, desires, and intentions of rational agents.

No doubt you will have noticed, and been distracted by, a serious flaw in our thought experiment: the Martian is presumed to treat his Earthling opponent as an intelligent being like himself, with whom communication is possible, a being with whom one can make a wager, against whom one can compete. In short, a being with beliefs (such as the belief he expressed in his prediction) and desires (such as the desire to win the prediction contest). So if the Martian sees the pattern in one Earthling, how can he fail to see it in the others? As a bit of narrative, our example could be strengthened by supposing that our Earthling cleverly learned Martian (which is transmitted by X-ray modulation) and disguised himself as a Martian, counting on the species-chauvinism of these otherwise brilliant aliens to permit him to pass as an intentional system while not giving away the secret of his fellow human beings. This addition might get us over a bad twist in the tale, but might obscure the moral to be drawn: namely, *the unavoidability of the intentional stance with regard to oneself and one's fellow intelligent beings.* This unavoidability is itself interest relative; it is perfectly possible to adopt a physical stance, for instance, with regard to an intelligent being, oneself included, but not to the exclusion of main-taining at the same time an intentional stance with regard to oneself at a minimum, and one's fellows *if* one intends, for instance, to learn what they know (a point that has been powerfully made by Stuart Hampshire in a number of writings). We can perhaps suppose our super-intelligent Martians fail to recognize *us* as intentional systems, but we cannot suppose them to lack the requisite concepts.[2] If they observe, theorize, predict, communicate, they view *themselves* as intentional systems.[3] Where there are intelligent beings, the patterns must be there to be described, whether or not we care to see them.

It is important to recognize the objective reality of the intentional patterns discernible in the activities of intelligent creatures, but also import-ant to recognize the incompleteness and imperfections in the patterns. The objective fact is that the intentional strategy *works as well as it does*, which is not perfectly. No one is perfectly rational, perfectly unforgetful, all-observant, or invulnerable to fatigue, malfunction, or design imperfec-tion. This leads inevitably to circumstances beyond the power of the intentional strategy to describe, in much the same way that physical damage to an artifact, such as a telephone or an automobile, may render it inde-scribable by the normal design terminology for that artifact. How do you draw the schematic wiring diagram of an audio amplifier that has been partially melted, or how do you characterize the program state of a malfunctioning computer? In cases of even the mildest and most familiar cognitive pathology – where people seem to hold contradictory beliefs or to be deceiving themselves, for instance – the canons of interpretation of the intentional strategy fail to yield clear, stable verdicts about which beliefs and desires to attribute to a person.

Now a *strong* realist position on beliefs and desires would claim that in these cases the person in question really does have some particular beliefs and desires which the intentional strategy, as I have described it, is simply unable to divine. On the milder sort of realism I am advocating, there is no fact of the matter of exactly which beliefs and desires a person has in these degenerate cases, but this is not a surrender to relativism or subjectivism, for *when* and *why* there is no fact of the matter is itself a matter of objective fact. On this view one can even acknowledge the *interest relativity* of belief attributions and grant that given the different interests of different cultures, for instance, the beliefs and desires one culture would attribute to a member might be quite different from the beliefs and desires another culture would attribute to that very same person. But supposing that were so in a particular case, there would be the further facts about *how well* each of the rival intentional strategies worked for predicting the behavior of that person. We can be sure in advance that no intentional interpretation of an individual will work to perfection, and it may be that two rival schemes are about equally good, and better than any others we can devise. That this is the case is itself something about which there can be a fact of the matter. The objective presence of one pattern (with whatever imperfections) does not rule out the objective presence of another pattern (with whatever imperfections).

The bogey of radically different interpretations with equal warrant from the intentional strategy is theoretically important – one might better say metaphysically important – but practically negligible once one restricts one's attention to the largest and most complex intentional systems we know: human beings.[4]

Until now I have been stressing our kinship to clams and thermostats, in order to emphasize a view of the logical status of belief attribution, but the time has come to acknowledge the obvious differences and say what can be made of them. The perverse claim remains: *all there is* to being a true believer is being a system whose behavior is reliably predictable via the intentional strategy, and hence *all there is* to really and truly believing that *p* (for any proposition *p*) is being an intentional system for which *p* occurs as a belief in the best (most predictive) interpretation. But once we turn our attention to the truly interesting and versatile intentional systems, we see that this apparently shallow and instrumentalistic criterion of belief puts a severe constraint on the internal constitution of a genuine believer, and thus yields a robust version of belief after all.

Consider the lowly thermostat, as degenerate a case of an intentional system as could conceivably hold our attention for more than a moment. Going along with the gag, we might agree to grant it the capacity for about half a dozen different beliefs and fewer desires – it can believe the room is too cold or too hot, that the boiler is on or off, and that if it wants the room warmer it should turn on the boiler, and so forth. But surely this is imputing too much to the thermostat; it has no concept of heat or of a boiler, for instance. So suppose we *de-interpret* its beliefs and desires: it can believe the A is too F or G, and if it wants the A to be more F it should do K, and so forth. After all, by attaching the thermostatic control mechanism to different input and output devices, it could be made to regulate the amount of water in a tank, or the speed of a train, for instance. Its attachment to a heat-sensitive transducer and a boiler is too impoverished a link to the world to grant any rich semantics to its belief-like states.

But suppose we then enrich these modes of attachment. Suppose we give it more than one way of learning about the temperature, for instance. We give it an eye of sorts that can distinguish huddled, shivering occupants of the room and an ear so that it can be told how cold it is. We give it some facts about geography so that it can conclude that it is probably in a cold place if it learns that its spatio-temporal location is Winnipeg in December. Of course giving it a visual system that is multipurpose and general – not a mere shivering-object detector – will require vast complications of its inner structure. Suppose we also give our system more behavioral versatility: it chooses the boiler fuel, purchases it from the cheapest and most reliable dealer, checks the weather stripping, and so forth. This adds another dimension of internal complexity; it gives individual belief-like states *more to do*, in effect, by providing more and different occasions for their derivation or deduction from other states, and by providing more and different occasions for them to serve as premises for further reasoning. The cumulative effect of enriching these connections between the device and the world in which it resides is to enrich the semantics of its dummy predicates, F and G and the rest. The more of this we add, the less amenable our device becomes to serving as the control structure of anything other than a room-temperature maintenance system. A more formal way of saying this is that the class of indistinguishably satisfactory models of the formal system embodied in its internal states gets smaller and smaller as we add such complexities; the more we add, the richer or more demanding or specific the semantics of the system, until eventually we reach systems for which a unique semantic interpretation is practically (but never in principle) dictated (cf. Hayes 1979).

At that point we say this device (or animal or person) has beliefs *about heat* and *about this very room*, and so forth, not only because of the system's actual location in, and operations on, the world, but because we cannot imagine another niche in which it could be placed *where it would work* (see also Dennett 1987).

Our original simple thermostat had a state we called a belief about a particular boiler, to the effect that it was on or off. Why about *that* boiler? Well, what other boiler would you want to say it was about? The belief is about the boiler because it is *fastened* to the boiler.[5] Given the actual, if minimal, causal link to the world that happened to be in effect, we could endow a state of the device with *meaning* (of a sort) and *truth conditions*, but it was altogether too easy to substitute a different minimal link and completely change the meaning (in this impoverished sense) of that internal state. But as systems become perceptually richer and behaviorally more versatile, it becomes harder and harder to make substitutions in the actual links of the system to the world without changing the organization of the system itself. If you change its environment, it will *notice*, in effect, and make a change in its internal state in response. There comes to be a two-way constraint of growing specificity between the device and the environment. Fix the device in any one state and it demands a very specific environment in which to operate properly (you can no longer switch it easily from regulating temperature to regulating speed or anything else); but at the same time, if you do not *fix* the state it is in, but just plonk it down in a changed environment, its sensory attachments will be sensitive and discriminative enough to respond appropriately to the change, driving the system into a new state, in which it will operate effectively in the new environment. There is a familiar way of alluding to this tight relationship that can exist between the organization of a system and its environment: you say that the organism continuously *mirrors* the environment, or that there is a *representation* of the environment in – or implicit in – the organization of the system.

It is not that we attribute (or should attribute) beliefs and desires only to things in which we find internal representations, but rather that when we discover some object for which the intentional strategy works, we endeavor to interpret some of its internal states or processes as internal representations. What makes some internal feature of a thing a representation could only be its role in regulating the behavior of an intentional system.

Now the reason for stressing our kinship with the thermostat should be clear. There is no magic moment in the transition from a simple thermostat to a system that *really* has an internal representation of the world around it. The thermostat has a minimally demanding representation of the world, fancier thermostats have more demanding representations of the world, fancier robots for helping around the house would have still more demanding representations of the world. Finally you reach us. We are so multifariously and intricately connected to the world that almost no substitution is possible – though it is clearly imaginable in a thought experiment. Hilary Putnam imagines the planet Twin Earth, which is just like Earth right down to the scuff marks on the shoes of the Twin Earth replica of your neighbor, but which differs from Earth in some property that is entirely beneath the thresholds of your capacities to discriminate. (What they call water on Twin Earth has a different chemical analysis.) Were *you* to be whisked instantaneously to Twin Earth and exchanged for your Twin Earth replica, you would never be the wiser – just like the simple control system that cannot tell whether it is regulating temperature, speed, or volume of water in a tank. It is easy to devise radically different Twin Earths for something as simple and sensorily deprived as a thermostat, but your internal organization puts a much more stringent demand on substitution. Your Twin Earth and Earth must be virtual replicas or you will change state dramatically on arrival.

So which boiler are *your* beliefs about when you believe the boiler is on? Why, the boiler in your cellar (rather than its twin on Twin Earth, for instance). What other boiler would your beliefs be about? The completion of the semantic interpretation of your beliefs, fixing the referents of your beliefs, requires, as in the case of the thermostat, facts about your actual embedding in the world. The principles, and problems, of interpretation that we discover when we attribute beliefs to people are the *same* principles and problems we discover when we look at the ludicrous, but blessedly simple, problem of attributing beliefs to a thermostat. The differences are of degree, but nevertheless of such great degree that understanding the internal organization of a simple intentional system gives one very little basis for understanding the internal organization of a complex intentional system, such as a human being.

Why does the intentional strategy work?

When we turn to the question of *why* the intentional strategy works as well as it does, we find that the question is ambiguous, admitting of two very different sorts of answers. If the intentional system is a simple thermostat, one answer is simply this: the intentional strategy works because the thermostat is well designed; it was designed to be a system that could be easily and reliably comprehended and manipulated from this stance. That is true, but not very informative, if what we are after are the actual features of its design that explain its performance. Fortunately, however, in the case of a simple thermostat those features are easily discovered and understood, so the other answer to our *why* question, which is really an answer about *how the machinery works*, is readily available.

If the intentional system in question is a person, there is also an ambiguity in our question. The first answer to the question of why the intentional strategy works is that evolution has designed human beings to be rational, to believe what they ought to believe and want what they ought to want. The fact that we are products of a long and demanding evolutionary process guarantees that using the intentional strategy on us is a safe bet. This answer has the virtues of truth and brevity, and on this occasion the additional virtue of being an answer Herbert Spencer would applaud, but it is also strikingly uninformative. The more difficult version of the question asks, in effect, how the machinery which Nature has provided us works. And we cannot yet give a good answer to that question. We just do not know. We do know how the *strategy* works, and we know the easy answer to the question of why it works, but knowing these does not help us much with the hard answer.

It is not that there is any dearth of doctrine, however. A Skinnerian behaviorist, for instance, would say that the strategy works because its imputations of beliefs and desires are shorthand, in effect, for as yet unimaginably complex descriptions of the effects of prior histories of response and reinforcement. To say that someone wants some ice cream is to say that in the past the ingestion of ice cream has been reinforced in him by the results, creating a propensity under certain background conditions (also too complex to describe) to engage in ice-cream-acquiring behavior. In the absence of detailed knowledge of those historical facts we can nevertheless make shrewd guesses on inductive grounds; these guesses are embodied in our intentional stance claims. Even if all this were true, it would tell us very little about the way such propensities were regulated by the internal machinery.

A currently more popular explanation is that the account of how the strategy works and the account of how the mechanism works will (roughly) *coincide*: for each predictively attributable belief, there will be a functionally salient internal state of the machinery, decomposable into functional parts in just about the same way the sentence expressing the belief is decomposable into parts – that is, words or terms. The inferences we attribute to rational creatures will be mirrored by physical, causal processes in the hardware; the *logical* form of the propositions believed will be copied in the *structural* form of the states in correspondence with them. This is the hypothesis that there is a *language of thought* coded in our brains, and our brains will eventually be understood as symbol manipulating systems in at least rough analogy with computers. Many different versions of this view are currently being explored, in the new research program called cognitive science, and provided one allows great latitude for attenuation of the basic, bold claim, I think some version of it will prove correct.

But I do not believe that this is *obvious*. Those who think that it is obvious, or inevitable, that such a theory will prove true (and there are many who do), are confusing two different empirical claims. The first is that intentional stance description yields an objective, real pattern in the world – the pattern our imaginary Martians missed. This is an empirical claim, but one that is confirmed beyond skepticism. The second is that this real pattern is *produced by* another real pattern roughly isomorphic to it within the brains of intelligent creatures. Doubting the existence of the second real pattern is not doubting the existence of the first. There *are* reasons for believing in the second pattern, but they are not overwhelming. The best simple account I can give of the reasons is as follows.

As we ascend the scale of complexity from simple thermostat, through sophisticated robot, to human being, we discover that our efforts to design systems with the requisite behavior increasingly run foul of the problem of *combinatorial explosion*. Increasing some parameter by, say, ten percent – ten percent more inputs or more degrees of freedom in the behavior to be controlled or more words to be recognized or whatever – tends to increase the internal complexity of the system being designed by orders of magnitude. Things get out of hand very fast and, for instance, can lead to computer programs that will swamp the largest, fastest machines. Now somehow the brain has solved the problem of combinatorial explosion. It is a gigantic network of billions of cells, but still finite, compact, reliable, and swift, and capable of learning new behaviors, vocabularies, theories, almost without limit. Some elegant, *generative*, indefinitely extendable principles of representation must be responsible. We have only one model of such a representation system: a human language. So the argument for a language of thought comes down to this: what else could it be? We have so far been unable to imagine any plausible alternative in any detail. That is a good enough reason, I think, for recommending as a matter of scientific tactics that we pursue the hypothesis in its various forms as far as we can.[6] But we will engage in that exploration more circumspectly, and fruitfully, if we bear in mind that its inevitable rightness is far from assured. One does not understand even a true empirical hypothesis so long as one is under the misapprehension that it is necessarily true.

Notes

1   The idea that most of anyone's beliefs *must* be true seems obvious to some people. Support for the idea can be found in works by Quine, Putnam, Shoemaker, Davidson, and myself. Other people find the idea equally

incredible – so probably each side is calling a different phenomenon belief. Once one makes the distinction between belief and opinion (in my technical sense – see "How to Change Your Mind" in Dennett 1978, chapter 16), according to which opinions are linguistically infected, relatively sophisticated cognitive states – *roughly* states of betting on the truth of a particular, formulated sentence – one can see the near triviality of the claim that most beliefs are true. A few reflections on peripheral matters should bring it out. Consider Democritus, who had a systematic, all-embracing, but (let us say, for the sake of argument) entirely false physics. He had things *all wrong*, though his views held together and had a sort of systematic utility. But even if every *claim* that scholarship permits us to attribute to Democritus (either explicit or implicit in his writings) is false, these represent a vanishingly small fraction of his *beliefs*, which include both the vast numbers of humdrum standing beliefs he must have had (about which house he lived in, what to look for in a good pair of sandals, and so forth) and also those occasional beliefs that came and went by the millions as his perceptual experience changed.

But, it may be urged, this isolation of his humdrum beliefs from his science relies on an insupportable distinction between truths of observation and truths of theory; all Democritus's beliefs are theory-laden, and since his theory is false, they are false. The reply is as follows: Granted that all observation beliefs are theory laden, why should we choose Democritus's *explicit*, sophisticated theory (couched in his *opinions*) as the theory with which to burden his quotidian observations? Note that the least theoretical compatriot of Democritus also had myriads of theory-laden observation beliefs – and was, in one sense, none the wiser for it. Why should we not suppose Democritus's observations are laden with the same (presumably innocuous) theory? If Democritus forgot his theory, or changed his mind, his observational beliefs would be *largely* untouched. To the extent that his sophisticated theory played a discernible role in his routine behavior and expectations and so forth, it would be quite appropriate to couch his humdrum beliefs in terms of the sophisticated theory, but this will not yield a *mainly false* catalogue of beliefs, since so few of his beliefs will be affected. (The effect of theory on observation is nevertheless often underrated. See Churchland 1979 for dramatic and convincing examples of the tight relationship that can sometimes exist between theory and experience. [The discussion in this note was distilled from a useful conversation with Paul and Patricia Churchland and Michael Stack.])

2   A member of the audience in Oxford pointed out that if the Martian included the Earthling in his physical stance purview (a possibility I had not explicitly excluded), he would not be surprised by the Earthling's prediction. He would indeed have predicted exactly the pattern of X-ray modulations produced by the Earthling speaking Martian. True, but as the Martian wrote down the results of his calculations, his prediction of the Earthling's prediction would appear, word by Martian word, as on a Ouija board, and what would be baffling to the Martian was how this chunk of mechanism, the Earthling predictor dressed up like a Martian, was able to yield this *true* sentence of Martian when it was so informationally isolated from the events the Martian needed to know of in order to make his own prediction about the arriving automobile.

3   Might there not be intelligent beings who had no use for communicating, predicting, observing . . . ? There might be marvelous, nifty, invulnerable

entities lacking these modes of action, but I cannot see what would lead us to call them *intelligent.*

4   John McCarthy's analogy to cryptography nicely makes this point. The larger the corpus of cipher text, the less chance there is of dual, systematically unrelated decipherings. For a very useful discussion of the principles and presuppositions of the intentional stance applied to machines – explicitly including thermostats – see McCarthy 1979.

5   This idea is the ancestor in effect of the species of different ideas lumped together under the rubric of *de re* belief. If one builds from this idea toward its scions, one can see better the difficulties with them, and how to repair them. (For more on this topic, see Dennett 1987, chapter 5.)

6   The fact that all *language of thought* models of mental representation so far proposed fall victim to combinatorial explosion in one way or another should temper one's enthusiasm for engaging in what Fodor aptly calls "the only game in town."

References

Cherniak, C. (1986) *Minimal Rationality*, Cambridge, Mass.: MIT Press.

Churchland, P.M. (1979) *Scientific Realism and the Plasticity of Mind*, Cambridge: Cambridge University Press.

Dennett, D.C. (1969) *Content and Consciousness*, London: Routledge and Kegan Paul.

—— (1978) *Brainstorms*, Cambridge, Mass.: MIT Press.

—— (1987) *The Intentional Stance*, Cambridge, Mass.: MIT Press.

Feyerabend, P. (1978) *Science in a Free Society*, London: New Left Bank Publications.

Hayes, P. (1979) "The Naïve Physics Manifesto," in D. Michie (ed.) *Expert Systems in the Microelectronic Age*, Edinburgh: Edinburgh University Press.

McCarthy, J. (1979) "Ascribing Mental Qualities to Machines," in M. Ringle (ed.) *Philosophical Perspectives on Artificial Intelligence*, Atlantic Highlands, N.J.: Humanities Press.

19

Paul M. Churchland, "Eliminative Materialism and the Propositional Attitudes"*

Eliminative materialism is the thesis that our commonsense conception of psychological phenomena constitutes a radically false theory, a theory so fundamentally defective that both the principles and the ontology of that theory will eventually be displaced, rather than smoothly reduced, by completed neuroscience. Our mutual understanding and even our introspection may then be reconstituted within the conceptual framework of completed neuroscience, a theory we may expect to be more powerful by far than the common-sense psychology it displaces, and more substantially integrated within physical science generally. My purpose in this paper is to explore these projections, especially as they bear on (1) the principal elements of common-sense psychology: the propositional attitudes (beliefs, desires, etc.), and (2) the conception of rationality in which these elements figure.

This focus represents a change in the fortunes of materialism. Twenty years ago, emotions, qualia, and "raw feels" were held to be the principal stumbling blocks for the materialist program. With these barriers dissolving,[1] the locus of opposition has shifted. Now it is the realm of the intentional, the realm of the propositional attitude, that is most commonly held up as being both irreducible to and ineliminable in favor of anything from within a materialist framework. Whether and why this is so, we must examine.

Such an examination will make little sense, however, unless it is first appreciated that the relevant network of common-sense concepts does

* An earlier draft of this paper was presented at the University of Ottawa, and to the *Brain, Mind, and Person* colloquium at SUNY/Oswego. My thanks for the suggestions and criticisms that have informed the present version.

Paul M. Churchland, "Eliminative Materialism and the Propositional Attitudes," *The Journal of Philosophy*, 78(2) (1981): 67–90.

indeed constitute an empirical theory, with all the functions, virtues, *and perils* entailed by that status. I shall therefore begin with a brief sketch of this view and a summary rehearsal of its rationale. The resistance it encounters still surprises me. After all, common sense has yielded up many theories. Recall the view that space has a preferred direction in which all things fall; that weight is an intrinsic feature of a body; that a force-free moving object will promptly return to rest; that the sphere of the heavens turns daily; and so on. These examples are clear, perhaps, but people seem willing to concede a theoretical component within common sense only if (1) the theory and the common sense involved are safely located in antiquity, and (2) the relevant theory is now so clearly false that its speculative nature is inescapable. Theories are indeed easier to discern under these circumstances. But the vision of hindsight is always 20/20. Let us aspire to some foresight for a change.

I. Why folk psychology is a theory

Seeing our common-sense conceptual framework for mental phenomena as a theory brings a simple and unifying organization to most of the major topics in the philosophy of mind, including the explanation and prediction of behavior, the semantics of mental predicates, action theory, the other-minds problem, the intentionality of mental states, the nature of introspection, and the mind–body problem. Any view that can pull this lot together deserves careful consideration.

Let us begin with the explanation of human (and animal) behavior. The fact is that the average person is able to explain, and even predict, the behavior of other persons with a facility and success that is remarkable. Such explanations and predictions standardly make reference to the desires, beliefs, fears, intentions, perceptions, and so forth, to which the agents are presumed subject. But explanations presuppose laws – rough and ready ones, at least – that connect the explanatory conditions with the behavior explained. The same is true for the making of predictions, and for the justification of subjunctive and counterfactual conditional concerning behavior. Reassuringly, a rich network of common-sense laws can indeed be reconstructed from this quotidian commerce of explanation and anticipation; its principles are familiar homilies; and their sundry functions are transparent. Each of us understands others, as well as we do, because we share a tacit command of an integrated body of lore concerning the law-like relations holding among external circumstances, internal states, and overt behavior. Given its nature and functions, this body of lore may quite aptly be called "folk psychology."[2]

This approach entails that the semantics of the terms in our familiar mentalistic vocabulary is to be understood in the same manner as the semantics of theoretical terms generally: the meaning of any theoretical term is fixed or constituted by the network of laws in which it figures. (This position is quite distinct from logical behaviorism. We deny that the relevant laws are analytic, and it is the lawlike connections generally that carry the semantic weight, not just the connections with overt behavior. But this view does account for what little plausibility logical behaviorism did enjoy.)

More importantly, the recognition that folk psychology is a theory provides a simple and decisive solution to an old skeptical problem, the problem of other minds. The problematic conviction that another individual is the subject of certain mental states is not inferred deductively from his behavior, nor is it inferred by inductive analogy from the perilously isolated instance of one's own case. Rather, that conviction is a singular *explanatory hypothesis* of a perfectly straightforward kind. Its function, in conjunction with the background laws of folk psychology, is to provide explanations/predictions/understanding of the individual's continuing behavior, and it is credible to the degree that it is successful in this regard over competing hypotheses. In the main, such hypotheses are successful, and so the belief that others enjoy the internal states comprehended by folk psychology is a reasonable belief.

Knowledge of other minds thus has no essential dependence on knowledge of one's own mind. Applying the principles of our folk psychology to our behavior, a Martian could justly ascribe to us the familiar run of mental states, even though his own psychology were very different from ours. He would not, therefore, be "generalizing from his own case."

As well, introspective judgments about one's own case turn out not to have any special status or integrity anyway. On the present view, an introspective judgment is just an instance of an acquired habit of conceptual response to one's internal states, and the integrity of any particular response is always contingent on the integrity of the acquired conceptual framework (theory) in which the response is framed. Accordingly, one's *introspective* certainty that one's mind is the seat of beliefs and desires may be as badly misplaced as was the classical man's *visual* certainty that the star-flecked sphere of the heavens turns daily.

Another conundrum is the intentionality of mental states. The "propositional attitudes," as Russell called them, form the systematic core of folk psychology; and their uniqueness and anomalous logical properties have inspired some to see here a fundamental contrast with anything that mere physical phenomena might conceivably display. The key to this matter lies again in the theoretical nature of folk psychology. The intentionality of mental states here emerges not as a mystery of nature, but as a structural

393

feature of the concepts of folk psychology. Ironically, those same structural features reveal the very close affinity that folk psychology bears to theories in the physical sciences. Let me try to explain.

Consider the large variety of what might be called "numerical attitudes" appearing in the conceptual framework of physical science: "... has a $mass_{kg}$ of n," "... has a velocity of n," "... has a $temperature_k$ of n," and so forth. These expressions are predicate-forming expressions: when one substitutes a singular term for a number into the place held by "n," a determinate predicate results. More interestingly, the relations between the various "numerical attitudes" that result are precisely the relations between the numbers "contained" in those attitudes. More interesting still, the argument place that takes the singular terms for numbers is open to quantification. All this permits the expression of generalizations concerning the lawlike relations that hold between the various numerical attitudes in nature. Such laws involve quantification over numbers, and they exploit the mathematical relations holding in that domain. Thus, for example,

(1) (x) (f) (m) [((x has a mass of m) & (x suffers a net force of f))
$$\supset (x \text{ accelerates at } f/m)]$$

Consider now the large variety of propositional attitudes: "... believes that p," "... desires that p," "... fears that p," "... is happy that p," etc. These expressions are predicate-forming expressions also. When one substitutes a singular term for a proposition into the place held by "p," a determinate predicate results, e.g., "... believes that Tom is tall." (Sentences do not generally function as singular terms, but it is difficult to escape the idea that when a sentence occurs in the place held by "p," it is there functioning as or like a singular term. On this, more below.) More interestingly, the relations between the resulting propositional attitudes are characteristically the relations that hold between the propositions "contained" in them, relations such as entailment, equivalence, and mutual inconsistency. More interesting still, the argument place that takes the singular terms for propositions is open to quantification. All this permits the expression of generalizations concerning the lawlike relations that hold among propositional attitudes. Such laws involve quantification over propositions, and they exploit various relations holding in that domain. Thus, for example,

(2) (x) (p) [(x fears that p) $\supset$ (x desires that $\sim p$)]
(3) (x) (p) [(x hopes that p) & (x discovers that p))
$$\supset (x \text{ is pleased that } p)]$$
(4) (x) (p) (q) [((x believes that p) & (x believes that (if p then q)))
$$\supset (\text{barring confusion, distraction, etc., } x \text{ believes that } q)]$$

(5) (x) (p) (q) $[((x$ desires that $p)$ & $(x$ believes that (if q then $p))$
& $(x$ is able to bring it about that $q))$
⊃ (barring conflicting desires or preferred strategies,
x brings it about that $q)]^3$

Not only is folk psychology a theory, it is so *obviously* a theory that it must be held a major mystery why it has taken until the last half of the twentieth century for philosophers to realize it. The structural features of folk psychology parallel perfectly those of mathematical physics; the only difference lies in the respective domain of abstract entities they exploit – numbers in the case of physics, and propositions in the case of psychology.

Finally, the realization that folk psychology is a theory puts a new light on the mind–body problem. The issue becomes a matter of how the ontology of one theory (folk psychology) is, or is not, going to be related to the ontology of another theory (completed neuroscience); and the major philosophical positions on the mind–body problem emerge as so many different anticipations of what future research will reveal about the inter-theoretic status and integrity of folk psychology.

The identity theorist optimistically expects that folk psychology will be smoothly *reduced* by completed neuroscience, and its ontology preserved by dint of transtheoretic identities. The dualist expects that it will prove *ir*reducible to completed neuroscience, by dint of being a nonredundant description of an autonomous, nonphysical domain of natural phenomena. The functionalist also expects that it will prove irreducible, but on the quite different grounds that the internal economy characterized by folk psychology is not, in the last analysis, a law-governed economy of natural states, but an abstract organization of functional states, an organization instantiable in a variety of quite different material substrates. It is therefore irreducible to the principles peculiar to any of them.

Finally, the eliminative materialist is also pessimistic about the prospects for reduction, but his reason is that folk psychology is a radically inadequate account of our internal activities, too confused and too defective to win survival through intertheoretic reduction. On his view it will simply be displaced by a better theory of those activities.

Which of these fates is the real destiny of folk psychology, we shall attempt to divine presently. For now, the point to keep in mind is that we shall be exploring the fate of a theory, a systematic, corrigible, speculative *theory.*

II. Why folk psychology might (really) be false

Given that folk psychology is an empirical theory, it is at least an abstract possibility that its principles are radically false and that its ontology is an illusion. With the exception of eliminative materialism, however, none of the major positions takes this possibility seriously. None of them doubts the basic integrity or truth of folk psychology (hereafter, "FP"), and all of them anticipate a future in which its laws and categories are conserved. This conservatism is not without some foundation. After all, FP does enjoy a substantial amount of explanatory and predictive success. And what better grounds than this for confidence in the integrity of its categories?

What better grounds indeed? Even so, the presumption in FP's favor is spurious, born of innocence and tunnel vision. A more searching examination reveals a different picture. First, we must reckon not only with FP's successes, but with its explanatory failures, and with their extent and seriousness. Second, we must consider the long-term history of FP, its growth, fertility, and current promise of future development. And third, we must consider what sorts of theories are *likely* to be true of the etiology of our behavior, given what else we have learned about ourselves in recent history. That is, we must evaluate FP with regard to its coherence and continuity with fertile and well-established theories in adjacent and overlapping domains – with evolutionary theory, biology, and neuroscience, for example – because active coherence with the rest of what we presume to know is perhaps the final measure of any hypothesis.

A serious inventory of this sort reveals a very troubled situation, one which would evoke open skepticism in the case of any theory less familiar and dear to us. Let me sketch some relevant detail. When one centers one's attention not on what FP can explain, but on what it cannot explain or fails even to address, one discovers that there is a very great deal. As examples of central and important mental phenomena that remain largely or wholly mysterious within the framework of FP, consider the nature and dynamics of mental illness, the faculty of creative imagination, or the ground of intelligence differences between individuals. Consider our utter ignorance of the nature and psychological functions of sleep, that curious state in which a third of one's life is spent. Reflect on the common ability to catch an outfield fly ball on the run, or hit a moving car with a snowball. Consider the internal construction of a 3-D visual image from subtle differences in the 2-D array of stimulations in our respective retinas. Consider the rich variety of perceptual illusions, visual and otherwise. Or consider the miracle of memory, with its lightning capacity for relevant retrieval. On these and many other mental phenomena, FP sheds negligible light.

One particularly outstanding mystery is the nature of the learning process itself, especially where it involves large-scale conceptual change, and especially as it appears in its pre-linguistic or entirely nonlinguistic form (as in infants and animals), which is by far the most common form in nature.

396

FP is faced with special difficulties here, since its conception of learning as the manipulation and storage of propositional attitudes founders on the fact that how to formulate, manipulate, and store a rich fabric of propositional attitudes is itself something that is learned, and is only one among many acquired cognitive skills. FP would thus appear constitutionally incapable of even addressing this most basic of mysteries.[4]

Failures on such a large scale do not (yet) show that FP is a false theory, but they do move that prospect well into the range of real possibility, and they do show decisively that FP is *at best* a highly superficial theory, a partial and unpenetrating gloss on a deeper and more complex reality. Having reached this opinion, we may be forgiven for exploring the possibility that FP provides a positively misleading sketch of our internal kinematics and dynamics, one whose success is owed more to selective application and forced interpretation on our part than to genuine theoretical insight on FP's part.

A look at the history of FP does little to allay such fears, once raised. The story is one of retreat, infertility, and decadence. The presumed domain of FP used to be much larger than it is now. In primitive cultures, the behavior of most of the elements of nature were understood in intentional terms. The wind could know anger, the moon jealousy, the river generosity, the sea fury, and so forth. These were not metaphors. Sacrifices were made and auguries undertaken to placate or divine the changing passions of the gods. Despite its sterility, this animistic approach to nature has dominated our history, and it is only in the last two or three thousand years that we have restricted FP's literal application to the domain of the higher animals.

Even in this preferred domain, however, both the content and the success of FP have not advanced sensibly in two or three thousand years. The FP of the Greeks is essentially the FP we use today, and we are negligibly better at explaining human behavior in its terms than was Sophocles. This is a very long period of stagnation and infertility for any theory to display, especially when faced with such an enormous backlog of anomalies and mysteries in its own explanatory domain. Perfect theories, perhaps, have no need to evolve. But FP is profoundly imperfect. Its failure to develop its resources and extend its range of success is therefore darkly curious, and one must query the integrity of its basic categories. To use Imre Lakatos' terms, FP is a stagnant or degenerating research program, and has been for millennia.

Explanatory success to date is of course not the only dimension in which a theory can display virtue or promise. A troubled or stagnant theory may merit patience and solicitude on other grounds; for example, on grounds that it is the only theory or theoretical approach that fits well with other theories about adjacent subject matters, or the only one that promises to reduce to or be explained by some established background theory whose domain encompasses the domain of the theory at issue. In sum, it may rate credence because it holds promise of theoretical integration. How does FP rate in this dimension?

It is just here, perhaps, that FP fares poorest of all. If we approach *homo sapiens* from the perspective of natural history and the physical sciences, we can tell a coherent story of his constitution, development, and behavioral capacities which encompasses particle physics, atomic and molecular theory, organic chemistry, evolutionary theory, biology, physiology, and materialistic neuroscience. That story, though still radically incomplete, is already extremely powerful, outperforming FP at many points even in its own domain. And it is deliberately and self-consciously coherent with the rest of our developing world picture. In short, the greatest theoretical synthesis in the history of the human race is currently in our hands, and parts of it already provide searching descriptions and explanations of human sensory input, neural activity, and motor control.

But FP is no part of this growing synthesis. Its intentional categories stand magnificently alone, without visible prospect of reduction to that larger corpus. A successful reduction cannot be ruled out, in my view, but FP's explanatory impotence and long stagnation inspire little faith that its categories will find themselves neatly reflected in the framework of neuroscience. On the contrary, one is reminded of how alchemy must have looked as elemental chemistry was taking form, how Aristotelian cosmology must have looked as classical mechanics was being articulated, or how the vitalist conception of life must have looked as organic chemistry marched forward.

In sketching a fair summary of this situation, we must make a special effort to abstract from the fact that FP is a central part of our current *Lebenswelt*, and serves as the principal vehicle of our interpersonal commerce. For these facts provide FP with a conceptual inertia that goes far beyond its purely theoretical virtues. Restricting ourselves to this latter dimension, what we must say is that FP suffers explanatory failures on an epic scale, that it has been stagnant for at least twenty-five centuries, and that its categories appear (so far) to be incommensurable with or orthogonal to the categories of the background physical science whose long-term claim to explain human behavior seems undeniable. Any theory that meets this description must be allowed a serious candidate for outright elimination.

We can of course insist on no stronger conclusion at this stage. Nor is it my concern to do so. We are here exploring a possibility, and the facts demand no more, and no less, than it be taken seriously. The distinguishing feature of the eliminative materialist is that he takes it very seriously indeed.

III. Arguments against elimination

Thus the basic rationale of eliminative materialism: FP is a theory, and quite probably a false one; let us attempt, therefore to transcend it.

The rationale is clear and simple, but many find it uncompelling. It will be objected that FP is not, strictly speaking, an *empirical* theory; that it is not false, or at least not refutable by empirical considerations; and that it ought not or cannot be transcended in the fashion of a defunct empirical theory. In what follows we shall examine these objections as they flow from the most popular and best-founded of the competing positions in the philosophy of mind: functionalism.

An antipathy toward eliminative materialism arises from two distinct threads running through contemporary functionalism. The first thread concerns the *normative* character of FP, or at least of that central core of FP which treats of the propositional attitudes. FP, some will say, is a characterization of an ideal, or at least praiseworthy mode of internal activity. It outlines not only what it is to have and process beliefs and desires, but also (and inevitably) what it is to be rational in their administration. The ideal laid down by FP may be imperfectly achieved by empirical humans, but this does not impugn FP as a normative characterization. Nor need such failures seriously impugn FP even as a descriptive characterization, for it remains true that our activities can be both usefully and accurately understood as rational *except for* the occasional lapse due to noise, interference, or other breakdown, which defects empirical research may eventually unravel. Accordingly, though neuroscience may usefully augment it, FP has no pressing need to be displaced, even as a descriptive theory; nor could it be replaced, qua normative characterization, by any descriptive theory of neural mechanisms, since rationality is defined over propositional attitudes like beliefs and desires. FP, therefore, is here to stay.

Daniel Dennett has defended a view along these lines.[5] And the view just outlined gives voice to a theme of the property dualists as well. Karl Popper and Joseph Margolis both cite the normative nature of mental and linguistic activity as a bar to their penetration or elimination by any descriptive/materialist theory.[6] I hope to deflate the appeal of such moves below.

The second thread concerns the *abstract* nature of FP. The central claim of functionalism is that the principles of FP characterize our internal states in a fashion that makes no reference to their intrinsic nature or physical constitution. Rather, they are characterized in terms of the network of causal relations they bear to one another, and to sensory circumstances and overt behavior. Given its abstract specification, that internal economy may therefore be realized in a nomically heterogeneous variety of physical systems. All of them may differ, even radically, in their physical constitution, and yet at another level, they will all share the same nature. This view, says Fodor, "is compatible with very strong claims about the ineliminability of mental language from behavioral theories."[7] Given the real possibility of multiple instantiations in heterogeneous physical substrates, we cannot eliminate the functional characterization in favor of any theory peculiar to one such substrate. That would preclude our being able to describe the (abstract) organization that any one instantiation shares with all the other. A functional characterization of our internal states is therefore here to stay.

This second theme, like the first, assigns a faintly stipulative character to FP, as if the onus were on the empirical systems to instantiate faithfully the organization that FP specifies, instead of the onus being on FP to describe faithfully the internal activities of a naturally distinct class of empirical systems. This impression is enhanced by the standard examples used to illustrate the claims of functionalism – mousetraps, valve-lifters, arithmetical calculators, computers, robots, and the like. These are artifacts, constructed to fill a preconceived bill. In such cases, a failure of fit between the physical system and the relevant functional characterization impugns only the former, not the latter. The functional characterization is thus removed from empirical criticism in a way that is most unlike the case of an empirical theory. One prominent functionalist – Hilary Putnam – has argued outright that FP is not a corrigible theory at all.[8] Plainly, if FP is construed on these models, as regularly it is, the question of its empirical integrity is unlikely ever to pose itself, let alone receive a critical answer.

Although fair to some functionalists, the preceding is not entirely fair to Fodor. On his view the aim of psychology is to find the *best* functional characterization of ourselves, and what that is remains an empirical question. As well, his argument for the ineliminability of mental vocabulary from psychology does not pick out current FP in particular as ineliminable. It need claim only that *some* abstract functional characterization must be retained, some articulation or refinement of FP perhaps.

His estimate of eliminative materialism remains low, however. First, it is plain that Fodor thinks there is nothing fundamentally or interestingly wrong with FP. On the contrary, FP's central conception of cognitive activity – as consisting in the manipulation of propositional attitudes – turns up as the central element in Fodor's own theory on the nature of thought (*The Language of Thought*, *op. cit.*). And second, there remains the point that, whatever tidying up FP may or may not require, it cannot be displaced by any naturalistic theory of our physical substrate, since it is the abstract functional features of his internal states that make a person, not the chemistry of his substrate.

All of this is appealing. But almost none of it, I think, is right. Function-alism has too long enjoyed its reputation as a daring and *avant garde* position. It needs to be revealed for the short-sighted and reactionary position it is.

IV.   The conservative nature of functionalism

A valuable perspective on functionalism can be gained from the following story. To begin with, recall the alchemists' theory of inanimate matter. We have here a long and variegated tradition, of course, not a single theory, but our purposes will be served by a gloss.

The alchemists conceived the "inanimate" as entirely continuous with animated matter, in that the sensible and behavioral properties of the various substances are owed to the ensoulment of baser matter by various spirits or essences. These nonmaterial aspects were held to undergo devel-opment, just as we find growth and development in the various souls of plants, animals, and humans. The alchemist's peculiar skill lay in knowing how to seed, nourish, and bring to maturity the desired spirits enmattered in the appropriate combinations.

On one orthodoxy, the four fundamental spirits (for "inanimate" matter) were named "mercury," "sulphur," "yellow arsenic," and "sal ammoniac." Each of these spirits was held responsible for a rough but characteristic syndrome of sensible, combinatorial, and causal properties. The spirit mercury, for example, was held responsible for certain features typical of metallic substances – their shininess, liquefiability, and so forth. Sulphur was held responsible for certain residual features typical of metals, and for those displayed by the ores from which running metal could be distilled. Any given metallic substance was a critical orchestration principally of these two spirits. A similar story held for the other two spirits, and among the four of them a certain domain of physical features and transformations was rendered intelligible and controllable.

The degree of control was always limited, of course. Or better, such prediction and control as the alchemists possessed was owed more to the manipulative lore acquired as an apprentice to a master, than to any genuine insight supplied by the theory. The theory followed, more than it dictated, practice. But the theory did supply some rhyme to the practice, and in the absence of a developed alternative it was sufficiently compelling to sustain a long and stubborn tradition.

The tradition had become faded and fragmented by the time the elemental chemistry of Lavoisier and Dalton arose to replace it for good. But let us suppose that it had hung on a little longer – perhaps because the four-spirit orthodoxy had become a thumb-worn part of everyman's common sense – and let us examine the nature of the conflict between the two theories and some possible avenues of resolution.

No doubt the simplest line of resolution, and the one which historically took place, is outright displacement. The dualistic interpretation of the four essences – as immaterial spirits – will appear both feckless and unnecessary given the power of the corpuscularian taxonomy of atomic chemistry. And a reduction of the old taxonomy to the new will appear impossible, given the extent to which the comparatively toothless old theory cross-classifies things relative to the new. Elimination would thus appear the only alternative – *unless* some cunning and determined defender of the alchemical vision has the wit to suggest the following defense.

Being "ensouled by mercury," or "sulphur," or either of the other two so-called spirits, is actually a *functional* state. The first, for example, is defined by the disposition to reflect light, to liquefy under heat, to unite with other matter in the same state, and so forth. And each of these four states is related to the others, in that the syndrome for each varies as a function of which of the other three states is also instantiated in the same substrate. Thus the level of description comprehended by the alchemical vocabulary is abstract: various material substances, suitably "ensouled," can display the features of a metal, for example, or even of gold specifically. For it is the total syndrome of occurrent and causal properties which matters, not the corpuscularian details of the substrate. Alchemy, it is concluded, comprehends a level of organization in reality distinct from and irreducible to the organization found at the level of corpuscularian chemistry.

This view might have had considerable appeal. After all, it spares alchemists the burden of defending immaterial souls that come and go; it frees them from having to meet the very strong demands of a naturalistic reduction; and it spares them the shock and confusion of outright elimination. Alchemical theory emerges as basically all right! Nor need they appear too obviously stubborn or dogmatic in this. Alchemy as it stands, they concede, may need substantial tidying up, and experience must be our guide. But we need not fear its naturalistic displacement, they remind us, since it is the particular orchestration of the syndromes of occurrent and causal properties which makes a piece of matter gold, not the idiosyncratic details of its corpuscularian substrate. A further circumstance would have made this claim even more plausible. For the fact is, the alchemists *did* know how to make gold, in this relevantly weakened sense of "gold," and they could do so in a variety of ways. Their "gold" was never as perfect, alas, as the "gold" nurtured in nature's womb, but what mortal can expect to match the skills of nature herself?

What this story shows is that it is at least possible for the constellation of moves, claims, and defenses characteristic of functionalism to constitute an outrage against reason and truth, and to do so with a plausibility that is frightening. Alchemy is a terrible theory, well-deserving of its complete elimination, and the defense of it just explored is reactionary, obfuscatory, retrograde, and wrong. But in historical context, that defense might have seemed wholly sensible, even to reasonable people.

The alchemical example is a deliberately transparent case of what might well be called "the functionalist strategem," and other cases are easy to imagine. A cracking good defense of the phlogiston theory of combustion can also be constructed along these lines. Construe being highly phlogisti-cated and being dephlogisticated as functional states defined by certain syndromes of causal dispositions; point to the great variety of natural substrates capable of combustion and calxification; claim an irreducible functional integrity for what has proved to lack any natural integrity; and bury the remaining defects under a pledge to contrive improvements. A similar recipe will provide new life for the four humors of medieval medi-cine, for the vital essence or archeus of pre-modern biology, and so forth.

If its application in these other cases is any guide, the functionalist strategem is a smokescreen for the preservation of error and confusion. Whence derives our assurance that in contemporary journals the same charade is not being played out on behalf of FP? The parallel with the case of alchemy is in all other respects distressingly complete, right down to the parallel between the search for artificial gold and the search for artificial intelligence!

Let me not be misunderstood on this last point. Both aims are worthy aims: thanks to nuclear physics, artificial (but real) gold is finally within our means, if only in submicroscopic quantities; and artificial (but real) intelligence eventually will be. But just as the careful orchestration of super-ficial syndromes was the wrong way to produce genuine gold, so may the careful orchestration of superficial syndromes be the wrong way to produce genuine intelligence. Just as with gold, what may be required is that our science penetrate to the underlying *natural* kind that gives rise to the total syndrome directly.

In summary, when confronted with the explanatory impotence, stagnant history, and systematic isolation of the intentional idioms of FP, it is not an adequate or responsive defense to insist that those idioms are abstract, func-tional, and irreducible in character. For one thing, this same defense could have been mounted with comparable plausibility no matter *what* haywire network of internal states our folklore had ascribed to us. And for another, the defense assumes essentially what is at issue: it assumes that it is the intentional idioms of FP, plus or minus a bit, that express the *important* features shared by all cognitive systems. But they may not. Certainly it is wrong to assume that they do, and then argue against the possibility of a materialistic displacement on grounds that it must describe matters at a level that is different from the important level. This just begs the question in favor of the older framework.

Finally, it is very important to point out that eliminative materialism is strictly *consistent* with the claim that the essence of a cognitive system resides in the abstract functional organization of its internal states. The eliminative materialist is not committed to the idea that the correct account of cognition *must* be a naturalistic account, though he may be forgiven for exploring the possibility. What he does hold is that the correct account of cognition, whether functionalistic or naturalistic, will bear about as much resemblance to FP as modern chemistry bears to four-spirit alchemy.

Let us now try to deal with the argument, against eliminative materialism, from the normative dimension of FP. This can be dealt with rather swiftly, I believe.

First, the fact that the regularities ascribed by the intentional core of FP are predicated on certain logical relations among propositions is not by itself grounds for claiming anything essentially normative about FP. To draw a relevant parallel, the fact that the regularities ascribed by the classical gas law are predicated on arithmetical relations between numbers does not imply anything essentially normative about the classical gas law. And logical relations between propositions are as much an objective matter of abstract fact as are arithmetical relations between numbers. In this respect, the law

(4) $(x) (p) (q) [((x$ believes that $p) \& (x$ believes that (if p then $q)))$
$\supset$ (barring confusion, distraction, etc., x believes that $q)]$

is entirely on a par with the classical gas law

(6) $(x) (P) (V) (\mu) [((x$ has a pressure $P) \& (x$ has a volume $V)$
$\& (x$ has a quantity $\mu)) \supset$ (barring very high pressure
or density, x has a temperature of $PV/\mu R)]$

A normative dimension enters only because we happen to *value* most of the patterns ascribed by FP. But we do not value all of them. Consider

(7) $(x) (p) [((x$ desires with all his heart that $p) \& (x$ learns that $\sim p))$
$\supset$ (barring unusual strength of character,
x is shattered that $\sim p)]$

Moreover, and as with normative convictions generally, fresh insight may motivate major changes in what we value.

Second, the laws of FP ascribe to us only a very minimal and truncated rationality, not an ideal rationality as some have suggested. The rationality characterized by the set of all FP laws falls well short of an ideal rationality. This is not surprising. We have no clear or finished conception of ideal rationality anyway; certainly the ordinary man does not. Accordingly, it is just not plausible to suppose that the explanatory failures from which FP suffers are owed primarily to human failure to live up to the ideal standard it provides. Quite to the contrary, the conception of rationality it provides appears limping and superficial, especially when compared with the dialectical complexity of our scientific history, or with the ratiocinative virtuosity displayed by any child.

Third, even if our current conception of rationality – and more generally, of cognitive virtue – is largely constituted within the sentential/propositional framework of FP, there is no guarantee that this framework is adequate to the deeper and more accurate account of cognitive virtue which is clearly needed. Even if we concede the categorial integrity of FP, at least as applied to language-using humans, it remains far from clear that the basic parameters of intellectual virtue are to be found at the categorial level comprehended by the propositional attitudes. After all, language use is something that is learned, by a brain already capable of vigorous cognitive activity; language use is acquired as only one among a great variety of learned manipulative skills; and it is mastered by a brain that evolution has shaped for a great many functions, language use being only the very latest and perhaps the least of them. Against the background of these facts, language use appears as an extremely peripheral activity, as a racially idiosyncratic mode of social interaction which is mastered thanks to the versatility and power of a more basic mode of activity. Why accept then, a theory of cognitive activity that models its elements on the elements of human language? And why assume that the fundamental parameters of intellectual virtue are or can be defined over the elements at this superficial level?

A serious advance in our appreciation of cognitive virtue would thus seem to *require* that we go beyond FP, that we transcend the poverty of FP's conception of rationality by transcending its propositional kinematics entirely, by developing a deeper and more general kinematics of cognitive activity, and by distinguishing within this new framework which of the kinematically possible modes of activity are to be valued and encouraged (as more efficient, reliable, productive, or whatever). Eliminative materialism thus does not imply the end of our normative concerns. It implies only that they will have to be reconstituted at a more revealing level of understanding, the level that a matured neuroscience will provide.

What a theoretically informed future might hold in store for us, we shall now turn to explore. Not because we can foresee matters with any special

clarity, but because it is important to try to break the grip on our imagination held by the propositional kinematics of FP. As far as the present
section is concerned, we may summarize our conclusions as follows. FP is
nothing more and nothing less than a culturally entrenched theory of how
we and the higher animals work. It has no special features that make it
empirically invulnerable, no unique functions that make it irreplaceable, no
special status of any kind whatsoever. We shall turn a skeptical ear then,
to any special pleading on its behalf.

V.   Beyond folk psychology

What might the elimination of FP actually involve – not just the comparatively straightforward idioms for sensation, but the entire apparatus of
propositional attitudes? That depends heavily on what neuroscience might
discover, and on our determination to capitalize on it. Here follow three
scenarios in which the operative conception of cognitive activity is progressively divorced from the forms and categories that characterize natural
language. If the reader will indulge the lack of actual substance, I shall try
to sketch some plausible form.

First suppose that research into the structure and activity of the brain,
both fine-grained and global, finally does yield a new kinematics and correlative dynamics for what is now thought of as cognitive activity. The
theory is uniform for all terrestrial brains, not just human brains, and it
makes suitable conceptual contact with both evolutionary biology and non-
equilibrium thermodynamics. It ascribes to us, at any given time, a set
or configuration of complex states, which are specified within the theory as
figurative "solids" within a four- or five-dimensional phase space. The laws
of the theory govern the interaction, motion, and transformation of these
"solid" states within that space, and also their relations to whatever sensory
and motor transducers the system possesses. As with celestial mechanics, the
exact specification of the "solids" involved and the exhaustive accounting
of all dynamically relevant adjacent "solids" is not practically possible,
for many reasons, but here also it turns out that the obvious approxima-
tions we fall back on yield excellent explanations/predictions of internal
change and external behavior, at least in the short term. Regarding long-
term activity, the theory provides powerful and unified accounts of the
learning process, the nature of mental illness, and variations in character
and intelligence across the animal kingdom as well as across individual
humans.

Moreover, it provides a straightforward account of "knowledge," as
traditionally conceived. According to the new theory, any declarative
sentence to which a speaker would give confident assent is merely a one-

dimensional *projection* – through the compound lens of Wernicke's and Broca's areas onto the idiosyncratic surface of the speaker's language – a one-dimensional projection of a four- or five-dimensional "solid" that is an element in his true kinematical state. (Recall the shadows on the wall of Plato's cave.) Being projections of that inner reality, such sentences do carry significant information regarding it and are thus fit to function as elements in a communication system. On the other hand, being *sub*dimensional projections, they reflect but a narrow part of the reality projected. They are therefore *un*fit to represent the deeper reality in all its kinematically, dynamically, and even normatively relevant respects. That is to say, a system of propositional attitudes, such as FP, must inevitably fail to capture what is going on here, though it may reflect just enough superficial structure to sustain an alchemy-like tradition among folk who lack any better theory. From the perspective of the newer theory, however, it is plain that there simply are no law-governed states of the kind FP postulates. The real laws governing our internal activities are defined over different and much more complex kinematical states and configurations, as are the normative criteria for developmental integrity and intellectual virtue.

A theoretical outcome of the kind just described may fairly be counted as a case of elimination of one theoretical ontology in favor of another, but the success here imagined for systematic neuroscience need not have any sensible effect on common practice. Old ways die hard, and in the absence of some practical necessity, they may not die at all. Even so, it is not inconceivable that some segment of the population, or all of it, should become intimately familiar with the vocabulary required to characterize our kinematical states, learn the laws governing their interactions and behavioral projections, acquire a facility in their first-person ascription, and displace the use of FP altogether, even in the marketplace. The demise of FP's ontology would then be complete.

We may now explore a second and rather more radical possibility. Everyone is familiar with Chomsky's thesis that the human mind or brain contains innately and uniquely the abstract structures for learning and using specifically human natural languages. A competing hypothesis is that our brain does indeed contain innate structures, but that those structures have as their original and still primary function the organization of perceptual experience, the administration of linguistic categories being an acquired and additional function for which evolution has only incidentally suited them.[9] This hypothesis has the advantage of not requiring the evolutionary saltation that Chomsky's view would seem to require, and there are other advantages as well. But these matters need not concern us here. Suppose, for our purposes, that this competing view is true, and consider the following story.

Research into the neural structures that fund the organization and processing of perceptual information reveals that they are capable of administering a great variety of complex tasks, some of them showing a complexity far in excess of that shown by natural language. Natural languages, it turns out, exploit only a very elementary portion of the available machinery, the bulk of which serves far more complex activities beyond the ken of the propositional conceptions of FP. The detailed unraveling of what that machinery is and of the capacities it has makes it plain that a form of language far more sophisticated than "natural" language, though decidedly "alien" in its syntactic and semantic structures, could also be learned and used by our innate systems. Such a novel system of communication, it is quickly realized, could raise the efficiency of information exchange between brains by an order of magnitude, and would enhance epistemic evaluation by a comparable amount, since it would reflect the underlying structure of our cognitive activities in greater detail than does natural language.

Guided by our new understanding of those internal structures, we manage to construct a new system of verbal communication entirely distinct from natural language, with a new and more powerful combinatorial grammar over novel elements forming novel combinations with exotic properties. The compounded strings of this alternative system – call them "übersatzen" – are not evaluated as true or false, nor are the relations between them remotely analogous to the relations of entailment, etc., that hold between sentences. They display a different organization and manifest different virtues.

Once constructed, this "language" proves to be learnable; it has the power projected; and in two generations it has swept the planet. Everyone uses the new system. The syntactic forms and semantic categories of so-called "natural" language disappear entirely. And with them disappear the propositional attitudes of FP, displaced by a more revealing scheme in which (of course) "übersatzenal attitudes" play the leading role. FP again suffers elimination.

This second story, note, illustrates a theme with endless variations. There are possible as many different "folk psychologies" as there are possible differently structured communication systems to serve as models for them.

A third and even stranger possibility can be outlined as follows. We know that there is considerable lateralization of function between the two cerebral hemispheres, and that the two hemispheres make use of the information they get from each other by way of the great cerebral commissure – the corpus callosum – a giant cable of neurons connecting them. Patients whose commissure has been surgically severed display a variety of behavioral deficits that indicate a loss of access by one hemisphere to information it used to get from the other. However, in people with callosal agenesis (a congenital defect in which the connecting cable is simply absent), there is little or no behavioral deficit, suggesting that the two hemisphere have learned to exploit the information carried in other less direct pathways connecting them through the subcortical regions. This suggests that, even in the normal case, a developing hemisphere *learns* to make use of the information the cerebral commissure deposits at its doorstep. What we have then, in the case of a normal human, is two physically distinct cognitive systems (both capable of independent function) responding in a systematic and learned fashion to exchanged information. And what is especially interesting about this case is the sheer amount of information exchanged. The cable of the commissure consists of $\approx$200 million neurons,[10] and even if we assume that each of these fibers is capable of one of only two possible states each second (a most conservative estimate), we are looking at a channel whose information capacity is $>2 \times 10^8$ binary bits/second. Compare this to the <500 bits/second capacity of spoken English.

Now, if two distinct hemispheres can learn to communicate on so impressive a scale, why shouldn't two distinct brains learn to do it also? This would require an artificial "commissure" of some kind, but let us suppose that we can fashion a workable transducer for implantation at some site in the brain that research reveals to be suitable, a transducer to convert a symphony of neural activity into (say) microwaves radiated from an aerial in the forehead, and to perform the reverse function of converting received microwaves back into neural activation. Connecting it up need not be an insuperable problem. We simply trick the normal processes of dendretic arborization into growing their own myriad connections with the active microsurface of the transducer.

Once the channel is opened between two or more people, they can learn (*learn*) to exchange information and coordinate their behavior with the same intimacy and virtuosity displayed by your own cerebral hemispheres. Think what this might do for hockey teams, and ballet companies, and research teams! If the entire population were thus fitted out, spoken language of any kind might well disappear completely, a victim of the "why crawl when you can fly?" principle. Libraries become filled not with books, but with long recordings of exemplary bouts of neural activity. These constitute a growing cultural heritage, an evolving "Third World," to use Karl Popper's terms. But they do not consist of sentences or arguments.

How will such people understand and conceive of other individuals? To this question I can only answer, "In roughly the same fashion that your right hemisphere 'understands' and 'conceives of' your left hemisphere – intimately and efficiently, but not propositionally!"

These speculations, I hope, will evoke the required sense of untapped possibilities, and I shall in any case bring them to a close here. Their function is to make some inroads into the aura of inconceivability that commonly surrounds the idea that we might reject FP. The felt conceptual strain even finds expression in an argument to the effect that the thesis of eliminative materialism is incoherent since it denies the very conditions presupposed by the assumption that it is meaningful. I shall close with a brief discussion of this very popular move.

As I have received it, the reductio proceeds by pointing out that the statement of eliminative materialism is just a meaningless string of marks or noises, unless that string is the expression of a certain *belief*, and a certain *intention* to communicate, and a *knowledge* of the grammar of the language, and so forth. But if the statement of eliminative materialism is true, then there are no such states to express. The statement at issue would then be a meaningless string of marks or noises. It would therefore *not* be true. Therefore it is not true. Q.E.D.

The difficulty with any nonformal reductio is that the conclusion against the initial assumption is always no better than the material assumptions invoked to reach the incoherent conclusion. In this case the additional assumptions involve a certain theory of meaning, one that presupposes the integrity of FP. But formally speaking, one can as well infer, from the incoherent result, that this theory of meaning is what must be rejected. Given the independent critique of FP leveled earlier, this would even seem the preferred option. But in any case, one cannot simply assume that particular theory of meaning without begging the question at issue, namely, the integrity of FP.

The question-begging nature of this move is most graphically illustrated by the following analogue, which I owe to Patricia Churchland.[11] The issue here, placed in the seventeenth century, is whether there exists such a substance as *vital spirit*. At the time, this substance was held, without significant awareness of real alternatives, to be that which distinguished the animate from the inanimate. Given the monopoly enjoyed by this conception, given the degree to which it was integrated with many of our other conceptions, and given the magnitude of the revisions any serious alternative conception would require, the following refutation of any anti-vitalist claim would be found instantly plausible.

> The anti-vitalist says that there is no such thing as vital spirit. But this claim is self-refuting. The speaker can expect to be taken seriously only if his claim cannot. For if the claim is true, then the speaker does not have vital spirit and must be *dead*. But if he is dead, then his statement is a meaningless string of noises, devoid of reason and truth.

410

The question-begging nature of this argument does not, I assume, require elaboration. To those moved by the earlier argument, I commend the parallel for examination.

The thesis of this paper may be summarized as follows. The propositional attitudes of folk psychology do not constitute an unbreachable barrier to the advancing tide of neuroscience. On the contrary the principled displacement of folk psychology is not only richly possible, it represents one of the most intriguing theoretical displacements we can currently imagine.

Notes

1   See Paul Feyerabend, "Materialism and the Mind–Body Problem," *Review* of *Metaphysics*, XVII.1, 65 (September 1963): 49–66; Richard Rorty, "Mind–Body Identity, Privacy, and Categories," *ibid.*, XIX.1, 73 (September 1965): 24–54; and my *Scientific Realism and the Plasticity of Mind* (New York: Cambridge, 1979).

2   We shall examine a handful of these laws presently. For a more comprehensive sampling of the laws of folk psychology, see my *Scientific Realism and Plasticity of Mind, op. cit.*, ch. 4. For a detailed examination of the folk principles that underwrite action explanations in particular, see my "The Logical Character of Action Explanations," *Philosophical Review*, LXXIX, 2 (April 1970): 214–236.

3   Staying within an objectual interpretation of the quantifiers, perhaps the simplest way to make systematic sense of expressions like ⌜x believes that p⌝ and closed sentences formed therefrom is just to construe whatever occurs in the nested position held by "p," "q," etc. as there having the function of a singular term. Accordingly, the standard connectives, as they occur between terms in that nested position, must be construed as there functioning as operators that form compound singular terms from other singular terms, and not as sentence operators. The compound singular terms so formed denote the appropriate compound propositions. Substitutional quantification will of course underwrite a different interpretation, and there are other approaches as well. Especially appealing is the prosentential approach of Dorothy Grover, Joseph Camp, and Nuel Belnap, "A Prosentential Theory of Truth," *Philosophical Studies*, XXVII, 2 (February 1975): 73–125. But the resolution of these issues is not vital to the present discussion.

4   A possible response here is to insist that the cognitive activity of animals and infants is linguaformal in its elements, structures, and processing right from birth. J.A. Fodor, in *The Language of Thought* (New York: Crowell 1975), has erected a positive theory of thought on the assumption that the innate forms of cognitive activity have precisely the form here denied. For a critique of Fodor's view, see Patricia Churchland, "Fodor on Language Learning," *Synthese*, XXXVIII, 1 (May 1978): 149–159.

5   Most explicitly in "Three Kinds of Intentional Psychology" (in R. Healy (ed.) *Reduction, Time and Reality* (Cambridge: Cambridge University Press, 1981)), but this theme of Dennett's goes all the way back to his "Intentional Systems," *Journal of Philosophy*, LXVIII, 4 (Feb. 25, 1971): 87–106; reprinted in his *Brainstorms* (Montgomery, Vt.: Bradford Books, 1978).

6 Popper, *Objective Knowledge* (New York: Oxford, 1972); with J. Eccles, *The Self and Its Brain* (New York: Springer Verlag, 1978). Margolis, *Persons and Minds* (Boston: Reidel, 1978).

7 *Psychological Explanation* (New York: Random House, 1968), p. 116.

8 "Robots: Machines or Artificially Created Life?," *Journal of Philosophy*, LXI, 21 (Nov. 12, 1964): 668–691, pp. 675, 681 ff.

9 Richard Gregory defends such a view in "The Grammar of Vision," *Listener*, LXXXIII, 2133 (February 1970): 242–246; reprinted in his *Concepts and Mechanisms of Perception* (London: Duckworth, 1975), pp. 622–629.

10 M.S. Gazzaniga and J.E. LeDoux, *The Integrated Mind* (New York: Plenum Press, 1975).

11 "Is Determinism Self-Refuting?," *Mind*, XC, 357 (Jan. 1981): 99—101.

QUESTIONS

1   We can, it seems, think about future objects and events, such as next year's winner of the Academy Award for Best Picture, or the ultimate fate of the universe. Yet the future is causally isolated from us. No future object or event – obscure features of the quantum world aside – can causally influence the present. Does this automatically spell doom for naturalist theories of intentionality, at least those with a causal component? Or is it possible, without appealing to temporally "backwards" causality, to give a causal account of our thoughts about the future?

2   When he's answering various replies to the Chinese Room thought-experiment, Searle doesn't consider a view such as Dretske's. What would a Dretske-inspired response to Searle look like? That is, what features would Dretske add to the Chinese Room to give it (original) intentionality? How would Searle respond?

3   Interpretation plays a central role in the theories of Davidson and Dennett. But to interpret others, I must be able to think about them and their behavior. Interpretation, that is, *presupposes* intentionality, and so cannot explain it. How would Davidson and Dennett respond to this objection? What do their replies reveal about the way they approach the problem of intentionality?

4   In spite of not being a language-user, a squirrel, say, surely has internal, information-bearing states that track the way its environment changes, and such states are responsible for the squirrel's behavior. So why, exactly, can't these internal states count as *beliefs* on Davidson's view?

5   Try to envision, with Churchland, a time in the future when the concepts of folk psychology have been replaced by the more sophisticated, fine-grained concepts of a completed neuroscience. Under these circumstances, will we – *could* we – adopt what Dennett calls the "design stance" (or perhaps the "physical stance") toward one another? If so, is this a scenario in which we no longer have, and perhaps never did have, beliefs?

PART IV

CONSCIOUSNESS

INTRODUCTION

There are many metaphysical puzzles about the human mind and its relationship to the brain and its physical environment. Some that have been considered previously in this volume are: what kind of thing a mind is; how mental causation works in relation to physical causation; and how minds are able to represent their environment, or even non-existing possibilities. In contemporary philosophy of mind, it is widely thought that the hardest puzzle concerns the nature of conscious experience and its relationship to physical processes of the brain. There are a family of puzzles in the neighborhood, in fact, though they appear to be intimately related. All are puzzles for those inclined to suppose that materialism is true. (So for the dualist, these "puzzles" are actually disguised *arguments* for some form or other of dualism.)

I. Some puzzles about consciousness

One puzzle about consciousness was raised in Part II, by Kripke. Kripke's argument is specifically focused on pain, but it readily generalizes to other types of conscious experience, such as the visual experience of looking at this page. If *pain = C-fiber firing pattern 257*, then this identity statement must be absolutely necessary. It must be impossible for pain to occur in the absence of that C-fiber firing, or for the firing to occur without the pain. But while it is no doubt true that pains in human beings are intimately associated with certain types of neural events, it is possible, argues Kripke, for either one to occur without the other. The conclusion drawn is that the type–type identity form of materialism, at least, must be false.

In Chapter 20, Joseph Levine softens Kripke's argument by contending only that there is an *explanatory gap* in the assertion of any such identity statement (see also Levine 2001). In coming to infer such a statement from a well-confirmed theory, we would not have learned why the statement is necessarily true. Unlike other necessary identities, such as *Samuel Clemens = Mark Twain*, or *water = H₂O*, which can, on a little reflection, be *seen* to be

417

necessary, the appearance of possibility for pains existing in the absence of C-fibers, or any other physical structure, is stubborn, impervious to philosophical dissolution. Furthermore, according to Levine, this is not just a problem for the identity theorist. A functional-state identity claim will have the same air of contingency about it as a physical-type identity claim. In either case, the theoretical problem remains of relating phenomenal concepts such as pain to the relevant physical or functional concepts in a way that enables us to see their necessary link. Absent a solution to this problem, we'll be hard-pressed to motivate a simple, bold identity claim of the form, *pain = F*, for some narrowly defined F (such as C-fiber firing pattern 257). Pain might, instead, be identical to the *disjunction* of F with various other properties. Until we come to "see" that pain just is F, of necessity, as we see that water necessarily is H_2O, we will not be able to say that F exhausts the realization possibilities for pain – and, again, that goes for functional types, too.

In Chapter 21, Colin McGinn suggests that the apparent-contingency problem is insoluble, but not serious. He notes that we can see how various cognitive systems simpler than humans are "cognitively closed" to certain concepts. He then argues that there is reason to think that we may face a similar inherent limitation when it comes to the physical basis of conscious experience. While there is some physical basis or other, we are "cut off" from that natural property of the brain which intelligibly explains the dependency of consciousness on the brain.

Thomas Nagel (1974) contends that even an ideal and complete understanding of the neurophysiology of bat experience would not show us *what it is like* to be a bat. We can surmise that some of the fundamental qualities of bat experience (involving echo-location) are quite different from those of human experience, to an extent that it seems difficult, if not impossible, for me to imaginatively "step inside a bat's shoes." Even clever simulations, which might provide a rough analogy to the sensory modalities I lack, could not disclose to me what it would be like *simply* to be a bat, as opposed to a (cognitively more sophisticated) human being trying to better appreciate such experience via simulation. So one form of the puzzle about consciousness is why a full appreciation for the qualities of a *kind* of conscious experience should require one to have the very experiential capacities in question. After all, human investigators face no similar limits when trying to understand a bat's unfolding neurophysiology from a purely physical point of view.

A related puzzle is raised by Frank Jackson in Chapter 22. Jackson imagines a future expert (Mary) in the neurophysiology of *human* color experience. The materialist holds that there is, in principle, an exhaustive and purely physical explanation to be had of all the features of such experience. So let us suppose that Mary possesses this account. Give Mary complete information in suitable form of the physical aspects of a subject's visual experience of a red apple, *and nothing else*, and she can correctly tell you exactly what the subject is experiencing, color-wise. There is just one peculiar fact about Mary: she herself has never had color experience apart from shades of black and white, having lived her entire life in a black-and-white environment – until, that is, the fateful day arrives when she strolls outside and experiences for the first time a bright red rose. Says Jackson: in doing so, Mary has come to *learn* something about the color experience of others: *that* is what it is like for them to see a red object. This is a new piece of information about those red experiences she had previously studied, information about features of those experiences beyond those posited in her theory. Since, *ex hypothesi*, Mary had already known all the *physical* facts concerning others' color experience, materialism is false.

II. Materialist strategies

Our readings offer three materialist strategies for dissolving one or other version of the puzzle of consciousness. In Chapter 23, David Lewis (responding to Jackson 1982) questions Jackson's description of the Mary case. Mary does not acquire new information about the experiences of others (there is none), but instead a new ability to represent those experiences. After she left her chromatically challenged environment, she acquired the ability to have color experiences herself, and thereby to imagine the experiences of others. It is a different way to recognize such experiences from the neurophysiological perspective, but in each case the same (utterly physical) set of *facts* are the objects of attention. Lewis motivates this reading of the case by arguing that Jackson's line will force one – even the dualist – to become *epiphenomenalist* about the alleged phenomenal facts: they make no causal difference to the rest of the unfolding experience, not even to the subject's claims about the phenomenal character of his experience! We shall not reconstruct Lewis's subtle argument on this point, but the reader should note that it requires the controversial metaphysical assumption that the nature of a given natural property (whether physical or not) is independent of the causal power it "happens" to confer on its object. (So there might have been negatively charged particles that don't have a tendency to attract positively charged particles.)

A second materialist response (Harman, Chapter 24) to Jackson's "knowledge" argument starts by denying that we are aware of any of the intrinsic properties of our experiences. Instead, our experiences are awarenesses of external objects and their properties. (We are aware of the redness of the *rose*, not a redness of our experience.) Put another way, we are aware of the properties of the object our experience represents, but not of the properties of the representation of the object. This is in contrast to a case where we observe a presentational portrait, of Julius Caesar, say. We get a sense both of Caesar's facial features (the objects represented) and the intrinsic features – flatness, streaks of paint, etc. – of the representation (the portrait). But in the case of our own representational experience, says Harman, the only features of the experience we are aware of are *intentional* – what the experience discloses about its object, such as a red rose. (For a counter-argument to Harman, see Block 1990.)

So how does this bear on Jackson's argument? Harman actually concedes that Mary comes to learn a new fact when she steps outside her room. But Jackson is mistaken in supposing that, prior to leaving her room, Mary could know everything *physical* there is to know about color experience. Harman accepts a functionalist account of concepts. On this account, the inexperienced Mary lacks a concept of redness, since having the concept of redness depends in part on one's having been affected by red things in the right way. So Mary only later comes to know what it is like to see something red, because this requires that one is "capable of representing something's being red." Jackson's error, then, is to think that knowing all the physical facts is possible even for one who has not activated certain recognitional capabilities, or lacks them altogether. Such capacities are in fact necessary for understanding corresponding concepts, and of course factual knowledge requires the use of concepts.

Our final reading from a materialist perspective is not a direct response to any of the above puzzles. Instead, it seeks to give a general account of what makes a mental state conscious to begin with. It belongs to a family of views that center on the capacity to represent one's own mental states (first-order states) within distinct, higher-order states. On some views, consciously believing or desiring something involves a form of "perception-like awareness of [these] states and activities in our own minds" (Armstrong 1981, p. 724) – that is, the conscious mind is equipped with an internal monitor of our first-order states. This capacity does not involve, as the dualist contends, an infallible, "naked" grasp of the intrinsic properties of experiences (these are neurophysiological), but it does enable us to recognize, non-inferentially, at least some of our current mental states, in terms of their relational and intentional properties. For example, I can non-inferentially "perceive" that I have a belief – a type of state that is characterized relationally, in terms of causal role – and that it is about philosophy – its intentional content. I do not perceive the intrinsic, neurophysiological properties of this state, at least not as such.

Call Armstrong's account a higher-order *perception* account of consciousness. In Chapter 25, Carruthers offers instead a higher-order *thought* account, on which "a mental state is one that is available to conscious thought." (Compare the even stronger condition given by Rosenthal 1990, p. 741, that "a mental state is conscious when, and only when, it is accompanied by a suitable [higher-order thought].") Carruthers believes that this account is actually independent of debates about the nature of intrinsic qualities of our experience ("qualia"), though in repudiating the dualist's primitive-grasp model of conscious awareness of one's own mental states, he is undercutting the appeal of qualia-based arguments for dualism.

III. Alternative dualist strategies

Suppose one finds materialist approaches to consciousness to be unsatisfactory, perhaps for the reasons adduced by Kripke or Jackson. The puzzle then becomes one of understanding how non-physical conscious states can causally interact with physical states. The problem seems especially acute for the Cartesian dualist, for whom mind and body are two distinct substances, complete in their own right, that systematically interact as a matter of basic causal law. It is puzzling, as Kim argued in Chapter 4, how individual minds and bodies become permanently paired as they do, such that the conscious states of a particular mind always and only act on and react to the neural states of a particular brain.

In Chapter 26, William Hasker proposes that we modify the traditional Cartesian picture of the mind as a wholly independent substance which happens, as a contingent matter of fact, to interact with a specific brain. He supposes instead that the nonphysical mind *emerges* from the brain. The notion of emergence here is philosophically controversial, dating to mid-nineteenth century discussions of the relationship of living systems to their underlying physico-chemical constituents. The core idea is that when matter achieves a certain threshold of organized complexity, the emergent entity appears. Its continuing existence is wholly dependent on the persistence of the organized system which generates it, but its nature and activity are "novel," or irreducible, with respect to the fundamental properties and relations of the system. From the standpoint of an idealized observer who has complete knowledge of how the microphysical entities behave when organized below the threshold level of complexity, the first appearance of an emergent entity would be totally unexpected. After one observes emergence occurring regularly under such conditions, it would then be wholly predictable. (See O'Connor and Wong 2002 for a lengthy survey of more precise construals and applications of emergence.) Hasker contends that if one's mind is a substance which in this sense emerges from and depends on one's brain for its existence and functioning, then it is not mysterious that it should causally interact with it.

Hasker's notion of emergence is an especially strong one: the emergence of a complete *substance*, radically distinct in kind, from a complex physical system. Other emergentists suggest that human beings are biological substances with emergent conscious states. This view is a substance-monist, property (or event) dualism. On this picture, specific configurations of the brain generate conscious mental states, which in turn affect subsequent states of the brain and other conscious states. (This view is defended in O'Connor 2000; see Lockwood's Chapter 27 for an argument that appeal to emergence will get us only part of the way towards an understanding of the relation of conscious states to brain states.) In Chapter 21, McGinn objects to this account of consciousness that it does not render *intelligible* why neural states of the brain should generate radically distinct types of states. It may happen with the regularity of natural law, but it still appears to be wholly contingent, admitting no further explanation. Property emergentists will respond that conscious states are ontologically basic states, in the way that states involving mass and electric charge may turn out to be fundamental. It may well be a brute fact that qualities of mass and charge dynamically interact in accordance with the laws of fundamental physics. These laws cannot now be made "intelligible" by being explained as instances of some more basic phenomena. Furthermore, even if they do turn out to admit of reductive analysis, some physical interactions or other are basic – describable by dynamical laws which themselves are inexplicable. Just so, says the emergentist, laws governing the emergence of conscious states are ultimate, having no further explanation (at least none in purely naturalistic terms).

Other dualists believe that no form of mental–physical interactionism is tenable, either on the grounds of conceptual incoherence or empirical implausibility. One alternative is to embrace epiphenomenalism, the thesis that conscious states, though irreducible to physical states, have no causal effects. (This view is indicated in Jackson's Chapter 22; see also Jackson 1982.) This at first seems a desperate measure, requiring us to suppose that our beliefs and desires, for example, do not affect how we behave. But Jackson sharply separates propositional attitude states (beliefs, desires, intentions, hopes, and so on) from the purely qualitative aspects of conscious experiences. The former he believes to be functional, physical states, and so causally efficacious. But even epiphenomenalism restricted to "qualia" is counterintuitive; it must say that the occurrence of qualia has nothing to do with our beliefs and reports about them! (For an attempt to mitigate this consequence, see Chalmers 1996: Ch. 5.)

Another approach to bridge the gap between subjective conscious states and physical states of the brain is known as *panpsychism*. As with the idea of emergence, this notion admits a variety of interpretations (see Seager 2002). The version of the view considered in our reading from Michael Lockwood (Chapter 27) begins from the position that fundamental science (physics) reveals the abstract *structure* of the physical universe, but tells us nothing about the intrinsic character of the properties it describes in causal/functional terms. Consider what you know about the property of negative charge. We do not observe this property directly, and so cannot characterize it in intrinsic terms. Instead, we describe the power it confers on entities, such as electrons, to affect the future states of neighboring particles. In general, through complex theoretical inference grounded in experiment, physics posits certain kinds of basic qualities (charge, mass, and so on) of varying magnitude and gives us dynamical equations that describe the continuous evolution of systems from one state to the next. Our scientific understanding of these basic properties is exhausted by the role they play within such equations.

The panpsychist's central idea is that conscious experience opens a window on that *intrinsic character of the physical* that is undisclosed by formal dynamical theories. In conscious experience, we are immediately aware of at least certain intrinsic aspects of complex physical states of our brains. (And since the fundamental physical properties of the constituents of our brains are no different from those of any physical system whatever, we are gleaning intrinsic aspects of matter quite generally.) Qualia, then, are not dual to physical properties, and so there is no question of the interaction of qualia and physical properties. However, experiential *awareness* of qualia is fundamentally dual to the causal, relational understanding given by physical theory. Lockwood argues that the chief obstacle to this view is the "grain problem." Physics posits structure, and the physical structure of our brains is, in quantum-mechanical terms, enormous. There *is* structure to the qualities of our experience – think of the distribution of the look of colors and shapes in your current visual field – but that structure does not seem to match the nested, structural complexity of brains posited by our physical and biological theories. In a discussion that will be challenging for those uninitiated in the categories of fundamental physics, Lockwood seeks to show how the apparent mismatch might be circumnavigated through a consideration of certain striking features of current physical theories.

Finally, our volume concludes with a difficult, absorbing philosophical exploration by Peter Unger (Chapter 28) on what is required, by way of a general theory of properties, for a comprehensive understanding of the physical world. Although Unger does not endorse a determinate account, he (like Lockwood) advocates giving a central role in any such account to the qualities of our experience. (So the puzzle of consciousness, by Unger's lights, is the puzzle of adapting notions of the physical to our first-person grasp of the qualities of experience, rather than the other way around.) The resulting theory might be panpsychist, idealist, or dualist, but it will not in any recognizable sense be materialist.

PART IV: CONSCIOUSNESS

FURTHER READING

Armstrong, D.M. (1981) "What is Consciousness?," reprinted in Block *et al.* (1997).

Block, N. (1990) "Inverted Earth," reprinted in Block *et al.* (1997).

Block, N., Flanagan, O., and Güzeldere, G. (eds) (1997) *The Nature of Consciousness: Philosophical Debates*, Cambridge, Mass.: MIT Press.

Chalmers, D. (1996) *The Conscious Mind*, New York: Oxford University Press.

—— (1999) "Materialism and the Metaphysics of Modality," *Philosophy and Phenomenological Research* 59: 473–96.

Dretske, F. (1995) *Naturalizing the Mind*, Cambridge, Mass.: MIT Press.

Hill, C. and McLaughlin, B. (1999) "There Are Fewer Things in Reality Than Are Dreamt of in Chalmers's Philosophy," *Philosophy and Phenomenological Research* 59: 445–54.

Jackson, F. (1982) "Epiphenomenal Qualia," *Philosophical Quarterly* 32: 127–36.

Levine, J. (2001) *Purple Haze: The Puzzle of Consciousness*, New York: Oxford University Press.

Nagel, T. (1974) "What is it Like to be a Bat?," reprinted in Block *et al.* (1997).

O'Connor, T. (2000) *Persons and Causes: The Metaphysics of Free Will*, New York: Oxford University Press, Ch. 6.

O'Connor, T. and Wong, H.Y. (2002) "Emergent Properties," in E. Zalta (ed.), *The Stanford Encyclopedia of Philosophy*, URL = http://plato.stanford.edu/entries/emergent-properties/

Rosenthal, D. (1990) "A Theory of Consciousness," reprinted in Block *et al.* (1997).

Seager, W. (2002) "Panpsychism," in E. Zalta (ed.), *The Stanford Encyclopedia of Philosophy*, URL = http://plato.stanford.edu/entries/panpsychism/

Shoemaker, S. (1981) "The Inverted Spectrum," reprinted in Block *et al.* (1997).

Tye, M. (1995) *Ten Problems of Consciousness*, Cambridge, Mass.: MIT Press.

Unger, P. (currently unpublished) *All the Power in the World*.

IVA

THE PROBLEM OF
PHENOMENAL CONSCIOUSNESS

20

Joseph Levine, "Materialism and Qualia: The Explanatory Gap"

In "Naming and Necessity"[1] and "Identity and Necessity,"[2] Kripke presents a version of the Cartesian argument against materialism. His argument involves two central claims: first, that all identity statements using rigid designators on both sides of the identity sign are, if true at all, true in all possible worlds where the terms refer; second, that psycho-physical identity statements are conceivably false, and therefore, by the first claim, actually false.

My purpose in this paper is to transform Kripke's argument from a metaphysical one into an epistemological one. My general point is this. Kripke relies upon a particular intuition regarding conscious experience to support his second claim. I find this intuition important, not least because of its stubborn resistance to philosophical dissolution. But I don't believe this intuition supports the metaphysical thesis Kripke defends – namely, that pyscho-physical identity statements must be false. Rather, I think it supports a closely related epistemological thesis – namely, that psycho-physical identity statements leave a significant *explanatory gap*, and, as a corollary, that we don't have any way of determining exactly which psycho-physical identity statements are true.[3] One cannot conclude from my version of the argument that materialism is false, which makes my version a weaker attack than Kripke's. Nevertheless, it does, if correct, constitute a problem for materialism, and one that I think better captures the uneasiness many philosophers feel regarding that doctrine.

I will present this epistemological argument by starting with Kripke's own argument and extracting the underlying intuition. For brevity's sake, I am going to assume knowledge of Kripke's general position concerning necessity and the theory of reference, and concentrate only on the argument

Joseph Levine, "Materialism and Qualia: The Explanatory Gap," *Pacific Philosophical Quarterly*, 64 (1983): 354–61.

against materialism. To begin with, let us assume that we are dealing with a physicalist type-identity theory. That is, our materialist is committed to statements like:

(1)   Pain is the firing of C-fibers.

On Kripke's general theory, if (1) is true at all it is necessarily true. The same of course, is the case with the following statement:

(2)   Heat is the motion of molecules.

That is, if (2) is true at all it is necessarily true. So far so good.

The problem arises when we note that, with both (1) and (2), there is a felt contingency about them. That is, it seems conceivable that they be false. If they are necessarily true, however, that means there is no possible world in which they are false. Thus, imagining heat without the motion of molecules, or pain without the firing of C-fibers, must be to imagine a logically impossible world. Yet these suppositions *seem* coherent enough. Kripke responds that the felt contingency of (2) can be satisfactorily explained away, but that this can't be done for (1). Thus, there is an important difference between psycho-physical identities and other theoretical identities, and this difference makes belief in the former implausible.

The difference between the two cases is this. When it seems plausible that (2) is contingent, one can become disabused of this notion by noting that instead of imagining *heat* without the motion of molecules, one is really imagining there being some phenomenon that affects our senses the way heat in fact does, but is not the motion of molecules. The truly contingent statement is not (2) but

(2')   The phenomenon we experience through the sensations of warmth and cold, which is responsible for the expansion and contraction of mercury in thermometers, which causes some gases to rise and others to sink, etc., is the motion of molecules.

However, this sort of explanation will not work for (1). When we imagine a possible world in which a phenomenon is experienced as pain but we have no C-fibers, that is a possible world in which there *is* pain without there being any C-fibers. This is so, argues Kripke, for the simple reason that the experience of pain, the sensation of pain, counts as pain itself. We cannot make the distinction here, as we can with heat, between the way it appears to us and the phenomenon itself. Thus, we have no good account of our intuition that (1) is contingent, unless we give up the truth of (1) altogether.

Now, there are several responses available to the materialist. First of all, the most popular materialist view nowadays is functionalism, which is not committed to even the contingent truth of statements like (1). Rather than identifying types of mental states with types of physical states, functionalists identify the former with types of functional, or what Boyd calls "configurational" states.[4] Functional states are more abstract than physical states, and are capable of realization in a wide variety of physical constitutions. In terms of the computer metaphor, which is behind many functionalist views, our mentality is a matter of the way we are "programmed," our "software," whereas our physiology is a matter of our "hardware." On this view, the intuition that pain could exist without C-fibers is explained in terms of the multiple realizability of mental states. This particular dilemma, then, doesn't appear to arise for functionalist materialists.

However, this reply won't work. First of all, a Kripke-style argument can be mounted against functionalist identity statements as well. Ned Block, in "Troubles with Functionalism,"[5] actually makes the argument. He asks us to imagine any complete functionalist description of pain (embedded, of course, in a relatively complete functionalist psychological theory). Though we have no idea as yet exactly what this description would be, insofar as it is a *functionalist* description, we know roughly what form it would take. Call this functionalist description "F." Then functionalism entails the following statement:

(3)   To be in pain is to be in state F.

Again, on Kripke's theory of reference, (3) is necessarily true if true at all. Again, it seems imaginable that in some possible world (perhaps even in the actual world) (3) is false. Block attempts to persuade us of this by describing a situation where some object is in F but it is doubtful that it is in pain. For instance, suppose F were satisfied by the entire nation of China – which, given the nature of functional descriptions, is logically possible. Note that all the argument requires is that it should be *possible* that the entire nation of China, while realizing F, not be in pain. This certainly does seem possible.

Furthermore, some adherents of functionalism have moved back toward physicalist reductionism for qualia, largely in response to considerations like those put forward by Block. The idea is this. What Block's example seems to indicate is that functional descriptions are just *too* abstract to capture the essential features of qualitative sensory experiences. The so-called "inverted spectrum" argument – which involves the hypothesis that two people could share functional descriptions yet experience different visual qualia when viewing the same object – also points up the excessive abstractness of functional descriptions. Now one way some functionalists propose to deal with this problem is to return to a physicalist type-identity theory for sensory qualia, or at least for particular kinds of sensory qualia.[6] The gist of the latter proposal is this. While it's sufficient for being conscious (for having qualia at all) that an entity realize the appropriate functional description, the particular way a qualitative state is experienced is determined by the nature of the physical realization. So if, while looking at a ripe McIntosh apple, I experience the visual quality normally associated with looking at ripe McIntosh apples, and my inverted friend experiences the quality normally associated with looking at ripe cucumbers, this has to do with the difference in our physical realizations of the same functional state. Obviously, if we adopt this position Kripke's original argument applies.

So far, then, we see that the move to functionalism doesn't provide materialists with a way to avoid the dilemma Kripke poses: either bite the bullet and deny that (1), or (3), is contingent, or give up materialism. Well, what about biting the bullet? Why not just say that, intuition notwithstanding, statements like (1) and (3) are not contingent? In fact, Kripke himself, by emphasizing the gulf between epistemological possibility and metaphysical possibility, might even seem to give the materialist the ammunition she needs to attack the legitimacy of the appeal to this intuition. For what seems intuitively to be the case is, if anything, merely an epistemological matter. Since epistemological possibility is not sufficient for metaphysical possibility, the fact that what is intuitively contingent turns out to be metaphysically necessary should not bother us terribly. It's to be expected.

In the end, of course, one can just stand pat and say that. This is why I don't think Kripke's argument is entirely successful. However, I do think the intuitive resistance to materialism brought out by Kripke (and Block) should not be shrugged off as *merely* a matter of epistemology. Though clearly an epistemological matter, I think this intuitive resistance to materialism should bother us a lot. But before I can defend this claim, the intuition in question requires some clarification.

First of all, let's return to our list of statements. What I want to do is look more closely at the difference between statement (2) on the one hand, and statements (1) and (3) on the other. One difference between them, already noted, was the fact that the felt contingency of (2) could be explained away while the felt contingency of the others could not. But I want to focus on another difference, one which I think underlies the first one. Statement (2), I want to say, expresses an identity that is *fully explanatory*, with nothing crucial left out. On the other hand, statements (1) and (3) do seem to leave something crucial unexplained, there is a "gap" in the explanatory import of these statements. It is this explanatory gap, I claim, which is responsible for their vulnerability to Kripke-type objections. Let me explain what I mean by an "explanatory gap."

What is explanatory about (2)? (2) states that heat is the motion of molecules. The explanatory force of this statement is captured in statements like (2′) above. (2′) tells us by what mechanism the causal functions we associate with heat are effected. It is explanatory in the sense that our knowledge of chemistry and physics makes intelligible how it is that something like the motion of molecules could play the causal role we associate with heat. Furthermore, antecedent to our discovery of the essential nature of heat, its causal role, captured in statements like (2′), exhausts our notion of it. Once we understand how this causal role is carried out there is nothing more we need to understand.

Now, what is the situation with (1)? What is explained by learning that pain is the firing of C-fibers? Well, one might say that in fact quite a bit is explained. If we believe that part of the concept expressed by the term "pain" is that of a state which plays a certain causal role in our interaction with the environment (e.g. it warns us of damage, it causes us to attempt to avoid situations we believe will result in it, etc.), (1) explains the mechanisms underlying the performance of these functions. So, for instance, if penetration of the skin by a sharp metallic object excites certain nerve endings, which in turn excite the C-fibers, which then causes various avoidance mechanisms to go into effect, the causal role of pain has been explained.

Of course, the above is precisely the functionalist story. Obviously, there is something right about it. Indeed, we do feel that the causal role of pain is crucial to our concept of it, and that discovering the physical mechanism by which this causal role is effected explains an important facet of what there is to be explained about pain. However, there is more to our concept of pain than its causal role, there is its qualitative character, how it feels; and what is left unexplained by the discovery of C-fiber firing is *why pain should feel the way it does*! For there seems to be nothing about C-fiber firing which makes it naturally "fit" the phenomenal properties of pain, any more than it would fit some other set of phenomenal properties. Unlike its functional role, the identification of the qualitative side of pain with C-fiber firing (or some property of C-fiber firing) leaves the connection between it and what we identify it with completely mysterious. One might say, it makes the way pain feels into merely a brute fact.

Perhaps my point is easier to see with the example above involving vision. Let's consider again what it is to see green and red. The physical story involves talk about the various wave-lengths detectable by the retina, and the receptors and processors that discriminate among them. Let's

431

call the physical story for seeing red "R" and the physical story for seeing green "G." My claim is this. When we consider the qualitative character of our visual experiences when looking at ripe McIntosh apples, as opposed to looking at ripe cucumbers, the difference is not explained by appeal to G and R. For R doesn't really explain why I have the one kind of qualitative experience – the kind I have when looking at McIntosh apples – and not the other. As evidence for this, note that it seems just as easy to imagine G as it is to imagine R underlying the qualitative experience that is in fact associated with R. The reverse, of course, also seems quite imaginable.

It should be clear from what's been said that it doesn't help if we actually identify qualia with their functional roles. First of all, as I mentioned above, some functionalists resist this and prefer to adopt some form of type-physicalism for qualia. So when seeking the essence of how it feels to be in a certain functional state, they claim we must look to the essence of the physical realization. Secondly, even if we don't take this route, it still seems that we can ask why the kind of state that performs the function performed by pain, whatever its physical basis, should *feel* the way pain does. The analogous question regarding heat doesn't feel compelling. If someone asks why the motion of molecules plays the physical role it does, one can properly reply that an understanding of chemistry and physics is all that is needed to answer that question. If one objects that the phenomenal properties we associate with heat are not explained by identifying it with the motion of molecules, since being the motion of molecules seems compatible with all sorts of phenomenal properties, this just reduces to the problem under discussion. For it is precisely phenomenal properties – how it is for us to be in certain mental (including perceptual) states – which seem to resist physical (including functional) explanations.

Of course, the claim that (1) and (3) leave an explanatory gap in a way that (2) doesn't cannot be made more precise than the notion of explanation itself. Obviously, the D-N model of explanation is not sufficient for my purposes, since (1) and (3) presumably support counter-factuals and could be used, along with other premises, to deduce all sorts of particular facts.[7] What we need is an account of what it is for a phenomenon to be made *intelligible*, along with rules which determine when the demand for further intelligibility is inappropriate. For instance, I presume that the laws of gravity explain, in the sense at issue here, the phenomena of falling bodies. There doesn't seem to be anything "left out." Yet I am told that the value of G, the gravitational constant, is not derived from any basic laws. It is a given, a primitive, brute fact about the universe. Does this leave us with a feeling that something which ought to be explained is not? Or do we expect that some facts of nature should appear arbitrary in this way?

I am inclined to take the latter attitude with respect to G. So, one may ask, why does the connection between what it's like to be in a particular functional (or physical) state and the state itself demand explanation, to be made intelligible?

Without a theoretical account of the notion of intelligibility I have in mind, I can't provide a really adequate answer to this question. Yet I think there are ways to at least indicate why it is reasonable to seek such an explanation. First of all, the phenomenon of consciousness arises on the macroscopic level. That is, it is only highly organized physical systems which exhibit mentality. This is of course what one would expect if mentality were a matter of functional organization. Now, it just seems odd that primitive facts of the sort apparently presented by statements like (1) and (3) should arise at this level of organization. Materialism, as I understand it, implies explanatory reductionism of at least this minimal sort: that for every phenomenon not describable in terms of the fundamental physical magnitudes (whatever they turn out to be), there is a mechanism that is describable in terms of the fundamental physical magnitudes such that occurrences of the former are intelligible in terms of occurrences of the latter. While this minimal reductionism does not imply anything about the reducibility of theories like psychology to physics, it does imply that brute facts – of the sort exemplified by the value of G – will not arise in the domain of theories like psychology.

Furthermore, to return to my original point, the claim that statements (1) and (3) leave an explanatory gap accounts for their apparent contingency, and, more importantly, for the failure to explain away their apparent contingency in the standard way. After all, why is it that we can account for the apparent contingency of (2) in a theoretically and intuitively satisfactory manner, but not for that of (1) and (3)? Even if one believes that we don't have to take this intuitive resistance seriously, it is still legitimate to ask why the problem arises in these particular cases. As I claimed above, I think the difference in this regard between (2) on the one hand, and (1) and (3) on the other, is accounted for by the explanatory gap left by the latter as opposed to the former. Since this is the crucial connection between Kripke's argument and mine, let me belabor this point for a bit.

The idea is this. If there is nothing we can determine about C-fiber firing that explains why having one's C-fibers fire has the qualitative character that it does – or, to put it another way, if what it's particularly like to have one's C-fibers fire is not explained, or made intelligible, by understanding the physical or functional properties of C-fiber firings – it immediately becomes imaginable that there be C-fiber firings without the feeling of pain, and *vice versa*. We don't have the corresponding intuition in the case of heat and the motion of molecules – once we get clear about the right way to characterize what we imagine – because whatever there is to explain about heat is explained by its being the motion of molecules. So, how could it be anything else?

The point I am trying to make was captured by Locke[8] in his discussion of the relation between primary and secondary qualities. He states that the simple ideas which we experience in response to impingements from the external world bear no intelligible relation to the corpuscular processes underlying impingement and response. Rather, the two sets of phenomena – corpuscular processes and simple ideas – are stuck together in an arbitrary manner. The simple ideas go with their respective corpuscular configurations because God chose to so attach them. He could have chosen to do it differently. Now, so long as the two states of affairs seem arbitrarily stuck together in this way, imagination will pry them apart. Thus it is the non-intelligibility of the connection between the feeling of pain and its physical correlate that underlies the apparent contingency of that connection.

Another way to support my contention that psycho-physical (or psycho-functional) identity statements leave an explanatory gap will also serve to establish the corollary I mentioned at the beginning of this paper; namely, that even if some psycho-physical identity statements are true, we can't determine exactly which ones are true. The two claims, that there is an explanatory gap and that such identities are, in a sense, unknowable, are interdependent and mutually supporting. First I will show why there is a significant problem about our ever coming to know that statements like (1) are true, then I will show how this is connected to the problem of the explanatory gap.

So suppose, as a matter of fact, that having the feeling of pain is identical with being in a particular kind of physical state. Well, which physical state? Suppose we believed it to be the firing of C-fibers because that was the state we found to be correlated with the feeling of pain in ourselves. Now imagine we come across alien life which gives every behavioral and functional sign of sharing our qualitative states. Do they have the feeling of pain we have? Well, if we believed that to have that feeling is to have one's C-fibers fire, and if the aliens don't have firing C-fibers, then we must suppose that they can't have this feeling. But the problem is, even if it is true that creatures with physical constitutions radically different from ours do not share our qualitative states, how do we determine what measure of physical similarity/dissimilarity to use? That is, the fact that the feeling of pain is a kind of physical state, if it is, doesn't itself tell us how thickly or thinly to slice our physical kinds when determining which physical state it is identical to. For all we know, pain is identical to the disjunctive state, the firing of C-fibers *or* the opening of D-valves (the latter disjunct realizing pain (say) in creatures with a hydraulic nervous system).[9]

This objection may seem like the standard argument for functionalism. However, I am actually making a quite different argument. First of all, the same objection can be made against various forms of functionalist identity statements. That is, if we believe that to have the feeling of pain is to be in some functional state, what measure of functional similarity/dissimilarity do we use in judging whether or not some alien creature shares our qualitative states? Now, the more inclusive we make this measure, the more pressure we feel about questions of inverted qualia, and therefore the more reason we have to adopt a physicalist-reductionist position concerning particular kinds of qualia. This just brings us back where we started. That is, if having a radically different physical constitution is sufficient for having different qualia, there must be some fact of the matter about *how* different the physical constitution must be. But what possible evidence could tell between the hypothesis that the qualitative character of our pain is a matter of having firing C-fibers, and the hypothesis that it is a matter of having either firing C-fibers or opening D-valves?[10]

Now, if there were some intrinsic connection discernible between having one's C-fibers firing (or being in functional state F) and what it's like to be in pain, by which I mean that experiencing the latter was intelligible in terms of the properties of the former, then we could derive our measure of similarity from the nature of the explanation. Whatever properties of the firing of C-fibers (or being in state F) that explained the feel of pain would determine the properties a kind of physical (or functional) state had to have in order to count as feeling like our pain. But without this explanatory gap filled in, facts about the kind or the existence of phenomenal experiences of pain in creatures physically (or functionally) different from us become impossible to determine. This, in turn, entails that the truth or falsity of (1), while perhaps metaphysically factual, is nevertheless epistemologically inaccessible. This seems to be a very undesirable consequence of materialism.

There is only one way in the end that I can see to escape this dilemma and remain a materialist. One must either deny, or dissolve, the intuition which lies at the foundation of the argument. This would involve, I believe, taking more of an eliminationist line with respect to qualia than many materialist philosophers are prepared to take. As I said earlier, this kind of intuition about our qualitative experience seems surprisingly resistant to philosophical attempts to eliminate it. As long as it remains, the mind/body problem will remain.[11]

Notes

1 Saul Kripke, "Naming and Necessity," reprinted in *Semantics of Natural Language*, second edition, edited by Donald Davidson and Gilbert Harmon, D. Reidel Publishing Co., 1972; excerpts from this work are reprinted as Chapter 7 in this volume.
2 Saul Kripke, "Identity and Necessity," reprinted in *Naming, Necessity and Natural Kinds*, edited by Stephen Schwartz, Cornell University Press, 1977.
3 My argument in this paper is influenced by Thomas Nagel's in his paper "What Is It Like To Be a Bat?" (reprinted in *Readings in the Philosophy of Psychology*, vol. 1, edited by Ned Block, Harvard University Press, 1980), as readers who are familiar with Nagel's paper will notice as it develops.
4 Richard Boyd, "Materialism Without Reductionism," reprinted in *Readings in the Philosophy of Psychology*, vol. 1.
5 Ned Block, "Troubles with Functionalism," reprinted in *Readings in the Philosophy of Psychology*, vol. 1; excerpts from this paper are reprinted as Chapter 12 in this volume.
6 Cf. Sydney Shoemaker, "The Inverted Spectrum," *The Journal of Philosophy*, vol. LXXIX, no. 7, July 1982.
7 To elaborate a bit, on the D-N model of explanation, a particular event *e* is explained when it is shown to be deducible from general laws together with whatever description of the particular situation is relevant. Statements (1) and (3) could obviously be employed as premises in a deduction concerning (say) someone's psychological state. Cf. Carl Hempel, "Aspects of Scientific Explanation," reprinted in Hempel, *Aspects of Scientific Explanation*, Free Press, 1968.
8 Cf. Locke, *An Essay Concerning Human Understanding*, edited by J. Yolton, Everyman's Library, 1971 (originally published 1690); Bk. II, Ch. VIII, sec. 13, and Bk. IV, Ch. III, secs. 12 and 13.
9 This point is similar to an argument of Putnam's in the chapter of *Reason, Truth, and History* (Cambridge University Press, 1981) entitled "Mind and Body." Putnam uses the argument to serve a different purpose from mine, however. The example of the hydraulic nervous system is from David Lewis, "Mad Pain and Martian Pain," reprinted in *Readings in the Philosophy of Psychology*, vol. 1.
10 Shoemaker, in "The Inverted Spectrum," *op. cit.*, explicitly tries to deal with this problem. He proposes a fairly complicated principle according to which disjunctive states like the one mentioned in the text do not qualify for identification with (or realization of) qualitative states. I cannot discuss his principle in detail here. However, the main idea is that we look to the causal role of a quale for its individuation conditions. That is, if the causal effects of pain in human beings are explained by their C-fiber firings *alone*, then the state of having one's C-fibers fire *or* having one's D-valves open is not a legitimate candidate for the physical realization of pain. Viewed from the standpoint of my argument in this paper, Shoemaker's principle begs the very question at issue; namely, whether the qualitative character of pain is explained by its causal role. For if it isn't, there is no reason to presume that the identity conditions of the physical state causally responsible for pain's functional role would determine the presence or absence of a particular kind

of qualitative character. So long as the nature of that qualitative character is not explained by anything peculiar to any particular physical realization of pain, we have no way of knowing whether or not a different physical realization of pain, in a different creature, is associated with the same qualitative character.

11 An earlier version of this paper, under the title "Qualia, Materialism, and the Explanatory Gap," was delivered at the APA Eastern Division meetings, 1982. I would like to thank Carolyn McMullen for her comments on that occasion. I would also like to thank Louise Antony, Hilary Putnam, and Susan Wolf for their helpful comments on even earlier versions.

21

Colin McGinn, "Can We Solve the Mind–Body Problem?"

> How it is that anything so remarkable as a state of consciousness comes about
> as a result of initiating nerve tissue, is just as unaccountable as the appear-
> ance of the Djin, where Aladdin rubbed his lamp in the story . . .
>
> (Thomas Huxley)

We have been trying for a long time to solve the mind–body problem. It
has stubbornly resisted our best efforts. The mystery persists. I think the
time has come to admit candidly that we cannot resolve the mystery. But I
also think that this very insolubility – or the reason for it – removes the
philosophical problem. In this paper I explain why I say these outrageous
things.

The specific problem I want to discuss concerns consciousness, the hard
nut of the mind–body problem. How is it possible for conscious states to
depend upon brain states? How can technicolour phenomenology arise
from soggy grey matter? What makes the bodily organ we call the brain so
radically different from other bodily organs, say the kidneys – the body
parts without a trace of consciousness? How could the aggregation of
millions of individually insentient neurons generate subjective awareness?
We know that brains are the *de facto* causal basis of consciousness, but we
have, it seems, no understanding whatever of how this can be so. It strikes
us as miraculous, eerie, even faintly comic. Somehow, we feel, the water of
the physical brain is turned into the wine of consciousness, but we draw a
total blank on the nature of this conversion. Neural transmissions just seem
like the wrong kind of materials with which to bring consciousness into the
world, but it appears that in some way they perform this mysterious feat.
The mind–body problem is the problem of understanding how the miracle
is wrought, thus removing the sense of deep mystery. We want to take the
magic out of the link between consciousness and the brain.[1]

Colin McGinn, "Can We Solve the Mind–Body Problem?," *Mind*, 98(391) (1989):
349–66.

Purported solutions to the problem have tended to assume one of two forms. One form, which we may call constructive, attempts to specify some natural property of the brain (or body) which explains how consciousness can be elicited from it. Thus functionalism, for example, suggests a property – namely, causal role – which is held to be satisfied by both brain states and mental states; this property is supposed to explain how conscious states can come from brain states.[2] The other form, which has been historically dominant, frankly admits that nothing merely natural could do the job, and suggests instead that we invoke supernatural entities or divine interventions. Thus we have Cartesian dualism and Leibnizian pre-established harmony. These "solutions" at least recognize that something pretty remarkable is needed if the mind–body relation is to be made sense of; they are as extreme as the problem. The approach I favour is naturalistic but not constructive: I do not believe we can ever specify what it is about the brain that is responsible for consciousness, but I am sure that whatever it is it is not inherently miraculous. The problem arises, I want to suggest, because we are cut off by our very cognitive constitution from achieving a conception of that natural property of the brain (or of consciousness) that accounts for the psychophysical link. This is a kind of causal nexus that we are precluded from ever understanding, given the way we have to form our concepts and develop our theories. No wonder we find the problem so difficult!

Before I can hope to make this view plausible, I need to sketch the general conception of cognitive competence that underlies my position. Let me introduce the idea of *cognitive closure*. A type of mind M is cognitively closed with respect to a property P (or theory T) if and only if the concept-forming procedures at M's disposal cannot extend to a grasp of P (or an understanding of T). Conceiving minds come in different kinds, equipped with varying powers and limitations, biases and blindspots, so that properties (or theories) may be accessible to some minds but not to others. What is closed to the mind of a rat may be open to the mind of a monkey, and what is open to us may be closed to the monkey. Representational power is not all or nothing. Minds are biological products like bodies, and like bodies they come in different shapes and sizes, more or less capacious, more or less suited to certain cognitive tasks.[3] This is particularly clear for perceptual faculties, of course: perceptual closure is hardly to be denied. Different species are capable of perceiving different properties of the world, and no species can perceive every property things may instantiate (without artificial instrumentation anyway). But such closure does not reflect adversely on the reality of the properties that lie outside the representational capacities in question; a property is no less real for not being reachable from a certain kind of perceiving and conceiving mind. The

COLIN MCGINN

invisible parts of the electromagnetic spectrum are just as real as the visible parts, and whether a specific kind of creature can form conceptual representations of these imperceptible parts does not determine whether they exist. Thus cognitive closure with respect to P does not imply irrealism about P. That P is (as we might say) *noumenal* for M does not show that P does not occur in some naturalistic scientific theory T – it shows only that T is not cognitively accessible to M. Presumably monkey minds and the property of being an electron illustrate this possibility. And the question must arise as to whether human minds are closed with respect to certain true explanatory theories. Nothing, at least, in the concept of reality shows that everything real is open to the human concept-forming faculty – if, that is, we are realists about reality.[4]

Consider a mind constructed according to the principles of classical empiricism, a Humean mind. Hume mistakenly thought that human minds were Humean, but we can at least conceive of such a mind (perhaps dogs and monkeys have Humean minds). A Humean mind is such that perceptual closure determines cognitive closure, since "ideas" must always be copies of "impressions"; therefore the concept-forming system cannot transcend what can be perceptually presented to the subject. Such a mind will be closed with respect to unobservables; the properties of atoms, say, will not be representable by a mind constructed in this way. This implies that explanatory theories in which these properties are essentially mentioned will not be accessible to a Humean mind.[5] And hence the observable phenomena that are explained by allusion to unobservables will be inexplicable by a mind thus limited. But notice: the incapacity to explain certain phenomena does not carry with it a lack of recognition of the theoretical problems the phenomena pose. You might be able to appreciate a problem without being able to formulate (even in principle) the solution to that problem (I suppose human children are often in this position, at least for a while). A Humean mind cannot solve the problems that our physics solves, yet it might be able to have an inkling of what needs to be explained. We would expect, then, that a moderately intelligent enquiring Humean mind will feel permanently perplexed and mystified by the physical world, since the correct science is forever beyond its cognitive reach. Indeed, something like this was precisely the view of Locke. He thought that our ideas of matter are quite sharply constrained by our perceptions and so concluded that the true science of matter is eternally beyond us – that we could never remove our perplexities about (say) what solidity ultimately is.[6] But it does not follow for Locke that nature is itself inherently mysterious; the felt mystery comes from our own cognitive limitations, not from any objective eeriness in the world. It looks today as if Locke was wrong about our capacity to fathom the nature of the physical world, but we can still learn from his fundamental thought – the insistence that our cognitive faculties may not be up to solving every problem that confronts us. To put the point more generally: the human mind may not conform to empiricist principles, but it must conform to *some* principles – and it is a substantive claim that these principles permit the solution of every problem we can formulate or sense. Total cognitive openness is not guaranteed for human beings and it should not be expected. Yet what is noumenal for us may not be miraculous in itself. We should therefore be alert to the possibility that a problem that strikes us as deeply intractable, as utterly baffling, may arise from an area of cognitive closure in our ways of representing the world.[7] That is what I now want to argue is the case with our sense of the mysterious nature of the connection between consciousness and the brain. We are biased away from arriving at the correct explanatory theory of the psychophysical nexus. And this makes us prone to an illusion of objective mystery. Appreciating this should remove the philosophical problem: consciousness does not, in reality, arise from the brain in the miraculous way in which the Djin arises from the lamp.

I now need to establish three things: (i) there exists some property of the brain that accounts naturalistically for consciousness; (ii) we are cognitively closed with respect to that property; but (iii) there is no philosophical (as opposed to scientific) mind–body problem. Most of the work will go into establishing (ii).

Resolutely shunning the supernatural, I think it is undeniable that it must be in virtue of *some* natural property of the brain that organisms are conscious. There just *has* to be some explanation for how brains subserve minds. If we are not to be eliminativists about consciousness, then some theory must exist which accounts for the psychophysical correlations we observe. It is implausible to take these correlations as ultimate and inexplicable facts, as simply brute. And we do not want to acknowledge radical emergence of the conscious with respect to the cerebral: that is too much like accepting miracles *de re*. Brain states cause conscious states, we know, and this causal nexus must proceed through necessary connections of some kind – the kind that would make the nexus intelligible *if* they were understood.[8] Consciousness is like life in this respect. We know that life evolved from inorganic matter, so we expect there to be some explanation of this process. We cannot plausibly take the arrival of life as a primitive brute fact, nor can we accept that life arose by some form of miraculous emergence. Rather, there must be some natural account of how life comes from matter, whether or not we can know it. Eschewing vitalism and the magic touch of God's finger, we rightly insist that it must be in virtue of some natural property of (organized) matter that parcels of it get to be alive. But consciousness itself is just a further biological development, and so it too must be susceptible of some natural explanation – whether or not human beings are capable of arriving at this explanation. Presumably there exist objective natural laws that somehow account for the upsurge of consciousness. Consciousness, in short, must be a natural phenomenon, naturally arising from certain organizations of matter. Let us then say that there exists some property P, instantiated by the brain, in virtue of which the brain is the basis of consciousness. Equivalently, there exists some theory T, referring to P, which fully explains the dependence of conscious states on brain states. If we knew T, then we would have a constructive solution to the mind–body problem. The question then is whether we can ever come to know T and grasp the nature of P.

Let me first observe that it is surely *possible* that we could never arrive at a grasp of P; there is, as I said, no guarantee that our cognitive powers permit the solution of every problem we can recognize. Only a misplaced idealism about the natural world could warrant the dogmatic claim that everything is knowable by the human species at this stage of its evolutionary development (consider the same claim made on behalf of the intellect of cro-Magnon man). It *may* be that every property for which we can form a concept is such that *it* could never solve the mind–body problem. We *could* be like five-year-old children trying to understand Relativity Theory. Still, so far this is just a possibility claim: what reason do we have for asserting, positively, that our minds are closed with respect to P?

Longstanding historical failure is suggestive, but scarcely conclusive. Maybe, it will be said, the solution is just around the corner, or it has to wait upon the completion of the physical sciences? Perhaps we simply have yet to produce the Einstein-like genius who will restructure the problem in some clever way and then present an astonished world with the solution?[9] However, I think that our deep bafflement about the problem, amounting to a vertiginous sense of ultimate mystery, which resists even articulate formulation, should at least encourage us to explore the idea that there is something terminal about our perplexity. Rather as traditional theologians found themselves conceding cognitive closure with respect to certain of the properties of God, so we should look seriously at the idea that the mind–body problem brings us bang up against the limits of our capacity to understand the world. That is what I shall do now.

There seem to be two possible avenues open to us in our aspiration to identify P: we could try to get to P by investigating consciousness directly, or we could look to the study of the brain for P. Let us consider these in turn, starting with consciousness. Our acquaintance with consciousness could hardly be more direct; phenomenological description thus comes (relatively) easily. "Introspection" is the name of the faculty through which we catch consciousness in all its vivid nakedness. By virtue of possessing this cognitive faculty we ascribe concepts of consciousness to ourselves; we thus have "immediate access" to the properties of consciousness. But does the introspective faculty reveal property P? Can we tell just by introspecting what the solution to the mind-body problem is? Clearly not. We have direct cognitive access to one term of the mind-brain relation, but we do not have such access to the nature of the link. Introspection does not present conscious states *as* depending upon the brain in some intelligible way. We cannot therefore introspect P. Moreover, it seems impossible that we should ever augment our stock of introspectively ascribed concepts with the concept P – that is, we could not acquire this concept simply on the basis of sustained and careful introspection. Pure phenomenology will never provide the solution to the mind-body problem. Neither does it seem feasible to try to extract P from the concepts of consciousness we now have by some procedure of conceptual analysis – any more than we could solve the life-matter problem simply by reflecting on the concept *life*.[10] P has to lie outside the field of the introspectable, and it is not implicitly contained in the concepts we bring to bear in our first-person ascriptions. Thus the faculty of introspection, as a concept-forming capacity, is cognitively closed with respect to P; which is not surprising in view of its highly limited domain of operation (*most* properties of the world are closed to introspection).

But there is a further point to be made about P and consciousness, which concerns our restricted access to the concepts of consciousness themselves. It is a familiar point that the range of concepts of consciousness attainable by a mind M is constrained by the specific forms of consciousness possessed by M. Crudely, you cannot form concepts of conscious properties unless you yourself instantiate those properties. The man born blind cannot grasp the concept of a visual experience of red, and human beings cannot conceive of the echolocatory experiences of bats.[11] These are cases of cognitive closure within the class of conscious properties. But now this kind of closure will, it seems, affect our hopes of access to P. For suppose that we were cognitively open with respect to P; suppose, that is, that we had the solution to the problem of how specific forms of consciousness depend upon different kinds of physiological structure. Then, of course, we would understand how the brain of a bat subserves the subjective experiences of bats. Call this type of experience B, and call the explanatory property that links B to the bat's brain P_I. By grasping P_I it would be perfectly intelligible to us how the bat's brain generates B-experiences; we would have an explanatory theory of the causal nexus in question. We would be in possession of the same kind of understanding we would have of our own experiences if we had the correct psychophysical theory of them. But then it seems to follow that grasp of the theory that explains B-experiences would *confer* a grasp of the nature of those experiences: for how could we understand that theory without understanding the concept *B* that occurs in it? How could we grasp the *nature* of *B*-experiences without grasping the *character* of those experiences? The true psychophysical theory would seem to provide a route to a grasp of the subjective form of the bat's experiences. But now we face a dilemma, a dilemma which threatens to become a reductio: either we *can* grasp this theory, in which case the property *B* becomes open to us; or we *cannot* grasp the theory, simply because property *B* is *not* open to us. It seems to me that the looming reductio here is compelling: our concepts of consciousness just *are* inherently constrained by our own form of consciousness, so that any theory the understanding of which required us to transcend these constraints would *ipso facto* be inaccessible to us. Similarly, I think, any theory that required us to transcend the finiteness of our cognitive capacities would *ipso facto* be a theory we could not grasp – and this despite the fact that it might be needed to explain something we can see needs explaining. We cannot simply stipulate that our concept-forming abilities are indefinitely plastic and unlimited just because they would have to be to enable us to grasp the truth about the world. We constitutionally lack the concept-forming capacity to encompass all possible types of conscious state, and this obstructs our path to a general solution to the mind–body problem. Even if we could solve it for our own case, we could not solve it for bats and Martians. *P* is, as it were, too close to the different forms of subjectivity for it to be accessible to all such forms, given that one's form of subjectivity restricts one's concepts of subjectivity.[12]

I suspect that most optimists about constructively solving the mind–body problem will prefer to place their bets on the brain side of the relation. Neuroscience is the place to look for property *P*, they will say. My question then is whether there is any conceivable way in which we might come to introduce *P* in the course of our empirical investigations of the brain. New concepts have been introduced in the effort to understand the workings of the brain, certainly: could not *P* then occur in conceivable extensions of this manner of introduction? So far, indeed, the theoretical concepts we ascribe to the brain seem as remote from consciousness as any ordinary physical properties are, but perhaps we might reach *P* by diligent application of essentially the same procedures: so it is tempting to think. I want to suggest, to the contrary, that such procedures are inherently closed with respect to *P*. The fundamental reason for this, I think, is the role of *perception* in shaping our understanding of the brain – the way that our perception of the brain constrains the concepts we can apply to it. A point whose significance it would be hard to overstress here is this: the property of consciousness itself (or specific conscious states) is not an observable or perceptible property of the brain. You can stare into a living conscious brain, your own or someone else's, and see there a wide variety of unstantiated properties – its shape, colour, texture, etc. – but you will not thereby *see* what the subject is experiencing, the conscious state itself. Conscious states are simply not potential objects of perception: they depend upon the brain but they cannot be observed by directing the senses onto the brain. In other words, consciousness is noumenal with respect to perception of the brain.[13] I take it this is obvious. So we know there *are* properties of the brain that are necessarily closed to perception of the brain; the question now is whether *P* is likewise closed to perception.

My argument will proceed as follows. I shall first argue that *P* is indeed perceptually closed; then I shall complete the argument to full cognitive closure by insisting that no form of *inference* from what is perceived can lead us to *P*. The argument for perceptual closure starts from the thought that nothing we can imagine perceiving in the brain would ever convince us that we have located the intelligible nexus we seek. No matter what recondite property we could see to be instantiated in the brain we would always be baffled about how it could give rise to consciousness. I hereby invite you to try to conceive of a perceptible property of the brain that might allay the feeling of mystery that attends our contemplation of the brain–mind link: I do not think you will be able to do it. It is like trying to conceive of a perceptible property of a rock that would render it perspicuous that the rock was conscious. In fact, I think it is the very impossibility of this that lies at the root of the felt mind–body problem. But why is this? Basically, I think, it is because the senses are geared to representing a spatial world; they essentially present things in space with spatially defined properties. But it is precisely *such* properties that seem inherently incapable of resolving the mind–body problem: we cannot link consciousness to the brain in virtue of spatial properties of the brain. There the brain is, an object of perception, laid out in space, containing spatially distributed processes; but consciousness defies explanation in such terms. Consciousness does not seem made up out of smaller spatial processes; yet perception of the brain seems limited to revealing such processes.[14] The senses are responsive to certain *kinds* of properties – those that are essentially bound up with space – but these properties are of the wrong sort (the wrong *category*) to constitute *P*. Kant was right, the form of outer sensibility is spatial; but if so, then *P* will be noumenal with respect to the senses, since no spatial property will ever deliver a satisfying answer to the mind–body problem. We simply do not understand the idea that conscious states might intelligibly arise from spatial configurations of the kind disclosed by perception of the world.

I take it this claim will not seem terribly controversial. After all, we do not generally expect that every property referred to in our theories should be a potential object of human perception: consider quantum theory and cosmology. Unrestricted perceptual openness is a dogma of empiricism if ever there was one. And there is no compelling reason to suppose that the property needed to explain the mind–brain relation should be in principle perceptible; it might be essentially "theoretical," an object of thought not sensory experience. Looking harder at nature is not the only (or the best) way of discovering its theoretically significant properties. Perceptual closure does not entail cognitive closure, since we have available the procedure of hypothesis formation, in which *un*observables come to be conceptualized.

I readily agree with these sentiments, but I think there are reasons for believing that no coherent method of concept introduction will ever lead us to *P*. This is because a certain principle of *homogeneity* operates in our introduction of theoretical concepts on the basis of observation. Let me first note that consciousness itself could not be introduced simply on the basis of what we observe about the brain and its physical effects. If our data, arrived at by perception of the brain, do not include anything that brings in conscious states, then the theoretical properties we need to explain these data will not include conscious states either. Inference to the best explanation of purely physical data will never take us outside the realm of the physical, forcing us to introduce concepts of consciousness.[15] Everything physical has a purely physical explanation. So the property of consciousness is cognitively closed with respect to the introduction of concepts by means of inference to the best explanation of perceptual data about the brain.

Now the question is whether *P* could ever be arrived at by this kind of inference. Here we must be careful to guard against a form of magical emergentism with respect to concept formation. Suppose we try out a relatively clear theory of how theoretical concepts are formed: we get them by a sort of analogical extension of what we observe. Thus, for example, we arrive at the concept of a molecule by taking our perceptual representations of macroscopic objects and conceiving of smaller scale objects of the same general kind. This method seems to work well enough for unobservable material objects, but it will not help in arriving at *P*, since analogical extensions of the entities we observe in the brain are precisely as hopeless as the original entities were as solutions to the mind–body problem. We would need a method that left the base of observational properties behind in a much more radical way. But it seems to me that even a more unconstrained conception of inference to the best explanation would still not do what is required: it would no more serve to introduce *P* than it serves to introduce the property of consciousness itself. To explain the observed physical data we need only such theoretical properties as bear upon those data, not the property that explains consciousness, which does not occur in the data. Since we do not need consciousness to explain those data, we do

446

not need the property that explains consciousness. We will never get as far away from the perceptual data in our explanations of those data as we need to get in order to connect up explanatorily with consciousness. This is, indeed, why it seems that consciousness is theoretically epiphenomenal in the task of accounting for physical events. No concept needed to explain the workings of the physical world will suffice to explain how the physical world produces consciousness. So if P is perceptually noumenal, then it will be noumenal with respect to perception-based explanatory inferences. Accordingly, I do not think that P could be arrived at by empirical studies of the brain alone. Nevertheless, the brain *has* this property, as it has the property of consciousness. Only a magical idea of how we come by concepts could lead one to think that we can reach P by first perceiving the brain and then asking what is needed to explain what we perceive.[16] (The mind–body problem tempts us to magic in more ways than one.)

It will help elucidate the position I am driving towards if I contrast it with another view of the source of the perplexity we feel about the mind–brain nexus. I have argued that we cannot know which property of the brain accounts for consciousness, and so we find the mind–brain link unintelligible. But, it may be said, there is another account of our sense of irremediable mystery, which does not require positing properties our minds cannot represent. This alternative view claims that, even if we *now* had a grasp of P, we would *still* feel that there is something mysterious about the link, because of a special epistemological feature of the situation. Namely this: our acquaintance with the brain and our acquaintance with consciousness are necessarily mediated by distinct cognitive faculties, namely perception and introspection. Thus the faculty through which we apprehend one term of the relation is necessarily distinct from the faculty through which we apprehend the other. In consequence, it is not possible for us to use one of these faculties to apprehend the nature of the psychophysical nexus. No single faculty will enable us ever to apprehend the fact that consciousness depends upon the brain in virtue of property P. Neither perception alone nor introspection alone will ever enable us to witness the dependence. And this, my objector insists, is the real reason we find the link baffling: we cannot make sense of it in terms of the deliverances of a single cognitive faculty. So, even if we now had concepts for the properties of the brain that explain consciousness, we would still feel a residual sense of unintelligibility; we would still take there to be something mysterious going on. The necessity to shift from one faculty to the other produces in us an illusion of inexplicability. We might in fact have the explanation right now but be under the illusion that we do not. The right diagnosis, then, is that we should recognize the peculiarity of the epistemological situation and stop trying to make sense of the psychophysical nexus in the way we make sense of other sorts of nexus. It only *seems* to us that we can never discover a property that will render the nexus intelligible.

I think this line of thought deserves to be taken seriously, but I doubt that it correctly diagnoses our predicament. It is true enough that the problematic nexus is essentially apprehended by distinct faculties, so that it will never reveal its secrets to a single faculty; but I doubt that our intuitive sense of intelligibility is so rigidly governed by the "single-faculty condition." Why *should* facts only seem intelligible to us if we can conceive of apprehending them by one (sort of) cognitive faculty? Why not allow that we can recognize intelligible connections between concepts (or properties) even when those concepts (or properties) are necessarily ascribed using different faculties? Is it not suspiciously empiricist to insist that a causal nexus can only be made sense of by us if we can conceive of its being an object of a single faculty of apprehension? Would we think this of a nexus that called for touch and sight to apprehend each term of the relation? Suppose (*per impossible*) that we were offered P on a plate, as a gift from God: would we still shake our heads and wonder how that could resolve the mystery, being still the victims of the illusion of mystery generated by the epistemological duality in question? No, I think this suggestion is not enough to account for the miraculous appearance of the link: it is better to suppose that we are permanently blocked from forming a concept of what accounts for that link.

How strong is the thesis I am urging? Let me distinguish *absolute* from *relative* claims of cognitive closure. A problem is absolutely cognitively closed if no possible mind could resolve it; a problem is relatively closed if minds of some sorts can in principle solve it while minds of other sorts cannot. Most problems we may safely suppose, are only relatively closed: armadillo minds cannot solve problems of elementary arithmetic but human minds can. Should we say that the mind–body problem is only relatively closed or is the closure absolute? This depends on what we allow as a possible concept-forming mind, which is not an easy question. If we allow for minds that form their concepts of the brain and consciousness in ways that are quite independent of perception and introspection, then there may be room for the idea that there are possible minds for which the mind–body problem is soluble, and easily so. But if we suppose that *all* concept formation is tied to perception and introspection, however loosely, then *no* mind will be capable of understanding how it relates to its own body – the insolubility will be absolute. I think we can just about make sense of the former kind of mind, by exploiting our own faculty of a priori reasoning. Our mathematical concepts (say) do not seem tied either to perception or to introspection, so there does seem to be a mode of concept formation that operates without the constraints I identified earlier. The suggestion might then be that a mind that formed all of its concepts in this way – including its concepts of the brain and consciousness – would be free of the biases that prevent *us* from coming up with the right theory of how the two connect. Such a mind would have to be able to think of the brain and consciousness in ways that utterly prescind from the perceptual and the introspective – in somewhat the way we now (it seems) think about numbers. This mind would conceive of the psychophysical link in totally a priori terms. Perhaps this is how we should think of God's mind, and God's understanding of the mind–body relation. At any rate, something pretty radical is going to be needed if we are to devise a mind that can escape the kinds of closure that make the problem insoluble for us – if I am right in my diagnosis of our difficulty. *If* the problem is only relatively insoluble, then the type of mind that can solve it is going to be very different from ours and the kinds of mind we can readily make sense of (there may, of course, be cognitive closure here too). It certainly seems to me to be at least an open question whether the problem is absolutely insoluble; I would not be surprised if it were.[17]

My position is both pessimistic and optimistic at the same time. It is pessimistic about the prospects for arriving at a constructive solution to the mind–body problem, but it is optimistic about our hopes of removing the philosophical perplexity. The central point here is that I do not think we need to do the former in order to achieve the latter. This depends on a rather special understanding of what the philosophical problem consists in. What I want to suggest is that the nature of the psychophysical connection has a full and non-mysterious explanation in a certain science, but that this science is inaccessible to us as a matter of principle. Call this explanatory scientific theory *T*: *T* is as natural and prosaic and devoid of miracle as any theory of nature; it describes the link between consciousness and the brain in a way that is no more remarkable (or alarming) than the way we now describe the link between the liver and bile.[18] According to *T*, there is nothing eerie going on in the world when an event in my visual cortex causes me to have an experience of yellow – however much it seems to *us* that there is. In other words, there is no intrinsic conceptual or metaphysical difficulty about how consciousness depends on the brain. It is not that the correct science is compelled to postulate miracles *de re*; it is rather that the correct science lies in the dark part of the world for us. We confuse our own cognitive limitations with objective eeriness. We are like a Humean mind trying to understand the physical world, or a creature without spatial concepts trying to understand the possibility of motion. This removes the philosophical problem because it assures us that the entities *themselves* pose no inherent philosophical difficulty. The case is unlike, for example, the problem of how the abstract world of numbers might be intelligibly related

449

to the world of concrete knowing subjects: here the mystery seems intrinsic to the entities, not a mere artefact of our cognitive limitations or biases in trying to understand the relation.[19] It would not be plausible to suggest that there exists a science, whose theoretical concepts we cannot grasp, which completely resolves any sense of mystery that surrounds the question how the abstract becomes an object of knowledge for us. In this case, then, eliminativism seems a live option. The *philosophical* problem about consciousness and the brain arises from a sense that we are compelled to accept that nature contains miracles – as if the merely metallic lamp of the brain could really spirit into existence the Djin of consciousness. But we do not need to accept this: we can rest secure in the knowledge that some (unknowable) property of the brain makes everything fall into place. What creates the philosophical puzzlement is the assumption that the problem must somehow be scientific but that any science *we* can come up with will represent things as utterly miraculous. And the solution is to recognize that the sense of miracle comes from us and not from the world. There is, in reality, nothing mysterious about how the brain generates consciousness. There is no *metaphysical* problem.[20]

So far that deflationary claim has been justified by a general naturalism and certain considerations about cognitive closure and the illusions it can give rise to. Now I want to marshall some reasons for thinking that consciousness is actually a rather simple natural fact; objectively, consciousness is nothing very special. We should now be comfortable with the idea that our own sense of difficulty is a fallible guide to objective complexity: what is hard for us to grasp may not be very fancy in itself. The grain of our thinking is not a mirror held up to the facts of nature.[21] In particular, it may be that the extent of our understanding of facts about the mind is not commensurate with some objective estimate of their intrinsic complexity: we may be good at understanding the mind in some of its aspects but hopeless with respect to others, in a way that cuts across objective differences in what the aspects involve. Thus we are adept at understanding action in terms of the folk psychology of belief and desire, and we seem not entirely out of our depth when it comes to devising theories of language. But our understanding of how consciousness develops from the organization of matter is non-existent. But now, think of these various aspects of mind from the point of view of evolutionary biology. Surely language and the propositional attitudes are more complex and advanced evolutionary achievements than the mere possession of consciousness by a physical organism. Thus it seems that we are better at understanding some of the more complex aspects of mind than the simpler ones. Consciousness arises early in evolutionary history and is found right across the animal kingdom. In some respects it seems that the biological engineering required for consciousness is less fancy than that needed for certain kinds of complex motor behaviour. Yet we can come to understand the latter while drawing a total blank with respect to the former. Conscious states seem biologically quite primitive, comparatively speaking. So the theory T that explains the occurrence of consciousness in a physical world is very probably less objectively complex (by some standard) than a range of other theories that do not defy our intellects. If only we could know the psychophysical mechanism it might surprise us with its simplicity, its utter naturalness. In the manual that God consulted when he made the earth and all the beasts that dwell thereon the chapter about how to engineer consciousness from matter occurs fairly early on, well before the really difficult later chapters on mammalian reproduction and speech. It is not the *size* of the problem but its *type* that makes the mind–body problem so hard for us. This reflection should make us receptive to the idea that it is something about the tracks of our thought that prevents us from achieving a science that relates consciousness to its physical basis: the enemy lies within the gates.[22]

The position I have reached has implications for a tangle of intuitions it is natural to have regarding the mind–body relation. On the one hand, there are intuitions, pressed from Descartes to Kripke, to the effect that the relation between conscious states and bodily states is fundamentally contingent.[23] It can easily seem to us that there is no necessitation involved in the dependence of the mind on the brain. But, on the other hand, it looks absurd to try to dissociate the two entirely, to let the mind float completely free of the body. Disembodiment is a dubious possibility at best, and some kind of necessary supervenience of the mental on the physical has seemed undeniable to many. It is not my aim here to adjudicate this longstanding dispute; I want simply to offer a diagnosis of what is going on when one finds oneself assailed with this flurry of conflicting intuitions. The reason we feel the tug of contingency, pulling consciousness loose from its physical moorings, may be that we do not and cannot grasp the nature of the property that intelligibly links them. The brain has physical properties we can grasp, and variations in these correlate with changes in consciousness, but we cannot draw the veil that conceals the manner of their connection. Not grasping the nature of the connection, it strikes us as deeply contingent; we cannot make the assertion of a necessary connection intelligible to ourselves. There *may* then be a real necessary connection; it is just that it will always strike us as curiously brute and unperspicuous. We may thus, as upholders of intrinsic contingency, be the dupes of our own cognitive blindness. On the other hand, we are scarcely in a position to assert that there *is* a necessary connection between the properties of the brain we can grasp and states of consciousness, since we are so ignorant (and irremediably so) about the character of the connection. For all we know, the connection may be contingent, as access to *P* would reveal if we could have such access. The link between consciousness and property *P* is not, to be sure, contingent – virtually by definition – but we are not in a position to say exactly how *P* is related to the "ordinary" properties of the brain. It may be necessary or it may be contingent. Thus it is that we tend to vacillate between contingency and necessity; for we lack the conceptual resources to decide the question – or to understand the answer we are inclined to give. The indicated conclusion appears to be that we can never really know whether disembodiment is metaphysically possible, or whether necessary supervenience is the case, or whether spectrum inversion could occur. For these all involve claims about the modal connections between properties of consciousness and the ordinary properties of the body and brain that we can conceptualize; and the real nature of these connections is not accessible to us. Perhaps *P* makes the relation between C-fibre firing and pain necessary or perhaps it does not: we are simply not equipped to know. We are like a Humean mind wondering whether the observed link between the temperature of a gas and its pressure (at a constant volume) is necessary or contingent. To know the answer to that you need to grasp atomic (or molecular) theory, and a Humean mind just is not up to attaining the requisite theoretical understanding. Similarly, we are constitutionally ignorant at precisely the spot where the answer exists.

I predict that many readers of this paper will find its main thesis utterly incredible, even ludicrous. Let me remark that I sympathize with such readers: the thesis is not easily digestible. But I would say this: if the thesis *is* actually true, it will still strike us as hard to believe. For the idea of an explanatory property (or set of properties) that is noumenal for us, yet is essential for the (constructive) solution of a problem we face, offends a kind of natural idealism that tends to dominate our thinking. We find it taxing to conceive of the existence of a real property, under our noses as it were, which we are built not to grasp – a property that is responsible for phenomena that we observe in the most direct way possible. This kind of realism, which brings cognitive closure so close to home, is apt to seem both an affront to our intellects and impossible to get our minds around. We try to think of this unthinkable property and understandably fail in the effort; so we rush to infer that the very supposition of such a property is nonsensical. Realism of the kind I am presupposing thus seems difficult to hold in focus, and any philosophical theory that depends upon it will also seem to rest on something systematically elusive.[24] My response to such misgivings, however, is unconcessive: the limits of our minds are just not the limits of reality. It is deplorably anthropocentric to insist that reality be constrained by what the human mind can conceive. We need to cultivate a vision of reality (a metaphysics) that makes it truly independent of our given cognitive powers, a conception that includes these powers as a proper part. It is just that, in the case of the mind–body problem, the bit of reality that systematically eludes our cognitive grasp is an aspect of our own nature. Indeed, it is an aspect that makes it possible for us to have minds at all and to think about how they are related to our bodies. This particular transcendent tract of reality happens to lie within our own heads. A deep fact about our own nature as a form of embodied consciousness is thus necessarily hidden from us. Yet there is nothing inherently eerie or bizarre about this embodiment. We are much more straightforward than we seem. Our weirdness lies in the eye of the beholder.

The answer to the question that forms my title is therefore "No and Yes."[25]

Notes

1 One of the peculiarities of the mind–body problem is the difficulty of formulating it in a rigorous way. We have a sense of the problem that outruns our capacity to articulate it clearly. Thus we quickly find ourselves resorting to invitations to look inward, instead of specifying precisely *what* it is about consciousness that makes it inexplicable in terms of ordinary physical properties. And this can make it seem that the problem is spurious. A creature without consciousness would not properly appreciate the problem (assuming such a creature could appreciate other problems). I think an adequate treatment of the mind–body problem should explain why it is so hard to state the problem explicitly. My treatment locates our difficulty in our inadequate conceptions of the nature of the brain and consciousness. In fact, if we knew their natures fully we would already have solved the problem. This should become clear later.

2 I would also classify panpsychism as a constructive solution, since it attempts to explain consciousness in terms of properties of the brain that are as natural as consciousness itself. Attributing specks of proto-consciousness to the constituents of matter is not supernatural in the way postulating immaterial substances or divine interventions is; it is merely extravagant. I shall here be assuming that panpsychism, like all other extant constructive solutions, is inadequate as an answer to the mind–body problem – as (of course) are the supernatural "solutions." I am speaking to those who still feel perplexed (almost everyone, I would think, at least in their heart).

3 This kind of view of cognitive capacity is forcefully advocated by Noam Chomsky in *Reflections on Language*, Pantheon Books, 1975, and by Jerry Fodor in *The Modularity of Mind*, Cambridge, Mass., MIT Press, 1983. Chomsky distinguishes between "problems," which human minds are in principle equipped to solve, and "mysteries," which systematically elude our understanding; and he envisages a study of our cognitive systems that would chart these powers and limitations. I am here engaged in such a study, citing the mind–body problem as falling on the side of the mysteries.

4 See Thomas Nagel's discussion of realism in *The View From Nowhere*, Oxford, Oxford University Press, 1986, ch. VI. He argues there for the possibility of properties we can never grasp. Combining Nagel's realism with

COLIN MCGINN

Chomsky–Fodor cognitive closure gives a position looking very much like Locke's in the *Essay Concerning Human Understanding*: the idea that our God-given faculties do not equip us to fathom the deep truth about reality. In fact, Locke held precisely this about the relation between mind and brain: only divine revelation could enable us to understand how "perceptions" are produced in our minds by material objects.

5 Hume, of course, argued, in effect, that no theory essentially employing a notion of objective causal necessitation could be grasped by our minds – and likewise for the notion of objective persistence. We might compare the frustrations of the Humean mind to the conceptual travails of the pure sound beings discussed in Ch. II of P.F. Strawson's *Individuals*, London, Methuen, 1959; both are types of mind whose constitution puts various concepts beyond them. We can do a lot better than these truncated minds, but we also have our constitutional limitations.

6 See the *Essay*, Book II, ch. IV. Locke compares the project of saying what solidity ultimately is to trying to clear up a blind man's vision by talking to him.

7 Some of the more arcane aspects of cosmology and quantum theory might be thought to lie just within the bounds of human intelligibility. Chomsky suggests that the causation of behaviour might be necessarily mysterious to human investigators: see *Reflections on Language*, p. 156. I myself believe that the mind–body problem exhibits a qualitatively different level of mystery from this case (unless it is taken as an aspect of that problem).

8 Cf. Nagel's discussion of emergence in "Panpsychism," in *Mortal Questions*, Cambridge, Cambridge University Press, 1979. I agree with him that the apparent radical emergence of mind from matter has to be epistemic only, on pain of accepting inexplicable miracles in the world.

9 Despite his reputation for pessimism over the mind–body problem, a careful reading of Nagel reveals an optimistic strain in his thought (by the standards of the present paper): see, in particular, the closing remarks of "What is it Like to be a Bat?," in *Mortal Questions*. Nagel speculates that we might be able to devise an "objective phenomenology" that made conscious states more amenable to physical analysis. Unlike me, he does not regard the problem as inherently beyond us.

10 This is perhaps the most remarkably optimistic view of all – the expectation that reflecting on the ordinary concept of pain (say) will reveal the manner of pain's dependence on the brain. If I am not mistaken, this is in effect the view of common-sense functionalists: they think that P consists in causal role, and that this can be inferred analytically from the concepts of conscious states. This would make it truly amazing that we should ever have felt there to be a mind–body problem at all, since the solution is already contained in our mental concepts. What optimism!

11 See Nagel, "What is it Like to be a Bat?" Notice that the fugitive character of such properties with respect to our concepts has nothing to do with their "complexity"; like fugitive colour properties, such experiential properties are "simple." Note too that such properties provide counter-examples to the claim that (somehow) rationality is a faculty that, once possessed, can be extended to encompass all concepts, so that if *any* concept can be possessed then *every* concept can.

454

12 It might be suggested that we borrow Nagel's idea of "objective phenomenology" in order to get around this problem. Instead of representing
experiences under subjective descriptions, we should describe them in entirely
objective terms, thus bringing them within our conceptual ken. My problem
with this is that, even allowing that there could be such a form of description,
it would not permit us to understand how the subjective aspects of experience
depend upon the brain – which is really the problem we are trying to solve.
In fact, I doubt that the notion of objective phenomenology is any more
coherent than the notion of subjective physiology. Both involve trying to bridge
the psychophysical gap by a sort of stipulation. The lesson here is that the
gap cannot be bridged just by applying concepts drawn from one side to items
that belong on the other side; and this is because neither sort of concept could
ever do what is needed.

13 We should distinguish two claims about the imperceptibility of consciousness:
(i) consciousness is not perceivable by directing the senses onto the brain;
(ii) consciousness is not perceivable by directing the senses anywhere, even
towards the behaviour that "expresses" conscious states. I believe both theses,
but my present point requires only (i). I am assuming, of course, that perception cannot be unrestrictedly theory-laden; or that if it can, the infusions of
theory cannot have been originally derived simply by looking at things
or tasting them or touching them or . . .

14 Nagel discusses the difficulty of thinking of conscious processes in the spatial
terms that apply to the brain in *The View From Nowhere*, pp. 50–1, but he
does not draw my despairing conclusion. The case is exactly unlike (say) the
dependence of liquidity on the properties of molecules, since here we do think
of both terms of the relation as spatial in character; so we can simply employ
the idea of spatial composition.

15 Cf. Nagel: "it will never be legitimate to infer, as a theoretical explanation of
physical phenomena alone, a property that includes or implies the consciousness of its subject," "Panpsychism," p. 183.

16 It is surely a striking fact that the microprocesses that have been discovered
in the brain by the usual methods seem no nearer to consciousness than the
gross properties of the brain open to casual inspection. Neither do more
abstract "holistic" features of brain function seem to be on the right lines to
tell us the nature of consciousness. The deeper science probes into the brain
the more remote it seems to get from consciousness. Greater knowledge of the
brain thus destroys our illusions about the kinds of properties that might be
discovered by travelling along this path. Advanced neurophysiological theory
seems only to deepen the miracle.

17 The kind of limitation I have identified is therefore not the kind that could
be remedied simply by a large increase in general intelligence. No matter how
large the frontal lobes of our biological descendants may become, they will
still be stumped by the mind–body problem, so long as they form their (empirical) concepts on the basis of perception and introspection.

18 Or again, no more miraculous than the theory of evolution. Creationism is an
understandable response to the theoretical problem posed by the existence
of complex organisms; fortunately, we now have a theory that renders this
response unnecessary, and so undermines the theism required by the
creationist thesis. In the case of consciousness, the appearance of miracle

455

might also tempt us in a "creationist" direction, with God required to perform the alchemy necessary to transform matter into experience. Thus the mind–body problem might similarly be used to prove the existence of God (no miracle without a miracle-maker). We cannot, I think, refute this argument in the way we can the original creationist argument, namely by actually producing a non-miraculous explanatory theory, but we can refute it by arguing that such a naturalistic theory must *exist*. (It is a condition of adequacy upon any account of the mind–body relation that it avoid assuming theism.)

19 See Paul Benacerraf, "Mathematical Truth," *Journal of Philosophy*, 1973, for a statement of this problem about abstract entities. Another problem that seems to me to differ from the mind–body problem is the problem of free will. I do not believe that there is some unknowable property *Q* which reconciles free will with determinism (or indeterminism); rather, the concept of free will contains internal incoherencies – as the concept of consciousness does not. This is why it is much more reasonable to be an eliminativist about free will than about consciousness.

20 A test of whether a proposed solution to the mind–body problem is adequate is whether it relieves the pressure towards eliminativism. If the data can only be explained by postulating a miracle (i.e. not explained), then we must repudiate the data – this is the principle behind the impulse to deny that conscious states exist. My proposal passes this test because it allows us to resist the postulation of miracles; it interprets the eeriness as merely epistemic, though deeply so. Constructive solutions are not the only way to relieve the pressure.

21 Chomsky suggests that the very faculties of mind that make us good at some cognitive tasks may make us poor at others; see *Reflections on Language*, pp. 155–6. It seems to me possible that what makes us good at the science of the purely physical world is what skews us away from developing a science of consciousness. Our faculties bias us towards understanding matter in motion, but it is precisely this kind of understanding that is inapplicable to the mind–body problem. Perhaps, then, the price of being good at understanding matter is that we cannot understand mind. Certainly our notorious tendency to think of everything in spatial terms does not help us in understanding the mind.

22 I get this phrase from Fodor, *The Modularity of Mind*, p. 121. The intended contrast is with kinds of cognitive closure that stem from exogenous factors – as, say, in astronomy. Our problem with *P* is not that it is too distant or too small or too large or too complex; rather, the very structure of our concept-forming apparatus points us away from *P*.

23 Saul Kripke, *Naming and Necessity*, Oxford, Blackwell, 1980. [Excerpts from this work are reprinted as Chapter 7 in this volume.] Of course, Descartes explicitly argued from (what he took to be) the essential natures of the body and mind to the contingency of their connection. If we abandon the assumption that we know these natures, then agnosticism about the modality of the connection seems the indicated conclusion.

24 This is the kind of realism defended by Nagel in ch. VI of *The View From Nowhere*: to be is not to be conceivable by us. I would say that the mind–body problem provides a demonstration that there *are* such concept-transcending properties – not merely that there *could* be. I would also say that realism of

this kind should be accepted precisely because it helps solve the mind–body problem; it is a metaphysical thesis that pulls its weight in coping with a problem that looks hopeless otherwise. There is thus nothing "epiphenomenal" about such radical realism: the existence of a reality we cannot know can yet have intellectual significance for us.

25 Discussions with the following people have helped me work out the ideas of this paper: Anita Avramides, Jerry Katz, Ernie Lepore, Michael Levin, Thomas Nagel, Galen Strawson, Peter Unger. My large debt to Nagel's work should be obvious throughout the paper: I would not have tried to face the mind–body problem down had he not first faced up to it.

22

Frank Jackson, "What Mary Didn't Know"*

Mary is confined to a black-and-white room, is educated through black-and-white books and through lectures relayed on black-and-white television. In this way she learns everything there is to know about the physical nature of the world. She knows all the physical facts about us and our environment, in a wide sense of "physical" which includes everything in *completed* physics, chemistry, and neurophysiology, and all there is to know about the causal and relational facts consequent upon all this, including of course functional roles. If physicalism is true, she knows all there is to know. For to suppose otherwise is to suppose that there is more to know than every physical fact, and that is just what physicalism denies.

Physicalism is not the noncontroversial thesis that the actual world is largely physical, but the challenging thesis that it is entirely physical. This is why physicalists must hold that complete physical knowledge is complete knowledge simpliciter. For suppose it is not complete: then our world must differ from a world, *W(P)*, for which it is complete, and the difference must be in nonphysical facts; for our world and *W(P)* agree in all matters physical. Hence, physicalism would be false at our world [though contingently so, for it would be true at *W(P)*].[1]

It seems, however, that Mary does not know all there is to know. For when she is let out of the black-and-white room or given a color television, she will learn what it is like to see something red, say. This is rightly described as *learning* – she will not say "ho, hum." Hence, physicalism is false. This is the knowledge argument against physicalism in one of its manifestations.[2] This note is a reply to three objections to it mounted by Paul M. Churchland.[3]

* I am much indebted to discussions with David Lewis and with Robert Pargetter.

Frank Jackson, "What Mary Didn't Know," *The Journal of Philosophy*, 83(5) (1986): 291–5.

I. Three clarifications

The knowledge argument does not rest on the dubious claim that logically you cannot imagine what sensing red is like unless you have sensed red. Powers of imagination are not to the point. The contention about Mary is not that, despite her fantastic grasp of neurophysiology and everything else physical, she *could not imagine* what it is like to sense red; it is that, as a matter of fact, she *would not know*. But if physicalism is true, she would know; and no great powers of imagination would be called for. Imagination is a faculty that those who *lack* knowledge need to fall back on.

Secondly, the intensionality of knowledge is not to the point. The argument does not rest on assuming falsely that, if *S* knows that *a* is *F* and if *a* = *b*, then *S* knows that *b* is *F*. It is concerned with the nature of Mary's total body of knowledge before she is released: is it complete, or do some facts escape it? What is to the point is that *S* may know that *a* is *F* and *know* that *a* = *b*, yet arguably not know that *b* is *F*, by virtue of not being sufficiently logically alert to follow the consequences through. If Mary's lack of knowledge were at all like this, there would be no threat to physicalism in it. But it is very hard to believe that her lack of knowledge could be remedied merely by her explicitly following through enough logical consequences of her vast physical knowledge. Endowing her with great logical acumen and persistence is not in itself enough to fill in the gaps in her knowledge. On being let out, she will not say "I could have worked all this out before by making some more purely logical inferences."

Thirdly, the knowledge Mary lacked which is of particular point for the knowledge argument against physicalism is *knowledge about the experiences of others*, not about her own. When she is let out, she has new experiences, color experiences she has never had before. It is not, therefore, an objection to physicalism that she learns *something* on being let out. Before she was let out, she could not have known facts about her experience of red, for there were no such facts to know. That physicalist and nonphysicalist alike can agree on. After she is let out, things change; and physicalism can happily admit that she learns this; after all, some physical things will change, for instance, her brain states and their functional roles. The trouble for physicalism is that, after Mary sees her first ripe tomato, she will realize how impoverished her conception of the mental life of *others* has been *all along*. She will realize that there was, all the time she was carrying out her laborious investigations into the neurophysiologies of others and into the functional roles of their internal states, something about these people she was quite unaware of. All along their experiences (or many of them, those got from tomatoes, the sky, . . .) had a feature conspicuous to them but until now hidden from her (in fact, not in logic). But she knew all the physical facts about them all along; hence, what she did not know until her release is not a physical fact about their experiences. But it is a fact about them. That is the trouble for physicalism.

II. Churchland's three objections

(i)   Churchland's first objection is that the knowledge argument contains a defect that "is simplicity itself" (23). The argument equivocates on the sense of "knows about." How so? Churchland suggests that the following is "a conveniently tightened version" of the knowledge argument:

(1)   Mary knows everything there is to know about brain states and their properties.
(2)   It is not the case that Mary knows everything there is to know about sensations and their properties.
Therefore, by Leibniz's law,
(3)   Sensations and their properties ≠ brain states and their properties (23).

Churchland observes, plausibly enough, that the type or kind of knowledge involved in premise 1 is distinct from the kind of knowledge involved in premise 2. We might follow his lead and tag the first "knowledge by description," and the second "knowledge by acquaintance"; but, whatever the tags, he is right that the displayed argument involves a highly dubious use of Leibniz's law.

My reply is that the displayed argument may be convenient, but it is not accurate. It is not the knowledge argument. Take, for instance, premise 1. The whole thrust of the knowledge argument is that Mary (before her release) does *not* know everything there is to know about brain states and their properties, because she does not know about certain qualia associated with them. What is complete, according to the argument, is her knowledge of matters physical. A convenient and accurate way of displaying the argument is:

(1′)   Mary (before her release) knows everything physical there is to know about other people.
(2′)   Mary (before her release) does not know everything there is to know about other people (because she *learns* something about them on her release).
Therefore,
(3′)   There are truths about other people (and herself) which escape the physicalist story.

What is immediately to the point is not the kind, manner, or type of knowledge Mary has, but *what* she knows. What she knows beforehand is ex hypothesi everything physical there is to know, but is it everything there is to know? That is the crucial question.

There is, though, a relevant challenge involving questions about kinds of knowledge. It concerns the *support* for premise 2'. The case for premise 2' is that Mary learns something on her release, she acquires knowledge, and that entails that her knowledge beforehand (*what* she knew, never mind whether by description, acquaintance, or whatever) was incomplete. The challenge, mounted by David Lewis and Laurence Nemirow, is that on her release Mary does *not* learn something or acquire knowledge in the relevant sense. What Mary acquires when she is released is a certain representational or imaginative ability; it is knowledge how rather than knowledge that. Hence, a physicalist can admit that Mary acquires something very significant of a knowledge kind – which can hardly be denied – without admitting that this shows that her earlier factual knowledge is defective. She knew all *that* there was to know about the experiences of others beforehand, but lacked an ability until after her release.[4]

Now it is certainly true that Mary will acquire abilities of various kinds after her release. She will, for instance, be able to imagine what seeing red is like, be able to remember what it is like, and be able to understand why her friends regarded her as so deprived (something which, until her release, had always mystified her). But is it plausible that that is *all* she will acquire? Suppose she received a lecture on skepticism about other minds while she was incarcerated. On her release she sees a ripe tomato in normal conditions, and so has a sensation of red. Her first reaction is to say that she now knows more about the kind of experiences others have when looking at ripe tomatoes. She then remembers the lecture and starts to worry. Does she really know more about what their experiences are like, or is she indulging in a wild generalization from one case? In the end she decides she does know, and that skepticism is mistaken (even if, like so many of us, she is not sure how to demonstrate its errors). What was she to-ing and fro-ing about – her abilities? Surely not; her representational abilities were a known constant throughout. What else then was she agonizing about than whether or not she had gained factual knowledge of others? There would be nothing to agonize about if ability was *all* she acquired on her release.

I grant that I have no *proof* that Mary acquires on her release, as well as abilities, factual knowledge about the experiences of others – and not just because I have no disproof of skepticism. My claim is that the knowledge argument is a valid argument from highly plausible, though admittedly not demonstrable, premises to the conclusion that physicalism is false. And that, after all, is about as good an objection as one could expect in this area of philosophy.

(ii) Churchland's second objection (24/5) is that there must be something wrong with the argument, for it proves too much. Suppose Mary received a special series of lectures over her black-and-white television from a full-blown dualist, explaining the "laws" governing the behavior of "ectoplasm" and telling her about qualia. This would not affect the plausibility of the claim that on her release she learns something. So if the argument works against physicalism, it works against dualism too.

My reply is that lectures about qualia over black-and-white television do not tell Mary all there is to know about qualia. They may tell her some things about qualia, for instance, that they do not appear in the physicalist's story, and that the quale we use "yellow" for is nearly as different from the one we use "blue" for as is white from black. But why should it be supposed that they tell her everything about qualia? On the other hand, it is plausible that lectures over black-and-white television might in principle tell Mary everything in the physicalist's story. You do not need color television to learn physics or functionalist psychology. To obtain a good argument against dualism (attribute dualism; ectoplasm is a bit of fun), the premise in the knowledge argument that "Mary has the full story according to physicalism before her release, has to be replaced by a premise that she has the full story according to dualism. The former is plausible; the latter is not. Hence, there is no "parity of reasons" trouble for dualists who use the knowledge argument.

(iii) Churchland's third objection is that the knowledge argument claims "that Mary could not even *imagine* what the relevant experience would be like, despite her exhaustive neuroscientific knowledge, and hence must still be missing certain crucial information" (25), a claim he goes on to argue against.

But, as we emphasized earlier, the knowledge argument claims that Mary would not know what the relevant experience is like. What she could imagine is another matter. If her knowledge is defective, despite being all there is to know according to physicalism, then physicalism is false, whatever her powers of imagination.

Notes

1   The claim here is not that, if physicalism is true, only what is expressed in explicitly physical language is an item of knowledge. It is that, if physicalism is true, then if you know everything expressed or expressible in explicitly physical language, you know everything. *Pace* Terence Horgan, "Jackson on Physical Information and Qualia," *Philosophical Quarterly*, XXXIV, 135 (April 1984): 147–152.

2 Namely, that in my "Epiphenomenal Qualia," *ibid.*, XXXII, 127 (April 1982): 127–136. See also Thomas Nagel, "What Is It Like to Be a Bat?," *Philosophical Review*, LXXXIII, 4 (October 1974): 435–450, and Howard Robinson, *Matter and Sense* (New York: Cambridge, 1982).

3 "Reduction, Qualia, and the Direct Introspection of Brain States," *The Journal of Philosophy*, LXXXII, 1 (January 1985): 8–28. Unless otherwise stated, future page references are to this paper.

4 See Laurence Nemirow, "Review of Thomas Nagel, *Mortal Questions*," *Philosophical Review*, LXXXIX, 3 (July 1980): 473–477, and David Lewis, "Postscript to 'Mad Pain and Martian Pain,'" *Philosophical Papers*, vol. I (New York: Oxford, 1983). Churchland mentions both Nemirow and Lewis, and it may be that he intended his objection to be essentially the one I have just given. However, he says quite explicitly (bottom of p. 23) that his objection does not need an "ability" analysis of the relevant knowledge.

IVB

MATERIALIST THEORIES
OF CONSCIOUSNESS

23

David Lewis, "What Experience Teaches"

Experience the best teacher

They say that experience is the best teacher, and the classroom is no substitute for Real Life. There's truth to this. If you want to know what some new and different experience is like, you can learn it by going out and really *having* that experience. You can't learn it by being told about the experience, however thorough your lessons may be.

Does this prove much of anything about the metaphysics of mind and the limits of science? I think not.

Example: skunks and Vegemite. I have smelled skunks, so I know what it's like to smell skunks. But skunks live only in some parts of the world, so you may never have smelled a skunk. If you haven't smelled a skunk, then you don't know what it's like. You never will, unless someday you smell a skunk for yourself. On the other hand, you may have tasted Vegemite, that famous Australian substance; and I never have. So you may know what it's like to taste Vegemite. I don't, and unless I taste Vegemite (what, and spoil a good example!), I never will. It won't help at all to take lessons on the chemical composition of skunk scent or Vegemite, the physiology of the nostrils or the taste-buds, and the neurophysiology of the sensory nerves and the brain.

Example: the captive scientist.[1] Mary, a brilliant scientist, has lived from birth in a cell where everything is black or white. (Even she herself is painted all over.) She views the world on black-and-white television. By television she reads books, she joins in discussion, she watches the results of experiments done under her direction. In this way she becomes the world's leading

David Lewis, "What Experience Teaches," in William G. Lycan (ed.) *Mind and Cognition: A Reader* (Blackwell, Oxford, 1990), pp. 499–519.

expert on color and color vision and the brain states produced by exposure to colors. But she doesn't know what it's like to see color. And she never will, unless she escapes from her cell.

Example: the bat.[2] The bat is an alien creature, with a sonar sense quite unlike any sense of ours. We can never have the experiences of a bat; because we could not become bat-like enough to have those experiences and still be ourselves. We will never know what it's like to be a bat. Not even if we come to know all the facts there are about the bat's behavior and behavioral dispositions, about the bat's physical structure and processes, about the bat's functional organization. Not even if we come to know all the same sort of physical facts about all the other bats, or about other creatures, or about ourselves. Not even if we come to possess all physical facts whatever. Not even if we become able to recognize all the mathematical and logical implications of all these facts, no matter how complicated and how far beyond the reach of finite deduction.

Experience is the best teacher, in this sense: having an experience is the best way or perhaps the only way, of coming to know what that experience is like. No amount of scientific information about the stimuli that produce that experience and the process that goes on in you when you have that experience will enable you to know what it's like to have the experience.

. . . but not necessarily

Having an experience is surely one good way, and surely the only practical way, of coming to know what that experience is like. Can we say, flatly, that it is the only *possible* way? Probably not. There is a change that takes place in you when you have the experience and thereby come to know what it's like. Perhaps the exact same change could in principle be produced in you by precise neurosurgery, very far beyond the limits of present-day technique. Or it could possibly be produced in you by magic. If we ignore the laws of nature, which are after all contingent, then there is no necessary connection between cause and effect: anything could cause anything. For instance, the casting of a spell could do to you exactly what your first smell of skunk would do. We might quibble about whether a state produced in this artificial fashion would deserve the *name* "knowing what it's like to smell a skunk," but we can imagine that so far as what goes on within you is concerned, it would differ not at all.[3]

Just as we can imagine that a spell might produce the same change as a smell, so likewise we can imagine that science lessons might cause that same change. Even that is possible, in the broadest sense of the word. If we ignored all we know about how the world really works, we could not say what might happen to someone if he were taught about the chemistry of scent and the physiology of the nose. There might have been a causal mechanism that transforms science lessons into whatever it is that experience gives us. But there isn't. It is not an absolutely necessary truth that experience is the best teacher about what a new experience is like. It's a contingent truth. But we have good reason to think it's true.

We have good reason to think that something of this kind is true, anyway, but less reason to be sure exactly what. Maybe some way of giving the lessons that hasn't yet been invented, and some way of taking them in that hasn't yet been practiced, could give us a big surprise. Consider sight-reading: a trained musician can read the score and know what it would be like to hear the music. If I'd never heard that some people can sight-read, I would never have thought it humanly possible. Of course the moral is that new music isn't altogether new – the big new experience is a rearrangement of lots of little old experiences. It just might turn out the same for new smells and tastes *vis-à-vis* old ones; or even for color vision *vis-à-vis* black and white;[4] or even for sonar sense experience *vis-à-vis* the sort we enjoy. The thing we can say with some confidence is that we have no faculty for knowing on the basis of mere science lessons what some *new enough* experience would be like. But how new is "new enough"? – There, we just might be in for surprises.

Three ways to miss the point

The first way. A literalist might see the phrase "know what it's like" and take that to mean: "know what it resembles." Then he might ask: what's so hard about that? Why can't you just be told which experiences resemble one another? You needn't have had the experiences – all you need, to be taught your lessons, is some way of referring to them. You could be told: the smell of skunk somewhat resembles the smell of burning rubber. I have been told: the taste of Vegemite somewhat resembles that of Marmite. Black-and-white Mary might know more than most of us about the resemblances among color-experiences. She might know which ones are spontaneously called "similar" by subjects who have them; which gradual changes from one to another tend to escape notice; which ones get conflated with which in memory; which ones involve roughly the same neurons firing in similar rhythms; and so forth. We could even know what the bat's sonar experiences resemble just by knowing that they do not at all resemble any experiences of humans, but do resemble – as it might be – certain experiences that occur in certain fish. This misses the point. *Pace* the literalist, "know what it's like" does not mean "know what it resembles." The most that's true is that knowing what it resembles *may* help you to know what it's like. If you are taught that experience A resembles B and C closely, D less, E not at all, that will help you know what A is like – *if* you know already what B and C and D and E are like. Otherwise, it helps you not at all. I don't know any better what it's like to taste Vegemite when I'm told that it tastes like Marmite, because I don't know what Marmite tastes like either. (Nor do I know any better what Marmite tastes like for being told it tastes like Vegemite.) Maybe Mary knows enough to triangulate each color experience exactly in a network of resemblances, or in many networks of resemblance in different respects, while never knowing what any node of any network is like. Maybe we could do the same for bat experiences. But no amount of information about resemblances, just by itself, does anything to help us know what an experience is like.

The second way. In so far as I don't know what it would be like to drive a steam locomotive fast on a cold, stormy night, part of my problem is just that I don't know what experiences I would have. The firebox puts out a lot of heat, especially when the fireman opens the door to throw on more coal; on the other hand, the cab is drafty and gives poor protection from the weather. Would I be too hot or too cold? Or both by turns? Or would it be chilled face and scorched legs? If I knew the answers to such questions, I'd know much better what it would be like to drive the locomotive. So maybe "know what it's like" just means "know what experiences one has." Then again: what's the problem? Why can't you just be told what experiences you would have if, say, you tasted Vegemite? Again, you needn't have had the experiences – all you need, to be taught your lessons, is some way of referring to them. We have ways to refer to experiences we haven't had. We can refer to them in terms of their causes: the experience one has upon tasting Vegemite, the experience one has upon tasting a substance of such-and-such chemical composition. Or we can refer to them in terms of their effects: the experience that just caused Fred to say "Yeeuch!" Or we can refer to them in terms of the physical states of the nervous system that mediate between those causes and effects: the experience one has when one's nerves are firing in such-and-such pattern. (According to some materialists, I myself for one, this means the experience which is identical with such-and-such firing pattern. According to other materialists it means the experience which is realized by such-and-such firing pattern. According to many dualists, it means the experience which is merely the lawful companion of such-and-such firing pattern. But whichever it is, we get a way of referring to the experience.) Black-and-white Mary is in a position to refer to color-experiences in all these ways. Therefore you should have no problem in telling her exactly what experiences one has upon seeing the colors. Or rather, your only problem is that you'd be telling her what she knows very well already! In general, to know what is the X is to know that the X is the Y, where it's not too obvious that the X is the Y. (Just knowing that the X is the X won't do, of course, because it is too obvious.) If Mary knows that the experience of seeing green is the experience associated with such-and-such pattern of nerve firings, then she knows the right sort of unobvious identity. So she knows what experience one has upon seeing green.

(Sometimes it's suggested that you need a "rigid designator": you know what is the X by knowing that the X is the Y only if "the Y" is a term whose referent does not depend on any contingent matter of fact. In the first place, this suggestion is false. You can know who is the man on the balcony by knowing that the man on the balcony is the Prime Minister even if neither "the Prime Minister" nor any other phrase available to you rigidly designates the man who is, in fact, the Prime Minister. In the second place, according to one version of Materialism (the one I accept) a description of the form "the state of having nerves firing in such-and-such a pattern" *is* a rigid designator, and what it designates is in fact an experience; and according to another version of Materialism, a description of the form "having some or other state which occupies so-and-so functional role" is a rigid designator of an experience. So even if the false suggestion were granted, still it hasn't been shown, without begging the question against Materialism, that Mary could not know what experience one has upon seeing red.)

Since Mary *does* know what experiences she would have if she saw the colors, but she *doesn't* know what it would be like to see the colors, we'd better conclude that "know what it's like" does not after all mean "know what experiences one has." The locomotive example was misleading. Yes, by learning what experiences the driver would have, I can know what driving the locomotive would be like; but only because I already know what those experiences are like. (It matters that I know what they're like under the appropriate descriptions – as it might be, the description "chilled face and scorched legs." This is something we'll return to later.) Mary may know as well as I do that when the driver leans out into the storm to watch the signals, he will have the experience of seeing sometimes green lights and sometimes red. She knows better than I what experiences he has when signals come into view. She can give many more unobviously equivalent descriptions of those experiences than I can. But knowing what color-experiences the driver has won't help Mary to know what his job is like. It will help me.

The third way. Until Mary sees green, here is one thing she will never know: she will never know that she is seeing green. The reason why is just that until she sees green, it will never be true that she is seeing green. Some knowledge is irreducibly egocentric, or *de se.*[5] It is not just knowledge about what goes on in the world; it is knowledge of who and when in the world one is. Knowledge of what goes on in the world will be true alike for all who live in that world; whereas egocentric knowledge may be true for one and false for another, or true for one at one time and false for the same one at another time. Maybe Mary knows in advance, as she plots her escape, that 9 a.m. on the 13th of May, 1997, is the moment when someone previously confined in a black-and-white cell sees color for the first time. But until that moment comes, she will never know that she herself is then seeing color – because she isn't. What isn't true isn't knowledge. This goes as much for egocentric knowledge as for the rest. So only those of whom an egocentric proposition is true can know it, and only at times when it is true of them can they know it. That one is then seeing color is an egocentric proposition. So we've found a proposition which Mary can never know until she sees color – which, as it happens, is the very moment when she will first know what it's like to see color! Have we discovered the reason why experience is the best teacher? And not contingently after all, but as a necessary consequence of the logic of egocentric knowledge?

No; we have two separate phenomena here, and only some bewitchment about the "first-person perspective" could make us miss the difference. In the first place, Mary will probably go on knowing what it's like to see green after she stops knowing the egocentric proposition that she's then seeing green. Since what isn't true isn't known she must stop knowing that proposition the moment she stops seeing green. (Does that only mean that we should have taken a different egocentric proposition: that one *has* seen green? No; for in that case Mary could go on knowing the proposition even after she forgets what it's like to see green, as might happen if she were soon recaptured.) In the second place, Mary might come to know what it's like to see green even if she didn't know the egocentric proposition. She might not have known in advance that her escape route would take her across a green meadow, and it might take her a little while to recognize grass by its shape. So at first she might know only that she was seeing some colors or other, and thereby finding out what some color-experiences or other were like, without being able to put a name either to the colors or to the experiences. She would then know what it was like to see green, though not under that description, indeed not under any description more useful than "the color-experience I'm having now"; but she would not know the egocentric proposition that she is then seeing green, since she wouldn't know which color she was seeing. In the third place, the gaining

472

of egocentric knowledge may have prerequisites that have nothing to do with experience. Just as Mary can't know she's seeing green until she *does* see green, she can't know she's turning 50 until she *does* turn 50. But – I hope! – turning 50 does not involve some special experience. In short, though indeed one can gain egocentric knowledge that one is in some situation only when one is in it, that is not the same as finding out what an experience is like only when one has that experience.

We've just rejected two suggestions that don't work separately, and we may note that they don't work any better when put together. One knows what is the X by knowing that the X is the Y, where the identity is not too obvious; and "the Y" might be an egocentric description. So knowledge that the X is the Y might be irreducibly egocentric knowledge, therefore knowledge that cannot be had until it is true of one that the X is the Y. So one way of knowing what is the X will remain unavailable until it comes true of one that the X is the Y. One way that I could gain an unobvious identity concerning the taste of Vegemite would be for it to come true that the taste of Vegemite was the taste I was having at that very moment – and that would come true at the very moment I tasted Vegemite and found out what it was like! Is this why experience is the best teacher? – No; cases of gaining an unobvious egocentric identity are a dime a dozen, and most of them do not result in finding out what an experience is like. Suppose I plan ahead that I will finally break down and taste Vegemite next Thursday noon. Then on Wednesday noon, if I watch the clock, I first gain the unobvious egocentric knowledge that the taste of Vegemite is the taste I shall be having in exactly 24 hours, and thereby I have a new way of knowing what is the taste of Vegemite. But on Wednesday noon I don't yet know what it's like. Another example: from time to time I find myself next to a Vegemite-taster. On those occasions, and only those, I know what is the taste of Vegemite by knowing that it is the taste being had by the person next to me. But on no such occasion has it ever yet happened that I knew what it was like to taste Vegemite.

The Hypothesis of Phenomenal Information

No amount of the physical information that black-and-white Mary gathers could help her know what it was like to see colors; no amount of the physical information that we might gather about bats could help us know what it's like to have their experiences; and likewise in other cases. There is a natural and tempting explanation of why physical information does not help. That is the hypothesis that besides physical information there is an irreducibly different kind of information to be had: *phenomenal information*. The two are independent. Two possible cases might be exactly alike physically, yet differ phenomenally. When we get physical information we narrow down the physical possibilities, and perhaps we narrow them down all the way to one, but we leave open a range of phenomenal possibilities. When we have an experience, on the other hand, we acquire phenomenal information; possibilities previously open are eliminated; and that is what it is to learn what the experience is like.

(Analogy. Suppose the question concerned the location of a point within a certain region of the x–y plane. We might be told that its x-coordinate lies in certain intervals, and outside certain others. We might even get enough of this information to fix the x-coordinate exactly. But no amount of x-information would tell us anything about the y-coordinate; any amount of x-information leaves open all the y-possibilities. But when at last we make a y-measurement, we acquire a new kind of information; possibilities previously open are eliminated; and that is how we learn where the point is in the y-direction.)

What might the subject matter of phenomenal information be? *If* the Hypothesis of Phenomenal Information is true, then you have an easy answer: it is information about experience. More specifically, it is information about a certain part or aspect or feature of experience. But if the Hypothesis is false, then there is still experience (complete with all its parts and aspects and features) and yet no information about experience is phenomenal information. So it cannot be said in a neutral way, without presupposing the Hypothesis, that information about experience is phenomenal information. For if the Hypothesis is false and Materialism is true, it may be that all the information there is about experience is physical information, and can very well be presented in lessons for the inexperienced.

It makes no difference to put some fashionable new phrase in place of "experience." If instead of "experience" you say "raw feel" (or just "feeling"), or "way it feels," or "what it's like," then I submit that you mean nothing different. Is there anything it's like to be this robot? Does this robot have experiences? – I can tell no difference between the new question and the old. Does sunburn feel the same way to you that it does to me? Do we have the same raw feel? Do we have the same experience when sunburned? – Again, same question. "Know the feeling," "know what it's like" – interchangeable. (Except that the former may hint at an alternative to the Hypothesis of Phenomenal Information.) So if the friend of phenomenal information says that its subject matter is raw feels, or ways to feel, or what it's like, then I respond just as I do if he says that the subject matter is experience. Maybe so, *if* the Hypothesis of Phenomenal Information is true; but if the Hypothesis is false and Materialism is true, nevertheless there is still information about raw feels, ways to feel or what it's like; but in that case it is physical information and can be conveyed in lessons.

We might get a candidate for the subject matter of phenomenal information that is not just experience renamed, but is still tendentious. For instance, we might be told that phenomenal information concerns the intrinsic character of experience. A friend of phenomenal information might indeed believe that it reveals certain special, non-physical intrinsic properties of experience. He might even believe that it reveals the existence of some special non-physical thing or process, *all* of whose intrinsic properties are non-physical. But he is by no means alone in saying that experience has an intrinsic character. Plenty of us materialists say so too. We say that a certain color-experience is whatever state occupies a certain functional role. So if the occupant of that role (universally, or in the case of humans, or in the case of certain humans) is a certain pattern of neural firing, then that pattern of firing *is* the experience (in the case in question). Therefore the intrinsic character of the experience is the intrinsic character of the firing pattern. For instance, a frequency of firing is part of the intrinsic character of the experience. If we materialists are right about what experience is, then black-and-white Mary knows all about the intrinsic character of color-experience; whereas most people who know what color-experience is like remain totally ignorant about its intrinsic character.[6]

To say that phenomenal information concerns "qualia" would be tendentious in much the same way. For how was this notion introduced? Often thus. We are told to imagine someone who, when he sees red things, has just the sort of experiences that we have when we see green things, and vice versa; and we are told to call this a case of "inverted qualia." And then we are told to imagine someone queerer still, who sees red and responds to it appropriately, and indeed has entirely the same functional organization of inner states as we do and yet has no experiences at all; and we are told to call this a case of "absent qualia." Now a friend of phenomenal information might well think that these deficiencies have something to do with the non-physical subject matter of phenomenal information. But others can understand them otherwise. Some materialists will reject the cases outright, but others, and I for one, will make sense of them as best we can. Maybe the point is that the states that occupy the roles of experiences, and therefore *are* the experiences, in normal people are inverted or absent in victims of inverted or absent qualia. (This presupposes, what might be false, that most people are enough alike.) Experience of red – the state that occupies that role in normal people – occurs also in the victim of "inverted qualia," but in him it occupies the role of experience of green; whereas the state that occupies in him the role of experience of red is the state that occupies in normal people the role of experience of green. Experience of red and of green – that is, the occupants of those roles for normal people – do not occur at all in the victim of "absent qualia"; the occupants of those roles for him are states that don't occur at all in the normal. Thus we make good sense of inverted and absent qualia; but in such a way that "qualia" is just the word for role-occupying states taken *per se* rather than *qua* occupants of roles. Qualia, so understood, could not be the subject matter of phenomenal information. Mary knows all about them. We who have them mostly don't.[7]

It is best to rest content with an unhelpful name and a *via negativa*. Stipulate that "the phenomenal aspect of the world" is to name whatever is the subject matter of phenomenal information, if there is any such thing; the phenomenal aspect, if such there be, is that which we can become informed about by having new experiences but never by taking lessons. Having said this, it will be safe to say that information about the phenomenal aspect of the world can only be phenomenal information. But all we really know, after thus closing the circle, is that phenomenal information is supposed to reveal the presence of some sort of non-physical things or processes within experience, or else it is supposed to reveal that certain physical things or processes within experience have some sort of non-physical properties.

The Knowledge Argument

If we invoke the Hypothesis of Phenomenal Information to explain why no amount of physical information suffices to teach us what a new experience is like, then we have a powerful argument to refute any materialist theory of the mind. Frank Jackson (see note 1) calls it the "Knowledge Argument." Arguments against one materialist theory or another are never very conclusive. It is always possible to adjust the details. But the Knowledge Argument, if it worked, would directly refute the bare minimum that is common to *all* materialist theories.

It goes as follows. First in a simplified form; afterward we'll do it properly. Minimal Materialism is a supervenience thesis: no difference without physical difference. That is: any two possibilities that are just alike physically are just alike *simpliciter*. If two possibilities are just alike physically, then no physical information can eliminate one but not both of them. If two possibilities are just alike *simpliciter* (if that is possible) then no information whatsoever can eliminate one but not both of them. So if there is a kind of information – namely, phenomenal information – that can eliminate possibilities that any amount of physical information leaves open, then there must be possibilities that are just alike physically, but not just alike *simpliciter*. That is just what minimal Materialism denies.

(Analogy. If two possible locations in our region agree in their x-coordinate, then no amount of x-information can eliminate one but not both.

If, *per impossible*, two possible locations agreed in all their coordinates, then no information whatsoever could eliminate one but not both. So if there is a kind of information – namely, y-information – that can eliminate locations that any amount of x-information leaves open, then there must be locations in the region that agree in their x-coordinate but not in all their coordinates.)

Now to remove the simplification. What we saw so far was the Knowledge Argument against Materialism taken as a necessary truth, applying unrestrictedly to all possible worlds. But we materialists usually think that Materialism is a contingent truth. We grant that there are spooky possible worlds where Materialism is false, but we insist that our actual world isn't one of them. If so, then there might after all be two possibilities that are alike physically but not alike *simpliciter*; but one or both of the two would have to be possibilities where Materialism was false. Spooky worlds could differ with respect to their spooks without differing physically. Our minimal Materialism must be a *restricted* supervenience thesis: within a certain class of worlds, which includes our actual world, there is no difference without physical difference. Within that class, any two possibilities just alike physically are just alike *simpliciter*. But what delineates the relevant class? (It is trivial that our world belongs to *some* class wherein there is no difference without physical difference. That will be so however spooky our world may be. The unit class of our world is one such class, for instance. And so is any class that contains our world, and contains no two physical duplicates.) I think the relevant class should consist of the worlds that have nothing wholly alien to this world. The inhabitants of such a non-alien world could be made from the inhabitants of ours, so to speak, by a process of division and recombination. That will make no wholly different kinds of things, and no wholly different fundamental properties of things.[8] Our restricted materialist supervenience thesis should go as follows: throughout the non-alien worlds, there is no difference without physical difference.

If the Hypothesis of Phenomenal Information be granted, then the Knowledge Argument refutes this restricted supervenience nearly as decisively as it refutes the unrestricted version. Consider a possibility that is eliminated by phenomenal information, but not by any amount of physical information. There are two cases. Maybe this possibility has nothing that is alien to our world. In that case the argument goes as before: actuality and the eliminated possibility are just alike physically, they are not just alike *simpliciter*; furthermore, both of them fall within the restriction to non-alien worlds, so we have a counterexample even to restricted supervenience. Or maybe instead the eliminated possibility does have something X which is alien to this world – an alien kind of thing, or maybe an alien fundamental property of non-alien things. Then the phenomenal information gained by having a new experience has revealed something negative: at least in part, it is the information that X is *not* present. How can that be? If there is such a thing as phenomenal information, presumably what it reveals is positive: the presence of something hitherto unknown. Not, of course, something alien from actuality itself; but something alien from actuality as it is inadequately represented by the inexperienced and by the materialists. If Mary learns something when she finds out what it's like to see the colors, presumably she learns that there's *more* to the world than she knew before – not *less*. It's easy to think that phenomenal information might eliminate possibilities that are impoverished by comparison with actuality, but that would make a counterexample to the restricted supervenience thesis. To eliminate possibilities without making a counterexample, phenomenal information would have to eliminate possibilities less impoverished than actuality. And how can phenomenal information do that? Compare ordinary perceptual information. Maybe Jean-Paul can just *see* that Pierre is absent from the café, at least if it's a small café. But how can he just see that Pierre is absent from Paris, let alone from the whole of actuality?

(Is there a third case? What if the eliminated possibility is in one respect richer than actuality, in another respect poorer? Suppose the eliminated possibility has X, which is alien from actuality, but also it lacks Y. Then phenomenal information might eliminate it by revealing the actual presence of Y, without having to reveal the actual absence of X – But then I say there ought to be a third possibility, one with neither X nor Y, poorer and in no respect richer than actuality, and again without any physical difference from actuality. For why should taking away X automatically restore Y? Why can't they vary independently?[9] But this third possibility differs *simpliciter* from actuality without differing physically. Further, it has nothing alien from actuality. So we regain a counterexample to the restricted supervenience thesis.)

The Knowledge Argument works. There is no way to grant the Hypothesis of Phenomenal Information and still uphold Materialism. Therefore I deny the Hypothesis. I cannot refute it outright. But later I shall argue, first, that it is more peculiar, and therefore less tempting, that it may at first seem; and, second, that we are not forced to accept it, since an alternative hypothesis does justice to the way experience best teaches us what it's like.

Three more ways to miss the point

The Hypothesis of Phenomenal Information characterizes information in terms of eliminated possibilities. But there are other conceptions of "information." Therefore the Hypothesis has look-alikes: hypotheses which say that experience produces "information" which could not be gained otherwise, but do not characterize this "information" in terms of eliminated possibilities. These look-alikes do not work as premises for the Knowledge Argument. They do not say that phenomenal information eliminates possibilities that differ, but do not differ physically, from uneliminated possibilities. The look-alike hypotheses of phenomenal "information" are consistent with Materialism, and may very well be true. But they don't make the Knowledge Argument go away. Whatever harmless look-alikes may or may not be true, and whatever conception may or may not deserve the name "information," the only way to save Materialism is fix our attention squarely on the genuine Hypothesis of Phenomenal Information, and deny it. To avert our eyes, and attend to something else, is no substitute for that denial.

Might a look-alike help at least to this extent: by giving us something true that well might have been confused with the genuine Hypothesis, thereby explaining how we might have believed the Hypothesis although it was false? I think not. Each of the look-alikes turns out to imply not only that experience can give us "information" that no amount of lessons can give, but also that lessons in Russian can give us "information" that no amount of lessons in English can give (and vice versa). I doubt that any friend of phenomenal information ever thought that the special role of experience in teaching what it's like was on a par with the special role of Russian! I will have to say before I'm done that phenomenal information is an illusion, but I think I must look elsewhere for a credible hypothesis about what sort of illusion it might be.

The fourth way. If a hidden camera takes photographs of a room, the film ends up bearing traces of what went on in the room. The traces are distinctive: that is, the details of the traces depend on the details of what went on, and if what went on had been different in any of many ways, the traces would have been correspondingly different. So we can say that the traces bear information, and that he who has the film has the information. That might be said because the traces, plus the way they depend on what went on, suffice to eliminate possibilities; but instead we might say "information" and just mean "distinctive traces." If so, it's certainly true that new experience imparts "information" unlike any that can be gained from lessons. Experience and lessons leave different kinds of traces. That is so whether or not the experience eliminates possibilities that the lessons leave open. It is equally true, of course, that lessons in Russian leave traces unlike any that are left by lessons in English, regardless of whether the lessons cover the same ground and eliminate the same possibilities.

The fifth way. When we speak of transmission of "information," we often mean transmission of text. Repositories of "information," such as libraries, are storehouses of text. Whether the text is empty verbiage or highly informative is beside the point. Maybe we too contain information by being storehouses of text. Maybe there is a language of thought, and maybe the way we believe things is to store sentences of this language in some special way, or in some special part of our brains. In that case, we could say that storing away a new sentence was storing away a new piece of "information," whether or not that new piece eliminated any possibilities not already eliminated by the sentences stored previously. Maybe, also, the language of thought is not fixed once and for all, but can gain new words. Maybe, for instance, it borrows words from public language. And maybe, when one has a new experience, that causes one's language of thought to gain a new word which denotes that experience – a word which could not have been added to the language by any other means. If all this is so, then when Mary sees colors, her language of thought gains new words, allowing her to store away new sentences and thereby gain "information." All this about the language of thought, the storing of sentences, and the gaining of words is speculation. But it is plausible speculation, even if no longer the only game in town. If it is all true, then we have another look-alike hypothesis of phenomenal "information." When Mary gains new words and stores new sentences, that is "information" that she never had before, regardless of whether it eliminates any possibilities that she had not eliminated already.

But again, the special role of experience turns out to be on a par with the special role of Russian. If the language of thought picks up new words by borrowing from public language, then lessons in Russian add new words, and result in the storing of new sentences, and thereby impart "information" that never could have been had from lessons in English. (You might say that the new Russian words are mere synonyms of old words, or at least old phrases, that were there already; and synonyms don't count. But no reason has been given why the new inner words created by experience may not also be synonyms of old phrases, perhaps of long descriptions in the language of neurophysiology.)

The sixth way. A philosopher who is skeptical about possibility, as so many are, may wish to replace possibilities themselves with linguistic ersatz possibilities: maximal consistent sets of sentences. And he may be content to take "consistent" in a narrowly logical sense, so that a set with "Fred is married" and "Fred is a bachelor" may count as consistent, and only an overt contradiction like "Fred is married" and "Fred is not married" will be ruled out."[10] The ersatz possibilities might also be taken as sets of sentences of the language of thought, if the philosopher believes in it. Then if someone's language of thought gains new words, whether as a result of new experi-ence or as a result of being taught in Russian, the ersatz possibilities become richer and more numerous. The sets of sentences that were maximal before are no longer maximal after new words are added. So when Mary sees colors and her language of thought gains new words, there are new ersatz possibilities; and she can straightway eliminate some of them. Suppose she knows beforehand that she is about to see green, and that the experience of seeing green is associated with neural firing pattern F. So when she sees green and gains the new word G for her experience, then straightway there are new, enriched ersatz possibilities with sentences saying that she has G without F, and straightway she knows enough to eliminate these ersatz possibilities. (Even if she does not know beforehand what she is about to see, straightway she can eliminate at least those of her new-found ersatz possibilities with sentences denying that she then has G.) Just as we can characterize information in terms of elimination of possibilities, so we can characterize ersatz "information" in terms of elimination of ersatz "possibilities." So here we have the closest look-alike hypothesis of all, provided that language-of-thoughtism is true. But we still do not have the genuine Hypothesis of Phenomenal Information, since the eliminated ersatz possibility of G without F may not have been a genuine possibility at all. It may have been like the ersatz possibility of married bachelors.

Curiouser and curiouser

The Hypothesis of Phenomenal Information is more peculiar than it may at first seem. For one thing, because it is opposed to more than just Materialism. Some of you may have welcomed the Knowledge Argument because you thought all along that physical information was inadequate to explain the phenomena of mind. You may have been convinced all along that the mind could do things that no physical system could do: bend spoons, invent new jokes, demonstrate the consistency of arithmetic, reduce the wave packet, or what have you. You may have been convinced that the full causal story of how the deeds of mind are accomplished involves the causal interactions not only of material bodies but also of astral bodies; not only the vibrations of the electromagnetic field but also the good or bad vibes of the psionic field; not only protoplasm but ectoplasm. I doubt it, but never mind. It's irrelevant to our topic. The Knowledge Argument is targeted against you no less than it is against Materialism itself.

Let *parapsychology* be the science of all the non-physical things, prop-erties, causal processes, laws of nature, and so forth that may be required to explain the things we do. Let us suppose that we learn ever so much parapsychology. It will make no difference. Black-and-white Mary may study all the parapsychology as well as all the psychophysics of color vision, but she still won't know what it's like. Lessons on the aura of Vegemite will do no more for us than lessons on its chemical composition. And so it goes. Our intuitive starting point wasn't just that *physics* lessons couldn't help the inexperienced to know what it's like. It was that *lessons* couldn't help. If there is such a thing as phenomenal information, it isn't just independent of physical information. It's independent of every sort of information that could be served up in lessons for the inexperienced. For it is supposed to eliminate possibilities that any amount of lessons leave open. Therefore phenomenal information is not just parapsychological information, if such there be. It's something very much stranger.

The genuine Hypothesis of Phenomenal Information, as distinguished from its look-alikes, treats information in terms of the elimination of possibilities. When we lack information, several alternative possibilities are open, when we get the information some of the alternatives are excluded. But a second peculiar thing about phenomenal information is that it resists this treatment. (So does logical or mathematical "information." However, phenomenal information cannot be logical or mathematical, because lessons in logic and mathematics no more teach us what a new experience is like than lessons in physics or parapsychology do.) When someone doesn't know what it's like to have an experience, where are the alternative open possibilities? I cannot present to myself in thought a range of alternative possibilities about what it might be like to taste Vegemite. That is because I cannot imagine either what it *is* like to taste Vegemite, or any alternative way that it *might* be like but in fact isn't. (I could perfectly well imagine that Vegemite tastes just like peanut butter, or something else familiar to me, but let's suppose I've been told authoritatively that this isn't so.) I can't even pose the question that phenomenal information is supposed to answer: is it this way or that? It seems that the alternative possibilities must be unthinkable beforehand; and afterward too, except for the one that turns out to be actualized. I don't say there's anything altogether impossible about a range of unthinkable alternatives; only something peculiar. But it's peculiar enough to suggest that we may somehow have gone astray.

From phenomenal to epiphenomenal

A third peculiar thing about phenomenal information is that it is strangely isolated from all other sorts of information; and this is so regardless of whether the mind works on physical or parapsychological principles. The phenomenal aspect of the world has nothing to do with explaining why people seemingly talk about the phenomenal aspect of the world. For instance, it plays no part in explaining the movements of the pens of

482

philosophers writing treatises about phenomenal information and the way experience has provided them with it.

When Mary gets out of her black-and-white cell, her jaw drops. She says "At last! So this is what it's like to see colors !" Afterward she does things she couldn't do before, such as recognizing a new sample of the first color she ever saw. She may also do other things she didn't do before: unfortunate things, like writing about phenomenal information and the poverty of Materialism. One might think she said what she said and did what she did because she came to know what it's like to see colors. Not so, if the Hypothesis of Phenomenal Information is right. For suppose the phenomenal aspect of the world had been otherwise, so that she gained different phenomenal information. Or suppose the phenomenal aspect of the world had been absent altogether, as we materialists think it is. Would that have made the slightest difference to what she did or said then or later? I think not. Making a difference to what she does or says means, at least in part, making a difference to the motions of the particles of which she is composed. (Or better: making a difference to the spatiotemporal shape of the wave-function of those particles. But let that pass.) For how could she do or say anything different, if none of her particles moved any differently? But if something non-physical sometimes makes a difference to the motions of physical particles, then physics as we know it is wrong. Not just silent, not just incomplete – wrong. Either the particles are caused to change their motion without benefit of any force, or else there is some extra force that works very differently from the usual four. To believe in the phenomenal aspect of the world, but deny that it is epiphenomenal, is to bet against the truth of physics. Given the success of physics hitherto, and even with due allowance for the foundational ailments of quantum mechanics, such betting is rash! A friend of the phenomenal aspect would be safer to join Jackson in defense of *epiphenomenal* qualia.

But there is more to the case than just an empirical bet in favor of physics. Suppose there is a phenomenal aspect of the world, and suppose it does make some difference to the motions of Mary's jaw or the noises out of her mouth. Then we can describe the phenomenal aspect, if we know enough, in terms of its physical effects. It is that on which physical phenomena depend in such-and-such way. This descriptive handle will enable us to give lessons on it to the inexperienced. But in so far as we can give lessons on it, what we have is just parapsychology. That whereof we cannot learn except by having the experience still eludes us. I do not argue that *everything* about the alleged distinctive subject matter of phenomenal information must be epiphenomenal. Part of it may be parapsychological instead. But I insist that *some* aspect of it must be epiphenomenal. Suppose that the Hypothesis of Phenomenal Information is true and suppose that V_1 and V_2

are all of the maximally specific phenomenal possibilities concerning what it's like to taste Vegemite; anyone who tastes Vegemite will find out which one obtains, and no one else can. And suppose that P_1 and P_2 are all the maximally specific physical possibilities. (Of course we really need far more than two Ps, and maybe a friend of phenomenal information would want more than two Vs, but absurdly small numbers will do for an example.) Then we have four alternative hypotheses about the causal independence or dependence of the Ps on the Vs. Each one can be expressed as a pair of counterfactual conditionals. Two hypotheses are patterns of dependence:

K_1: if V_1 then P_1, if V_2 then P_2
K_2: if V_1 then P_2, if V_2 then P_1

The other two are patterns of independence:

K_3: if V_1 then P_1, if V_2 then P_1
K_4: if V_1 then P_2, if V_2 then P_2

These dependency hypotheses are, I take it, contingent propositions. They are made true, if they are, by some contingent feature of the world, though it's indeed a vexed question what sort of feature it is.[11] Now we have eight joint possibilities:

$K_1V_1P_1$	$K_3V_1P_1$	$K_3V_2P_1$	$K_2V_2P_1$
$K_2V_1P_2$	$K_4V_1P_2$	$K_4V_2P_2$	$K_1V_2P_2$

Between the four on the top row and the four on the bottom row, there is the physical difference between P_1 and P_2. Between the four on the left and the four on the right, there is the phenomenal difference between V_1 and V_2. And between the four on the edges and the four in the middle there is a parapsychological difference. It is the difference between dependence and independence of the physical on the phenomenal; between efficacy and epiphenomenalism, so far as this one example is concerned. There's nothing ineffable about that. Whether or not you've tasted Vegemite, and whether or not you can conceive of the alleged difference between V_1 and V_2, you can still be told whether the physical difference between P_1 and P_2 does or doesn't depend on some part of the phenomenal aspect of the world.

Lessons can teach the inexperienced which parapsychological possibility obtains, dependence or independence. Let it be dependence: we have either K_1 or K_2. For if we had independence, then already we would have found our epiphenomenal difference: namely, the difference between V_1 and V_2. And lessons can teach the inexperienced which of the two physical possibilities obtains. Without loss of generality let it be P_1. Now two of our original eight joint possibilities remain open: $K_1V_1P_1$ and $K_2V_2P_1$. The difference between those is not at all physical, and not at all parapsychological: it's P_1, and it's dependence, in both cases. The difference is entirely phenomenal. And also it is entirely epiphenomenal. Nothing physical, and nothing parapsychological, depends on the difference between $K_1V_1P_1$ and $K_2V_2P_1$. We have the same sort of pattern of dependence either way; it's just that the phenomenal possibilities have been swapped. Whether it's independence or whether it's dependence, therefore, we have found an epiphenomenal part of the phenomenal aspect of the world. It is the residue left behind when we remove the parapsychological part.

Suppose that someday I taste Vegemite, and hold forth about how I know at last what it's like. The sound of my holding forth is a physical effect, part of the realized physical possibility P_1. This physical effect is exactly the same whether it's part of the joint possibility $K_1V_1P_1$ or part of its alternative $K_2V_2P_1$. It may be caused by V_1 in accordance with K_1, or it may instead be caused by V_2 in accordance with K_2, but it's the same either way. So it does not occur because we have K_1V_1 rather than K_2V_2, or vice versa. The alleged difference between these two possibilities does nothing to explain the alleged physical manifestation of my finding out which one of them is realized. It is in that way that the difference is epiphenomenal. That makes it very queer, and repugnant to good sense.

The Ability Hypothesis

So the Hypothesis of Phenomenal Information turns out to be very peculiar indeed. It would be nice, and not only for materialists, if we could reject it. For materialists, it is essential to reject it. And we can. There is an alternative hypothesis about what it is to learn what an experience is like: the *Ability Hypothesis*. Laurence Nemirow summarizes it thus:

> some modes of understanding consist, not in the grasping of facts, but in the acquisition of abilities . . . . As for understanding an experience, we may construe that as an ability to place oneself, at will, in a state representative of the experience. I understand the experience of seeing red if I can at will visualize red. Now it is perfectly clear why there must be a special connection between the ability to place oneself in a state representative of a given experience and the point of view of experiencer: exercising the ability just *is* what we call "adopting the point of view of experiencer." . . . We can, then, come to terms with the subjectivity of our understanding of experience without positing subjective facts as the objects of our understanding. This account

explains, incidentally, the linguistic incommunicability of our subjective understanding of experience (a phenomenon which might seem to support the hypothesis of subjective facts). The latter is explained as a special case of the linguistic incommunicability of abilities to place oneself at will in a given state, such as the state of having lowered blood pressure, and the state of having wiggling ears.[12]

If you have a new experience, you gain abilities to remember and to imagine. After you taste Vegemite, and you learn what it's like, you can afterward remember the experience you had. By remembering how it once was, you can afterward imagine such an experience. Indeed, even if you eventually forget the occasion itself, you will very likely retain your ability to imagine such an experience.

Further, you gain an ability to recognize the same experience if it comes again. If you taste Vegemite on another day, you will probably know that you have met the taste once before. And if, while tasting Vegemite, you know that it is Vegemite you are tasting, then you will be able to put the name to the experience if you have it again. Or if you are told nothing at the time, but later you somehow know that it is Vegemite that you are then remembering or imagining tasting, again you can put the name to the experience, or to the memory, or to the experience of imagining, if it comes again. Here, the ability you gain is an ability to gain information if given other information. Nevertheless, the information gained is not phenomenal, and the ability to gain information is not the same thing as information itself.

Earlier, I mentioned "knowing what an experience is like under a description." Now I can say that what I meant by this was having the ability to remember or imagine an experience while also knowing the egocentric proposition that what one is then imagining is the experience of such-and-such description. One might well know what an experience is like under one description, but not under another. One might even know what some experience is like, but not under any description whatever – unless it be some rather trivial description like "that queer taste that I'm imagining right now." That is what would happen if you slipped a dab of Vegemite into my food without telling me what it was: afterward, I would know what it was like to taste Vegemite, but not under that description, and not under any other non-trivial description. It might be suggested that "knowing what it's like to taste Vegemite" really means what I'd call "knowing what it's like to taste Vegemite under the description 'tasting Vegemite'"; and if so, knowing what it's like would involve both ability and information. I disagree. For surely it would make sense to say: "I know this experience well, I've long known what it's like, but only today have I found out that it's the experience of tasting Vegemite." But this verbal question is unimportant. For the information involved in knowing what it's like under a description, and allegedly involved in knowing what it's like, is anyhow not the queer phenomenal information that needs rejecting.

(Is there a problem here for the friend of phenomenal information? Suppose he says that knowing what it's like to taste Vegemite means knowing that the taste of Vegemite has a certain "phenomenal character." This requires putting the name to the taste, so clearly it corresponds to our notion of knowing what it's like to taste Vegemite under the description "tasting Vegemite." But we also have our notion of knowing what it's like *simpliciter*, and what can he offer that corresponds to that? Perhaps he should answer by appeal to a trivial description, as follows: knowing what it's like *simpliciter* means knowing what it's like under the trivial description "taste I'm imagining now," and that means knowing that the taste one is imagining now has a certain phenomenal character.)

As well as gaining the ability to remember and imagine the experience you had, you also gain the ability to imagine related experiences that you never had. After tasting Vegemite, you might for instance become able to imagine tasting Vegemite ice cream. By performing imaginative experiments, you can predict with some confidence what you would do in circumstances that have never arisen – whether you'd ask for a second helping of Vegemite ice cream, for example.

These abilities to remember and imagine and recognize are abilities you cannot gain (unless by super-neurosurgery, or by magic) except by tasting Vegemite and learning what it's like. You can't get them by taking lessons on the physics or the parapsychology of the experience, or even by taking comprehensive lessons that cover the whole of physics and parapsychology. The Ability Hypothesis says that knowing what an experience is like just *is* the possession of these abilities to remember, imagine, and recognize. It isn't the possession of any kind of information, ordinary or peculiar. It isn't knowing that certain possibilities aren't actualized. It isn't knowing-that. It's knowing-how. Therefore it should be no surprise that lessons won't teach you what an experience is like. Lessons impart information; ability is something else. Knowledge-that does not automatically provide know-how.

There are parallel cases. Some know how to wiggle their ears; others don't. If you can't do it, no amount of information will help. Some know how to eat with chopsticks, others don't. Information will help up to a point – for instance, if your trouble is that you hold one chopstick in each hand – but no amount of information, by itself, will bring you to a very high level of know-how. Some know how to recognize a C-38 locomotive by sight, others don't. If you don't, it won't much help if you memorize a detailed geometrical description of its shape, even though that does all the eliminating of possibilities that there is to be done. (Conversely, knowing the shape by sight doesn't enable you to write down the geometrical description.) Information very often contributes to know-how, but often it doesn't contribute enough. That's why music students have to practice.

Know-how is ability. But of course some aspects of ability are in no sense knowledge: strength, sufficient funds. Other aspects of ability are, purely and simply, a matter of information. If you want to know how to open the combination lock on the bank vault, information is all you need. It remains that there are aspects of ability that do *not* consist simply of possession of information, and that we *do* call knowledge. The Ability Hypothesis holds that knowing what an experience is like is that sort of knowledge.

If the Ability Hypothesis is the correct analysis of knowing what an experience is like, then phenomenal information is an illusion. We ought to explain that illusion. It would be feeble, I think, just to say that we're fooled by the ambiguity of the word "know": we confuse ability with information because we confuse knowledge in the sense of knowing-how with knowledge in the sense of knowing-that. There may be two senses of the word "know," but they are well and truly entangled. They mark the two pure endpoints of a range of mixed cases. The usual thing is that we gain information and ability together. If so, it should be no surprise if we apply to pure cases of gaining ability, or to pure cases of gaining information, the same word "know" that we apply to all the mixed cases.

Along with information and ability, acquaintance is a third element of the mixture. If Lloyd George died too soon, there's a sense in which Father never can know him. Information won't do it, even if Father is a most thorough biographer and the archives are very complete. (And the trouble isn't that there's some very special information about someone that you can only get by being in his presence.) Know-how won't do it either, no matter how good Father may be at imagining Lloyd George, seemingly remembering him, and recognizing him. (Father may be able to recognize Lloyd George even if there's no longer any Lloyd George to recognize – if *per impossible* he did turn up, Father could tell it was him.) Again, what we have is not just a third separate sense of "know." Meeting someone, gaining a lot of information about him that would be hard to gain otherwise, and gaining abilities regarding him usually go together. The pure cases are exceptions.

A friend of phenomenal information will agree, of course, that when we learn what an experience is like, we gain abilities to remember, imagine, and recognize. But he will say that it is because we gain phenomenal information that we gain the abilities. He might even say the same about other cases of gaining know-how: you can recognize the C-38 when you have phenomenal information about what it's like to see that shape, you can eat with chopsticks or wiggle your ears when you gain phenomenal information about the experience of doing so, and so on. What should friends of the Ability Hypothesis make of this? Is he offering a conjecture, which we must reject, about the causal origin of abilities? I think not. He thinks, as we do, that experiences leave distinctive traces in people, and that these traces enable us to do things. Likewise being taught to recognize a C-38 or to eat with chopsticks, or whatever happens on first wiggling the ears, leave traces that enable us to do things afterward. That much is common ground. He also interprets these enabling traces as representations that bear information about their causes. (If the same traces had been caused in some deviant way they might perhaps have carried misinformation.) We might even be able to accept that too. The time for us to quarrel comes only when he says that these traces represent special phenomenal facts, facts which cannot be represented in any other way, and therefore which cannot be taught in physics lessons or even in parapsychology lessons. That is the part, and the *only* part, which we must reject. But that is no part of his psychological story about how we gain abilities. It is just a gratuitous metaphysical gloss on that story.

We say that learning what an experience is like means gaining certain abilities. If the causal basis for those abilities turns out also to be a special kind of representation of some sort of information, so be it. We need only deny that it represents a special kind of information about a special subject matter. Apart from that it's up for grabs what, if anything, it may represent. The details of stimuli: the chemical composition of Vegemite, reflectances of surfaces, the motions of well-handled chopsticks or of ears? The details of inner states produced by those stimuli: patterns of firings of nerves? We could agree to either, so long as we did not confuse "having information" represented in this special way with having the same information in the form of knowledge or belief. Or we could disagree. Treating the ability-conferring trace as a representation is optional. What's essential is that when we learn what an experience is like by having it, we gain abilities to remember, imagine, and recognize.

Acknowledgment

Part of this paper derives from a lecture at LaTrobe University in 1981. I thank La Trobe for support in 1981, Harvard University for support under a Santayana Fellowship in 1988, and Frank Jackson for very helpful discussion.

Notes

1 See Frank Jackson, "Epiphenomenal qualia," *Philosophical Quarterly* 32 (1982), pp. 127–36: "What Mary didn't know," *Journal of Philosophy* 83 (1986), pp. 291–5; reprinted as Chapter 22 in this volume.

2 See B.A. Farrell, "Experience," *Mind* 59 (1950), pp. 170–98; and Thomas Nagel, "What is it like to be a bat?," *Philosophical Review* 83 (1974), pp. 435–50, also in Thomas Nagel, *Mortal Questions* (Cambridge: Cambridge University Press, 1979).

3 See Peter Unger, "On experience and the development of the understanding," *American Philosophical Quarterly* 3 (1966), pp. 1–9.

4 For such speculation, see Paul M. Churchland, "Reduction, qualia, and the direct introspection of brain states," *Journal of Philosophy* 82 (1985), pp. 8–28.

5 See my "Attitudes *de dicto* and *de se*," *Philosophical Review* 88 (1979), pp. 513–43, also in my *Philosophical Papers*, vol. 1 (New York: Oxford University Press, 1983); and Roderick Chisholm, *The First Person: An Essay on Reference and Intentionality* (Minneapolis: University of Minnesota Press, 1981).

6 See Gilbert Harman, "The intrinsic quality of experience," *Philosophical Perspectives* 4 (1990); reprinted as Chapter 25 in this volume.

7 See Ned Block and Jerry A. Fodor, "What psychological states are not," *Philosophical Review* 81 (1972), pp. 159–81, also in Ned Block (ed.), *Readings in Philosophy of Psychology*, vol. I (Cambridge, Mass.: Harvard University Press, 1980); and my "Mad pain and Martian pain," in *Readings in Philosophy of Psychology*, vol. 1, and in my *Philosophical Papers*, vol. 1.

8 See my "New work for a theory of universals," *Australasian Journal of Philosophy* 61 (1983), pp. 343–77, especially pp. 361–4. For a different view about how to state minimal Materialism, see Terence Horgan, "Supervenience and microphysics," *Pacific Philosophical Quarterly* 63 (1982), pp 29–43.

9 On recombination of possibilities, see my *On the Plurality of Worlds* (Oxford: Blackwell, 1986), pp. 87–92. The present argument may call for a principle that also allows recombination of properties; I now think that would not necessarily require treating properties as non-spatiotemporal parts of their instances. On recombination of properties, see also D.M. Armstrong, *A Combinatorial Theory of Possibility* (Cambridge: Cambridge University Press, 1989).

10 See *On the Plurality of Worlds*, pp. 142–65, on linguistic ersatz possibilities.

11 On dependency hypotheses, see my "Causal decision theory," *Australasian Journal of Philosophy* 59 (1981), pp. 5–30, reprinted in my *Philosophical Papers*, vol. II (New York: Oxford University Press, 1986).

12 Laurence Nemirow, "Review of Nagel's *Mortal Questions*," *Philosophical Review* 89 (1980), pp. 475–6. For a fuller statement, see Nemirow, "Physicalism and the cognitive role of acquaintance"; and *Functionalism and the Subjective Quality of Experience* (doctoral dissertation, Stanford, 1979). See also Michael Tye, "The subjective qualities of experience," *Mind* 95 (1986), pp. 1–17.

   I should record a disagreement with Nemirow on one very small point. We agree that the phrase "what experience E is like" does not denote some "subjective quality" of E, something which supposedly would be part of the subject matter of the phenomenal information gained by having E. But whereas I have taken the phrase to denote E itself, Nemirow takes it to be a syncategorematic part of the expression "know what experience E is like." See "Physicalism and the cognitive role of acquaintance," section III.

24

Gilbert Harman, "The Intrinsic Quality of Experience"*

The problem

Many philosophers, psychologists, and artificial intelligence researchers accept a broadly functionalist view of the relation between mind and body, for example, viewing the mind in the body as something like a computer in a robot, perhaps with massively parallel processing (as in Rumelhart and McClelland 1986). But this view of the mind has not gone unchallenged. Some philosophers and others object strenuously that functionalism must inevitably fail to account for the most important part of mental life, namely, the subjective feel of conscious experience.

The computer model of mind represents one version of functionalism, although it is not the only version. In its most general form, functionalism defines mental states and processes by their causal or functional relations to each other and to perceptual inputs from the world outside and behavioral outputs expressed in action. According to functionalism, it is the functional relations that are important, not the intrinsic qualities of the stuff in which these relations are instanced. Just as the same computer programs can be run on different computers made out of different materials, so functionalism allows for the same mental states and events in beings with very different physical constitutions, since the very same functional relations might be instantiated in beings with very different physical makeups. According to functionalism, beliefs, desires, thoughts, and feelings are not limited to beings that are materially like ourselves. Such psychological states

*The preparation of this paper was supported in part by research grants to Princeton University from the James S. McDonnell Foundation and the National Science Foundation.

Gilbert Harman, "The Intrinsic Quality of Experience," *Philosophical Perspectives*, 4 (1990): 31–52.

and events might also occur, for example, in silicon based beings, as long as the right functional relations obtained.

Functionalism can allow for the possibility that something about silicon makes it impossible for the relevant relations to obtain in silicon based beings, perhaps because the relevant events could not occur fast enough in silicon. It is even conceivable that the relevant functional relations might obtain only in the sort of material that makes up human brains (Thagard 1986; Dennett 1987, Chapter 9). Functionalism implies that in such a case the material is important only because it is needed for the relevant functional relations and not because of some other more mysterious or magical connection between that sort of matter and a certain sort of consciousness.

Various issues arise within the general functionalist approach. For one thing, there is a dispute about how to identify the inputs to a functional system. Should inputs be identified with events in the external environment (Harman 1988) or should they instead be identified with events that are more internal such as the stimulation of an organism's sensory organs (Block 1986)? There is also the possibility of disagreement as to how deterministic the relevant functional relations have to be. Do they have to be completely deterministic, or can they be merely probabilistic? Or might they even be simply nondeterministic, not even associated with definite probabilities (Harman 1973, pp. 51–53)?

I will not be concerned with these issues here. Instead, I will concentrate on the different and more basic issue that I have already mentioned, namely, whether this sort of functionalism, no matter how elaborated, can account for the subjective feel of experience, for "what it is like" (Nagel 1974) to undergo this or that experience. Furthermore, I will not consider the general challenge, "How does functionalism account for X?" for this or that X. Nor will I consider negative arguments against particular functionalist analyses. I will instead consider three related arguments that purport to demonstrate that functionalism cannot account for this aspect of experience. I will argue that all three arguments are fallacious. I will say little that is original and will for the most part merely elaborate points made many years ago (Quine 1960, p. 235; Anscombe 1965; Armstrong 1961, 1962, and especially 1968; Pitcher 1971), points that I do not think have been properly appreciated. The three arguments are these:

> First, when you attend to a pain in your leg or to your experience of the redness of an apple, you are aware of an intrinsic quality of your experience, where an intrinsic quality is a quality something has in itself, apart from its relations to other things. This quality of experience cannot be captured in a functional definition, since such a definition is concerned entirely with relations, relations between mental

states and perceptual input, relations among mental states, and relations between mental states and behavioral output. For example, "An essential feature of [Armstrong's functionalist] analysis is that it tells us nothing about the intrinsic nature of mental states. . . . He never takes seriously the natural objection that we must know the intrinsic nature of our own mental states since we experience them directly" (Nagel 1970).

Second, a person blind from birth could know all about the physical and functional facts of color perception without knowing what it is like to see something red. So, what it is like to see something red cannot be explicated in purely functional terms (Nagel 1974; Jackson 1982, 1986).

Third, it is conceivable that two people should have similarly functioning visual systems despite the fact that things that look red to one person look green to the other, things that look orange to the first person look blue to the second, and so forth (Lycan 1973; Shoemaker 1982). This sort of spectrum inversion in the way things look is possible but cannot be given a purely functional description, since by hypothesis there are no functional differences between the people in question. Since the way things look to a person is an aspect of that person's mental life, this means that an important aspect of a person's mental life cannot be explicated in purely functional terms.

Intentionality

In order to assess these arguments, I begin by remarking on what is sometimes called the intentionality of experience. Our experience of the world has content – that is, it represents things as being in a certain way. In particular, perceptual experience represents a perceiver as in a particular environment, for example, as facing a tree with brown bark and green leaves fluttering in a slight breeze. One thing that philosophers mean when they refer to this as the intentional content of experience is that the content of the experience may not reflect what is really there. Although it looks to me as if I am seeing a tree, that may be a clever illusion produced with tilted mirrors and painted backdrops. Or it may be a hallucination produced by a drug in my coffee.

There are many other examples of intentionality. Ponce de Leon searched Florida for the Fountain of Youth. What he was looking for was a fountain whose waters would give eternal youth to whoever would drink them. In fact, there is no such thing as a Fountain of Youth, but that does not mean Ponce de Leon wasn't looking for anything. He was looking for something. We can therefore say that his search had an intentional object.

But the thing that he was looking for, the intentional object of his search, did not (and does not) exist. A painting of a unicorn is a painting of something; it has a certain content. But the content does not correspond to anything actual; the thing that the painting represents does not exist. The painting has an intentional content in the relevant sense of "intentional."

Imagining or mentally picturing a unicorn is usefully compared with a painting of a unicorn. In both cases the content is not actual; the object pictured, the intentional object of the picturing, does not exist. It is only an intentional object.

This is not to suppose that mentally picturing a unicorn involves an awareness of a mental picture of a unicorn. I am comparing mentally picturing something with a picture of something, not with a perception of a picture. An awareness of a picture has as its intentional object a picture. The picture has as its intentional object a unicorn. Imagining a unicorn is different from imagining a picture of a unicorn. The intentional object of the imagining is a unicorn, not a picture of a unicorn.

It is very important to distinguish between the properties of a represented object and the properties of a representation of that object. Clearly, these properties can be very different. The unicorn is pictured as having four legs and a single horn. The painting of the unicorn does not have four legs and a single horn. The painting is flat and covered with paint. The unicorn is not pictured as flat or covered with paint. Similarly, an imagined unicorn is imagined as having legs and a horn. The imagining of the unicorn has no legs or horn. The imagining of the unicorn is a mental activity. The unicorn is not imagined as either an activity or anything mental.

The notorious sense datum theory of perception arises through failing to keep these elementary points straight. According to that ancient theory, perception of external objects in the environment is always indirect and mediated by a more direct awareness of a mental sense datum. Defenders of the sense datum theory argue for it by appealing to the so-called argument from illusion. This argument begins with the uncontroversial premise that the way things are presented in perception is not always the way they are. Eloise sees some brown and green. But there is nothing brown and green before her; it is all an illusion or hallucination. From this the argument fallaciously infers that the brown and green Eloise sees is not external to her and so must be internal or mental. Since veridical, nonillusory, nonhallucinatory perception can be qualitatively indistinguishable from illusory or hallucinatory perception, the argument concludes that in all cases of perception Eloise is directly aware of something inner and mental and only indirectly aware of external objects like trees and leaves.

An analogous argument about paintings would start from the premise that a painting can be a painting of a unicorn even though there are no unicorns. From this it might be concluded that the painting is "in the first instance" a painting of something else that is actual, for example, the painter's idea of a unicorn.

In order to see that such arguments are fallacious, consider the corresponding argument applied to searches: "Ponce de Leon was searching for the Fountain of Youth. But there is no such thing. So he must have been searching for something mental." This is just a mistake. From the fact that there is no Fountain of Youth, it does not follow that Ponce de Leon was searching for something mental. In particular, he was not looking for an idea of the Fountain of Youth. He already had the idea. What he wanted was a real Fountain of Youth, not just the idea of such a thing.

The painter has painted a picture of a unicorn. The picture painted is not a picture of an idea of a unicorn. The painter might be at a loss to paint a picture of an idea, especially if he is not familiar with conceptual art. It may be that the painter has an idea of a unicorn and tries to capture that idea in his painting. But that is to say his painting is a painting of the same thing that his idea is an idea of. The painting is not a painting of the idea, but a painting of what the idea is about.

In the same way, what Eloise sees before her is a tree, whether or not it is a hallucination. That is to say, the content of her visual experience is that she is presented with a tree, not with an idea of a tree. Perhaps, Eloise's visual experience involves some sort of mental picture of the environment. It does not follow that she is aware of a mental picture. If there is a mental picture, it may be that what she is aware of is whatever is represented by that mental picture; but then that mental picture represents something in the world, not something in the mind.

Now, we sometimes count someone as perceiving something only if that thing exists. So, if there is no tree before her and Eloise is suffering from a hallucination, we might describe this either by saying that Eloise sees something that is not really there or by saying that she does not really see anything at all but only seems to see something. There is not a use of "search for" corresponding to this second use of "see" that would allow us to say that, because there was and is no such thing as the Fountain of Youth, Ponce de Leon was not really searching for anything at all.

But this ambiguity in perceptual verbs does not affect the point I am trying to make. To see that it does not, let us use "see†" ("see-dagger") for the sense of "see" in which the object seen might not exist, as when Macbeth saw a dagger before him.[1] And let us use "see*" ("see-star") for the sense of "see" in which only things that exist can be seen. Macbeth saw† a dagger but he did not see* a dagger.

The argument from illusion starts from a case in which Eloise "sees" something brown and green before her, although there is nothing brown and green before her in the external physical world. From this, the argument infers that the brown and green she sees must be internal and mental. Now, if "see" is "see†" here, this is the fallacy already noted, like that of concluding that Ponce de Leon was searching for something mental from the fact that there is no Fountain of Youth in the external world. On the other hand, if "see" is "see*" here, then the premise of the argument simply begs the question. No reason at all has so far been given for the claim that Eloise sees* something brown and green in this case. It is true that her perceptual experience represents her as visually presented with something brown and green; but that is to say merely that she sees† something brown and green, not that she sees* anything at all. (From now on I will suppress the † and * modification of perceptual verbs unless indication of which sense is meant is crucial to the discussion.)

Here, some philosophers (e.g. Jackson 1977) would object as follows:

> You agree that there is a sense in which Eloise sees something green and brown when there is nothing green and brown before her in the external world. You are able to deny that this brown and green thing is mental by taking it to be a nonexistent and merely intentional object. But it is surely more reasonable to suppose that one is in this case aware of something mental than to suppose that one is aware of something that does not exist. How can there be anything that does not exist? The very suggestion is a contradiction in terms, since "be" simply means "exist," so that you are really saying that there exists something that does not exist (Quine 1948). There are no such things as nonexistent objects!

In reply, let me concede immediately that I do not have a well worked out theory of intentional objects. Parsons (1980) offers one such theory, although I do not mean to express an opinion as to the success of Parsons' approach. Indeed, I am quite willing to believe that there are not really any nonexistent objects and that apparent talk of such objects should be analyzed away somehow. I do not see that it is my job to resolve this issue. However this issue is resolved, the theory that results had better end up agreeing that Ponce de Leon was looking for something when he was looking for the Fountain of Youth, even though there is no Fountain of Youth, and the theory had better *not* have the consequence that Ponce de Leon was looking for something mental. If a logical theory can account for searches for things that do not, as it happens, exist, it can presumably also allow for a sense of "see" in which Macbeth can see something that does not really exist.

Another point is that Eloise's visual experience does not just present a tree. It presents a tree as viewed from a certain place. Various features that the tree is presented as having are presented as relations between the viewer and the tree, for example, features the tree has from here. The tree is presented as "in front of" and "hiding" certain other trees. It is presented as fuller on "the right." It is presented as the same size "from here" as a closer smaller tree, which is not to say that it really looks the same in size, only that it is presented as subtending roughly the same angle from here as the smaller tree. To be presented as the same in size from here is not to be presented as the same in size, period.

I do not mean to suggest that the way the tree is visually presented as being from here is something that is easily expressed in words. In particular, I do not mean to suggest that the tree can thus be presented as subtending a certain visual angle only to someone who understands words like "subtend" and "angle" (as is assumed in Peacocke 1983, Chapter 1). I mean only that this feature of a tree from here is an objective feature of the tree in relation to here, a feature to which perceivers are sensitive and which their visual experience can somehow represent things as having from here.

Now, perhaps, Eloise's visual experience even presents a tree as seen by her, that is, as an object of her visual experience. If so, there is a sense after all in which Eloise's visual experience represents something mental: it represents objects in the world as objects of visual experience. But this does not mean that Eloise's visual experience in any way reveals to her the intrinsic properties of that experience by virtue of which it has the content it has.

I want to stress this point, because it is very important. Eloise is aware of the tree as a tree that she is now seeing. So, we can suppose she is aware of some features of her current visual experience. In particular, she is aware that her visual experience has the feature of being an experience of seeing a tree. That is to be aware of an intentional feature of her experience; she is aware that her experience has a certain content. On the other hand, I want to argue that she is not aware of those intrinsic features of her experience by virtue of which it has that content. Indeed, I believe that she has no access at all to the intrinsic features of her mental representation that make it a mental representation of seeing a tree.

Things are different with paintings. In the case of a painting Eloise can be aware of those features of the painting that are responsible for its being a painting of a unicorn. That is, she can turn her attention to the pattern of the paint on the canvas by virtue of which the painting represents a unicorn. But in the case of her visual experience of a tree, I want to say that she is not aware of, as it were, the mental paint by virtue of which her experience is an experience of seeing a tree. She is aware only of the intentional or relational features of her experience, not of its intrinsic nonintentional features.

Some sense datum theorists will object that Eloise is indeed aware of the relevant mental paint when she is aware of an arrangement of color, because these sense datum theorists assert that the color she is aware of is inner and mental and not a property of external objects. But, this sense datum claim is counter to ordinary visual experience. When Eloise sees a tree before her, the colors she experiences are all experienced as features of the tree and its surroundings. None of them are experienced as intrinsic features of her experience. Nor does she experience any features of anything as intrinsic features of her experience. And that is true of you too. There is nothing special about Eloise's visual experience. When you see a tree, you do not experience any features as intrinsic features of your experience. Look at a tree and try to turn your attention to intrinsic features of your visual experience. I predict you will find that the only features there to turn your attention to will be features of the presented tree, including relational features of the tree "from here."

The sense datum theorists' view about our immediate experience of color is definitely not the naive view; it does not represent the viewpoint of ordinary perception. The sense datum theory is not the result of phenomenological study; it is rather the result of an argument, namely, the argument from illusion. But that argument is either invalid or question-begging, as we have seen.

It is very important to distinguish what are experienced as intrinsic features of the intentional object of experience from intrinsic features of the experience itself. It is not always easy to distinguish these things, but they can be distinguished. Consider the experience of having a pain in your right leg. It is very tempting to confuse features of what you experience as happening in your leg with intrinsic features of your experience. But the happening in your leg that you are presented with is the intentional object of your experience; it is not the experience itself. The content of your experience is that there is a disturbance of a certain specific sort in your right leg. The intentional object of the experience is an event located in your right leg. The experience itself is not located in your right leg. If the experience is anywhere specific, it is somewhere in your brain.

Notice that the content of your experience may not be true to what is actually happening. A slipped disc in your back may press against your sciatic nerve making it appear that there is a disturbance in your right leg when there really is not. The intentional object of your painful experience may not exist. Of course, that is not to say there is no pain in your leg. You do feel something there. But there is a sense in which what you feel in your leg is an illusion or hallucination.

It is true that, if Melvin hallucinates a pink elephant, the elephant that Melvin sees does not exist. But the pain in your leg resulting from a slipped disc in your back certainly does exist.[2] The pain is not an intentional object in quite the way the elephant is. The pain in your leg caused by the slipped disc in your back is more like the afterimage of a bright light. If you look at a blank wall, you see the image on the wall. The image is on the wall, the pain is in your leg. There is no physical spot on the wall, there is no physical disturbance in your leg. The afterimage exists, the pain exists. When we talk about afterimages or referred pains, some of what we say is about our experience and some of what we say is about the intentional object of that experience. When we say the pain or afterimage exists, we mean that the experience exists. When we say that the afterimage is on the wall or that the pain is in your leg, we are talking about the location of the intentional object of that experience.

Assessment of the first objection

We are now in a position to reject the first of the three arguments against functionalism which I now repeat:

> When you attend to a pain in your leg or to your experience of the redness of an apple, you are aware of an intrinsic quality of your experience, where an intrinsic quality is a quality something has in itself, apart from its relations to other things. This quality of experience cannot be captured in a functional definition, since such a definition is concerned entirely with relations, relations between mental states and perceptual input, relations among mental states, and relations between mental states and behavioral output.

We can now see that this argument fails through confounding a quality of the intentional object of an experience with a quality of the experience itself. When you attend to a pain in your leg or to your experience of the redness of an apple, you are attending to a quality of an occurrence in your leg or a quality of the apple. Perhaps this quality is presented to you as an intrinsic quality of the occurrence in your leg or as an intrinsic quality of the surface of the apple. But it is not at all presented as an intrinsic quality of your experience. And, since you are not aware of the intrinsic character of your experience, the fact that functionalism abstracts from the intrinsic character of experience does not show it leaves out anything you are aware of.

To be sure, there are possible complications. Suppose David undergoes brain surgery which he watches in a mirror. Suppose that he sees certain intrinsic features of the firing of certain neurons in his brain and suppose that the firing of these neurons is the realization of part of the experience he is having at that moment. In that case, David is aware of intrinsic features of his experience. But that way of being aware of intrinsic features of experience is not incompatible with functionalism. Given a functionalist account of David's perception of trees, tables, and the brain processes of other people, the same account applies when the object perceived happens to be David's own brain processes. The awareness David has of his own brain processes is psychologically similar to the awareness any other sighted perceiver might have of those same brain processes, including perceivers constructed in a very different way from the way in which David is constructed.

According to functionalism, the psychologically relevant properties of an internal process are all functional properties. The intrinsic nature of the process is relevant only inasmuch as it is responsible for the process's having the functional properties it has. I have been considering the objection that certain intrinsic features of experience must be psychologically relevant properties apart from their contribution to function, since these are properties we are or can be aware of. The objection is not just that we can become aware of intrinsic features of certain mental processes in the way just mentioned, that is, by perceiving in a mirror the underlying physical processes that realize those mental processes. That would not be an objection to functionalism. The objection is rather that all or most conscious experience has intrinsic aspects of which we are or can be aware in such a way that these aspects of the experience are psychologically significant over and above the contribution they make to function.

Of course, to say that these aspects are psychologically significant is not to claim that they are or ought to be significant for the science of psychology. Rather, they are supposed to be psychologically significant in the sense of mentally significant, whether or not this aspect of experience is susceptible of scientific understanding. The objection is that any account of our mental life that does not count these intrinsic properties as mental or psychological properties leaves out a crucial aspect of our experience.

My reply to this objection is that it cannot be defended without confusing intrinsic features of the intentional object of experience with intrinsic features of the experience. Apart from that confusion, there is no reason to think that we are ever aware of the relevant intrinsic features of our experiences.

There are other ways in which one might be aware of intrinsic features of our experience without that casting any doubt on functionalism. For example, one might be aware of intrinsic features of experience without being aware of them as intrinsic features of experience, just as Ortcutt can be aware of a man who, as it happens, is a spy without being aware of the man as a spy. When Eloise sees a tree, she is aware of her perceptual experience as an experience with a certain intentional content. Suppose that her experience is realized by a particular physical event and that certain intrinsic features of the event are in this case responsible for certain intentional features of Eloise's experience. Perhaps there is then a sense in which Eloise is aware of this physical process and aware of those intrinsic features, although she is not aware of them as the intrinsic features that they are.

Even if that is so, it is no objection to functionalism. The intrinsic features that Eloise is aware of in that case are no more psychologically significant than is the property of being a spy to Ortcutt's perception of a man who happens to be a spy. The case gives no reason to think that there is a psychologically significant difference between Eloise's experience and the experience of any functional duplicate of Eloise that is made of different stuff from what Eloise is made of.

Similarly, if Eloise undertakes the sort of education recommended by Paul Churchland (1985) so that she automatically thinks of the intentional aspects of her experience in terms of their neurophysiological causes, then she may be aware of intrinsic features of her experience as the very features that they are. But again that would be no objection to functionalism, since it gives no reason to think that there is a psychological difference between Eloise after such training and a robot who is Eloise's functional duplicate and who has been given similar training (Shoemaker 1985). The duplicate now wrongly thinks of certain aspects of its experience as certain features of certain neurological processes – wrongly, because the relevant processes in the duplicate are not neurological processes at all.

Observe, by the way, that I am not offering any sort of positive argument that Eloise and her duplicate must have experiences that are psychologically similar in all respects. I am only observing that the cases just considered are compatible with the functionalist claim that their experiences are similar.

The objections to functionalism that I am considering in this paper claim that certain intrinsic properties of experience so inform the experience that any experience with different intrinsic properties would have a different psychological character. What I have argued so far is that this objection is not established by simple inspection of our experience.

Perception and understanding

Now, let me turn to the second objection, which I repeat:

> A person blind from birth could know all about the physical and functional facts of color perception without knowing what it is like to see something red. So, what it is like to see something red cannot be explicated in purely functional terms.

In order to address this objection, I have to say something about the functionalist theory of the content of mental representations and, more particularly, something about the functionalist theory of concepts. I have to do this because to know what it is like to see something red is to be capable of representing to yourself something's being red. You can represent that to yourself only if you have the relevant concept of what it is for something to be red. The blind person lacks the full concept of redness that a sighted person has; so the blind person cannot fully represent what it is for a sighted person to see something red. Therefore, the blind person cannot be said to know what it is like to see something red.

One kind of functionalist account of mental representation supposes that mental representations are constructed from concepts, where the content of a representation is determined by the concepts it contains and the way these concepts are put together to form that representation (Harman 1987). In this view, what it is to have a given concept is functionally determined. Someone has the appropriate concept of something's being red if and only if the person has available a concept that functions in the appropriate way. The relevant functioning may involve connections with the use of other concepts, connections to perceptual input, and/or connections to behavioral output. In this case, connections to perceptual input are crucial. If the concept is to function in such a way that the person has the full concept of something's being red, the person must be disposed to form representations involving that concept as the natural and immediate consequence of seeing something red. Since the blind person lacks any concept of this sort, the blind person lacks the full concept of something's being red. Therefore, the blind person does not know what it is like to see something red.

It is not easy to specify the relevant functional relation precisely. Someone who goes blind later in life will normally retain the relevant concept of something's being red. Such a person has a concept that he or she would be able to use in forming such immediate visual representations except for the condition that interferes in his or her case with normal visual perception. So, the right functional relation holds for such a person. I am supposing that the person blind from birth has no such concept; that is, the person has no concept of something's being red that could be immediately brought into service in visual representations of the environment if the person were suddenly to acquire sight.

We are now in a position to assess the claim that the person blind from birth could know all the physical and functional facts about color perception without knowing what it is like to see something red. I claim that there is one important functional fact about color perception that the blind person cannot know, namely, that there is a concept R such that when a normal perceiver sees something red in good lighting conditions, the perceiver has visual experience with a representational structure containing this concept *R*. The person blind from birth does not know that fact, because in order to know it the person needs to be able to represent that fact to him or herself, which requires having the relevant concepts. A key concept needed to represent that fact is the concept of something's being red, because the fact in question is a fact about what happens when a normal perceiver sees something red. Since the person blind from birth does not have the full concept of something's being red, the person cannot fully understand that fact and so cannot know that fact.

The blind person might know something resembling this, for example, that there is a concept *R* such that, when a normal perceiver sees something that reflects light of such and such a frequency, the perceiver has visual experience with a representational structure containing this concept *R*. But that is to know something different.

The person blind from birth fails to know what it is like to see something red because he or she does not fully understand what it is for something to be red, that is, because he or she does not have the full concept of something's being red. So, contrary to what is assumed in the second objection, the person blind from birth does not know all the functional facts, since he or she does not know how the concept *R* functions with respect to the perception of things that are red.

This response to the second objection appeals to a functionalism that refers to the functions of concepts, not just to the functions of overall mental states. There are other versions of functionalism that try to make do with references to the functions of overall mental states, without appeal to concepts. Some of these versions identify the contents of such states with sets of possible worlds (or centered possible worlds). These versions of functionalism cannot respond to the objection in the way that I have responded. It is unclear to me whether any satisfactory response is possible on behalf of such theories. For example, Lewis (1983) is forced to say that although the person blind from birth lacks certain skills, e.g., the ability to recognize red objects just by looking at them in the way that sighted people can, this person lacks no information about visual perception. I am not happy with that response, since it is clearly false to say that the person blind from birth does not lack any information.

Inverted spectrum

I now turn to the third objection to functionalism, which I repeat:

> It is conceivable that two people should have similarly functioning visual systems despite the fact that things that look red to one person

503

look green to the other, things that look orange to the first person look blue to the second, and so forth. This sort of spectrum inversion in the way things look is possible but cannot be given a purely functional description, since by hypothesis there are no functional differences between the people in question. Since the way things look to a person is an aspect of that person's mental life, this means that there is an important aspect of a person's mental life that cannot be explicated in purely functional terms.

In order to discuss this objection, I need to say something more about how perceptual states function. In particular, I have to say something about how perceptual states function in relation to belief.

Perceptual experience represents a particular environment of the perceiver. Normally, a perceiver uses this representation as his or her representation of the environment. That is to say, the perceiver uses it in order to negotiate the furniture. In still other words, this representation is used as the perceiver's belief about the environment. This sort of use of perceptual representations is the normal case, although there are exceptions when a perceiver inhibits his or her natural tendency and refrains from using a perceptual representation (or certain aspects of that representation) as a guide to the environment, as a belief about the surroundings. The content of perceptual representation is functionally defined in part by the ways in which this representation normally arises in perception and in part by the ways in which the representation is normally used to guide actions (Armstrong 1961, 1968; Dennett 1969; Harman 1973).

The objection has us consider two people, call them Alice and Fred, with similarly functioning visual systems but with inverted spectra with respect to each other. Things that look red to Alice look green to Fred, things that look blue to Alice look orange to Fred, and so on. We are to imagine that this difference between Alice and Fred is not reflected in their behavior in any way. They both call ripe strawberries "red" and call grass "green" and they do this in the effortless ways in which normal perceivers do who have learned English in the usual ways.

Consider what this means for Alice in a normal case of perception. She looks at a ripe strawberry. Perceptual processing results in a perceptual representation of that strawberry, including a representation of its color. She uses this representation as her guide to the environment, that is, as her belief about the strawberry, in particular, her belief about its color. She expresses her belief about the color of the strawberry by using the words, "it is red." Similarly, for Fred. His perception of the strawberry results in a perceptual representation of the color of the strawberry that he uses as his belief about the color and expresses with the same words, "it is red."

Now, in the normal case of perception, there can be no distinction between how things look and how they are believed to be, since how things look is given by the content of one's perceptual representation and in the normal case one's perceptual representation is used as one's belief about the environment. The hypothesis of the inverted spectrum objection is that the strawberry looks different in color to Alice and to Fred. Since everything is supposed to be functioning in them in the normal way, it follows that they must have different beliefs about the color of the strawberry. If they had the same beliefs while having perceptual representations that differed in content, then at least one of them would have a perceptual representation that was not functioning as his or her belief about the color of the strawberry, which is to say that it would not be functioning in what we are assuming is the normal way.

A further consequence of the inverted spectrum hypothesis is that, since in the normal case Alice and Fred express their beliefs about the color of strawberries and grass by saying "it is red" and "it is green," they must mean something different by their color words. By "red" Fred means the way ripe strawberries look to him. Since that is the way grass looks to Alice, what Fred means by "red" is what she means by "green."

It is important to see that these really are consequences of the inverted spectrum hypothesis. If Alice and Fred meant the same thing by their color terms, then either (a) one of them would not be using these words to express his or her beliefs about color or (b) one of them would not be using his or her perceptual representations of color as his or her beliefs about color. In either case, there would be a failure of normal functioning, contrary to the hypothesis of the inverted spectrum objection.

According to functionalism, if Alice and Fred use words in the same way with respect to the same things, then they mean the same things by those words (assuming also that they are members of the same linguistic community and their words are taken from the common language). But this is just common sense. Suppose Alice and Humphrey are both members of the same linguistic community, using words in the same way, etc. Alice is an ordinary human being and Humphrey is a humanoid robot made of quite a different material from Alice. Common sense would attribute the same meanings to Humphrey's words as to Alice's, given that they use words in the same way. Some sort of philosophical argument is needed to argue otherwise. No such argument has been provided by defenders of the inverted spectrum objection.

Shoemaker (1982) offers a different version of the inverted spectrum objection. He has us consider a single person, call him Harry, at two different times, at an initial time of normal color perception and at a later time after Harry has suffered through a highly noticeable spectrum inversion (perhaps as the result of the sort of brain operation described in Lycan 1973, in which nerves are switched around so that red things now have the perceptual consequences that green things used to have, etc.) and has finally completely adapted his responses so as to restore normal functioning. Shoemaker agrees that Harry now has the same beliefs about color as before and means the same things by his color words, and he agrees that there is a sense in which strawberries now look to Harry the same as they looked before Harry's spectrum inversion. But Shoemaker takes it to be evident that there is another sense of "looks" in which it may very well be true that things do not look the same as they looked before, so that in this second sense of "looks" red things look the way green things used to look.

In other words, Shoemaker thinks it is evident that there may be a psychologically relevant difference between the sort of experience Harry had on looking at a ripe strawberry at the initial stage and the experience he has on looking at a ripe strawberry at the final stage (after he has completely adapted to his operation). That is, he thinks it is evident that there may be a psychologically relevant difference between these experiences even though there is no functional difference and no difference in the content of the experiences.

Now, this may seem evident to anyone who has fallen victim to the sense datum fallacy, which holds that one's awareness of the color of a strawberry is mediated by one's awareness of an intrinsic feature of a perceptual representation. But why should anyone else agree? Two perceptual experiences with the same intentional content must be psychologically the same. In particular, there can be nothing one is aware of in having the one experience that one is not aware of in having the other, since the intentional content of an experience comprises everything one is aware of in having that experience.

I suggest that Shoemaker's inverted spectrum hypothesis will seem evident only to someone who *begins* with the prior assumption that people have an immediate and direct awareness of intrinsic features of their experience, including those intrinsic features that function to represent color. Such a person can then go on to suppose that the intrinsic feature of experience that represents red for Alice is the intrinsic feature of experience that represents green for Fred, and so forth. This prior assumption is exactly the view behind the first objection, which I have argued is contrary to ordinary experience and can be defended only by confusing qualities of the intentional objects of experience with qualities of the experience itself. Shoemaker's inverted spectrum hypothesis therefore offers no independent argument against functionalism.[3]

Conclusion

To summarize briefly, I have described and replied to three related objections to functionalism. The first claims that we are directly aware of intrinsic features of our experience and argues that there is no way to account for this awareness in a functional view. To this, I reply that when we clearly distinguish properties of the object of experience from properties of the experience, we see that we are not aware of the relevant intrinsic features of the experience. The second objection claims that a person blind from birth can know all about the functional role of visual experience without knowing what it is like to see something red. To this I reply that the blind person does not know all about the functional role of visual experience; in particular, the blind person does not know how such experience functions in relation to the perception of red objects. The third objection claims that functionalism cannot account for the possibility of an inverted spectrum. To this I reply that someone with the relevant sort of inverted spectrum would have to have beliefs about the colors of things that are different from the beliefs others have and would have to mean something different by his or her color terms, despite being a functionally normal color perceiver who sorts things by color in exactly the way others do and who uses color terminology in the same way that others do. Functionalism's rejection of this possibility is commonsensical and is certainly not so utterly implausible or counter-intuitive that these cases present an objection to functionalism. On the other hand, to imagine that there could be relevant cases of inverted spectrum without inversion of belief and meaning is to fall back onto the first objection and not to offer any additional consideration against functionalism.

Notes

1   W. Shakespeare, *Macbeth*, Act II, Scene I: "Is this a dagger which I see before me, The handle toward my hand? Come let me clutch thee. I have thee not, and yet I see thee still. Art thou not, fatal vision, sensible To feeling as to sight? or art thou but A dagger of the mind, a false creating, Proceeding from the heat oppressed brain? ... ... I see thee still; And on thy blade and dudgeon gouts of blood, Which was not so before. There's no such thing; it is the bloody business which informs Thus to mine eyes."

2   I am indebted to Sydney Shoemaker for emphasizing this to me.

3   I should say that Shoemaker himself does not offer his case as an objection to what he calls functionalism. He claims that his version of functionalism is compatible with his case. But I am considering a version of functionalism that is defined in a way that makes it incompatible with such a case.

References

Anscombe, G.E.M. (1965) "The intentionality of sensation: a grammatical feature," *Analytical Philosophy*, second series, edited by R.J. Butler (Oxford, Blackwell); reprinted in Anscombe, G.E.M., *Metaphysics and the Philosophy of Mind: Collected Philosophical Papers, Volume II* (Minneapolis, Minnesota; University of Minnesota Press: 1981), pp. 3–20.

Armstrong, David M. (1961) *Perception and the Physical World* (London: Routledge and Kegan Paul).

Armstrong, David M. (1962) *Bodily Sensations* (London: Routledge and Kegan Paul).

Armstrong, David M. (1968) *The Materialist Theory of Mind* (London: Routledge and Kegan Paul).

Block, Ned (1986) "Advertisement for a semantics for psychology," *Midwest Studies in Philosophy* 10: 615–678.

Churchland, Paul (1985) "Reduction, qualia, and the direct introspection of mental states," *Journal of Philosophy* 82: 8–28.

Dennett, Daniel C. (1969) *Content and Consciousness* (London: Routledge and Kegan Paul).

Dennett, Daniel C. (1987) *The Intentional Stance* (Cambridge, Massachusetts: MIT Press).

Harman, Gilbert (1973) *Thought* (Princeton, New Jersey: Princeton University Press).

Harman, Gilbert (1987) "(Nonsolipsistic) conceptual role semantics," *New Directions in Semantics*, edited by Ernest LePore (London, Academic Press), pp. 55–81.

Harman, Gilbert (1988) "Wide functionalism," *Cognition and Representation*, edited by Stephen Schiffer and Susan Steele (Boulder, Colorado: Westview Press), pp. 11–20.

Jackson, Frank (1977) *Perception: A Representative Theory* (Cambridge, England: Cambridge University Press).

Jackson, Frank (1982) "Epiphenomenal qualia," *Philosophical Quarterly* 32: 127–132.

Jackson, Frank (1986) "What Mary didn't know," *Journal of Philosophy* 83: 291–295; reprinted as Chapter 22 in this volume.

Lewis, David K. (1983) "Postscript to 'Mad pain and Martian pain,'" *Philosophical Papers*, Volume 1, (New York: Oxford University Press), pp. 130–132.

Lycan, William G. (1973) "Inverted spectrum," *Ratio* 15.

Nagel, Thomas (1970) "Armstrong on the mind," *Philosophical Review* 79, reprinted in *Reading in the Philosophy of Psychology*, Volume 1, edited by Ned Block (Cambridge, Massachusetts: Harvard University Press).

Nagel, Thomas (1974) "What is it like to be a bat?," *Philosophical Review* 83: 435–450.

Parsons, Terence (1980) *Nonexistent Objects* (New Haven: Yale University Press).

Peacocke, Christopher (1983) *Sense and Content* (Oxford: Oxford University Press).

Pitcher, George (1971) *A Theory of Perception* (Princeton, New Jersey: Princeton University Press).

Quine, W.V. (1948) "On what there is," *Review of Metaphysics*, reprinted in *From a Logical Point of View* (Cambridge, Massachusetts: Harvard University Press: 1953).

Quine, W.V. (1960) *Word and Object* (Cambridge, Massachusetts: MIT Press).

Rumelhart, David E., and McClelland, James L. (1986) *Parallel Distributed Processing*, 2 volumes (Cambridge, Massachusetts: MIT Press).

Shoemaker, Sydney (1982) "The inverted spectrum," *Journal of Philosophy* 79: 357–381.

Shoemaker, Sydney (1985) "Churchland on reduction, qualia, and introspection," *PSA 1984*, Volume 2 (Philosophy of Science Association), pp. 799–809.

Thagard, Paul T. (1986) "Parallel computation and the mind–body problem," *Cognitive Science* 10: 301–318.

25

Peter Carruthers, "Brute Experience" *†

The question whether brutes have experiences has been granted as obvious
in recent times, and in one sense of the term "experience" no doubt it is
so. But not, I shall argue, in the sense that makes their experiences an
appropriate object of moral concern.

I

Since Thomas Nagel's seminal paper "What is it Like to be a Bat?,"[1] it has
become generally accepted that a creature may be said to have experiences
if and only if there is something that it is like to be that thing (even if we
cannot know what). But this identification of experience with subjective feel
is false. There are, in fact, many experiences that do not feel like anything.

Consider some familiar examples. While driving the car over a route
I know well, my conscious attention may be wholly abstracted from my
surroundings. I may be thinking deeply about a current piece of writing
of mine, or phantasizing about my next summer's holiday, to the extent of
being unaware of what I am doing on the road. It is common in such cases
that one may suddenly "come to," returning one's attention to the task at
hand with a startled realization that one has not the faintest idea what one
has been doing or seeing for some minutes past. Yet there is a clear sense

* I am grateful to Clare McCready for discussions that stimulated the writing of
this paper, and to A.D. Smith for his comments on an earlier draft.
† The author of this article no longer endorses the "reflexive thinking" theory of
consciousness which it contains. For his current view, see his book *Phenomenal
Consciousness* (Cambridge: Cambridge University Press, 2000). Nor does the author
agree any longer that non-conscious pains cannot be appropriate objects
of sympathy. See his article, "Sympathy and Subjectivity," *Australasian Journal of
Philosophy*, 77 (1999): 465–482.

Peter Carruthers, "Brute Experience," *The Journal of Philosophy*, 86(5) (1989):
258–69.

in which I must have been seeing, or I should have crashed the car. My passenger sitting next to me may correctly report that I had seen the lorry double parked by the side of the road, since I had deftly steered the car around it. But I was not aware of seeing that lorry, either at the time or later in memory.

Another example: when washing up dishes I generally put on music to help pass the time. If it is a piece that I love particularly well, I may become totally absorbed, ceasing to be conscious of what I am doing at the sink. Yet someone observing me position a glass neatly on the rack to dry between two coffee mugs would correctly say that I must have seen that those mugs were already there, or I should not have placed the glass where I did. Yet I was not aware of seeing those mugs, or of placing the glass between them. At the time I was swept up in the finale of Schubert's "Arpeggione Sonata," and if asked even a moment later I should have been unable to recall at what I had been looking.

Let us call such experiences *nonconscious experiences*. What does it feel like to be the subject of a nonconscious experience? It feels like nothing. It does not *feel like anything* to have a nonconscious visual experience, as of a lorry parked at the side of the road or as of two coffee mugs placed on a draining rack, precisely because to have such an experience is not to be conscious of it. Only conscious experiences have a distinctive phenomenology, a distinctive feel. Nonconscious experiences are those which may help to control behavior without being felt by the conscious subject.

These points – intuitive as they are – are already sufficient to show that Nagel is wrong to identify the question whether a creature has experiences with the question whether there is something that it feels like to be that thing. For there is a class – perhaps a large class – of nonconscious experiences that have no phenomenology. So, the fact that a creature has sense organs, and can be observed to display sensitivity in its behavior to the salient features of its surrounding environment, is insufficient to establish that it feels like anything to be that thing. It may be that the experiences of brutes (that is, of some or all nonhuman animals) are wholly of the nonconscious variety. It is an open question whether there is anything that it feels like to be a bat or a dog or a monkey. If consciousness is like the turning on of a light, then it may be that their lives are nothing but darkness. In order to make progress with this issue, we need to understand the nature of the distinction between conscious and nonconscious mental states.

Before proceeding to that task, however, it is worth noticing a somewhat less familiar example of nonconscious experience, since this will help us to see how the conscious/nonconscious distinction may have a physical realization in the neurological structure of the human brain. The phenomenon I have in mind is that of blindsight.[2] Human subjects who have suffered

511

lesions in the striate cortex (the visual center in the higher part of the
brain) may lose all conscious experience in an area of their visual field.
They insist that they can see nothing at all within that region. Nevertheless,
if asked to guess, they prove remarkably good at describing features of
objects presented to them in that area, such as the orientation of a line, or
at pointing out the direction of a light source. They can also reach out and
grasp objects. Indeed, if asked to try to catch a ball thrown toward them
from their blind side, they often prove successful.[3]

The conclusion to be drawn from these studies is that, while blindsight
patients lack conscious visual experience within an area of their visual field,
they nevertheless have nonconscious experiences which are somehow
made available to help in the control of their actions. It seems that the
neurological explanation for the phenomenon is that information from the
eye is not only mapped on to the striate cortex (in normal subjects) but is
also sent to a second mapping in the midbrain. It is presumably this latter
mapping which is made available, in blindsight patients, to be integrated
with the subject's goals and other perceptions in controlling behavior. It is
also possible that it is this midbrain information which underlies the
everyday examples of nonconscious experience outlined above. But we
should beware of concluding that any creature with a striate cortex will be
the subject of conscious visual experiences. The phenomenon of hindsight
shows only that a functioning striate cortex is a physically necessary condition for conscious visual experience, not that it is sufficient. It may be that
in the case of everyday nonconscious experience the striate cortex is indeed
active, but that its information is not made available to whatever structures
in the human brain underlie consciousness. And it may be that nonhuman
animals with a striate cortex do not possess those structures at all.

It is worth stressing that the various nonconscious experiences we have
considered do genuinely deserve to be counted as a species of *experience*.
For not only is incoming information processed to quite a high degree of
sophistication, but the states in question conform to the practical-reasoning
model of explanation. Thus, the car driver behaved as he did because he
wanted to reach his destination safely and *saw* that the lorry was an obstacle
in his path. And the blindsight patient picked up the ball because he *wanted*
to comply with the request of the experimenter and *saw* that the ball was
on the edge of the desk. But if someone really insists that experiences are
conscious states *by definition*, then the conclusion of this section may simply
be rephrased. It is that, since there exist in humans similar levels of cognitive processing and behavior control to those displayed by brutes, which
do not involve experiences, it is an open question whether brutes have
experiences at all. In the discussion that follows, however, I shall assume,
as seems most natural, that not all experiences are conscious ones.

II

What distinguishes conscious from nonconscious experiences? The question is best raised in connection with the distinction between conscious and nonconscious mental states generally. Since David Armstrong's[4] early work, it has been usual to characterize conscious mental states as those which give rise (noninferentially) to an activated second-order belief in their own existence. Thus, a conscious belief that P is one which, besides being available to enter into the causation of the subject's behavior, is apt to cause in them the activated belief that they believe that P.[5] Similarly, a conscious visual experience is one that, besides causing beliefs about the matter to which the experience relates, and being made available to nonconscious motor control processes, is apt to give rise to the belief that just such an experience is taking place.

If such an account were correct, then it would be very doubtful whether many species of animal could be said to enjoy conscious experiences. For only the most anthropomorphic of us is prepared to ascribe second-order beliefs to toads and mice; and many of us would have serious doubts about ascribing such states even to higher mammals such as chimpanzees.[6] At any rate, behavioral evidence for the possession of such states in higher mammals is contentious, whereas their absence from lower mammals, birds, reptiles, and fish is surely uncontentious. I shall show, however, that the proposed account is definitely incorrect. But this result is not a defense of conscious experience for brutes. Quite the contrary: the account of consciousness which emerges will make it even less likely that any non-human animals have conscious experiences.

I begin with an example I owe to Tim Williamson, designed to show that one cannot equate conscious believing that P with an activated second-order belief that one believes that P. In the course of a discussion of the merits and demerits of functionalism in the philosophy of mind, I might realize that I had for some time been speaking of functionalists as "we," also becoming angry when the views of functionalists were maligned, thus manifesting the activated second-order belief that I believe myself to believe in functionalism. But this might strike me with the force of self-discovery. If anyone had asked me previously whether I were a functionalist, I might have expressed uncertainty. In which case it would seem that the possession of activated second-order beliefs is not sufficient for conscious believing.

Another argument with the same conclusion is that the proposed account gets the focus of attention of conscious believing quite wrong. Conscious belief is surely world-directed in precisely the way that belief itself is. If I entertain the conscious belief that the world is getting warmer, then the primary object of my belief is the earth and its likely future temperature.

513

Whereas if the proposed account were correct, the primary object of the conscious belief would be myself (I should be believing of myself that I possess a particular first-order belief), only focusing on the world indirectly, via the content of the first-order belief in question.

This point holds also for the proposed account of the distinction between conscious and nonconscious experience. Conscious visual experiences, too, are primarily world-directed. When I consciously see that there is a dagger on the desk before me, the primary focus of my attention is the dagger itself. In normal cases of conscious perception, our experiences are, as it were, transparent: representing the world to us without themselves being objects of attention. It is of course possible to pay attention to one's conscious experiences, as when I attempt a phenomenological description of my visual field. But this is a sophisticated and relatively unusual thing to do. Whereas on the proposed account it is the normal case: to perceive consciously that there is a dagger on the desk would be to have activated the belief about myself that I have an experience of there being a dagger on the desk.

Is it possible to do better? Indeed it is.[7] A conscious, as opposed to a non-conscious, mental state is one that is available to conscious thought – where a conscious act of thinking is itself an event that is available to be thought about in turn. (When we think things consciously to ourselves, the events that express our thoughts are themselves available to be objects of further thoughts – I can think to myself that my thought was poorly formulated, or hasty, or confused, or whatever.) In the case of belief, a conscious belief (qua standing state) is one that is apt to emerge in a conscious thinking with the same content. This is then able to handle Williamson's example: the reason why I had not consciously believed functionalism to be true is that I failed to have any disposition to think to myself, "Functionalism is true." The account also has the advantage that conscious beliefs have the same primary world-directedness as beliefs. For the conscious act of thinking, aptness to emerge in which is the distinctive mark of a conscious belief, is an event with the very same (world-directed) content as that belief itself. What makes my belief that the earth is getting warmer a conscious one is that I am disposed in suitable circumstances to think to myself, "The earth is getting warmer"; in both cases, the direction of focus is on the world, rather than on myself.

In the case of experience, a conscious experience is a state whose content is available to be consciously thought about (that is, which is available for description in acts of thinking which are themselves made available to further acts of thinking). In this case, I say "available to be thought *about*," rather than "apt to emerge in thinkings with the same content," because it is plausible to claim that most experiences have a degree of complexity and richness which may outreach our powers of accurate description.

Nevertheless, every aspect of the perceived scene is made available to thought, even if only the thought that things are now subtly different. (Although the manner in which the leaves of a tree are shimmering in the breeze may defy description, I must at least be able to think to myself that the pattern of movement is now slightly altered, if it is.) Here, too, we can retain the primary world-directedness of conscious experience, since the normal way for information that is made available to thought through perception to emerge in acts of thinking is in thoughts about the object perceived – as when I think to myself that the dagger on the desk is richly ornamented.

When we turn to consider, not conscious experience of something in the world, but the more sophisticated state of consciousness of that experience itself, it is important to note that the suggested account is consistent with the existence of unanalyzable qualia. It may indeed be the case that the distinctive feel of my experience of a warm shade of red is incapable of further analysis, or even of nonrelational description. But I claim that what constitutes that feeling as a conscious rather than a nonconscious state is that it is available to be consciously thought about. It is the status of qualia as conscious states, not the individual qualia themselves, which is being analyzed on the proposed account.

Besides the virtues mentioned above, my account provides a natural treatment of the examples of nonconscious experience with which we began. The reason why my perception of the double-parked lorry was not conscious, is that, while information about the lorry was somehow made available for integration into my actions, it was not available to my conscious thoughts. Similarly in the example of nonconscious perception of mugs on a draining board, what makes the experience nonconscious is that there was, in the circumstances, nothing available for me to think spontaneously about those mugs.

The issue of spontaneity is important in handling the blindsight examples. For although in these cases the visual information is, in a sense, available to be thought about (since if asked to guess what is there, subjects will generally guess correctly), it is not apt to give rise to spontaneous thoughts in the way that conscious experiences do. In the normal course of events, blindsighted people will have no thoughts whatever about objects positioned in the blind portion of their visual field. Indeed, when they do think about the matter, they are strongly inclined to believe that they see nothing.

One final virtue of my account is that it is able to explain why so many philosophers have been inclined to connect possession of conscious mental states with the ability to speak a natural language. For such a connection is at its most plausible (though still denied by many) where conscious thinkings are concerned. The idea that the ability to think things consciously to oneself is tied to the possession of a natural language has an immediate (if defeasible) plausibility. Whereas a similar thesis applied to the capacity for conscious experience seems much more puzzling. For why should it be supposed that language mastery is a necessary condition for a creature to enjoy conscious visual experiences? If the account sketched above is correct, then there may indeed be such a connection, but at one remove: it is because conscious experiences are those which are available to conscious thinkings. Now, although I am in fact one of those who maintain that language mastery is at least contingently connected with the capacity for conscious thought, I shall not argue for this here.[8] Nor is such a thesis necessary in what follows.

Are there any other alternatives to my account? I can think of only three. First, it might be said that the distinctive feature of a conscious experience is that it is recorded in short-term memory (this being the *explanation* of why such experiences are, in humans, available to be thought about). But the trouble with this is that there is nothing here to distinguish conscious from nonconscious short-term memory. (My own account, in contrast, is reflexive: conscious thinkings are ones that are themselves available to be consciously thought about.) Second, it might be said that a conscious state is one that is available to the organism as a whole. But the trouble here is that the experiences of any earth worm or slug will turn out to be conscious ones, on this account, whereas the experiences of my car driver are not. Third, it might be claimed that the distinction between conscious and nonconscious states is simple and unanalyzable. But this surely cannot be right. It cannot be merely that we are capable of recognizing, straight off, whether or not a given state is conscious (in the way that we are capable of recognizing whether or not a given shade of color is green); for nonconscious states, precisely because they *are* nonconscious, cannot be immediately recognized as such. Yet if it is said to be the availability for such immediate recognition which constitutes a state as a conscious one, then we appear to have returned to a version of my own proposal.

If my account of the distinction between conscious and nonconscious mental states may be taken as established, then the nonconscious status of most animal experiences follows with very little further argument. For if it is implausible to ascribe second-order beliefs to mice or fish, it is even more unlikely that they should be thinking things consciously to themselves – that is, that they should engage in acts of thinking which are themselves made available for the organism to think about. Indeed, it seems highly implausible to ascribe such activities to any but the higher primates; and, even then, many of us would entertain serious doubts.[9] In the discussion that follows, I shall confine attention to those species for which I take it the above thesis will be noncontroversial. I shall assume that no one would seriously maintain that dogs, cats, sheep, cattle, pigs, or chickens consciously think things to themselves (let alone that fish or reptiles do). In which case, if my account of the distinction between conscious and nonconscious experience is correct, the experiences of all these creatures will be of the nonconscious variety.

III

It goes without saying that pains, too, are experiences. Then two questions remain. First, does pain, like any other experience, admit of a conscious/nonconscious distinction? If so, then the pains of brutes will be nonconscious ones, according to my general account of this distinction. Second, are nonconscious pains an appropriate object of sympathy and moral concern? If not, then the sufferings of brutes will make no moral claims upon us.

There are no noncontroversial examples of nonconscious pain in humans to parallel our everyday examples of nonconscious visual experience. There is an obvious reason for this, since part of the function of pain is to intrude upon consciousness, in order that one may give one's full attention to taking evasive action. But possible examples come from cases where someone is concentrating very intently upon a task, and where they later report having felt no pain upon injury, but where they nevertheless display aversive behavior. For instance, a soldier in the midst of battle may be too caught up in the fighting to notice any pain when he badly burns his hand on the red-hot barrel of a gun, but an observer would see him jerk his hand away in the manner characteristic of someone in pain. Should we feel sympathy in such a case? Clearly we would be sympathetic for the soldier's injury; but not for his suffering, since he in fact felt no pain. This sort of example is incapable of carrying very great weight, however, because the pain behavior displayed is hardly paradigmatic. Since the episode is so brief and unstructured, it may perhaps be thought of as a mere reflex, rather than a genuine instance of non-conscious pain perception.

Can there be cases of pain parallel to those of blindsight? That is, cases where the full (or nearly full) range of pain behavior is displayed, but in which the subject is not conscious of any pain. So far as I am aware, no such cases have actually occurred; but the neurophysiology of pain perception suggests that they are, in principle, possible.[10] Pain in humans is mediated through two types of nerve, which generate distinct projections in the brain subserving distinct functions. Very roughly, the "new path" is fast; it is projected into the higher centers of the brain, and is responsible for precise pain location and fine discriminations of feel. The "old path" is, by contrast, slow; it is projected primarily to the more ancient limbic system in the brain, and gives rise to aversion (the desire for the pain to cease).

Some types of morphine can suppress the activity of the old path, while leaving the new path fully functioning. Patients report that their pain is still just as intense (it feels the same), but that it no longer bothers them (they no longer want it to stop). It seems unlikely, in contrast, that there will be any drug, or any naturally-occurring lesions, which suppress the activity of the new path while leaving the old path functioning. For, unlike the case of vision, the nerves of the new path have no specialized projection area in the higher cortex, but seem rather to be mapped in a complex way into many different regions throughout it.[11] This suggests that phenomena similar to blindsight could only occur as a result of direct surgical intervention. But they do seem to be possible, in principle.

Let us then imagine a case for pain similar to that of blindsight. Suppose that a particular subject, Mary, is never conscious of any pains in her legs. But when she suffers injury in that region, she displays much of normal pain behavior. If we jab pins into her feet, she tends to try very hard to make us stop, she grimaces and groans, and severe damage causes her to scream. But she sincerely declares that she feels nothing. Perhaps she initially found her own behavior disquieting, but now she understands its basis and merely finds it a nuisance. When she twists her ankle, she does not ask for something to alleviate the pain (she says she feels none), but for something to help her relax, and to stop her from grinding her teeth and limping when she walks.

This case is clearly imaginable. It is a possible example (physically possible as well as logically so) of nonconscious pain – that is, of events which otherwise occupy the normal causal role of pain,[12] but which are not available to be thought about consciously and spontaneously by the subject. Ought we to feel sympathy for Mary? We might perhaps feel sympathy for her general condition, since it is in many ways a disturbing situation in which to find oneself. But we should not feel sympathy on specific occasions of injury, since it is clear that she does not suffer. Not being conscious of any pain, her mental state is not an appropriate object of moral concern. (Her injury itself might be, however, because of its indirect effects upon her life, and hence her conscious desires and disappointments. There are many things that you cannot do with a twisted ankle, even if you feel no pain.) Similarly then in the case of brutes: since their experiences, including their pains, are nonconscious ones, their pains are of no immediate moral concern. Indeed, since all the mental states of brutes are nonconscious, their injuries are lacking even in indirect moral concern. Since the disappointments caused to a dog through possession of a broken leg are themselves nonconscious in their turn, they, too, are not appropriate objects of our sympathy. Hence, neither the pain of the broken leg itself, nor its further effects upon the life of the dog, have any rational claim upon our sympathy.

Of course, it is one thing to reach an intellectual acceptance of such a position, and quite another to put it into practice. Are we really capable of suppressing our sympathy when we see an animal (especially a cuddly one) in severe pain? Not only is it possible that this should occur – after all, the history of mankind is replete with examples of those who have eradicated all feelings of sympathy even for members of other races, by telling themselves that they are not "really human" – but it is a moral imperative that it ought to. Much time and money is presently spent on alleviating the pains of brutes which ought properly to be directed toward human beings, and many are now campaigning to reduce the efficiency of modern farming methods because of the pain caused to the animals involved. If the arguments presented here have been sound, such activities are not only morally unsupportable but morally objectionable.[13]

Consider once again the case of Mary. Suppose that you are a doctor who knows the details of her condition, and that you happen to be on the scene of an accident in which her legs have been badly injured. A number of other people are obviously injured and in pain, but Mary is screaming the loudest. Ought you to treat her first? Clearly not, other things being equal (e.g., provided that she is not bleeding badly); indeed, it would be moral weakness in you to do so. For you know that she is not really suffering, since her pains are nonconscious, whereas the sufferings of the others are real. Similarly then in the case of brutes: since their pains are nonconscious (as are all their mental states), they ought not to be allowed to get in the way of any morally-serious objective.

It is worth drawing a contrast at this point with the case of very young children. I presume that the pains of babies, too, are nonconscious; for no one will seriously maintain that they consciously think things to themselves. Nevertheless, it is important that they should continue to evoke our sympathy. For a baby's pains and injuries, and our attitudes toward them, are likely to have a significant effect upon the person the baby will one day become. There is a parallel here with the case of language development. As every parent knows, one naturally becomes possessed by a sort of necessary insanity, talking to young children as if they could understand. This is no doubt essential if children are to develop into skilled practitioners of their native tongue. In both cases, one engages, and should engage, in a useful fiction: ascribing to the baby thoughts that it does not in fact possess.

There is no such rationale in the case of brutes. For our sympathy and concern for their pains and injuries cannot be said to have an effect on the persons they will one day become. Nevertheless, it is hard, especially in a culture such as ours where animals are often used as exemplars in moral training (we tell children that it is *cruel* to pull the whiskers out of the cat), to eradicate our feelings toward them. Indeed, in such a culture we may have reason to look askance at people who can be wholly indifferent to an animal writhing in agony before their very eyes. (We say, "How can you be so inhuman?") But what should be said is that we are obliged to set such feelings aside whenever they threaten to have a morally significant effect upon other humans. And it also follows that there is no moral criticism to be leveled at the majority of people who are indifferent to the pains of factory-farmed animals, which they know to exist but do not themselves observe.

Notes

1 *Philosophical Review*, LXXXIII, 4 (1974): 435–451.
2 This has been researched by a number of investigators. See in particular L. Weiskrantz, "Varieties of Residual Experience," *Quarterly Journal of Experimental Psychology*, XXXIII, 3 (1980): 365–386.
3 For these last two facts, I rely upon personal communication from A.J. Marcel, Applied Psychology Unit, Cambridge, who will be publishing details shortly. Subjects displayed 80%–90% of normal accuracy in reaching out for objects of varying sizes and orientations, placed at varying distances. For examples of other experimental data suggesting the existence of nonconscious perceptions of quite a sophisticated sort, see Marcel, "Conscious and Unconscious Perception," *Cognitive Psychology*, XV, 2 (1983): 197–300.
4 *A Materialist Theory of the Mind* (London: Routledge, 1968). Similar accounts have been defended recently in Peter Smith and O.R. Jones, *The Philosophy of Mind* (New York: Cambridge, 1986), and in my own *Introducing Persons* (Albany: SUNY, 1986).
5 A belief is activated when it becomes engaged in the subject's current mental processes.
6 For a useful review of the evidence of various levels of cognitive organization in a range animal species, see Stephen Walker *Animal Thought* (New York: Routledge & Kegan Paul, 1983).
7 The account that follows is modelled on some of Daniel Dennett's suggestions in "Toward a Cognitive Theory of Consciousness," in *Brainstorms* (Montgomery, VT: Bradford, 1978), 149–173. But Dennett, implausibly, connects consciousness directly with the ability to give verbal reports. If there is such a connection, it needs to be established at least in part by empirical investigation, not fixed by definition.
8 See ch. 10 of my *Tractarian Semantics* (New York: Blackwell, 1989).
9 See the very sensible discussion of the cognitive powers of chimpanzees in Walker, *op. cit.*
10 In what follows, I rely largely upon the account provided by Dennett in "Why You Can't Make a Computer that Feels Pain," in *Brainstorms*, ch. 10.
11 Here I rely upon J.Z. Young, *Philosophy and the Brain* (New York: Oxford, 1986).

12 This is not strictly correct, since part of the normal causal role of pain is to give rise to a conscious desire that the pain should cease, whereas I am supposing that Mary's avoidance behavior is motivated by desires that are nonconscious. (This is merely for ease of presentation: Mary cannot consciously desire that her *pain* should stop, since she feels none. But she might in fact have a conscious desire that whatever is going on in her ankle should cease.) The adjustment is allowable in this context, since the desires of brutes, as well as their pains, will be nonconscious ones.

13 Peter Singer has been prominent in defending the moral significance of animals, from a broadly utilitarian perspective. See, for example, his *Practical Ethics* (New York: Cambridge, 1979). But he makes no attempt to take account of the distinction between conscious and nonconscious experience. Indeed, he does not notice it. There are, of course, other moral perspectives, from the standpoint of some of which the moral significance of animals may be attacked; for example, versions of contractualism which place a premium upon rational agency. But my argument is the more fundamental, since even contractualists should find a place for compassion.

IVC

CONSCIOUSNESS AND ALTERNATIVE VARIETIES OF DUALISM

26

William Hasker, "Emergent Dualism"

Anyone who finds traditional dualisms implausible, yet is unsatisfied with eliminativist or strongly reductive views of the mind, is likely to find congenial the idea that somehow or other the mind emerges from the functioning of the brain and nervous system. This idea was an integral part of the "emergent evolution" espoused early in this century by Samuel Alexander, C. Lloyd Morgan, and C.D. Broad.[1] The notion of emergence, however, has been employed with a variety of different meanings, so it is necessary at this point to say something about those differing uses and to clarify the way emergence is to be understood in the present discussion. We will then proceed to consider two recent emergentist views of the mind, offer a constructive proposal, and conclude by raising some additional questions.

Concepts of emergence

We begin with some intriguing (but, as we shall see, incomplete) remarks of John Searle about different concepts of emergence. He writes:

> Suppose we have a system, S, made up of elements a, b, c .... For example, S might be a stone and the elements might be molecules. In general, there will be features of S that are not, or not necessarily, features of a, b, c .... For example, S might weigh ten pounds, but the molecules individually do not weigh ten pounds. Let us call such features "system features." The shape and the weight of the stone are system features. Some system features can be deduced or figured out or calculated from the features of a, b, c ... just from the way these

William Hasker, "Emergent Dualism" (excerpts), Chapter 7 of *The Emergent Self* (Cornell University Press, Ithaca, 1999), pp. 171–8, 185–95.

are composed and arranged (and sometimes from their relations to the rest of the environment). Examples of these would be shape, weight, and velocity. But some other system features cannot be figured out just from the composition of the elements and environmental relations; they have to be explained in terms of the causal interactions among the elements. Let's call these "causally emergent system features." Solidity, liquidity, and transparency are examples of causally emergent system features.

On these definitions, consciousness is a causally emergent property of systems. It is an emergent feature of certain systems of neurons in the same way that solidity and liquidity are emergent features of systems of molecules. The existence of consciousness can be explained by the causal interactions between elements of the brain at the micro level, but consciousness cannot itself be deduced or calculated from the sheer physical structure of the neurons without some additional account of the causal relations between them.

This conception of causal emergence, call it "emergent$_1$," has to be distinguished from a much more adventurous conception, call it "emergent$_2$." A feature F is emergent$_2$ if F is emergent$_1$, and F has causal powers that cannot be explained by the causal interactions of $a, b, c \ldots$. If consciousness were emergent$_2$, then consciousness could cause things that could not be explained by the causal behavior of the neurons. The naive idea here is that consciousness gets squirted out by the behavior of the neurons in the brain, but once it has been squirted out, it then has a life of its own.

It should be obvious from the previous chapter that on my view consciousness is emergent$_1$ but not emergent$_2$. In fact, I cannot think of anything that is emergent$_2$, and it seems unlikely that we will be able to find any features that are emergent$_2$, because the existence of any such features would seem to violate even the weakest principle of the transitivity of causation.[2]

This remarkable (but somewhat less than perspicuous) passage calls for comment at several points. First, consider the system features that are explainable merely in terms of the features of the elements and the way they are arranged. Apparently Searle doesn't find it appropriate to describe these features as emergent in any sense; there just isn't enough that is "new" in the system feature to warrant such a description. We should note, however, that these features can on occasion be quite interesting and surprising. Consider, for example, the complex and beautiful properties exhibited by fractal patterns, which surely are wondrous enough in spite of being "mere" logical consequences of the equations that generate the patterns. Perhaps we can term such features (at least when they are striking enough to get our attention) as "logical emergents," or as "emergent$_0$."

To be distinguished from these are the causally emergent system features – emergent$_1$ features – which are the main topic of Searle's discussion. But before considering these there are some points about "explanation" that need to be clarified. First, I think Searle is using this notion in such a way that if A is the cause of B, then A explains B; there is no further requirement on explanation beyond what is already implied in causation. But, second, Searle clearly is talking about both causation and explanation *as they would be in a completed science.* In saying that "the existence of consciousness can be explained by the causal interactions between elements of the brain at the micro level" he clearly doesn't mean that we can *now* give such explanations; it's obvious we can't do this, since we don't yet know even the Humean-type correlations that govern the emergence of consciousness.

According to Searle, emergent$_1$ features are those which "cannot be figured out just from the composition of the elements and environmental relations; they have to be explained in terms of the causal interactions among the elements."[3] And such, Searle claims, are liquidity, solidity, transparency – and consciousness. But there is a further, important distinction that needs to be made here. In order to grasp this distinction, consider the case of biological life, which is clearly an emergent$_1$ feature. And let's consider two scenarios with respect to the explanation of life. In both scenarios, we assume that physics and chemistry, including organic chemistry, have been studied and understood to the point that we have completely adequate theories to explain and predict everything that happens in the absence of biological life. In the first scenario, these theories also enable us to explain and predict what occurs on the biological level; the "causal interactions among the elements," described according to the ordinary laws of physics and chemistry, suffice to explain life as well as everything that happens on the pre-biological levels. Whether or not this is true about life, we are confident it is true of solidity and liquidity. Emergent features of this sort we term "ordinary causal emergents," or "emergent$_1$."

But not all of Searle's emergent$_1$ features need be of this sort. In fact, it is clear that emergentists have typically wanted to assert more than this. And it is at least conceivable that, in the case of life, the most complete understanding possible of the causal interactions of nonliving matter will *not* enable us to explain life itself. On this second scenario, the processes of life would indeed be explained by causal interactions among the elements, but *the laws that govern these interactions are different because of the influence of the new property that emerges in consequence of the higher-level organization.* So if (for example) consciousness is emergent in this sense, the behavior of the physical components of the brain (neurons, and substructures within neurons) will be *different*, in virtue of the causal influence of consciousness, than it would be without this property; the ordinary causal laws that govern the operations of such structures apart from the effects of consciousness will no longer suffice. If, then, the behavior of the system continues to be law-governed, we will have to reckon with the existence of *emergent laws*, laws whose operation is discernible only in the special sorts of situations in which the higher-level emergent properties manifest themselves.[4] Features which are emergent in this more robust sense may be termed "emergent$_{1b}$"; they involve "emergent causal powers" whose operation is described by the emergent laws.[5]

According to Timothy O'Connor, emergentists often have wanted to claim for the emergent properties they recognize "novel causal influence" – in effect, emergence$_{1b}$. O'Connor explains novel causal influence as follows: "This term is intended to capture a very strong sense in which an emergent's causal influence is irreducible to that of the micro-properties on which it supervenes: It bears its influence in a direct, 'downward' fashion, in contrast to the operation of a simple structural macro-property, whose causal influence occurs *via* the activity of the micro-properties that constitute it."[6] The notion of "downward" causal influence – a notion that is quite popular in recent discussions of emergence – is of course a metaphor; the "levels" involved are levels of organization and integration, and the downward influence means that *the behavior of the "lower" levels – that is, of the components of which the "higher-level" structure consists – is different than it would otherwise be, because of the influence of the new property that emerges in consequence of the higher-level organization.*[7]

This is what "downward causation" *needs* to mean, if the notion is to make coherent sense. But the terminology of levels and of downward causation has, I want to suggest, a definite tendency to mislead one into thinking of the different levels as concrete and as capable of exerting, on their own, distinct kinds of causal influence. It's as though one were thinking of a multistoried building, in which almost everything that reaches the upper stories comes in through the ground floor, but occasionally something comes down from the upper stories – say, a telephone call containing orders or instructions – that makes things on the ground floor go differently than they would otherwise have done. It's obvious, though, that this kind of picture is seriously misleading. The only concrete existents involved are the ultimate constituents and combinations thereof; the only causal influences are those of the ultimate constituents in their interactions with each other, and the only way the "higher levels" can make a difference is by *altering or superseding the laws* according to which the elements interact. To think otherwise is to fall into confusion on the basis of an inadequate grasp of what "levels" and "downward causation" involve.

The kind of emergence we've been considering here – emergence$_{1b}$, the emergence of novel causal powers – has been discussed by Jaegwon Kim in several essays. Kim views emergentism as, in effect, a special form of supervenience theory.[8] Even more interesting, however, is his general claim that "nonreductive physicalism . . . is best viewed as a form of emergentism."[9] Kim would reject such a view because it violates the "causal closure of the physical."[10] This becomes part of Kim's case against nonreductive physicalism, a view which seeks to maintain the reality and causal efficacy of mental properties, yet uphold the physicalist commitment to the causal closure of the physical realm. Kim recognizes, however, that the classical emergentists were not committed to the closure of the physical, and thus would not be deterred by this objection.[11]

There remains Searle's suggestion – and dismissal – of the "more adventurous" conception of emergence he dubs "emergent$_2$." On the one hand, his remarks about the transitivity of causation make the view seem just incoherent: if A causes B, and B causes C, then A causes C, and how could anyone deny this? And yet, the image of consciousness being "squirted out" by the behavior of the neurons, and then acquiring a "life of its own," strikes one as intelligible even if a bit bizarre. Just what is going on here?

In fact, Searle seems to be talking about two different things. According to his formal definition, consciousness is emergent$_2$ iff the existence of consciousness is emergent$_1$ and consciousness has causal powers that can't be explained in terms of the causal interactions of the neurons. And that does seem incoherent: if the neurons, by their causal interactions, generate consciousness, then in so doing they generate whatever causal powers consciousness may possess. But Searle goes on to say, "If consciousness were emergent$_2$, then consciousness could cause things that could not be explained by the causal behavior of the neurons." Here the problem is not that the neurons' behavior doesn't explain the *causal powers* of consciousness, but that it doesn't explain the *things that are caused* by consciousness in the exercise of those powers. And that is quite a different matter; at least it is if we don't assume that the causal operations of consciousness must be deterministic. If there is an indeterministic element in the operations of consciousness, so that consciousness can cause things it isn't caused to cause – if, for instance, consciousness should happen to be endowed with libertarian freedom – then it might very well be the case that "consciousness could cause things that could not be explained by the causal behavior of the neurons." Understood in this way, there is nothing incoherent about the idea that consciousness might possess "emergent$_2$" features. Since free

WILLIAM HASKER

will seems to be the most plausible example of an emergent$_2$ feature, we will label this sort of emergence as the "emergence of freedom."

Still further issues arise when we confront these concepts of emergence with the principle of reducibility discussed previously. What we have to ask is whether the emergent property of an object is one that can consist of properties of, and relations between, the parts of the object. In the case of what we have termed "logical emergents," there is no reason to doubt that this is the case. For causal emergents, Searle's "emergent$_1$" properties, the situation is more complex. Keep in mind that the principle of reducibility is synchronic rather than diachronic; it concerns the relationship between properties of parts and wholes at a given time, not with the relationship over time or with the genesis of the emergent properties. Understood in this way, there seems to be no reason in general why both "emergent$_{1a}$" properties, ordinary causal emergents, and "emergent$_{1b}$" properties, involving novel, emergent causal powers, might not pass muster when scrutinized in terms of the principle. However, some putative emergent properties may fail the test. Sellars would argue, for example, that there is no satisfactory way to treat phenomenal color as an emergent property. Since this is so, being colored must be a property of base-level objects. He maintains that "the being colored of colored objects (in the naive realist sense) does not consist in a relationship of non-colored parts."[12] Furthermore, "unless we introduce Cartesian minds as scientific objects, individual scientific objects cannot be meaningfully said to sense-redly. Nor can the scientific objects postulated by the theory of inorganic matter be meaningfully said to be, in a relevant sense, colored."[13] Because of this, Sellars introduces a new category of scientific objects, called "sensa," to be the subjects of the color predicates[14] which are the successors in the Scientific Image of the color predicates of the Manifest Image. Sensa, then, are *emergent individuals*, individuals whose genesis is governed by emergent laws. Such individuals are of necessity emergent$_{1b}$; the ordinary causal laws that govern the operations of neural structures in the absence of sensa will not account either for the existence of sensa or for their causal influence on the perceptual states of persons and on their resulting behavior.[15]

Finally, what of the properties Searle terms "emergent$_2$"? The most plausible example we have seen of an emergent$_2$ property is libertarian free will, and it seems clear that this cannot be a property that consists of the properties of, and relations between, the parts that make up a system of objects. If we are to include libertarian free will as an attribute of persons, it seems we shall need to recognize persons, or minds, or souls, as unitary subjects, not analyzable as complexes of parts. And if creationist versions of dualism are rejected, as the previous chapter suggests they should be, this

530

means we shall have to acknowledge the existence of minds as *emergent individuals* – similar in this respect (but perhaps only in this respect) to Sellars's sensa.

A recent emergentist

. . .

Karl Popper

Probably the most significant philosophical voice for emergentism in the last half-century has been that of Karl Popper. Interestingly, Popper is discussed more extensively by Sperry than any other philosopher,[16] and Popper in turn indicates awareness of Sperry's work.[17] Popper's views on this topic have been less influential than his well-known contributions to the study of scientific method, but they provide some provocative insights and are well worth discussing.

Popper refers to the emergent evolutionists, and indicates general agreement with their approach. He opposes the philosophical dogma expressed by the saying "There is no new thing under the sun," and suggests instead "that the universe, or its evolution, is creative, and that the evolution of sentient animals with conscious experiences has brought about something new" (p. 15). He never gives a precise analysis of "emergence" (Popper frequently expresses his distaste for discussing the meanings of words), but by attending to context it is possible to get a fair idea of what he has in mind. In general, one may say that for Popper the point of emergence is that the course of the universe's development gives rise to new characteristics, not able to be anticipated or predicted on the basis of what has gone before. He lays considerable stress on *indeterminism* in this connection, apparently because this guarantees the unpredictability, and therefore the genuine novelty, of the outcome of the process. (This contrasts with Sperry, who emphasizes that his concept of emergence is fully compatible with determinism.) He considers the objection that "if something new seems to emerge in the course of the evolution of the universe . . . then the physical particles or structures involved must have possessed beforehand what we may call the 'disposition' or 'possibility' or 'potentiality' or 'capacity' for producing the new properties, under appropriate conditions" (p. 23). His reply is that this is either trivial or misleading: trivial, in the sense that there obviously must be something in evolutionary history that preceded and prepared the way for the appearance of the new feature; but misleading if it is assumed that the precursor must be something very similar to the new, emergent characteristic. (It is for this reason that he opposes panpsychism, which he treats as a rival and alternative to emergentism.) He writes, "We know of processes in nature which are 'emergent' in the sense that they lead, not gradually but by something like a leap, to a property which was not there before" (p. 69).

Popper does appeal to the notion of "downward causation," and it has to be said that his employment of this idea is not as careful or as precise as one might wish. He wants to establish the idea for use in connection with mind–body interaction, but he applies it very broadly, sometimes in contexts where the implications are far from clear. Thus he says,

> There are many ... macro structures which are examples of down-ward causation: every simple arrangement of negative feedback, such as a steam engine governor, is a macroscopic structure that regulates lower level events, such as the flow of the molecules that constitute the steam.
>
> Downward causation is of course important in all tools and machines which are designed for some purpose. When we use a wedge, for example, we do not arrange for the action of its elementary particles, but we use a structure, relying on it to guide the actions of its constituent elementary particles to act, in concert, so as to achieve the desired result (p. 19).

It is a little difficult to see what is meant here by "downward causation": presumably Popper does not want to claim that the higher-level structures in these cases operate in some way other than through molecular inter-actions! In general, downward causation as Popper speaks of it does not necessarily imply "novel causal influence" on the part of the emergent feature, though neither does it exclude this. Nor does downward causation exclude in principle the possibility of explanation in terms of "bottom-up" microcausation (see p. 23), though he clearly does not think such explan-ations can be given in all cases.

How then does Popper's theory of emergence stand in relation to the alternative conceptions developed in the first section of this chapter? Probably the best answer is that he is thinking in terms of causal emergence, Searle's emergence$_1$. Popper's use of "emergence" does not necessarily imply emergence$_{1b}$, the emergence of novel causal powers, although some of the cases he mentions, especially those involving consciousness, clearly are in that category. And his advocacy of libertarian freedom means that the mind, in particular, has features that are emergent$_2$.

The mind, of course, emerges from the functioning of the brain and is closely tied to it; Popper conjectures that "the flawless transplantation of a brain, were it possible, would amount to a transference of the mind, of the self" (p. 117). He is skeptical about the existence of minds after death (see p. 556), though he never claims this is logically impossible. He thinks "the very idea of substance is based on a mistake" (p. 105), and does not use the word "substance" in stating his own view.[18] Nevertheless, it seems clear that he thinks of the mind or self as a continuing individual entity, distinct from the brain and interacting with it; in our terms, he is a substance dualist. While affirming the liaison between the self and its brain to be extremely close, he nevertheless warns against assuming "too close and too mechanical a relationship" (p. 118). As evidence against such an assumption, he points out that "at least some outstanding brain scientists have pointed out that the development of a new speech centre in the undamaged hemisphere reminds them of the reprogramming of a computer. The analogy between brain and computer may be admitted; and it may be pointed out that the computer is helpless without the programmer" (p. 119). In some cases brain functions stand in a one-to-one relationship with experience, but in other cases "this kind of relationship cannot be empirically supported." In another passage he returns to the computer metaphor, and also displays some of his affinities with traditional dualism: "I have called this section 'The Self and Its Brain,' because I intend here to suggest that the brain is owned by the self, rather than the other way round.[19] The self is almost always active. The activity of selves is, I suggest, the only genuine activity we know. The active, psycho-physical self is the active programmer to the brain (which is the computer), it is the executant whose instrument is the brain. The mind is, as Plato said, the pilot" (p. 120). Still another passage puts the emergence of mind in a broad evolutionary perspective:

> The emergence of full consciousness, capable of self-reflection, which seems to be linked to the human brain and to the descriptive function of language, is indeed one of the greatest of miracles. But if we look at the long evolution of individuation and of individuality, at the evolution of a central nervous system, and at the uniqueness of individuals . . . then the fact that consciousness and intelligence and unity are linked to the biological individual organism (rather than, say, to the germ plasm) does not seem so surprising. For it is in the individual organism that the germ plasm – the genome, the programme for life – has to stand up to tests (p. 129).

Emergent dualism

In the remainder of this chapter I will sketch out a theory of the mind which makes the mind both emergent$_{1b}$, since it is endowed with novel causal powers, and also emergent$_2$, since it possesses libertarian free will. I shall not claim either that this theory provides the only possible solution to the problem of the nature of persons, or that it is without difficulties of its own. I will count myself successful if I can leave the reader with the perception that this is a view that merits further consideration – that it may offer a way forward through the thicket of difficulties which perplex us.

We begin by stipulating that we take the well-confirmed results of natural science, including research on neurophysiology, just as we find them. Attempts to resolve the problem through a nonrealistic interpretation of the sciences, as in idealism and some forms of phenomenology, are deeply implausible and provide no lasting solution to our problems.[20] We need not assume that the sciences give us a *complete account* of the nature of the world, even an "in-principle" complete account. But what they do give us, in the form of their well-confirmed results, must be acknowledged as in the main true (or at least approximately true), and as informative about the real nature of things.

But if our theory should be realist about the results of the sciences, it should also be realist about the phenomena of the mind itself. John Searle has noted that a great deal of recent philosophy of mind is extremely implausible because of its denial of apparently "obvious facts about the mental, such as that we all really do have subjective conscious mental states and that these are not eliminable in favor of anything else."[21] It's true that we do not, in the case of the mind, have well-confirmed scientific theories comparable to the powerful theories that have been developed in the physical sciences. But we do have a vast amount of *data* concerning mental processes, events, and properties, and we should begin with the presumption that we are going to take these data as they stand (subject of course to correction), rather than truncate them in order to tailor them to the requirements of this or that philosophical scheme.

So far, perhaps, so good. But stating that we are realists both about the physical and about the mental brings to the fore once again the vast differences between the two: the chasm opens beneath our feet. Cartesian dualism simply accepts the chasm, postulating the soul as an entity of a completely different nature than the physical, an entity with no essential or internal relationship to the body, which must be added to the body *ab extra* by a special divine act of creation. This scheme is not entirely without plausibility, at least from a theistic point of view, but I believe that it carries with it serious difficulties.

In rejecting such dualisms, we implicitly affirm that *the human mind is produced by the human brain and is not a separate element "added to" the brain from outside.* This leads to the further conclusion that mental properties are "emergent" in the following sense: they are properties that manifest themselves when the appropriate material constituents are placed in special, highly complex relationships, but these properties are not observable in simpler configurations nor are they derivable from the laws which describe the properties of matter as it behaves in these simpler configurations. Which is to say: *mental properties are emergent*$_{1b}$; they involve emergent causal powers that are not in evidence in the absence of consciousness.

But while property emergence is necessary for the kind of view being developed here, it is not sufficient. For the unity-of-consciousness argument spelled out in Chapter 5 [of *The Emergent Self*] claims to show not only that the properties of the mind cannot be explained in terms of the properties exhibited by matter in simpler, nonbiological configurations; it claims that these properties cannot be explained in terms of – that is, they are not logical consequences of – *any* combination of properties of, and relations between, the material constituents of the brain. A conscious experience simply *is* a unity, and to decompose it into a collection of separate parts is to falsify it. So it is not enough to say that there are emergent properties here; what is needed is an *emergent individual*, a new individual entity which comes into existence as a result of a certain functional configuration of the material constituents of the brain and nervous system. Endowed, as we take it to be, with libertarian freedom, this individual is able, in Searle's words, to "cause things that could not be explained by the causal behavior of the neurons"; in virtue of this, consciousness is indeed emergent$_2$. As an analogy which may assist us in grasping this notion, I suggest the various "fields" with which we are familiar in physical science – the magnetic field, the gravitational field, and so on. A magnetic field, for example, is a real, existing, concrete entity, distinct from the magnet which produces it. (This is shown by the fact that the field normally occupies – and is detectable in – a region of space considerably larger than that occupied by the magnet.) The field is "generated" by the magnet in virtue of the fact that the magnet's material constituents are arranged in a certain way – namely, when a sufficient number of the iron molecules are aligned so that their "micro-fields" reinforce each other and produce a detectable overall field. But once generated, the field exerts a causality of its own, on the magnet itself as well as on other objects in the vicinity. (In an electric motor, the armature moves partly because of the magnetic fields produced by itself.) Keeping all this in mind, we can say that *as a magnet generates its magnetic field so the brain generates its field of consciousness.* The mind, like the magnetic field, comes into existence when the constituents of its "material base" are arranged in a suitable way – in this case, in the extremely complex arrangement found in the nervous systems of humans and other animals. And like the magnetic field, it exerts a causality of its own; certainly on the brain itself, and conceivably also on other minds (telepathy) or on other aspects of the material world (telekinesis).

535

To be sure, this analogy has its limitations, and it is important to keep in mind that it *is* an analogy rather than an attempt at causal explanation. In order to take the analogy in the right way, try to think of the generation of the magnetic field naively, somewhat as follows: to begin with, we have a coil of wire, with no associated magnetic field. We then cause an electric current to pass through the wire, and the presence of the current "causes a field of force to appear in previously empty space."[22] A new individual (however short-lived) has come into existence. In a somewhat similar way, on the present hypothesis, the organization and functioning of the nervous system bring into existence the "field of consciousness." One difference, of course, is that we know quite accurately the necessary and sufficient conditions for the generation of a magnetic field, whereas we know very little about the conditions for the emergence of consciousness.

Admittedly, the suggested way of thinking about the magnetic field *is* naive, and one might reasonably ask what becomes of the analogy when we view it in terms of the *real* ontology of fields, as opposed to the over-simplified version just presented. The problem with this is that the "real ontology of fields" has been a matter of debate ever since the introduction of the field concept (and its conceptual cousin, action at a distance) into physics.[23] As for the situation today, we need only recall the continuing controversy about the right way to interpret quantum mechanics. As Richard Feynman has observed, quantum electrodynamics is a theory that makes remarkably precise predictions (the theoretically calculated value for Dirac's number agrees with experiment to ten decimal places), but "nobody understands ... why Nature behaves in this peculiar way."[24] If this situation is someday resolved, so that a stable consensus on the ontology of fields is arrived at, it will certainly be necessary to reexamine the use of the field analogy in the philosophy of mind in the light of our new knowledge.

The limitations of the analogy are further shown in the fact that the properties of the magnetic field and the other fields identified by physics do not seem to be emergent in the strong sense required for the properties of the mind. Nor does it seem that these fields possess the kind of unity that is required for the mind, as shown by the unity-of-consciousness argument. And there is no reason to suppose that the fields of physics are endowed with inherent teleology, much less libertarian freedom. The analogy with the magnetic field is of some value in helping us to conceive of the ontological status of the mind according to the present theory. But it is *only* an analogy, and as such it can't bear the full weight of the theory, which must rather commend itself in virtue of its inherent advantages over both materialism and Cartesian dualism.

The theory's advantages over Cartesian dualism result from the close natural connection it postulates between mind and brain, as contrasted with the disparity between mind and matter postulated by Cartesianism. In view of this close connection, it is natural to conclude that the emergent consciousness is itself a spatial entity. If so, it would seem that emergent dualism is well placed in relation to Kim's "pairing problem." That problem asks about the basis of the connection whereby a particular soul and body are able to causally interact with each other. Timothy O'Connor speculates in this regard that "what is needed, perhaps, is an asymmetrical dependency-of-existence relation – most likely, this body (at the right stage of development) generating that mind. If this kind of baseline dependency relation is intelligible, the fact that these two entities should also interact in more specific ways over time does not seem to be a *further* mystery."[25] This seems correct, and it allows us to say a bit more about the spatial nature of the emergent mind: the volume of space within which the emergent mind exists must be *at least* sufficient to encompass those parts of the brain with which the mind interacts. It was argued in the previous chapter [of *The Emergent Self*] that the difficulty of conceiving mind–body interaction is not a conclusive objection against Cartesian dualism. But there seems little doubt that such interaction is *more readily* intelligible for emergent dualism, and this would seem to constitute a significant advantage for the latter theory.

There is evidence both from subhuman animals and from human beings (e.g., commissurotomy) that the field of consciousness is capable of being divided as a result of damage to the brain and nervous system.[26] This fact is a major embarrassment to Cartesianism, but it is a natural consequence of emergent dualism. Beyond this, the theory makes intelligible, as Cartesian dualism does not, the intimate dependence of consciousness and mental processes on brain function. The detailed ways in which various mental processes depend on the brain must of course be discovered (and are in fact being discovered) by empirical research. Philosophy should be wary of attempting to anticipate these conclusions, lest it reenact the tragicomedy of the pineal gland. But there is no reason to think the kind of theory here proposed will have any difficulty in accommodating the results as they emerge. It needs to be kept in mind, however, that the mind is not merely the passive, epiphenomenal resultant of brain activity; instead, the mind actively influences the brain at the same time as it is being influenced by it. And, finally, this theory is completely free of embarrassment over the souls of animals. Animals have souls, just as we do: their souls are less complex and sophisticated than ours, because generated by less complex nervous systems.

The theory's advantages over materialism will depend on which variety of materialism is in view. As compared with eliminativist and strongly reductive varieties of materialism, our theory has the advantage that it takes the phenomena of mental life at face value instead of denying them or mutilating them to fit into a Procrustean bed. In contrast with mind–body identity theories and supervenience theories that maintain the "causal closure of the physical," the view here presented recognizes the necessity of recognizing both teleology and intentionality as basic-level phenomena; they are not the result of an "interpretation" (by what or by whom, one might ask?) of processes which in their intrinsic nature are neither purpose-driven nor intentional. The view proposed here has more affinity with "property dualism" and views which postulate a strong form of property emergence – but these already are views to which many will hesitate to accord the label "materialist." Be that as it may, the present view differs from property dualism and property-emergence views in its postulation of the mind as an *emergent individual*, thus providing it with an answer, which those views lack, to the problem posed by the unity-of-consciousness argument.

The resemblance to property-emergence views does, however, suggest a suitable name for the theory. At one time I referred to it simply as "emergentism,"[27] but that label could lead to misunderstanding because it is most commonly used for theories of property emergence. I suggest, then, "emergent dualism" as a name which brings to the fore both the theme of emergence and the undeniable affinities between the "soul-field" postulated here and the mind as conceived by traditional dualism.

I have described the advantages of emergent dualism, but what of the costs? So far as I can tell, there is only one major cost involved in the theory, but some will find that cost to be pretty steep. The theory requires us to maintain, along with the materialists, that the potentiality for conscious life and experience really does exist in the nature of matter itself.[28] And at the same time we have to admit, as Colin McGinn has pointed out, that we have no insight whatever into how this is the case.[29] It is not necessary to endorse McGinn's assertion that the brain–mind link is "cognitively closed" to us – that is, that human beings are inherently, constitutionally incapable of grasping the way in which matter produces consciousness – though that possibility deserves serious consideration. And yet, in purely physiological terms, what is required for consciousness – or at least, some kind of sentience – to exist, must not be all that complex, since the requirements are apparently satisfied in relatively simple forms of life. As McGinn puts it, "In the manual that God consulted when he made the earth and all the beasts that dwell thereon the chapter about how to engineer consciousness from matter occurs fairly early on, well before the really difficult later chapters on mammalian reproduction and speech."[30]

While emergent dualism shares with (nonreductive) materialism the claim that ordinary matter contains within itself the potentiality for consciousness, it actually goes some way beyond materialism in the powers it attributes to matter. For standard materialism, the closure of the physical guarantees that consciousness does not "make a difference" to the way matter itself operates; all of the brain-processes are given a mechanistic explanation which would be just the same whether or not the processes were accompanied by conscious experience. Emergent dualism, on the other hand recognizes that a great many mental processes are *irreducibly* teleological, and cannot be explained by or supervenient upon brain processes that have a complete mechanistic explanation. So the power attributed to matter by emergent dualism amounts to this: when suitably configured, it generates a field of consciousness that is able to function teleologically and to exercise libertarian free will, and *the field of consciousness in turn modifies and directs the functioning of the physical brain.* At this point, it must be admitted, the tension between the apparently mechanistic character of the physical basis of mind and the irreducibly teleological nature of the mind itself becomes pretty severe, and the siren song of Cartesian dualism once again echoes in our ears.

. . .

Notes

1 For a brief overview see T.A. Goudge, "Emergent Evolutionism," in *The Encyclopedia of Philosophy*, 2:474–77. A fuller treatment is found in Brian P. McLaughlin, "The Rise and Fall of British Emergentism," in A. Beckerman, H. Flohr, and J. Kim, eds., *Emergence or Reduction? Essays on the Prospects of Nonreductive Physicalism* (Berlin: de Gruyter, 1992), pp. 49–93.

2 Searle, *The Rediscovery of the Mind* (Cambridge: MIT Press, 1992), pp. 111–12.

3 Although he doesn't say so, I am sure Searle means to include here also possible causal interactions between the elements and the environment.

4 Presumably these laws would be formulated in such a way as to have the ordinary, non-emergent laws as a special case. The possibility of such laws is the principal theme of P.E. Meehl and Wilfrid Sellars, "The Concept of Emergence," in H. Feigl *et al.*, eds., *Minnesota Studies in the Philosophy of Science*, vol. 1 (Minneapolis: University of Minnesota Press, 1956), pp. 239–52. (Meehl and Sellars are discussing a paper by Stephen Pepper in which he claims to show that emergent properties are of necessity epiphenomenal. Their reply, in effect, is that these properties will not be epiphenomenal if there are emergent laws, a possibility Pepper mistakenly dismissed.)

5 Note that while this concept of emergence is defined in relation to an ideal, completed science, our estimate concerning which (if any) properties will turn out to be emergent in this sense is likely to be influenced by the science we currently have available. Brian McLaughlin attributes the demise of classical emergentism to the rise of quantum mechanics, which made it more feasible than before to derive macro-properties (including chemical and biological properties) from micro-properties (McLaughlin, "Rise and Fall of British Emergentism," pp. 54–5).

6 Timothy O'Connor, "Emergent Properties," *American Philosophical Quarterly* 31 (April 1994): 98.

7 For an argument that downward causation is ultimately an incoherent concept, see Jaegwon Kim, "Making Sense of Emergence," *Philosophical Studies* 95 (1999), pp. 3–36, and "'Downward Causation' in Emergentism and Nonreductive Physicalism," in Beckerman, Flohr, and Kim, *Emergence or Reduction*, pp. 119–38. Kim, however, does not consider the possibility of emergent laws, which are essential to the notions of emergence$_{1b}$ and downward causation as explained here. Brian McLaughlin, on the other hand, comes very close to the idea of emergent laws in his conception of "configurational forces" (see "Rise and Fall of British Emergentism," pp. 52–3). McLaughlin considers the idea coherent, though he says "there seems not a scintilla of evidence that there is downward causation from the psychological, biological, or chemical levels" (p. 55).

8 See Jaegwon Kim, "The Nonreductivist's Troubles with Mental Causation," in *Supervenience and Mind: Selected Philosophical Essays* (Cambridge: Cambridge University Press, 1993), pp. 336–57.

9 Ibid., p. 344. And compare: "It is no undue exaggeration to say that we have been under the reign of emergentism since the early 1970s" (Kim, "Making Sense of Emergence").

10 Kim also suspects that the notion of downward causal influence is ultimately incoherent; see note 7 above.

11 Kim, "Nonreductivist's Troubles with Mental Causation," p. 356.

12 Wilfrid Sellars, "Science, Sense Impressions, and Sensa: A Reply to Cornman," *Review of Metaphysics* 24 (March 1971): 408.

13 Ibid., p. 409.

14 And other predicates; sensa are shaped as well as colored.

15 It follows from this, interestingly, that Sellars rejects the causal closure of the physical, in the sense in which this is understood by Kim.

16 In Roger Sperry, *Science and Moral Priority: Merging Mind, Brain, and Human Values* (New York: Columbia University Press, 1983).

17 See Karl R. Popper and John C. Eccles, *The Self and Its Brain: An Argument for Interactionism* (New York: Springer-Verlag, 1977), p. 209. Part I of this book, written by Popper, is the primary source for his views on emergentism and the mind–body problem. (Page references in this section are to this work.)

18 Popper writes: "I conjecture that the acceptance of an '*interaction*' of mental and physical states offers the only satisfactory solution of Descartes's problem" ("Of Clouds and Clocks," in *Objective Knowledge: An Evolutionary Approach* [Oxford: Clarendon, 1972], p. 252); he does not say what the "mental states" are states *of*.

19 It was at Eccles's suggestion (see p. 473) that this was made the title for the book as a whole.

20 The mind–body problem arises, in large part, because of the apparent incongruity between the well-confirmed results of the natural sciences and what seems experientially to be the case with regard to the mind. Giving a nonrealistic interpretation of the sciences simply moves the incongruity to another place, between the manifest content of the scientific disciplines and the philosophical interpretation that is given of that content.

21 Searle, *Rediscovery of the Mind*, p. 3.

22 See Mary Hesse, *Forces and Fields: The Concept of Action at a Distance in the History of Physics* (London: Thomas Nelson, 1961), p. 250.

23 The history is well documented in Hesse, *Forces and Fields*.

24 Richard Feynman, *QED: The Strange Theory of Light and Matter* (Princeton: Princeton University Press, 1985), p. 10.

25 Timothy O'Connor, "Comments on Jaegwon Kim, 'Causality and Dualism'" (paper delivered at the University of Notre Dame, March 7, 1998). In fairness, I should quote also O'Connor's next remark: "But the idea of a natural emergence of a whole substance is perhaps a lot to accept."

26 There are, of course, numerous organisms (e.g., starfish) that can be divided into parts, with each part subsequently developing into a complete organism. As yet (and many of us hope this will not change) nothing of the sort has been done with human beings, though recent examples of the cloning of mammals suggest that the cloning of humans is a technologically possible. Even more telling are the split-brain data. Eccles admits that in split-brain cases "there is remarkable evidence in favour of a limited self-consciousness of the right hemisphere" (*Evolution of the Brain: Creation of the Self* [London: Routledge, 1989], p. 210). This is especially significant coming from Eccles, who is essentially a Cartesian dualist: it is hardly intelligible that a Cartesian consciousness should be divided by an operation on the brain, so Eccles's admission has to reflect strong empirical pressure from the experimental data.

27 See Hasker, "The Souls of Beasts and Men," *Religious Studies* 10 (1974): 265–77, and "Emergentism," *Religious Studies* 18 (1982): 473–88.

28 David Chalmers has suggested in discussion that the emergence doctrine would not force us to revise our conception of matter, if we consider the laws of emergence as contingent laws of nature that merely specify what happens under given circumstances. This seems to be correct, but I find this conception of laws implausible; it immediately invites the question, What is the ontological grounding of the causal powers involved? The view taken here is that laws of nature formulate causal powers that inhere in the natures of natural causal agents.

29 See Colin McGinn, *The Problem of Consciousness* (Oxford: Blackwell, 1991), Chapter 1; reprinted as Chapter 21 in this volume.

30 McGinn, *Problem of Conciouness*, p. 19. (McGinn's fairly frequent references to God are to be taken heuristically and not as expressions of actual belief.)

27

Michael Lockwood, "The Grain Problem"[1]

Think of what consciousness feels like, what it feels like at this moment. Does that *feel* like billions of tiny atoms wiggling in place?

(Carl Sagan[2])

How can technicolour phenomenology arise from soggy grey matter?

(Colin McGinn[3])

There is, today, no glimmer of a consensus amongst philosophers about the mind–body problem. Nevertheless, an increasing number of philosophers find themselves occupying a middle ground between physicalist reductionism, on the one hand, and dualism on the other. Physicalist reductionism I take to be the view that the physical story about what is going on in the brain and the world with which it interacts is in some sense the whole story. If there really are such things as mental states and processes – which eliminative materialists notoriously deny – then their existence must be logically implicit in facts stable in the language of physics. Space does not permit a detailed rebuttal of reductionist physicalism; nor do the arguments I have elsewhere presented[4] admit of brief summary. But the simple intuitive argument is that a being provided with a description of you or me couched purely in the language of physics – even if it possessed unlimited powers of ratiocination – would have no way of deducing that our bodies were associated with awareness at all, much less what specifically it was *like* to be you or me.[5] There is, of course, a lot more to be said on the matter; but attempts to disarm such intuitive arguments seem to me, in the end, uniformly unsuccessful. Indeed, for those not blinded by science, the falsity of reductionist physicalism will probably seem almost too obvious to require argument: Galen Strawson aptly describes it as "moonshine."[6]

Michael Lockwood, "The Grain Problem," in Howard Robinson (ed.), *Objections to Physicalism* (Clarendon Press, Oxford, 1993), pp. 271–91.

Dualism, on the other hand, is unattractive to most philosophers because embracing such a doctrine seems more like giving up on the mind–body problem than providing a genuine solution to it. Dualism does little or nothing to satisfy our cravings for an integrated world view. It remains obscure, on the dualist theory, just how the material is supposed to dovetail with immaterial mind. For, on the face of it, there are no mind-shaped gaps in the material fabric; the material world offers no explanatory or descriptive slots into which immaterial minds could comfortably fit. (One pictures matter saying to Cartesian mind: "This universe ain't big enough for both of us"!)

Anyway, I shall be assuming in this paper that, though reductionist physicalism is false, some form of materialism is nevertheless true. Conscious states and events are, on the view I favour, states of, or events within, the brain. But the very existence of consciousness shows that there is more to the matter of the brain (and hence presumably to matter in general) than is currently capable of being captured in the language of physics or physiology. How, then, is this "more" to be conceived? Well, Bertrand Russell suggested, in the 1920s, that, in respect of the brain, awareness might be providing content, where science provides only form.[7] All that we really know of the physical world, on the basis either of sense perception or of physical theory, Russell argued, is that it possesses a certain *causal structure*. Any attribute of a physical system, whether it be shape, size, or electric charge, is really known to us only as whatever it is that occupies a certain logical niche within a causal-explanatory system. We have no way of knowing what the external world is like *in itself*; its intrinsic character is systematically hidden from the gaze of ordinary observation or experiment. But now, the brain is itself a part of the physical world, and we are assuming that conscious states are brain states. We certainly seem to know, from introspective awareness, the intrinsic character of an itch or the sound of middle C, played on the piano, or a patch of phenomenal yellow. So if conscious states *are* brain states, do we not here have a corner of the physical world whose intrinsic nature precisely *is* made manifest to us, albeit in a very limited way? This was Russell's suggestion: that in consciousness, a fragment of physical reality is, so to speak, being apprehended from within.

This idea – which seems to me the only approach to the philosophical mind–body problem, currently on offer, that holds out the slightest promise – can be thought of as a neat inversion of a celebrated theory put forward some thirty years ago by J.J.C. Smart. Smart suggested that mental state terms were, as he put it, "topic neutral." According to Smart, when I say that I am experiencing a yellowish-orange patch in my visual field, I am saying something like this: "There is something going on which is like what is going on when I have my eyes open, am awake, and there is an orange illuminated in good light in front of me, that is, when I really see an orange."[8] This then leaves it open for the physiologist to discover what, in relevant respects, actually is going on under such conditions, physiologically speaking, and identify it with the occurrence of phenomenal yellow-orange. But of course this isn't at all what I am saying when I report that I am experiencing phenomenal yellow-orange; if it were, it would follow, absurdly, that there was nothing to prevent a congenitally blind person from having as rich and complete an understanding of such introspective reports as a sighted person. Russell's view turns this unworkable theory on its head: for him it is the *physical* descriptions, rather than the mental ones, which are topic neutral.

It is at this point that we encounter the *grain problem* (a difficulty attributed to Wilfrid Sellars[9]). For if the immediate objects of introspective awareness just are states of, or events within, the brain, seen as they are in themselves, why do they *appear to be* so radically different from anything that a knowledge of the physiology of the brain would lead one to expect?

That rather vague intuitive thought may be resolved into three more specific difficulties, each of which can be regarded as an aspect of the grain problem, as I conceive it. First is the fact that the phenomenal objects of introspective awareness are far less finely structured than are any plausible physiological correlates. Consider, for example, a phenomenally flawless auditory experience, of a note, say, on a violin. Its physiological substrate, presumably, is a highly structured, not to say messy, concatenation of changes in electrical potential within billions of neurons in the auditory cortex, mediated by the migration of sodium and potassium ions across cell membranes, and of molecules of transmitter substances within the chemical soup at the synapses. How do all these microstructural discontinuities and inhomogeneities come to be *glossed over*, in such a way as to generate the elegant perfection of auditory phenomenology that we associate with the playing of a Yehudi Menuhin? How are we to make philosophical sense of such phenomenological *coarse-graining*?

The second problem is that the structure we do encounter at the phenomenal level seems not to match, even in coarse-grained fashion, that of the underlying physiology, as revealed by scientific investigation. The phenomenal contents of awareness don't appear to have the *right kind* of structure; what is ostensibly lacking, here, is even the most approximate isomorphism between states of awareness and the underlying physiological goings-on that, on my view, they are supposed to be mirroring. In particular, three-dimensional spatial arrangement, and changes therein, seem central to all physical structure. Where, then, are their phenomenological counterparts? Of course, there is the visual field, and auditory and somatic-sensory space. But these are local, modality-specific *representations*, merely, of regions of the external world. We search in vain for some global, over-arching mode of phenomenological organization that could plausibly be equated with introspectively encountered spatial layout. It is all very well to insist that the scientist's characterization of the brain, as of the physical world in general, is ultimately topic neutral; so that the terms of the characterization are, in the final analysis, mere placeholders for unspecified intrinsic natures. The problem is that the phenomenal pegs, as John Foster neatly puts it, seem not to be the right shape to fit these holes in the topic-neutral characterization.[10]

Someone may see in these difficulties an argument for functionalism. The functionalist would regard the relation between a phenomenological description of the contents of consciousness and a physiological description of the corresponding brain-processes as analogous to that between a description of the workings of a computer in software terms, on the one hand, and in terms, say, of the electronic configuration of the underlying circuits, on the other. Thus, brain states, for the functionalist, impinge on awareness only *qua* possessors of certain high-level causal-functional roles. Precisely what, in physiological terms, are playing those roles, and how they do so, is, at the level of phenomenology, essentially irrelevant.

Functionalism, however, has its own problems – most notably its inability to explain why functional roles should be associated with any phenomenal qualities – *qualia* – at all. And in any case, it would seem, intu-itively, perfectly possible for there to be a system functionally equivalent to a human mind, in which the corresponding functional roles were associated with different *qualia* from those associated with these roles in our own case.[11] Functionalism may have some plausibility in accounting for mental structure but, on the face of it, fails utterly to account for phenomenal *content*. Moreover, all arguments one could mount against reductionist physicalism apply *a fortiori* to functionalism; since if functionalism were true, reductionist physicalism clearly *could be* true also. If a physical system is, so to speak, running the right programs, then it follows, for the func-tionalist, that it has certain mental states; and this is something that a being with sufficient ratiocinative power could presumably read off from a description of the system couched in the language of physics. If, as I have been suggesting, reductionist physicalism is essentially a non-starter, then so too is functionalism – at least if put forward as a global theory of mind.

The third aspect of the grain problem that I wish to consider is raised by the profligate *qualitative diversity* of the phenomenal realm, which seems flatly at odds with the comparative qualitative homogeneity of the physical ingredients out of which any corresponding brain state could realistically be composed. There are two levels at which this might be argued. Both visual and auditory information, according to the current wisdom, are encoded – albeit in different parts of the brain – by firing rates within certain batteries of neurons. But there is (as far as I am aware) nothing qualitatively distinctive about a neuron in the auditory cortex, or the corresponding action potential, to mark it out from a neuron, or the firing of a neuron, in the visual cortex. So how, on this basis, is one to account, say, for the fundamental phenomenological difference between a sound and a flash?

The other level at which the point could be argued is that of particle physics. The most promising currently available candidate for a so-called *theory of everything* (TOE) is something known as *superstring theory*.[12] According to this theory, everything is ultimately composed of incredibly minute loops – the "strings" – with length and tension, but no thickness; everything that happens is ultimately a matter of the motion and interaction of these strings; elementary particles are strings in different vibratory states. These strings are held to inhabit a ten-dimensional space–time, in which six of the spatial dimensions are curled up in such a tight radius that they are effectively undetectable *as spatial dimensions*, though their presence manifests itself in the form of forces. The details of the theory scarcely matter, for our purposes. What does matter is that, once again, it seems incomprehensible that different combinations of collective or individual string states could generate the qualitative diversity that is manifest at the phenomenal level. It seems inconceivable in much the same way, and for much the same reasons, that it is inconceivable that an artist, however skilled, should conjure the simulacrum of a Turner sunset from a palette containing only black and white paints.

What is ostensibly lacking, both at the neuronal level and at the level of particle physics, is, most obviously, the requisite qualitative potential – just as black and white paints provide the potential for an infinite number of shades of grey, but not for a yellow or a red. But there is also (as John Foster has pointed out[13]) a subtler difficulty having to do with the possibility of securing, at the fundamental level, the required qualitative *flexibility*. One might, in speculative vein, attempt some wholesale enrichment of the physical microstructure – crediting the basic ingredients of the physicist's ontology with intrinsic attributes way beyond what are called for by their explanatory roles within physical theory, but which are specifically tailored to the demands of phenomenology. The trouble then, however, is that it seems scarcely deniable that, at some level, these fundamental ontological ingredients, whatever they are, must be broadly *interchangeable*. What, one may ask, is the use of attributing, say, embryonic colour to the ultimate physical components involved in the neuronal goings-on that are supposed to be constitutive of a phenomenal patch of red, if these self-same constituents are also to be capable of figuring in auditory or olfactory experiences which are wholly devoid of visual phenomenology? Little is gained if what one does in order to account for the *presence* of phenomenal qualities in one place has the effect of making a mystery of their ostensible *absence* elsewhere.

With regard to the first of these three difficulties, a concrete analogy may help to fix ideas. Consider a (monochrome) newspaper photograph. Seen at very close quarters, or through a magnifying glass, it stands revealed as a rectangular array of different-sized black dots on a white background. But casual inspection shows, rather, lines, edges, and patches of black, white, and varying shades of grey. Let the latter appearance correspond, in our analogy, to the phenomenal aspects of an experience, and the array of dots to the nitty-gritty of ion exchange and so forth, which is constitutive of the corresponding brain-process.

The very word "introspection" invokes a supposed analogy with perception: the metaphor of the "inner eye." (Compare Kant's talk of an "inner sense," complementary to the "outer senses.") Now if there really were a close parallel here, this first aspect of the grain problem would scarcely be troubling. Just as, with the photograph, the limited resolving power of the eyes ensures that, if we stand back sufficiently, we shall have the illusion of continuity, so we could envisage the mind, in introspection, as standing back from the underlying brain-processes – again, with consequent loss of resolution. Particulate and discontinuous physico-chemical activity will yield perceived continuity, just as the discrete patches of ink on paper give way to ostensibly continuous lines and patches of black, white, and grey. But of course, this picture is simply incoherent. For the mind is not supposed to exist *over and above* the relevant brain activity. And no literal sense can be attached to the notion of the conscious mind being distanced, in this fashion, *from itself.*

Coarse-graining within ordinary perception is ultimately to be explained via the concept of a *mental representation.* It is a mental representation of the external object, rather than the object itself, that is directly before the mind in ordinary perception. And this mental representation is linked to the external object by an information-conveying causal chain. Degree of resolution is largely a matter of *how much* information about the external object is conserved in transmission; though, more generally, it is also a matter of how the information is encoded and reprocessed. (Thus, "smoothing" of the data is presumably, in part, a product of specific processing; it could hardly be accounted for on the basis merely of information degradation.)

But, as I say, there is no such story to be told in regard to introspective awareness. Introspection is not a distinct sensory modality whose objects differ from those of "outer sense" by being internal instead of external to the conscious mind. Rather, it is distinguished by one's cognitive or intentional *focus*. Thus, any of the ordinary five senses may be exercised in introspective mode; and doing so is a matter of taking as one's cognitive focus the mental representations themselves, instead of the external objects (if any) which they represent. (Compare the way in which, while watching the Wimbledon men's finals on television, one could switch one's mental focus from the players themselves to the corresponding images on the screen – in the context, say, of wondering whether one should adjust the contrast.) Hence, there are no distinctively introspective meta-mental representations, which stand to introspection as do ordinary visual, auditory, etc. representations to sight and hearing – and whose separation from their mental objects could help us resolve this aspect of the grain problem. And even if there were, the original problem would simply re-emerge at the level of these meta-representations themselves. Our difficulties begin at the point where the perceptual buck stops.

The force of these arguments will, I suspect, be lost on some people. Clearly, someone might protest, there are macroscopic qualities, and there is macroscopic structure: consider liquidity, for example, or temperature, or sphericity. These are perfectly genuine features of physical reality; so why shouldn't it be correspondingly macroscopic features of brain activity that manifest themselves in awareness? But macroscopic features such as those cited are not genuinely *emergent* attributes of the physical world. On the contrary, high-level descriptions like "liquid," "hot," or "spherical" apply – so it would seem – entirely in virtue of what holds true at the microlevel. And if so, it appears to follow that external physical reality can, in thought and perception, present itself to the mind in such high-level terms only by courtesy of the mediating role of mental representations.

I am not, of course, suggesting that the objects of direct awareness come unconceptualized. Thus the presence, within one's visual field, of a number of black dots – even if, in contrast to the dots in our newspaper photograph, they are individually perceived as such – may inescapably carry with it the interpretation *circle*. But that does nothing to explain how what is presented to awareness can, in another instance, just *be* a phenomenally continuous circle, when the physical substrate of the experience consists of a discontinuous array of, say, discrete centres of electrical activity.

Grover Maxwell (whose statement of the grain problem is the most lucid I have come across in the published literature) suggests that, if we are looking for physical structure that is isomorphic to the phenomenal structure encountered in awareness, we might find it at what he dubs the "middle-sized" level.[14] What he has in mind is a level of structure intermediate between, and less familiar than, quantum microstructure and quasi-classical macrostructure: a level the better understanding of which might, he thinks, hold the key to the elusive goal of bringing together, into a consistent whole, quantum mechanics and general relativity. But there is a fundamental philosophical unclarity in Maxwell's proposal. For what exactly is "middle-sized" structure supposed to consist in? Is it supposed to be structure which is, in the above sense, *high-level* with respect to electrons and the like – albeit low-level with respect to, say, blizzards, buffaloes, ball-bearings, and bacteria, hamsters, ham sandwiches, and housing estates? If so, then all he's really talking about – so it's tempting to argue – is microstructure under a (relatively) high-level description. And all the considerations invoked in the past few paragraphs still apply; it will remain a complete mystery how direct introspective contact with brain activity – unmediated by intervening mental representations – can reveal middle-sized structure to the total exclusion of the microstructure which is ultimately constitutive of it.

Perhaps, however, what Maxwell means by middle-sized structure is not merely high-level structure, with respect to the quantum microstructure, but something genuinely *emergent*, in a sense in which liquidity, temperature, and the like are not. The only sense I can attach, in the present context, to Maxwell's middle-sized structure being emergent is that it is structure which is instantiated – in part or in whole – by *emergent qualities*. By emergent qualities, I mean intrinsic attributes which are qualitatively distinct from any attributes possessed either by the low-level constituents of physical reality, considered individually, or by any configurations of them that involve relatively small numbers of these constituents, or which have a relatively low level of organization or complexity. The idea is that, at a certain number/density/complexity (or whatever) *threshold*, new qualities emerge which are different in kind from any that are present in sub-threshold phenomena involving these same constituents; and *pari passu* with these new qualities, new behaviour also. One can imagine possessing a dynamical theory which is ostensibly equal to the task of describing the fundamental constituents, and explaining and predicting their behaviour, *up to the threshold* – at which point, however, the theory begins to prove inadequate.

Well, I daresay that something roughly along these lines may be true. Indeed, it is difficult to see how *awareness itself* could be anything other than an emergent phenomenon, in something like the above sense, assuming the truth of materialism. Nor does such emergence threaten to compromise the unity of physical science. Whatever emerged, at and above the associated threshold, would – by hypothesis – have been *latent*, all along, in the low-level constituents. Hence, a complete description of these constituents would have to include reference to dispositional properties, of which the emergent qualities and behaviour constituted a manifestation. If we assume – as is very plausible – that all dispositions must have a *categorical base*

549

(as the disposition of a key to draw the bolt of a given lock has *shape* as its categorical base), then a description of these constituents need contain no reference to these dispositions as such. It would suffice to cite their intrinsic (non-dispositional) attributes, together with the fundamental laws; a disposition, on the part of any low-level constituent, would hold in virtue of the combination of its intrinsic, categorical attributes and laws which related these attributes to the emergent ones. And incidentally, even if awareness, say, is an emergent phenomenon in the sense just indicated (involving emergent properties and relations), it does not follow that the fundamental low-level constituents need possess any intrinsic, categorical attributes other than those which current physical theory would credit them with – at least, under the conditions prevailing in ordinary physics experiments. Their potential for generating awareness could be a matter of the application of certain currently unknown *laws* to their familiar physical attributes (in which laws, of course, there *would* be an essential reference to the emergent attributes). This fairly elementary point would appear to have escaped those authors who have argued that, if we are made out of electrons, quarks, gluons, and the like, then – given that we are conscious – electrons, quarks, and so forth must themselves be possessed of some sort of primitive proto-consciousness. As I see it, this is a complete *non sequitur.*

So, as I say, emergence in this sense seems to me wholly unobjectionable, philosophically speaking. But, having said that, I doubt very much whether such emergence could, realistically, be expected by itself to offer a solution to the grain problem. For we need to ask: is it really *scientifically* plausible to suppose that the distribution of these emergent qualities would possess any less microstructural complexity than that of the non-emergent ones? Let us go back to our earlier schematic example, involving a circular array of discrete centres of electrical activity in the brain. How, by appealing to emergence, might one explain how this array could present itself to consciousness as an *unbroken* circle? Well, one might suppose that, under the right conditions, such an array would give rise to an emergent field, in the immediately surrounding space, which was continuous, homogeneous, and bounded, in such a way as to match the associated phenomenal presentation, and the innate quality of which was registered in awareness. (See Figure 27.1.)[15]

In short, we should have to suppose that the microstructural arrangement of the fundamental constituents was capable of giving rise to emergent distributions of qualities which were *truly* smooth and homogeneous, where their source was anything but – in stark contrast to any actual field known to science, and in clear violation of the theoretical demands of quantum mechanics. Well I, for one, simply don't believe it; and I doubt if many people would. Where emergence may indeed come into its own is in

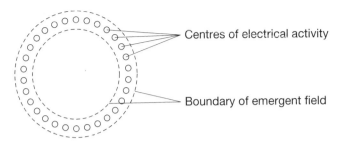

Figure 27.1 How a circular array of discrete centres of electrical activity in the brain might give rise to an emergent field

accounting for the qualitative diversity that is in evidence within the phenomenal realm: McGinn's problem of how "technicolour phenomenology [can] arise from soggy grey matter." But as regards the problem of phenomenal coarse-graining, it seems to me that it has little or nothing to offer. A solution – if such is to be found within the confines of philosophical materialism – must be sought elsewhere.

Before we proceed further, I should make clear just what I take to be required of a solution to the grain problem. The premiss of the problem is that sensory phenomenology belongs, so to speak, to that tip of the neurophysiological iceberg which projects above the surface of awareness. We are to regard it as a part or aspect of the reality of the brain that is directly present to the conscious mind, without benefit of any intervening representation: in awareness, the intrinsic nature of some part or aspect of what is to be found within the skull stands revealed. From this it follows that the phenomenal objects of sensory awareness must be thought of as somehow *embedded* within that tract of physical reality consisting of the brain and its doings. Assuming this position to be correct, consciousness, at the phenomenal level, can only make selections from the underlying neurophysiology. There is, as we have seen, no possibility of interposing any further stage of reprocessing between awareness and the neurophysiological substrate of its phenomenal objects; for sensory phenomenology is located precisely at the point where the *output* of all processing of sensory data is delivered to the conscious mind. The challenge posed by the grain problem is, therefore, the challenge of showing how *mere selectivity*, as applied to the physical reality of the brain, can yield the form and qualitative content characteristic of sensory phenomenology.

It is often said that philosophers are better at asking questions than at answering them; and I fear that this philosopher is no exception. All that I shall try to do now (and all that space really permits) is to provide a few hints towards a solution.

Underlying the grain problem, it seems to me, are a number of tacit assumptions about the nature of reality and our relationship to it which, though intuitively natural, are philosophically far from compelling. First, I suspect that most people, when it is put to them that in awareness we are immediately aware of some part or aspect of our own brain states, will think that, on this view, the relation between what is going on in one's brain as a whole and the phenomenal contents of awareness must be something like that between a painting and a detail of that painting. But to suppose that is to make the natural but nevertheless unwarranted assumption that the *principle of selection* underlying consciousness must be purely spatial location. There is, *a priori*, no reason to assume that *any* purely *spatial* cordoning of the brain at a given time would capture all *and only* that of which the subject was directly aware. With respect to any spatially defined region, the subject could surely be aware of some but not all aspects or attributes of what lay within it. Secondly and relatedly, there is no good reason to assume that the contents of a given state of awareness correspond to *simultaneous* goings-on in the brain. Indeed, in the context of relativity, no absolute sense can be attached to the notion of spatially separated events being simultaneous. From a relativistic viewpoint, the brain corresponds to a four-dimensional *world-tube*. And it is as likely as not that what is, so to speak, *given together* in awareness is spread throughout a segment of this world-tube, rather than being confined to a time-slice. In some ways, that would square better, in any case, with the psychological phenomenon of the *specious present* – the fact that, subjectively speaking, states of awareness seem to possess a measure of temporal "depth."

These are assumptions relating to us in relation to the world. But there is, thirdly, an assumption about the nature of reality itself which one might wish to question. Kronecker once said, apropos of arithmetic, that the natural numbers were created by God and that everything else is the work of man. In a similar way, it seems to me, people are very apt to suppose that only micro-structure is, so to speak, God-given, and that any higher level of structure is, at best, ontologically or metaphysically derivative, and at worst, a mere conceptual artefact. That assumption, in effect, was the basis of our earlier attack on Maxwell's suggestions regarding "middle-sized structure." But perhaps, after all, this notion of the ontological primacy of the microstructural is a dogma which should be rejected; perhaps the dilemma on whose horns we attempted to impale Maxwell is a false one. (I shall shortly advance some considerations which suggest that it is.)

None of these observations, however, penetrates to what I conceive to be the real heart of the matter, which is that the grain problem is one manifestation of a more general philosophical puzzle having to do with *subjectivity* and *objectivity*. The world of modern science, it is sometimes said, is a *centreless* world, a world which abstracts from the *point of view* of any particular observer. As Nagel neatly puts it, science is in the business of describing "the view from nowhere."[16] Awareness, by contrast, is inescapably centred on a point of view. What is directly present to awareness must, therefore, be conceived as a *perspective* on the brain. I wish to argue that the apparent dissonance between a physiologist's description of brain activity and the contents of our introspective judgements is to be seen, in part, as a consequence of the (relatively) perspective-transcendent character of the former.

If what is true "subjectively" is true relative to a point of view, then the only way of reconciling subjectivity and objectivity is by incorporating *points of view* within one's objective inventory of the world. Any metaphysical theory which does not somehow include points of view in its ontology is to that extent inadequate, as a comprehensive conception of reality. One philosopher who saw this very clearly was Leibniz, who went to the extreme lengths of supposing, in effect, that the universe was entirely composed of points of view – his *monads*.

What I have just said applies as much to physics as it does to metaphysics. Indeed, it is in some sense as much a condition of the explanatory adequacy of a physical theory that one be able to locate, within it, the point of view of the observer, as it is of the practical efficacy of a map that one be able to pinpoint, on the map, one's own position.

In classical physics it was unnecessary to address this requirement explicitly, since the associated conceptual scheme was essentially continuous with that of common sense. In the theory of relativity, however, the requirement is met quite explicitly via the notion of a *frame of reference*. The currently favoured language of space–time and four-vectors would be intuitively unintelligible without the auxiliary notion of an *observer* as situated at the origin of a set of spatial co-ordinates with respect to which he is invariably at rest, with a personal flow of time which corresponds to integration of the space–time *interval* along his own *world-line*. (Einstein sometimes put this very concretely, imagining the observer as carrying around with him an apparatus consisting of three rigid, mutually perpendicular measuring-rods, clutching it at the point where the three rods intersect – the "origin" – to which is attached an ideal clock.)

Via this notion of a frame of reference, one comes to see how, from the observer's own point of view, space–time comes to be partitioned into the distinct space and time of common sense. Thus, the space–time interval (that is, four-dimensional separation) between two events comes to be decomposed into spatial and temporal intervals corresponding, respectively, to the *projections* of the space–time interval on to the three-dimensional space defined by the spatial co-ordinates (or the set of mutually perpendicular measuring-rods) and the one-dimensional space defined by the time co-ordinate (or the ideal clock). And, in general, a four-vector is decomposed into a three-vector and a scalar component – the four-momentum, for example, into a three-vector momentum and a scalar energy.

It is tempting to think of an observer, in the context of relativity, as the *concrete embodiment* of a frame of reference (rather than merely as "carry-ing around" such a frame, à la Einstein). A description of objects and events *relative to* this frame of reference – couched, therefore, in the language of space and time, rather than of space–time – may then be thought of as corre-sponding to the observer's perspective: how things are from his own "subjective" point of view.

The conception of physical science as giving us a centreless account of the world chimes well with its aim, in modern times, of finding things that remain *invariant* with respect to different ways of representing physical reality. (Einstein, it is alleged, originally wanted to call his theory the *theory of invariants*.) This notion of invariance is perhaps the single most powerful idea in modern physics and crops up everywhere – gauge invari-ance, in field theory, being one of its most prominent recent manifestations. But in particular, it crops up at the foundations of *quantum mechanics*. States of a physical system, in quantum mechanics, correspond to vectors in an abstract space known as *Hilbert space*. And just as the four-dimensional space of relativity can be seen through the eyes of any of an infinity of different *frames of reference*, so the Hilbert space of a quantum-mechanical system can be seen through the eyes of any of an infinity of different so-called *vector bases*. Every quantum-mechanical *observable*, that is to say, question one can ask of a quantum-mechanical system, sus-ceptible of being answered by a suitable measurement – or more generally, every set of *compatible* observables, that is, questions capable of being simultaneously answered – corresponds to a vector basis for Hilbert space, known as the *eigenbasis* of the corresponding observable or set of observ-ables. A set of observables, via its eigenbasis, defines a co-ordinate system for Hilbert space, just as a frame of reference defines a co-ordinate system for space–time. (The key things that remain invariant with respect to differ-ent bases are the respective probabilities of getting various outcomes, when carrying out measurements on the quantum-mechanical system in question.)

Quantum mechanics was discovered independently, in the mid-1920s, by Heisenberg and Schrödinger. But so different, in their mathematical formu-lation, were Heisenberg's *matrix mechanics* and Schrödinger's *wave mech-anics*, that they were at first thought to be distinct, rival theories. Only subsequently were they found (by Schrödinger himself, in the first instance) to be essentially equivalent, the difference in form being due, in large part, to different choices of basis. Roughly speaking, Heisenberg chose the eigenbasis corresponding to the energy observable, and Schrödinger the eigenbasis corresponding to the position observable.

That said, I am now in a position to convey the essence of my own favoured approach to the grain problem. (Again, space does not permit more than a very approximate and compressed rendering.) First, the brain, I suggest, may legitimately be regarded as a quantum-mechanical system. (There is nothing in the formalism of quantum mechanics that prevents it from being applied to macroscopic systems.) As with most complex quantum-mechanical systems, the brain may be conceptually decomposed (doubtless, in several alternative ways) into *subsystems*, which can be treated as quantum-mechanical systems in their own right. One of these subsystems I take to coincide with the neurophysiological substrate of conscious mental functioning. (This dividing-up of the brain into subsystems need not, as remarked earlier, correspond to anything that would seem intuitively at all natural; nor need the subsystem in question correspond to what would ordinarily be thought of as a *part* of the brain. The dividing-up would not, in general, be a *spatial*, or even a *spatio-temporal* division, so much as a partitioning of the *degrees of freedom* of the larger brain system – the distinct ways in which it can change state or store energy.)

Anyway, there is, I take it, such a brain subsystem. And from the point of view of consciousness, I contend, there is (at any given time, at least) a preferred set of compatible observables on that system. The conscious observer views his or her own brain through the eyes, so to speak, of this preferred set of observables, much as the observer, in relativity, views the world through the eyes of his own frame of reference. Indeed, just as, in relativity, the observer can, in a sense, be regarded as a concrete embodiment of a particular frame of reference, so, I suggest, may a conscious subject be thought of as, in some sense, the concrete embodiment of a set of compatible observables. Every quantum-mechanical observable has a so-called *spectrum of eigenvalues*, associated, respectively, with the eigenvectors comprising its eigenbasis; these are numbers corresponding to the possible results of measuring the observable in question. If we consider a *set* of observables, then their spectra can themselves be thought of as co-ordinate axes, jointly defining a further abstract space. And a value of each co-ordinate, corresponding to an eigenvalue of each observable in the set, will define a point or vector in this abstract space. When the set of observables is the set preferred by, or embodied in, consciousness, then this space may be equated with phenomenal or experiential space: points or vectors in the space correspond to distinct possible states of awareness. And the various *qualia* spaces of sense-perception – colour space, for example – are simply sub-spaces of this abstract space; specific *qualia*, as they figure in awareness, represent points or regions of such spaces encountered, so to speak, in the flesh. It is precisely here that the intrinsic character of the concrete reality that the abstract mathematical formalism of quantum mechanics purports to describe makes itself manifest.

But how does all this address the problem of how awareness is able to gloss over the complex microstructure which presumably underlies the phenomenal contents of any experience? Well quite simply, there are, in quantum mechanics, no observables, or sets thereof, which are *a priori* privileged. In particular, there is, in terms of quantum-mechanical observables, no rock-bottom level of structure to be discerned in the world. In quantum field theory, no sense can be attached, for example, to the notion of measuring the values of the field variables at a precise point – only their average values over some finite spatio-temporal region (which one can make as small as one wishes); indeed, no sense can be attached to their *possessing* a precise value at any precise point. (No more, in elementary quantum mechanics, can an electron be said to have, let alone be measured as having, a precisely defined position or momentum.) In quantum mechanics there is a sense in which all observables, and in particular observables corresponding to every level of structure, are to be regarded as equal in the sight of God, as are different frames of reference, relativistically conceived.[17] As I intimated earlier, quantum mechanics seems to be telling us that it is a classical prejudice to suppose that the world is not *intrinsically* structured at anything but the level of elementary particles, and their actions and interactions.

According to this approach, then, the apparent dissonance between brain activity, as seen through the eyes (and concepts) of the neurophysiologist, on the one hand, and the conscious subject, on the other, is to be attributed to three distinct considerations. First, this brain activity is revealed to the awareness of the corresponding conscious subject – as it is not to the probings of the neurophysiologist – *as it is in itself* (albeit only from a certain point of view). Second, introspective awareness is focused on a *subsystem* of the brain, selected according to principles that, from the standpoint of physiology, would seem very unnatural. And finally, the contents of consciousness correspond to eigenvalues of a set of *observables* which, again, are distinct from anything that the physiologist is likely to settle on: the dissonance between the subject's view, and that of the physiologist, might be conceived as analogous to that between, say, Schrödinger's wave mechanics and Heisenberg's matrix mechanics. Thinking in terms of co-ordinate systems for the Hilbert space of the relevant brain system, it is as though the co-ordinate system of the conscious subject were, so to speak, rotated with respect to that of the external observer.[18]

The state of a physical system – on the view that I am proposing – might be compared to a block of wood, distinct cross-sections of which can reveal strikingly different sorts of patterns, depending on the angle at which it is sliced: concentric rings at one extreme, roughly parallel, gently undulating lines at the other. Though the analogy is very imperfect, one might think of the neurophysiologist, and the conscious subject in introspection, as likewise being confronted, so to speak, with different "cross-sections" of what are in fact the same brain states. My claim is that, by appealing to the quantum-mechanical concept of an observable, we can render it intelligible, as with the grain of the wood, that a common underlying structure should manifest itself in superficially very different ways. On the side of introspection, moreover, such a conception removes the need to appeal to any inner representation, distinct from the state itself. For to be directly acquainted with a "cross-section" of something is *a fortiori* to be directly acquainted with the thing itself, not merely some cognitive surrogate of it – in spite of the fact that what is thereby revealed to consciousness is revealed only under a certain aspect.

What, then, finally, is consciousness telling us about the nature of physical reality? Well, first (assuming materialism to be true), that there is more to matter than meets the physicist's eye. For there is nothing in the physicist's account of the world to explain why there should *exist* conscious points of view – why the world should contain such concrete embodiments of sets of quantum-mechanical observables. Thus we are in a position to know *a priori* that something like superstring theory, whatever its other merits, cannot literally be a theory of everything – since there is nothing in the theory that could, even in principle, explain how matter, suitably combined, is able to generate awareness. But on the positive side, it follows from what I have been saying that our states of awareness, corresponding as they do, on my account, to sequences of eigenvalues of brain observables, are providing us with the answers to specific questions concerning the intrinsic nature of a corner of the physical world – something that (as Russell rightly insisted) can never be revealed in ordinary measurement or observation. For our own awareness, so I have been urging, embodies a preferred set of observables, which in turn amounts to saying that its contents, at any given time, embody the answers to a set of questions about the state (the intrinsic state) of the underlying brain system. Sadly, however, we here find ourselves in a predicament akin to that of the characters in *The Hitch Hiker's Guide to the Galaxy*, on being told that the answer to life, the universe, and everything was 42. We know the *answers* to these questions, in a way that a scientist, merely by examining our brains from without, never could. But unfortunately, we have, as yet, no idea what the questions are!

557

Notes

1 In writing this article, I have benefited greatly from an excellent critique of my views – as set out in ch. 10 of my *Mind, Brain and the Quantum: The Compound "I"* (Oxford, 1989) – which appears in J.A. Foster's *The Immaterial Self* (London, 1991), 119–30. My statement of the grain problem, in particular, owes much to this discussion.

2 *Contact: A Novel* (New York, 1985), 255.

3 "Can We Solve the Mind–Body Problem?," *Mind*, 98 (1989), 349; reprinted as Chapter 21 in this volume.

4 *Mind, Brain and the Quantum*, ch. 8.

5 See T. Nagel, "What is it Like to be a Bat?," *Philosophical Review*, 83 (1974), 435–50; repr. in id., *Mortal Questions* (Cambridge, 1979), 165–80.

6 G. Strawson, "Consciousness, Free Will, and the Unimportance of Determinism," *Inquiry*, 32 (1989), 3.

7 See esp. B. Russell, *The Analysis of Matter* (London, 1927).

8 J.J.C. Smart, "Sensations and Brain Processes," *Philosophical Review*, 68 (1959), 141–56; reprinted as Chapter 6 in this volume.

9 W. Sellars, "The Identity Approach to the Mind–body Problem," *Review of Metaphysics*, 18 (1965), 430–51.

10 Foster, *The Immaterial Self*, 126.

11 See N. Block, "Troubles with Functionalism," in *Minnesota Studies in the Philosophy of Science*, 9, ed. C.W. Savage (Minneapolis, 1978), 261–325, and also my *Mind, Brain and the Quantum*, ch. 3. [Excerpts from the former are reprinted as Chapter 12 in this volume.]

12 See M.B. Green, "Superstrings," *Scientific American*, 255 (Sept. 1986), 44–56.

13 Foster, *The Immaterial Self*, 127–8.

14 G. Maxwell, "Rigid Designators and Mind–Brain Identity," in *Minnesota Studies in the Philosophy of Science*, 9, ed. C.W. Savage (Minneapolis, 1978), 399.

15 I am here imagining that phenomenal spatial relations, say within the visual field, reflect – indeed, in some sense just *are* – actual spatial relations within the appropriate region of the cerebral cortex. But this is only for the sake of concreteness; I do not advance it as a serious hypothesis.

16 T. Nagel, *The View from Nowhere* (Oxford, 1986).

17 For the benefit of those familiar with quantum mechanics, let me say that I am, of course, glossing over the distinction between so-called *maximal* and *non-maximal* (or *degenerate)* observables, or sets thereof. (A maximal observable, or set of observables, is one corresponding to a measurement, or set of simultaneous measurements, which yields a state of *maximum information* about the system in question – one that cannot be improved upon by the performance of further measurements.) In case someone thinks that maximal observables, or maximal sets of compatible observables, are privileged with respect to non-maximal ones, in a way that vitiates my argument, it should be pointed out that one could imagine the space of possible states of awareness of the conscious observer being generated, so to speak, in two stages. Any non-maximal set of compatible observables can, after all, be turned into a maximal set simply by adding observables to the original set. So suppose, to

begin with, that there is (from the perspective of consciousness, though not of the world) a preferred maximal set of compatible observables (having the requisite non-maximal set as a subset). The spectra of eigenvalues of the observables in the set could then be thought of as co-ordinate axes, defining a state space, with respect to which the range of possible states of awareness could then be regarded as constituting a preferred subspace.

18 Here I have been able to do no more than sketch the bare bones of the theory I favour. In *Mind, Brain and the Quantum*, I develop these ideas in far greater detail, and also, for the sake of those unversed in modern physics, provide an elementary account of quantum mechanics itself.

28

Peter Unger, "The Mystery of the Physical and the Matter of Qualities: A Paper for Professor Shaffer"*

1. Introduction: a Russellian respect for the mystery of the physical

For some fifty years now, nearly all work in mainstream analytic philosophy has made no serious attempt to understand the *nature of physical reality*, even though most analytic philosophers take this to be all of reality, or nearly all. Whereas we've worried much about the nature of our own experiences and thoughts and languages, we've worried little about the nature of the vast physical world that, as we ourselves believe, has them all as only a small part.

In this central respect, we've been very different from the man emerging as the century's preeminent analytic philosopher, Bertrand Russell. Although Russell thought hard about the things that have preoccupied us, *he also thought hard about the nature of physical reality*. Why has there been such a great disparity?

By contrast with Russell, most contemporary workers in core analytic areas just assume that, largely as a legacy from the physical sciences, we have been granted a happily adequate conception of physical reality: Thanks to physics, we have a pretty good understanding of physical reality, even if there may be some serious deficiencies in our understanding.

When in this frame of mind, we philosophers aren't moved to think hard about the nature of physical reality, even if we believe it to be all of reality. Rather, we're much more moved by thoughts like this: "Let's leave such

Peter Unger, "The Mystery of the Physical and the Matter of Qualities: A Paper for Professor Shaffer," in Peter A. French and Howard K. Wettstein (eds), *Midwest Studies in Philosophy* 23: *New Directions in Philosophy* (Blackwell, Oxford, 1999). pp. 75–99.

terribly large matters to so many successful scientists, and to the few philosophers so concerned to interpret the work of the many."

Just so, when we trouble ourselves about what's what with things grossly physical, or with physical reality that's extralinguistic, and extramental, and so on, our concerns are with quite superficial matters. For example, we may reflect on the apparent fact that, if an ordinary rock should be split down the middle, with the two resulting "halves" never even coming close to being rejoined, the rock that was split ceases to exist, while two substantially smaller rocks then begin to exist. And, then, we may reflect on the apparent fact that, when a rock that's as famous as Plymouth Rock is similarly bisected, there's still that rock that's then in two salient pieces, whether or not there are also two smaller rocks then coming into existence. Based on these two reflections, we may aspire to a complex theory that "capturing intuitions" about both cases will serve to illuminate the "persistence conditions" for rocks in general, both the famous and also the obscure. But won't such a theory reflect our own interests more than it will tell us about the nature of physical reality? At all events, it won't deliver anything very deep, or very illuminating, about physical reality.

Even while knowing all that very well, we still don't trouble ourselves to be more searching. Rather, we're still affected by thoughts like, "Let's leave such terribly large matters to so many successful scientists, and our few colleagues who know their science." Especially in this fearfully complacent philosophical day and age, we do well to remember what Russell counseled: About the rest of concrete reality, we don't know anything nearly so intimately, nor nearly so fully, as we know our experience or, maybe better, as we know the phenomena apprehended in experience. (This remains true, of course, even if what we know most fully, and intimately, might be known less fully, and less intimately, than it can often appear.) And, we do well to recall that Russell did not exaggerate much, if at all, when, in a generally robust epistemological spirit, he said, "as regards the world in general, both physical and mental, everything that we know of its intrinsic character is derived from the mental side."[1] Nor did he exaggerate very much when, in a specifically materialistic spirit, he said, "we know nothing about the intrinsic quality of physical events except when these are mental events that we directly experience."[2]

If there's to be appropriately ambitious analytic philosophy done any time soon, then we'd best pay heed to such Russellian reminders. And though our philosophical efforts might diverge from his in many respects, they should be guided by the same realization that so greatly moved Russell: Except for what little of the physical world we might apprehend in conscious experience, which is available if materialism should be true, *the physical is mysterious to us.*

561

So we should wonder: To what extent, if any at all, do we have a philosophically adequate conception of physical reality? Do we have a conception well enough related to the human mind for it to ground a metaphysic in terms of which physical reality can be understood, at all well, by us very limited human thinkers?

Inspired by Russell and others, I'll try to give decent answers to such daunting questions. In the course of the effort, I may do more toward raising further questions than toward giving decent answers. But if they are fresh questions, that might be all to the good.

2.   A brief exposition of the scientifical metaphysic

As a first step in this effort, I'll sketch, very briefly, what I take to be the metaphysical worldview that, for several centuries and with no letup anywhere in sight, has been the dominant metaphysic of the highly educated in cultures much affected by the development of the natural sciences. It will be useful to have a memorable name for this dominant worldview, but not a name loaded with positive connotations, like "the scientific metaphysic," or with negative ones, like "the scientistic metaphysic." For a name that's reasonably memorable and neutral, I'll introduce a word that's meant to parallel "philosophical" and, with it, I'll coin the naming phrase "the *scientifical* metaphysic."

Though various modifications of it appear required by certain twentieth-century scientific developments, notably, by quantum mechanics and relativity theory, the heart of our scientifical metaphysic is, apparently, essentially the same as before the advent of the twentieth century. So, even if folks versed in contemporary physics would rightly prefer esoteric analogues of the ordinary terms I feel most comfortable using for the job, for my main philosophical purposes the following few paragraphs may serve to express our dominant worldview.

First, differently distributed in space at different times, there is physical stuff or *matter*. Placing aside the thought that this matter may have been, very long ago, created by some Extraordinarily Powerful Mind (or Minds), and placing aside thoughts of how such a SuperMind might, even nowadays, occasionally affect matter, this matter is *independent of minds*: To exist, the matter needn't be sensed by, or be thought about by, sentient beings.

Second (again placing to the side all such "theological" ideas, which from now on will generally be done only implicitly), insofar as it's determined by anything at all and isn't merely random, the distribution of this matter at any given time is determined by the distribution of the matter at earlier times, with the determination proceeding in line with our world's basic natural laws, which are physical laws.

562

Third, owing to the variety in these material distributions, at certain times some of the world's matter, or possibly much of the matter, is configured so as to compose various complex material structures and systems, ranging from the slightly complex through the fairly complex to the highly complex. Among the more complex of even these highly complex material structures and systems are living entities, or those serving to constitute living entities.

Fourth, among the more complex of even these living material entities, and possibly even among some (very distant) nonliving material complexes, there are those that are thinking, feeling, experiencing physical entities. Or, more cautiously, complexly composed of some matter, there are the living physical bodies of such thinking physical entities.

Fifth, there are certain properties that are the *naturally important* properties of matter, both matter that's involved in composing a highly complex material system and, equally, matter that's never so interestingly involved. To date, it's mainly been the work of physics to discover what actually are these properties.

Sixth, beyond what physics aims to discover, there are other naturally important properties. The most salient of these properties are to be found in a most intimate connection with the minds of the sentient beings of the world: These salient properties will qualify the conscious immediate experiences of these beings; or, if not quite that, they'll qualify whatever it is that such beings most immediately experience, perhaps manifolds of qualia. So, these properties will include (absolutely specific) phenomenal color properties and, just as well, (absolutely specific) phenomenal pain properties. None of these properties are, of course, even remotely like mere powers of material bodies to promote, in finite minds, any sort of experience. Because they figure prominently in my inquiry, I'll refer to the phenomenal properties as the *Qualities*, which capitalized term I'll reserve for them and only such other properties as are strongly and deeply analogous to phenomenal properties.

Seventh, the six preceding paragraphs are to be understood as implying that our scientifical metaphysics conflicts with many traditional metaphysical systems, even though it's not in conflict with many others. Thus, whereas Berkeley's subjective idealism conflicts with our scientifical metaphysic, other metaphysical views comport with it well. For example, Descartes's dualism, or at least a view much like the Cartesian metaphysic, provides a consistent line for further specification of our scientifical metaphysic. And it appears a materialistic worldview provides a quite different consistent line.

Although I've sketched the main thrust of our scientifical metaphysic in the seven paragraphs just preceding, I've ignored some very large matters.

For example, I've offered nothing about what this metaphysic might say, or might not say, regarding questions of genuine choice, or free will. Still, even with only as much of the scientifical metaphysic as what's been presented, there may be raised questions of philosophical importance. In this paper, we'll explore some of them.

3. This metaphysic, three kinds of property, and the restriction of qualities to minds

For a discussion that we may hope to be as profitable as it's protracted, I'll move deliberately toward displaying a doctrine that's assumed true by most who embrace the scientifical metaphysic, even if it might not be so much as actually implied by the dominant worldview. Toward succinctly presenting this popular proposition, which I'll call the *Restriction of Qualities to Minds*, it will be useful to notice *three categories of basic natural property* (of whatever entities, or entity, might serve to constitute physical reality).

First, I'll take note of what might be called the purely *Spatiotemporal properties* or, for short, the *Spatiotemporals*. Central to this group are, with one exception, what Descartes regarded as "the primary or real properties of matter . . . shape, size, position, duration, movability, divisibility and number. This list we can immediately diminish by one, because it is clear that *number* is an interloper here."[3] As concrete reality might have very many dimensions, this group may include, in addition to geometric properties, topological properties and, perhaps, other such "mathematically recognized" properties. Of course, even such determinables as Descartes's are just a starting point here; more to the concrete point are such absolutely specific determinate properties as, say, *being perfectly spherical*.

As I'm understanding the Spatiotemporals, even absolutely empty regions will, at least when limited in some dimensions or respects, have Spatiotemporal properties whether at an instant or over time, even if they might be devoid of all other basic properties. And, at least in many possible worlds, there's nothing more to the having of Spatiotemporal properties than what a perfectly empty region has, at an instant or over time.

As I'm painfully aware, the scientifical metaphysic *might not* help provide us with any understanding of concrete reality that's even modestly adequate. But, if it does profit us in that large regard, then we must think of very much of this reality, even if not absolutely all of it, as having Spatiotemporal properties. Indeed, though I'm far less confident of it, I suggest that we should accept even this much more ambitious proposition: For the scientifical metaphysic to do much *for our understanding* of concrete reality, there must be *some* truth in the thought that much of this reality has the three-dimensional nondirectional spatial structure, and the correlative one-dimensional directional temporal structure that, in our conscious perception of reality, are Spatiotemporal properties that physical reality appears to have. For although such perception might provide us with only a *very partial perspective* on reality, and with a *quite superficial* perspective, still and all, unless there's *something about physical reality* in virtue of which it has these familiar Spatiotemporal properties, the scientifical metaphysic will, I think, do far more toward providing intellectual illusion than toward giving us even a very modestly adequate understanding of reality. But in the present essay, I will rely only on less ambitious propositions. At all events, so much for my first category of basic natural properties, the Spatiotemporals.

Second, I'll notice what, for want of a better expression, I'll call the *propensity properties* or, more briefly, the *Propensities*. Often, these properties, or some of them, have been called "powers"; but inappropriately for us, that term connotes positive force. Others have called the properties "dispositions"; but despite the valiant efforts of C.B. Martin and others, that term has been so badly abused that it will arouse, in the minds of too many, undue confusion.[4]

Now, at least for the meanwhile, we'll understand the Propensities as being distinct from, even if they might be importantly related to, the Spatiotemporals. On this understanding, regions of absolutely empty space, or perfect vacuums, can have Spatiotemporal properties; but as it at least appears, no such physically empty regions will themselves have any powers or, as I'll say, any Propensities. By contrast with such vacuums, we may envision a finite spatial region that's precisely occupied by an electron, where our supposed electron is well suited to making true an early theory of such supposedly simple physical things. Then what's in that small finite region will be something that has, in addition to its Spatiotemporal properties, *unit negative electric charge*. Its having *that* property is, we may suppose, the electron's having a certain complex Propensity or, perhaps the same, its having a cluster of simpler Propensities. The complex Propensity of our electron will include, for salient examples, its Propensity to repel any other electron with such-and-such a force in so-and-so a direction, and its Propensity to attract any proton with such-and-such a force in so-and-so a direction. As with any entity's having any Propensity, the electron's having this one is not dependent, not even in the minutest degree, on there ever actually being any protons, or there being any other electrons. In contradistinction to there being any *chance for* the Propensity of our electron to be *manifested*, which does require there to be things external to it, the electron's *just having* the indicated Propensity doesn't depend on there ever being *any* such external entity.

Third, and last, I'll notice what I call the *Qualities*, a group of properties whose most accessible members are the phenomenal properties available in our conscious experience. But the Qualities may also include other properties: Beyond the properties experientially available to us, and even beyond those available to any of the world's finite minds, there may be properties that are *deeply analogous to* at least some of the phenomenal properties. Through *extrapolative analogical thinking*, perhaps we might get some grasp as to the nature of some of these farther-fetched properties, even if, perhaps, never a grasp that's very rich, firm, or clear.

So on the one hand, consider those phenomenal properties best suited to filling space, or to being spread through space. Here, we may consider a perfectly specific sort of translucent red, and an equally specific "colorless transparency," as with what's apprehended in experience of, say, a typical windowpane, and an equally specific "silveriness," as with what's experienced in, say, seeing some shiny silver. Since they're so well suited to filling space, we'll call these *Extensible Qualities*. Now, and on the other hand, consider some phenomenal properties that seem *unsuited* to filling space. Here we may consider a perfectly specific sort of taste of sweet chocolate, and a perfectly specific sort of pleasant sound, as with what's apprehended in one's experience of, say, a certain rendition of a favorite song, and a perfectly specific sort of elation, as with what's experienced upon, say, hearing some wonderful news. Since they're so unsuited to filling space, suppose, we'll call them *Nonextensible Qualities*. Now, we can have a conception, it appears, of properties that, though they're *not* available in experience to the world's finite minds, are very much *more like each* of our indicated Extensible Qualities than they're like *any* of our indicated Nonextensible Qualities.

The qualities we're analogically contemplating are very much more like our indicated Extensibles than our indicated Nonextensibles both overall and, as well, in those respects, whatever precisely they may be, that have our Extensibles be so very much more suited to filling space than are our Nonextensibles. By way of such extrapolative analogical thinking, I'm suggesting, we may have a contentful conception of (even if not yet any reason to believe in) a world featuring many instantiations of Extensible Qualities that can't, at least as a matter of natural fact, be experienced by any of the world's finite minds. In parallel, we can also conceive of properties that, though they're likewise unavailable to experience, are much more like each of our indicated *Nonextensible* Qualities than they're like any of our indicated Extensible Qualities. Here, too, there may be properties that, though they're not properly phenomenal properties, are among a world's farther-fetched Qualities.

In marked contrast with how things were fifty years ago, nowadays it appears almost universally believed by analytic philosophers that the phenomenal properties are properties of, and only of, conscious experiences; and, rather than being any mere contingent truth, this belief runs, it's conceptually and necessarily true that the phenomenal properties are all properties of, and only of, the mental, and even just the experiential. Let's suppose this belief is correct. Then it might be that, though the phenomenal color properties *seem well suited* to filling space, that's an illusory appearance. For as far as any of us can tell, it might be that conscious experiences can't literally occupy spatial regions.

Let's further suppose that, whether or not for that reason, none of the phenomenal properties are actually Extensible, are Qualities well suited to filling space. Well, even in such an event, it's still true to say this: The phenomenal properties may be peculiarly helpful leads for our only quite partially grasping, through extrapolative analogical thinking, Qualities whose instances *are* so prevalent in our mind-independent spatiotemporal reality.

Having said that, I'll also say this: Apparently against almost all other contemporary analytic philosophers, I *don't* believe that the phenomenal properties are features only of conscious experiences. Rather, I'm quite agnostic. Toward explaining this unfashionable agnosticism, in the next section I'll offer two sorts of consideration. Here it suffices to note that the present project doesn't depend on what's the best approach to this interesting issue. To indicate what's much more relevant, I display this from Russell:

> To assert that the material *must* be very different from percepts is to assume that we know a great deal more than we do in fact know of the intrinsic character of physical events. If there is any advantage in supposing that the light-wave, the process in the eye, and the process in the optic nerve, contain events qualitatively continuous with the final visual percept, nothing that we know of the physical world can be used to disprove the supposition.
>
> The gulf between percepts and physics is not a gulf as regards intrinsic quality, for we know nothing of the intrinsic quality of the physical world, and therefore do not know whether it is, or is not, very different from that of percepts. The gulf is as to what we know about the two realms. We know the quality of percepts, but we do not know their laws so well as we could wish. We know the laws of the physical world, in so far as these are mathematical, pretty well, but we know nothing else about it. If there is any intellectual difficulty in supposing that the physical world is intrinsically quite unlike

that of percepts, this is a reason for supposing that there is not this complete unlikeness. And there is a certain ground for such a view, in the fact that percepts are part of the physical world, and are the only part that we can know without the help of rather elaborate and difficult inferences.[5]

At all events, at least for the meanwhile we may understand the Qualities as being distinct from, though perhaps importantly related to, both the Spatiotemporals and the Propensities. On this understanding, whereas the Spatiotemporal properties can be possessed by regions of absolutely empty space, it is at least somewhat doubtful that any of the Qualities, including even any of the Extensible Qualities, can be possessed by an *absolutely* perfect vacuum. For now, that's all for this last sort of basic natural property.

With this threefold classification providing the context for it, I can briefly display the doctrine that, at this section's start, I said was assumed by most who hold with the scientifical metaphysic, even if it's not actually implied by the dominant worldview:

> *The Restriction of Qualities to Minds.* Unlike the Spatiotemporal properties and the Propensities, which are so widely instantiated in what's physical, there are not (any instantiations of) any of the Qualities in physical reality, with the possible exception, at any given time, of such a small part as may subserve the minds of sentient beings.

According to the *Restriction*, to use this doctrine's short name, all the world's matter, or almost all, has no Qualities, whatever might be its Spatiotemporal properties and its Propensities.

Though they need fleshing out if they're ever to be of much philosophical interest, here are a couple of questions that, I'll suggest, may already be of some interest: If we *add* the Restriction to our scientifical metaphysic and, thus, obtain a *deeply segregated* worldview, what will be, for us, the advantages of, and the disadvantages of, such a view of the world? On the opposite hand, if we add the *Denial* of the Restriction to our scientifical metaphysic, obtaining a *deeply integrated* worldview, what will be the advantages and disadvantages?

4. Might phenomenal qualities outrun experience?

Before inquiring into the implications of the Restriction, which will soon be my main order of business, I'll offer two groups of ideas, each complementing the other, that serve to motivate this pretty unusual philosophical stance of mine: Apparently against almost all my analytically philosophical contemporaries, I *don't* believe that the phenomenal properties are possessed only by experiences. Rather, I'm agnostic about the matter. Though providing motivation for this unfashionable stance isn't crucial for my project, my doing that will help contemporary readers appreciate, rather well, what I mean to say about the implications of the Restriction.

For the first group of motivating ideas, I'll quote at length from Michael Lockwood's wonderfully stimulating book, *Mind, Brain and the Quantum*:

> I find it plausible to suppose that the phenomenal qualities themselves are less fickle than one's attention, and may persist even when one's awareness of them lapses. On this view, phenomenal qualities are neither realized by/being sensed nor sensed by being realized . . . . The realization of a phenomenal quality is one thing, I contend; its being an object of awareness is something else, . . .
>
> At first hearing, the present proposal may seem wildly eccentric . . .
>
> . . . But now consider the following example. Suppose we have three colour patches projected close together on to a screen; call them *L* (left), *M* (middle) and *R* (right). Suppose, further, that in the absence of *R*, *L* is indistinguishable from *M*, and that in the absence of *L*, *M* is indistinguishable from *R*. *L*, however (in the presence or absence of *M*), *is* distinguishable from *R* . . . . So what are we to suppose happens if we start with a screen containing only *L* and *M*, which are *ex hypothesi* indistinguishable, then add *R*, so that all three patches are present, and finally remove *L*, leaving *M* and *R*, which are likewise indistinguishable?
>
> There are only two possibilities, surely. By far the more plausible, to my mind, is that the phenomenal colours corresponding to *L* and *M* are distinct, even in the absence of *R*: there *is* a phenomenal difference here, but one too small to register in consciousness, no matter how closely the subject attends. Adding together two phenomenal differences of this magnitude does, however, produce a difference that registers in consciousness; hence the subject's ability to distinguish *L* from *R*. The only alternative is to suppose that the effect, either of adding *R* or of removing *L*, is to induce a qualitative change in the phenomenal colour corresponding to one or the other of the remaining patches. But it surely won't *seem* to the subject that this is what happens. So on this supposition too, there would be phenomenal differences – or at least, phenomenal *transitions* – that defied conscious detection.
>
> Not only, in such perceptual cases, does the phenomenal character of what one is immediately aware of outrun one's awareness of it; it actually seems to do so . . . . What I am suggesting, in effect, is that

we should allow phenomenal qualities quite generally to outrun awareness. Those who think they understand what it is for phenomenal qualities to inhere in portions of their visual field of which . . . they are not currently conscious, now have a model for what, . . . the unsensed portion of the physical world is like in itself, quite generally – even in regions beyond the confines of the brains of sentient beings, where awareness, as far as we know, never intrudes.[6]

These passages provide extremely suggestive argumentation, even if no decisive argumentation, to the effect that there are instances of phenomenal color qualities that outrun experience (and also *fairly* suggestive reasoning that these Qualities outrun even nonconscious mentality).

Much as the quotation from Lockwood indicates, insofar as philosophers now think they have difficulty understanding the suggestion that phenomenal qualities may outrun mentality, it's generally because they think they have difficulties with the suggestion that phenomenal qualities might ever outrun *conscious* mentality. But what's just been quoted serves to confute the latter thought. So most of these philosophers should reject the former as well.

While many may still find it hard to *believe* phenomenal properties outrun all of mentality, myself included, by now few should have trouble with the thought that the suggestion is a *coherent* proposition. With that said, there's enough from the first group of motivating ideas.

For the second group of ideas, I'll relate the results of some bouts of phenomenological thinking, and some analysis pertaining thereto: When lying still in silence and darkness, sometimes I vividly experience my body as filling space. Then, it appears, I apprehend *Qualities felt as suffusing space*. Naturally enough, I'll call these Extensible Qualities the *Felt Bodily Qualities*. Now, with the Felt Bodily Qualities I can conceive *only* of there being such instances as are *experienced*; indeed, with *these* Qualities, I conceive only of such instances as are *experienced as extending through space occupied by (some of) a being that experiences them*.

By contrast with the Felt Bodily Qualities, it seems clear, I can conceive of there being instances of *color* Qualities that *aren't* ever experienced; indeed, I can do that about as well, it appears, as I can conceive instances that *are* experienced. (To me, this has been intuitive for as long as I can remember, long before any encounter with *arguments* in support of such an idea, like what's just been displayed from Lockwood.)

In marked contrast to the phenomenal colors, it appears, the Felt Bodily Qualities are *essentially mental* Qualities, which can be instanced only when they figure in experience. By that same contrast, the phenomenal colors, and the Extensibles strongly analogous with them, *aren't essentially mental*

Qualities, and can be instanced *even when they don't* figure in experience. So as it appears, we have tolerably clear conceptions of two quite different sorts of Extensible Quality. Considerations like these serve to motivate my agnosticism as to whether the phenomenal qualities may outrun experience, or even mentality.

Having had both groups of motivating ideas presented, perhaps readers will be sympathetic to the idea that the phenomenal qualities can outrun experience. And with that reasonably open-minded stance, perhaps they'll appreciate, rather well, what I'll now say about the implications of the Restriction. At all events, it's high time for that main order of business.

5. The Restriction, Particles in space and spaces in a plenum

For the scientifical metaphysic to provide us with a reasonably adequate view of our world, do its bare bones need such Qualitative flesh as can be had only with the Denial of the Restriction? My conjecture is that the question receives an affirmative answer.

Toward motivating this conjecture, I'll *suppose that the Restriction holds* and, in terms of the scientifical metaphysic as thus limited, I'll begin two *extremely simple attempts to characterize* our world. (Toward the Restriction's being fully in force, I'll stipulate that both are mainly aimed at characterizing the world well before there were any [finite] minds.)

First, and familiarly, I'll begin an attempt to characterize physical reality in generally Newtonian terms: Moving about in what's otherwise uniformly empty space, there are many particles of matter, grandiosely labeled Particles, whose motion is governed by physical laws. In that we're supposing the Restriction to hold, we must suppose that, in this *Particulate World*, the laws concern only Nonqualitative properties that the Particles might have, not Qualities.

Second, and unusually, I begin this attempt to characterize physical reality: In what's otherwise a continuous material plenum, or a continuous field of matter, there are little perfectly empty spaces, or absolute vacua, or *Bubbles*: As regards both shape and size, each Bubble is precisely similar to a certain Particle, its *counterpart* Particle, in the Particulate World. And, wherever there's a Particle in our Particulate World, there's a counterpart place with a counterpart Bubble in this *Plenumate World*. So, if there are eight spherical Particles arrayed in a quite cubical pattern in a certain region of our Particulate World, then in the counterpart region of our Plenumate World there'll be eight such Bubbles arrayed in just such a pattern.

Even as various Particles may instance certain physical properties that will have them be suited for governance by certain physical laws, so various regions of a physical Plenum may have certain correlative physical properties that will have them be correlatively suited for governance by apt parallels of, or nice inversions of, the Particle-governing laws. So, in a nice parallel with the law-governed behavior of the Particles in our Particulate World, this Plenumate World features laws governing the distribution of its Plenum throughout all its time. And, since its Bubbles always *are* at just the places in the World where there *isn't* any Plenum, this World's laws also serve to determine the distribution of all its *Bubbles* over time. So, our Plenumate World's Bubbles will move through its material field along trajectories that, over time, perfectly parallel the trajectories of the Particulate World's Particles through its empty space.

Always supposing the Restriction holds, I'd make two extremely simple attempts, it appears, at starting to characterize our world. Before concluding the section, it may be useful to comment on what may be the two most salient respects in which my attempts were so simple.

First, there's the point that my attempts were conducted in the general framework of classical physics, with its quite intuitive conceptions of space and of time, rather than the framework of more recent physics, with its quite *unintuitive* conceptions, like the notion of *spacetime*. One reason for this, I blush to confess, is that I know precious little about contemporary physical science. A more important reason is that I'm engaged in an endeavor that's meant to transcend the differences between classical physics and more recent scientific developments. And it's perfectly possible, it appears, for there to be an endeavor that succeeds in being that comprehensive: Since recent scientific developments make no Completely Revolutionary Break with earlier science, what's new in the recent scientific conceptions doesn't affect the question of how we might, with the Restriction fully in force, ever have an intelligible worldview that, far from being any sort of idealism, is an adequate specification of the scientifical metaphysic.

Apparently with complete sincerity, that's what I've been told by philosophers knowledgeable about contemporary physics. So apparently, my employing the framework of classical physics means no loss of generality for these philosophical exercises.

Second, there's the point that, in trying to characterize a Particulate World, and also a Plenumate World, I forswore saying anything about complex material structures or systems, much less anything about any minds that any material complexes might subserve. That was done for several reasons, the most important being that such a simplification would be helpful toward having the Restriction be fully in force. Even if it might be unnecessary, I'll again implore my readers: When trying to think of a Particulate World, *don't do anything even remotely like*, say, thinking of *light grey* spheres moving through a *dark grey* space or field; and, when attempting thoughts of a Plenumate World, don't do anything even remotely like thinking of dark grey spheres moving through a light grey space or field!

For holding to this supposition, it will be useful to discuss some relations regarding the scientifical metaphysic, the instantiation of Qualities, and "the place of mind in the world order," or, as it might turn out, what just appear to be some such relations: Even while they try to have the Restriction be in force, some may have these following thoughts regarding the scientifical metaphysic. As our dominant metaphysic seems fully to allow, where and when a World features creatures with conscious minds, there and then there'll be someplace in the World for Qualities to be instantiated. So, if we should endeavor to characterize, say, a Particulate World, at greater length, then, as we may make specifications for complex living material creatures, and so consciously experiencing creatures, we may thus characterize a part of the world in which Qualities will be instanced, even while supposing the Restriction to hold. So, if we just go further in our attempts to characterized Worlds, even while supposing the Restriction, won't we do quite a lot toward characterizing a Particulate World, and also a Plenumate World?

No, we won't, for the situation is this: Whenever there's something that seems to characterize an experiencing creature as constituted of many Particles, there's also something, in correlative Plenumate terms, that seems to characterize that creature, with just as much propriety, as not being so constituted. Let me explain.

In an attempt to characterize an experiencing creature that features a body as well as a mind with *Particulate* terms, we may say this: Ever so many material Particles, perhaps billions and billions, serve to *constitute* the material creature with a mind. Or at the very least, they all serve to constitute the body of the creature; and because so many of this body's Particles are going through an appropriately complex sequence of arrangements, this body, it may then be said, subserves the creature's mind. When the duly constituted creature has experiences, Qualities are, through or in the creature's mind, instanced in the Particulate World.

But using *Plenumate* terms, we can say *this* about any materially realized experiencing creature: Ever so many Bubbles in the Plenum, perhaps billions and billions, serve to *institute* the physical creature with a mind, to coin a euphonious Plenumate term. Or at least they serve to institute the body of the creature, which body subserves the creature with a mind. When the duly instituted creature has experiences, Qualities are, through or in the creature's mind, instanced in the Plenumate World.

In this section, serious questions were raised about any attempt to contemplate physical reality within the confines of the Restriction. Initially, it may have appeared that each of my attempts to characterize physical reality, one with Particulate wording and one with the Plenumate terms, clearly contrasted with the other. But mightn't it be that I actually made just one extremely insubstantial start twice over, first using one mutually connected group of terms, the "Particulate terms," and then using another, the "Plenumate terms"? Mightn't it be that, as long as any attempt to conceive of our world is limited by the Restriction, it will be doomed to futility?

6. When limited by the Restriction, how to conceive a Particle's Propensities?

In my two attempts at characterizing Worlds, I tried to attribute Spatiotemporal properties to the objects of the Worlds. For example, I said that, in one sort of World, there are spherical Particles and, in the other, there are spherical Bubbles. By contrast, I did little, or nothing, as regards the other basic natural properties of the intended objects, the Propensities and the Qualities. Of course, as the Restriction was fully in force, it was forbidden to attribute any Quality to a Particle or to a Plenum. But what about Propensities?

On this we can hardly do better, I should think, than to consider what, historically, appears the propensity most saliently proposed for philosophical consideration, the supposed *solidity* of things material. And, on that, we can hardly do better than to begin with book 2, chapter 4 of the *Essay Concerning Human Understanding,* which is "Of Solidity," in which Locke aims to present an "Idea" that serves to distinguish material Bodies from the mere Space they may occupy:

> That which thus hinders the approach of two Bodies, when they are moving one towards another, I call *Solidity* . . . but if any one think it better to call it *Impenetrability,* he has my Consent. . . . This of all other, seems the *Idea* most intimately connected with, and essential to Body, so as no where else to be found or imagin'd, but only in matter: . . . the Mind, . . . considers it, as well as Figure, in the minutest Particle of Matter, that can exist; and finds it inseparably inherent in Body, where-ever, or however modified.
>
> This is the *Idea,* belongs to Body, whereby we conceive it *to fill space.*[7]

As with other passages, we should understand Locke here as assuming, if not affirming, that the Restriction holds. Even as Newton's physics ignores Qualities, Locke excludes them from the world's vast material realm, restricting them to our Minds (*Essay,* 136–37).

For Locke, solidity is impenetrability. But, with the Restriction in force, what can such solidity do for our conception of a Particle? An excellent discussion of the question can be found in John Foster's terribly difficult but at least occasionally brilliant book, *The Case for Idealism*. According to Foster:

> Locke ... thought that the nature of solidity is revealed in tactual experience. But in this Locke was clearly mistaken. ... The tactual experience of solidity is no more nor less than the experience of voluminous resistance, and, in so far as our concept of solidity is acquired through tactual experience, the specification of matter as solid is opaque. All it adds to the specification of matter as a voluminous substance is that there is *something* in its intrinsic nature (it does not say *what*) which makes material objects mutually obstructive.[8]

Now, I do not know that Foster is right in his suggestion that Locke thought that solidity was not a Power of material objects. More likely, it seems to me, in "Of Solidity" Locke was involved in muddles: How could *Impenetrability*, which Locke says is the very same as Solidity, *not* be a Power of resistance on the part of Impenetrable Bodies. But philosophically, there's no more to be gained from Locke here than what Foster contends, nothing much at all. Indeed, insofar as Foster's reading of Locke may be mistaken, his error will be, apparently, *undue charity* toward the old philosopher.

At all events, where Foster is most helpful is in his own discussion of the quite general question of the "Powers of Material Bodies." This occurs in an appendix to chapter 4 of the book. As Foster's thinking there is so very helpful, I'll quote this appendix at length:

> The only properties of fundamental particles which can be transparently specified in physical terms are (1) Spatiotemporal properties, such as shape, size and velocity and (2) causal and dispositional properties, such as mutual obstructiveness, gravitational power and electric charge. From this, I have concluded that ... the intrinsic nature of the particles can, in physical terms, only be specified opaquely, as that on which their behavioural dispositions and causal powers are grounded. But, is this conclusion justified? An alternative would be to say that ... each particle is, in itself, no more than a mobile cluster of causal powers, there being no "substantial" space-occupant which possesses the powers and on whose categorical nature the powers are grounded. Such a thesis has been endorsed, in different forms, by a number of distinguished scientists and philosophers. [Here, Foster has

PETER UNGER

a note naming such intellectual heavyweights as Leibniz, Boscovich, Kant, Priestley and Faraday.] If it is coherent, this thesis certainly has some appeal . . . .

But is the powers-thesis (PT) coherent? The main problem is that if all the fundamental particles are construed in this way, there seem to be no physical items in terms of whose behaviour the content of the powers could be specified, and consequently, it seems that, in the last analysis, there is nothing which the powers are powers to do. Let us begin with a concrete example. We will assume that the atoms are the only fundamental particles and that all atoms are of exactly the same type. Now each atom has a number of causal powers. It has a power of resistance, whereby any two atoms are mutually obstructive. It has a power of gravitational attraction, whereby, between any two atoms, there is a force of attraction inversely proportional to the square of their distance. . . . And it has a number of other powers which we need not list. For PT to be true, it is necessary some subset of these powers constitutes the essential nature of an atom. Let us suppose, for simplicity, we select the power of resistance as the only (putatively) essential atomic power and leave the other powers to depend on the contingent laws of nature governing the behavior of atoms. Thus each atom is construed as a mobile sphere of impenetrability, the behavior and causal interaction of these spheres, apart from their mutual obstructiveness, being governed by additional laws. The problem arises when we ask: "To what is a sphere of impenetrability impenetrable?" The answer is: "To other atoms, i.e., to other spheres of impenetrability." But this means that the specification of the content of the atom-constituting power is viciously regressive: each atom is a sphere of impenetrability to any other sphere of impenetrability to any other sphere of impenetrability . . . and so on *ad infinitum*. From which it follows that the notion of such a power is incoherent, since there is nothing which the power is a power to do. . . .

The problem is not avoided if we include further powers in the essential nature of the atom. Thus we might take the atomic nature to combine a power of resistance with a power of attraction, so that each atom is constituted by a mobile sphere of impenetrability surrounded by a more extensive (perhaps infinitely extended) field of gravitational potential (the field being structured, in accordance with the inverse-square-law, around the centre of the sphere). We could then try to specify the content of the power of resistance in terms of the behavior of gravitational fields or specify the content of the power of attraction in terms of the behavior of spheres of impenetrability. But neither specification blocks the regress, since it merely specifies the content of one power in terms of another. The only way of avoiding the regress, it seems, is to construe at least one of the powers as a power to affect the behavior of some . . . space occupant . . . with an intrinsic nature independent of its causal powers and dispositions. But such occupants are just what PT excludes (67–69).

My conclusion, therefore, is that the powers-thesis is incoherent. And consequently, I stand by my previous conclusion that, apart from their shape and size, the intrinsic nature of the fundamental space-occupants (assuming there are occupants at all) cannot be empirically discovered or transparently specified in physical terms (72).

Now, I'm not sure that the considerations Foster marshals show that the powers-thesis is so much as *incoherent*. But, it does seem clear that they show there to be grave difficulties, perhaps even insuperable ones, with the thought we can understand certain regions of space, or certain entities occupying the regions, to have just so many Spatiotemporal properties and Propensity properties without their having any Qualities at all.

To take full advantage of them, I'll conjoin Foster's ideas with some complementary considerations. Toward setting out these considerations, I'll quote from "Of the Modern Philosophy," a marvelous section of Hume's *Treatise*:

The idea of solidity is that of two objects, which being impell'd by the utmost force, cannot penetrate each other; but still maintain a separate and distinct existence. Solidity, therefore, is perfectly incomprehensible alone, and without the conception of some bodies, which are solid, and maintain this separate and distinct existence. Now what idea have we of these bodies? The ideas of colours, sounds, and other secondary qualities are excluded. The idea of motion depends on that of extension, and the idea of extension on that of solidity. 'Tis impossible, therefore, that the idea of solidity can depend on either of them. For that wou'd be to run in a circle, and make one idea depend on another, while at the same time the latter depends on the former. Our modern philosophy, therefore, leaves us no just nor satisfactory idea of solidity; nor consequently of matter.

Add to this, that, properly speaking, solidity or impenetrability is nothing, but an impossibility of annihilation, ... An impossibility of being annihilated cannot exist, and can never be conceived to exist, by itself; but necessarily requires some object or real existence, to which it may belong. Now the difficulty still remains, how to form an idea of this object or existence, without having recourse to the secondary and sensible qualities.[9]

We should now understand Hume, like Locke before him, as assuming the Restriction to hold. And as these passages then serve to show, in fixing on solidity, or on *what's left of that notion when the Restriction has been supposed*, Locke found nothing to distinguish adequately between Particles of Matter and Bubbles in a material Plenum.

Now, right before the quote just displayed, there are these sentences:

> The idea of extension is a compound idea; but as it is not compounded of an infinite number of parts or inferior ideas, it must at last resolve itself into such as are perfectly simple and indivisible. Those simple and indivisible parts, not being ideas of extension, must be non-entities, unless conceiv'd as colour'd or solid. Colour is excluded from any real existence. The reality, therefore, of our idea of extension depends upon the reality of that of solidity, nor can the former be just while the latter is chimerical. Let us, then, lend our attention to the examination of the idea of solidity (228).

As Hume's here suggesting, without phenomenal colors available, or any similarly helpful Qualities, we'll lack the resources for an adequate conception of something's being physically solid or impenetrable. As Hume also seems rightly to suggest, the same pertains to any other alleged physical Propensity. (Except that Locke fixed on solidity as his favorite, there's nothing very special about that candidate, as the passages from Foster can be seen to show.)

In light of what's been presented in this section, we may be able to make useful comments concerning the questions that, at the just previous section's end, arose for my attempts to characterize a Particulate World, and also a Plenumate World: Though it may have appeared that each of my attempts to characterize physical reality, one with Particulate wording and one with the Plenumate terms, clearly contrasted with the other, mightn't it be that I actually made just one extremely insubstantial start twice over, first using one mutually connected group of terms and then using another? Indeed, it may now be so plain that those questions have affirmative answers that the whole matter's no longer interesting.

What may still be interesting, I think, is to notice these further points: With those attempts, even my *very talk of particles* may have been badly misleading, as was my *talk of a plenum*. As I'm suggesting, it may be that something's *being a particle* isn't ever a completely Nonqualitative matter, and the question of whether there's *a plenum* might not be wholly Nonqualitative. With the *Restriction in place*, it may be that we're unable to think of a World as containing any *particles*; when supposing the Restriction to hold while trying to think of a "Particulate World," perhaps the most we can do is think, very abstractly indeed, about a physical World where "Quality-purged correlates of true particles" are to play a certain role in the history of the World. And, with the Restriction in place while trying to think of a "Plenumate World," perhaps the most we can do is think, just as abstractly, about a World where "Quality-purged correlates of a true plenum" play a perfectly parallel role, or maybe even the very same role, in the history of the World. With thoughts so abstract, perhaps there's no significant difference between what we're thinking at the one time and at the other.

7. Extensible Qualities and intelligible Propensities

With the Restriction in force and no Qualities available, we'll have no adequate conception of physical reality. By contrast, with Qualities having "real existence" in the physical realm, we may have a systematically rich variety of physical conceptions, perhaps far beyond anything imagined by Locke or Hume. Directly, I'll explain.

Whether or not we scientifically educated philosophers now can *believe* that any matter is a certain Qualitative color, say, that it's a certain Absolutely Specific shade of phenomenal red, it certainly seems that we can *conceive* of there being matter, even perfectly insensate matter, that's entirely just such a red, and that has no other Absolutely Specific Quality. As I'll say, we're to contemplate matter that is *Red*.

It may also be helpful to have our considered stuff be, through and through, *pretty highly phenomenally transparent* (and *somewhat phenomenally translucent*). As with any Quality our matter may have, it's (degree of) transparency must be Absolutely Specific. So, it's Red Transp-Taso matter that we're to conceive. For easy exposition, we'll call our matter just by its first name, Red.

Though it might not be believable for you and me, it's perfectly conceivable, even to us, that all of a World's matter be Red. In particular, it's conceivable that all of a World's matter be distributed so as to comprise eight Red congruent material spheres, each separated from the others by Qualityless empty space, and with nothing else in such a region having any Qualities, while what's where any sphere is has just the color Quality we're contemplating.

Consonant with such a conception, there may be clear content in *each of several different ideas of impenetrability*. For just one salient way of cutting the conceptual pie, we may have clear content both in (1) the idea of a sphere that's impenetrable to, or by, *all* the matter that's external to it and in (2) the idea of a sphere that's impenetrable to *some*, but *not all*, the matter external to it. In turn, I'll illustrate both ideas.

1. We may think of an infinity of Red spheres each of which is absolutely impenetrable to every other, with the matter of these spheres comprising all the matter of the World in which there are the spheres. When two such spheres collide, then each directly recedes from the other, without either making any intrusion into the bounds of the other.

2. In addition to all our Red spheres, we may contemplate an infinity of spheres that are each an Absolutely Specific shade of phenomenal blue and a certain Absolutely Specific phenomenal transparency, an infinity of *Blue* spheres. Now, just as each Red sphere is completely impenetrable to all other Red spheres, each Blue sphere is impenetrable to all other Blue spheres. More interestingly, each *Red* sphere will be *perfectly penetrable* by any *Blue* sphere, and *vice versa*; so without even the least resistance or temporal delay in trajectory, Red spheres and Blue spheres will pass through each other, as will parts of such Qualitatively different spheres. To conceive such a "perfect passing" most vividly, we may think of a region where a Blue and a Red sphere overlap as suffused with a certain Absolutely Specific transparent purple, as being *Purple* regions.

As this discussion of impenetrability suggests, any intelligible conception of physical Propensities, and any adequate conception of physical entities, has a central place for Extensible Qualities. At the same time, there's an abundance of such good conceptions that do that.

It's not surprising, then, to observe that, just as thought of Extensible Qualities allows us to have intelligible ideas of physical objects, variously distributed through spacetime and disposed toward various possible interactions, so it allows us to make intelligible specifications of Particulate Worlds, and clearly contrasting characterizations of Plenumate Worlds.

With attempts at Worldly characterization, we'll now have there be instanced some Extensible Quality *wherever there is matter*, from the minutest particle to a material expanse infinitely extensive in all directions. And, it's *only where* there's matter, or only where there's physical reality, that there'll be Extensible Quality instantiated.

In a Particulate World, there'll be Extensible Quality where, and only where, there are Particles, these being relatively small bounded regions of materially filled space, or spacetime. Each suffused with Extensible Quality, each particle is surrounded by a region that, as it's completely devoid of Quality, will also lack any real physical Propensity.

In a Perfectly Plenumate Physical World, Extensible Quality is instanced everywhere, and always, in the whole space (or spacetime) of the World. And, this Qualified space will be equally pervaded with physical Propensities; so, then, the World is filled with matter.

In a Plenumate World with Bubbles, finally, such well-Qualified materially filled space won't exhaust the space of the World. Rather, with each separated from the others by well-Qualified matter, there'll be many regions without Quality, and without anything of physical reality.

8. Intelligible physical reality and a principle of contingency

In terms of our three kinds of basic property, what's required for there to be a humanly intelligible mind-independent *physical* reality, whether or not it's the World's only realm of reality? Without much detail, I'll try to give the question a serviceable answer.

First, some words about some necessary relations: For a World to feature *physical* reality, it *must* include at least one entity such that (1) it has *some* Spatiotemporal properties – even if it may be, in a quite extreme case, only the property of being, in all directions, infinitely extensive, and (2) it has *some* Extensible Qualities – even if it may be, in a quite extreme case, only the property of being, everywhere and always, the very same Quality, and also (3) it has *some* Propensities – even if it may be, in a quite extreme case, only the Propensity to exemplify, in each place at each time, exactly the same Quality it exemplifies right there at the just previous time. The necessity just stressed is the same as with this more familiar proposition: As does any Euclidean geometrical closed solid, a physical entity precisely bounded by such a figure *must* be such that (1) it has *some* shape and also (2) it has *some* size.

As far as its being required of a physical entity that it instantiate some Extensible Quality, we need only recall the discussion of the previous section. As far as its being required that it instantiate some Spatiotemporal Property, we need only note that, for any thing to exemplify any Extensible Quality, there must be some space (or spacetime) that's occupied by that thing and suffused with that Quality. And as far as its being required that our physical entity instantiate some Propensity, we've already observed the point to hold even in the extreme case of a physically homogeneous reality.

Second, some complementary words about some contingent relations: Even with regard to something that's a *physical* entity, there is *no necessary connection* between (1) *which* Spatiotemporal properties the thing has, and (2) *which* Qualities the thing has, and (3) *which* Propensities are those of that physical thing. The *lack* of necessity just stressed, and the *contingency* just indicated, is the same as with this proposition: As is true of the Euclidean closed solid figures that precisely bound them, physical entities precisely bounded by such figures may be a certain given *shape* even while being *any* one of *numerous distinct sizes* and, equally, they *may* be a certain given *size* even while being *any* one of *numerous distinct shapes*. As seems fitting, I'll call the proposition this paragraph aims to express the *Principle of Contingency (of Relations among the Basic Properties)*.

For an easy appreciation of this Principle, recall the most recent remarks on characterizing Particulate and Plenumate Worlds. Perfectly in line with them all, for each of numerous Particulate Worlds, for example, there may be specified distinct exemplifications of Extensible Qualities. Even with a World specified as being "fully monochromatic" in Extensible Quality, there are numerous Particulate Worlds to countenance: Some are some Worlds where all the Particles are Red; others have all Blue Particles, and so on. Equally, just as there are Plenumate Worlds where the Plenum is Red, there are others with a Blue Plenum, and so on.

For ease of exposition, we'll focus on Particulate Worlds, and we'll narrow the focus to Worlds whose Particles are like the Newtonian entities familiar from the quote from Foster. In these Worlds, each of enormously many Particles has the same "mass" and the same "amount of matter," and each will attract the others with a force that varies inversely with the square of the distance between the centers of the interacting Particles. In some of these monochromatic Newtonian Worlds, all the Particles are Red; in others, all are Blue Particles, and so on. Whereas that's old hat, we newly notice this: In *Tutti-Frutti* Particulate Worlds, many Particles are Red and many others Blue, with yet many others being Yellow, and also Green, and Brown, and Grey, and Silvery, and Goldenish, and so on. (Along with such Qualitative variety, in many Tutti-Frutti Worlds there's also much Qualitative stability; there, any Particle that's Red will always be Red, and it will never have any other Quality, not Blue, not Yellow, and so on.)

Our supposition of Tutti-Frutti Worlds is as perfectly intelligible as it's vividly imaginable. So, as I'll suggest, our Principle of Contingency may be both perfectly intelligible and entirely unobjectionable.

9. Qualities as a factor in the development of physical reality: a problem

As it often appears, the Qualities of physical things won't be much of a factor in determining the development of any physical reality. The problematic appearance is most acute with physically well-behaved Worlds that, while otherwise heterogeneous, lack Qualitative variation, as with many monochromatic Worlds. What are we to make of this appearance? This question poses the *Problem of the Roles for Qualities (in Physical Reality)*.

Without thinking long and hard about the possible relations between physical entities and Qualities, there's little likelihood of encountering this Problem. So, as I expect, most contemporary philosophers will find this to be their first encounter with it. But many may quickly come to appreciate the puzzle quite well.

To that purpose, we'll focus on the comparison between a monochromatic Newtonian World and, on the other hand, a Tutti-Frutti Newtonian World. Except that the first has no Qualitative variety and the second has a great deal, the two Worlds may be exceedingly similar. So the behavior of the Tutti-Frutti World's Particles may precisely parallel the behavior of the Particles in the monochromatic World. And then all its Qualitative variety will make no difference to the physical development of the Tutti-Frutti World. But, then, are there *any* Worlds where Qualitative variety means much more than that for the development of the World's physical reality? All too often, it seems there are none. So, our Problem often appears acute.

To appreciate this Problem properly, however, it's also important that we not overestimate the apparent predicament: Our Problem is *not* to show how it might be true that, in *every* World with physical reality, all the Qualities of physical things are very significant factors in the physical development of the World. Nor is it to show even how it might be that, in every such World, *at least some* such Qualities are such significant factors. Indeed, it follows from the Principle of Contingency (of Relations among the Basic Properties) that there's no more chance of doing such a thing than of drawing a perfectly round square. Rather than any of that, our Problem asks us to show how it might be that, in *some* Worlds with physical reality, some Qualities of physical things are quite significant factors in the development of that reality.

10. The Problem of the Roles for Qualities in physical reality: a solution

At least since Galileo, physics has made great progress by ignoring, it appears, thoughts as to Qualities. Because we're so impressed by that, when we contemplate physical Propensities such thoughts are excluded from our consideration. For progress with the Problem of the Roles for Qualities, we must rectify this intellectually restrictive situation.

To that end, I'll first characterize a World whose salient Propensities we find it easy to take seriously. Using this *Size-Propensity* World as a model for further characterization, I'll then characterize various *Quality-Propensity* Worlds, whose quite different Propensities we can also take seriously. When we fully acknowledge these Quality-directed Propensities, perhaps we'll have found a solution to our Problem.

First, we'll contemplate a monochromatic Particulate World: Whereas all the World's Particles have the very same Extensible Quality, perhaps *Grey*, these spherical Particles come in ten different Sizes, with many Particles of each Size. As regards both its volume and its "amount of matter," each of the smallest Particles is one-tenth as great as each of the largest Particles; each of the next smallest is two-tenths as great as a largest Particle, and so on. Now, each Particle has the Propensity to attract each of the others, and to be attracted by each of the others, with a force that varies directly with its Size (and, say, inversely with the square of the distance between its center and the centers of each of the other Particles). It's easy enough to take seriously the thought that a World might work in that way.

Next, we'll contemplate a *multichromatic* Particulate World: Whereas all this World's Particles have the very same Size, perhaps the Size of the smallest Particles in the foregoing monochromatic World, these spherical Particles come in ten different "Achromatic Colors," with many Particles of each such Color. The lightest Particles, each of them Snow White, each have one-tenth "the amount of matter" of the darkest, each of which is Jet Black; each of the next lightest Particles, each of them Very Light Grey, is two-tenths as "massive" as the darkest, and so on. Here, each Particle has the Propensity to attract each of the others, and to be attracted by each of the others, with a force that varies directly with its *Qualitative Darkness* (and, say, inversely with the square of the distance). Though there might be *no good reason for it*, as I'll suggest, it maybe quite hard to take seriously the thought that a World might work in *this* way.

To make progress on our Problem, we must overcome this difficulty. We must take seriously not only the thought that physical entities have Qualities, but also the thought that, at least in some Worlds, such entities have Propensities *with respect to Qualities*. In other words, we must adopt a *more inclusive mode of thinking* than the one that, apparently, proved so successful for Galileo and so many successors. For adopting such more inclusive thinking, what's most helpful, I imagine, is more experience with such thinking.

Accordingly, we may do well to contemplate a different contrasting pair of Particulate Worlds, again one a Size-Propensity World and the other a Quality-Propensity World. In both of these Worlds, there are four sorts of spherical Particles: Each exactly the same as the other in Quality, there are Large Red Particles and Small Red Particles, with the former being ten times the Size of the latter. And, each of them having a Quality very different from that of any Red Particle, there are Large Blue Particles and Small Blue Particles, the former being exactly the same size as the Large Red Particles and the latter the same as the Small Red Particles.

Now, in the first of our two Worlds, each Particle will have a Propensity to attract any Particle that's different from it in Size, and a Propensity to repel any Particle that's the same Size. In this World, the Large Red Particles and the Large Blue Particles will repel each other, as will the Small Red and the Small Blue Particles. And the Large Particles, both Red and Blue, will attract, and will be attracted by, the Small Particles, Red and Blue. As I'm envisioning this World, when Particles attract, or repel, other Particles, it's *because* the former have Propensities *with respect to the very Size* the latter possess.

In the second World, no Particle will have any of those Propensities. Rather, each will have a Propensity to attract any Particle that's different from it in *Quality*, and a Propensity to repel any Particle that's the same Quality. In this World, the Red Particles, Large and Small, will attract, and will be attracted by, the Blue Particles, Large and Small. Far from repelling each other, here the Large Red Particles and the Large Blue Particles will *attract* each other. As I'm envisioning this other World, when Particles attract, or repel, other Particles, it's *because* the former have Propensities *with respect to the very Quality* the latter possess.

Toward gaining comfort with the good thought that, in addition to their having Qualities, many physical entities have Propensities *with respect to Qualities*, I've considered a couple of relevantly contrasting pairs of Particulate Worlds. Although the job is a tad more complex, we can do as well with, say, apt pairs of Plenumate Worlds. But even without actually encountering such a variety of illustrative examples, we see how the Qualities of physical entities can be a very significant factor in the development of physical reality.

11. Concluding and continuing questions

In comparison with most recent papers in philosophy, this one has been quite ambitious. But it is not nearly so ambitious as might appear. So it might sometimes seem that I have attempted an argument, very largely a priori, to the effect that, in this actual world, certain sorts of properties are basic properties, to wit, Spatiotemporals, Propensities, and Qualities. But of course, it's futile for anyone to argue, in such an a priori fashion, to any such substantial effect. And of course, I haven't really attempted anything like that much.

Much more modestly, I've argued only for conditional propositions. Conspicuous among them is this: If the scientifical metaphysic provides us with a tolerably accurate understanding of this world, then, as basic properties instanced in the actual world, there are Spatiotemporal Properties, and Propensities, and also Qualities. As we should bear in mind, it *might* be that this dominant worldview provides us with no such thing.

When the limits of the present essay are appreciated, we see large questions for future inquiry. Salient among them is this: If the scientifical metaphysic should be inadequate, then what might we best suppose are the basic properties of concrete reality? As a first pass at this fearful question, I hazard the conjecture that we should still countenance Qualities and Propensities, and perhaps Temporal Properties but no Spatial Properties.

In the present climate, I may be a greater friend of qualities than any other admittedly ambitious metaphysician. Yet I have doubts about that. Now, especially as this essay is dedicated to Jerome Shaffer, for a most salient example of work that fuels these doubts it's especially fitting to consider work from a most salient student of Professor Shaffer's. So, I ask: What does David Lewis denote with "qualities" in this schematic metaphysical passage?

> Many of the papers, here and in Volume I, seem to me in hindsight to fall into place within a prolonged campaign on behalf of the thesis I call "Humean supervenience." . . .
>
> Humean supervenience is named in honor of the greater denier of necessary connections. It is the doctrine that all there is to the world is a vast mosaic of local matters of particular fact, just one little thing and then another. (But it is no part of the thesis that these local matters are mental.) We have geometry: a system of external relations of spatio-temporal distance between points. Maybe points in spacetime itself, maybe point-sized bits of matter or aether or fields, maybe both. And at those points we have local qualities: perfectly natural intrinsic properties which need nothing bigger than a point at which to be instantiated. For short: we have an arrangement of qualities. And that is all. There is no difference without difference in the arrangement of qualities. All else supervenes on that.[10]

Though Lewis clearly uses "qualities" for *some* metaphysically basic properties, it's not clear what these properties are. Are his qualities much like our Qualities?

Following Russell, who followed Hume, in characterizing the Qualities I wanted there to be *some* connection, however indirect and tenuous, between the properties targeted and what we might experience, if only with the experience enjoyed in imaginative understanding. Without *any* connection to *any* such aid to intelligibility, what are we humans to understand by *anyone's* metaphysical reference to qualities? So it is that, in trying to say *something intelligible about what are* Qualities, I referred us to phenomenal qualities. Anyway, as Lewis's qualities are absolutely basic in his metaphysics, it should be asked: In humanly intelligible terms, what's there to say as to *what are* these items on whose arrangement, perhaps, all else supervenes?

This paper serves also to raise questions about the work of other students of Shaffer's, including the work in this very paper itself: When I said that, if the Extensible Qualities don't include phenomenal colors, then they should be strongly and deeply analogous to such colors, what sort of analogy could I sensibly have had in mind? More specifically, *in what respects* are such Extensible Qualities to be so analogous to phenomenal colors?

The previous section's discussion promotes the appearance that, for an intelligible conception of the actual world as comprising a heterogeneous physical reality, we need only a very few Qualities, and these may bear very much the same relations to each other as obtain among a *very few achromatic* phenomenal colors, perhaps much as obtain between just a certain Light Grey, say, and a certain Dark Grey. So, perhaps we can do a fair amount to sharpen our questions, and even to place limits on the range of sensible answers: What is it about the relations among, or even between, a few colors that, at least to a quite significant degree, must find a parallel in relations among Extensible Qualities, if thinking in terms of these Qualities will do much toward our having an adequate conception of physical reality?

As I've just observed, there's been the appearance that an adequate conception of what seems most of our world requires us to conceive only a very few Qualities as basic properties, perhaps just two Extensible Qualities. But that appearance might be illusory. To do justice to even just the Qualities apparently available in, or through, our immediate experience, perhaps we must regard as basic all the known phenomenal qualities, both such as seem Extensible and such as seem Nonextensible. Now, insofar as it may come to seem that the truth lies in such a more expansive vein, then, however restricted the academically respectable options of the time, serious philosophers will have to confront such extensive considerations as this final question: Might it possibly be that, rather than with the scientifical metaphysic, only with a more mentalistic worldview, maybe one where neither the physical nor the mental is most basic, will we have anything like an adequate conception of what's actually concrete reality?

Notes

*In 1995, David Lewis dedicated a paper to Professor Jerome Shaffer, his undergraduate philosophy teacher, for the occasion of Jerry Shaffer's retirement from teaching philosophy: "Should a Materialist Believe in Qualia?," *Australasian Journal of Philosophy*, Vol. 73, 1995, 140–44, and *Faith and Philosophy*, 1995, 467–71. Now, I much more belatedly dedicate this paper to Shaffer, who was also my undergraduate philosophy teacher. Not only for his understanding and encouragement, but especially for that, I'll always be grateful to Jerry Shaffer.

For many years, Shaffer has thought hard about the relation between the mental and the physical. Now, I try to write usefully about part of what may be sustaining his thinking.

With this effort, help came from many others: In the fall of 1997, it was discussed by those regularly attending the graduate seminar I gave at New York University with John Gibbons. In addition to Gibbons, I gratefully thank Mark Bajakian, David Barnett, Geoff Helmreich, Peter Kung, Brian Leftow, Barbara Montero, and Sebastien Pennes. Grateful thanks also go to Robert Adams, David Armstrong, Gordon Belot, Michael Della Rocca, Hartry Field, Kit Fine, Brian Loar, Michael Lockwood, Barry Loewer, Graham Priest, Michael Rea, and Galen Strawson. For almost incredible efforts, very special great thanks go to John Carroll, John Heil, and C.B. (Charlie) Martin.

1   Bertrand Russell, *The Analysis of Matter* (London: Kegan Paul, 1927), 407. My own copy of the work is a reprinting by Dover Publications, New York, 1954. In that, see p. 402. Anyway, the quoted words are from the book's penultimate sentence.
2   Bertrand Russell, "Mind and Matter," in *Portraits from Memory* (Nottingham, England: Spokesman, 1956), 153. Until recently, truths like those just quoted were, for centuries, influential with serious philosophers. For a seminal example, "the father of modern philosophy" advances some in Descartes' *Principles of Philosophy*, part I, paragraph 11: "How our mind is better known than our body," as in *The Philosophical Writings of Descartes*, trans. J. Cottingham, R. Stoothoff, and D. Murdoch, Vol. 1 (Cambridge: Cambridge University Press, 1985).
3   The quote is from David Armstrong, *Perception and the Physical World* (London: Routledge and Kegan Paul, New York: Humanities Press, 1961), 184. For Descartes' list, Armstrong refers us to "the second paragraph in the Fifth Meditation, and elsewhere."
4   Though some of Martin's writings on this subject are very hard to understand, others are helpfully clear. For work that helps clarify the fact that *dispositions are as categorical as anything,* see C.B. Martin, "Dispositions and Conditionals," *Philosophical Quarterly*, Vol. 44, 1994, and Martin's contribution to D.M. Armstrong, C.B. Martin, and U.T. Place, *Dispositions: A Debate*, ed. Tim Crane (London and New York: Routledge, 1996).
5   Bertrand Russell, *The Analysis of Matter* (London: Kegan Paul, 1927). My copy is a reprinting by Dover Publications, New York, 1954. In this reprinting, see pp. 263–64.
6   Michael Lockwood. *Mind, Brain and the Quantum* (Oxford: Basil Blackwell, 1989), 164–65.
7   In P.H. Nidditch's edition of John Locke's *An Essay Concerning Human Understanding* (Oxford: Oxford University Press, 1975), the quoted words can be found on p. 123.
8   John Foster, *The Case for Idealism* (London: Routledge and Kegan Paul, 1982), 63. By contrast with the passages from it that I'll cite, much of the book is written in a very difficult technical style. From the parts I've managed to understand, I'm convinced that the work deserves serious study. A few of its last words convey the thrust of the courageous book: "I hope one day to . . . make the case for mentalism irresistible. But until then, I must be content with a Defence of idealism in its anti-realist and phenomenalist forms."

With his paper, "The Succinct Case for Idealism," in H. Robinson (ed.), *Objections to Physicalism* (Oxford: Oxford University Press, 1993), Foster gives an overview of the difficult work.

9 David Hume, *A Treatise of Human Nature*, book 1, part 4, section IV. My copy of the *Treatise* is the P.H. Nidditch edition, based on L.A. Selby-Bigge's earlier edition, from the Oxford University Press (Oxford, 1978). In this edition, the quoted words are on pp. 228–29.

10 David Lewis, "Introduction," *Philosophical Papers*, Vol. 2 (New York: Oxford University Press, 1986), *ix.*

QUESTIONS

1   Levine argues that the puzzle of conscious experience is epistemic, not metaphysical: we are not yet in a position to see the necessity of certain mental–physical identity claims. What sort of conceptual development or empirical information would the materialist need in order to solve the puzzle? Is such a solution even *possible*?

2   Lewis claims that Mary does not learn new information about color perception, but instead acquires a new imaginative ability. Is the thrust of Jackson's reply to Lewis epistemic, as Levine's is, or metaphysical?

3   Consider Harman's view that in conscious experience we are aware only of the intrinsic properties of the objects of our experiences, not those of the experiences themselves. How might he best respond to cases involving after-images, or hallucination, where we seem to be aware of intrinsic qualities of *something*, but there is no *physical* object of the experience?

4   Lockwood argues that science delivers a purely causal-structural understanding of the world, identifying properties only relationally, in terms of the role they play in determining subsequent physical states. He then suggests that there are qualities disclosed in experience that may be thought to be (structures of) the very qualities science conceives in dispositional terms. What if a materialist were to counter that such a hypothesis is unnecessary, since all there is to properties is causal role – i.e., they are *pure* dispositions?

INDEX

observation 53–4, 168–9, 290, 359,
543, 557; beliefs 389; concepts 295,
302; sentences 296; terms 285,
287–8, 302; see also access,
privileged; acquaintance, direct;
introspection; privacy
Occam's Razor see Ockham's Razor
Ockham's Razor 122, 135; see also
simplicity
O'Connor, Timothy 421–2, 528, 537,
541
ontology 95, 395, 407, 536, 546, 553;
see also dualism; monism; Unger,
Peter
other minds 344, 392–3, 461

pairing problem 9, 69–76, 537
parallelism 54
parapsychology 205, 481–3, 487,
489
parsimony see Ockham's Razor;
simplicity
particulars 50, 264–5; see also objects;
substance
parts, arrangement of 122, 123, 199,
535, 544, 586
perception 4, 289, 313, 444–8,
514–17, 565; and causation 71;
color 493–4, 501–7; clear and
distinct 6; and idealism 88–94;
nonconscious 520; of one's own
states 21–2, 420, 500 (see also
introspection); and representation
547–8
persistence, conditions of 22, 454; see
also individuation
physical stance 374, 382, 389, 413; see
also design stance; intentional
stance
pineal gland 53, 58, 75, 537
Place, U.T. 121, 131, 135
Popper, Karl 63, 85, 399, 409, 531–3,
540
power see disposition
predicates 133, 142, 172, 384, 530;
and concepts 180, 211; disjunctive
167, 169–70, 183, 283; extension of
326; functional 160, 179; kind
166–7; numerical 394; psychological

217, 336, 394; well-behaved 172;
see also properties
preference 215, 359–62, 375
privacy 4, 38, 40, 129, 131, 368 (see
also introspection); and behaviorism
108, 355
privileged access see access,
privileged
processes 88–93, 539; brain 121–37,
263, 314, 455, 500, 545–7; causal
107, 345, 481; computational 115,
342; corpuscular 434; evolutionary
30, 36, 387, 441; formal 351;
internal 385; mental 50–1, 57–8, 63,
107, 491, 534–7; physical 45, 181,
417, 500–1; rational 241–2; spatial
445
projectibility 168–9, 174
properties 4, 88, 139, 197, 211, 260,
564–8; categorical 95, 549–50,
588; disjunctive 165–71, 178, 208,
284; dispositional 95, 156, 549,
575 (see also disposition); emergent
126, 525–41, 550; first-order
163–4; functional 237, 249, 433,
500; fundamental 83, 197–8, 421,
477; instantiation of 35, 163,
197–8, 271–303, 346, 586; intrinsic
73, 420, 500–1, 586, 590; material
66; mental 17, 26, 41–2, 163–4,
173–4, 178–81; psychophysical
291–2; physical 5, 38, 160–5, 198,
234, 423 (see also properties,
material); qualitative aspects of
147–53, 178, 225, 228–9, 267,
422, 429–36; relational 94–5,
420, 590; second-order 171,
178–9
propositional attitudes 232, 263–7,
272, 300, 355–69, 391–412, 422;
language of 450
propositions 263, 265, 321, 365, 387,
394, 404; compound 411; contingent
112, 126; egocentric 472, 486;
identity 10
publicity 31–2, 92, 108, 129, 136,
368
Putnam, Hilary 114, 160–2, 165,
210–21, 230–2, 386